GLIMPSES OF ONEIDA LIFE

Glimpses of Oneida Life is a remarkable compilation of modern stories of community life at the Oneida Nation of the Thames Settlement and the surrounding area. With topics ranging from work experiences and Oneida customs to pranks, humorous encounters, and ghost stories, these fifty-two unscripted narrations and conversations in Oneida represent a rare collection of first-hand Iroquoian reflections on aspects of daily life and culture not found in print elsewhere.

Each text is presented in Oneida with both an interlinear, word-by-word translation and a more colloquial translation in English. The book also contains a grammatical sketch of the Oneida language by Karin Michelson, co-author of the *Oneida-English/English-Oneida Dictionary*, that describes how words are structured and combined into larger linguistic structures, thus allowing *Glimpses* to be used as a teaching text as well.

The engrossing tales in *Glimpses of Oneida Life* will be a valuable resource for linguists and language learners, a useful source for those studying the history and culture of Iroquois people in the twentieth-century, and an entertaining read for anyone interested in everyday First Nations life in southern Ontario.

KARIN MICHELSON is a professor in the Department of Linguistics at the University at Buffalo. She has worked with speakers of the Oneida language for over thirty-five years and has published theoretical linguistics articles on Oneida, reference works, and practical guides.

NORMA KENNEDY has taught the Oneida language in New York and Ontario for more than twenty-five years. She is a master speaker at the Oneida Language and Cultural Center at the Oneida Nation of the Thames.

MERCY DOXTATOR (1936–2005) taught the Oneida language for almost twenty-five years at the Oneida Nation of the Thames, where she was the founder and director of the Oneida Language and Cultural Center.

GLIMPSES OF ONEIDA LIFE

Karin Michelson, Norma Kennedy, and Mercy Doxtator

Stories told by
Rose Antone, Margaret Antone, Clifford Cornelius, Hazel Cornelius,
Pearl Cornelius, Verland Cornelius, Mildred Cutcut, Ruben Cutcut,
Mercy Doxtator, Olive Elm, Ray George, Norma Kennedy,
Georgina Nicholas, Barbara Schuyler

UNIVERSITY OF TORONTO PRESS
Toronto Buffalo London

ISBN 978-1-4426-5030-5 (cloth)   ISBN 978-1-4426-2833-5 (paper)

Library and Archives Canada Cataloguing in Publication

Glimpses of Oneida life / Karin Michelson, Norma Kennedy, and Mercy
Doxtator, authors; stories told by Rose Antone, Margaret Antone,
Clifford Cornelius, Hazel Cornelius, Pearl Cornelius, Verland Cornelius,
Mildred Cutcut, Ruben Cutcut, Mercy Doxtator, Olive Elm, Ray George,
Norma Kennedy, Georgina Nicholas, Barbara Schuyler.

Includes bibliographical references and index.
Includes text in English and Oneida.
ISBN 978-1-4426-5030-5 (cloth)   ISBN 978-1-4426-2833-5 (paper)

1. Oneida language − Texts. 2. Oneida language – Texts − Translations into
English. 3. Oneida Indians − Ontario, Southern − Social life and customs.
4. Oneida Indians − Ontario, Southern − Humour. 5. Oneida language − Grammar.
I. Michelson, Karin, 1953−, author II. Kennedy, Norma, 1934−, author
III. Doxtator, Mercy, 1936−2005, author

PM2073.Z77G65 2016   497'.5546   C2015-907981-0

University of Toronto Press acknowledges the financial assistance to its publishing
program of the Canada Council for the Arts and the Ontario Arts Council, an agency
of the Government of Ontario.

Canada Council   Conseil des Arts
for the Arts   du Canada

ONTARIO ARTS COUNCIL
CONSEIL DES ARTS DE L'ONTARIO
an Ontario government agency
un organisme du gouvernement de l'Ontario

Funded by the   Financé par le
Government   gouvernement
of Canada   du Canada

Contents

Tables   ix

Acknowledgments   xi

Abbreviations   xiii

PART I: PRELIMINARIES

1. Introduction   3

    1.1 The Recordings   3
    1.2 Text Presentation and Format   4
    1.3 Variation in Spoken Oneida   6
    1.4 The English Translations   6

2. Oneida Sounds and Orthography   7

    2.1 Consonants and Vowels   7
    2.2 Accent and Vowel Length   7
    2.3 Utterance-Final Processes   8
    2.4 Use of Punctuation   9

PART II: STORIES

Language   13

    A Man Tells Off His Boss   14
    Berries and Bellies   16
    Why Berries Are Bellies in Oneida   17
    Kastes Buys a Face   19
    The Bean Game   22
    The Fat Cat   27

Lessons   31

   The Flirt   32
   Why the Bat Travels at Night   35
   The Crow   38
   Some Woodcutters Get a Visitor   39
   Why Dogs Don't Talk   46
   The Bird   50
   A Jealous Husband   53
   The Story of Birch Bark   55

Ghostly Tales   59

   Ghost Sightings at the Language Centre   60
   Ghosts, Flirts, and Scary Beings   65
   My Father's Encounter   72
   The Girl with the Bandaged Fingers   79
   An Unwanted Passenger   86
   A Scary Light   92
   A Ghost on the Tracks   96
   A Night Visitor   99
   What My Brother Leo Saw   103

Pranks and Mishaps   105

   Visits to My Auntie's   106
   A Pig in the Window   110
   An Unusual Spittoon   115
   Worms in the Soup   117
   My First Christmas Tree   121
   A Steamy Story   126
   How I Learned to Swear   130

More Favourite Memories   136

   A Wish Comes True   137
   My Dog Blackie   139
   A Hairy Adventure   142
   A Scary Hairy Adventure   146
   Friday Nights   151
   Wintertime   154

Customs   157

   The Spoiled Child   158
   The Dreamer   165
   Forecasting Things to Come   174
   Starting Life Together   178
   After a Loss   182

Getting Hoyan   191
Beaver, Let's Trade Teeth!   195
How to Divert a Storm   198

Growing Up and Working   200

An Oneida Childhood   201
A Lifetime Working   216
Learning to Work in Tobacco   238
All about Tobacco   246
My First Job in Tobacco   266

Reflections   276

My Childhood   277
Family and Friends   298
A Lifetime of Memories   311

PART III: GRAMMAR   341

1. Introduction   343

2. Word Structure   343

2.1 Verbs   343
2.2 Particles   355
    2.2.1 Pronouns and Identification of Participants   356
    2.2.2 Certainty and Emphasis   357
    2.2.3 Location and Time   358
    2.2.4 Connectives   359
2.3 Nouns   359
2.4 Noun Incorporation   362
2.5 Kinship Terms   365

3. Possession   366

3.1 Verbal Possession with Alienable Nouns   366
3.2 Nominal Possession with Alienable Nouns   367
3.3 Verbal Possession with Inalienable Nouns   369
3.4 Nominal Possession with Inalienable Nouns   370

4. Clauses   371

4.1 Clauses, Utterances, and Constructions   371
4.2 Clauses as Arguments   373
4.3 Introduction and Mention of Discourse Referents   376
4.4 Mismatches between Verbal and Nominal Prefixes   380

viii

5. Negation — 381

6. Questions — 386
6.1 Content Questions — 386
6.2 Yes-No Questions — 388
6.3 Embedded Questions — 390

7. Indefinites — 392
7.1 Positive Indefinites — 392
7.2 Negative Indefinites — 394

8. Free Relatives and Correlatives — 397

9. Counting — 403
9.1 Counting One — 403
9.2 Counting Two — 404
9.3 Counting Three or More — 405
9.4 Counting Possessed Entities — 408
9.5 Age and Time — 409

10. Degree and Comparison — 412
10.1 Degree — 412
10.2 Comparison 'more,' 'less' — 415

11. Possibility and Necessity — 417
11.1 Possibility — 417
11.2 Necessity — 420

12. Other Linkages between Clauses — 422
12.1 kanyó· ok 'so that' — 424
12.2 tá·t 'if, maybe, whether, or' — 424
12.3 ati 'no matter, although, even though' — 426
12.4 khále?, tahnú· 'and' — 427
12.5 nók tsi?, kwah nók (tsi?) 'but, only, just' — 427
12.6 né· tsi? 'because' — 428

Appendix 1: List of Particles — 429

Appendix 2: Segmented texts — 435

References — 455

Index — 457

Tables

Table 1. Distinctions made by pronominal prefixes	346
Table 2. C-stem pronominal prefixes	348
Table 3. i-stem pronominal prefixes	349
Table 4. o- and u-stem pronominal prefixes	350
Table 5. e- and ʌ-stem pronominal prefixes	351
Table 6. a-stem pronominal prefixes	352
Table 7. Noun structure	363
Table 8. Possessive prefixes	368
Table 9. Possessive structures	371
Table 10. Negation	386
Table 11. Questions	391
Table 12. Indefinite expressions	398
Table 13. Counting expressions	410
Table 14. Expressions of possibility and necessity	423
Table 15. Constructions in segmented texts	436

Acknowledgments

This volume is the culmination of many years, in fact decades, of work. We are grateful to the storytellers and to others for inspiration and encouragement. We thank Karin's husband Russell Deer for unwavering support, proofreading, and endless conversations about grammar, meaning, and how to word things. We thank Norma's sister Joan Doxtator for her always enthusiastic interest and Karin's sister Iris Michelson for valuable discussions about various ways to think about translations. Deep felt thanks are due also to Leslie Elm, a constant supporter of the Oneida language. We thank David Maracle, of the Centre for Research and Teaching of Native Languages at the University of Western Ontario for turning over materials on Oneida from 1980–2 for our use, including tape recordings of Mildred Cutcut and Ruben Cutcut. Thanks go to Carolyn O'Meara, Poornima Farrar, and Eunkyung Yi for digitizing tape recordings made before 2007. Recordings from 1993–5 were made with support from the National Science Foundation, which we also gratefully acknowledge. We would like too to acknowledge the efficient and congenial correspondence with Siobhan McMenemy, our editor at the University of Toronto Press.

Karin Michelson wrote Parts I and III; these sections use the first person ('I' or 'we') since avoiding the first person often resulted in convoluted and unnecessarily impersonal phrasing. The presentation of some of the topics in Parts I and III has been enriched and clarified as a result of conversations with Iroquoian colleagues Cliff Abbott, Wally Chafe, Mike Foster, Marianne Mithun, and Hanni Woodbury. Finally, Part III would have been far less informed without the innumerable fruitful and sometimes frenzied discussions with Jean-Pierre (JP) Koenig, Karin's colleague and collaborator at the University at Buffalo. Hanni Woodbury's and JP Koenig's readings of drafts of Parts I and III has lead to many improvements.

The following are remembered with deep regard for their knowledge, experiences, and thoughts: Clifford Cornelius, Hazel Cornelius, Mildred Cutcut, Ruben Cutcut, Mercy Doxtator, and Georgina Nicholas.

Abbreviations

A	Agent	JN	Joiner vowel
BEN	Benefactive	LOC	Locative
CAUS	Causative	M	Masculine
COIN	Coincident	NEG	Negative
CONT	Continuative	NMZR	Nominalizer
CONTR	Contrastive	NPF	Noun Prefix
CSL	Cislocative	NSF	Noun Suffix
DISL	Dislocative	OPT	Optative
DISTR	Distributive	P	Patient
DL	Dualic	PART	Partitive
DP	Dual/plural (nonsingular)	PL	Plural
DU	Dual	PNC	Punctual
EMPTY	Empty Noun Root	POSS	Possessive
EPEN	Epenthetic	PRES	Present
EX	Exclusive	PROG	Progressive
FACT	Factual	REFL	Reflexive
FI	Feminine-indefinite	REP	Repetitive
FUT	Future	REV	Reversative
FZ	Feminine-zoic	SG	Singular
HAB	Habitual	SRF	Semi-reflexive
IMP	Imperative	STV	Stative
IN	Inclusive	TRL	Translocative
INCH	Inchoative	Z/N	Feminine-zoic/neuter
INST	Instrumental		

PART I: PRELIMINARIES

1. Introduction

This volume contains fifty-two stories told by fourteen speakers. They tell ghost stories and stories that have a lesson, they relate pranks and hilarious happenings, and they talk about the way things used to be. They range from a few minutes in length, to ten or twenty minutes, or in a few cases longer. They are called "stories" because that seemed like a good label but they were not told from a script and most do not come from a stock of "traditional" stories. Almost all have some direct speech, and a few include some conversation. There is no specific theme that runs through them except that they are about people's lives and their encounters with other people or animals or scary beings, and they recall what life was like growing up and working at and around the Oneida Nation of the Thames settlement from about 1940 onwards. The stories are special in that they are amusing and warm and upbeat even when they report hardship.

The rest of this introduction gives some background on the recordings and explains the choice of presentation for the written texts; it also says something about the variation to expect in the Oneida texts as well as in the English translations of Oneida words and sentences. Section 2 describes the sounds of Oneida and the orthography used to represent them. Part II comprises the stories. Part III is titled "Grammar," but it is not intended as a comprehensive reference grammar as that deserves a volume all on its own. Rather it describes structures and patterns that occur in these stories, particularly those structures that typically involve several words. It is more usual in the linguistic tradition to give the grammar first, and then texts. However, presenting the stories first also makes sense, without diminishing the importance of studying the structure of Oneida for a full appreciation of the intricacies of the language.

1.1 The Recordings

A few of the stories were recorded when I first began to study the Oneida language in 1979 and got to know the late Georgina Nicholas, a masterful speaker and superb storyteller. She recorded three stories in 1980 (these were traditional stories), as well as an introduction that talked about her hearing stories when she was young; these were published as Michelson and Nicholas (1981). One of the three stories was recorded twice and the version that was not published in 1981 is included in the collection here. Another contribution by Georgina Nicholas to this volume is a longer story in which she compares her life as a child to the lives of children in contemporary times; sadly Georgina passed away before she was able to complete her story. Also from the 1980s there are two stories by Ruben and Mildred Cutcut. During the summers of 1980, 1981, and 1982 The Centre for the Research and Teaching of Canadian Native Languages at the University of Western Ontario obtained funding from the National Museum of Man in Ottawa for projects that would employ three university students and three young people from the Oneida community. Mercy Doxtator supervised these projects with the goal to develop materials that could be used in her Oneida classes at Standing Stone School. Ruben and Mildred Cutcut recorded some stories and recipes as part of the 1982 project. David Maracle, the current director of the Centre, kindly turned over these recordings to me several years ago. A transcription of Ruben Cutcut's story about the bat appears, without an English translation, in Cornelius et al. (1985). (The first publication to come out of these projects was Antone et al. [1981].) The version here is a revised transcription and it includes an English translation.

About half of the stories were recorded as part of a project whose goal was to figure out when so-called "utterance-final" forms in Oneida are used. Oneida is unique in the extent to which words that occur at the end of "utterances" undergo some modification. The most pervasive modification is that the final syllable of an utterance-final word is devoiced or "whispered." That means that a word spoken in isolation, which is also the final word in an utterance, has to be heard in an utterance-medial context in order to identify properties of the final syllable, such as whether the word ends in a vowel or a glottal stop, whether a word-final vowel is long or short, and what the vowel quality is. (The various utterance-final changes are described in Lounsbury [1942] and Michelson [1988].) In order to learn more about when speakers use an utterance-final form, outside of speaking a word in isolation, I obtained funding in 1993 from the National Science Foundation to record different people speaking Oneida. Mercy Doxtator, with whom I had taught a course on Oneida at the University of Western Ontario in 1979 and who had recently retired from teaching, was Co-Principal Investigator on the project. From 1993 – 5 she (or in some cases, she and I) recorded several speakers and she did an initial transcription and translation of the recordings. The speakers who contributed their stories were Margaret Antone, Clifford Cornelius, Hazel Cornelius, Pearl Cornelius, Verland Cornelius, Olive Elm, and Norma Kennedy. Transcribing the stories was challenging and time consuming, so thinking that it might provide a kind of break I suggested to Mercy that she record some of her own stories too. Over the years that Mercy and I worked together she recorded eighteen stories, all but one of which are included in this volume.

The rest of the stories were recorded after Mercy Doxtator, my good friend and reliable collaborator, passed away in January 2005. Rose Antone, Verland Cornelius, Olive Elm, Ray George, and Barbara Schuyler contributed these later stories. Since 2007, Norma (Jamieson) Kennedy has been working diligently and indefatigably with me to review all the stories—checking the transcriptions, improving the translations, brainstorming to explicate constructions, and also recording some of her own stories.

1.2 Text Presentation and Format

Texts can be presented in several different ways depending on the language and the audience. The simplest presentation gives just the native or source language and an English translation, often in two columns or on facing pages. Another kind of presentation provides an interlinear word-by-word translation in addition to a sentence-by-sentence translation. This is the format used for the stories published here, with the running English translation separate and at the bottom of the page. Just a short excerpt from Norma Kennedy's story about a little girl who turns into a bird is given in this interlinear format below.

(1.1)   Kanyó· onʌ́ ʌkanaʔtala·lí·   nʌ kwí· yʌkúhʌleʔ   ókhnaʔ
         As soon as   bread will get cooked   so then   I will call you   and then

         tʌtehsatáwyahteʔ   ʌtyatekhu·ní·.
         you will come back in   you and I will eat.

         'As soon as the bread gets cooked I will call you and then you will come back in and we will eat.'

A linguistically more informative presentation includes an analysis of words into component parts by placing a dash between components and then identifying each of the components with an abbreviated grammatical label. The division between components is not always straightforward in languages like Oneida and therefore a more abstract representation of the components is considered useful. This more abstract representation shows the segmentation into components and it is given on a separate line below the native language. In this type of presentation the word-by-word gloss is often omitted. An example of this more elaborated interlinear format is given in (1.2). We will use this format in Part III since this part of the volume deals with language structure, but for the presentation of the texts in Part II we will use the simpler interlinear format as in (1.1).

(1.2)　　**Kanyó·　onʌ́　ʌkanaʔtala·lí·　nʌ　kwí·　yʌkúhʌleʔ　ókhnaʔ　tʌtehsatáwyahteʔ　ʌtyatekhu·ní·.**

kanyó· onʌ́　ʌ-ka-naʔtal-a-li-ʔ　　　　　　　　　　　　nʌ kwí·
as soon as　FUT-3Z/N.SG A-bread-JN-ripe,cooked-PNC　so then

y-ʌ-ku-hʌl-eʔ　　　　　　　ókhnaʔ　t-ʌ-te-hs-atawyaʔt-eʔ
TRL-FUT-1SG>2SG-call-PNC　and then　DL-FUT-CSL-2SG.A-enter-PNC

ʌ-ty-ate-khw-uni-ʔ
FUT-1IN.DU.A-SRF-food-make-PNC

'As soon as the bread gets cooked I will call you and then you will come back in and we will eat.'

There are a number of practical reasons for choosing the simpler interlinear format for Part II. Foremost is that, although not obvious just from the example sentence above, the linguistically analyzed version takes up considerably more space. Another reason is that it is probably true that this format will appeal to the largest audience. Aside from these practical considerations, segmented texts of languages that have a complex word structure on a par with Oneida and other Iroquoian languages give *all* the details (as well they should), but the detail does not allow one to distinguish between what has, through time, acquired a meaning beyond the literal meaning and thus has become a distinct lexical entry in a dictionary, and what is relevant for understanding the syntactic and discourse patterns of the language. For example, in the excerpt above the word **ʌtyatekhu·ní·** 'you and I will eat' is built on a complex stem **-atekhuni-**. This stem is composed of the semi-reflexive prefix **-ate-**, the incorporated noun root **-khw-** 'food,' and the verb root **-uni- 'make.'** The fact that this particular combination of elements has become lexicalized with the meaning 'eat (a meal)' does not bear on how this verb combines with other words in the sentence. Fortunately, there are two large dictionaries of Oneida (Abbott, Christjohn, and Hinton [1996] and Michelson and Doxtator [2002]), and both of these give the internal composition of stems and even of many whole words. (The first of these dictionaries is also available at www.uwgb.edu/Oneida/Dictionary.html.) Moreover, the fact that **ʌtyatekhu·ní·** has an inclusive pronominal prefix (**-ty-**) is indicated by the translation 'you and I will eat,' and the fact that the verb is in the future (**ʌ-**) is also evident from the interlinear translation. However, for those who find it more satisfying and fruitful to study analyzed texts, segmented versions of three of the texts are given in Appendix 2 and additional segmented texts are available (by contacting Michelson at kmich@buffalo.edu).

1.3 Variation in Spoken Oneida

Another question that comes up when presenting spoken language from several speakers is how much standardization should be imposed on the written text. Variation in spoken language is due to (1) regular and predictable differences between speakers and (2) how fast someone is speaking. In at least some cases it seemed sensible to "regularize" the written text. For example, some speakers say **thok náhte?** 'something' while others say **tok náhte?**. We always write **thok náhte?**. Most of the speakers pronounced the particle **yakʌ?** 'reportedly' as two syllables, but a few pronounced it as if it was written **ye?**. We decided to write this particle **yakʌ?** everywhere. Another example, this time partly dependent on speech rate, is verbs that begin in the factual prefix **wa?-** plus the first person exclusive plural prefix **yakwa**. This combination is pronounced variously as **wa?akwa-** or **wa?yakwa-** or **wa?kwa-** or even **wae?kwa-**. In this case we always write **wa?akwa-**. Perhaps the greatest variation that is dependent on rate of speech is the pronunciation of some common particles. For example, the connective particle **kwí·** (see section 2.2.4) is often unaccented and often the vowel is short (thus pronounced as if written **kwi**). We consistently represent a particle as accented or unaccented, but such decisions are not always easy. An example of a word that we do not standardize is the particle **to·kʌ́ske?** or its shortened variant **tú·ske?** 'truly.' The two pronunciations are different enough and both are so frequent that we decided not to regularize these.

1.4 The English Translations

Sometimes it was challenging to convey the syntactic and discourse structure of Oneida, or to know how to treat constructions that are unlike those commonly used in English, or to decide on glosses for those hard-to-translate particles, and yet provide an English version that did not sound stilted. For the free translation we have aimed to achieve a balance between literal translation and literary translation so that the discourse structure of Oneida is (usually) still evident but the English has some natural flow to it as well. In the interlinear version we have translated (and written) most constructions or particles the same way each time they occur, but in some cases the translation can vary depending on context. For example, the particles **úhka?** and **náhte?** are translated as 'who' and 'what' when they occur in questions, as 'anyone' or 'anything' when they occur in negative contexts (thus, **yah úhka?** 'not anyone' and **yah náhte?** 'not anything'), and as 'someone' or 'something' when they occur with the particles **ok** or **thok** (thus, **úhka? ok** 'someone,' **thok náhte?** 'something'). Another example is the particle **tho**, which is translated 'there' unless it occurs in certain structures. With a classificatory word such as **nú·** 'where' or **nikú** 'how much,' **tho** is translated 'that's' (for example, **tho nú·** 'that's where'); with a following verb that begins in the partitive prefix, it is translated 'thus' (for example, **tho niyawʌ́·u** 'thus it has happened'). A final example is the translation of the particle **tsi?**. This particle is most often translated as 'that,' but it is also translated as 'at' in expressions for locations, 'as' in expressions of time, 'because' in the combination **né· tsi?**, 'how' in expressions of intensity when the following verb begins in the **n-** partitive prefix, and 'what' with certain verbs that begin in the **n-** partitive prefix (for example, **tsi? nihatyélha?** 'what he is doing').

2. Oneida Sounds and Orthography

This section provides an overview of the sound system of Oneida and the letters and symbols used in writing Oneida. While the orthography for Oneida is well established, the use of punctuation varies widely and so this section ends with a description of how periods and commas are used in the written texts.

2.1 Consonants and Vowels

The Oneida orthography employs fifteen symbols for consonant and vowel sounds and two additional symbols for accent and vowel length. The consonant sounds are written with the letters **k t s n l w y h ʔ** and the vowel sounds with **a e ʌ i o u**. Oneida does not have a voicing distinction, so the obstruent sounds **k t s** are most strongly voiced before vowels and least voiced before another obstruent. What this means is that these sounds are perceived closer to the sounds written in English as **g d z** when the sounds occur before another voiced sound, namely vowels and the consonants **n l w y**. They sound most like English **g d z** between two vowels. Before other consonants and at the ends of words, the sounds written **k t s** are perceived as sounding very much like English **k t s**. The glottal stop **ʔ** (the sound in English uh-oh!) is written with an apostrophe in some other sources on Oneida. The cluster **tsy**, as well as the cluster **ts** when it is followed by the vowel **i**, represent a voiced palatoalveolar affricate as in English g̲em, ed̲ge, or j̲am. In some written works, including Lounsbury (1953), this sound is written with a **j**. The corresponding voiceless sound, the sound in English chur̲ch, also occurs, though less frequently; it is written **tshy** or **tts** (before **i**).

 The vowel written **a** is similar to the vowel in the English word fa̲ther, the vowel written **e** sounds sometimes like English be̲t and sometimes like ba̲it, **i** sounds like English be̲e, and **o** sounds like English so̲. The vowels **ʌ** and **u** are nasal vowels. The vowel **ʌ** is a mid, central, nasal vowel which sounds close to English so̲n but without the n̲, or like some people's pronunciation of the question hu̲h?! The vowel **u** is a lower-high, back, mildly rounded, nasal vowel, similar to English so̲on but again without the n̲, or like English oo̲mph without the m̲. In the speech of some speakers the two nasal vowels are difficult to distinguish. At the beginning of utterances, words that begin in vowels are pronounced with either an **h** or a **ʔ** before the vowel. Whether there is an **h** versus a **ʔ** seems to depend on a number of factors—for example, whether the utterance is a word spoken in isolation or whether the word is focused in some way. Speakers who pronounce an **h** at the beginnings of words spoken in isolation are tempted to write the initial **h**.

2.2 Accent and Vowel Length

Accent is written with an acute accent mark over the accented vowel. A long vowel is written with a raised period after the vowel in this volume, as in previous works such as Lounsbury (1953) and both the dictionaries by Abbott, Hinton, and Christjohn (1996) and Michelson and Doxtator (2002). However, most of the resource materials on Oneida use a colon for vowel length.

 The accent mark is located on the syllable that is considered most prominent by speakers who are confident about identifying the most prominent syllable. Mercy Doxtator described the accented syllable as one where the voice "goes up," referring to an initial rise in pitch, which is confirmed by instrumental study. The most common patterns of accent and vowel length are described below; see Michelson (1988) for a detailed description.

One pattern is that the second-to-last syllable in the word is accented. The vowel of the accented syllable can be short or long. Examples of words with long accented vowels are **tsyeyá·tat** 'one person' and **wahʌ́·luʔ** 'he said.' An example of a word with a short accented vowel is **yutátyats** 'her name is.' The vowel in a short accented syllable is usually (but not always) followed by two or more consonants. For most speakers, when the vowel is long there is a steady rise in pitch over the duration of the accented syllable; for other speakers the long vowel ends with a (slight) fall in pitch.

Another common pattern is the last syllable of the word is accented. In this case both the vowel of the accented syllable and the vowel of the preceding syllable can be long, as in **wahakhlo·lí·** 'he told me.' Or both vowels can be short, as in **ʌtilú** 'raccoon.' Or the vowel of the syllable preceding the accented syllable is long, but the accented syllable itself is short, as in **ni·yót** 'how it is.' This pattern applies to words that end in one or more consonants. A less common pattern is a final accented vowel that is long, and the accented vowel is the only long vowel. An example is **tshikeksá·** 'when I was a child.'

There are other patterns due to phenomena that interact with accent. The most common phenomenon that interacts with accent is that the final syllable of a great many words contains a *weightless* vowel, usually the vowel **e** followed by a word-final **ʔ**. Examples of words that have a weightless **e** in the final syllable are **tyutʌhni·núheʔ** 'store' (literally, 'one sells things there') and **shakónhahseʔ** 'he hires her or them, the boss.' The word for 'store' has the same pattern as one described above: the vowel of the syllable preceding the accented syllable is long, but the accented syllable itself is short (**ni·yót**). But in **tyutʌhni·núheʔ**, because of the weightless vowel in the final syllable, it is not the final syllable that is accented but the second-to-last syllable. So the pattern "long vowel plus accented short vowel" is shifted one syllable to the left in **tyutʌhni·núheʔ** as compared with **ni·yót**. The long syllable in these kinds of examples tends to have a falling pitch, then the pitch rises on the accented syllable, and the pitch continues to rise so that the pitch peak occurs in the final syllable with the weightless vowel. We also described a pattern where the second-to-last syllable is accented (**yutátyats**). If the final syllable contains a weightless vowel, the accent is on the third-to-last syllable instead of the second-to-last; for example, **shakónhahseʔ** 'he hires her or them, the boss.' The pitch begins to rise on the accented syllable, and it continues to rise so that the pitch peak is realized on the syllable following the accented one.

Another phenomenon that bears on the accent pattern is that what was once pronounced at the end of a word as a sequence **CyVʔ**, where the **V** stands for any vowel and the **C** stands for any consonant, has come to be pronounced most of the time as **Ciʔ**. For example, **lotshanunihátyeʔ** 'he's going along happy' is now pronounced by almost everyone as **lotshanunihátiʔ**. Thus whereas at an earlier time the accented vowel was followed by two consonants, now the accented vowel is followed by only one consonant.

2.3 Utterance-Final Processes

Oneida is unique for the extent to which many (or most) final syllables of words that occur at the end of an *utterance* (see below) undergo some modification. The most pervasive modification is that a final syllable is devoiced or whispered; for some speakers no sound is emitted at all. The sounds that are devoiced are underlined.

There are a number of other modifications. For example, some words have a vowel **e** that is absent in the utterance-medial form. So compare **othé·tsli?** 'flour' with **othé·tshe<u>li?</u>**. The second-to-last syllable can be lengthened, as in **ʌti·lú** 'raccoon' (compare utterance-medial **ʌtilú**). If the utterance-medial form has a long accented vowel, as in **aknulhá·** 'my mother,' the final form ends in a breathy-sounding **h** and the vowel is short, thus **aknulháh**. Additional utterance-final changes are described in Michelson (1988).

At this point in our study of Oneida it is still unclear exactly what an utterance is. A single word spoken in isolation is an utterance on its own. At the other extreme, a string of sentences that in English would be considered a paragraph can be an utterance in the sense that it is only the last word in the string that has the utterance-final modification.

2.4 Use of Punctuation

Three punctuation symbols occur in the texts: a period (.), comma (,), and relatively infrequently a semicolon (;). The period is used after all utterance-final forms. It is also used occasionally after a word that does not have distinct utterance-final and utterance-medial forms but where, for other reasons, an utterance-final form would be expected. So, periods mark the ends of "utterances" regardless of how long the utterance is. A comma signals that the following phrase begins at a higher pitch as compared with the end of the phrase that has the comma after it. Commas usually, but by no means always, coincide with a pause. Most of the time, it was easy to decide whether or not a phrase should end in a comma, but in some cases it was not so easy and someone else listening to the stories might have used more or fewer commas. Finally, a semicolon is used relatively infrequently, when a speaker uses an utterance-medial form but manipulates loudness and rate of speech in a way that suggests a break that is more significant than one marked by a comma.

Of course, the best way to get a sense of the prosody, and all the sounds, of Oneida is to listen to the recordings. We recommend starting with the seven currently available at the first author's website at linguistics.buffalo.edu, and continue listening as more recording are made available in the coming year.

PART II: STORIES

Language

The stories in this first section all have to do with language. They come from two different eras. The first four stories are from a time when Oneidas spoke mostly Oneida and very little, if any, English. It was also a time when Oneidas did seasonal work—picking berries or cutting wood for example—and usually they were hired by white people, who of course spoke only English. These stories, then, are about what can happen when someone speaks only very little of someone else's language.

The last two stories are situated in the present time, when many Oneidas speak only English and those who are still fluent and teach the language are always trying to find ways to make learning the Oneida language more fun. *The Bean Game* describes one such strategy. *The Fat Cat* has a lot of repetition, which is intended to be helpful to the beginning student.

These stories include a lot of direct speech, and although this is not the same thing as a conversation between two (or more) people it does give an idea of what dialogue in Oneida is like. Even when there isn't direct speech the storytellers were speaking quite naturally and so they often use conversational expressions such as **o·ké·**, which is loosely equivalent to 'Oh my!' in English, or **yáts** 'Gee! Geez!' The stories often begin or end with a phrase that means 'it really happened that way.' Another frequent way of ending a story is with **thok ni·kú̱** or **tho kati? ok wí· ni·kú̱** 'that's all.'

A notable feature about the Oneida language is that there is not much borrowing of English vocabulary. But there is some. Borrowed English words are mostly nouns and they are treated in one of two ways. One way is to add to the English noun the NOMINALIZER, which has the forms **-hsl-**, **-sl-**, **-?tsl-**, or **-tsl-**. An example is **countertslá·ke** 'on the counter' from the story *Kastes Buys a Face*. In this case the LOCATIVE ending **á·ke** has been added to the nominalizer **-tsl-** (thus **counter-tsl-á·ke**). The other way that borrowed words are treated is to add the SEMI-REFLEXIVE element **-at-** to the beginning of the word—then additional elements such as a POSSESSIVE prefix (see section 3 in Part III) can be added before the **-at-**. An example of this is from the story *The Bean Game*; the word **akwatlighter** 'my lighter' has the possessive prefix **akw-** (thus **akw-at-lighter**).

Note that occasionally Mercy Doxtator recorded a story while I was not present. When this is the case the story is identified simply as *Told by Mercy Doxtator*.

A Man Tells Off His Boss

(Told by Mercy Doxtator to Karin Michelson on June 6, 1994)

(1) Ú·waʔ yá·yaʔk tshiskaha·wí· kʌ́· awʌ́hihteʔ, né· kaʔikʌ́ tsiʔ náhteʔ
    Now six when again it brings y'know strawberry, it's this that what

i·kélheʔ a·kka·látu, aknulhá· yukkalatuní kaʔikʌ́, né· wí· n
I want I would tell a story, my mother she has told me a story this, so it's

tshiwahu·níseʔ kʌ́·, né· kyuhte wí· kaʔikʌ́ aknulhá· onulhaʔkʌ́
a long time ago see, it's supposedly this my mother her late mother

tekyatahnútlahkweʔ né· teyutateshnyé·u tsiʔ nʌ né· tshiyakawʌheyú n
the two were sisters it's she has cared for her since then it's when she has died

aknulhá· onulhaʔkʌ́, ya·wét kwí· né· kwí· kaʔikʌ́ aksotkʌ́
my mother her late mother, it's like so it's this my late grandmother

tekyatahnútlahkweʔ, né· kwí· kaʔikʌ́ lónaʔ, kátshaʔ ok wí· nú·
the two were sisters, so it's this man and wife, somewhere

Ukwehuwé·ne nihninákleʔ kʌ́·, oʔsluní·taku kátshaʔ ok nú·
at the Native people's the two reside y'know, among the white man somewhere

nihoyo·té· kaʔikʌ́ lo·né· kʌ́·, né· s katiʔ wí· nʌ sá·laweʔ náleʔ
he is working this spouse see, well then it's when he got home then again

wahathlolyániʔ n tsiʔ niyo·lé· nihonaʔku·níheʔ kaʔikʌ́ n lónhah<u>se</u>ʔ.
he told all about it how far he makes him mad this he hires him.

(2) Tyótkut thok náhteʔ lolihwatshʌ́li kʌ́·, tsyoʔk nahté·shuʔ
    Constantly something he has found fault see, all different things

yah teʔtkaye·lí· tsiʔ nihatyél<u>ha</u>ʔ. (3) Né· s katiʔ wí· nʌ sá·laweʔ kháleʔ?
not it is not right what he is doing. Well then it's then he got back and

(1) Today is the sixth of June, the time of the strawberry, this story I want to tell, my mother told me this story, it was a long time ago, I guess it was my mother's late mother's sister, she cared for her [my mother] when my mother's late mother died, so like this was my late grandmother's sister, so she and her husband, they lived somewhere on the Reserve, her husband was working at some white people's somewhere, well then when he got home he would tell all about how much this guy who hired him was making him mad. (2) He was constantly finding fault with something, all these things that weren't right what he was doing. (3) So anyway then he would get home and

wa?shakohlolyáni? lo·né· kʌ́h, khále? kwí· onʌ́ wa?akono·lú·se? wa?í·lu?
he told her all about it spouse y'know, and then she tired of it she said

yakʌ?, "tutahetshatátyahse? s kwí· ne? kʌ́h, a·hetshlo·lí· tsi? yah
reportedly, "you should answer him back right, you should tell him that not

te?tisa?nikuhliyó tsi? náhte? yʌ́·nihe?." (4) Wahʌ́·lu? yakʌ? ka?ikʌ́
you are not content that what he belittles you." He said reportedly this

lokstʌ́ha, "tutakata·tí· nʌ ki? nʌ?ú·wa?." (5) Nʌ kwí· né· tú·ske?
old man, "I did answer back actually this time." So then it's truly

yakonehlakwʌ́·u ka?ikʌ́ n lo·né·, náhte? uhte né· onʌ́ a·hakwe·ní·
she is amazed this spouse, what possibly it's now he would be able

a·hʌ́·lu? n o?sluni?ké·ne yah se? tehahlúkha?. (6) Nʌ kwí· wa?í·lu?
he could say white man's way not too he doesn't speak. So then she said

yakʌ? thikʌ́ n akokstʌ́ha, "náhte? kati? wahsí·lu?, náhte? wahetshlo·lí·."
reportedly that old woman, "what well then you said, what you told him."

(7) "Wa?kí·lu? ki?, 'You German'." (8) Thok né· nikú thikʌ́
    "I said actually, 'You German'." That's only it's how much that

lonúhte? kʌ́·, nʌ wá·lelhe? nʌ kwí· né· tú·ske? wahohloli?kó· thok náhte?,
he knows see, then he thought so then it's truly he told him big something,

yah se? né· náhte? só·tsi? tehawʌ́ kʌ́h. (9) Tho kati? wí· ka?ikʌ́
not too it's anything too much he hasn't said y'know. Well that's this

niwakkaló·tʌ tsi? náhte? yukkalatuní aknulháh.
the kind of story I have that what she has told me a story my mother.

(10) Tho kati? ok wí· ni·kú.
     That's then only how much.

he would tell his wife all about it, and then she got tired of it, she said, "you should talk back to him, right? you should tell him that you are not happy that he keeps saying things to put you down." (4) The old man said, "I did answer back this time actually." (5) So then truly his wife was amazed, what could he possibly say in English, no way he could speak any [English]. (6) So then the old lady said, "Well what did you say? What did you tell him?" (7) "I said, 'You German'!" (8) That's all [the English] he knew, he thought then truly he told him off something big, [but] he didn't really say anything too much. (9) Well that's my story, the story my mother told me. (10) That's all then.

Berries and Bellies

(Told by Mercy Doxtator to Karin Michelson on June 21, 1994)

(1) Shekólih. (2) Ú·waʔ tekníhatut tewáshʌ úska tshískaleʔ   awʌ́hih<u>teʔ</u>.
Hello.   Now   Tuesday   twenty   one   it's that time again strawberry.

(3) Tsiʔ kwí· nikakaló·tʌ   kaʔikʌ́ i·kélheʔ a·kka·látu,   tshiwahu·níseʔ s wí·
What   kind of story it is this   I want   I would tell a story, a long time ago

lonuʔwéskwaniheʔ Ukwehuwé,   kwáh kwí· tsiʔ náhteʔ niyotyelʌ́ tho kwí·
they enjoy   Native people, just   that   what   it is doing there

wahotiyoʔtʌ́hsaʔ, né· katiʔ wí· kaʔikʌ́ teknukwé,   nʌ kyaleʔ wí· nyaʔkáheweʔ n
they went to work, well then it's this   two women,   so again   it came time

a·yuhyákhaʔ   kʌ́·, nʌ kwí· waʔkyahyákhaʔ   kiʔwáh,
one should go and pick berries see,   so then   the two went to pick berries indeed,

kátshaʔ ok nú· oʔsluní·ta<u>ku</u>.   (4) Né·n,   nʌ kwí· né· kaʔikʌ́ tú·skeʔ
somewhere   among the white man.   It's that, so then it's this   truly

kyahyákwas   nʌ   tho   yahá·laweʔ   shakónhahseʔ kʌ́·,
the two are picking berries then   there he got over there he hires them   see,

latkʌʔsé·neʔ   náhteʔ ni·yót tsiʔ yotiyo·té·   kʌ́h. (5) Wahʌ́·luʔ wí·
he's come to see what   how it is that they are working see.   He said

thikʌ́ laʔslu·ní·, "katkʌʔsé·neʔ," wahʌ́·luʔ, "náhteʔ ni·yót tsiʔ
that   white man, "I've come to see," he said,   "what   how it is that

tsyahyákwas,"   wahʌ́·luʔ kwí·, "I came to see your berries." (6) Nʌ kwí·
you two are picking berries," he said,   "I came to see your berries."   So then

né· kaʔikʌ́ tsyeyá·tat tsiʔ ka·yʌ́· yakoʔnikuhlayʌ·tá·seʔ n oʔsluniʔké·ne, waʔí·luʔ
it's this   she is one the one that she understands   white man's way, she said

(1) Hello. (2) Today is Tuesday, the twenty-first of June, the time of the strawberry. (3) This is the story I want to tell, a long time ago the Indians enjoyed going off to work at whatever was happening, well then there were these two ladies, and the time came again to go and pick berries, so then indeed the two went to pick berries somewhere around some white people. (4) So then they were really at it picking berries when the one who does the hiring [the boss] got there, he came to see how they were working. (5) So he said, that white man, "I've come to see," he said, "how it is with your berry picking," he said, "I came to see your berries." (6) So then this one lady, the one who understood some English, she said,

yakʌʔ   thikʌ́, tsyutathlo·líheʔ kwíʔ n onatʌ·ló·, "Yáts tehanahalawʌ́lyeheʔ thikʌ́
reportedly that,   again she is telling her   her friend, "Geez he is crazy   that

laʔslu·ní·, í·lelheʔ   né· a·hatkátho   tninikwʌʔté·<u>ne</u>."   (7) Né· uhte wí·   né·
white man, he wants it's   he would see your and my bellies."   It's   supposedly it's

wá·knelheʔ   wahʌ́·luʔ? "I wanna see your bellies." (8) Né· katiʔ wí· kaʔikʌ́,
the two thought he said   "I wanna see your bellies."   Well then it's   this,

tho kwíʔ niwakkaló·tʌ   kaʔikʌ́ wá·kelheʔ a·kwaka·látus.
so that's   the kind of story I have this   I thought   I would tell you all a story.

she's telling her friend, "Geez, that white man is crazy, he wants to see our bellies." (7) I
guess what they thought he said was "I want to see your bellies." (8) Well anyway that's the
story I have, that I thought I would tell you.

Why Berries Are Bellies in Oneida

(Told by Mercy Doxtator on August 20, 1998)

(1) Yah ní· teʔwakanúhteʔ nʌ   uhte   kʌ   kukalatú·se   kaʔikʌ́
     Not   me I don't know   now possibly question   I have told you a story   this

tsiʔ   núwaʔ   niswakkaló·tʌ.   (2) Né· kwí· né· kaʔikʌ́ tekniyáshe otikstʌ́ha,
what   this time   kind of story I have again.   So it's   it's   this   two   old ladies,

waʔkyahyákhaʔ   kátshaʔ ok wí· nú· oʔsluní·ta<u>ku</u>.   (3) Aggie Elijah
the two went to pick berries   somewhere   among the white man.   Aggie Elijah

kʌs   yutátyats   thikʌ́ tsyeyá·tat, kháleʔ thikʌ́ n onatʌ·ló·, né· s kwí· né·
customarily   is her name   that   she is one,   and   that   her friend,   so it's   it's

yah teʔské·yaleʔ   náhteʔ uhte   né· yutátyats.   (4) Nók tsiʔ
not   I don't remember anymore what   possibly it's   is her name.   But

kátshaʔ ok wí· nú· kaʔikʌ́ yekyahyákwas   awʌ́hih<u>teʔ</u>.
somewhere   this   over there the two are picking berries   strawberry.

(1) I don't know whether I already told you the story I have this time. (2) So these two old
ladies, they went to pick berries somewhere around some white people. (3) Aggie Elijah
was the name of one of them, and her friend, I don't remember anymore what her name was.
(4) But somewhere the two were off picking strawberries.

(5) Nʌ kwí· tú·ske? yotitsyakʌ́   ka?ikʌ́   kyahyákwas.   (6) Nʌ
     So then   truly   they excel at   this   the two are picking berries.   Then

yakʌ?   tho   wá·lawe?   thikʌ́   tsi? ka·yʌ́·   shakónhahse?   kʌ́·,   wahʌ́·lu?
reportedly there he got there   that   the one that   he hires them   y'know, he said

yakʌ?   thikʌ́   la?slu·ní·,   "I wanna see your berries."   (7) Nʌ kwí· né·n
reportedly   that   white man,   "I wanna see your berries."   So then   it's that

tahnú· ka?ikʌ́   otikstʌ́ha,   tsyeyá·tat   ok   uhte wí·   yuhlúkha?
and   this   old ladies,   she is one   only   supposedly   she knows a language

o?sluni?ké·ne,   nʌ kwí· wa?utathlo·lí· n   onatʌ·ló·,   wa?í·lu? yakʌ?   thikʌ́ n
white man's way,   so then   she told her   her friend,   she said   reportedly that

Aggie,   "Yáts   tehanahalawʌ́lyehe? thikʌ́   la?slu·ní·,   í·lelhe?   yakʌ?
Aggie,   "Geez   he is crazy   that   white man,   he wants   reportedly

a·hatkátho   tninikwʌ?té·<u>ne</u>."   (8) Tho   né· ni·yót   tsi? wa?ako?nikuhlayʌ·táne?
he would see   your and my bellies."   That's   it's   how it is   that   she understood it

tsi? í·lelhe?   se? kninikwʌ?té·ne nukwá· a·hatkátho   kʌ́h.   (9) Né· kyale?
that   he wants   too   their two bellies   where   he would see   y'know.   It's   again

né· thikʌ́   suknehla·kó·   tsi?   ni·yót   tsi?   wa?akothu·táne? thikʌ́ n   Aggieha.
it's   that   I was surprised   how   it is so   that   she heard it   that   Aggie dear.

(10) Né· s kwí· wá·kelhe?,   né· s kati? wí·   né·n   kwáh   tsi? nú· thikʌ́ n
      So it's   I thought,   well then it's   it's that   just   where   that

niyonathu·té· n 'r,' nʌ ki? ok né· 'l,' né· tho   utáyahte? tsi?   yah se? ní·
they hear it   'r,'   at once   it's 'l,'   it's there   it came in   because   not   too   us

te?twayʌtelí   aetwaná·tu?   'r's, wé·ne kwí· tsi? óksa?
you and we don't recognize   you and we would call   'r's, evidently   that   right away

(5) So then they were truly excelling at picking berries. (6) Then the one who does the hiring [the boss] got there, he said, that white man, "I wanna see your berries." (7) So then, and these old ladies, only one of them knew some English I guess, so then she told her friend, Aggie said, "Geez, that white man is crazy, he wants to see our bellies." (8) That's the way she understood it, that he wanted to see their bellies. (9) Then I was surprised at the way Aggie heard it. (10) So I thought, well whenever they hear 'r,' at once it's an 'l,' it comes in there because we don't recognize 'r's, so it must be that right away

né·   tho   ni·yót   tsi?   yonathu·té·   tsi?   '1.'   (11)   Né·   aolí·wa?   wá·knelhe? kwí·
it's   that's   how it is   that   they hear   as   '1.'   It's   the reason   the two thought

né·   wahʌ́·lu?   tho   la?slu·ní·,   "I wanna see your bellies."   (12)   Tho kwí·   né·
it's   he said   there   white man,   "I wanna see your bellies."   So that's   it's

ni·yót   tsi?   wa?oti?nikuhlayʌ·táne?.   (13)   Nók tsi?   tho   ki?
how it is   that   they understood it.   But   that's   actually

niwakkaló·tʌ   ka?i·kʌ́.   (14)   Nʌ kyale?   thok   nʌkúhake?
the kind of story I have   this.   Again   that's only   how much it will be

kwáh   nʌ?ú·wa?.
just   this time.

the way they heard it was as an '1.' (11) It's the reason why they thought it's that the white
man said, "I want to see your bellies." (12) That's the way they understood it. (13) But
that's the story I have. (14) That'll be all this time.

Kastes Buys a Face

(Told by Mercy Doxtator to Karin Michelson on July 8, 1994)

(1)   Shekólih.   (2)   Wá·kelhe?   a·kka·látu   ka?ikʌ́   wʌhnisla·té·,   ú·wa?   wí·
      Hello.   I thought   I would tell a story   this   a day exists,   now

núwa?   téklu?   tshiskaha·wí·   ohyótsheli?.   (3)   Né· kati? wí·   ka?ikʌ́   tsi?
this time   eight   when again it brings   string bean.   Well then it's   this   what

niwakkaló·tʌ   kʌ́·,   wahu·níse?   ka?ikʌ́   latiyʌtákwas   yakʌ?
kind of story I have   see,   a long time ago   this   they are cutting wood   reportedly

kátsha? ok nú·   lʌnukwé   kʌ́·,   né·   kati?   tsha?tutahonahtʌtyuháti?,
somewhere   men   see,   it's   well   as they are on the way home again,

(1) Hello. (2) I thought I would tell a story today, today is the eighth of July, the time of the
string bean. (3) Well then this is the story I have, a long time ago the men were cutting
wood somewhere, as they were on their way home again,

wahʌ·nélheʔ kwíˑ aʔéˑ kwíˑ tʌthati·táneʔ   thikʎ Talbotville, tho s
they thought   far away   they will stop there that   Talbotville,   there

thuteʔwahlahni·núheʔ kʎˑ,   wahʌ·nélheʔ kwíˑ thok náhteʔ tʌthatihni·nú·
they sell meat   y'know, they thought   something   there again they will buy it

tsiʔ niyo·léˑ nʌ   tʌthutu·kóhteʔ.   (4) Néˑ katiʔ wíˑ kaʔikʎ
until   then   again they will keep passing this way.   Well then it's   this

shayá·tat Kastes Bread kʌs   luwanaʔtúkhwaʔ kʎˑ, kháleʔ oyáˑ
he is one Kastes Bread customarily what they call him see, and   other

Tá·wet Sumas néˑ luwa·yátskweʔ, néˑ kwíˑ ló·sleʔ   kaʔikʎ Tá·wet nʌ   tho
Dave Summers it's was his name,   so it's   he is driving this   Dave   when   there

tshaʔtutahʌ·néweʔ,   nʌ   waʔtha·táneʔ kwíˑ n yahatáyahteʔ, kalóˑ tsiʔ niyo·léˑ
when they got back there, then he stopped   he went in,   before until

nʌ   tshihatitahkó·neʔ   kʎˑ, ókhnaʔ wahʎ·luʔ n Kastes, néˑ kwíˑ wahʎ·luʔ
when   when he is going to get out see, and then he said   Kastes, so it's   he said

thikʎ "utasknutsistahawíhtʌʔ   kóskos onu·tsí." (5) Wahʎ·luʔ, wahʎ·luʔ kiʔ wíˑ
that   "you should bring me a head pig head."   He said,   he said   actually

Tá·wet, "iséˑ kwíˑ neʔ kʎh yaʔsatáyaʔt kʎˑ, iséˑ shninú·na."   (6) Nʌ kwíˑ néˑ
Dave,   "you   okay   you go in   eh,   you   you go and buy it."   So then   it's

wahatitáhkoʔ n Kastes, í·neʔ kwíˑ   yahyatáyahteʔ. (7) Né·n   nʌ kwíˑ néˑ
he got out   Kastes, the two are walking the two went in.   It's that so then   it's

tshaháhsaneʔ   Tá·wet tsiʔ náhteʔ lahninúnyuheʔ,   nʌ   wahʎ·luʔ n Kastes,
when he finished Dave   that what   he is buying things, then   he said   Kastes,

"néˑ kiʔ   ní·" wahʎ·luʔ "tewakatuhutsyoní thikʎ kóskos onu·tsí." (8) Nʌ kwíˑ
"it's actually me" he said   "I want   that   pig head."   So then

they thought they would stop way over in Talbotville, they sold meat there, and they thought
they would buy something before they would keep passing this way. (4) Well this one fellow, Kastes Bread they used to call him, and the other one, Dave Summers was his name, so
Dave was the one driving when they got there, then he stopped and he went in, but before he
was about to get out, then Kastes said, he said "bring me a pig head." (5) He said, Dave
said, "okay you, you go in eh, you go and buy it." (6) So then Kastes got out, and the two of
them went walking in. (7) So then when Dave was done buying things, then Kastes said,
"me," he said, "I want that pig head." (8) So then

né· tho wahá·lʌʔ n latʌhni·núheʔ kʌ́·, nʌ kwí· wahahweʔnu·ní· kiʔwáh.
it's there he set it down he sells y'know, so then he wrapped it up right.

(9) Nʌ sahniya·kʌ́neʔ kʌ́·, yusahyatítaneʔ kʌ́·,
Then the two went out again y'know, over there the two got in again see,

nʌ uhte aleʔ wí· kaʔikʌ́ n Kastes tehoʔnikúlhaleʔ, só·tsiʔ wahonehla·kó·,
then supposedly again this Kastes it bothers him, too much he got surprised,

só·tsiʔ kano·lú· kaʔikʌ́ n kóskos onu·tsí. (10) Kwáh kʌʔ náheʔ nʌ
too much it is expensive this pig head. Just some while then

wahʌ́·luʔ, "Tá·wet," wahʌ́·luʔ, "a·kúnhaneʔ," wahʌ́·luʔ, "usahsyʌ·hná·
he said, "Dave," he said, "I would hire you," he said, "you should take it back

kaʔikʌ́, yah thaʔtewakatuhutsyoní, só·tsiʔ kano·lú·." (11) Nʌ kwí· né·n
this, not I don't want it, too much it is expensive." So then it's that

Tá·wet, wahʌ́·luʔ, "isé· kiʔ satsyʌ·ná." (12) "Kwah nók tsiʔ tho
Dave, he said, "you actually you take it back." "Just there

yʌséshlʌʔ, ʌhetshlo·lí· tsiʔ yah thaʔtesatuhutsyoní, só·tsi
you will set it over there again, you will tell him that not you don't want it, too much

kano·lú·." (13) Nʌ kyaleʔ wí· shotitahkwʌhátiʔ kaʔikʌ́ n Kastes,
it is expensive." So again he is getting back out this Kastes,

yusahatáyahteʔ kʌ́·, tahnú· tho kwí· íthlateʔ thikʌ́ n latʌhni·núheʔ kʌ́·,
he went in again see, and there he is standing there that he sells see,

tahnú· tho kwí· shaha·wí· kaʔikʌ́ n kóskos onutsí kʌ́·, ókhnaʔ
and there again he is carrying this pig head y'know, and then

kwáh seʔ wí· tho tusahlo·yʌ́hteʔ kʌ́· kaʔikʌ́ countertslá·ke n Kastes.
just too there he slammed with it y'know this on the counter Kastes.

the storekeeper set it down, and then he wrapped it up. (9) Then the two went out again, they got back in [the car], then I suppose it bothered Kastes, he was so surprised the pig head was so expensive. (10) It wasn't that long and then he said, "Dave," he said, "I'd like to get you to take it back, I don't want it, it's too expensive." (11) So then Dave said, "you, you take it back." (12) "All you do is set it down again over there, you tell him that you don't want it, it's too expensive." (13) So Kastes got back out, he went back in, and the storekeeper was standing there, and there he [Kastes] was carrying the pig head, and then Kastes just slammed it right down on the counter.

(14) Nʌ sok   wahʌ́·luʔ yakʌʔ   kaʔikʌ́ n,   wahʌ́·luʔ n Kastes,
     So then too he said   reportedly this,   he said   Kastes,

"I don't want this Goddamn face."   (15) Ne·né· wahʌ́·luʔ n Kastes, né· wí· tsiʔ yah
"I don't want this Goddamn face."   It's that he said   Kastes, because   not

tehahlúkhaʔ   kʌ́·, thok kwí· né· nikú   lonúhteʔ kʌ́·   tsiʔ náhteʔ
he doesn't know a language see,   that's only it's   how much he knows y'know that   what

wahʌ́·luʔ kʌ́·, yah kwí· thaʔtehotuhutsyoní n onutsí kʌ́h.   (16) Tahnú· kyaleʔ wí·
he said   see,   not   he doesn't want it   head   see.   And   so again

kaʔikʌ́ kwahotokʌ́·u tho   niyawʌ́·u   kaʔikʌ́ tshiwahu·níseʔ, né· s wí· tsiʔ yah
this   just for real   thus it has happened this   a long time ago,   because   not

tehuhlúkhaʔ   kʌ́·   Ukwehuwé,   tahnú· lʌ·nélheʔ tsyoʔk nahté·shuʔ
they don't know a language y'know Native people, and   they want   all different things

a·hatihninúni   kʌ́·, kwáh katiʔ wí· kwahotokʌ́·u tsiʔ tho   niyawʌ́·u
they would buy things see,   well then   just for real   that thus   it has happened

kaʔikʌ́ tsiʔ niwakkaló·tʌ.   (17) Tahnú· to·kʌ́skeʔ tho   nihotiyaʔtawʌ́·u.
this   what kind of story I have.   And   it's true   thus   it has happened to them.

(18) Tho   katiʔ   ok wí· niwakkaló·tʌ   kaʔikʌ́ nʌʔú·waʔ.
     That's anyway only   the kind of story I have this   this time.

(14) And he said, Kastes said, "I don't want this Goddamn face!" (15) That's what Kastes said, because he didn't know the language [English], that's all he knew, what he said, that he didn't want the head. (16) And it really happened that way a long time ago, because the Indians didn't speak [English], and they wanted to buy all these things, well anyway it really happened like in my story. (17) And it's true that happened to them. (18) That's my story this time.

The Bean Game

(Told by Norma Kennedy to Karin Michelson on July 16, 2008)

(1) Shekólih.   (2) Norma, Norma Kennedy ní· yúkyats   oʔsluniʔké·ne.
     Greetings.   Norma,   Norma Kennedy me   is my name white man's way.

(1) Greetings. (2) Norma, Norma Kennedy is my English name.

(3) Thiwé·sa?   yúkyats   Ukwehuwehnéha?.   (4) Ohkwalí   niwaki?taló·tʌ.
     She Wanders   is my name   Native people's way.   Bear   is my clan.

(5) Onʌyote?a·ká·   niwakuhutsyó·tʌ.   (6) I·kélhe?
     People of the Standing Stone   is my nation.   I want

a·kwaka·látus   ka?ikʌ   a?é·   tshyewakyo·té·   Otstʌhlonú·ke
I would tell you all a story   this   far away   when I am working over there   at United States

Onʌyote?a·ká·   tsi?   thatinákele?.   (7)   Tho kwí· nú·   thikʌ   yewakyó·tehkwe?
Oneida   at   they reside there.   That's where   that   I used to work over there

khelihunyʌ·níhe?   Onʌyote?a·ká·   a·hutwʌnu·táhkwe?.   (8)   Tsyóhslat
I am teaching them   Oneida   that they speak in a language.   One year

uhte i·kélhe?   tsi? náhe?   tho   yehe·ké·se?   thikʌ,   kwa?kʌnhé·ke   ki?   nú·
I think   while   there   I am over there   that,   summertime   actually   where

nikaha·wí·   ka?ikʌ   nʌ   wahuwatíkwahte?   ka?ikʌ   Kolahkowánhe
it comes time   this   then   they invited them   this   Canada

nithonenú   Onʌyote?a·ká·   utahatinatá·la?.   (9)   Yah   te?ské·yale?
they have come from   Oneida   they should come visit.   Not   I don't remember

oye·lí   tá·tkʌ   úksa yawʌ·lé·   nihatí   thikʌ   tho   yahʌ·néwe?
ten   or maybe   eleven   how many they are   that   there   they got over there

Onʌyote?a·ká·,   kʌh   Kolahkowánhe   yehonahtʌ́ti.   (10)   Nók tsi?
Oneida,   over here   Canada   they have left for there.   But

wa?tyakwátyeste?   ki?   ka?ikʌ,   ukyulha?tsíwa?   kwí·   ka?ikʌ,   oskánhe
we mixed together   actually   this,   all by ourselves   this,   together

wa?ukwata·tʌ́le?   swʌ·tát   tsi? náhe?.   (11)   Kwáh ki? otokʌ́·u   tsi? niwʌhnísles
we were left   one week   while.   Just for real   during the day

khále?   tsi? niwahsu·tés,   tho kwí· nú·   thikʌ   oskánhe   wa?ukwata·tʌ́le?.   (12)   Né·
and   during the night,   that's where   that   together   we were left.   It's

(5) I am of the Oneida nation. (6) I want to tell you this story about when I was working
way over in the United States where the Oneida live. (7) That's where I used to work teaching them to speak the Oneida language. (8) I think I was there one year, then come summer
they invited some Oneidas from Canada to come visit. (9) I don't remember, ten or maybe
eleven Oneidas went there, they left from over here in Canada. (10) But we mingled together, all by ourselves, we were left together for one whole week. (11) All during the day
and all during the night, we were together.

ka?ikʌ́   wʌhnisla·té·   wa?akwatnutólyahte?,   né·   kyuhte wí·   a·hsná·tuhkwe?
this   a day exists   we played,   it's   supposedly   you would call it

wa?akwatnutólyahte?,   wísk niwáshʌ   nikasahé·take   tayukhi·yú·   tsyukwé·tat.
we played,   fifty   beans amount to   they gave us   one person.

(13) Né·   thikʌ́   tá·t   o?slu·ní·   a·yakwatwʌnu·táhkwe?   nʌ ki? ok   nok ʌwa·tú·
      It's   that   if   white man   we would speak in a language   right then   it has to be

tsi? ka·yʌ́·   ʌyúttoke?   tsi?   o?slu·ní·   wa?akwatwʌnu·táhkwe?,   né·   ki?
the one that   one will notice   that   white man   we spoke in a language,   it's   actually

thikʌ́   nok ʌwa·tú·   ʌtyakhi·yú·   skasahé·tat.   (14) Né· wí·   yákwelhe?
that   it has to be   we will give someone   one bean.   It's   we want

kwáh kwí· nók   Onʌyote?a·ká·   kwí·   nikawʌnó·tʌ   a·yakwatwʌnu·táhkwe?.
just only   Oneida   kind of word   we would speak in a language.

(15) Nʌ kwí·   tayukhiyawíni?   ka?ikʌ́   osahé·ta?,   nʌ kwí·   tutáhsawʌ?   ka?ikʌ́
      So then   they distributed to us   this   bean,   so then   it started   this

wa?akwatnutólyahte?.   (16) Né·n   kwáh   kok náhe?   thok náhte?   wa?kí·lu?,
we played.   It's that   just   a little while   something   I said,

o?slu·ní·   wa?katwʌnu·táhkwe?,   nʌ ki? ok wí·   ukwa·tí·   skasahé·tat.   (17) Ókhale? n
white man   I spoke in a language,   so right then   I lost   one bean.   And

tsyeyá·tat   tho   yehe·yʌ́·se?,   Marlene   yutátyats,   né·   thikʌ́   tsi? nikú
one person   there   she is over there,   Marlene   is her name,   it's   that   how much

wa?kheste·líste?,   kok né· náhe?   ókhna?   né·   yahútsha?ahte?   tsi? nikú   yako·yʌ́·
I laughed at her,   a little while   and then   it's   it got used up   how much   she has

osahé·ta?.   (18) Né·   thikʌ́   wa?khekahkʌ·ní·,   wa?í·lu?,   "kátsha?   né·n
bean.   It's   that   I caught her at it,   she said,   "where   it's that

(12) This one day we played [a game], I suppose you would call it 'we played,' they gave each of us fifty beans. (13) If we spoke in English then right away it had to be the one who would notice that we spoke in English, we had to give that person one bean. (14) We wanted to speak nothing but the Oneida language. (15) So then they handed out the beans, and then our game got started. (16) In just a little while I said something, I spoke in English, so right away I lost one bean. (17) And one person who was over there, Marlene is her name, did I ever laugh at her, in a little while all the beans she had got used up. (18) I caught her, she said "where is

akwatlighter."   (19)   Nʌ kiʔ ok wíˑ   néˑ   waʔkhesteˑlísteʔ,   waʔkíˑluʔ   "Marlene,
my lighter."   So right then   it's   I laughed at her,   I said   "Marlene,

takú   skasahéˑtat."   (20)   Nʌ kiʔ ok wíˑ   néˑ   waʔíˑluʔ,   "oˑkéˑ,"   waʔíˑluʔ,
give me   one bean."   So right then   it's   she said,   "golly,"   she said,

"yah   kiʔ   níˑ   shekú   oyáˑ   náhteʔ   thusakíˑluʔ."   (21)   Nók wíˑ tsiʔ
"not   actually   me   even   another   anything   I won't say again."   But

yah   Ukwehuwé   teʔyakotwʌnutáhkwʌ.   (22)   Waʔíˑluʔ   néˑ,   "oˑkéˑ,
not   Native people   she didn't speak in a language.   She said   it's,   "golly,

I'm not going to say anything in English anymore."   (23)   Nʌ kiʔ ok wíˑ   néˑ   kwáh
I'm not going to say anything in English anymore."   So right then   it's   just

kok náheʔ   sʌ́haʔ   eˑsóˑ   waʔakosaheʔtuˑtíˑ.   (24)   Kʌʔ kiʔ ok   néˑ   náheʔ   thikʌ́
a little while   more   lots   she lost beans.   Only a little   it's   a while   that

yahútshaʔahteʔ   tsiʔ nikú   yakosahéˑtayʌʔ,   néˑ tsiʔ   kok náheʔ   kháleʔ   oʔsluˑníˑ
it got used up   how much   she has beans,   because   a little while   and   white man

teyakoyéstu   thikʌ́   Ukwehuwé   yakotwʌnutáhkwʌ.   (25)   Néˑ   kiʔ
she has mixed in   that   Native people   she is speaking in a language.   It's   actually

néˑ   tsiʔ nikú   waʔshakotisteˑlísteʔ   tsiʔ   yah   thaˑyekweˑníˑ   Onʌyoteʔaˑkáˑ
it's   how much   they laughed at her   because   not   she won't be able   Oneida

ok   aˑyutwʌnuˑtáhkweʔ.   (26)   Tahnúˑ   toˑkʌ́skeʔ   thikʌ́   wʌtoˑléˑ   seʔ wíˑ
only   that she speaks in a language.   And   truly   that   it is hard   too

utaskuˑtáhkweʔ   thikʌ́   Onʌyoteʔaˑkáˑ   ok   aˑhsatwʌnuˑtáhkweʔ,   néˑ tsiʔ   néˑ
for you to persist   that   Oneida   only   that you speak in a language,   because   it's

níˑ   sʌ́haʔ   yukwalʌʔnháˑu   thikʌ́ n   oʔsluniʔkéhaʔ wíˑ   taetwayéstaniʔ   tsiʔ
us   more   we know how   that   white man's way   that you and we mix in   as

'akwatlighter' [my lighter]?" (19) So right away I laughed at her, I said "Marlene, give me one bean." (20) So right away she said "golly," she said, "I'm not even going to say anything anymore." (21) But she wasn't speaking in Indian. (22) What she said was, "golly, I'm not going to say anything in English anymore." (23) So then in just a little while she lost more beans. (24) In a little while all her beans were gone, because in a little while she was mixing in English as she was speaking Indian. (25) They laughed at her a lot because she couldn't speak Oneida only. (26) And it's really hard to persist in speaking Oneida only, because we are more used to mixing in English as

yukwáthale?. (27) Né· ki? nʌ kwáh tho ni·yót ka?ikʌ́ wʌhnisla·té·
we are talking. It's actually then just that's how it is this a day exists

shekú tsi? ka·yʌ́· luhlúkhahse?, a·kí·lu? kwí· lotikstʌhokúha, né· s ní·
still the one that they are fluent, I'd say old people, it's me

wakahkwíshlu? ya?khewʌ·nálane? Ukwehuwé kwí· wakatwʌnutáhkwʌ.
I make an effort I spoke to them Native people I am speaking in a language.

(28) Né·n o?sluni?kéha? né· tayuklihwa?slákwahse?. (29) Wʌto·lé· ki?
It's that white man's way it's they answered me. It is hard actually

thikʌ́ tsi? tyótkut nók ní· yukwathu·té· o?slu·ní· lotitha·lé·,
that because always only us we hear white man they are talking,

o?sluni?kéha? lútsta? tsi? lotitha·lé·. (30) Nók tsi? wa?akwatu?wéskwahte?
white man's way they use it as they talk. But we had fun

ki? tsi? náhe? tho yehotinatahlenʌ́, kwáh kwí· tsyo?k náhte?
actually while there they are visiting over there, all kinds of things

na?tetyukwatyelʌ́ né· wí· a·yakwatu?wéskwahte? ki?wáh. (31) Nók tsi? né·
we have done it's that we have fun indeed. But it's

ki? ní· tuku?wéskwʌ? thikʌ́ n osahé·ta? wa?akwatnutólyahte?. (32) Tákʌ?
actually me I enjoyed that bean we played. So as not

o?slu·ní· wí· a·hsatwʌnu·táhkwe?. (33) Kwáh ki? otokʌ́·u tsi?
white man you should speak in a language. Just for real that

ya?weskwa?tú·ne? ne? thó·ne?. (34) Kwáh ya?tewʌhnislaké oyá· núwa?
it was fun at that time. Quite every day another this time

náhte? nitsyukwatye·lʌ́. (35) Ya?weskwa?tú·ne? ki? thikʌ́ ne? thó·ne?.
what we have done it again. It was fun actually that at that time.

we talk. (27) That's how it is today with those who are still fluent, the older people I'd say, I make an effort when I talk to them to speak in Indian. (28) They answer me in English. (29) It's hard because we always only hear them talking English, they use English when they talk. (30) But we had fun while they were visiting over there, we were doing all kinds of things so that we could have fun. (31) But I enjoyed playing that bean [game]. (32) So as not to speak English. (33) It was really fun at that time. (34) Every single day we did something different. (35) It was fun at the time.

(36) Né· kyuhte wí· tho   nikaka·lés   ka?ikʌ́ wá·kelhe? a·kwahlo·lí·.
      It's   supposedly that's how long the story is this   I wanted   I would tell you all.

(37) Thok   ni·kú.
      That's   how much.

(36) I guess that's how long the story is that I wanted to tell you. (37) That's it!

The Fat Cat

(Told by Norma Kennedy to Karin Michelson on July 6, 2007)

(1) Né· ka?ikʌ́ i·kélhe? a·kuka·látuhse?   lólehsʌ? takó·s kuwa·yáts. (2) Úska
     It's   this   I want   I would tell you a story he is fat   cat   is its name.   One

útlatste? ka?ikʌ́ akokstʌ́ha ohnekákli? wa?utu·ní·. (3) Tsi? náhe? yutu·níhe?
time   this   old woman   soup   she made.   While   she is making

ka?ikʌ́ ohnekákli? nʌ   sayakehyá·lane? tsi? yah thya·ya·wʌ́· tsi? kanatá·ke
this   soup   then   she remembered   that   it has to be   that   town

yʌhʌ·yʌ́.   (4) Nʌ kwí· wahuwali?wanu·tú·se? takó·s, wa?í·lu?, "takó·s
over there she will go.   So then   she asked him   cat,   she said,   "cat

ʌhsathu·táte?   kʌ   ʌhsatʌ?nikú·lalʌ? ka?ikʌ́ ohnekákli?, yah thya·ya·wʌ́· tsi?
you will consent   question   you will look after   this   soup,   it has to be   that

kanatá·ke yʌhʌ·ké·."   (5) Wahʌ́·lu? takó·s, "tó·   né· na·katshanu·ní·."
town   over there I will go."   He said   cat,   "how   it's   I would become joyful."

(6) Nʌ kwí· wa?uhtʌ·tí·, kanatá·ke nyahá·yʌ?   ka?ikʌ́ akokstʌ·ha.
     So then   she left,   town   over there she went this   old woman.

(1) I want to tell you a story called the fat cat. (2) Once upon a time this old woman made some soup. (3) While she was making the soup she remembered that she had to go to town. (4) So then she asked the cat, she said, "cat, would you agree to look after the soup? I have to go to town." (5) The cat said, "oh, joy!" (6) So then she left, the old woman went to town.

(7) Né·n   tsi? náhe? yakohtʌ́ti,   nʌ   né· wahatuhkályahke? ka?ikʌ́ takó·s.
     So it's while   she has gone away,   then it's he got hungry   this   cat.

(8) Nʌ sok wí· wá·lake?   ohnekákeli?.   (9) Tho   né· nihatuhkálya?ks thikʌ́ n
     So then too he ate   soup.   That's it's how hungry he is   that

takó·s, wahatekhwísane? ohnekákli?, shekú n kaná·tsi? wá·lake?.   (10) Nʌ
cat,   he finished the food soup,   even   kettle   he ate.   When

tshahóhtane?   nʌ   wá·lelhe? tʌhatawʌlyéhsa?   ki?wáh.   (11) Nʌ kwí·
when he ate his fill   then   he thought   he will go for a stroll right.   So then

wa?thatawʌlyéhsa? ka?ikʌ́ takó·s.   (12) Tho   wa?thyátlane? yeksáh.   (13) Wa?í·lu?
he went for a stroll   this   cat.   There   the two met   girl.   She said

yeksá·, "takó·s, náhte? íhseks, só·tsi?   sálehsʌ?."   (14) Wahʌ́·lu? takó·s,
girl,   "cat,   what   you eat,   too much you are fat."   He said   cat,

"ohnekákli? wakatekhwísu?,   shekú n kaná·tsi? wake·kú."   (15) "Isé· ki?
"soup   I have eaten it up,   even   kettle   I have eaten."   "You   actually

núwa?   ʌsku?wá·lake?."   (16) Nʌ sok wí· wa?shako?wá·lake?.   (17) Nʌ kyale? wí·
this time I will devour you."   So then too   he devoured her.   So again

wahatu·kóhte? ka?ikʌ́ takó·s, tehotawʌlyeháti?.   (18) Nʌ   tho   wa?thyátlane?
he went on   this   cat,   he is strolling along.   Then   there   the two met

laksáh.   (19) Wahʌ́·lu? thikʌ́ laksá·, "takó·s, náhte? íhseks, só·tsi?   sálehsʌ?."
boy.   He said   that   boy,   "cat,   what   you eat,   too much you are fat."

(20) Wahʌ́·lu? takó·s, "ohnekákli? wakatekhwísu?,   shekú n kaná·tsi? wake·kú,
      He said   cat,   "soup   I have eaten it up,   even   kettle   I have eaten,

yeksá· khe?wahla·kú,   isé· ki?   núwa?   ʌsku?wá·lake?."
girl   I have devoured her, you   actually   this time   again I will devour you."

(7) So while she was gone, the cat got hungry. (8) So then he ate the soup. (9) The cat was
that hungry he finished the soup, he even ate the kettle. (10) When he was done eating he
thought he would go for a walk. (11) So then the cat went for a walk. (12) There he met up
with a little girl. (13) The little girl said, "cat, what do you eat, you're so fat." (14) The cat
said, "I finished the soup, I even ate the kettle." (15) "And now, I'm going to eat you."
(16) And so then he ate her. (17) So again the cat went on, he's strolling along. (18) Then
he met a little boy. (19) The boy said, "cat, what do you eat, you're so fat." (20) The cat
said, "I finished the soup, I even ate the kettle, I ate the little girl, and now I'm going to eat
you next."

(21) Nʌ sok wíꞏ waho?wáꞏlake?.   (22) Wahóhtane? kwíꞏ ka?ikʌ́ takóꞏs,
      So then too he devoured him.   He ate his fill   this   cat,

nʌ kyale? wíꞏ wahatuꞏkóhte?.   (23) Kwáh kʌ? náhe? latsihʌ́statsi? núwa?
so again   he went on.   Just   a little while preacher   this time

tusahyátlane?.   (24) Wahʌ́ꞏlu? latsihʌ́statsi?, "takóꞏs, náhte? íhseks, sóꞏtsi?
again the two met.   He said   preacher,   "cat,   what   you eat, too much

sálehsʌ?."   (25) Wahʌ́ꞏlu? takóꞏs, "ohnekákli? wakatekhwísu?,   shekú n kanáꞏtsi?
you are fat."   He said   cat,   "soup   I have eaten it up, even   kettle

wakeꞏkú,   yeksáꞏ khe?wahlaꞏkú,   khále? laksáꞏ li?wahlaꞏkú,   iséꞏ ki?
I have eaten, girl   I have devoured her, and   boy   I have devoured him, you actually

núwa?   ʌsku?wáꞏlake?."   (26) Nʌ sok wíꞏ waho?wáꞏlake? ka?ikʌ́ latsihʌ́statsi?.
this time   again I will devour you."   So then too he devoured him this   preacher.

(27) Nʌ kyale? wíꞏ wahatuꞏkóhte?, yakukwé yeya?taséha   núwa?
      So again   he went on,   woman   pretty young girl this time

tusahyátlane?.   (28) Wa?íꞏlu? ka?ikʌ́ yeya?taséha,   "takóꞏs, náhte? íhseks,
again the two met.   She said,   this   pretty young girl, "cat,   what   you eat,

sóꞏtsi?   sálehsʌ?."   (29) Wahʌ́ꞏlu? takóꞏs, "ohnekákli? wakatekhwísu?, shekú n
too much   you are fat."   He said   cat,   "soup   I have eaten it up, even

kanáꞏtsi? wakeꞏkú,   yeksáꞏ khe?wahlaꞏkú,   khále? laksáꞏ li?wahlaꞏkú,
kettle   I have eaten, girl   I have devoured her, and   boy   I have devoured him,

khále? latsihʌ́statsi? sʌ́ꞏ li?wahlaꞏkú,   iséꞏ ki?   núwa?
and   preacher   also I have devoured him, you actually this time

ʌsku?wáꞏlake?."   (30) Nʌ sok wíꞏ wa?shako?wáꞏlake? ka?ikʌ́ yeya?taséha.
again I will devour you."   So then too he devoured her   this   pretty young girl.

(21) And so then he ate him. (22) The cat got done eating, and again he went on. (23) In a
little while he met up with a preacher next. (24) The preacher said, "cat, what do you eat,
you're so fat." (25) The cat said, "I finished the soup, I even ate the kettle, I ate the little
girl, and I ate the little boy, now I'm going to eat you." (26) And so then he ate the
preacher. (27) So he went on again, and he met this pretty young girl. (28) The pretty girl
said, "cat, what do you eat, you're so fat." (29) The cat said, "I finished the soup, I even ate
the kettle, I ate the little girl, and I ate the little boy, and I ate the preacher, and now I'm going to eat you next." (30) And so then he ate the pretty girl.

(31) Wahóhtane?, nʌ kyale? wí· wahatu·kóhte?. (32) Kwáh kok niyo·lé·
He ate his fill, so again he went on. Just a little ways

nyehawenú, layʌtákwas núwa? tusahyátlane?. (33) Wahʌ́·lu? ka?ikʌ́
he has gone on, he cuts wood this time again the two met. He said this

layʌtákwas, "takó·s, náhte? íhseks, só·tsi? sálehsʌ?." (34) Wahʌ́·lu? takó·s,
he cuts wood, "cat, what you eat, too much you are fat." He said cat,

"ohnekákli? wakatekhwísu?, shekú n kaná·tsi? wake·kú, yeksá·
"soup I have eaten it up, even kettle I have eaten, girl

khe?wahla·kú, khále? laksá· li?wahla·kú, khále? latsihʌ́statsi?
I have devoured her, and boy I have devoured him, and preacher

li?wahla·kú, khále? yeya?taséha khe?wahla·kú, isé· ki? núwa?
I have devoured him, and pretty young girl I have devoured her, you actually this time

ʌsku?wá·lake?." (35) Nʌ sok wí· ka?ikʌ́ layʌtákwas wahʌ́·lu?, "yah wí· né·
again I will devour you." So then too this he cuts wood he said, "not it's

tha·kathu·táte? a·ske?wá·lake?." (36) Nʌ sok wí· laoto·kʌ́· wá·latste? tahá·sʌhte?,
I won't allow that you devour me." So then too his axe he used it he lowered it,

kwáh lanikwʌ?té·ne nú· ka?ikʌ́ takó·s naho?áshʌ?. (37) Nʌ sok wí· né· tho
just his belly where this cat he stabbed him. So then too it's there

sahatiya·kʌ́ne? tsi? nihatí shako?wahlakú, thikʌ́ latsihʌ́statsi? khále?
they went out again how many they are he has devoured them, that preacher and

yeya?taséha khále? laksá· khále? yeksá· khále? ohnekákeli?, shekú n kaná·tsi?,
pretty young girl and boy and girl and soup, even kettle,

akwekú tho sahotiké·tohte?. (38) Thok ni·kú.
all there they appeared again. That's only how much.

(31) He got done eating and he went on again. (32) He hadn't gone too far when he met up
with a woodcutter. (33) The woodcutter said, "cat, what do you eat, you're so fat."
(34) The cat said, "I finished the soup, I even ate the kettle,I ate the little girl, and I ate the
little boy, and I ate the preacher, and I ate the pretty young girl, and now I'm going to eat
you." (35) And so then this woodcutter said, "I'm not going to let you eat me." (36) So
then he used his axe, he lowered it, he just stabbed the cat in his belly. (37) And then all
those he had eaten came out, the preacher and the pretty girl and the little boy and the little
girl and the soup, even the kettle, all of them appeared again. (38) That's all.

Lessons

While some stories are intended to make us laugh, like some of the stories in the section on language, others are supposed to teach a lesson; they "have a moral." Sometimes the lesson is delivered in the context of how something has come to have particular characteristics; this is the case with Ruben Cutcut's story about the bat, Mercy Doxtator's story about dogs, and Norma Kennedy's stories about a species of bird and the bark of the birch tree. In other stories, like *The Flirt* told by Georgina Nicholas, *Some Woodcutters Get a Visitor* told by Mercy Doxtator, and *A Jealous Husband* told by Ray George, it takes an unusual (and frightening) encounter or experience to change people's ways.

A slightly different Oneida version of the story titled *The Bird* may be found on Clifford Abbott's Oneida Language website (www.uwgb.edu/Oneida/Texts. html), and a Seneca version was told by Lena Snow to Wallace Chafe (Chafe and Snow [1980]). In the three versions, the species of bird is different. In Snow and Chafe, it is suggested that the bird is a chickadee. The title on the Oneida Language website is *Whippoorwill*. In the version that Norma Kennedy tells, the bird asks a question that mimics the bird's song. Norma couldn't think of the name of the bird but she recalls hearing it a lot. From the way she says (or sings) the bird's song **nʌ kʌ yolí**, it sounds like it could be a red-winged blackbird.

These stories, like most of the stories in this volume, include a lot of direct speech, and this is often introduced by either **wahʌ́·luʔ** 'he said' or **waʔí·luʔ** 'she said.' **Waʔí·luʔ** is actually a shortened form of **waʔyaí·luʔ**, but since everyone pronounces this form consistently as **waʔí·luʔ**, this is the form we write.

A traditional story opening is the word **Ihéh**, and this is the way that Ruben Cutcut and Mildred Cutcut begin their stories.

The Flirt

(Told by Georgina Nicholas in Spring, 1980)

(1) Oyá·   né· yakʌʔ   né·n   kʌʔ nithotiyʌ́·saʔ, tsiʔ tyutʌhni·núheʔ kaʔikʌ́
     Another it's it is said it's that young men,   at   there one sells   this

tho   latikʌ́nyate̲ʔ.   (2) Tehotitha·lú·   kiʔwáh.   (3) Né· kwí·
there they are standing around.   They are conversing right.   So it's

shakonathlolí   laotiyaʔtaseʔtsliʔo·kú·, úhkaʔ katiʔ   sʌ́haʔ
they are telling about them all their girlfriends,   who   anyway more

thoyaʔtaseʔtsli·y o̲.   (4) Shayá·tat kaʔikʌ́ kʌʔ nithoyʌ́ha, yah kwí· teʔwé·ni
his girlfriend is the best.   He is one   this   young man,   it's amazing

nihatatnikʌ́htele̲ʔ.   (5) Nʌ   oniʔ né· tahatáhsawʌ̲ʔ. (6) Tsiʔ kwí·
how he thinks himself handsome.   Then too   it's he started.   How

né· nihoyaʔtaseʔtslaká·teʔ, ati   né· úhkaʔ   á·neʔ   kih.
it's he has many girlfriends, no matter it's anyone the two would go actually.

(7) Swatyelʌ́ s oniʔ yakʌʔ   tóhkaʔ nahatyaʔtaseʔtslate·ní· tsiʔ niwahsu·tés.
     Sometimes even they say a few   he changed girlfriends   through the night.

(8) Tho kwí· nihuwanú·wehseʔ kaʔikʌ́ kunu·kwé̲. (9) Tsiʔ katiʔ náheʔ?
     That's   how they like him   this   women.   Well then while

tho   latikʌ́nyateʔ   tehotíthaleʔ   thikʌ́ nʌ   washakoti·kʌ́·
there they are standing around they are talking that   then   they saw her

tayakothahitákheʔ   kaʔikʌ́ kʌʔ nityakoyʌ́ha. (10) Yah teʔwé·ni
she is coming down the road   this   young woman.   It's amazing

niyakotyaʔtahslu·ní̲.   (11) Kwahikʌ́ teyostaláth eʔ teyakohtáli̲ʔ.
how she is dressed up.   Just really it is shiny   she has on shoes.

(1) Another one [story] is these young people, they were standing around at the store.
(2) They were talking, right. (3) They were talking about their girlfriends, who has the nic-
est-looking girlfriend. (4) This one young fellow, he thought he was so handsome. (5) And
then he got started. (6) He had so many girlfriends, he would go out with just anybody.
(7) Sometimes even, it is said, he would have a few different girlfriends through the night.
(8) That's how much these women liked him. (9) While they were standing around talking,
they saw this young girl coming down the road. (10) It was amazing how dressed up she
was. (11) She had on really shiny shoes.

(12) Katsistohkwiyó   yakota?kóhsute?.   (13) Wahsohkwiyó   ka?nhehsatʌ́sha
      It is nicely dotted   she has on a skirt.   It is a nice colour   taffeta or silk

yakotyá·tute?.   (14) A?é· kwí· na?teyota·lá·   yakona?alo·lú.
she has on a blouse.   Great   is the size of the brim   she has on a hat.

(15) Yah kwí· thau·tú· a·shakoti·kʌ́·   niyeya?tó·tʌ.   (16) A?é· kwí·
      It can't be   that they see her   how she looks.   Great

niyakonuhkwísles, kwáh teyakonuhklíkhu?.   (17) Nʌ kyale? wí· ka?ikʌ́
her hair is long,   quite her hair is curly.   So again   this

kʌ? nithoyʌ́ha, wahʌ́·lu?, "nʌ kyale? wí· oyá·   sakatya?tase?tslo·lʌ́ne?."
young man,   he said,   "so again   another again I found a girlfriend."

(18) Wahʌ́·lu? "swatló·lok."   (19) Kwáh se? sahateyʌ?túni? tsi? lotsluní,
      He said   "you all watch."   Just   too he arranged   at   he is dressed,

tusahatnathálho?   thikʌ́; nʌ   kwáh ákta?   i·yʌ́·   thikʌ́, nʌ
again he combed his hair that;   then just   close by she is walking that,   then

tho kwí· yahata·tí.   (20) Yah kwí· thutayutkátho?   thikʌ́, yakotukohtuháti?.
there   he spoke up.   Not   she won't look there   that,   she keeps going by.

(21) Nʌ kwí· washakóhsle? thikʌ́, tho kwí· lothaláti?,
      So then   he chased her   that,   there   he is going along speaking,

shako?tehslu·níhe?.   (22) Yah kwí· thikʌ́ thutayutkátho?,   kwáh ok onʌ́
he is flirting with her.   Not   that   she won't look there,   just the same

yakothahitákhe?.   (23) Khále? kʌs   nʌ   né· lonehlákwas   ka?ikʌ́
she is going down the road.   And   usually then   it's   he is surprised this

tsi? yah thau·tú· utahuwalihwáshnyehse?.   (24) Tho kwí· thikʌ́ shakohnutláti?,
that   it can't be   that she would encourage him.   There   that   he is following her,

(12) The skirt she had on was a nice calico print. (13) She had on a taffeta blouse that was a
pretty colour. (14) And she was wearing a hat with a really broad brim. (15) [But] they
couldn't see what she looked like. (16) She had long hair, and it was quite curly. (17) So
again this young fellow said, "I found another girlfriend." (18) He said "you watch."
(19) He fixed his clothes, he combed his hair; then just as she was walking close by, then he
spoke up. (20) She would not look his way, she kept right on going. (21) So then he chased
after her, he went along talking, flirting with her. (22) She wouldn't look his way, she kept
on going down the road just the same. (23) And then he was surprised that it couldn't be
that she was willing and encouraging him. (24) He kept following her,

nʌ kwí· wahonúhtuhkeʔ   kaʔikʌ́ utayutkáthoʔ,   nʌ sók   yahatyaʔtu·tí·,
so then   he became impatient this   for her to look there,   then too he reached out,

yashakoye·ná·   thikʌ́, kwáh tahatá·layʌʔ,   yahatkáthoʔ kwí· tsiʔ
he grabbed hold of her that,   just   he set his sight, he looked that way what

niyeyaʔtó·tʌ.   (25) Óstyʌʔ ok   né· yekúksne.   (26) Yéskʌn nʌʔ né·.
she looks like.   Bones   only it's her face.   Skeleton that one.

(27) Tho   nahayaʔtakʌ́heyeʔ   kaʔikʌ́, yah tha·hakwe·ní· usahatolyá·nluʔ,
      That's how weak he became this,   not   he is not able   that he moves again,

yah oniʔ tha·hakwe·ní· a·hata·tí·,   tho kwí· í·lateʔ   thikʌ́ waʔutu·kóhteʔ.
not even he is not able   that he speaks, there   he is standing that   she passed by.

(28) Nʌ   né· kʌʔ nukwá· kaʔikʌ́ thatikʌ́nyateʔ   kʌʔ nithotiyʌ́·saʔ,
      Then   it's right there this   they are standing around young men,

nʌ   tú·skeʔ wahotilihwi·yó·seʔ, nʌ sók   wahatiste·lísteʔ.   (29) Tho   kʌs kwí·
then   truly   they were amused,   then too they laughed.   There   habitually

thatistelístaʔ   kaʔikʌ́, nʌ   luwastelístaʔ kwí·   tsiʔ   nʌ   utetshʌ·lí·
they are laughing   this,   then they are laughing at him because then it was found

úhkaʔ ok wahuwatluhyá·tahkweʔ.   (30) Kwahotokʌ́·u oskanʌ́ha u·tú·
someone someone repelled him.   Just for real   slowly   it could be

sahatolyá·nluʔ, tho kwí· nyusá·leʔ   tsiʔ thatikʌ́nyateʔ,
he moved again, there   he went back over there at   they are standing around,

yah kiʔ   tha·hakwe·ní· a·hathlo·lí·   nahoyá·tawʌʔ,   yah tha·hakwe·ní·
not actually he is not able   that he tells about what happened to him, not   he is not able

shekú usahata·tí·.   (31) Neʔ thó·neʔ katiʔ   né· tetyotá·u   kaʔikʌ́
still   that he speaks again.   At that time so then it's   there it stopped this

so then he became impatient for her to look his way, so then he reached out, he grabbed hold
of her, he really looked closely, he looked to see what she looked like. (25) Her face was
only bones. (26) She was a skeleton. (27) He became so weak, he wasn't able to move, he
couldn't even speak, he was standing there [as] she passed by. (28) The young fellows
standing around right there, they were really amused, and then they started to laugh.
(29) They were laughing there, they were laughing at him because then it was found someone that repelled him. (30) Ever so slowly he could move again, he went back over to where
they were standing around, but he wasn't able to tell them what happened to him, he still
couldn't speak. (31) It was at that time then

tsi? nahana·yé·   ka?ikʌ́ kʌ? nithoyʌ́<u>ha</u>.
that   how he is cocky   this   young man.

this young fellow stopped being so cocky.

Why the Bat Travels at Night

(Told by Ruben Cutcut to Mercy Doxtator in Summer, 1982)

(1) Ihéh.   (2) Né· wí· ka?ikʌ́ tsi?   nikakaló·tʌ   yotlátstu   yakʌ?
     Hark.   So it's   this   what   kind of story it is   there was a time   reportedly

wahutli·yó· tsi? ka·yʌ́·   lotistó·slote?   khále? kályo?   nahatiya?tó·tʌ<u>?</u>.
they fought   the one that   they have feathers   and   wild animals   they are that kind.

(3) Nʌ kwí· tho s yakʌ?   kwa?nyóh wahutkwe·ní· tsi? ka·yʌ́·   tehati·tʌ́he?;
     So then   there reportedly   seems   they won   the one that   they fly;

nʌ   ka?ikʌ́ tsi?kla?wístal, nʌ   a?é· nukwá·   nahahkwata·sé·, tho nukwá·
then   this   bat,   now   way over there   he went around,   that's where

sahatyá·talʌ?,   sashakotya?tálhahse? tsi? nukwá· lonatkwenyuháti<u>?</u>. (4) Kwáh
again he joined in,   again he joined them   where   they are winning.   Just

kʌ? náhe? nʌ   sahuwʌnáktahte?,   nʌ   sahuwatikwe·ní·   ka?ikʌ́
some while   then   they pushed them back,   then   again they bested them   this

kályo?,   né· kwa?nyóh nʌ   né· sahutkwe·<u>ní·</u>. (5) Nʌ sók ale?   ka?ikʌ́
wild animals,   it's   seems   then   it's   again they won.   Then again too   this

tsi?kla?wístal, tó·k niyo·lé·   nahahkwata·sé·, tho nukwá· tutahoké·tohte?,
bat,   some distance   he went around,   that's where   again he showed up,

(1) Hark! (2) The way the story goes is that once upon a time, it is said, the ones that have feathers and the wild animals were fighting. (3) So then it seems that the ones that fly were winning; then the bat, he went way around over [to their side], that's where he joined in, he joined them [on the side] where they were winning. (4) In a little while they made them retreat, now the animals were gaining on them, it seems now they were winning. (5) Then again the bat, he went a ways around, that's where he showed up again,

khále? oná wahuwali?wanu·tú·se?, wahʌní·lu?, "kwa·kʌ́he? thikʌ́ lotistó·slote?,
and   then they asked him,   they said,   "we see you that   they have feathers,

tho nukwá· tehsya?talátye?skwe?, náhte? nihsatyélha? tsi? kʌ? séhsehse?
that's where you used to go among, what   you are doing that here again you are around

kʌ́h." (6) Wahʌ́·lu? yakʌ?,   "wakenhwa·lóte? ni?í·," khále? wahʌ́·lu?
eh."   He said   reportedly, "I have fur   me,"   and   he said

"ʌkkwe·ní·   ʌkahtʌ·tí·,   isé· kati? wí· ka?ikʌ́ yah thya·ya·wʌ́ne? tsi?
"I will be able I will get underway, you well then this   it has to be   that

ʌskwaye·ná·   ka?i·kʌ́." (7) Kwáh kʌ? náhe? nále?   sahuwʌnáktahte?,
you all will accept me this."   Just   some while then again they pushed them back,

nʌ sok ale? wí· kʌ? nishátye?   kʌ́·,   elʌ́ nukwá·   tutahatukóhtahkwe?
then again too   here he is flying back y'know, other direction again he got on a side

tsi? nukwá· lotistó·slote?   tehati·tʌ́he?, khále? oná wahuwakahkʌ·ní·
where   they have feathers they fly,   and   then they caught on to him

tsi?   nihatyélha?, kwáh tsyo?k nukwá· tethotukohtáhkwʌ.   (8) Nʌ kwí·
what   he is doing,   every direction   again he has gotten on a side.   So then

wahuwali?wanu·tú·se?, wahʌní·lu?, "ot   ni·yót ka?ikʌ́ tsi? tho nukwá·
they asked him,   they said,   "how it is so this   that that's where

tehsya?talátyehse?," wahʌ́·lu?, "né· kwí· tsi? teki·tʌ́he? se? ni?í·, yah né·
you go among,"   he said,   "because   I fly   too   me,   not it's

tha·hatikwe·ní· ta·hati·tʌ́· thikʌ́ tho thʌ·né·se?,   nʌ   kati? wí·
they are not able that they fly that   there they walk around, now   well then

yah thya·ya·wʌ́ne? tsi? ʌskwaye·ná·   ka?ikʌ́, a·kwaya?takénha? tsi?
it has to be   that you all will accept me this,   I may help you all   at

and then they asked him, they said, "we see you with the feathered ones, that's where you used to go among [them], what are you doing that you are over here again?" (6) He said, "I have fur," and he said "I am able to walk, so it's up to you to accept me." (7) In a little while they made them retreat again, then again he was flying back, he got back on the other side where the feathered ones were flying, and now they caught on to what he was doing, he would get on every side [whatever side was winning]. (8) So then they asked him, they said, "how come that's where you go among [them]?," he said, "because me too, I fly, they can't fly, the ones who are walking around over there, so now you have to accept me, I may help you

swatli·yó."   (9) Khále? onʌ́ nʌ   skʌ·nʌ́· sahʌnu·ní·   thikʌ́ tehati·tʌ́he?
you all are fighting."   And   now   then   peace   again they made   that   they fly

khále? kályo?,   sahutlihwahslu·ní·, nʌ   ka?ikʌ́ wa?thuwaya?to·léhte?
and   wild animals, they reconciled,   then   this   they judged him

ka?ikʌ́ tsi?kla?wístal tsi?   yah te?thalihwaye·lí·.   (10) Elók nukwá·
this   bat   because not   he is not trustworthy.   Back and forth

tethotukohtáhkwʌ.   (11) Nʌ kwí· wahuwaté·kwahte?,   wahʌní·lu?,
again he has gotten on a side.   So then   they chased him away,   they said,

"yah shekú tha?tutáhse?,   nʌ kati? wí· ʌkwahle·wáhte?,
"not   even   you should not come back this way,   well then   we will punish you,

yah   tha?tusahsatawʌ́li?   kwʌ?té·ke, kwah nók kwa?ahsuté·ke   nisé·
not   again you would not travel   daytime,   only   throughout the night   you

tʌhsatawʌlyéhe<u>ke?</u>."   (12) "Tahnú· tho   ni·yót   tsi?   ʌkwahle·wáhte?,   yah
you will be travelling."   "And   that's   how it is   that   we will punish you,   not

tha·hsatná·skwayʌ?   kwáh ok skʌ·nʌ́·,   kwáh nisé· nók tʌhsani?takétskwahte?
you should not settle down   just   in peace,   just   you   only   you will flip upside down

tsi? kánhke onʌ́ ʌhsatolíshʌ?, kʌh nú·   nʌhsya?tiha·láke? kʌ́h."
whenever   now   you will rest,   over this way   you will be hanging   y'know."

(13) Nʌ kati? wí· tho   ni·yót   ka?ikʌ́ nikakaló·tʌ,   a·yukwalihúni?   tsi?
        Well then   that's   how it is   this   is the kind of story,   it should teach us   that

a·yukwalihwatokʌ́hake? tsi? náhte? utayukwehtahkwʌ́hake?. (14) Thok
we should be honest   that   what   we should believe in.   That's only

niwakatkwéni.
so I am best able.

with your fight." (9) And now the ones that fly and the wild animals made peace, they reconciled, then they judged the bat because he was not trustworthy. (10) He was going from
one side to the other and back again. (11) So then they chased him away, they said, "you
should not ever come back here again, and then we are going to punish you, you won't
travel in the daytime again, it's only at night that you will be travelling." (12) "And this is
how we will punish you, you won't ever settle down in peace, you will just flip upside down
whenever you rest, you will be hanging over this way." (13) Well that's how the story goes,
it should teach us that we should be honest in our dealings, it's what we should believe in.
(14) That's the best I can do.

The Crow

(Told by Mildred Cutcut to Mercy Doxtator in Summer, 1982)

(1) Ihéh. (2) Ukyatyóha,   kwahikʌ́ tsiʔ lauʔweskwaníhahkweʔ aʔhato·láteʔ.
    Hark.   My brother-in-law, just really that he used to enjoy   that he hunts.

(3) Tho   ni·yót   tsiʔ tehotawʌlyeháti?   oska·wáku, thahatye·lʌ́·   né·
    That's how it is that he is wandering around in the bush, suddenly he noticed it's

ká·ka, tho   tehuwahwánhʌ,   luwanu·túheʔ.   (4) Né· kaʔikʌ́ n ká·ka,
crow,   there they have surrounded him, they are feeding him.   It's   this   crow,

só·tsiʔ   wahotsiʔyo·háneʔ, khe·lé· wahokstʌ·háneʔ sʌ́·, yah thusahakwe·ní·
too much   he became sickly,   I guess he became old   also, not   he is no longer able

laulhá· usahatshʌ·lí·   aʔhatekhu·ní·. (5) Nʌ kwí· kaʔikʌ́ lotithóskaʔ né·
him   he would find it that he eats.   So then this   young ones   it's

luwanu·túheʔ.   (6) Kwáh sʌ́· yakʌʔ lolʌʔnhá·u   kaʔikʌ́ n lokstʌ́ha
they are feeding him.   Just   also reportedly he knows how this   old one

ká·ka, tho   kʌs   tehotskalá·wʌ,   lolha·lé· kwí· tsiʔ náhteʔ aʔhatekhu·ní·,
crow,   there habitually he has his mouth open, he is ready   whatever   that he eats,

lolha·lé· kwí· utahʌ·né·   tho   aʔhuwanhúthuʔ.   (7) Wahʌ́·luʔ kwí·
he is ready   that they come there   that they put food in his mouth.   He said

né·n   ukyatyóha,   yah nuwʌtú teʔthotkáthu   tho   ni·yót   oska·wáku.
it's that my brother-in-law, not   never   there he has not seen   that's how it is in the bush.

(8) Kwáh kwí· nók tsiʔ wá·lelheʔ,   tho kwí· naʔtehutatnolúkhwaʔ n katshe·nʌ́· oniʔ
     Just   he thought, that's   how they love each other animal   too

(1) Hark! (2) My brother-in-law, he used to really enjoy hunting. (3) The way it was is that
he was wandering around in the bush, suddenly he noticed a crow, he was surrounded [by
other crows], they were feeding him. (4) This crow, he had become too sickly, I guess he
had gotten old as well, he was no longer able to find [food] to eat on his own. (5) So then
these young ones were feeding him. (6) This old crow knew too to have his mouth open, he
was ready to eat anything, he was ready for them to come to put food in his mouth. (7) My
brother-in-law said he had never seen anything like that in the bush. (8) He just thought
that's how much they love one another, the animals

né·n   kalha·kú.   (9) Wé·ne kwí·   tho   ni·yót   tsiʔ teshukwáshnyeheʔ,   tho
it's that   in the forest.   Evidently   that's   how it is   that   he looks after us,   that's

ni·yót   tsiʔ   shakoyaʔtísuʔ   oniʔ né·n   katshe·<u>nʌ́</u>.   (10) Tsiʔ ni·yót   ukwé,
how it is   that   he has created them   too   it's that   animal.   As   how it is   man,

tho   oniʔ   né· nihatiyélhaʔ,   tehuwatíshnyeheʔ kwí· n tsiʔ ka·yʌ́·   yah
thus   too   it's   how they do it,   they take care of them   the one that   not

thusahatikwe·<u>ní·</u>.   (11) Né·   kiʔ   né· wahʌ́·luʔ, wahatshanu·ní· tsiʔ
they are no longer able.   It's   actually   it's   he said,   he got happy   that

tho   ni·yót   tsiʔ waʔshakokahkʌ·ní· né·n   katshe·<u>nʌ́·</u>.   (12) Né· kiʔ   ní·
that's   how it is   that   he caught them at it   it's that   animal.   It's   actually   me

kwahikʌ́   twakkalanʌ́steʔ   kaʔikʌ́, tsiʔ   náhteʔ wahatkáthoʔ ukyatyóha.
just really   I treasure most a story   this,   that   what   he saw   my brother-in-law.

in the forest. (9) It must be that's the way he [The Creator] looks after us, that's the way he
created the animals too. (10) Like the way it is with humans, that's how they do it too, they
take care of those that can't do [for themselves] anymore. (11) He said he was happy that
that's how he caught sight of the animals. (12) This is my favourite story, what my brother-
in-law saw.

Some Woodcutters Get a Visitor

(Told by Mercy Doxtator to Karin Michelson on June 28, 1996)

(1) Ú·waʔ kwí· June 28, wé·ne   wísk yawʌ·lé· yotukóhtu   oye·<u>lí·</u>.
      Today   June 28,   evidently   fifteen   it has gone by   ten.

(2) Né· kwí· núwaʔ   kaʔikʌ́ tsiʔ niwakkaló·tʌ.   (3) Aknulhá· kaʔikʌ́
      So it's   this time   this   what kind of story I have.   My mother   this

yukkalatuní   tsiʔ   uhte wí·   nihotiyaʔtawʌ́·u   tshiwahu·<u>níseʔ</u>.
she has told me a story   what   supposedly   has happened to them   a long time ago.

(1) Today is June 28, it must be fifteen past ten. (2) So this is my story this time. (3) My
mother told me this story about what happened to them a long time ago.

(4) Né· s wí· né·n tshiwahu·níseʔ lonuʔwéskwaniheʔ a·hatiyʌtakó·naʔ   kʌ́·,
     So it's   a long time ago they enjoy   that they go cut wood see,

tahnú· s kwí· kwahotokʌ́·u tsiʔ wahunakla·kó·   tho   yahunáklateʔ   tsiʔ nú·
and   just for real   that they moved away there over there they settled where

yehotiyoʔtʌ́staʔ.   (5) Tho kwí· yeyaʔtalátiʔ kaʔikʌ́ aknulhá·,   wé·ne kwí·
over there they work.   There   she is among   this   my mother, evidently

tá·t núwaʔ shakotinhá·u   né· a·huwatikhúniʔ   kaʔikʌ́ latiyʌtákwas.
maybe   they have hired her it's that she cooks for them this   they cut wood.

(6) Nók tsiʔ né· wí· tsiʔ ni·yót tsiʔ ʌkuka·látuhseʔ,   né· s katiʔ kaʔikʌ́
     But   it's   how   it is so that I will tell you a story, well then   this

nʌ   wahatikhwʌ·táneʔ yoʔkaláshʌ kʌ́·, kháleʔ kwah nók sayeksaló·lokeʔ
then they finished eating evening   see, and   just   again she gathered up dishes

kháleʔ tahutáhsawʌʔ waʔthatihyatúhslay<u>ʌ</u>ʔ. (7) Né· kwí· onʌ́ kaʔikʌ́ tsiʔ ka·yʌ́·
and   they started   they played cards.   So it's   then this   the one that

ʌho·tí·   kʌ́·, né· katiʔ thok náhteʔ nok ʌwa·tú· nʌhátyeleʔ tá·t núwaʔ nok ʌwa·tú·
he will lose see, it's then   something   it has to be   he will do it maybe   it has to be

ʌhatsyʌ́·naʔ   kʌ́h. (8) Tá·thuniʔ tsiʔ ka·yʌ́· oyá·   ʌsho·tí·,   né· kwí·
he will go get water y'know.   Or else   the one that another he will lose, so it's

núwaʔ nʌ   nok ʌwa·tú· tʌhayʌtá·lihteʔ   kʌ́·, ʌhuteká·tahkweʔ n   astéhtsiʔ
this time then it has to be he will cut up wood see, they will make a fire with it morning

kʌ́h. (9) Tá·thuniʔ úhkaʔ ok sʌ́· nok ʌwa·tú· ísiʔ nyʌhohnekutyéhslaʔ, kwáh s
y'know.   Or else   someone also it has to be   he will go throw out water, just

kyuhte wí· tsyoʔk nihotitsyapsló·tʌ, swatyelʌ́ oniʔ nok ʌwa·tú· úhkaʔ ok
supposedly they have all kinds of jobs, sometimes too   it has to be   someone

(4) A long time ago they used to like to go cut wood, and so they would move away and they would settle over there where they were working. (5) My mother was going along, I guess maybe these woodcutters hired her to cook for them. (6) But it's how I'm going to tell you the story, well then they would get done eating in the evening, and as soon as she cleared the dishes they would start playing cards. (7) Then the one who lost, he would have to do something, maybe he had to go get water. (8) Or else another one that lost, he would be the one to have to cut kindling, they used that to start the fire in the morning. (9) Or else someone would have to go throw out the water, they had all kinds of jobs, sometimes too someone would have to

Λtsyeksohaléni?,   tá·thuni? Λhutuhewáni?,   kwáh s kyuhte wí·
someone will wash dishes again,   or else   they will sweep,   just   supposedly

tsyo?k náhte? kanyó· ok ta·hatihyatúhslayΛ? ka?ikΛ, né· kwí· tsi? ka·yΛ·   Λyako·tí·
what all   so that   they may play cards   this,   so it's   the one that   one will lose

tá·thuni? Λho·tí·,   né· kwí· thok náhte? Λhotiyʌ·táne?   náhte? na·hútye_le_?.
or else   he will lose, so it's   something   they will receive   what   they should do.

(10) Tho kwí· niyohtuháti? ka?ikΛ oyá·   sayólhΛne?   sayó·kalawe?,
      That's   how it's going this   another   it became the next day   it got dark again,

nΛ ki? ok ale? wí· wahatikhwΛ·táne? kΛ· ókhale? wa?thatihyatúhslay_ΛA_?. (11) Né·n
just then again   they finished eating eh   and   they played cards.   It's that

ka?ikΛ úska wahsuta·té·   tho   kyale? wí· na?a·wΛne?, kwáh kyale? wí· nók
this   one   a night exists thus   again   it happened,   just again

wa?eksaló·loke?   khále? tahutáhsawΛ? wa?thatihyatúhslay_ΛA_?. (12) Kwáh
she gathered dishes   and   they started   they played cards.   Just

uhte wí·   kwahikΛ tsi? tyo?kalá·u ka?ikΛ, nΛ   áhsok   yakΛ?   nΛ
supposedly just really late at night   this,   then   all of a sudden reportedly   then

lonathu·té·, tahnú· kwahikΛ tsi? tuhkwíshlu?   uta?klo·kó· khále? tyotho·lé·   sΛh.
they hear,   and   just really that it did it intensely it snowed   and   it is very cold also.

(13) Né·n   kwah nók né· thahutye·lΛ·   úhka? ok tayenhohaya?ákhu?.
      It's that just   it's suddenly they realized someone   someone knocked.

(14) Tahnú· lonanúhte? ka?ikΛ tsi? kwáh yah kátsha?   tehonathu·té·
      And   they know   this   that just   not   anywhere they don't hear

utayo?slehta·kálele?, kátsha? kati? né· nú·   ta·yΛ·   tá·thuni? kátsha? kati?
that a vehicle sounds,   where   then   it's where one is coming   or else   where   then

wash dishes, or sweep, I guess all kinds [of excuses] so that they could play cards, the one who lost would get something what they should do. (10) That's the way it was from one night to the next, once they finished eating they would play cards. (11) So this one night that's what happened again, as soon as she [my mother] gathered up the dishes they started to play cards. (12) I guess it was really late at night, all of a sudden they heard something, and it really started to snow hard and it was very cold too. (13) Suddenly they realized someone was knocking at the door. (14) And they knew that they hadn't heard anywhere the sound of a vehicle, where then did someone come from, or where

né· nú· tá·le?   tho   niwahsutó·tʌ.   (15) Nók tsi? tho   ki?   thikʌ́
it's where he is coming thus kind of night.   But   there actually that

lati?tlu·tú·   kʌ́·   lonathu·té· úhka? ok tayenhohaya?ákhu?, nʌ kwí·
they are sitting around y'know they hear   someone someone knocked,   so then

úhka? ok wí· tayuta·tí·,   né·n   úhka? ok né· tahatáyahte? kʌ́·,
someone   someone spoke up, it's that someone   it's he entered   see,

kʌ? nithoyʌ́ha kʌ́·,   kwáh tshikʌ́ ka?ikʌ́ tsi? lotya?tahsluní   khále?
young man   y'know, just really   this   that he is all dressed up and

kwahikʌ́ tsi? lahsʌ·ná·   kʌ́h.   (16) Kwáh o?swʌ́·ta? niwahsohkó·tʌ
just really that he is well-dressed y'know.   Just   black   is the kind of colour

ka?ikʌ́ suit lótstu,   kwáh yah te?wé·ne tsi? nihahsʌ·<u>ná·</u>.   (17) Shekú
this   suit he is wearing, just   it's incredible how he is well-dressed.   Even

né· ka?ikʌ́ tehohtáli?,   kwahikʌ́ teyostaláthe?, yu·té· s kwí· aknulhá·
it's this   he has on shoes, just really it is shiny,   she says   my mother

wé·ne   tsi? kwa?nyóh tho   niwahtahkó·tʌhse? thikʌ́ tsi? ni·yót   patent leather.
evidently that seems like thus is the kind of shoes that   as   how it is patent leather.

(18) Yah kwí· te?wé·ne tsi?   nihahsʌ·ná·   kʌ́·,   né·n   wahali?wanu·tʌ́·
       It's incredible   how he is well-dressed y'know, it's that he asked

yakʌ?   ka?ikʌ́, wa?shakoli?wanu·tú·se? tho   lati?tlu·tú·,   yah kʌ
reportedly this,   he asked them   there they are sitting around, not   question

úhka?   te?yakotsístayʌ?   a·huwatsistúthahse?,   í·lelhe?
anyone one doesn't have a light one should provide him with a light, he wants

a·hahlo·tʌ́.   (19) Nʌ kwí· né· ka?ikʌ́ úhka? ok kyuhte wí· tahatkʌ́·lahte?
he would smoke.   So then it's this   someone   supposedly he gave it up

did he come from, on such a night? (15) But those who were sitting around, they heard
someone knock, so then someone spoke up, and so someone came in, a young fellow, he
was all dressed up, and really well-dressed. (16) He was wearing a black suit, it was something the way he was dressed. (17) He even had on these shoes, really shiny ones, my
mother said that it seemed like the shoes were patent leather. (18) It was something how
well-dressed he was, so he asked, he asked those sitting around there, no one had a light for
him? he wanted to smoke. (19) So then I guess someone must have given up

matches, nʌ kwí· wahattsisto·tʌ́· kwí· wahahlo·<u>tʌ́</u>·. (20) Kwáh se? yah úhka?
matches, so then he lit it up he smoked. Just too not anyone

te?yakóthale? kʌ́·, nʌ se? uhte wí· né· ka?ikʌ́ lutto·kás tsi? wé·ne
one isn't talking y'know, then too supposedly it's this they realize that evidently

se? tsi? só·tsi? nʌ wahatiye·lá·te? ka?ikʌ́, kwáh tsi? nikú yo?kalá·u khále?
too that too much then they overdid it this, however many night and

wa?thatihyatúhslayʌ?, kwáh kwí· otokʌ́·u tsi? tehoti·yʌ́· kʌ́h; tsi? ka·yʌ́·
they played cards, just for real that they are gambling see; the one that

ʌho·tí· né· kwí· nok ʌwa·tú· ʌhayʌtakó·na?, tá·thuni? ʌhatsyʌ́·na?,
he will lose so it's it has to be he will go get wood, or else he will go get water,

tá·thuni? tsyo?k wí· náhte?, tʌhayʌtá·lihte? sʌ́h; kwáh kwí· otokʌ́·u tsi?
or else different things, he will cut up wood also; just for real that

teka·yʌ́· kʌ́h. (21) Nʌ kwí· ka?ikʌ́ lutto·kás tsi? wé·ne tsi?
it is gambling y'know. So then this they realize that evidently that

tehona?kalu·tú· ka?ikʌ́ tho wá·lawe?. (22) Né·n nʌ ka?ikʌ́ tshahattsisto·tʌ́·
he has horns this there he arrived. It's that then this when he set light to

laocigarette, nʌ kwí· né· sahaya·kʌ́<u>ne</u>?. (23) Né·n kwáh kʌs kwí· nók
his cigarette, so then it's he went out again. It's that just as usual just

tho tshihatí·tlu?, nʌ yah úhka? te?tsyakóthale?, nók
there when they are sitting around, then not anyone one isn't talking anymore, only

teshutatká·nle? kʌ́h. (24) Úhka? ok yakʌ? wa?í·lu?,
they are looking at one other y'know. Someone reportedly someone said,

"sathu·té· kʌ nisé· thikʌ́ tsi? ka?ikʌ́ sahaya·kʌ́ne? kʌ́·,
"you hear question as for you that that this he went out again eh,

some matches, so then he lit up and he started to smoke. (20) No one spoke, they must have realized that they had gone too far, every night they were playing cards, for real they were gambling, the one that lost would have to get wood, or go after water, or different things, split wood too, for sure it was gambling. (21) So then they realized that it must have been the devil who got there. (22) Then he lit his cigarette, and then he went out again. (23) So they were still just sitting there, no one was talking anymore, they were just looking at one another. (24) Someone said, "you, did you hear that he went out again,

sathu·té· kʌ   kʌʔ tshyusá·leʔ   kʌ́h.”   (25) Kwáh kiʔ
you hear   question here when he walked out again   eh.”   Just   actually

tahata·tí·,   “yah kiʔ   ní· teʔwakathu·<u>té·</u>.”   (26) Tahnú· wí· tsiʔ niyotho·lé·,
he answered, “not   actually me   I didn't hear.”   And   how   it is cold,

kwáh s kwí· thikʌ́ thiwé·ne   tsiʔ tá·t yotho·lé· tsiʔ ni·yót tsiʔ ʌtehsatlata·kóʔ,
just   that   just seems as if   it is cold how   it is like that   you will take a step,

ʌsathu·táneʔ kwí· tsiʔ kwaʔnyóh s waʔola·káleleʔ onyʌ́h<u>taku</u>. (27) Tahnú·
you will hear   that   seems like   it made a sound   in the snow.   And

yah tho   té·yot   kaʔi·<u>kʌ́</u>. (28) Úhkaʔ ok yakʌʔ   wahuwánhaneʔ
not   that's not how it is this.   Someone   reportedly someone got him to do it

ya·hatkeʔto·tʌ́·,   kwáh yah kátshaʔ   thaʔtehaya·ná<u>leʔ</u>.   (29) Náleʔ
he should look out,   just   not   anywhere   he has no footprints.   Then again

sahotinehla·kó·   tsiʔ yah kátshaʔ   thaʔtehaya·náleʔ,   kháleʔ yah sʌ́·
they were amazed again   that   not   anywhere   he has no footprints,   and   not   also

kátshaʔ   teʔkaʔsléhtayʌʔ,   kháleʔ tsiʔ ok   ni·yót tsiʔ lotsluní   kʌ́·,
anywhere there is no vehicle,   and   how   only   it is so that   he is dressed   y'know,

suit ok   lótstu,   yah kátshaʔ   a·kí·luʔ tá·t kwaʔnyóh overcoat
suit only he is wearing,   not   anywhere   I'd say   if   seems like   overcoat

a·hotstúhakeʔ   tsiʔ seʔ niyotho·lé·, kháleʔ yah náhteʔ   teʔyonyʌ́htaleʔ
he would be wearing   how   too   it is so cold,   and   not   anything   there is no snow

tehohtáli<u>ʔ</u>.   (30) Kwáh katiʔ wí· akwekú tsiʔ wahotinehlakoha·tú·   tsiʔ
he has on shoes.   Just   so then   all   how   they were all surprised   how

ni·yót.   (31) Né· katiʔ wí· kaʔikʌ́ wahʌ·nélheʔ, né· wé·ne kwí· nʌ   nok ʌwa·tú·
it is so.   Well then it's this   they thought,   it's   evidently   then   it has to be

did you hear him leave?” (25) He answered, "not me, I didn't hear it." (26) And it was so
cold, just seems as if it was so cold that what it was like if you took a step, you would hear it
make like a noise in the snow. (27) And that's not how it was [it didn't happen like that].
(28) They got someone to look out, there were no footprints of his anywhere. (29) Then
they were amazed that there were no footprints of his anywhere, and also there was no vehicle anywhere, and the way only he was dressed, he was wearing only a suit, no way I'd say
for him to be wearing an overcoat [and] it was so cold, and there was no snow on his shoes.
(30) They were all just so surprised how it was. (31) Well then they thought they have to

ʌhutkʌ·lahteʔ   kaʔikʌ   tsiʔ   tyótkut   tehoti·yʌ·   kʌ·,   nʌ   seʔ   waʔshakóktahseʔ
they will quit   this   that   always   they are gambling   eh,   now   too   he visited them

tehonaʔkalu·tú·,   tahnú·   tá·t   yah   tha·hutkʌ·lahteʔ   wé·ne kwí·   khále?   onʌ́
he has horns,   and   if   not   they won't quit   evidently   and   then

yʌshakoya?táha<u>we?</u>.   (32)   Né·   se?   s wí·   lu·té·   tshiwahu·níse?,   tá·t   só·tsi?
he will take them.   It's   too   they say   a long time ago,   if   too much

ʌhsye·lá·te?   thok náhte?   wahétkʌ?,   ʌ́thle?   ki?   thikʌ́   tehonaʔkalu·tú·
you will overdo   something   it is bad,   he will come   actually   that   he has horns

yʌhyaya?táha<u>we?</u>.   (33)   Né· s kwí·   né·   ka?ikʌ́ n   aknulhá·   tho s   niyakolihó·tʌ
he will take you.   It's   it's   this   my mother   thus   is her custom

náhte?   wa?tkatʌ́·nuke?   nále?   keksa?táksʌ,   "hányo   ka?ikʌ́,   tehsato·tát,"
anything   I did wrong   then again   I am a bad child,   "come on   this,   be still,"

tá·thuni?   "sateksa?ti·yóst,   a?tsyók   né·   tehonaʔkalu·tú·   yʌhyaya?táha<u>we?</u>."
or   "be a good child,   after a while   it's   he has horns   he will take you."

(34)   Né· kati? wí·   tho s   niyohtú·ne?   tshiwahu·níse?,   nók tsi?   kwáh kwí·
      Well then it's   that's   how it was   a long time ago,   but   just

ne? thó·ne?   wahutkʌ́·lahte?   ka?ikʌ́   tehatihyatúhslayʌhe?   kʌ́·,   yah   nuwʌtú   tho
at that time   they quit   this   they are playing cards   y'know,   not   never   thus

te?tsyawʌ́·u   ta·hatihyatúhslayʌ?   nʌ   ʌhatikhwʌ·táne<u>?</u>.   (35)   Tho
it hasn't happened again   that they play cards   when   they will finish eating.   That's

kati? ok wí·   ka?ikʌ́   niwakkaló·tʌ   aknulhá·   ka·té·   yukkalatuní,
then   only   this   the way my story is   my mother   I am saying   she has told me a story,

to·kʌ́ske?   kwahotokʌ́·u   tho   niyawʌ́·u,   kwáh s   kyuhte wí·   nók tsi?
it's true   just for real   thus   it has happened,   just   supposedly   but

quit gambling all the time, surely then the one with the horns had come to visit them, and if they didn't quit he would take them. (32) That's what they said a long time ago, if you overdo something that's bad, the horned one will come and he will take you. (33) That was my mother's way, I did anything wrong, when I was a bad child, [she'd say] "come on, be still," or "you be a good child, or after a while the horned one will take you." (34) Well that's how it was a long time ago, but it was at that time they quit playing cards, it never happened again that they played cards when they got done eating. (35) So that's all of my story, a story I'm saying my mother told me, it's true it really happened, but I guess

yanaʔtu·níheʔ   tsiʔ   nʌyukwalihoʔtʌ́hakeʔ   utetwalihwaye·líteʔ   tsiʔ
he is showing you   what   habits we should have   you and we should do honourably   that

náhteʔ   yukwatlihwahtʌtyé·tu.   (36) Tho katiʔ wí· kaʔikʌ́ nikú   né· ʌkí·luʔ kʌ́h.
what   we conduct our affairs.   So that's   this   how much   it's I will say eh.

he was just showing you [us] what habits we should have and that we should behave honourably in whatever we undertake. (36) So that's all I will say.

Why Dogs Don't Talk

(Told by Mercy Doxtator on May 12, 1998)

(1) Shekólih.   (2) Né· kwí· tsiʔ náhteʔ i·kélheʔ a·kka·látu   aknulhá·   kaʔikʌ́
     Hello.   So it's   that   what   I want   I would tell a story   my mother   this

yukkalatuní   tshikeksáh.   (3) Né· s wí· n yu·té·   lutatíhahkweʔ s
she has told me a story   when I was a child.   So it's   she says   they used to talk

é·lhal tshiwahu·níseʔ.   (4) Né· katiʔ wí· kaʔikʌ́ tsiʔ   niwakkaló·tʌ.
dog   a long time ago.   Well then it's   this   what   kind of story I have.

(5) Waknʌskwayʌ·táhkweʔ s kaʔikʌ́ é·lhal, tahnú· kwáh owísklaʔ nihayaʔtó·tʌ
     I had a pet   this   dog,   and   just   white   what kind he is

tahnú· kwaʔnyóh athéhsaʔ yottsistohkwa·lú·   kʌ́·,   Spot kʌs   linaʔtúkhwaʔ.
and   kind of like   brown   it is spotted all over y'know,   Spot habitually   what I call him.

(6) Né· katiʔ wí· kaʔikʌ́ lakeʔníha kʌ́·,   wahahni·nú· thikʌ́ lu·té· s kwí·
     Well then it's   this   my father   y'know,   he bought it   that   they say

teyehnaʔtatslatilúthaʔ kʌ́·,   kátshaʔ ok wí· nú· taháhaweʔ   kʌ́·;   né· katiʔ wí·
people stretch a pocket   see,   somewhere   he brought it from   y'know;   well then it's

(1) Hello. (2) The story I want to tell is a story my mother told me when I was a child.
(3) She said a long time ago dogs used to talk. (4) Well then this is my story. (5) I had this
pet dog, and he was white and he had kind of like brown spots, I called him Spot. (6) Well
anyway my father bought an accordion, they say 'people stretch a pocket,' he brought it
from somewhere; well

thikʌ́ wakatnutolyaʔtáhkwʌ, kwáh kwíˑ nók tsiʔ yah kwíˑ thaˑkkweˑníˑ
that I am playing with it, only not I am not able

aˑkatlʌnoˑtʌ́ˑ, kwáh kwíˑ nók tsiʔ wakatnutolyaʔtáhkwʌ. (7) Néˑn
that I make music, only I am playing with it. It's that

nʌ sók kʌs thikʌ́ kwahikʌ́ waʔthashʌ́thoʔ akitsheˑnʌ́ˑ, kwáh s thikʌ́
so then habitually that just really he cried my pet, just that

wahathaʔkwáweluʔ kʌ́ˑ, nʌ sók waʔthashʌ́tho̲ʔ. (8) Kwáh s kwíˑ nók
he tilted back his head y'know, so then he cried. Just

wakuʔweskwaníˑu kaʔikʌ́ tsiʔ waʔthahsʌ́thoʔ s akitsheˑnʌ́ˑ, kwáh kwíˑ tyotkutáhkwʌ
I was enjoying this that he cried my pet, just persistently

kaʔikʌ́ tewakatlakalehlástu, kyuhte wíˑ yah seʔ thaˑkkweˑníˑ aˑkatlʌnoˑtʌ́ˑ.
this I am making noise, supposedly not too I am not able that I make music.

(9) Néˑn tayeláthʌʔ thikʌ́ aknulháˑ éˑnik seʔ wíˑ kaʔikʌ́ iˑké̲se̲ʔ.
    It's that she climbed up that my mother upstairs too this I am around.

(10) Tayeláthʌʔ kʌ́ˑ, waʔkhehloˑlíˑ aknulháˑ, waʔkíˑluʔ, "teskáˑnlak kaʔikʌ́,
     She climbed up see, I told her my mother, I said, "watch this,

waʔthashʌ́thoʔ kʌs Spot táˑt náleʔ lothuˑté· kaʔikʌ́ waʔkatlʌnoˑtʌ́ˑ."
he cried habitually Spot if when again he hears this I made music."

(11) Nʌ sok wíˑ néˑ sakatlʌnoˑtʌ́ˑ kyaleʔ wíˑ nʌ sók aleʔ wíˑ
     So then too it's again I made music so again right then again

sahathaʔkwáweluʔ, waʔthohʌˑléhte̲ʔ. (12) Waʔíˑluʔ aknulháˑ, "yah katiʔ
he tilted back his head again, he howled. She said my mother, "not then

kʌ teʔsanúhteʔ tsiʔ luˑtéˑ s tshiwahuˑníseʔ lutatíhahkweʔ éˑlhal, tahnúˑ
question you don't know that they say a long time ago they used to talk dog, and

I was playing with it, but I couldn't make any music, I was just playing with it. (7) So then
my pet really cried, he tilted back his head, and then he cried. (8) And I was just enjoying
that my pet was crying, so I kept on making noise, I guess I really couldn't make any music.
(9) So my mother climbed to where I was upstairs. (10) She climbed up, and I told my
mother, I said, "Watch this! Spot starts to cry if he hears me make music." (11) So then I
played some music again and right away again he put back his head again and he howled.
(12) My mother said, "Don't you know that they say a long time ago dogs used to talk, and

kwáh s tshi·kʌ́· tsiʔ lonatkanuni·hné· kʌ́·,   yah teʔwé·ne tsiʔ nihotinúhsahseʔ
just really   that they were wealthy y'know, it's incredible how big their houses are

tsiʔ nú· nihatinákleʔ kʌ́·,   tsiʔ nihoti·kwáts."   (13) Nʌ kyaleʔ wí· tú·skeʔ
where   they reside   y'know, how they are well-off."   So again   truly

uknehla·kó·   kaʔikʌ́ tsiʔ náhteʔ waʔukka·látuhseʔ kʌ́h, waʔí·luʔ né· wí· tsiʔ
I became surprised this   that what she told me a story eh, she said because

kwaʔnyóh lonatkanuni·hné· kaʔikʌ́ é·lhal. (14) Nók tsiʔ tho kiʔ ok kwí·
seems like they were wealthy this   dog.   But   something

naʔa·wʌ́neʔ kaʔikʌ́ tsiʔ sahotitʌ́htaneʔ n é·lhal, tá·tkʌ né· thikʌ́ aolí·waʔ   thikʌ́
it happened this   that they lost out again dog,   maybe it's that   the reason that

tsiʔ   só·tsiʔ   lonatlihwatyé·ni, ya·wét   kyuhte wí· lonulhá· wahatilihu·ní·,
because too much   they are talkative, kind of like supposedly them   they became at fault,

waʔthotilihwaksʌ́·sluʔ tsiʔ latinákele̲ʔ. (15) Nʌ kwí· né·n   Shukwayaʔtísuʔ
they feuded   at   they reside.   So then it's that Our Creator

tethaká·nleʔ ki?wáh. (16) Kwáh né· neʔ thó·neʔ ok   thutatíhahkweʔ thikʌ́
he is watching right.   Just it's at that time only they used to speak that

é·lhal. (17) Kwáh akwekú waʔshakókhwaʔ   ʌhuta·tí·   kʌ́·, nʌ kwí·
dog.   Just all   he took it away from them they will speak see, so then

kwah nók tho   nikú   shotikwení   onʌ́ n, kwáh s kwí· nók wahatihnyáni̲ʔ.
just   that's how much they are able again now, just   they barked.

(18) Né· katiʔ wí· thikʌ́ tho   nikakaló·tʌ   kʌ́·,   aknulhá· waʔukka·látuhseʔ
     Well then it's that   that's the kind of story y'know, my mother she told me a story

they were really wealthy, it's incredible how big their houses were where they lived, they
were so well-off." (13) So I was really surprised at the story she told me, she said because it
seems like dogs used to be wealthy. (14) But something happened that the dogs lost out,
maybe the reason why was because they talked too much, kind of like I guess it was their
own fault, for feuding where they were living. (15) So then our Creator was watching, right.
(16) Back then was the very last time dogs used to speak. (17) He took away from all of
them the [ability to] speak, so then that's all they are able [to do] now, just bark. (18) Well
that's the story, the story my mother told me,

kʌ·,   wé·ne kwí· kwáh s kwí· tsyoʔk nihotikaló·tʌhseʔ tshiwahu·níseʔ kʌ·,
y'know,   evidently   all kinds of   they have stories   a long time ago   y'know,

nók tsiʔ né· kiʔ   thikʌ́ wá·kelheʔ a·kka·látuʔ   kʌ·, thoʔnʌ́   ʌwa·tú· kwí·
but   it's actually that   I wanted   I would tell a story see,   and then   it can be

né· sʌ́· aétyatsteʔ   a·yukniyo·tʌ́·.   (19) Tho   kyuhte i·kélheʔ kaʔikʌ́
it's   also that you and I use it we two would work.   That's I think   this

nikaka·lés.
is the length of the story.

   (20) Ostúha ukeʔnikúlhʌʔ kaʔikʌ́ tsiʔ   niwakkaló·tʌ.   (21) Né· wí· waʔí·luʔ
       A little   I forgot   this   what   kind of story I have.   So it's   she said

aknulhá·   tsiʔ né· s thikʌ́ náleʔ waʔthotihʌ·léhteʔ, waʔthushʌ́thoʔ kaʔikʌ́ é·lhal.
my mother that it's   that   then   they hollered,   they cried   this   dog.

(22) Né· s yakʌʔ   né· thikʌ́ sahʌnehyá·laneʔ? tsiʔ   nihonatkanuni·hné·
      It's   reportedly it's   that   they remembered   how   they were wealthy

tshiwahu·níseʔ, kháleʔ tyótkut seʔ s yakʌʔ wí· kalʌ·nóteʔ tsiʔ nú· nihʌ·né·seʔ,
a long time ago,   and   always   too   reportedly it is music   where   they are around,

né· s katiʔ aolí·waʔ   nʌ   lonathu·té· tekalihwáhkwʌ, tá·thuniʔ thok náhteʔ
well   the reason when   they hear   it is singing,   or else   something

utlʌno·tʌ́·   ókhaleʔ wahutati·tʌ́leʔ.   (23) Tho   nikú   thikʌ́
it played music and   they felt sorry for themselves.   That's how much that

ukeʔnikúlhʌʔ a·kathlo·lí· kʌ́h, nʌ kiʔ   tho   ni·kú.
I forgot   I should tell see, now actually that's how much.

they must have had all kinds of stories a long time ago, but I wanted to tell this story, and
then the two of us could use it also to work on. (19) That, I think, is the extent of the story.
   (20) I forgot a little bit of my story. (21) So my mother said that then they howl, when
dogs cry. (22) It's that they remember how wealthy they were a long time ago, and there
was always music where they were, well this is why when they hear singing, or some music
playing then they feel sorry for themselves. (23) That's all I forgot to tell, that's it.

The Bird

(Told by Norma Kennedy to Karin Michelson on April 21, 2008)

(1) Yah teʔské·yaleʔ   úhkaʔ náhteʔ yukkalatú·se   kaʔikʌ́ oka·lá·
     Not   I don't remember who   one has told me a story this   story

i·kélheʔ a·kuka·látus̲.   (2) Nʌ   kiʔ   né· tshiwahu·níseʔ kaʔikʌ́
I want   I would tell you a story.   Then actually it's a long time ago   this

tho   niyawʌ́·u.   (3) Úska yotlátstu   yotinuhsóta   kaʔikʌ́
thus it has happened.   One   there was a time they have a house together this

onatatyʌ́ha,   tahnú· nʌ   yaʔkáheweʔ a·kyatekhu·ní·,   yah kwí· thau·tú·
mother and daughter,   and   when it came time that the two eat,   not   it can't be

óksaʔ   a·kyatekhu·ní· tsiʔ niyo·lé· nok ʌwa·tú· ʌyenaʔtalu·ní·   kaʔikʌ́
right away   that the two eat until   it has to be she will make bread this

onulháh.   (4) Tahnú· yakʌʔ   tsiʔ niyutuhkályaʔks kaʔikʌ́ yeksáh.
her mother.   And   reportedly how   she is so hungry this   girl.

(5) Nʌ kwí· tayutáhsawʌʔ kaʔikʌ́ onulhá·   waʔutnaʔtalu·ní̲·. (6) Nʌ s né·
     So then   she started   this   her mother she made bread.   Then   it's

yakonúhtuʔks   kaʔikʌ́ yeksá·, né· wí· tsiʔ niyutuhkályaʔks. (7) Né·n
she is running out of patience this   girl,   because   she is so hungry.   It's that

waʔí·luʔ onulhá·,   "wá·s kwí· átste   satnutolyaʔtá·na tsiʔ náheʔ ʌkatnaʔtalu·ní̲·."
she said   her mother, "go   outside go and play   while   I will make bread."

(8) "Kanyó· onʌ́ ʌkanaʔtala·lí·   nʌ kwí· yʌkúhʌleʔ   ókhnaʔ
     "As soon as   bread will get cooked so then   I will summon you and then

tʌtehsatáwyahteʔ   ʌtyatekhu·ní̲·."   (9) Nʌ kwí· né· waʔutnutolyaʔtá·naʔ átste
you will come back in   you and I will eat."   So then   it's   she went to play   outside

(1) I don't remember who told me this story I want to tell you. (2) It was a long time ago
this happened. (3) Once upon a time this mother and daughter had a home together, and
when it came time for the two of them to eat, they couldn't eat right away until her mother
had to make some bread. (4) And the little girl was really hungry. (5) So then her mother
started to make bread. (6) Now the little girl was running out of patience, because she was
so hungry. (7) So her mother said, "Go, go and play outside while I make some bread."
(8) "As soon as the bread gets cooked I will call you and then you will come back in and we
will eat." (9) So then the little girl went to play outside.

kaʔikʌ́ yeksáh.　(10)　Nʌ　kyuniʔ wí·　né·　tayutáhsawʌʔ　kaʔikʌ́　onulhá·
this　　girl.　　　　　Then　too　　it's　she started　　this　　her mother

waʔutnaʔtalu·ní·.　(11)　Tahnú·　né·　tsiʔ　niyutuhkályaʔks　kaʔikʌ́　yeksá·,　kwáh　né·
she made bread.　　　And　　it's　how　she is so hungry　　this　　　girl,　just　it's

kʌʔ ok náheʔ　átste　yehe·yʌ́·seʔ　　　　　ókhnaʔ　yusayenhohayaʔákhuʔ,
a little while　outside　she is around over there　and then　she knocked on the door again,

waʔí·luʔ,　"nʌ　kʌ　　　yonaʔtala·lí."　　(12)　Waʔí·luʔ　onulhá·,　　"táh,
she said,　"now　question　bread is cooked."　　She said　her mother,　"no,

áhsu　kih."　　(13)　"Wá·s　satnutolyaʔtá·na,　yʌkúhʌleʔ　　　kiʔ　　nʌ
not yet　actually."　　"Go　go and play,　　I will summon you　actually　when

ʌkanaʔtala·lí·."　　(14)　Nʌ kyaleʔ wí·　sayeya·kʌ́neʔ　　　kaʔikʌ́　yeksá·
bread will get cooked."　　So again　　she went out again　this　　girl

sayutnutolyaʔtá·naʔ.　(15)　Né·n　tho kwí·　átste　　tyakotnutolyá·tu　thikʌ́,
she went to play again.　It's that　there　outside　she is playing　　that,

kok náheʔ　ókhnaʔ　wá·yʌlheʔ,　nʌ kyaleʔ　ʌtsyutatliʔwanu·tú·seʔ　nʌ　　kʌ
a little while　and then　she thought,　again　　she will ask her again　now　question

yonaʔtala·lí.　　(16)　Nʌ kyaleʔ wí·　yusayenhohayaʔákhuʔ,　　　waʔí·luʔ,
bread is cooked.　　So again　　she knocked on the door again,　she said,

"nʌ　kʌ　　　yonaʔtala·lí."　　(17)　Waʔí·luʔ　onulhá·,　"táh　áshu　kih."
"now　question　bread is cooked."　　She said　her mother,　"no　not yet　actually."

(18)　"Yʌkúhʌleʔ　kiʔ　　nʌ　ʌkanaʔtala·lí·."　　(19)　Nʌ kyaleʔ wí·
"I will call you　actually　when　bread will get cooked."　　So again

sayeya·kʌ́neʔ　　kaʔikʌ́ yeksá·　sayutnutolyaʔtá·naʔ.　(20)　Nʌ kwí·　né·　kaʔikʌ́
she went out again　this　girl　again she went to play.　　So then　it's　this

(10) Then too her mother started to make bread. (11) And the little girl was really hungry, she was outside only a little while and then she knocked on the door again, she said, "is the bread done?" (12) Her mother said, "no, not yet." (13) "Go, go play, I will call you when the bread gets done." (14) So again the little girl went out to play. (15) So she was outside playing, and in a little while she thought she would ask her again whether the bread was done. (16) So again she knocked on the door, she said, "is the bread done?" (17) Her mother said, "no, not yet." (18) "I will call you when the bread gets done." (19) So again the little girl went back out to play. (20) So then

wa?éhsane?   wa?utna?talu·ní·   ókhna?   wa?utna?talu·tʌ́·   kwí·   yutna?talutakhwá·tslaku
she finished   she made bread   and then   she baked bread   inside   it's used to bake bread

ya?étane?   ka?ikʌ́   kaná·talok.   (21)   Kwáh   ki?   né·   kʌ?   ok   náhe?   ókhna?
she put it in   this   bread.   Just   actually   it's   a little while   and then

yusayutke?to·tʌ́·,   nʌ   ki?   ok   né·   wa?kana?tala·lí·,   nʌ   ki?   ok   wí·
again she peered into it,   then   actually   just   it's   bread got cooked,   right then

wa?ekwe?talu·kó·   ka?ikʌ́   kaná·talok,   wa?utelhá·latste?   kwí·   a·kyatekhu·ní·.
she cut it into chunks   this   bread,   she got it ready   for the two to eat.

(22)   Nʌ   né·   wa?akonúhtuhke?   tutayutáwyahte?,   nʌ   kwí·   ya?utáthʌle?
      Then   it's   she grew impatient   for her to come in again,   so then   she summoned her

ka?ikʌ́   utatyʌ́ha,   wa?utathlo·lí·   tsi?   nʌ   ki?   wa?kana?tala·lí·.   (23)   Né·n
this   her daughter,   she told her   that   now   actually   bread got cooked.   It's that

wa?tyutkahtúni?   ka?ikʌ́   átste,   kwáh   ki?   né·   sayutatya?tátstale?
she looked all around   this   outside,   just   actually   it's   she was unable to find her

utatyʌ́ha,   wa?unuhtunyu·kó·   wa?í·lu?,   "kátsha?   uhte   niyakawe·nú."
her daughter,   she thought about it   she said,   "where   possibly   she has gone."

(24)   Né·n   tha?utye·lʌ́·   né·   tsi?   kalu·tóte?   tho   kʌtskwáhele?   otsi?tʌ́ha,
      It's that   she suddenly noticed   it's   at   there's a tree   there   it is perching   bird,

wa·té·,   "nʌ   kʌ   yolí,   nʌ   kʌ   yolí."   (25)   Kali?wanútha?
it says,   "now   question   it is cooked,   now   question   it is cooked."   It is asking

né·   ka?ikʌ́   otsi?tʌ́ha   nʌ   kʌ   yolí   kaná·talok.   (26)   Só·tsi?
it's   this   bird   now   question   it is cooked   bread.   Too much

wahu·níse?   wa?utnúhtuhte?   a·kana?tala·lí·,   nʌ   né·   otsi?tʌ́ha   ya?tyutte·ní·.
a long time   she waited   for bread to get cooked,   now   it's   bird   she turned into.

she finished making the bread and then she baked it, she put the bread in the oven. (21) In just a little while she looked in, just then the bread was done, so right then she cut the bread, and she got things ready for the two of them to eat. (22) Now she became impatient for her to come back inside, so then she called her daughter, she told her that now the bread was done. (23) She looked all around outside, she just couldn't find her daughter, she thought about it and she said, "I wonder where she's gone." (24) Then she suddenly noticed there was a tree with a bird perching on it, it was saying, "is it done, is it done?" (25) This bird was asking whether the bread was done. (26) She waited too long for the bread to get done, so she turned into a bird.

(27) Né· ki?   né· shekú kʌh wʌhnisla·té· ʌsathu·téke? thikʌ́ otsi?tʌ́ha wa·té·
    It's   actually   it's   still   here   a day exists   you will hear   that   bird   it says

"nʌ kʌ   yolí."
"now   question   it is cooked."

(27) Still to this day you will hear this bird say "nʌ kʌ yolí?"

A Jealous Husband

(Told by Ray George at the University at Buffalo on November 20, 2009)

(1) Ʌkwaka·látuhse?   okalakayú   aksótha   wa?ukka·látuhse?   tshiwahu·níse?.
    I will tell you all a story   an old story   my grandmother   she told me a story   a long time ago.

(2) Né· yakʌ?   ka?ikʌ́   kʌ? nithotiyʌ́ha wahotínyake?,   tahnú· ka?ikʌ́ lukwé
    It's   reportedly   this   young people   they got married,   and   this   man

kwahikʌ́   lotʌ?kéwhʌ.   (3) Wahahtʌ·tí· kʌs   yakʌ?   astéhtsi?
just really   he is jealous.   He left   habitually   reportedly   in the morning

wahoyo?tʌ́hsa?,   nók tsi? kalhakú   tkaluto·tú·   kalutowa·nʌ́·se?,
he went to work,   but   in the woods   there are trees around   large trees,

tho   kʌs   thotahséhtu.   (4) Ya?teshaká·nle?   tsi? tkanúhsote?
there   habitually   he has hidden.   He is looking back that way   at   there is a house

tsi? nú· ítyʌhse?   lo·né·.   (5) Yah kʌs   yakʌ?   né· te?wé·ne
where   she is around   spouse.   Not   habitually   reportedly   it's   incredible

niyakotshanuní,   tayeya·kʌ́ne? yakoyo·té·,   wa?enohaléni? atslunyákhwa?,   átste
how she is happy,   she came out   she is working,   she washed   clothes,   outside

ya?ehalúni?.   (6) Yusayutáwyahte?,   tho   ni·yót   tyótkut   yakotshanu·ní.
over there she hung them.   She went back in,   that's   how it is   always   she is happy.

(1) I will tell you a story, an old story my grandmother told me a long time ago. (2) These young people got married, and the man was really jealous. (3) He would leave in the morning to go to work, but in the woods with these large trees all around, there he hid. (4) He was looking back at the house where his wife was. (5) She was incredibly happy, she would come out and work, she washed the clothes, and she hung them up outside. (6) She would go back inside, and that's the way it was, she was always happy.

(7) Yusá·lawe?   yo?kaláshʌ   yakokhuní,   a·hatekhu·ní· tsi? nahté·shu?
     He arrived back there   in the evening   she is cooking,   he should eat   what all

yakokhu·ní.   (8) Né·n   oyá·   swʌhnisla·té·   khále? teyotuhutsyóhu
she is cooking.   It's that another   again a day exists   and   it is necessary

a·hoyo?tʌ́hsa?   wahahtʌ·tí·, khále? tsi? tkalu·tóte?   thotahséhtu.
that he goes to work   he left,   and   at   there is a tree   he has hidden.

(9) Tho   yakʌ?   kʌs   nihayélha?   thikʌ́ nya?tewʌhnislaké, tsi? niyo·lé·
     That's   reportedly habitually   what he is doing   that   every day,   until

wa?óhslate?,   wa?kanye·yʌ́·   utho·láte?, né·n   tsiléhkwa? yakʌ?   tho
it became winter,   snow got on the ground   it got cold,   it's that   almost   reportedly   there

utahowisto?kwanʌ́stuke?,   tho   nyusá·le?   tsi? thohtʌ́ti.   (10) Nʌ
he would have gotten all frozen,   there   he went over there again   his home.   Then

sahatathle·wáhte? tsi?   niholihó·tʌ tsi?   nihotʌ?kéwhʌ, tsiléhkwa? a·hawʌhe·yúke?
he repented   what   is his way   how   he is jealous,   almost   he would have died

tsi?   nahawístoske?. (11) Tyótkut né· yakotshanuní lo·né·   yakokhuní,
how   he got cold.   Always   it's   she is happy   spouse   she is cooking,

né·n   tyótkut late?nyʌ́tha? a·halihwatshʌ·lí·   tsyo?k náhte? a·hotʌ?kewhʌ́hake?.
it's that always   he is trying   that he finds a reason   all kinds of   for him to be jealous.

(12) Né· ki?   thikʌ́ tho   nikakaló·tʌ   wa?ukhlo·lí· aksótha,   tsi?
      It's   actually   that   that's   the kind of story   she told me   my grandmother,   that

yah te?yoyánle? a·yakotʌ?kewhʌ́hake?. (13) Tho   ki?   nikawʌ·náke
not   it's not good   one should be jealous.   Thus   actually   the words amount to

ka?ikʌ́ n ako·kále? aksótha.   (14) Nʌ   kíh.
this   her story   my grandmother.   Then   actually.

(7) He would get back in the evening and she was cooking, for him to eat everything she
was cooking. (8) And then it was another day and he needed to go to work, he left and he
hid by a tree. (9) That's what he was doing every day, until winter came, the ground got
covered with snow and it got cold, so he almost froze, and so he went back home. (10) Then
he repented that he had such a jealous disposition, he almost died he got so cold. (11) His
wife was always happy, cooking, and he was always trying to find all kinds of reasons to be
jealous. (12) So that's the story my grandmother told me, that it's not good to be jealous.
(13) That's all of the words to my grandmother's story. (14) There you go.

The Story of Birch Bark

(Told by Norma Kennedy to Karin Michelson on September 14, 2007)

(1) Né· ka?ikʌ́ tsi? nikakaló·tʌ kalute?shúha i·kélhe? a·kuka·látu<u>s</u>.
It's this what kind of story it is trees I want I would tell you a story.

(2) Tshiwahu·níse? tshihatu·níhe? tsyo?k nahté·shu? Shukwaya?tísu?, né· tho
A long time ago when he makes all kinds of things He has created us, it's there

ka?ikʌ́ tsi? nikaha·wí· wahatunyáni? kalute?shúha. (3) Kwáh kwí· tsyo?k
this at that era he made several trees. Just every

nikalutó·tʌhse? wahatu·ní·, né· ki? ka?ikʌ́ úska ka·lúte? nʌ wahatu·ní·
kind of tree he made, it's actually this one tree then he made

ohnakwʌ́hsa? kuwa·yáts, o?sluni?kéha? 'white birch' kuwa·yáts. (4) Tahnú· wí·
white birch is its name, white man's way 'white birch' is its name. And

yotiya?tayʌ́stu ka?ikʌ́ kalute?shúha ka?ikʌ́ ohnakwʌ́hsa? na?kalutó·tʌ?.
they are nice-looking this trees this white birch is the species of tree.

(5) Tahnú· yonanúhte? kwí· tsi? nikalutiyó ka?ikʌ́ tho nikalutó·tʌ.
And they know how it is a beautiful tree this that's the kind of tree.

(6) Kwáh s kwí· tsyo?k na?tetyotiyelʌ́ thikʌ́, sʌ́ha? s kwí· nále? takáwelute?,
All kinds of they are doing that, more when again it got windy,

tho kwí· teyonatnʌtshalúni? tsi? yowelutú, kanyó· ki? ok wí· a·hutkátho?
there they are waving their arms as it is windy, so that they should see

tsi? niyotiya?tayʌ́stu. (7) Kwáh kwí· ikʌ́ tsi? kaluti·<u>y</u>ó. (8) Né·
how they are nice-looking. Just really that it is a beautiful tree. It's

núwa? áhsok né· nʌ wa?otishwá·tʌ? ka?ikʌ́ oyá· tho kaluto·tú·,
this time suddenly it's when they became annoyed this other there trees standing,

(1) I want to tell you a story, a story about the trees. (2) A long time ago when the Creator made all things, at that time he made the trees. (3) He made every kind of tree, he made this one tree called *ohnakwʌ́hsa?*, in English it's called 'white birch.' (4) And these trees were really nice-looking, the white birch. (5) And they knew what a beautiful tree they were. (6) And they were doing all kinds of things, more so when it got windy, they would wave their arms all around in the wind, so all should see how nice-looking they were. (7) It really was a beautiful tree. (8) Now suddenly all the other trees there became annoyed,

tyótkut ka?ikʌ́ ku·nélhe? onulhá· kwáh tkaluti·yó.   (9) Nʌ kwí·
always   this   they think they   quite it is the most beautiful tree.   So then

wa?kuwahlo·lí· tsi? yah te?kutinú·wehse? ka?ikʌ́ tsi? ni·yót tsi? ku·nélhe?
they told her   that not they don't like it   this   how   it is so that they think

onulhá· ok kʌ   kwáh tkaluti·yó.   (10) Nʌ kwí· wa?kuwahlo·lí·
they   only question quite it is the most beautiful tree.   So then   they told her

tsi? náhte? yah te?kutinú·wehse? oyá· kalute?shúha. (11) Wa?kuní·lu?, "oyá· se?
that what   not they don't like it   other trees.   They said,   "other too

sʌ́· kwáh tho nikaluti·yó·se?   tsi? nisé· ni·yót."   (12) "Yah ki?
also quite there they are beautiful trees as   you   how it is."   "Not   actually

te?yakwanú·wehse? thikʌ́ tsi? kwa?nyóh íhselhe?, isé· ok kʌ   kwáh
we don't like it   that   that just seems you think, you only question quite

tkaluti·yó."   (13) Nʌ kwí· né· unuhtunyu·kó·   ka?ikʌ́ ohnakwʌ́hsa?
it is the most beautiful tree."   So then   it's   she thought it over this   white birch

ka·lúte?, "to·kʌ́ske? kwí· tsi? náhte? wa?kuní·lu? thikʌ́, oyá· se? sʌ́·
tree,   "it's true   that what   they said   that,   other too also

kalutiyó,   kwáh tho nikalutiyó   tsi? ní· ni·yót."   (14) Nʌ kwí·
it is a beautiful tree,   quite there it is a beautiful tree as   we how it is."   So then

né· wa?kutkʌ́·lahte? ka?ikʌ́ ohnakwʌ́hsa? tsi? kwa?nyóh ku·nélhe?.
it's they quit   this   white birch   that just seems they think.

(15) Tóhka? ok niwʌhnislaké khále? né· sayoti?nikúlhʌ?, ókhale? tho
      A few   only days amount to and   it's again they forgot,   and   there

tetsyonatnʌtshalúni?   tsi? yowelutú, kwáh a?nyóh ku·nélhe? tsi?
again they are waving their arms as   it is windy, just seems   they think   how

they were always thinking THEY were the most beautiful tree. (9) So then they told her
[them] that they didn't like how they thought only THEY were the most beautiful tree.
(10) So then they told her [them] what it was the other trees didn't like. (11) They said,
"other trees too are quite as beautiful as you." (12) "We don't like how you are showing off,
that only you are so beautiful." (13) So then the white birch thought about it, "it's true what
they say, there are other beautiful trees too, just as beautiful as we are." (14) So then the
white birch quit being so conceited. (15) It was only a few days and again they forgot, and
again there they were waving their arms back and forth in the wind, they were showing off

nikaluti·yó·se̲ʔ.   (16) Ókhaleʔ   né·   óksaʔ ok   waʔkúttokeʔ   oyá·   tho
they are beautiful trees.   And   it's   right away   they noticed   other   there

kaluto·tú·   tsiʔ   kháleʔ   né·   sayoʔnikúlhʌʔ   náhteʔ   kuwaliʔwanutú·se,   tákʌʔ
trees standing   that   and   it's   again she forgot   what   they have asked her,   don't

thikʌ́   tho   na·ka·yél,   kwaʔnyóh   i·wélheʔ   tsiʔ   aulhá·   ok   kʌ
that   thus   she should do it,   just seems   she thinks   that   she   only   question

kaluti·yó̲.   (17)   Nʌ kyaleʔ   wí·   sakuwayehyahláhkwʌʔ   tsiʔ   náhteʔ
it is a beautiful tree.   So again   they reminded her   that   what

yotilihwísuʔ   tsiʔ   yah   wí·   tho   tha·yohtúhakeʔ,   a·wélhekeʔ   aulhá·   ok
they have promised   that   not   that's   not how it should be,   she should think   she   only

kʌ   kaluti·yó̲.   (18)   Nʌ kyaleʔ   wí·   kaʔikʌ́   utkʌ́·lahteʔ   tsiʔ   kwaʔnyóh
question   it is a beautiful tree.   So again   this   she quit   that   just seems

i·wélheʔ   kaʔikʌ́   ohnakwʌ́hsaʔ   ka·lúte̲ʔ.   (19)   Né·n   tóhkaʔ   ok   niwʌhnislaké
she thinks   this   white birch   tree.   It's that   a few   only   days amount to

kháleʔ   né·   sayotiʔnikúlhʌʔ   tsiʔ   náhteʔ   yotilihwísu̲ʔ.   (20)   Ókháleʔ   tho
and   it's   again they forgot   that   what   they promised.   And   there

tetsyonatnʌtshalúniʔ   tsiʔ   yowelutú,   kwáh   kwaʔnyóh   ku·nélheʔ
again they are waving their arms   as   it is windy,   quite   just seems   they think

tsiʔ   nikaluti·yó̲.   (21)   Nʌ sok wí·   né·   tayotiná·khwʌʔ   kaʔikʌ́,   yah
how   it is a beautiful tree.   So then too   it's   they became angry   this,   not

teʔyotinuhwé·u   oyá·   tho   kaluto·tú·   tsiʔ   kháleʔ   né·   tsyotiʔnikulhʌ́·u
they don't like it   other   there   trees standing   that   and   it's   again they have forgotten

náhteʔ   yotilihwísu̲ʔ.   (22)   Nʌ sok wí·   kwahikʌ́   tsiʔ   waʔkáweluteʔ   thikʌ́
what   they have promised.   So then too   just really   that   it got windy   that

what beautiful trees they were. (16) And right away the other trees noticed that she had forgotten what they asked her, that she should not do like that, show off as if only she was a
beautiful tree. (17) So again they reminded her about what they [she] had promised, that
that's not how it should be, that she thinks she only is a beautiful tree. (18) So again the
birch tree stopped being so conceited. (19) And it was only a few days and they forgot once
again what they had promised. (20) And there they were waving their arms in the wind,
showing off how beautiful they were. (21) And so then they got angry, the other trees did
not like that they had forgotten again what they had promised. (22) And so then on that day
a big wind came up,

ne? thó·ne? wʌhnisla·té·, nʌ sok wí· kwahikʌ́ tsi? yo?shátste?, tho
at that time a day exists,   so then too just really that it is forceful,   there

teyonatnʌtshalúni?   ka?ikʌ́ n oyá· tho kaluto·tú·,   ya·wét kwí·
they are waving their arms this   other there trees standing, kind of like

wa?kuwanuwʌhsláli? ka?ikʌ́ ohnakwʌ́hsa? ka·lúte?, kwáh kwí· ikʌ́ tsi? yo?shátste?
they whipped her   this   white birch   tree,   just really   that it is forceful

wa?kuwanuwʌhsláli?. (23) Né· thikʌ́ tsi? yokwilu·tú· kwí· wa?ku·nútste? tsi?
they whipped her.   It's   that   at   saplings attached they used it   that

wa?kuwanuwʌhsláli? ka?ikʌ́ ohnakwʌ́hsa? ka·lúte?. (24) Ne? thó·ne? kwí· né·
they whipped her   this   white birch   tree.   At that time   it's

tyotáhsawʌ? thikʌ́, ya·wét kwí· wa?tyonatahsa·túne? ka?ikʌ́ ohnakwʌ́hsa?
it has begun   that,   kind of like   they got bruised   this   white birch

kalute?shúha. (25) Ne? thó·ne? kwí· tyotáhsawʌ? ka?ikʌ́ o?swʌ́·ta? kwí·
trees.   At that time   it has started   this   black

niwahsohkó·tʌ   ka?ikʌ́ watényu?, wé·ne   tsi? nikú   kwa?nyóh a·yʌ́lhe?
is the kind of colour this   it is striped, evidently as many as seems   one would think

yotinuhlyá·khu?   ka?ikʌ́ kaluto·tú·.   (26) Yah né· se? owisklósku?
they have gotten hurt this   trees standing.   Not   it's   too   all white

te?swahsohkó·tʌ.   (27) Né· ki?   né· thikʌ́ tho   niyawʌ́·u   tsi?
is not the colour anymore.   It's   actually it's   that   thus   it has happened that

o?swʌ́·ta? ni·yót tsi? tekayéstu n owískla? thikʌ́ n white birch, ohnawkʌ́hsa? kwí·
black   kind   that   it is mixed in white   that   white birch,   white birch

kuwa·yáts Ukwehuwehnéha?.   (28) Ne? thó·ne? tyotáhsawʌ? thikʌ́ tekayéstu
is its name Native people's way.   At that time   it has started   that   it is mixed in

o?swʌ́·ta? niwahsohkó·tʌ.   (29) Thok ni·kú.
black   is the kind of colour.   That's how much.

it was really fierce, and the other trees waved their arms all around, it's kind of like they
were whipping the white birch, they whipped her with a lot of force. (23) They used their
branches to whip the white birch. (24) And at that time it started, it's like the white birch
tree got bruises. (25) So at that time it started that it was striped [with] black, it must have
been so many [stripes] one would think these trees got hurt. (26) They weren't all white
anymore. (27) That's how it happened that black got mixed in with white in the white birch,
ohnakwʌ́hsa? in Indian. (28) At that time it started to have black mixed in. (29) That's all.

Ghostly Tales

The stories in this section are about encounters with ghostly beings. Some of the beings have been seen by more than one person and on more than one occasion. Some wear characteristic clothing, such as the ghost who wears a skirt and a red jacket, or the stranger who has on a long coat and a black hat. Some have a human body while others are just a part of a body, or a skeleton, or a light, or even just a sensation.

Several stories mention the old Number 3 School on Ball Park Road. This building functioned as the Oneida Language Centre for many years; just recently the Language Centre moved to a new building located closer to the Oneida administration buildings. The Anglican church, mentioned in the story *A Scary Light*, is located on Oneida Road between Ball Park Road and the fairgrounds. Anglicans are called **tehoti?kha·lúte?** in Oneida, literally 'they wear skirts.' The Baptist church used to be across from the fairgrounds before it burned down last year. Baptists, mentioned near the end of Verland Cornelius's story in the 'Reflections' section, are referred to as **shakotí·sko?s**, literally 'they drown or dunk them.'

An expression that occurs in these stories when someone can't remember some detail, like for instance the name of someone, is **náhte? akwáh** 'what the heck, whaddyamacallit.' Another expression people use when they are talking in a conversational way, as in these stories, is **nikʌ·** 'let me see,' which is used when someone isn't sure about what they're going to say next.

Some words are hard to translate into English, and sometimes it takes almost a sentence, or even an image. One example is the verb form **yakothlohóstu** from Olive Elm's story about a mysterious woman outside the Language Centre. It is translated 'she is shielding herself' but this is not quite adequate; the verb describes someone who is turned away and shielding their face from view.

Ghost Sightings at the Language Centre
(Told by Olive Elm to Karin Michelson on July 6, 2007)

(1) Wé·ni kwí· ʌkwaka·látuhseʔ   tsiʔ   niyukwayaʔtawʌ́·u, tá·t núwaʔ nʌ
     Evidently   I will tell you all a story   what   has happened to us,   maybe   then

kyuhte wí· kátshaʔ ok nú· wísk niyohslakehkʌ́ kaʔikʌ́ tho   nityawʌ́·u   aʔé·
probably   somewhere   five   years past   this   thus   it has happened   over there

kʌs   tsiʔ tyakhilihunyʌniʔtákhwaʔ   Language Centre, tho   kʌs   nú·
usually   at   there we use it to teach them Language Centre,   that's   usually   where

yaʔteyakwatlástaʔ yawʌtʌtá·u yoʔkalá·u, craft kʌs   yotiyó·tʌhseʔ, tsyoʔk náhteʔ
over there we meet   Monday   evening,   craft   usually   they work,   different things

kutunyányuheʔ.   (2) Né· katiʔ wí· kaʔikʌ́ úska útlatsteʔ yoʔkáláshʌ, wé·ni kwí·
they make.   Well then it's   this   one time   evening,   evidently

tá·t núwaʔ nʌ   kanʌnaʔké·ne tsiʔ   yoshno·lé· kʌs   tutayó·kalaweʔ.
maybe   then in the fall   because it is fast   usually   it got dark again.

(3) Nʌ kwí· né· kaʔikʌ́ Lana kʌs   yutátyats,   né· kuwatilihunyʌ·níheʔ
     So then   it's this   Lana   customarily is her name,   it's   she teaches them

kʌs   tsyoʔk náhteʔ   kutunyányuheʔ. (4) Né· katiʔ wí· yahá·yuweʔ   thikʌ́,
usually   all kinds of things they make.   Well then it's   she got over there   that,

waʔkhenhotúkwahseʔ   yaʔutáwyahteʔ, tahnú·   kʌs   ohná·kʌʔ nukwá· ne·né·
I opened the door for her she went in,   and   usually   in back   where   it's that

wheelchair tho nukwá· tkutawyaʔtákhwaʔ, waʔkhehlolí· Lana, waʔkí·luʔ,
wheelchair   that's where   they enter with it,   I told her   Lana,   I said,

"Wá·s yaʔsenhotukó   ohná·kʌʔ nukwá·, waʔtsyók   ʌku·néweʔ
"Go   open the door over there in back   where,   after a while   they will arrive

(1) So I guess I'll tell you the story about what happened to us, maybe about five years ago
this happened over at the Language Centre, that's where we used to meet on Monday nights,
the ladies were working on craft, making all kinds of things. (2) This one evening, I guess it
must have been in the fall because it got dark early. (3) So then Lana is her name, she was
the one who used to teach them to make different things. (4) Well anyway she got there, I
opened the door for her and she went in, and in the back is where they come in with a wheelchair, so I told Lana, I said, "Go open the back door, after a while they will get here,

ka?ikʌ,   tekniyáshe   kʌs   a·kí·lu?   yah thya·ya·wʌ́·   tsi?   kʌs   tho nukwá·
this,   two of them   usually   I'd say   it has to be   that   usually   that's where

ʌtkniláthʌ?   ka?ikʌ ramp   ʌtkyatáwyah<u>te</u>?."   (5) Nʌ kwí·   ya?eya·kʌ́ne?,   kwáh
the two will climb up   this   ramp   the two will enter."   So then   she went out,   just

nʌ   tutayó·kalawe?   ya?eya·kʌ́ne?   thikʌ,   ya?enhotu·kó·,   ya?utkátho?
then   it got dark again   she went out   that,   she opened the door,   she looked that way

yakʌ?,   tho   kwáh   yakothlohóstu   yakukwé   tho   i·yé<u>te</u>?.
reportedly,   there   just   she is shielding herself   a woman   there   she is standing.

(6) Kwáh   wa?í·lu?,   "kwáh   oni?   wakanúhte?   tsi?   ni·yót   tsi?   yakotsluní,
      Just   she said,   "just   even   I know   how   it is so   that   she is dressed,

yakó·khale?   khále?   yakotya?tawí·tu,   kwa?nyóh ok   onikwʌ́htala?   thi·yót
she has on a skirt   and   she has on a jacket,   seems just like   red   it's like

yakotya?tawí·tu."   (7) "Tho   i·yé<u>te</u>?."   (8) Wa?í·lu?   nʌ sok wí·
she has on a jacket."   "There   she is standing."   She said   so then too

wa?akonehla·kó·   ki?   né·n   Lana.   (9) Uhka? né· náhte?   kʌ? nú·
she was surprised   actually   it's that   Lana.   Who   right there

niyakotahséhtu   tá·t   tho   tyutawya?tá·ne?,   né·n,   wa?tyutkahkwílo?oke?
she is hiding   if   there   she is going to come in,   it's that,   she blinked

yakʌ?,   yusayutkátho?   ókhna?   né·   yah   kánike?
reportedly,   she looked over that way again   and then   it's   not   anywhere

té·tsye<u>te</u>?.   (10) Wé·ni kwí·   né·   tá·t núwa?   wa?akotyánlune?
she is not standing anymore.   Evidently   it's   maybe   it got her spooked

thikʌ   ne? thó·<u>ne</u>?.   (11) Né·n   yah   se? wí·   náhte?   te?yakawʌ́   thikʌ,
that   at that time.   It's that   not   too   anything   she didn't say   that,

that's where these two ladies have to get up the ramp to come in." (5) So then she went out, it had got dark again and she went out, she opened the door, she looked out, there shielding herself and turned the other way was a woman standing there. (6) She said, "I even know how she was dressed, she had on a skirt and a jacket, and the jacket she was wearing was kind of red." (7) "She was standing there." (8) She said so then she, Lana, was surprised. (9) Who would it be hiding right there if she was going to come in? and then she blinked, she looked out that way again, and then she wasn't there anymore. (10) I guess maybe it spooked her at the time. (11) She didn't say anything,

tutayutáwyahteʔ,   né·n,   kwáh   kʌʔ náheʔ   thikʌ́,   tá·t núwaʔ   swʌhní·tat   thikʌ́
she came in again, it's that, just   a while   that,   maybe   one month   that

nʌ   elhúwaʔ   waʔukhlo·lí·   náhteʔ   naʔakoyá·tawʌʔ.   (12) Tsiʔ   waʔutatatkátho?
then   just then   she told me   what   happened to her.   That   she saw her

kaʔikʌ́   yakukwé   tho   i·yéteʔ   yakothlohóstu   tsiʔ   kanúhsoteʔ.
this   a woman   there   she is standing   she is shielding herself   at   there is a building.

(13) Kháleʔ   né·   oniʔ   né·   tho   nihoyaʔtawʌ́·u,   né·n,   náhteʔ akwáh,
       And   it's   too   it's   thus   it has happened to him,   it's that,   what exactly,

James,   James Antone,   lokstʌ́ha,   né·   kʌs   tho   loyo·té·   thikʌ́   tsiʔ náheʔ
James,   James Antone,   old man,   it's   usually   there   he is working   that   while

Masyha   oskánhe   yukniyó·tʌhseʔ,   elhúwaʔ   tshaʔakwatáwyahteʔ   né·   tho   thikʌ́
dear Mercy   together   we two work,   recently   when we came   it's   there   that

Language Centre,   tsyoʔk náhteʔ   lacarpenter   kʌs kwí·   ya·wét,   lateyʌʔtúnyuheʔ.
Language Centre,   different things   carpenter   usually   kind of like,   he fixes things.

(14) Né· katiʔ wí·   waʔakyatolíshʌʔ   nʌ   né·   tutayakyahtʌ·tí·,   nʌ
       Well then it's   we two rested   then   it's   we two left to go home again,   then

laulhá·   tho   yusahatáwyahteʔ,   cupboards   wahatunyániʔ.   (15) Né·n,   thikʌ́
him   there   he went in again,   cupboards   he made several.   It's that,   that

tshaháhsaneʔ,   nʌ kwí·   tetyó·kalas   nʌ   sahaya·kʌ́neʔ,   kaʔsléhtaku   sahatítaneʔ
when he finished, so then   it is dark   then   he went out again,   in the car   he got in again

nʌ   yahatkátho?,   tutaháhkete?,   yahatkátho?   tsi?   tkanúhsote?,   tho
then   he looked that way,   he backed it up,   he looked that way   at   there is a building,   there

yakʌʔ   í·lateʔ   lukwé,   ya·wét   kwáh   aʔé· nukwá·   nihotyelá·tu.
reportedly   he is standing   a man,   kind of like   just   away   he is turned facing.

she came back in, and so it was a while, maybe a month before she told me what happened to her. (12) That she saw this lady standing there by the building, shielding herself and turned the other way. (13) And it happened to him too—who the heck—James, James Antone, the old man, he would be there working while Mercy and I were working together, right after we first came to the Language Centre, kind of like a carpenter, he was fixing different things. (14) Well the two of us would get done and we'd leave to go home, then he went in, he was making cupboards. (15) So then [one time] when he finished, so then it was dark and then he went out again, he got in his car and then he looked, he backed up and he looked over at the building, a man was standing there, kind of like facing away.

(16) Aʔé· naʔtehotkhótsles,   kwáh oniʔ oʔswʌ́·taʔ lonaʔalo·lú.
Great how long is his coat, just   too   black   he has on a hat.

(17) Né·n,   né· kyuhte   oniʔ wí· né· tho nahoyá·tawʌʔ,   tutaháhketeʔ
It's that, it's supposedly too   it's thus it happened to him, he backed it up

yusahattsisto·tʌ́·   ókhnaʔ né· yah kánikeʔ té·shlate̲ʔ.   (18) Né·
again he put on lights and then it's not   anywhere he is not standing anymore.   It's

kyuhte   oniʔ wí· né·, nʌ s kwí· luthlolyányuheʔ   thikʌ́ tshiwahuniseʔkʌ́ thikʌ́
supposedly too   it's, so then   they tell all about it that   a long time ago   that

tho nú·   niyohatátiʔ,   thikʌ́ yʌhsanutahalo·lʌ́·teʔ   tho   áktaʔ tsiʔ
that's where a road extends,   that   you will go to the bottom of a hill there   near   at

kanúhsoteʔ   Language Centre. (19) Tho s yakʌʔ?   nú·   nihuwa·kʌ́heʔ
there is a building Language Centre.   That's reportedly where   they see him

kaʔikʌ́ tho   ni·yót   tsiʔ lotsluní   tshiwahuniseʔkʌ́. (20) Wé·ni kwí· kaʔikʌ́
this   that's how it is that he is dressed a long time ago.   Evidently   this

tá·t núwaʔ né· tshahayá·tat   kaʔikʌ́ tsiʔ né· ka·yʌ́· waho·kʌ́·   neʔ thó·neʔ, kháleʔ
maybe   it's he is the same one this   the one that   he saw him at that time,   and

thikʌ́ tsiʔ ka·yʌ́· Lana waʔutatatkáthoʔ, né· oniʔ né· kʌs   luthlolyányuheʔ
that   the one that Lana she saw her,   it's too   it's usually   they tell all about it

tshiwahuniseʔkʌ́, né· kʌs   oniʔ né· thikʌ́ tho nú·   niyohatátiʔ,
a long time ago,   it's usually too   it's that   that's where a road extends,

tá·t núwaʔ aʔé·nukwá· sʌ́haʔ corner nukwá· Townline Road, tho   kʌs
maybe   far way   more   corner where   Townline Road,   that's habitually

yakʌʔ?   né· nú·   thikʌ́ tayuhtʌ·tí·   thikʌ́, swatyelʌ́   aʔé· nukwá· Southwold
reportedly it's where that   she left from   that,   sometimes far way   Southwold

(16) He had on a really long coat, he was wearing a black hat too. (17) So I guess what happened to him, he backed up and he turned on the [car] lights, and then he [the man] wasn't anywhere anymore. (18) I guess too, then they used to tell about it a long time ago where that road goes, you go to the bottom of the hill near the Language Centre. (19) That's where they used to see him a long time ago dressed like that. (20) I guess maybe he was the same one that he saw at that time, and the one that Lana saw, they used to tell about it too a long time ago, where that road goes, maybe more over towards the corner of Townline Road, that's where she would leave from, sometimes

nyʌhʌ·yʌ́·,   a·lé·   oni? swatyelʌ́ a·kí·lu? wí· tho   ʌyekalʌhla·kó·,
she will go over there,   at times   too   sometimes   I'd say   there   she will turn onto,

né· kwí· núwa?   a·kí·lu? wé·ni kwí· Ball Park Road kuwa·yáts o·nʌ́.   (21) Tho s
so it's   this time   I'd say   evidently   Ball Park Road   is its name   now.   There

yakʌ?   tho nú·   thikʌ́ swatyelʌ́   na?ekalʌhla·<u>kó·</u>. (22) Tho nukwá·
reportedly   that's where   that   sometimes   she turned onto.   That's where

nuta·yʌ́·   thi·<u>kʌ́</u>. (23) Khehlolyányuhe?   Lana, wa?kí·lu?, "tá·t núwa?
she is coming from   that.   I am telling her all about it   Lana,   I said,   "maybe

nʌ   ne·né· onʌ́ wa?she·kʌ́· n luthlolyányuhe?   kʌs   tshiwanunise?kʌ́
then   that's it   now   you saw her   they are telling all about it   usually   a long time ago

tho   owaha?késhu?   teyakotawʌ́li<u>?</u>." (24) Yah ki?   ní· nuwʌtú náhte?
there   all over the roads   she is travelling."   Not   actually   we   never   anything

te?yukyatkáthu   í·   khále? Masyha,   tahnú· se? kʌs   swatyelʌ́
we two have not seen   me   and   dear Mercy,   and   too   usually   sometimes

tó· ok nityo?kalá·u nále? elhúwa?   tutayakyahtʌ·tí·,   nók tsi? yah ki?
really late at night   again   right then   we two left to come home again,   but   not   actually

ní· nuwʌtú náhte?   a·yukyatká<u>tho?</u>. (25) Yáts, tho   ki?   ok   uhte wí·
we   never   anything   for us two to see.   Yikes, that's   actually   only   supposedly

niwakka·lés.
how long my story is.

she would go towards Southwold, sometimes also she would turn onto what I'd say is called Ball Park Road now. (21) That's where she would turn in sometimes. (22) That's the way she comes. (23) I'm telling Lana, I said, "maybe the one you saw, they used to tell about it a long time ago that she used to travel all over these roads." (24) But the two of us never ever saw anything, me and Mercy, and sometimes it was really late at night before we left, but it was never for us to see anything. (25) Yikes, I guess my story is long enough.

Ghosts, Flirts, and Scary Beings

(Told by Verland Cornelius to Karin Michelson and Norma Kennedy
on September 13, 2007)

(1) Né· núwaʔ   thikʌ́ aʔé·   tshityakninákleʔ   lakeʔníha
     It's this time that   way over there when we two reside there my father

lonulhaʔké·ne. (2) Tho nú·   yeyakní·tluʔ   sʌ́h. (3) Né·n   kaʔikʌ́
at his mother's.   That's where over there we two dwell also.   It's that this

Model T kwí· yukniʔsléhtayʌ?,   thikʌ́ kakʌ́hoteʔ   wáh. (4) Wákyʌʔ kiʔ
Model T   we two have a car,   that   a cloth standing right.   I have   actually

núwaʔ kayá·taleʔ.   (5) Kwáh tsiʔ nikú thikʌ́ corner, aʔé· nukwá· wí· ya·wét wí·
now   it is pictured.   However many that   corner, way over there kind of like

Marina Hillhné·ke corner, kwáh tsiʔ nikú tho   yʌyáknewe?   thikʌ́ kháleʔ
at Marina Hill's   corner, however many   there we two will get there that   and

knock knock knock knock, úhkaʔ ok tho   i·yʌ́·.   (6) At the side of the
knock knock knock knock,   someone there someone is walking.   At the side of the

road, úhkaʔ ok náhteʔ tho   i·yʌ́·,   kwahikʌ́   teyakoshlihʌʔuhátiʔ.
road, someone   there someone is walking, just really someone is hurrying along.

(7) Owísklaʔ yakó·khaleʔ.   (8) Kháleʔ onikwʌ́htalaʔ jacket, kwáh tsiʔ
     White   she has on a skirt.   And   red   jacket, just   as

ni·yót   thikʌ́ sátstu.   (9) Kháleʔ teyakonúhkliʔ,   kháleʔ onikwʌ́htalaʔ
how it is that   you are wearing.   And   she has curly hair, and   red

yakonaʔalo·lú.   (10) Kwáh nʌ   thikʌ́ a·yakhihnútlaneʔ,   nʌ sók
she has on a hat.   Just   when   that   we would catch up to her, and then too

(1) This time it's when the two of us [my mother and I] were living over at my father's
mother's place. (2) That's where we were staying. (3) We had a car, a Model T, with a
cloth top, right. (4) I have a picture of it. (5) Whenever [at] that corner, kind of like way
over at Marina Hill's corner, whenever the two of us got there, knock knock knock knock
(Verland knocks gently on the table four times), someone was walking. (6) At the side of
the road, someone was walking, they were really in a hurry. (7) She had on a white skirt.
(8) And a red jacket, just like the one you are wearing. (9) And she had curly hair, and she
had on a red hat. (10) Just when we were about to catch up to her—and then

tsi? s wí· nisé· nʌ́hsyele?   tʌhsanítskwahkwe? tʌhsate?kháhetste? kwí·
thus   you   how you will do it you will jump   you will take a long stride

ni?i·sé. (11) Ok ne?   ka?ikʌ́, kwáh né· otokʌ́·u tsi? kwáh né· yeyelu?takwekú
you.   But as for this,   just for real   that just it's her whole body

tʌyunítskwahkwe?, a?é·   na?kaná·tslati   ya?etsko·táne?.
she will jump,   way over there that side of the ditch over there she landed.

(12) Yah né· kʌ? tha·ye·yéle?. (13) Kwáh né· otokʌ́·u tsi? tʌyunítskwahkwe?
      Not   it's she won't do this.   Just for real   that   she will jump

a?é· niwa?slátii?. (14) Yah thau·tú· a·yakyatkátho? yekúksne. (15) Tho   niyo·lé·
great it is wide.   It can't be   that we two see her face.   That's as far as

yʌyúhkete?   thikʌ́ Willy Georgehnehkʌ́   wáh, khále? tʌtyúhkete?.
she will go up to that   at the late Willy George's right, and   she will come back.

(16) Go back and forth thikʌ́ tsi? niyo·lé· wí· corner, khále? kʌh nukwá·
      Go back and forth   that   as far as   corner, and   over this way

nʌtsyeye·lá·te?.   (17) Tsi? nukwá· í· tyakwanákele?. (18) Tho   kati? wí· ni·yót
again she will face.   Where   us we reside.   Thus   anyway   it is so

tyótkut thikʌ́, yotká·te? tho   yukní·sle?,   ókhale? tho   ki?   i·yʌ́·.
always   that,   often   there we two are driving, and   there actually she is walking.

(19) Nʌ kwí· aknulhá· wa?í·lu?, "náhte? uhte   né· aolí·wa? thikʌ́ úhka? ok
      So then   my mother she said, "what   supposedly it's the reason that   someone

tho   tetyakotawʌ́li?."   (20) Wahʌ́·lu? laksótha,   "wé·ni kwí·
there someone is wandering."   He said   my grandfather, "evidently

úhka? ok náhte? tho   shakotíli   thikʌ́ wí· corner nukwá·."
someone   there they have killed someone that   corner where."

the way you do it when you jump, YOU take a long stride. (11) But this one, she would just
jump with her whole body, and she would land on the other side of the ditch. (12) She
wouldn't do this (Verland shows with her hands how she jumps with both legs together instead of one leg out in front of the other). (13) She would jump real wide. (14) We couldn't
see her face. (15) She would go as far as the late Willy George's, and she would come back
again. (16) Go back and forth as far as the corner, and she would face this direction.
(17) Where WE live. (18) That's how it was always, often we're driving there, and she was
there walking. (19) So then my mother said, "I wonder why someone keeps wandering
around there?" (20) My grandfather said, "must be someone got killed there at that corner."

(21) Tó· nikú ohná·kʌʔ nú· Rol Christjohn tahanatá·laʔ, wahʌ́·luʔ, "shekú
How much back then Rol Christjohn he came to visit, he said, "still

kʌ yetshi·kʌ́heʔ thikʌ́ atyanlúhslaʔ owahá·<u>ke</u>." (22) Waʔí·luʔ aknulhá·
question you all see her that ghost on the road." She said my mother

"shekú kih, shekú kiʔ tho ítyʌh<u>se</u>ʔ." (23) Wahʌ́·luʔ, "nʌ kiʔ
"still actually, still actually there she goes." He said, "now actually

usahihnúksaʔ [name], kwahikʌ́ tyótkut shakonú·wehseʔ kunukweshúha, tahnú·
I should go fetch him [name], just really always he likes them female persons, and

ati úhkaʔ kanyó· ok ta·hatetshʌ·líˑ." (24) Né· kwíˑ thikʌ́ náhteʔ akwáh
no matter anyone so long as he would find one." So it's that what quite

a·hiná·tuhkweʔ, [name], wahohnúk<u>sa</u>ʔ. (25) Ó·, kwáh kiʔ kʌʔ náheʔ
I should call him, [name], he went to fetch him. Oh, just actually a while

nʌ sahotiké·toht<u>e</u>ʔ. (26) Tahnú· wahsuti·y<u>ó</u>. (27) Né· tho
then they showed up again. And it is a nice night. It's there

nyahá·neʔ thikʌ́ wahotí·sleʔ, tho yahyateʔsléhtayʌʔ
over there the two went that they drove, there over there the two set their vehicle

tó·k niyo·léˑ, nʌ sók tho nyahá·leʔ, né· kyaleʔ tho áleʔ ni·yót thikʌ́,
some distance, then too there over there he went, it's again thus again it is so that,

waʔshakóhsleʔ, ókhnaʔ nʌ́hkleʔ aʔé· nukwá· nyaha·<u>yʌ́</u>.
he chased her, and then and so then way over there over there she went.

(28) Tutá·leʔ ókhaleʔ tutahuwáhsel<u>e</u>ʔ. (29) Go back,
He came back this way and she followed him back this way. Go back,

kʌʔ kwíˑ niya·wʌ́·seʔ kʌ́h. (30) Kháleʔ onʌ́ yaʔthoshlíhʌʔ thikʌ́,
this is how it happens see. And then he is hurrying over there that,

(21) Whenever back then Rol Christjohn came to visit, he would say, "do you still see that ghost on the road?" (22) My mother said, "still, she's still there." (23) He said, "I could go get [name], he really always likes the ladies, and could be anyone so long as he finds one." (24) So what the heck is his name? [name], he went to get him. (25) Oh, not too long and they showed up again. (26) And it was a nice night. (27) They drove there, they parked the car not too far away, and then he went over there, and it was like this, he chased after her, and then she walked off that way. (28) He came back this way and she followed him back. (29) Go back, this is the way it's happening (Verland motioning with the hands back and forth). (30) And then he hurried,

ostúha sʌ́haʔ yaʔshakohnútlane<u>ʔ</u>.   (31) Kháleʔ onʌ́ tho niyo·lé·   u·tú·
a little   more   he caught up to her.   And   now   it is far enough   it could be

waʔteshakokalhate·ní·, skeleton né· kʌh yekúk<u>sne</u>.   (32) Kʌh né·
he turned her around,   skeleton   it's here her face.   This   it's

naʔteyeká·lah<u>seʔ</u>.   (33) Neʔ thó·neʔ nʌ   [name] he just freeze, kwáh olihwiyó
how big her eyes are.   At that time   then [name]   he just freeze,   just   a sure thing

tsiʔ tho naʔohnílhʌʔ tsiʔ lúnheʔ   wahotétsh<u>ʌ</u>ʔ.   (34) Shekú n usahatolyá·nluʔ
that   thus how it got stiff as   he is alive he got scared.   Even   could he move

yah tha·hakwe·n<u>í·</u>.   (35) Yaʔshakotkʌhlá·tahkweʔ, nʌ   kwáh kʌʔ náheʔ
not   he would not be able.   He quickly let go of her,   then   just   a while

tusahatkalhate·ní·,   ókhnaʔ   nʌ́hkleʔ   tusahaláhtatsteʔ Rol laó·slet,
he turned around again,   and then   and so then   he started it again Rol   his car,

waʔthatkalhate·ní· tahanhotu·kó·   tutahatítane<u>ʔ</u>.   (36) Nʌ sók   tutahaláhtateʔ
he turned around   he opened the door   he got in again.   Then too   he ran back again

yakʌʔ   tutahatítaneʔ yakʌʔ,   yah tha·hakwe·ní· náhteʔ   usahʌ́·<u>luʔ</u>.
reportedly   he got in again reportedly,   not   he is not able   anything   that he says anymore.

(37) Tsiʔ niyo·lé· laksothné·ke   nyusá·neweʔ,   nʌ
       Until   at my grandfather's   the two arrived over there again,   then

yusahyatáwyahteʔ   nʌ   u·tú·   sahata·tí· n   [name].   (38) Tsiʔ niyo·lé·
the two went in again   then   it could be   he spoke again [name].   As far as that

nahotétsh<u>ʌ</u>ʔ.   (39) Yah tha·hakwe·ní· usahata·tí·.   (40) "Náhteʔ
how scared he got.   Not   he is not able   that he speaks anymore.   "What

uhte   wahsatkáthoʔ," wahʌ́·luʔ, "kwáh kiʔ   nók skeleton, kwáh aʔé·
supposedly you saw,"   he said,   "just   actually only skeleton,   just   great

he's a little closer to catching up with her. (31) And then [he was] that close he could turn her around, here her face was a skeleton. (32) Her eyes were THIS big. (33) At that time [name], he just freeze, for sure that's how stiff his being got, did he get scared. (34) Even [if he tried] to move he couldn't. (35) He let go of her real quick, in just a little while he turned around again, and then Rol started his car again, he turned around, he opened the door and he got back in. (36) Then he ran, he got back in, he couldn't say anything. (37) Until they got back to my grandfather's, they went in again and then [name] could speak again. (38) That's how scared he got. (39) He wasn't able to speak anymore. (40) "What did you see?," he said "just a skeleton,

niyoshu·wá·seʔ   yekahlaʔkéshuʔ.”   (41) Waʔkí·luʔ “yah katiʔ   teʔshenuhwé·u
so big are the holes her eyes.”   I said   “not   so then you don't like her

waʔtehsatetshʌ·lí·,” wahʌ́·luʔ “yah kiʔ   teʔkhenuhwé·u.”   (42) Nók tsiʔ yah
you found one,”   he said   “not   actually I don't like her.”   But   not

kiʔ   teʔwakanúhteʔ tho kiʔ   ni·yót thikʌ́, wahu·níseʔ kiʔ   thikʌ́
actually I don't know   thus actually it is so that,   a long time actually that

tho   niyohtuhátiʔ,   tho ítyʌhseʔ   thikʌ́ yaku·kwé. (43) Tá·t núwaʔ
thus so it is going along, there she walks here that   a woman.   Maybe

shekú tho ni·yót tá·t kwahotokʌ́·u a·yakehsákhaʔ   she·kú. (44) Maybe
still   thus it is so if   just for real   one would go look for one still.   Maybe

it's still like that yet.   (45) Yah kʌ   téhselheʔ   a·sheyaʔtisákhaʔ.
it's still ike that yet.   Not   question you don't want you would go look for her.

(46) Onikwʌ́htalaʔ yakonaʔalolú   kháleʔ onikwʌ́htalaʔ ni·yót   teyakotkhot,
      Red   she has on a hat and   red   what kind she has on a coat,

kháleʔ owísklaʔ yakó·khaleʔ.   (47) Tahnú· kʌʔ ok   niyakoʔkha·lés   kʌ́h.
and   white   she has on a skirt.   And   this only how long is her skirt eh.

(48) Kánhke ok ʌshe·kʌ́·   atyanlúhslaʔ nʌʔ né·.
      Some time   you will see her ghost   that one.

  (49) Thoʔn ́ né· núwaʔ nikʌ́·,   kháleʔ kʌs   kʌh nukwá· nutayákneʔ,
      And then it's this time let me see, and   usually over this way we two came,

ya·wét kwí· thikʌ́ Number 3 School kwí· a·kí·luʔ ohlu·wáku kiʔwáh. (50) Tho
kind of like   that   Number 3 School   I'd say   in the gulley right.   That's

kʌs   sʌ́· nú· yah thya·ya·wʌ́· tsiʔ ehtaʔkéshuʔ kwí· yákneʔ,   yah
habitually also where it has to be   that on foot   we two walk, not

with two great big holes for her eyes.” (41) I said, “you don't like her then, the one you
found,” he said “I don't like her.” (42) I don't actually know but that's how it was, a long
time it was like that, this woman walking around here. (43) Maybe it's still like that if you
really want to go and look. (44) Maybe it's still like that yet. (45) Don't you want to go and
look for her? (46) She has on a red hat and a red coat, and she has on a white skirt.
(47) And her skirt is short. (48) If you should see her sometime, it's a ghost.

  (49) And then this time, let me see, and we came this way, kind of like [towards] Number
3 School, I'd say in the gulley. (50) That's where also the two of us had to walk,

teʔyukniʔsléhtayʌʔ   neʔ thó·neʔ, ehtaʔkéshuʔ kwí· yákneʔ,   tho   né·
we two don't have a car at that time, on foot   we two walk, there it's

íthlateʔ,   aʔé· naʔtehatkhótsles,   felt hat sʌ́· lonaʔalo·lú.   (51) Né·
he is standing, great how long is his coat, felt hat also he has on a hat.   It's

kyuhte wí· tshahayá·tat   thikʌ́ Mercy wí· luwatkáthos Number 3 School.
supposedly he is the same one   that Mercy   she sees him Number 3 School.

(52) Áhsok   yakʌʔ   náleʔ   átste   íthlateʔ,   lonaʔalolú   kháleʔ
      All of a sudden reportedly then again outside   he is standing,   he has on a hat and

aʔé· niyólhes   topcoat lótstu.   (53) Tho s nú·   thikʌ́ íthlateʔ,
great how long it is topcoat he is wearing.   That's where that   he is standing,

nʌ kyaleʔ wí· niyukyatetshʌʔuhátiʔ,   kʌh nukwá·   nutayuknenuhátiʔ.
so again   we two are going along so scared,   over this way   we two came along.

(54) Oskanʌʔshúha lohtʌtyuhátiʔ.   (55) Yah kwí· teʔyakninú·wehseʔ
      Slowly   he is on his way.   Not   we two don't like

a·shakyatukóhtʌʔ,   tá·t núwaʔ a·shukniye·ná·.   (56) Kwáh kwí· laulhá·
that we two pass him,   maybe   he may catch us two.   Just   him

wahanúhtuʔ   tsiʔ niyo·lé· waʔakwanutá·laneʔ.   (57) He just disappeared
he determined it   until   we got to the top of the hill.   He just disappeared

kanyó· onʌ́ wahanutá·laneʔ.   (58) Nʌ   uhte wí·   e·só· waʔukyatétshʌʔ.
as soon as   he got to the top of the hill.   Then   supposedly much   we two got scared.

   (59) And náhteʔ uhte   sʌ́· a·kka·látuʔ.   (60) Né· yakʌʔ wí· sʌ́· n,
          And what   supposedly also I should tell a story.   It's reportedly also,

lotiʔtéhahseʔ wí· sʌ́· yah teʔyoyáneleʔ. (61) Ne·né· tho   nihoyaʔtawʌ́·u
they flirt   also not it is not good.   It's   thus   how it has happened to him

we didn't have a car at that time, so we're walking, he's standing there, his coat is really long, also he has on a felt hat. (51) I guess he's the same one that Mercy used to see at Number 3 School. (52) All of a sudden he's standing outside, he has on a hat and he's wearing a really long topcoat. (53) That's where he's standing, and we're going along so scared, we're coming along over this way. (54) He's moving real slow. (55) We don't like for us to pass him, maybe he would catch us. (56) It was up to him [how fast we could go], until we got to the top of the hill. (57) He just disappeared as soon as he got to the top of the hill. (58) Then I guess we got very scared.

   (59) And, what other story should I tell? (60) Also, people flirting is not good. (61) This is how it happened to him,

thikʌ́, né· kyaleʔ wí· né·n   í· kwí· lakuhwatʌ́ha, [name] kwí· nʌʔ né·.
that,   it's so again   it's that me   my uncle,   [name]   that one.

(62) Kwáh yakʌʔ   ati   úhkaʔ   yakukwé kanyó· ok yakukwé
      Just   reportedly no matter anyone   a woman   so long as a woman

ta·hatetshʌ·lí·.   (63) Tyótkut wí· oyá·   tehatéhsaks. (64) Né·n,   náleʔ
he should find one.   Always   another   he looks for.   It's that, then again

né·n   ahsúthʌ   thikʌ́ aʔé·   Joneshné kwí· nú·,   ya·wét a·kí·luʔ
it's that midnight   that   over there at the Jones's   where,   like   I should say

Agnes Kennedyhné nú·.   (65) Tho   né· kwahikʌ́ wahsutiyó, thoʔnʌ́
at Agnes Kennedy's   where.   There   it's just really a nice night,   and then

lothu·té· yakʌʔ   "slap slap slap slap slap slap slap."   (66) Yahatkáthoʔ,
he hears   reportedly "slap slap slap slap slap slap slap."   He looked that way,

kʌh yakʌʔ   ni·yús   kʌ́·tho wí· nityótteʔ, kwáh olihwiyó   tsiʔ
here reportedly it is so long here   it is so high, just   a sure thing that

teyothweʔnuní, tahnú· kwahikʌ́ tsiʔ teyostalátheʔ, kwáh tsiʔ ni·yót   tho
it is round,   and   just really that it is shiny,   just   as   how it is thus

niwahsohkó·tʌ   ó·swʌʔ wáh. (67) Tho   niwaʔswʌʔti·yó.   (68) Kwah nók tsiʔ
the kind of colour coal   right.   That's how it is a nice black.   Only

tekahsinu·tú·. (69) Kwah nók tsiʔ ohná·tshaʔ. (70) Nʌ sok wí· né· tutahaté·koʔ
it has legs.   Only   hind end.   So then too it's he fled this way

waʔthaláhtateʔ waʔthaláhtateʔ waʔthaláhtateʔ, tho   kiʔ   thikʌ́ ohnaʔkʌ́·shuʔ
he ran   he ran   he ran,   there actually that   all along behind

"chok chok chok chok chok chok chok chok," wahóhseleʔ.   (71) Kháleʔ onʌ́
"chok chok chok chok chok chok chok chok,"   it chased him.   And   then

so me, MY uncle [name], that's the one. (62) It could be just about any woman so long as he found himself a woman. (63) He was always looking for another one. (64) So then, it was midnight and over by the Jones's (she makes a mistake, stops and continues), kind of like I should say at Agnes Kennedy's place. (65) It was a really nice night, and then he heard "slap slap slap slap slap slap slap." (Verland gently claps her hands as she says each "slap.") (66) He looked over that way, it was this long and this high (gestures with her hands to show how long and how high), and for sure it was round, and really shiny, just like the colour of coal. (67) That's how black it was, very black. (68) Only it had legs. (69) But it was only a hind end. (70) And then he ran away this way, he ran, he ran, he ran, and there all along behind [him], "chok chok chok chok chok chok chok chok," it chased him. (71) And then

kʌh   tutá·lawe?,   nʌ   kwáh ok o·nʌ́.   (72) Tu?swʌ?túti?.
over here   he arrived back,   then   just the same.   A black thing is coming.

(73) Né·n   ísi?   lonulha?ké·ne tutá·lawe?,   kwáh ok   yakʌ?
      It's that   there   at his mother's   he got back,   and just   reportedly

thyahanhohá·leke?,   tho   ya?thahyeskwʌ́htalane? oshu?kalá·ke.
he just pushed open the door,   there   he fell flat on his stomach   on the floor.

(74) Yah   thau·tú·   náhte?   oni?   né·   usahʌ́·lu?.   (75) Khále?   ki?
      Not   it can't be   anything   even   it's   that he says again.   And   actually

onʌ́   wahathlo·lí·   tsi?   náhte?   wahatkátho?.   (76) Ohná·tsha?.   (77) Wa?í·lu?
then   he told about   that   what   he saw.   Hind end.   She said

yakʌ?   aksótha,   "né· kwí·   tsi?   nisʌ?téha."   (78) "Tyótkut   kunukwé
reportedly   my grandmother,   "so it's   how   you are a flirt."   "Always   women

tesalelútyehse?."   (79) "Ati   niyukwe?tó·tʌ   né·   ki?   kanyó· ok wí·
you are racing along."   "No matter   what kind she is   it's   actually   so long as

ta·hsatetshʌ·lí·."   (80) "Tá· ni·yót kwí·   niwa?swʌ?tó·tʌ   i·wélhe?   aesaye·ná·."
you should find one."   "Now look'it   it is a black kind   it wants   it should catch you."

he got to over here, and just the same. (72) This black thing is coming. (73) So he got back
to his mother's place, he just pushed open the door, and he fell flat on the floor. (74) He
couldn't even say anything. (75) And finally he told what he saw. (76) A hind end.
(77) My grandmother said, "you are such a flirt." (78) "You're always racing after the
women." (79) "It doesn't matter what she is like, so long as you find yourself one."
(80) "Now look'it, this black thing wants to catch you."

My Father's Encounter

(Told by Norma Kennedy to Karin Michelson on September 14, 2007)

(1) A·kuka·látuhse?   kyuhte wí·   ka?ikʌ́   tsi?   náhte?   lakkalatú·se
     I could tell you a story   supposedly   this   that   what   he has told me a story

(1) I guess I could tell you a story that my late father told me

lake?nihkʌ́   kʌ? tshitwakyʌ́<u>ha</u>.   (2) Ya·wét kyuhte wí· kátsha? ok nú· wísk yawʌ·lé·
my late father   when I was young.   It's like   supposedly   somewhere   fifteen

tsha?tewakohsliyá·ku.   (3) Nʌ   wahaka·látu? ka?ikʌ́, né· kyuhte wí· n
when I have crossed over winters.   Then   he told a story   this,   it's   supposedly

onélu?uske? s yotityohkwanʌ́·ne? ka?ikʌ́ kʌh nú·   nikutináklehkwe? tshiwahu·ní<u>se</u>?.
witches   there were many   this   over here   they used to reside   a long time ago.

(4) Úska útlatste? yakʌ?   ka?ikʌ́, nʌ   kyuhte wí· kwáh kʌ? nityo?kalá·u
      One   time   reportedly this,   then   supposedly   really late at night

kátsha? ok nú· lawehtú·ne?   tutahohtʌtyuháti?,   ahsuhkʌ́ kwí·
somewhere   he had gone somewhere   he is on his way back home,   before when

né· tshiyukwattsisto·tú· ka?ikʌ́ owahaktúti<u>?</u>.   (5) Khále? ahsuhkʌ́
it's   when we have lights   this   along the road.   And   before when

tshiyukwa·yʌ́· wí· n hydro.   (6) Né· kwí· thikʌ́ coal oil kwí· yakwátsta?
when we have   hydro.   So it's   that   coal oil   we use it

tsi? yukwattsístote? ne? thó·ne? tshiwahu·ní<u>se</u>?.   (7) Kwáh kwí· ikʌ́ tsi?
at   we have light   at that time   a long time ago.   Just really   that

tetyó·kalas kwí· n átste,   tho kwí· n niwahsutó·tʌ   ka?ikʌ́, wa?kí·lu? wí·
it is dark   outside,   that's   the kind of night it is   this,   I said

kátsha? ok nú· lawehtú·ne?   lake?nihkʌ́.   (8) Tahnú· nʌ kwí·
somewhere   he had gone somewhere   my late father.   And   so then

kwáh kʌ? nityo?kalá·u thikʌ́ tsha?tutahohtʌtyuháti<u>?</u>.   (9) Tahnú· tho kwí·
really late at night   that   when he is on his way back home.   And   there

thikʌ́ kalista?késhu?   nú· tahathahítane?,   né· wí· tsi? tehoshlíhʌhse?
that   along the railway tracks   where he came down the route,   because   he is hurrying

when I was young. (2) Like I guess I was about fifteen years old. (3) Then he told this story, I guess there used to be a lot of witches living over here a long time ago. (4) One time, I guess it was really late at night, he had gone somewhere and he was on his way back home, that was before we had lights along the roads. (5) And it was before we had hydro. (6) We used coal oil for lights back then, a long time ago. (7) It was really dark out that night, and like I said my late father had gone somewhere. (8) And so then it was really late at night when he was on his way back home. (9) And the route he took was along the railway tracks, because he was in a hurry

usá·la<u>we</u>ʔ.   (10) Kalistaʔkéshuʔ kwí·   thikʌ́ nú·   tahathahítane<u>ʔ</u>.
for him to get home.   Along the railway tracks   that   where   he came down the route.

(11) Né·n   lothu·té· thikʌ́ tsiʔ úhkaʔ ok ohnaʔkʌ́·shuʔ ta·yʌ́·,   nʌ kwí·
      It's that he hears   that   that someone   along behind   someone is coming,   so then

waʔtha·táneʔ, wahatnúhtuhteʔ, tá·t núwaʔ ʌhuwahnútla<u>ne</u>ʔ.   (12) Né·n,
he stopped,   he waited,   maybe   someone will catch up to him.   It's that,

né· tsiʔ waʔtha·táneʔ kaʔikʌ́ tsiʔ í·leʔ,   waʔtka·táneʔ oniʔ né· thikʌ́ tsiʔ
it's as   he stopped   this   as   he is walking, it stopped   too   it's   that   that

lothu·té· wí· úhkaʔ ok ta·yʌ́·   ohnaʔkʌ́·shuʔ tsiʔ í·leʔ.
he hears   someone   someone is coming   along behind   as   he is walking.

(13) Né· kwí· wá·lelheʔ,   wé·ne kwí· yah úhkaʔ,   nók tsiʔ wá·lelheʔ lothu·té·
      So it's   he thought, evidently   not   anyone,   but   he thought he hears

kaʔikʌ́ úhkaʔ ok ta·<u>yʌ́·</u>.   (14) Nʌ kyaleʔ wí· wahatu·kó·teʔ   kaʔikʌ́,
this   someone   someone is coming.   So again   he continued on   this,

kháleʔ né· lothu·té· thikʌ́ tsiʔ úhkaʔ ok ta·yʌ́·   ohnaʔkʌ́·shuʔ,
and   it's   he hears   that   that someone   someone is coming   along behind,

lothu·té· wí· tsiʔ úhkaʔ ok i·yʌ́· wí·   kalistaʔkéshuʔ.
he hears   that someone   someone is walking   along the railway tracks.

(15) Né·n,   waʔtha·táneʔ kwí· thikʌ́ a·hatahúhsatateʔ, kháleʔ né· yah náhteʔ
      It's that, he stopped   that   that he may listen, and   it's   not   anything

teʔshothu·té·.   (16) Nʌ kwí· né· ostúha kaʔikʌ́ wahotétshʌʔ tsiʔ
he doesn't hear it anymore.   So then   it's   a little   this   he got scared   because

lonúhteʔ wí· tsiʔ kaʔikʌ́ onéluʔuskeʔ wí· yotityohkwanʌ́ kʌh nú·   nikutinákleʔ
he knows   that this   witches   there are many   over here   they reside

to get back home. (10) He came along the railway tracks. (11) And so he heard someone coming along behind, so then he stopped, he waited, maybe they would catch up to him. (12) So he stopped walking, it stopped too the [noise] he heard of someone coming along behind as he was walking. (13) So he thought, must be there is no one, but he thought he heard someone coming. (14) So he continued on again, and he heard someone coming along behind, he heard someone walking on the tracks. (15) So he stopped to listen, and he didn't hear anything anymore. (16) So then he got scared a bit because he knew that there were a lot of witches living over here

neʔ thó·neʔ tshiwahu·níseʔ. (17) Né· kwíʔ wá·lelheʔ, tá·t núwaʔ né· thikʌ tho
at that time a long time ago.   So it's   he thought,   maybe   it's   that   there

teyonatawʌliʔ.   (18) Nʌ kwíʔ né· kaʔikʌ wahotétshʌʔ, nʌ sok wíʔ kwahikʌ tsiʔ
they are wandering.   So then   it's   this   he got scared,   so then too just really   that

nʌ   waʔthaláhtateʔ, yoshno·lé· kwíʔ sá·laweʔ.   (19) Né· thikʌ nʌ
then   he started to run,   it is fast   he got home.   It's   that   then

tshusá·laweʔ   wahanuhtunyu·kó·, kwáh wíʔ olihwiyó   tsiʔ to·kʌske? thikʌ
when he got home   he thought it over,   quite   a sure thing that   it's true   that

úhkaʔ ok náhteʔ awéluʔuskeʔ thikʌ tho   teyotawʌliʔ   kalistaʔkéshuʔ.
someone   witch   that   there she is wandering   along the railway tracks.

(20) Tahnú· tsyeyá·tat kaʔikʌ shakoyʌtelí   úhkaʔ náhohteʔ.
        And   one person   this   he knows someone   who.

(21) Wahʌ́·luʔ, kwáh olihwiyó   tsiʔ né· thikʌ i·yʌ́lheʔ   a·huwatetshahníhtʌ.
        He said,   quite   a sure thing that   it's   that   she wants   she would scare him.

(22) Wahanuhtunyu·kó· thikʌ, wahʌ́·luʔ, "kwáh olihwiyó   tsiʔ Yakowín thi·kʌ́."
        He thought it over   that,   he said,   "quite   a sure thing that   Yakowín   that."

(23) Né· wíʔ tsiʔ shakoyʌtelí wíʔ thikʌ Yakowín. (24) Kwáh tsiʔ nikú
        Because   he knows her   that   Yakowín.   Whatever amount

tʌhyátlaneʔ   kátshaʔ ok nú·, waʔthnithalúniʔ s kwíʔ ostúha. (25) Tahnú·
the two will meet somewhere,   the two conversed   a little.   And

lolihwahlukú kwíʔ tsiʔ awéluʔuskeʔ yakʌʔ   kaʔikʌ Yakowín. (26) Né· kwíʔ
he has heard news   that   witch   reportedly this   Yakowín.   So it's

aolí·waʔ   thikʌ wá·lelheʔ, tsiʔ kwáh wíʔ olihwiyó   tsiʔ Yakowín thi·kʌ́.
the reason that   he thought, that   quite   a sure thing that   Yakowín   that.

a long time ago. (17) So he thought, maybe they're wandering around there. (18) So then
he got scared, and then he really started to run to get home fast. (19) When he got home he
thought about it, for sure it was true that some witch was wandering around there on the
railway tracks. (20) And he knew who one of them was. (21) He said, for sure she wants to
scare him. (22) He thought about it, he said, "for sure it's Yakowín." (23) Because he knew
Yakowín. (24) Every time they met somewhere, they talked a little. (25) And he heard that
Yakowín was a witch. (26) So that's why he thought that for sure it was Yakowín.

(27) Nʌ kwíˑ tóhkaʔ niwahsuˑtáke náleʔ sahahtʌˑtíˑ, néˑ kwíˑ
      So then a few nights amount to then again he went away again, so it's

thikʌ́ íˑlelheʔ kwáh olihwiyó aˑhluˑníˑ tsiʔ Yakowín thikʌ́ tho
that he wants quite a sure thing he would make that Yakowín that there

tetyotawʌ́liʔ kalistaʔkéshuʔ. (28) Nʌ kyaleʔ wíˑ thikʌ́ tho núˑ
she is wandering again along the railway tracks. So again that that's where

kalistáˑke wahathahítaneʔ kaʔikʌ́, kátshaʔ ok núˑ wáˑlehteʔ.
on the railway tracks he took the route this, somewhere he went somewhere.

(29) Nók aolíˑwaʔ thikʌ́ kalistaʔkéshuʔ nyaháˑleʔ tsiʔ íˑlelheʔ
      Only the reason that along the tracks he went that way because he wants

aˑhotoˑkʌ́ˑseʔ úhkaʔ náhteʔ kaʔikʌ́ luwáhslehseʔ. (30) Nʌ kwíˑ néˑ,
he would find out who this someone is chasing him. So then it's,

kwáh kiʔ néˑ kok náheʔ kaʔikʌ́, kalistaʔkéshuʔ lothahítakheʔ ókhnaʔ
just actually it's a little while this, along the tracks he is in the route and then

lothuˑtéˑ úhkaʔ ok ohnaʔkʌ́ˑshuʔ taˑyʌ́ˑ tsiʔ íleʔ.
he hears someone along behind someone is coming as he is walking.

(31) Nʌ kiʔ ok wíˑ óksaʔ ok waʔthaˑtáneʔ thikʌ́ wahatahúhsatateʔ, nʌ kiʔ ok néˑ
      Right then right away he stopped that he listened, right then it's

yah teʔshothuˑtéˑ wíˑ úhkaʔ náhteʔ kalistáˑke aˑyʌ́ˑshekeʔ.
not he doesn't hear anymore anyone railway tracks that one would be walking.

(32) Ókhaleʔ wahatuˑkóˑteʔ, kháleʔ néˑ shothuˑtéˑ tsiʔ úhkaʔ seʔ ok thikʌ́
      And he continued on, and it's again he hears that someone too that

tho tayakotawʌlyeháti? kalistaʔkéshuʔ. (33) Kwáh kʌʔ niyoˑléˑ
there someone is travelling this way along the railway tracks. Just some distance

(27) So then in a few nights he went away again, he wanted to make sure it was Yakowín wandering around there on the railway tracks. (28) So again he took the railway tracks, he went somewhere. (29) The only reason he went along the tracks was because he wanted to find out who kept chasing him. (30) So then he was going along the tracks for just a little while and already he heard someone coming along behind as he was walking. (31) Right away he stopped and listened, right then he didn't hear anyone anymore walking on the tracks. (32) And he went on and again he heard somebody travelling along the tracks.

nyahá·leʔ   thikʌ́, nʌ sók   watha·táneʔ   wahatahúhsatateʔ,   kháleʔ   né· kwáh
he went that way   that,   then too he stopped   he listened,   and   it's   just

yah náhteʔ   teʔshothu·té·,   wé·ne   tsiʔ yah úhkaʔ   kánikeʔ
not   anything he doesn't hear it anymore, evidently that   not   anyone   nowhere

té·yʌhseʔ.   (34) Kwáh kiʔ   kok náheʔ   thikʌ́ kháleʔ sahatu·kó·teʔ
one isn't there.   Just   actually a little while that   and   again he continued on

kháleʔ shothu·té·   thikʌ́ tsiʔ úhkaʔ seʔ ok tahuwáhseleʔ.
and   again he hears that   that someone too   someone is chasing him.

(35) Úhkaʔ ok ohnaʔkʌ́·shuʔ ta·yʌ́·   tsiʔ í·leʔ.   (36) Nʌ sok wí·
       Someone   along behind   someone is coming as   he is walking.   So then too

tutahatkalhatényahteʔ,   waʔthaláhtateʔ thikʌ́, kwáh tsiʔ niyoshno·lé· a·hakwe·ní·
he turned around real quick,   he ran   that,   just   however fast   he is able to

waʔthaláhtateʔ, tho   né· tú·skeʔ waʔshakohnútlaneʔ kaʔikʌ́ akawéluʔuskeʔ.
he ran,   there it's   truly   he caught up to her   this   witch.

(37) Waʔshakoye·ná·,   wahyatli·yó· kiʔ   né· thikʌ́, yah wí· té·yʌlheʔ
       He took hold of her,   the two fought actually   it's   that,   not   she doesn't want

a·háttok   úhkaʔ náhohteʔ. (38) Waʔshakoʔshʌ·ní·   kiʔ   sʌ́haʔ laʔshátsteʔ
that he realizes   who.   He overpowered her   actually   more   he is strong

tsiʔ né· ni·yót kaʔikʌ́ awéluʔuskeʔ. (39) Nén   wahoto·kʌ́·seʔ, né· kiʔ   né·
as   it's   how it is this   witch.   It's that   he found out,   it's   actually   it's

to·kʌ́skeʔ thikʌ́ Yakowín. (40) Nʌ kwí· né· waʔkʌ́·luʔ thikʌ́ Yakowín, "tákʌʔ
truly   that   Yakowín.   So then   it's   she said   that   Yakowín,   "don't

nuwʌtú úhkaʔ ʌshehlolí   kaʔikʌ́ tsiʔ nukyá·tawʌʔ."   (41) Waʔkʌ́·luʔ,
never   anyone   you will tell anyone   this   what   happened to me."   She said,

(33) He went a ways further and then he stopped and listened, and he didn't hear anything
anymore, must be that there was no one there. (34) And he continued on just a little while
and he heard it again, that someone was chasing him. (35) Someone was coming along behind as he was walking. (36) So then he turned around real quick, he started to run, he ran
just as fast as he could, he really caught up to this witch. (37) He caught hold of her, the two
fought, she didn't want him to find out who she was. (38) But he overpowered her, he was
stronger than this witch. (39) So he found out, it really was Yakowín. (40) So then Yakowín said, "don't you ever tell anyone what happened to me." (41) She said,

"tá·t ʌshehlo·lí·   úhkaʔ ok ʌkkwe·ní·   kiʔ   thikʌ́ thok
"if   you will tell someone someone   I will enable actually that   something

nʌsayá·tawʌ́ʔ."   (42) "Yah teʔyoyánleʔ nʌsayá·tawʌ́ʔ."   (43) Waʔkʌ́·luʔ
will happen to you."   "Not   it is not good   will happen to you."   She said

"ʌhsehyá·lakeʔ   tsiʔ tákʌʔ nuwʌtú ʌhsathlo·lí."   (44) "Tsiʔ naʔa·wʌ́neʔ
"you will remember   that   don't   never   you will tell about it."   "What happened

kaʔikʌ́ yoʔkalá·u."   (45) Nʌ kwí· né· wahalihwísaʔahseʔ kwí· tsiʔ yah nuwʌtú
this   night."   So then   it's   he promised her   that   not   never

náhteʔ   tha·hʌ́·luʔ.   (46) Nʌ kwí· né· sahatkʌ́·lahteʔ,   utu·kó·teʔ kwí·
anything he won't say.   So then   it's   he let go of her again,   she continued on

kaʔikʌ́ Yakowín.   (47) Kháleʔ laulhá·   sahahtʌ·tí·,   nʌ   seʔ wahonúhtaneʔ
this   Yakowín.   And   as for him he went home, then too   he got to know

úhkaʔ náhohteʔ. (48) Né·n   yah kiʔ   nuwʌtú úhkaʔ   teʔshakohlo·lí.
who.   It's that not actually never   anyone   he didn't tell anyone.

(49) Tsiʔ niyo·lé· nʌ   tóhkaʔ niyohslaké   tyawʌheyú kaʔikʌ́ Yakowín, nʌ
       Until   then a few   years amount to she has died this   Yakowín,   then

elhúwaʔ wahathlo·lí·, nʌ kwí· né· yah thusu·tú· wí·   náhteʔ
right then he told,   so then   it's   not   it can't be anymore anything

na·hoye·lá·seʔ,   nʌ   seʔ né· yawʌhe·yú́.   (50) Né· kiʔ   né· thikʌ́
that she does to him,   then too   it's   she has died.   It's   actually it's   that

tho   nikakaló·tʌ   lakkalatú·se   lakeʔnihkʌ́.   (51) Yah kiʔ   ní·
that's   the kind of story he has told me a story my late father.   Not   actually me

nuwʌtú té·kelheʔ   kalistaʔkéshuʔ   ta·katháhahkweʔ.   (52) Núwaʔ
never   I don't want along the railway tracks I would take a route.   This time

"if you tell anyone I can see to it that something will happen to you." (42) "Something not good will happen to you." (43) She said "remember not to ever tell." (44) "What happened tonight." (45) So then he promised her that he would never say anything. (46) So then he let her go, and Yakowín continued on. (47) And him, he went home, now that he knew who it was. (48) And he never told anyone. (49) Until a few years later after Yakowín had died, and then only he told about it, so then she couldn't do anything to him, now that she had died. (50) That's the story my late father told me. (51) I don't ever want to go along the railway tracks.

thok   naʔkayaʔtó·tʌʔ   awéluʔuskeʔ   ʌwakye·ná·.
some   she's a kind of   witch   she will catch me.

(53)   Shukeʔnikúlhʌʔ   a·kuhlo·lí·   tsiʔ   aohétkwalaʔ   kaʔikʌ́   awéluʔuskeʔ,
       I forgot   I should tell you   that   a naked person   this   witch,

Yakowín,   tshahaye·ná·   lakeʔnihkʌ́.   (54)   Tho s   yakʌʔ   ni·yót   tsiʔ
Yakowín,   when he caught her   my late father.   That's   reportedly   how it is   that

teyonatawʌ́liʔ   kaʔikʌ́   onéluʔuskeʔ,   yah   kwí·   teʔyonatslu·ní·.
they travel around   this   witches,   not   they are not dressed.

(55)   Aotihétkwalaʔ   kiʔwáh.
     Naked persons   right.

(52) Some kind of witch might get me.

   (53) I forgot to tell you that this witch was naked, Yakowín, when my late father caught her. (54) That's how they say the witches travel, they aren't dressed. (55) They're naked.

The Girl with the Bandaged Fingers

(Told by Norma Kennedy to Karin Michelson on May 22, 2010)

(1)   Shekóli   swakwe·kú.   (2)   Norma   ní·   yúkyats   oʔsluniʔké·ne.
    Hello   all of you.   Norma   me   is my name   white man's way.

(3)   Thiwé·saʔ   yúkyats   Ukwehuwehnéhaʔ.   (4)   Ohkwalí   niwakiʔtaló·tʌ.
    She Wanders   is my name   Native people's way.   Bear   is my clan.

(5)   Onʌyoteʔa·ká·   niwakuhutsyó·tʌ.   (6)   Tsiʔ   nikakaló·tʌ   kaʔikʌ́   i·kélheʔ
    Oneida   is my nation.   What   kind of story it is   this   I want

a·kwaka·látus,   kwáh   tsiʔ   tyotáhsawʌʔ   né·   kaʔikʌ́   laksá·,   yaʔtehayá·ti   kwí·   kaʔikʌ́
I would tell you all,   quite   at   it has begun   it's   this   a boy,   he is alone   this

(1) Hello all. (2) Norma is my name in English. (3) She Wanders is my Indian name. (4) I am Bear Clan. (5) I am Oneida nation. (6) The story I want to tell you, at the very beginning there was a boy, this boy was an only child,

laksá·, yah   thaʔtehatʌhnu·téleʔ,   kwáh   laulhaʔtsíwaʔ.   (7) Tahnú· kwahikʌ́
a boy,   not   he does not have siblings,   just   he is by himself.   And   just really

tsiʔ   lotkanuní n   lauhwatʌ́ha.   (8) Tahnú· tho kwí· ni·yót tsiʔ lokwatákwʌ
that   he is wealthy   his uncle.   And   thus   it is so   that   he has prepared

lauhwatʌ́ha tsiʔ nʌ   ʌhatu·kó·teʔ   kaʔikʌ́ kʌ́·tho yohwʌtsya·té· laulhá· kiʔ
his uncle   that   when   he will pass on   this   here   earth exists   him   actually

a·haye·ná·   lonúhsoteʔ.   (9) Tahnú· wí· tsiʔ   nihonuhsowanʌ́ kaʔikʌ́
he should receive it   he has a house.   And   how   his house is big   this

lauhwatʌ́ha, tho kwí· kanyataláktaʔ   lonúhsoteʔ.   (10) Kwahikʌ́   tsiʔ
his uncle,   there   close to the lake   he has a house.   Just really   that

kanuhsowanʌ́   kaʔikʌ́, e·só· yonuhsu·tú· thikʌ́, kwáh kwí· tsiléhkwaʔ a·hsí·luʔ
it is a big house this,   lots   it has rooms   that,   just   almost like   you would say

lanutiyó lonúhsoteʔ.   (11) Né·n,   nʌ   tshahatótyakeʔ   kaʔikʌ́ laksá· ókhnaʔ
king   he has a house.   It's that,   then   when he grew up   this   boy   and then

wahónyakeʔ.   (12) Nʌ kiʔ ok wí· tho   yahyátiʔ?   kaʔikʌ́ lauhwatʌ́ha
he got married.   Right then   there   the two moved over there   this   his uncle

lonuhso·táhkweʔ.   (13) Laulhá· kwí· loyenʌ́   kaʔikʌ́ laksá· nʌ
he used to have a house.   Him   he has received it   this   boy   when

tshahatu·kó·teʔ n   lauhwatʌ́ha. (14) Nʌ kwí· tóhkaʔ niyohslaké   kaʔikʌ́
when he passed on   his uncle.   So then   a few   years amount to   this

utu·kó·teʔ, nʌ kwí· áhsʌ nikutí   lotiwi·láyʌʔ   kaʔikʌ́ lónaʔ.
it went by,   so then   three   how many   they have children   this   man and wife.

(15) Tahnú· tsyeyá·tat,   tyótkut yakauʔwéskwaniheʔ thikʌ́ kanyataláktaʔ
          And   one person,   always   she enjoys   that   close to the lake

he didn't have any brothers or sisters, he was all by himself. (7) And his uncle was really
wealthy. (8) And the way that his uncle prepared for when he would pass on from this earth
is that he would be the one to inherit his house. (9) And his uncle's house was very big, and
his house was close to the lake. (10) It was a really big house, it had a lot of rooms, almost
like, you would say, a palace. (11) So when this boy grew up, he got married. (12) At once
the two moved into his uncle's house. (13) He was the one, this boy, who inherited it when
his uncle died. (14) So then a few years went by, and then the couple had three daughters.
(15) And one of them, she always enjoyed playing close to the lake.

yeyakotnutolyá·tu.   (16) Tho s kwí· sʌ́· ohnekanúshne yeyuta·wʌ́he?.
over there she is playing.   There   also in the water   over there she swims.

(17) Yakau?wéskwanihe? tho nú·   a·yutawʌ́hsla?.   (18) Né·n,   nʌ
      She enjoys   that's where that she goes and swims.   It's that, then

tsha?utótyake?   thikʌ́, sʌ́ha? tsha?utótyake?,   tá·t núwa? yá·ya?k yawʌ·lé· tá·tkʌ
when she grew up that,   more when she grew up,   maybe   sixteen   or maybe

tsya·ták yawʌ·lé· tsha?teyakaohsliyá·ku,   nʌ   tayutáhsawʌ? thikʌ́ nʌ
seventeen   when she has crossed over winters, then she started   that   when

yo?kalá·u, nʌ kwí· loti·tá·s.   (19) Tá·t núwa? kátsha? ok nú· yotukóhtu
night-time, so then they are sleeping.   Maybe   somewhere   it has passed

ahsúthʌ, nále?   wa?utkétsko? thikʌ́, a?é· kwí· wa?kanuhsatáti?   thikʌ́,
midnight, then again she got up   that,   great   it extends through the house that,

tho s nyahá·yʌ?.   (20) E·só· kwí· yonhokahlu·tú· ka?ikʌ́ kanuhsote?kó·.
there she went over there.   Lots   there are doors this   huge house.

(21) Tóhka? kwí· niyonhoká·lute? thikʌ́ tho   wa?tyutu·kó·te?   tsi? niyo·lé·
      A few   there are doors   that   there she passed through until

yahá·yuwe?   tsi? nú· wa?akawehtuháti?.   (22) Né·n   khále? né· onʌ́
she got over there where   she is on her way somewhere.   It's that and   it's then

thikʌ́ tóhka? niwʌ·táke   utu·kó·te?, nʌ   wa?úttoke? thikʌ́ tekyatʌhnu·téle?
that   a few   weeks amount to it went by, then she noticed that   she is sisters with her

tsi? yutkétskwas. (23) Kwáh nʌ   ʌwatu·kó·te? ahsúthʌ ókhale? wa?utkétsko?,
that she gets up.   Just   then it will go by   midnight and   she got up,

nʌ kwí· né· yakonehlákwas thikʌ́ tekyatʌhnu·téle?,   náhte? né· aolí·wa?   tsi?
so then it's she is surprised that   she is sisters with her, what   it's the reason that

(16) She would swim in the water there too. (17) She enjoyed going there to swim.
(18) Then when she grew up, when she was more grown, maybe when she was sixteen or
seventeen years old, then she started and it was at night, then they were sleeping.
(19) Maybe somewhere just past midnight, then she would get up, there was a long corridor
that went through the house, and she would go there. (20) And there were a lot of doors in
this huge house. (21) She went through a few doors, until she got to where she was going.
(22) And then a few weeks went by, then her sister noticed that she was getting up. (23) Just
past midnight she would get up, so then her sister was surprised, why

kwáh   nʌ   ʌwatu·kó·teʔ   ahsúthʌ   ókhnaʔ   waʔutkétskoʔ,   kátshaʔ   kwáh   nú·
just   when   it will go by   midnight   and then   she got up,   where   just   place

yakéthaʔ   khále?   náhteʔ   niyutyélha<u>ʔ</u>.   (24) Nʌ kwí·   waʔí·luʔ,   "ʌkhéhsleʔ
she is going there   and   what   she is doing.   So then   she said,   "I will follow her

kiʔ   núwaʔ   kaʔikʌ́   ʌyó·kalaweʔ,   ʌkato·kʌ́neʔ   náhteʔ   akwáh
actually this time   this   it will get dark,   it will be become known   what   exactly

niyutyélha<u>ʔ</u>."   (25) "Kháleʔ   kátshaʔ nú·   yeyúktus."   (26) Nʌ kwí·   thikʌ́
she is doing."   "And   where   she goes to."   So then   that

waʔó·kalaweʔ,   waʔutnúhtuhteʔ   tsiʔ niyo·léʔ   yakothu·téʔ,   náleʔ   waʔutkétsoʔ
it got dark,   she waited   until   she hears,   then again   she got up

kaʔikʌ́   tekyatʌhnu·té<u>leʔ</u>.   (27) Ókhnaʔ   waʔeya·kʌ́neʔ.   (28) Nʌ kiʔ ok uniʔ wí·
this   she is sisters with her.   And then   she went out.   At once also

né·   waʔutkétskoʔ   kaʔikʌ́ n   tekyatʌhnu·téleʔ   waʔutátshele<u>ʔ</u>.   (29) Aʔé· kwí·
it's   she got up   this   she is sisters with her   she followed her.   Great

niyo·léʔ   thikʌ́   nyehéknehseʔ   waʔkanuhsatáti<u>ʔ</u>.
distance   that   over there the two are going   it extends through the house.

(30) Tóhkaʔ kwí·   niyonhoká·luteʔ   tho   waʔtkyatukohtániʔ   thikʌ́   tsiʔ niyo·léʔ
       A few   door   there   the two passed through   that   until

yahá·kneweʔ   tsiʔ nú·   yeyúktus.   (31) Ok wí·   kaʔikʌ́   tekyatʌhnu·téleʔ,
the two got over there   where   she goes up to.   And   this   she is sisters with her,

waʔutnúhtuhteʔ tsiʔ niyo·léʔ   tóhkaʔ   minit   yeyakotawyá·tu,   nʌ   akaulhá·   sʌ́·
she waited   until   a few   minutes she has entered,   then   her   also

oskanʌ́ha   waʔenhotu·kó·,   yaʔutkeʔto·tʌ́·,   náhteʔ   akwáh   niyutyélhaʔ   thikʌ́
quietly   she opened the door,   she looked in,   what   exactly   she is doing   that

would she get up when it was just past midnight? where was she going and what was she
doing? (24) So then she said, "I will follow her tonight, it will come to light what exactly
she is up to." (25) "And where she goes to." (26) So then that night, she waited until she
heard her sister get up again. (27) And then she went out. (28) At once her sister also got
up and she followed her. (29) They went a long ways along the corridor through the house.
(30) They passed through a few doors until they got to where she was going. (31) And her
sister, she waited for a few minutes after she had gone in, then she also quietly opened the
door, she looked inside, what was it her sister was doing?

tekyatʌhnu·té<u>le</u>ʔ.   (32) Né·n   tshaʔutkeʔto·tʌ́·   thikʌ́,   thaʔutye·lʌ́·
she is sisters with her.   It's that   when she looked in   that,   she was struck suddenly

né· ótkuʔ, tóhkaʔ nikutí   thikʌ́ tho   yotinuʔké·lʌ   yesnuʔké<u>shu</u>ʔ.
it's snake, several how many   that   there   they are sucking   her fingers.

(33) Nʌ kwí· né· waʔunuhtunyu·kó·, náhteʔ né· o·n<u>ʌ́</u>. (34) Náhteʔ né· aolí·waʔ
      So then   it's she wondered,   what   it's now.   What   it's the reason

tsiʔ tho   ni·yót   tsiʔ waʔutká<u>tho</u>ʔ. (35) Nʌ kiʔ ok wí· né· tusayutkalhate·ní·,
that   that's how it is   that   she saw.   At once   it's she turned around again,

kwáh   yeʔnikú·laleʔ tákʌʔ   ta·yutlakalé·last.   (36) Sayenho·tú·
just   she is careful so as not   she should make noise.   She closed the door again

ókhnaʔ   né· tho nyusa·yʌ́·   tsiʔ tyakotnáktayʌ́ʔ. (37) Yah kwí·
and then   it's   that she went back over there at   she has her bed.   Not

teʔyakottokʌ́   tekyatʌhnu·téleʔ   tsiʔ waʔutkáthoʔ? náhteʔ niyutyé<u>lha</u>ʔ.
she did not notice   she is sisters with her   that   she saw   what   she is doing.

(38) Nʌ kwí· tóhkaʔ niwʌhnislaké kaʔikʌ́ utu·kó·teʔ, nʌ kwí· waʔelihwatshʌ·lí·
      So then   a few   days amount to this   it went by,   so then   she found the reason

náhteʔ aolí·waʔ   thikʌ́ yehwaʔestáníʔ,   kwáh tsiʔ nikú yesnúhsuteʔ wí· n
what   the reason   that   she has on bandages,   just   as many   she has fingers

tekyatʌhnu·té<u>le</u>ʔ.   (39) Ne·né· aolí·waʔ   tsiʔ thikʌ́ ótkuʔ kwí· tho
she is sisters with her.   It's that   the reason   that   that   snake   there

kutinuʔkélhaʔ tsiʔ yesnuhsu·tú·.   (40) Né· katiʔ wí· aolí·waʔ   yakosnuhsanú·waks,
they are sucking   at   she has fingers.   Well then it's   the reason   she has sore fingers,

nʌ kwí· nok u·tú·   yehwaʔéstu   kiʔwáh. (41) Né·n   thikʌ́
so then   it has to be   she has on a bandage   right.   It's that   that

(32) So when she looked in, she was struck suddenly, snakes, several of them were sucking at her fingers. (33) So then she wondered, what is this? (34) Why did she see something like that? (35) At once she turned around again, she was careful not to make a noise. (36) She closed the door again and then she went back to her bed. (37) Her sister didn't notice that she saw what she was doing. (38) So then a few days went by, and then she figured out the reason why her sister had bandages on all of her fingers. (39) The reason was that snakes were sucking at her fingers. (40) So that's why she had sore fingers, so then she had to be bandaged, right.

ya?tewʌhnislaké kwí· tho   kanyatalákta? yehe·yʌ́·se?,   nʌ kwí· ya·wét
every day   there near the lake   she goes over there, so then   kind of like

tshiyakotóti   ka?ikʌ́ tekyatʌhnu·téle?.   (42) Nʌ   se? ya·wét
when she has grown up this   she is sisters with her.   Then   too   kind of like

tsyakotahsawáti?   tsya·ták yawʌ·lé· na?ta·yakohsli·yá·ke?.   (43) Tyótkut ki?
she is about to start   seventeen   that she crosses over winters.   Always   actually

thikʌ́ kanyatalákta? tho   yehe·yʌ́·se?.   (44) Né·n   khále? onʌ́ thikʌ́
that   near the lake   there she goes over there.   It's that and   now   that

tsyóhslat uhte i·kélhe? thikʌ́ ya?káhawe?,   nʌ   tho   ále?   yahá·yʌ?
one year   I think   that   time has gone, then   there again she went over there

ka?ikʌ́ kanyatalákta?. (45) Ókhale? n thikʌ́ tekyatʌhnu·téle?,   né· kwí· nʌ
this   near the lake.   And   that   she is sisters with her,   so it's   when

kwáh ok onʌ́ yutate?nikú·lale?,   khále? kwahikʌ́ tsi? ye?nikú·lale? tákʌ?
just the same   she is watching over her, and   just really that   she is careful   so as not

a·yúttok   tsi? teyutatká·nle?   wáh. (46) Né·n,   nʌ kyale? wí· thikʌ́
that she notice that   she is looking at her   right.   It's that, so again   that

kanyatalákta? nyahá·yʌ?   tekyatʌhnu·téle?   ókhna?   wa?utátshele?.
near the lake   she went over there she is sisters with her and then   she followed her.

(47) Né·n,   tha?utye·lʌ́·   né· nʌ   tho   nyahá·yʌ?   ka?ikʌ́
       It's that, she was struck suddenly it's when   there she went over there this

ohnekanúshne. (48) Tho   nyahá·yʌ?   thikʌ́ kwáh tsi? niyo·lé·
in the water.   There she went over there that   quite   until

ya?akonuwi·léhte?.   (49) Nʌ kwí· né· to·kʌ́ske? wa?ako?nikuhláksʌ? ka?ikʌ́
she went out of sight.   So then   it's   truly   she became sad   this

(41) Every day she was by the lake, so kind of like when her sister had grown up. (42) Like when she was about to become seventeen. (43) She was always by the lake. (44) And then I think one year went by, she went to the lake again. (45) And her sister, the same as ever, she was watching her and she was really careful that she not notice that she was watching her. (46) So again her sister went by the lake and she followed her. (47) She was surprised suddenly when she went into the water. (48) She went in right until she went out of sight. (49) So then her sister became really sad

tekyatʌhnuˑtéleʔ   tsiʔ   wéˑne   tsiʔ   waʔéˑskoneʔ n   tekyatʌhnuˑté<u>le</u>ʔ.
she is sisters with her   because   evidently   that   she drowned   she is sisters with her.

(50) Néˑn   áhsok   néˑ   tho   uteʔskoˑkóˑ   onyaleʔkóˑ.   (51) Wéˑne
     It's that   all of a sudden   it's   there   it came out of water   sea monster.   Evidently

néˑ tsiʔ   néˑ   tho   waʔtyutteˑníˑ   onyaleʔkóˑ   waʔuˑ<u>túˑ</u>.   (52) Néˑ   tho
because   it's   there   she changed into   sea monster   she became.   It's   thus

niyawʌ́ˑu   tsiʔ   kʌh   wʌhnislaˑtéˑ   kanákleʔ   onyaleʔkóˑ.   (53) Yaˑwét kwíˑ
it has happened   that   here   a day exists   it resides   sea monster.   Kind of like

thok núˑ   nyʌhsyaʔtoˑlʌ́neʔ   néˑ   tho   nikayaʔtóˑtʌ   thikʌ́ n   onyaleʔkóˑ.
that's where   over there you will find it   it's   thus   kind of creature   that   sea monster.

(54) Néˑ kwíˑ   tho   niyawʌ́ˑu   tsiʔ   kanyatalaˑke   kwíˑ núˑ   tkanákleʔ   thikʌ́
     So it's   thus   it has happened   that   at the lake   where   it resides   that

onyaleʔkóˑ.   (55) Neʔ thóˑneʔ   kwíˑ   néˑ   yeskʌhá   seshakotikʌ́   kaʔikʌ́
sea monster.   At that time   it's   the last time   they have seen her   this

tsyeyáˑtat   shakotiyʌ́<u>ha</u>.   (56) Néˑ   kiʔ   tho   nikakalóˑtʌ   kaʔikʌ́, nók tsiʔ
one person   their daughter.   It's   actually   that's   the kind of story   this,   but

kʌh   wʌhnislaˑtéˑ   wéˑne kwíˑ   yah   teʔskanákleʔ   thikʌ́ onyaleʔkóˑ.
here   a day exists   evidently   not   it does not reside anymore   that   sea monster.

(57) Néˑ tsiʔ   yah   kiʔ   níˑ   nuwʌtú   teʔwaklihwahlakú   úhkaʔ náhteʔ
     Because   not   actually   me   never   I have not heard news of   anyone

aˑkuwatkathó<u>hake</u>ʔ.   (58) Néˑ   kiʔ   tho   nikakaˑlés   kaʔiˑ<u>kʌ́</u>.
one would have been seeing it.   It's   actually   that's   how long the story is   this.

(59) Nʌ kiʔwáh.
     So long.

because I guess her sister drowned. (50) So all of a sudden this sea monster rose up out of the water. (51) It must have been because she had turned into a sea monster. (52) That's the way it happened that these days there are sea monsters around. (53) It's kind of like that's the place you will find that kind of creature, the sea monster. (54) So that's how it happened that the sea monster lives in the lake. (55) And that was the last time they saw this one daughter. (56) That's the story, but these days that sea monster must not be around anymore. (57) Because I've never heard of anyone seeing it. (58) That's the extent of the story. (59) So long.

An Unwanted Passenger

(Told by Norma Kennedy to Karin Michelson on November 17, 2010)

(1) Shekólih.   (2) Norma ní· yúkyats.   (3) Ohkwalí niwaki?taló·tʌ.
Greetings.   Norma me is my name.   Bear   such is my clan.

(4) Onʌyote?a·ká·   niwakuhutsyó·tʌ.   (5) Né· ka?ikʌ́ tsi?   nikakaló·tʌ
People of the Standing Stone such is my nation.   It's this   what kind of story

i·kélhe? a·kwaka·látus,   né· kwí· n "lake?níha laó·slet" ʌkná·tuhkwe? ka?ikʌ́,
I want   I would tell you all, it's   "my father   his car"   I will call it   this,

tsi?   niyawʌ́·u   úska yotlátstu kʌ? tshiká·,   tá·t núwa? wísk uhte wí·
what   has happened   one time   when I was little, maybe   five   possibly

tsha?tewakohsliyá·ku   ne? thó·ne?. (6) Lake?níha wa?thotuhútsyohse?
when I have crossed over winters at that time.   My father   he wanted

oyá·   usaho?slehatayʌ·táne?.   (7) Né· tsi? kwáh tsi? nikú   astéhtsi?
another he would obtain a car again.   Because whatever amount morning

yah thau·tú· ta·haláhtatste?   laó·slet. (8) Sʌ́ha? kwí· n nále?   yotho·lé·.
it can't be   that he starts it running his car.   More   again when it is cold.

(9) Nʌ s kwí· né· lonolú·sehe? ka?ikʌ́ tsi?   ni·yót laó·slet. (10) Né· kwí·
So then   it's he tires of   this   how it is so his car.   So it's

aolí·wa?   wá·lelhe? oyá·   usaha?slehtahni·nú·.   (11) Tahnú· yah kwí·
the reason he wanted another he would buy a car again.   And   not

só·tsi?   e·só· tha?tehatá·tsha?as, né· tsi?   kwáh kwí· nók tsi? layʌtákwas   ki?wáh.
too much   lots   he does not earn,   because   just   but   he cuts wood   right.

(12) Tho   tshá·lawe?   lake?níha lónhahse?   wahohlo·lí· kwí· tsi? náhte?
There   when he got there   my father   he hires him he told him   that   what

(1) Hello. (2) My name is Norma. (3) I am Bear Clan. (4) Oneida is my nation. (5) The story I want to tell you, I will call it "my father's car," is what happened one time when I was little, I guess maybe I was five years old at that time. (6) My father wanted to get another car. (7) Because every morning he couldn't get his car started. (8) Especially when it was cold. (9) So then he got fed up with the way his car was. (10) So it's why he wanted to buy another car. (11) And he didn't earn too much, because he was only cutting wood. (12) When my father's boss got there he [my father] told him what

lanuhtúnyuhe? wí· oyá·   usaho?slehtayʌ·tá<u>ne?</u>.   (13) Nʌ kwí· n lónhahse?
he is thinking   another he would obtain a car again.   So then   he hires him

wahʌ́·lu?, "wakanúhte? úhka? náhte? lo?sléhtayʌ?," tahnú· wahʌ́·lu? "tsi?
he said,   "I know   who   he has a car,"   and   he said   "how

nika?slehtiyó, tahnú· yah só·tsi?   te?we·só· tha?tehotuhutsyo·ní̲." (14) Nʌ kwí·
it is a nice car, and   not too much not lots   he does not want."   So then

wahʌ́·lu?, "ʌkuya?takénha? kwí· tá·t ʌhse?slehtanú·wene?, ʌkuya?takénha? kwí·,
he said,   "I will help you   if   you will like a car,   I will help you,

í· ʌkkályahke?, tho?nʌ́ ʌseskkálya?kse?,   kwáh tsi? nikú ʌsatkálya?kse?
me I will pay,   and then you will pay me back, whatever amount you will get paid

ostúha kwí· ʌtekla·kó· tsi? niyo·lé· ʌseskaló·<u>ktʌ?</u>."   (15) Né· kwí· tho   ni·yót
a little   I will claim until   you will end the debt."   So it's   that's how it is

tsi? wahyatlihwísa<u>ne?</u>.   (16) Nʌ ki? ok wí· né· wahuwatkʌ?sé·na? ka?ikʌ́
that   the two planned the matter.   Right then   it's   they went to see him   this

tsi? ka·yʌ́· lo?sléhtay<u>ʌ?</u>. (17) Tho kwí· na?a·wʌ́ne? thikʌ́ tshahatkátho? thikʌ́
the one that he has a car.   Thus   it happened   that   when he saw   that

ká·slet, waha?slehtanú·wene? ki?wáh. (18) Nʌ ki? ok wí· né·n   lónhahse?
car,   he liked a car   indeed.   Right then   it's that he hires him

wahokálya?kse? kwí· ka?ikʌ́ lukwé waho?slehtahni·<u>nú·</u>.   (19) Né·n   yah kwí·
he paid him   this   man   he bought a car from him.   It's that not

né· te?wé·ne tsi? nishotshanuniháti?   lake?níha tshusá·lawe?
it's incredible how he is going along happy again my father   when he went home

né· tsi? oyá·   sho?slehtayʌtáti̲?.   (20) Kwáh ki?   né· kʌ? ok náhe?
because another he is having a car again.   Just   actually it's a little while

he was thinking, about getting another car. (13) So then his boss said, "I know of a person
who has a car," and he said "it's a nice car, and he doesn't want too much for it." (14) So
then he said, "I will help you if you like the car, I will help you, I will pay [for it], and then
you will pay me back, every time you get paid I will hold back a little until your debt ends."
(15) So that's how they planned it. (16) At once they went to see the one who had the car.
(17) And what happened was when he saw the car, he really liked it. (18) So right away his
boss paid this man he bought the car from. (19) My father was going along really happy
when he went home because he had another car.

tshiho?sléhtayʌ? ka?ikʌ o?sléhtase? ókhna? tutáhsawʌ? tsyo?k náhte? na?a·wʌ́.
when he has a car this a new car and then it began different things happened.

(21) Kwáh tsi? nikú wahó·sle? ka?ikʌ ká·slet nʌ yo?kaláshʌ, kwáh s wahʌ́·lu?
Whatever amount he drove this car when at night, just he said

tho niwate?shʌnó·tʌ tsi? úhka? se? ok tehyatiták<u>he?</u>. (22) Nʌ kwí·
thus is the sensation that someone too the two are riding. So then

yahatke?to·tʌ́· kwí· thikʌ́ yutke?totakhwá·tslaku, úhka? ok kʌ náhte? ohná·kʌ?
he peered that way that in the mirror, someone question what in the back

tahʌ?tlutáti<u>?</u>. (23) Tho kwí· yahatke?to·tʌ́· thikʌ́, né·n
he is sitting coming along. There he peered that way that, it's that

wahatkátho? ki? tsi? úhka? se? ok tho thʌ́·tlu? thikʌ́ ohná·kʌ?, nʌ kwí·
he saw actually that someone too there he is sitting that in the back, so then

kwahotokʌ́·u wa?thatkalhate·ní· yahatkátho?, yah ki? né· úhka? tho
just for real he turned around he looked that way, not actually it's anyone there

tehʌ?tlutáti<u>?</u>. (24) Khále? ne? thó·ne? ok oni? wí· tho na?a·wʌ́ne?
he is not sitting coming along. And at that time only too thus it happened

thikʌ́ niyo?kaláshʌ. (25) Né·n tóhka? ki? niwʌhnislaké thikʌ́ utu·kó·te?,
that night-time. It's that a few actually days amount to that it went by,

nʌ wahʌ́·lu?, nʌ kwí· tshaháhsane? loyo·té·, nʌ kwí· wa?shakohlo·lí·
then he said, so then when he finished he is working, so then he told her

aknulhá· tsi? yah thya·ya·wʌ́· tsi? tyutʌhni·núhe? yʌhʌ́·le?
my mother that it has to be at at the store he will go over there

ʌhatyenata?á·nha?, wahʌ́·lu? "nʌ thóha a·katyenó·<u>ktʌ?</u>." (26) Wa?í·lu?
he will go and fill it with gas, he said "now almost I would run out of gas." She said

(20) He had the new car for just a little while and then some things started happening. (21) Every time he drove the car at night, he said he had this sensation that someone was riding with him. (22) So then he looked into the mirror, was someone sitting in the back? (23) He looked there [into the mirror], and he saw someone sitting in the back, so then he turned all the way around and he looked over [to the back], no one was sitting there. (24) And this only happened at night. (25) So a few days went by, then he said, so when he finished working, so then he told my mother that he has to go to the store to get gas, he said "I'm almost out of gas." (26) My mother said,

aknulhá·,   "ʌtéshaweʔ kwí· kaná·talok khále? onú·taʔ," waʔí·luʔ "nʌ   thóha
my mother, "you will bring   bread   and   milk,"   she said "now almost

aetwató·ktʌʔ   kaná·talok khále? onú·taʔ."   (27) Nʌ kwí· né· wahahtʌ·tí·,
you and we would run out of bread   and   milk."   So then   it's   he left,

tyutʌhni·núheʔ wá·lehteʔ   wahatyenataʔá·nhaʔ.   (28) Nʌ katiʔ wí· thikʌ́
at the store   he went there he is going to fill it with gas.   Well then   that

tshaʔtutahohtʌtyuháti?   nále?   né· wí· tsi? nok ʌwa·tú· owahá·ke wí·
as he is on his way home from there then again because   it has to be   on the road

tʌhakahnláti?   tsi? ló·sele̠ʔ.   (29) Kwáh kʌs   wahʌ́·lu? tho
he will keep looking as   he is driving.   Just   usually he said   thus

niwateʔshʌnó·tʌ tsi? úhka? ok se? tehyatlaʔnekʌháti?.   (30) Nʌ kyale? wí·
is the sensation   that someone too the two are going along next to.   So again

tahatkalʌhlákwahte?   yahatkátho?,   yah ki? né· úhka?, a·kí·lu?   kyuhte wí·
he turned quickly to the side he looked that way, no one in fact,   I would say   supposedly

tó·k niyo·lé·   thikʌ́ nyahó·sle?,   nále?   wá·lelhe?,   úhka? ok nʌ   ki?
some distance that   he drove over there, then again he thought, someone   then actually

thikʌ́ tho   layaʔtitákhe? ohná·kʌ?.   (31) Nʌ kyale? wí· kwahotokʌ́·u
that   there he is in it riding in the back.   So again   just for real

waʔthatkalhate·ní· a·hatkátho?, yah ki?   né· úhka? tho   tehayá·tit.
he turned around   that he looks, not   actually it's   anyone there he is not in it.

(32) Yah ki?   né· úhka? tho   teʔyeyaʔtitákhe̠?.   (33) Nʌ kwí·
       Not   actually it's   anyone there one is not riding in it.   So then

tshyusá·lawe?   thikʌ́, nále?   waʔshakohlo·lí· aknulhá· náhte? nahoyá·tawʌ̠?.
when he got home   that,   then again he told her   my mother what   happened to him.

"bring back some bread and some milk," she said "we've almost run out of bread and milk."
(27) So then he left, he went to the store to get some gas. (28) Well then as he was on his
way home again he had to keep his eye on the road as he was driving. (29) He said he just
had this sensation that someone was next to him. (30) So again he turned quickly to the side
to look over that way, there was no one, I'd say he probably drove a ways, and again he
thought, someone is riding in the back. (31) So again he turned all the way around to look,
there was nobody. (32) There was no one riding in it. (33) So then when he got home, he
told my mother what happened to him.

(34) Kwáh   kiʔ   tsiʔ wakanúhteʔ yah kiʔ   teʔyokwéni   thikʌ́ tewʌ·táke,
      Just   actually I think   not   actually   it was not able that   two weeks,

nʌ   wahʌ́·luʔ lakeʔníha, "yah kiʔ   ní· tha·kkwe·ní· kaʔikʌ́ shekú
then   he said   my father,   "not   actually me   I am not able   this   still

usuké·sele<u>ʔ</u>."   (35) Nʌ kwí· wahohlo·lí· lónhahseʔ   tsiʔ   nahoyá·taw<u>ʌ</u>ʔ.
I would drive it again."   So then   he told him   he hires him   what   happened to him.

(36) Wahʌ́·luʔ, "i·kélheʔ ní· usakyʌhná   kaʔikʌ́ ká·slet." (37) Nʌ kiʔ ok wí·
      He said,   "I want   me   I would return it   this   car."   Right then

né· óksaʔ ok wahathu·táteʔ n lónhahseʔ   tho kwí· sá·nehteʔ   tsiʔ nú·
it's   right away he consented   he hires him   there   the two went back there   where

thotiʔslehtahni·<u>nú</u>·.   (38) Né· kwí· n lakeʔníha waʔthnitha·lʌ́·   kaʔikʌ́ tsiʔ ka·yʌ́·
they have bought a car.   So it's   my father   the two conversed   this   the one that

loʔslehtahni·<u>nú</u>·.   (39) Wahʌ́·luʔ, "sekyʌ·hné·"   wahʌ́·luʔ "kaʔikʌ́
he has bought a car from him.   He said,   "I am returning it"   he said   "this

ká·slet, yah tha·kkwe·ní· auké·sel<u>e</u>ʔ."   (40) Wahʌ́·luʔ, "thok kʌ náhteʔ
car,   not   I am not able   I would drive it."   He said,   "something question

niyawʌ́·u   thikʌ́ kaʔsléhta<u>ku</u>." (41) Wahʌ́·luʔ lakeʔníha, "tá·t núwaʔ úhkaʔ ok
has happened that   in the car."   He said   my father,   "maybe   someone

kʌ   tho   lawʌheyú, tá·t núwaʔ shekú tho   watákhehseʔ laotunhéts<u>la</u>ʔ."
question there he has died, maybe   still   there   it runs around   his soul."

(42) Nʌ kwí· né·n   kaʔikʌ́ tsiʔ ka·yʌ́· loʔslehtahni·nú·,   wahʌ́·luʔ
      So then   it's that   this   the one that   he has bought a car from him, he said

(34) I think it wasn't quite two weeks, then my father said, "I can't keep driving it." (35) So then he told his boss what happened to him. (36) He said, "I want to return this car." (37) Right away his boss consented and the two of them went back there to where they bought the car. (38) My father talked to the guy he bought the car from. (39) He said, "I'm returning this car," he said "I can't drive it." (40) He said, "did something happen in that car?" (41) My father said, "maybe someone died there? maybe his soul is still running around there." (42) So then the guy that he bought the car from, he said

"hʌ·, to·kʌ́ske? ki?   úhka? ok tho   lawʌheyú,   úhka? ok tho
"yes,   it's true   actually someone   there he has died,   someone   there

luwanahalyá·khu."   (43) Né· kwí· aolí·wa?   thikʌ́ yah kwí· só·tsi
someone has murdered him."   So it's   the reason that   not   too much

teha?nyákatste?   a·hate?slehtahni·nú·. (44) Né· tsi?   shekú n laulhá· yah
he doesn't charge   he would sell a car.   Because even   him   not

tehokwéni   a·hó·sele?.   (45) Nʌ kwí· né· tutaho·yú· kwí· n   lake?níha
he was not able   he would drive it.   So then   it's   he gave it back to him   my father

laohwísta?.   (46) Nʌ ki? ok wí· né· tutahyahtʌ·tí· n   lónhahse? kwí·
his money.   Right then   it's   the two left there again   he hires him

ka?ikʌ́, teshyatitákhe?   sahyahtʌ·tí·.   (47) Yah ki?   ní·
this,   the two are riding again the two left for home.   Not   actually   me

te?ské·yale?   thikʌ́ náhte? niyawʌ́·u   thikʌ́ ká·slet. (48) Thok
I don't remember anymore   that   what   has happened that   car.   That's only

niyo·lé· ní· ké·yale?   thikʌ́, shekú né· yah te?ké·yale?   oyá·   kʌ
how far   me   I remember that,   even   it's   not   I don't remember another question

saha?slehtahni·nú·   lake?níha. (49) Tho   ki?   ok   ní· niyo·lé· thikʌ́
he bought a car again   my father.   That's actually only me   as far as   that

ké·yale?.   (50) Tho   ki?   ok   niwakka·lés   ka?i·kʌ́.
I remember.   That's actually only   how long my story is   this.

"yes, it's true someone died there, someone was murdered." (43) It's why he didn't charge too much to sell the car. (44) Because even he couldn't drive it. (45) So then he gave my father back his money. (46) At once he left again with his boss, they were riding back together to go home. (47) I don't remember anymore what happened to that car. (48) That's only as much as I remember, I don't even remember whether my father bought another car. (49) That's only as far as I remember. (50) That's only how long my story is.

A Scary Light

(Told by Norma Kennedy to Karin Michelson on November 17, 2010)

(1) Nʌ kyaleʔ wíˑ iˑkélheʔ oyáˑ   núwaʔ   nikakalóˑtʌ usakwakaˑlátu<u>s</u>.
     So again   I want   another this time kind of story again I would tell you all a story.

(2) Toˑkʌ́skeʔ kaʔikʌ́ tho niyawʌ́ˑu.   (3) Néˑ s wíˑ tshiwahuˑníseʔ yah kwíˑ
     Truly   this   thus it has happened.   So it's   a long time ago   not

teʔyukwaˑyʌ́ˑ   electricity wíˑ aetwattsistoˑtʌ́ˑ.   (4) Néˑ s kwíˑ thikʌ́
we do not have   electricity   for you and we to turn on lights.   So it's   that

coal oil lamp kwíˑ yakwátstahkweʔ aˑyakwattsistoˑtʌ́ˑ.   (5) Tahnúˑ kʌs kwíˑ
coal oil lamp   we used to use   for us to turn on lights.   And   usually

yah thyaˑyaˑwʌ́ˑ tsiʔ táˑt núwaʔ tékni tewátlatsteʔ tsiʔ niwʌˑtés   thikʌ́ nok ʌwaˑtúˑ
it has to be   that maybe   two times   during the week   that   it has to be

ʌyakwahninúˑnaʔ coal oil. (6) Néˑ s kwíˑ thikʌ́ yakauʔweskwaníhahkweʔ
we will go and buy coal oil.   So it's   that   she used to enjoy

yuknulháˑ, Muncey tyutʌhniˑnúheʔ yaaˑyʌ́ˑ   aˑyeyenahninúˑ<u>na</u>ʔ.
my aunt,   Muncey   at the store   that she goes over there for her to go and buy oil.

(7) Tahnúˑ kʌs kwíˑ yoʔkáláshʌ kʌs kwíˑ thikʌ́ yakauʔwéskwaniheʔ Muncey
     And   usually   night-time   usually   that   she enjoys   Muncey

yaaˑ<u>yʌ́</u>ˑ.   (8) Néˑ katiʔ wíˑ kaʔikʌ́ úska útlatsteʔ waʔukékwahteʔ
that she goes over there.   Well then it's this   one time   she invited me

kiʔwáh. (9) Waʔíˑluʔ, "íhselheʔ kʌ   aétene̲."   (10) "Yah thyaˑyaˑwʌ́ˑ
right.   She said,   "you want   question you and I would go."   "It has to be

tsiʔ waʔkyenahninúˑnaʔ coal oil." (11) "Yah thyaˑyaˑwʌ́ˑ tsiʔ Muncey
that I'm on my way to buy coal oil."   "It has to be   that Muncey

(1) I want to tell you another story. (2) This really happened. (3) A long time ago we didn't have electricity for lights. (4) We used a coal oil lamp for lights. (5) And usually it had to be maybe two times a week we had to go and buy coal oil. (6) So my aunt used to like to go to the store in Muncey to buy coal oil (she had a boyfriend in Muncey). (7) And it was at night-time usually she liked to go to Muncey. (8) Well this one time she invited me, right. (9) She said, "do you want to come with me?" (10) "I have to go and buy coal oil." (11) "I have to go to Muncey."

yʌhʌ·ké·."   (12) Nʌ kwí· waʔkí·luʔ, "wé·ne kiʔwáh." (13) Nʌ kwí·
I will go over there."   So then   I said,   "I guess so."   So then

waʔakyahtʌ·tí· thikʌ́, Muncey waʔáknehteʔ.   (14) Kátshaʔ kiʔ ok uhte wí·
we two set out   that,   Muncey we two went there.   Somewhere   supposedly

nú·   tá·t núwaʔ yá·yaʔk mile tsiʔ niyo·lé· thikʌ́ tyutʌhni·núheʔ. (15) Tho kwí·
where maybe   six   mile   until   that   at the store.   There

yaʔákneweʔ   thikʌ́ waʔeyenahni·nú· kiʔwáh. (16) Nʌ kiʔ ok wí· né·
we two got over there that   she bought oil   right.   Right then   it's

tutayakyahtʌ·tí·   thikʌ́, tutayakyathahítaneʔ.   (17) Né· kiʔ
we two left there for home that,   we two came down the road again.   It's actually

thikʌ́ Oneida Road kwí· kuwa·yáts thikʌ́ tsiʔ nú· niyukyathahitákheʔ.
that   Oneida Road   is its name that   where   we two are travelling in a road.

(18) Kwáh kiʔ   thikʌ́ tshyusayákneweʔ   tyutlʌnayʌtákhwaʔ,
       Just   actually that   when we two got over there   at the church,

né· kwí· thikʌ́ tehotiʔkha·lúteʔ kwí· luwatinaʔtúkhwaʔ, né· wí· tho nú·
it's   that   they wear skirts   what they call them, it's   that's where

thutlʌnayʌtákhwaʔ.   (19) Ya·wét kwí· waʔakyanutahalo·nʌ́teʔ ostúha, thoʔnʌ́
they use it for praying.   Kind of like   we two went downhill   a bit,   and then

sayakyanutá·laneʔ.   (20) Nʌ katiʔ wí· thikʌ́ tó· kiʔ ok niyo·lé· thikʌ́
again we two went uphill.   So then it's   that   some distance   that

nityuknenú   tsiʔ wí· nú· tyutlʌnayʌtákhwaʔ, nʌ   aʔé· niyo·lé·
we two have come from where   church,   then   far in the distance

kahʌtá·ke   yaʔakyatkáthoʔ   thikʌ́, kwáh kʌʔ nikatsístaʔ thikʌ́
on the field we two saw it over there   that,   quite   a light some size that

(12) So then I said, "I guess so." (13) So then we set out, we went to Muncey. (14) I guess it was about six miles to the store. (15) So we got there and she bought some oil. (16) At once we left there to come home, we came down the road again. (17) It's called Oneida Road, the road we were travelling on. (18) [It was] right when we got to the church, the Anglicans, 'they wear skirts' is what they're called, that's their church. (19) We went kind of downhill a bit, and then we went up the hill again. (20) So then we had come so far from where the church is, then we looked way off in the field, we saw a light that was quite big,

waʔakyatkáthoʔ,   tahnú· wí· tsiʔ   nikatsistiyó,   teyothweʔnuní kiʔwáh.
we two saw,   and   how it is a nice light,   it is round   right.

(21) Teyottsistakweʔnu·ní.   (22) Né· thikʌ́ yaʔteyakniká·nleʔ   kʌs   thikʌ́
      It is a round light.   It's   that   we two are looking that way   habitually that

tsiʔ náheʔ waʔukyatukohtuhátiʔ   kiʔwáh.   (23) Né·n   kháleʔ onʌ́ waʔtyakni·táneʔ,
while   we two are moving along right.   It's that and   then   we two stopped,

tho kwí· yaʔteyakniká·neleʔ.   (24) Né·n   waʔtka·táneʔ seʔ wí· thikʌ́ o·tsísteʔ
there   we two are looking that way.   It's that it stopped   too   that   light

tsiʔ yotukohtuhátiʔ.   (25) Né·n   nʌ kyaleʔ wí· sayakyatu·kó·teʔ   thikʌ́ kháleʔ
as   it is moving along.   It's that so again   we two moved on again that   and

yaʔakyatkáthoʔ.   (26) Nʌ kiʔ ok oniʔ né· sutu·kó·teʔ   thikʌ́ o·tsísteʔ.
we two looked that way.   Right then too   it's it moved on again that   light.

(27) Nʌ kwí· kwahotokʌ́·u waʔí·luʔ, "tetsitni·tán."   (28) "Ʌkato·kʌ́neʔ
      So then   just for real   she said, "let's you and I stop again."   "It will be found out

ta·ka·táneʔ oniʔ kʌ   nʌʔ né·." (29) Nʌ kyaleʔ wí· waʔtyakni·táneʔ thikʌ́,
it would stop too   question that one."   So again   we two stopped   that,

yaʔakyatkáthoʔ,   nʌ kiʔ ok oniʔ né· waʔtka·táneʔ thikʌ́ o·tsísteʔ.
we two looked that way, at once   too   it's it stopped   that   light.

(30) Nʌ kyaleʔ wí· oniʔ waʔakyatu·kó·teʔ. (31) Nʌ sók aleʔ utu·kó·teʔ   oniʔ
      So again   too   we two moved on.   And again too it moved on   too

nʌʔ né·. (32) Nʌ kwí· kwahikʌ́ tsiʔ waʔtyuknishlíhʌʔ thikʌ́, waʔukyatétshʌʔ
that one.   So then   just really that we two hurried   that,   we two got afraid

and it was a real nice light, it was round, right. (21) It was a round light. (22) We were looking over there while we kept moving along. (23) And then we stopped, we were looking over there. (24) So the light stopped moving along too. (25) So again we moved on and we looked over that way. (26) At once that light moved on too. (27) So then she said really, "let's us two stop again!" (28) "Just to see whether IT will stop too." (29) So we stopped again, we looked over that way, right away the light stopped too. (30) So again we moved on. (31) And again IT moved on too. (32) So then we really hurried, we were afraid,

ki?wáh. (33) Náhte? né· nikatsistó·tʌ thikʌ́, wé·ne   tsi? i·wélhe?
right.   What   it's a kind of light that, evidently that it wants

a·yukníhsel<u>e</u>.   (34) Kwáh ki?   tsi? niyo·lé· thikʌ́ tewahahá·slʌ? nú·
it would chase us two.   Just   actually as far as that crossroads   where

tayáknewe?,   kaló· ná·wati thikʌ́ lu·té· s kwí· o?slu·ní· né· laohútsi? thikʌ́,
we two got there, this side   that they say   white man it's his land   that,

tho ki?   ok niyo·lé· thikʌ́ nuta·wé· thikʌ́ katsistotáti<u>?</u>.   (35) Ókhna?
that's actually only how far that   it came that   light extended along.   And then

né· tusutkalhate·ní·   súhkete?,   ok   ní· tayakyatu·kó·te?, né· s kyuhte wí·
it's it turned around again it went back, and as for us we two came on,   it's   supposedly

ísi?   ki?   ok onʌ́ niyo·lé· nʌ ʌtsyáknewe?   tsi? nú· yukwahtʌ́ti.
over there actually only now so far   then we two will get back where   is our home.

(36) Ne? thó·ne? kati? wí· ní· yeskʌhá   Muncey tsyuknehtú·n<u>e?</u>.
    At that time   well then us the last time Muncey we two have gone there again.

(37) Né· yo?kalásh<u>ʌ</u>. (38) Kwʌ?té·ke kʌs   nále?   wa?aknihninú·na?
    It's night-time.   Daytime   usually then again we two went to buy

thikʌ́ coal oil. (39) Yah ki?   nuwʌtú kwa?ahsuté·ke tho nú·
that   coal oil.   Not actually never night-time   that's where

thye?tsyukne·n<u>ú</u>.   (40) Né· ki?   thikʌ́ tho   nikaka·lés.
we two have not gone again.   It's actually that   that's how long the story is.

right. (33) What kind of light is it that it wants to chase us? (34) We got to as far as the crossroads, on this side they say the land belongs to a non-Indian, that's only how far that light came. (35) And then it turned around again and it went back, and the two of us, we kept coming, then it wasn't too far and we would get back home. (36) Well that's the last time we went to Muncey. (37) At night. (38) We went to buy coal oil during the daytime. (39) We never went there again at night-time. (40) That's how long the story is.

A Ghost on the Tracks

(Told by Barbara Schuyler to Karin Michelson and Norma Kennedy on July 16, 2008)

(1) KʌɁ tshityukwayʌ́·saɁ,   i·kélheɁ a·kuka·látus   kheɁkʌ́ha   kháleɁ
     When we were young people, I want   I would tell you a story my younger sister and

í·   kháleɁ tekniyáshe ukwatʌló·slaɁ, Mack Irelandhné, Mack kháleɁ Dorothy
me   and   two   our friends,   at Mack Ireland's, Mack and   Dorothy

Ireland lotiyʌ·táhkweɁ   yutʌhni·núhe̠Ɂ. (2) Tho nú·   waɁákwehte̠Ɂ.
Ireland they used to have one sells.   That's where we went somewhere.

(3) Nók tsiɁ nok u·tú· kalistaɁkéshuɁ   nyaɁákoweɁ.   (4) NeɁ thó·neɁ nʌ
     But   it had to be on the railway tracks we walked there.   At that time then

tsiɁ kʌs nú· thyatʌhninúhahkweɁ   kʌ́h,   Ball Park kuwa·yáts, tahnú· kwáh
where   there the two used to sell y'know, Ball Park it is named, and   just

kʌs   tho   áktaɁ kalistatáti̠Ɂ.   (5) Nʌ kwí· tho   nyaɁákweɁ   thikʌ́
habitually there   near   railway tracks extend.   So then   there we walked there that

kalistaɁkéshuɁ,   nʌ   uhte   tshaɁtewahsʌnʌ́ niyo·lé· niyukwe·nú̠.   (6) Nʌ
on the railway tracks, then supposedly half   how far   we have gone.   Then

kaɁikʌ́ kunukwé   waɁtyonatuhútsyohseɁ ta·kutnuso·tʌ́·.   (7) Nʌ kwí·
this   female persons they needed   they should squat.   So then

í· kwí· tho   i·kéteɁ   waɁkatʌɁnikú·lalʌɁ, a·khehlo·lí· kwí· tá·t úhkaɁ ok
me   there I am standing I watched out,   I should tell them if   someone

ʌ́tih.   (8) Tahnú· tetyó·kalas wí·, yah kwí· né· úhkaɁ tha·yutkátho̠Ɂ.
someone will come.   And   it is dark,   not   it's anyone one won't see.

(1) When we were teenagers—I want to tell you a story about my younger sister and me and our two friends, at Mack Ireland's, Mack and Dorothy Ireland used to have a store. (2) That's where we went. (3) But we had to walk there on the railway tracks. (4) At that time, where they used to have their store, it was called Ball Park [Road], and the tracks went right by there. (5) So then we were walking there on the tracks, and we had gone about halfway. (6) Then these girls needed to relieve themselves. (7) So then I'm the one standing there keeping a lookout, to tell them if someone is coming. (8) And it was dark [nighttime], nobody could see.

(9)   Ya?katkátho?   St. Thomas   nukwá·,   nitwʌ·té·   kaluhyá·ke   nukwá·;
    I looked over that way   St. Thomas   direction,   it is bright there   in the sky   direction;

nʌ   wa?khe·kʌ́·   úhka? ok   ta·yʌ́·.   (10) Nʌ kwí·   kwahotokʌ́·u
then   I saw someone   someone   someone is coming.   So then   just for real

wa?katʌ?nikú·lalʌ?.   (11) Tá·t núwa?   ó·   yah   ki?   só·tsi?   te?wi·nú.
I watched out.   Maybe   oh   not   actually   too much   it is not far.

(12) Ka?ikʌ́   úhka? ok   tá·le?.   (13) Wá·kelhe?   ki?   ní·,   lukwé   uhte.
    This   someone   he is coming.   I thought   actually   me,   a man   probably.

(14) Né· tsi?   a?é·   niwana?aló·tsla?   lona?alo·lú.   (15) Nʌ sok wí·
    Because   great   is the size of the hat   he has on a hat.   So then too

wa?twakhʌ·léhte?   wa?kí·lu?,   "teswashlíhʌ   úhka? ok   ta·yʌ́·."
I yelled   I said,   "you all hurry   someone   someone is coming."

(16) "Tá·thuni?   tá·le?."   (17) Nʌ sok wí·   né·   wa?tyakwaláhtate?.
    "Or   he is coming."   So then too   it's   we started to run.

(18) Tahnú·   tsi?   niwʌto·lé·   thikʌ́   tho   ta·hsaláhtate?   kalista?késhu?.
    And   how   it is hard   that   there   for you to run   on railway tracks.

(19) Niyoshno·lé·   wa?ukya?tu·tí·.   (20) Yah   te?wakanúhte?   tho   kʌ
    How quickly   they left me behind.   Not   I don't know   that's   question

na?teyotí·kat.   (21) Ya?ákwawe?   kwí·   tsi? nú·   wa?ukwehtuháti?.
how fast they move.   We got over there   where   we are on our way somewhere.

(22) Nʌ   tho   wa?akwatnúhtuhte?.   (23) Tá·t núwa?   kátsha? ok   tsha?tewahsʌnʌ́
    Then   there   we waited.   Maybe   somewhere   half

(9) I looked over towards St. Thomas, the sky that way was bright; then I saw someone coming. (10) So then I really watched out. (11) Maybe, oh, it wasn't too far. (12) Someone was coming. (13) I thought, a man probably. (14) Because he had on a great big hat. (15) So then I yelled, I said, "hurry, someone is coming." (16) "Or he is coming." (17) So then we took off running. (18) And it's really hard to run on railway tracks. (19) They left me behind real quick. (20) I didn't know they could go so fast. (21) So we got to where we were going. (22) Then we waited there. (23) Maybe about half

uhte   waʔkahwistá·eke?.   (24) Tsiʔ náheʔ tho   yákweteʔ   yukwatnuhtú·tu,
probably   the metal struck.   While   there we are standing we are waiting,

né·n   yah úhkaʔ tehokeʔtóhtu.   (25) Nʌ   waʔukwanehla·kó· thikʌ́ tsiʔ
it's that not   anyone he didn't appear.   Then   we were surprised   that   because

oyá· thaʔa·wʌ́·.   (26) Nʌ   waʔukwatétshʌʔ.   (27) Nʌ kwí· nok u·tú·
other differently it happened.   Then   we got scared.   So then   it had to be

tho   tyákwehseʔ   tsiʔ niyo·lé· wahutenho·tú·.   (28) Nʌ kwí· úhkaʔ ok
there   we are around   until   they closed the door.   So then   someone

sayukhiyaʔtítaneʔ.   (29) Oyá· ukwatʌloʔslaʔshúha.   (30) Wé·ne kwí·
someone gave us a ride again.   Other our friends.   Evidently

tsiʔ waʔukwatyánluneʔ.   (31) Né· s yukhihlo·líheʔ lotikstʌhokúha tsiʔ lutkáthos
that   we got haunted.   It's   they tell us   old persons   that   they see

kʌs   tá·thuniʔ lonathu·té· tsyoʔk náhteʔ thikʌ́ kalistá·ke.
habitually   or   they hear   different things that   on the railway tracks.

(32) Nʌ   kiʔ   yahá·keweʔ   tsiʔ ni·yót   tsiʔ waʔkka·látuʔ.
      Then   actually I arrived over there at   the way it is   that   I told a story.

(33) Tahnú· kwáh kwí· otokʌ́·u kaʔikʌ́ tho   niyukwayaʔtawʌ́·u.
      And   just   for real   this   thus it has happened to us.

an hour. (24) While we were standing waiting there, nobody showed up. (25) Then we
were surprised because something out of the ordinary happened. (26) Then we got scared.
(27) So then we had to stay there until they closed up. (28) And then someone gave us a
ride home. (29) Some of our other friends. (30) I guess we got haunted. (31) Some elders
tell us that they used to see or hear things on the tracks. (32) Now I have arrived over there
[at the end] of how I told the story. (33) And this really happened to us.

A Night Visitor

(Told by Rose Antone to Karin Michelson and Norma Kennedy on October 15, 2011)

(1) Wata·tíheʔ   ní·   yúkyats.   (2) Rose   yúkyats   oʔsluniʔké·<u>ne</u>.
    She Talks   me   is my name.   Rose   is my name   white man's way.

(3) Yusakehyá·laneʔ   thikʌ́   wahuniseʔkʌ́,   ó·   tá·t núwaʔ   kayé
    I remember way back   that   a long time ago,   oh   maybe   four

tshaʔtewakohsliyá·ku.   (4) Tho   kʌs   tyakwanákleʔ   aʔé·
when I have crossed over winters.   There   habitually   we reside   over there

Suzie Webster   tsiʔ   tyakonúhsoteʔ.   (5) Né·n   úska útlatsteʔ   thikʌ́   tsiʔ niwahsu·tés
Suzie Webster   at   she has a house.   It's that   one time   that   during the night

yotho·lé·,   nʌ kwí·   wahatkétskoʔ   lakeʔnihkʌ́.   (6) Tho   áktaʔ   wahátyʌʔ   thikʌ́,
it is cold,   so then   he got up   my late father.   There   near   he sat down   that,

tékni   kʌs   teyonhoká·luteʔ   thikʌ́,   úska pantry   nyeyawenú   kháleʔ   úska
two   habitually   two doors   that,   one   pantry   it has gone there   and   one

kanuhsowanʌ́   thikʌ́   tsiʔ   tyutolishʌtákhwaʔ   nukwá·.   (7) Né·n,   nʌ kwí·
it is a big room   that   at   one uses it to rest   where.   It's that,   so then

wahate·ká·teʔ   kʌ́·   yenʌstalihaʔtákhwaʔ   a·yukwayaʔtatalíhʌʔ.   (8) Nʌ kwí·   tho
he made a fire   y'know   stove   that it warms us up.   So then   there

lʌ́tskoteʔ   thikʌ́,   kwah nók tsiʔ   lotahúhsateʔ   yokʌno·lú.   (9) Kwáh   kʌʔ náheʔ?
he is perching   that,   just only   he is listening   it is raining.   Just   a while

nʌ   lothu·té·   yakʌʔ   thikʌ́   úhkaʔ ok náhteʔ   ta·yʌ́·   thikʌ́   tsiʔ nukwá·
then   he hears   reportedly   that   someone   someone is coming   that   where

kanuhsowanʌ́,   tahnú·   tho   lʌ́·tluʔ   kwáh   tsiʔ   yonhoká·lu<u>teʔ</u>.   (10) Né·
it is a big room,   and   there   he is sitting   just   at   door.   It's

(1) She Talks is my name. (2) Rose is my English name. (3) I remember way back a long time ago, oh, maybe when I was four years old. (4) We were living over there where Suzie Webster had a house. (5) So this one time it was cold during the night, so then my late father got up. (6) He sat down near where there were these two doors, one went to the pantry and one to a big room that was a living room. (7) So then he made a fire in the stove to warm us up. (8) So then he's sitting there, he's just listening to it rain. (9) In a while he heard someone coming from the big room, and he's sitting there right by the door.

wahʌ́·luʔ, "kwáh seʔ tho ni·yót tsiʔ i·yʌ́· thikʌ́ tsiʔ ni·yót tho
he said, "just too that's how it is that she is walking that as how it is there

yakonuhso·táhkweʔ kʌ́·, nʌ kwíʔ· né· tshiyakawʌhe·yú." (11) "Ta·yʌ́·
she had a house y'know, so then it's when she has died." "She is coming

thikʌ́, kwaʔnyóh tá·t núwaʔ yakotaʔwástaʔ ahtaʔshúha yakótstu."
that, seems like maybe she uses it to sleep shoes she is wearing."

(12) Wahotétshʌ? lonúhteʔ tsiʔ yah úhkaʔ oyá· tho té·yʌhseʔ, kwah nók
      He got scared he knows that not anyone other there one isn't around, just

í· kháleʔ aknulhá·, lakeʔníha kháleʔ lakeʔkʌhkʌ́ Leo. (13) Né·n tho
me and my mother, my father and my late older brother Leo. It's that there

yakʌʔ tayolakale·lé· thikʌ́, kwáh tsiʔ niyo·lé· tho ta·yúweʔ
reportedly it made a noise coming this way that, just until there she got there

tsiʔ yonhoká·luteʔ, nʌ utkʌ́·lah<u>te</u>ʔ. (14) Né·n kwahikʌ́ wahotétshʌʔ,
at door, then it ceased. It's that just really he got scared,

wahʌ́·luʔ, "tá·t núwaʔ otsiʔno·w<u>ʌ́</u>." (15) Né· tsiʔ kwáh kʌs kaná·nu thikʌ́
he said, "maybe mouse." Because just habitually it is filled that

tho nukwá· tyonúhsuteʔ, shekú n tsyoʔk náhteʔ yehwaʔektá·ke nityawenú,
that's where there is a room, still all kinds of things barn it has come from,

akwekú né· tho yehonahséhtu, akwekú tho yehonatahkwʌ·náy<u>ʌ</u>ʔ.
all it's there they have hidden it over there, all there they leave it for a while.

(16) Kok náheʔ kháleʔ tutayohyakwilakale·lé· thikʌ́ tho
      A little while and it is the sound of toes coming again that there

tuta·y<u>ʌ́</u>·. (17) Kwáh kyaleʔ tho tsiʔ tyonhoká·luteʔ, nʌ
someone is coming again. Just again there at door, then

(10) He said, "the way she walks is just like the one whose house this used to be, [but] she
has already died." (11) "She is coming, and it seems like maybe she is wearing slippers."
(12) He got scared knowing that there wasn't anyone else there, just me and my mother, my
father and my late brother Leo. (13) It was making a sound, all the way until she got to the
door, then it stopped. (14) So he got really scared, he said, "maybe [it's] a mouse."
(15) Because it was packed full there in that room with all kinds of things that came from
the barn, they had it all hidden in there, they left it all there for a while. (16) In a little while
there was the sound of toes coming again as someone was coming again [walking on their
toes]. (17) Right to the door again, then

utkʌ·lah<u>te</u>ʔ. (18) Nʌ kwíʔ washako·yéhteʔ Ma, wahʌ́·luʔ, nʌ   wahʌ́·luʔ,
it ceased.   So then   he woke her up   Ma, he said,   then he said,

"teyotuhutsyóhu ákteʔ   nú·   nyaéto<u>we</u>ʔ."   (19) "Wé·ni   tsiʔ
"it should be   different   where   you and we should go there."   "Evidently that

yakotyanlustákhwaʔ kʌ́·tho." (20) Wahʌ́·luʔ, "shekú né·n   kwahotokʌ́·u
someone is haunting it here."   He said,   "even   it's that just for real

ya·hsatkeʔto·tʌ́·   tho nukwá· yah kiʔ   thau·tú·   tsiʔ nikaná·nu."
should you look in   that's where not   actually   it can't be how   it is filled up."

(21) Né·n,   nʌ kwíʔ· waʔutkétskoʔ, waʔí·luʔ, "Simonhné kwíʔ nukwá· ʌwa·tú·
      It's that,   so then   she got up,   she said,   "Simon's place   where   it can be

nyʌhʌ́to<u>we</u>ʔ."   (22) Wahʌ·luʔ lakeʔnihkʌ́,   "kwáh kwíʔ· nók
you and we will go over there."   He said   my late father,   "just

okʌhaʔshúha, kháleʔ tsiʔ nikú   yukwatʌná·tslayʌʔ taetwatekhwáyesteʔ
blankets,   and   how much   we have groceries   you and we should combine

astéhtsiʔ, né· sʌ́· yʌtwáhawe<u>ʔ</u>."   (23) Nʌ kwíʔ· wahyathleʔnu·ní·
morning,   it's also you and we will take it there."   So then   the two packed

thikʌ́, tahnú· tho   kʌs   loteʔsléhtayʌʔ thikʌ́ kwáh tsiʔ yonhoká·luteʔ
that,   and   there habitually he sets the car   that   just   at   door

ohná·kʌʔ nukwá· tsiʔ kanúhso<u>te</u>ʔ.   (24) Nʌ kwíʔ· wahnikale·ní·   thikʌ́,
behind   where   at   there is a house.   So then   the two transported things that,

tho   yehnétaʔas   tsyoʔk náhoh<u>te</u>ʔ. (25) Wahʌ́·luʔ, "tákʌʔ kwíʔ·
there   the two are putting it in over there   different things.   He said,   "don't

né· yʌsheyaʔtáhaw   óksaʔ   tehniksá·   tsiʔ niyo·lé· ʌtníhsaneʔ
it's you will take them over there   right away two children until   you and I will finish

it stopped. (18) So then he woke up Ma, he said, then he said, "we should go some place
else." (19) "It must be haunted here." (20) He said, "even if really you could look in there
[the room] you can't actually because it's packed so full." (21) So then she got up, she said,
"we can go to Simon's place." (22) My late father said, "just the blankets, and we can con-
tribute all the groceries we have for breakfast, so we'll take that also." (23) So then the two
of them packed, and he used to park the car behind the house right by the door. (24) So then
they carried stuff back and forth and put all the things in [the car]. (25) He said, "don't take
the children right away until you and I are done

tyathle?nu·níhe?."   (26) Né·n,   yahaya·kʌ́·ne? thikʌ́ thok náhte? tho
you and I are packing."   It's that,   he went out   that   something   there

yeháta?as.   (27) Nʌ   né· tayeya·kʌ́·ne? Ma.   (28) Wá·yʌlhe?
he is putting it in over there.   Then   it's   she came out   Ma.   She thought

né· ka?ikʌ́ kwáh kʌ? ohʌtú í·late?   kʌ́·,   tahnú· tsi? niyokʌnolú,
it's   this   just   here   in front he is standing y'know,   and   how   it is raining,

ostúha kʌ? nyahuwa·yéle? ísi?   a·hátkwihte?,   nʌ sók   né·
a little   she touched him   yonder   he should move over,   and just then   it's

yahaya?tye·nʌ́·ne?, ka?sléhtaku nukwá· yahʌtáklane?, tutahatkátho?
he fell over,   in the car   where   he fell down,   he looked back this way

ókhna?   wa?í·lu? tsi? a?é· na?tehaká·lahse?   tsi? nihotetshʌ́·u. (29) Wá·lelhe?
and then she said   how   great is the size of his eyes how   he is scared.   He thought

né· kʌ n   kʌ? nukwá· kanúsku   tetyakotawʌ́li? né· yahuwá·leke?.
it's   question   right there   in the house   she is wandering   it's   she pushed him.

(30) U·tú·   tusahatkalhate·ní·   thikʌ́ nále?   yahníhsane?
      It could be   he turned around again   that   then again   over there the two finished

yathle?nu·níhe?.   (31) Né· thikʌ́ tú·ske? ki?   thikʌ́ wa?akwahtʌ·tí,
the two are packing.   It's   that   truly   actually   that   we left,

Simonhné nukwá· nya?ákwe?   ne? thó·ne?, yah ki?   nuwʌtú tho nú·
at Simon's   where   we went over there   at that time,   not actually   never   that's where

te?tyakwʌ́·tlu? thikʌ́, kwahotokʌ́·u tho nukwá· ya?akwanáklate?   Simon tsi?
we don't dwell   that,   just for real   that's where   we settled over there Simon   at

thonahtʌ́ti. (32) Tho   ki?   ok   ni·kú.
their home.   That's   actually   only how much.

packing." (26) So he went out and he was putting something in [the car]. (27) Then Ma came out. (28) She thought he was standing a bit in front [in her way], and it was raining so hard, she touched him a little so he would move over, and then he fell over, he fell down into the car, he looked back and she said his eyes were great big, he was so scared. (29) He thought it was the one who was wandering around right there in the house, she's the one that pushed him. (30) He could turn around again and then the two finished packing. (31) And really we left, we went to Simon's place at that time, we never lived there again, we moved in there, to Simon's home. (32) That's all.

What My Brother Leo Saw

(Told by Rose Antone to Karin Michelson and Norma Kennedy on October 15, 2011)

(1) Né· kiʔ   sʌ́· kaʔikʌ́ sakehyá·laneʔ,   tsiʔ náheʔ s thikʌ́ tyakwʌ́·tluʔ
It's   actually also this   again I remember, while   that   we dwell there

thikʌ́ tsiʔ tkanúhsoteʔ,   Suzie Webster akonúhsaʔ.   (2) Lakeʔkʌ́ha   Leo,
that   at   a house there, Suzie Webster her house.   My older brother Leo,

né· kʌs   né· wahatkáthoʔ thikʌ́ tsiʔ niwahsu·tés, nók tsiʔ yah kʌs kwí· né·
it's habitually it's he saw   that   during the night, but   not habitually it's

thutahnéhtahkweʔ Ma kháleʔ Dad. (3) Ínelheʔ   né· kwáh kʌ   nók tsiʔ
the two won't believe Ma and   Dad.   The two think it's just   question only that

yah tehauʔwéskwaniheʔ tsiʔ tetyó·kalas. (4) Wahʌ́·luʔ, "tho" wahʌ́·luʔ "kʌs
not he doesn't like   at   it is dark.   He said,   "there" he said   "habitually

thikʌ́ tsiʔ tyonhoká·luteʔ nutá·leʔ, tahnú· yah seʔ teʔyotenhotúkwʌ." (5) "Né·
that   at   door   he came, and   not too the door isn't open."   "It's

thikʌ́ tho   tahatáyahteʔ úhkaʔ ok." (6) "Kwaʔnyóh ok aʔé· énike nityótteʔ
that   there he came in   someone."   "Seems just like great above it is high up

lahnaʔtshí·ne, tsiʔ   oshuʔkalá·ke sʌ́· loyenawaʔkhútyeʔ   thikʌ́ tsiʔ áktaʔ
his bum,   because on the floor also he is going along holding onto that   as   near

nutá·leʔ, kwáh s oniʔ yakʌʔ   tho   katsistáheleʔ lahnaʔtshí·ne énike nukwá·,
he came,   just too reportedly there a light sits on his bum   above where,

onikwʌ́htalaʔ ni·yót." (7) Nʌ   áktaʔ nutá·leʔ thikʌ́, nʌ s yah kiʔ   né·
red   how it is."   Then near he came that, then not actually it's

tha·ho·kʌ́·,   yah tha·hatkáthoʔ lakúksne, né· kiʔ   ok thikʌ́ tsiʔ ostúha
he won't see him, not he won't see   his face,   it's actually only that   that a little

(1) One more thing I remember, while we were living at that house, Suzie Webster's house. (2) My older brother Leo, he would see something during the night, but Ma and Dad didn't believe it. (3) They thought it's only because he didn't like the dark. (4) He said, "there" he said "he came up to the door, and the door wasn't open." (5) "Someone came in." (6) "It seems like his bum was way up high, because also he was going along holding onto the floor [he's walking on all fours] as he came closer, there was a light on top of his bum too, a red one." (7) Then he came closer, he didn't actually see him, he didn't see his face, only a bit

yotahsa·tále?, ya·wét   tsi?   nihaya?tó·tʌ tsi? ni·yót   lukwé ki? wí· tho
it is a shadow, kind of like what   he looks like   as   how it is a man   actually there

í·le?.   (8) Tehoká·nle? s   yakʌ?   wé·ni   thikʌ́ tsi? né· tsi?
he is walking.   He is looking at him reportedly evidently that   that because

oshu?kalá·ke s lanuhwétsta? kʌ́·,   kwah nók mattress tho   ka·yʌ́·. (9) Kwáh s
on the floor   he sleeps   y'know, just   mattress   there it lies.   Just

kʌ? náhe? thikʌ́ tehoká·nle?,   tehoká·nle?,   nʌ   swatyelʌ́ s oni?
a while   that   he is looking at him, he is looking at him, then   sometimes   too

wahʌ́·lu? thikʌ́ kwáh s a?nyóh   úhka? ok náhte? tayeye·ná·   lakúksne,
he said   that   just   seems like someone   someone grabbed   his face,

yah thau·tú·   usahatu·lí·   kwahotokʌ́·u. (10) Nók tsi? khále? ki?   onʌ́
not   it can't be for him to breathe just for real.   But   and   actually   then

thikʌ́ nále? tusahatkalhate·ní·   thikʌ́, nʌ sók   sahaya·kʌ́·ne?,
that   again   he turned around again   that,   right then   he went out again,

shekú a?é· nukwá·   nyusá·le?   tsi? yonhoká·lute?, kwah nók
still   way over there he went back that way at   door,   just

yahá·lawe?   né·tho, khále? wí· yah kánike?   té·shlehse?,   yah
he got over there   there,   and   not   anywhere   he is not around anymore, not

thusahotkátho?.   (11) Nók tsi? yah ki? s   thutahnéhtahkwe?   thikʌ́
he won't see him anymore.   But   not   actually the two won't believe that

aknulhá·   khále? lake?níha tsi? niyo·lé· thikʌ́ laulhá· lake?nihkʌ́   wahotétshʌ?.
my mother and   my father   until   that   him   my late father he got scared.

(12) Tho   ki?   ok   ni·kú.
       That's actually only how much.

of a shadow, it kind of looked like a man walking there. (8) He [the ghost] was looking at
him [Leo], I guess because he was sleeping on the floor, there was just a mattress there.
(9) He was looking at him for just a while, he was looking at him, and he said that sometimes too it was as if someone grabbed him by the face, so he couldn't breathe really.
(10) But then he turned around again, he went out again, he walked back over to the door, as
soon as he got there, he wasn't there anymore, he didn't see him anymore. (11) But my
mother and father didn't believe it until my late father got scared himself. (12) That's all.

Pranks and Mishaps

The seven stories in this section are about events that were not always amusing to everyone involved at the time, but looking back, they are pretty funny.

The two young ladies Rina and Rita, who cooked beans for supper in the story *Worms in the Soup*, are pictured on the front cover of this volume.

In the remarks for the section 'Ghostly Tales,' it was mentioned that some words can be difficult to translate into English. The stem **-atyelʌ-**, which occurs several times in the stories in this section as well as the next section, is another example. The meaning of the stem involves becoming suddenly and unexpectedly aware or conscious of something, or suddenly and to one's surprise noticing or realizing something. But there is no really apt equivalent in English, and translations like 'be confronted by, be shocked by, be astounded, be taken aback, be suddenly surprised' are not satisfactory either. Lounsbury (1953, p. 96) translates the stem as 'suddenly and to one's surprise to encounter or observe,' and he translates the form **wahatye·lʌ́·** as 'did he suddenly confront.'

One additional example, which comes up in the next section, is **-ʔnyalhaʔt(e)-** (with the **te-** dualic prefix, so for example **teyakoʔnyalhá·teʔ** 'she is snoopy and touching everything'). This stem is usually used to describe children who are nosey and snooping around, but it's not just about being inquisitive, it also involves exploring by touching everything.

Visits to My Auntie's

(Conversation between Olive Elm and Mercy Doxtator,
with Karin Michelson on June 15, 1993)

(1) Wathahi·né· ní· yúkyats.   (2) Kwáh se? nók tsi? i·kélhe? a·kwahlolí
She Walks   me is my name.   Just   too only   I want   I would tell you all

kok tshi·ká·   tsi? niyo·lé· niskehya·lú·, aksothné·ke   kʌs   oskánhe
when I was small as far as   I remember,   at my grandmother's habitually together

yakwanákle?, aknulhá·   khále? lake?níha khále? yakyatʌno?sʌ́ha. (3) Khále?
we reside,   my mother and   my father   and   we two siblings.   And

onʌ́ wahatnuhsu·ní· lake?níha, áhsu   kwahotokʌ́·u te?yotéhsu?   ókhna?
then he built a house my father,   not yet just for real   it wasn't finished and then

ya?akwanáklate?.   (4) Yah te?yonhokahlu·tú·.   (5) Né· kʌs   nʌ
we settled over there.   Not   it doesn't have doors.   It's habitually when

wa?ó·kalawe? nʌ   wa?ukwʌtá·wha? kwáh kʌs nók tho   wahanhohanʌ·tákte?
it got dark   then we went to bed   just habitually   there he stuck a door against it

lake?níha tsi? nú· niyoká·lute?. (6) Wahu·níse? tho   ni·yót,   shekú s né·
my father   where   is an opening.   A long time   that's how it is, even   it's

yah tha?tekahná·net kanúsku   nukwá·, khále? onʌ́ nʌ   wahakalakwe·ní·
not   it is not doubled in the house towards, and   then when he could afford it

nʌ   wa?thahna?nétane?. (7) Kwáh olihwiyó   tsi? áhsʌ niyohslaké   nʌ
then   he doubled it.   Just   a sure thing that three years amount to   then

wa?ekalakwe·ní· aknulhá·   wa?uthyatuhslanʌ·tákte?, tahnú· tsi? na?knú·wene?,
she could afford it my mother she stuck paper against it,   and   how   I liked it,

(1) She Walks is my name. (2) I just want to tell you about when I was little, as far as I remember, we lived all of us together at my grandmother's, my mother and my father and my
brother. (3) And then my father built a house, it wasn't finished yet and already we moved
in. (4) It didn't have doors. (5) When it got dark and we went to bed my father just put
a door up against where there was an opening. (6) A long time it was like that, it didn't
even have walls in the house, and finally when he could afford it then he got the walls up.
(7) For sure it was three years before my mother could afford to put up wallpaper, and I
really liked it,

kwáh   ké·yale?   tsi?   nikahyatuhsló·tʌ,   otsí·nkwal   ni·yót   tahnú·   cherries
just   I remember   what   kind of paper it is,   yellow   how it is   and   cherries

kwáh   kaya?ta·lú·.   (8) Khále?   wa?akoyʌ·táne?   sʌ́·   yutekhwahla?tslohlókta?   né·
just   it is pictured.   And   she obtained it   also   one uses it to cover a table   it's

tshá·kat.   (9) Tsi?   niké·yale?   nʌ s   kwáh s nók   Christmas   wa?ákwatste?   thikʌ́
it is the same.   How   I remember   then   just   Christmas   we used it   that

yutekhwahla?tslohlókta?.   (10) Né· tsi?   niyakonʌ́ste?.
one uses it to cover a table.   Because   she treasures it so.

   (11) Nikʌ́·,   khále?   ké·yale?   kʌs   kwáh   olihwiyó   tsi?   tá·t núwa?
      Let me see,   and   I remember   habitually   just   a sure thing   that   maybe

téklu?   wí·   tsha?tewakohsliyá·ku,   áhsok   kʌs   nále?   aknulhá·
eight   when I have crossed over winters,   suddenly   habitually   again   my mother

wa?akwahtʌ·tí·   astéhtsi?,   wa?akwanatá·la?   tsi? né· nukwá·   tyakohtʌtyú·ne?   akaulhá·,
we left   morning,   we went to visit   where   her home used to be   her,

a?é· s   tyutʌhni·núhe?   ya?tyakwa·táne?   wa?akwatekhu·ní·   ice cream,
way over there   at the store   over there we stopped   we ate   ice cream,

í·   khále?   yakyatʌno?sʌ́ha   Oliver.   (12) Kwáh   kʌs   kwʌ?táti?   yukwahtʌ́ti
me   and   we two siblings   Oliver.   Just   habitually   all day   we are gone

tsi?   tekyatahnu·téle?   yeyákwehse?.   (13) Tahnú· s   né·n   tekyatahnu·téle?
at   the two siblings   over there we are around.   And   it's that   the two siblings

yako?sléhtayʌ?   kʌs   buggy   khále?   ponyha   yakonʌ́skwayʌ?.   (14) Úska
she has a vehicle   habitually   buggy   and   little pony   she has a pet.   One

kati? wí·   útlatste?   thikʌ́   wa?í·lu? n   Rose,   né· kwí· n   aknulhá·   tekyatahnu·téle?,
so then   time   that   she said   Rose,   so it's   my mother   the two siblings,

I remember just the kind of paper it was, it was yellow and it had pictures of cherries. (8) And she got a tablecloth that matched. (9) The way I remember it, it was only at Christmas that we used that tablecloth. (10) Because she treasured it so.

(11) Let me see, and I remember for sure I was maybe eight years old, my mother and us would just up and leave early in the morning, we went to visit where her own home used to be, and we would stop over there at the store and eat ice cream, me and my brother Oliver. (12) All day we were gone at her sister's. (13) And her sister had a buggy and a little pony. (14) One time, Rose said, that's my mother's sister,

waʔí·luʔ, "ʌsesheʔtlu·ná· kwí·   kaʔikʌ́ só·tsiʔ   tayokʌnoluháti̱ʔ." (15) Nʌ kwí·
she said, "you will take them home this   because rain is on the way."   So then

né· waʔkuwahlo·lí· n kuwayʌ́ha,   Audrey kuwa·yáts, waʔkʌ́·luʔ Audrey,
it's she told her   her daughter, Audrey is her name, she said   Audrey,

"háoʔ kiʔwáh." (16) Nʌ sok wí· né· waʔakoyaʔtotálhoʔ n akotshe·nʌ́· ponyha,
"okay then."   So then too it's she harnessed   her pet   little pony,

waʔakwatítaneʔ ká·slet, buggy tayukwá·sleʔ, kwáh kʌs   tayonuwʌhslályoʔ
we got in   vehicle, buggy we came riding, just   habitually there she whipped it

thikʌ́ n Audrey ponyha kok ní·laʔ kʌ́h. (17) Waʔí·luʔ aknulhá·, "satkʌ́·laht
that   Audrey little pony it is only little eh.   She said   my mother, "you cease

thikʌ́, tsiʔ úhte   na·yakoná·khwʌʔ   sanulhá· n   a·yesatkáthoʔ
that,   how supposedly she should get mad your mother should she see you

nihsyélhaʔ,   niyakonʌskwanʌ́steʔ akotpony." (18) Kwáh s nók waʔkaste·lísteʔ
what you are doing, she treasures a pet so her pony."   Just   she laughed

Audrey tayukwá·sele̱ʔ. (19) Né· né·n   tutayákwaweʔ   tsiʔ tyukwahtʌ́ti,
Audrey we came riding.   It's it's that we got home again at   our home,

tututhahalákwahteʔ,   tho   tayukwateʔslehtakalháthoʔ. (20) Aʔé· niyo·lé·
quickly again she turned in a road, there we turned over in the vehicle.   Great how far

yaʔakwʌtáklaneʔ, nók tsiʔ yah kwí· né· teʔyukwanuhlyá·ku, yah seʔ só·tsiʔ
over there we fell, but   not   it's we were not hurt,   not too too much

teʔyoshnolátiʔ   yukwá·sele̱ʔ. (21) Yah teʔwé·ne niyakonaʔkhwʌ́·u aknulhá·,
it is not going along fast we are riding.   It's amazing   how mad she is   my mother,

tahnú· kwáh kʌs   né· yakonaʔalolú s strawhat. (22) Yah teʔwé·ne
and   just   habitually it's she has on a hat straw hat.   It's amazing

she said, "you'd better take them home because there's rain on the way." (15) So then that's
what she told her daughter, Audrey was her name, and Audrey said, "okay then." (16) So
then she harnessed her [mother's] pony, we got in, and we came riding in the buggy, and
Audrey just whipped that pony and it was only little. (17) My mother said, "you quit that,
your mother would get so cross should she see what you doing, she really cares for her
pony." (18) Audrey just laughed as we came riding. (19) So we got back to our home, she
turned in the drive really fast, there we upset the buggy and turned over in it. (20) We fell
quite far over a ways, but we weren't hurt because we weren't going all that fast. (21) My
mother got SO mad, and she used to wear a straw hat. (22) She was so

niyakona?khwʌ·u a?é· niyo·lé· nika·yʌ́· akotstrawhat. (23) Tsi? uhte wí·
how mad she is great how far it is lying her straw hat. How supposedly

na?kuwattéhtʌ? Audrey, nʌ kwí· Oliverha wahaya?takénha? Audrey,
she scolded her Audrey, so then Oliver dear he helped her Audrey,

sahnikétsko? n buggy, sutítane?, nʌ sók suhtʌ·tí·. (24) Tho s
again the two set it upright buggy, she got in again, right then she went home. That's

ni·yót thikʌ́, a·kí·lu? once a week kʌs wa?akwanatá·la? tsi? niyo·lé·
how it is that, I would say once a week habitually we went to visit as far as

tyakohtʌ́ti, tahnú· kwáh kʌ? niyo·lé· ehta?késhu? s kwí· nya?áko?.
her home, and quite some distance on foot we went over there.

(25) Swatyelʌ́ s wa?uké·sle? buggy, tho wa?katítane? a?é· na?teksine·sú·se?,
Sometimes they rode me buggy, there I got in great how long my legs are,

kwáh kʌs ya?katʌna?tsláhawe?, né· wí· tsi? yah kʌs tha·kathu·táte?
just habitually I took lunch, because not habitually I won't agree

a·katekhu·ní· thikʌ́ akwatauntieha tsi? nú· tyenákle?, "só·tsi?" wa?kí·lu?, "yah
I should eat that my auntie where she resides, "because" I said, "not

ní· te?wake·ká·se? thikʌ́ só·tsi? teyakonuhsanú·yanit." (26) Nʌ kwí· wa?í·lu?
me I don't like the taste that because her house is dirty." So then she said

aknulhá·, "ʌkatʌna?tslu·ní· kwí·, né· nisé· ʌ́hseke?." (27) Wa?í·lu?, "tákʌ?
my mother, "I will make a lunch, it's you you will eat it." She said, "don't

oni? náhte? ʌhsí·lu thikʌ́, a·shehlo·lí· náhte? aolí·wa? yah téhselhe?
too anything you will say that, for you to tell her what the reason not you don't want

a·hsatekhu·ní." (28) Nʌ kyale? wí· wa?kí·lu? "háo?." (29) Né·n,
you would eat a meal." So again I said "alright." It's that,

cross her straw hat was lying far away. (23) I guess she really gave Audrey heck, so then
Oliver helped Audrey, they got the buggy upright again, she got back in, and then she went
right home. (24) That's the way it was, I'd say once a week we would go to visit at her
home, and it was kind of far to walk to go there. (25) Sometimes they would ride me in the
buggy, I would get in there with my great long legs, I would take a lunch, because I
wouldn't agree to eat where my auntie lived, "because," I said, "I don't find it appetizing,
because her house is so dirty." (26) So then my mother said, "I will make a lunch, you will
eat that." (27) She said, "don't say anything, that you tell her why you don't want to eat."
(28) So I said "alright."

né· s kwí· né· tsi?   nikeksa?táksʌ.   (30) Kwáh ké·yale? wí· kok náhe?
so it's   because how I am a bad child.   Just   I remember   a little while

thikʌ́ nʌ wa?í·lu? akwatauntieha, "háo? kwí·   tetwa·tút,
that   then she said   my auntie,   "come on then   let's you and we eat together,

twatekhu·ní."   (31) Nʌ   wa?í·lu?, "háo? ki?wáh." (32) Wa?í·lu?,
let's you and we eat a meal."   Then she said, "come on then."   She said,

"yah né· té·yʌlhe?   a·yutekhu·ní·   kʌ? niyaká·,   yutʌna?tslaha·wí·
"not   it's   she doesn't want   she would eat a meal   she is a little one,   she is bringing lunch

nʌ? né·." (33) Wa?kí·lu?, "hʌ́·, yah ní· te?wake·ká·se?,   só·tsi?
that one."   I said,   "yes,   not   me   I don't like the taste,   too much

teyakonuhsanú·yanit." (34) Tho   thiyu·té·   aknulhá·,   "satwá·nik satwá·nik."
her house is dirty."   There   she is just saying   my mother,   "shut up   shut up."

(35) Sʌ́ha? ok   yahá·ksane?   náhte? ka·túhe?.
      Nevertheless   over there I finished   what   I am saying.

(29) So it's because I was such a bad girl. (30) I just remember in a little while my auntie said, "come on, let's all eat, let's eat a meal." (31) She said, "come on then." (32) She [my mother] said, "the little one doesn't want to eat, she brought her own lunch." (33) I said, "yes, I don't find it appetizing, because her house is too dirty." (34) My mother just kept saying, "shut up shut up." (35) I went ahead anyway and finished what I was saying.

A Pig in the Window

(Told by Verland Cornelius to Karin Michelson and Norma Kennedy
on September 13, 2007)

(1) James Dakstete wí· lonuhso·táhkwe? ísi? nukwá· old house, tho nú·
     James Doxtator   he had a house   yonder   old house,   that's where

niyakotʌnihʌ́·ne? aknulháh, lonatʌnihʌ́·ne?.   (2) Tekanáktanet é·nik   sʌ́·
she used to rent   my mother, they used to rent.   It is doubled   upstairs also

(1) So James Doxtator used to have a house over there, an old house, that's where my mother rented, they [my parents] rented. (2) There was an upstairs too.

yu·ní.   (3) Kwahikʌ́ tsiʔ yukwʌ·tʌ́t, shekú né· yah teʔyako·yʌ́·   curtains.
it is made.   Just really how we are poor, even it's not she doesn't have curtains.

(4) Newspaper kʌs   né· yakolaʔnʌtáktu tshaʔtewahsʌnʌ́ niyo·lé·, aʔé· kwí·
    Newspaper habitually it's she has stuck it on half   it extends, great

nikawise·sú·seʔ.   (5) Ehtá·ke ok nukwá· kanyu·tú· newspaper, kanyó· ok
how long is the glass.   Below only where it is hanging newspaper, so that

tákʌʔ   utayutkeʔtotʌ́ úhkaʔ. (6) Né· thikʌ́ tá·t ehtá·ke   yukwanú·leʔ,
so as not one would look in anyone.   It's that if downstairs we are sleeping,

tahnú· mattress kwí· tayuhkwé·nʌtsteʔ. (7) Tahnú· s yah tehʌ́·tluʔ   lakeʔníha,
and mattress   she got it down.   And   not he is not home my father,

Kirbyha kʌs   wahuwákwahteʔ ta·hanuhwéthaʔ.   (8) Luwaʔkʌ́ha
Kirby dear habitually she invited him   he should sleep over.   Her younger brother

kiʔwáh. (9) Tahanuhwéthaʔ   ehtá·ke   yukwanú·leʔ.   (10) Thoʔnʌ́
right.   He came to sleep over downstairs we are sleeping.   And then

rocking chair tká·nyoteʔ é·nik.   (11) Yukwathu·té· thikʌ́ "wisht," úhkaʔ ok
rocking chair it is standing upstairs.   We hear   that "wisht," someone

teyakotkalʌ́·luʔ é·nik, tahnú· yah úhkaʔ tho té·tyʌhseʔ.
someone is rocking upstairs, and not anyone there one is not around.

(12) Tá·thuniʔ anitskwahlákhwaʔ yé·seleʔ.   (13) Né· s kwí·
    Or   chair   someone is dragging it.   So it's

yukwatkʌholú,   yukwatetshʌ́·u.   (14) Né·n   kháleʔ onʌ́
we have covered up with a blanket, we have become scared.   It's that and   then

aʔé· nukwá· kʌs kwí· kok né· nityotshuhtaká·lateʔ kʌ́·, ehtá·ke   sʌ́h.
over there habitually a little it's the window is raised y'know, downstairs also.

(3) We were really poor, she didn't even have curtains. (4) She stuck newspaper halfway up [the windows], and the windows were really tall. (5) The newspaper was hanging only on the bottom, so that no one could look in. (6) If we slept downstairs, then she would get the mattress down. (7) And my father wasn't home, she would invite Kirby to come to sleep there. (8) Her younger brother, right. (9) He came over to sleep and we slept downstairs. (10) And then there was a rocking chair upstairs. (11) We hear this "wisht" [whistling noise], someone is rocking upstairs, and no one is there. (12) Or someone is dragging the chair. (13) We have the blanket over our heads, we're scared. (14) And then over there, the windows were open just a little, it's the downstairs ones too.

(15) Tahnú·   newspaper   yako?lholú,   né·n   sʌ́ha? ok   kʌ? ok kwí·
And   newspaper   she has covered it,   it's that nevertheless   just small

nikatsísta?   tho   wa?katsistá·lane?,   "tóh."   (16) Nʌ kwí· núwa?
is the size of a light   there   a light landed,   "toh."   So then   this time

a·hsattsisto·tʌ́·,   wa?wʌ·té·ne? kwí·   kwáh   tsi?   nikanúhsa?;
should you put on a light,   it got bright   just   as   is the size of a house;

tá·t a·hsattsisto·tʌ́·.   (17) Ok ne?   thikʌ́, yah nʌ? né·.   (18) Kwáh
if   you should put on a light.   And as for   that,   not   that one.   Just

né· nók tsi? tho   wa?katsistá·lane? …,   yah kwí· tha·wé·nene?, kwah nók tsi?
it's only   there   a light landed …,   not   it didn't show,   just

tho   katsistáhele?.   (19) Tho   kati? ná·wati nále?   kyale? wí· tho
there   a light is sitting.   There   then   that side   then again   again   there

tayakonakalutyéhslu?   aknulhá·   tsi? yakotwisakalatatú,   yo?talíhʌ
she pounded all over with a stick my mother   at   she has raised the window   it is hot

ki?wáh.   (20) Yusu?swáhtahkwe?   né· thikʌ́, nʌ kyale? wí· wahʌ́·lu?
right.   Over there a light went out again it's   that,   so again   he said

Kirbyha,   "sʌ́ha? yoyánle? é·nik nukwá· yaétowe?."
Kirby dear, "more   it is good   upstairs   you and we should go over there."

(21) Nʌ kyale? wí· é·nik nukwá· nyusahníhawe?   mattress.   (22) Tahnú·
So again   upstairs   the two took it again   mattress.   And

shekú kʌs   né· ohne·kánus   a·yétane?   yah te?yakowi·sáyʌ?.
even   habitually   it's   drinking water for her to fill it   not   she doesn't have a glass.

(23) Ketchup kʌs   yakʌ?   yakokalhatení,   né· thikʌ́ wa?ehnekátane?
Ketchup   habitually   reportedly   she has emptied it,   it's that   she put water in

(15) And she had covered them with newspaper, nevertheless a small light landed there, "toh." (16) So then you turn on a light, it illuminates the whole house; if you turn on a light. (17) But not that one. (18) The light just landed there …(unfinished), it didn't get all bright, the light was just sitting there. (19) There on that side then my mother started banging around with a stick, where she had raised up the window, it was hot, right. (20) The light went out again, then Kirby said, "it's better that we go upstairs." (21) So then the two of them took the mattress upstairs again. (22) And she didn't even have glasses to put water in. (23) She would empty a ketchup [bottle], she put water in that

tá·t i·kélheʔ a·khnekí·la,   ketchup bottle.   (24) Ne·né· thikʌ́ yeha·wí·
if   I want   I would drink, ketchup bottle.   It's that that   she is carrying it

é·nik   yaʔutetsheʔto·tʌ́·.   (25) Tho kwí· é·nik nukwá· yetsyákwehseʔ.
upstairs   over there she stood a jar.   There   upstairs   we are over there again.

(26) Né· aleʔ   né· tho naʔa·wʌ́·neʔ, úhkaʔ ok aleʔ   anitskwahlákhwaʔ
      It's again it's thus it happened,   someone again a chair

yé·sleʔ   ehtá·ke.   (27) Dragging a chair around, úhkaʔ ok
someone is dragging it downstairs.   Dragging a chair around,   someone

yé·sleʔ   kʌ́h. (28) Just like this, yolakaléluʔ.   (29) Tho kwí·
someone is dragging it see.   Just like this,   there was a noise.   There

waʔakwahsuti·yá·keʔ,   tho kwí· yukwatetshʌ́·u, kháleʔ onʌ́ wahʌ́·luʔ, "aʔnyóh
we crossed over the night, there   we are scared,   and   then he said,   "seems like

wahu·níseʔ a·yólhʌneʔ,   niyóhtlut." (30) Né·n,   sayólhʌneʔ sayó·kalaweʔ,
a long time it would be daylight, it is scary."   It's that, the next day it got dark again,

nʌ   tsyuknulhaʔtsíwaʔ   aknulhá·,   sahahtʌ·tí·   né·n   Kirby.
then   we two are alone again my mother,   he went home it's that Kirby.

(31) Tsyuknulhaʔtsíwaʔ   nʌʔú·waʔ. (32) Nók tsiʔ elhúwaʔ kwí· tutayó·kalaweʔ.
      We two are alone again this time.   But   right then   it got dark again.

(33) Tho kwí· yaknitskwáheleʔ, shekú né·n   é·lhal yah teʔyukninʌ́skwayʌʔ.
      There   we two are sitting, even   it's that dog   not   we two don't have an animal.

(34) Tayola·káleleʔ tsiʔ tyohsuhtaká·luteʔ,   "tóh." (35) Tho   yaʔutkáthoʔ,
      It made a noise at   an opening in the wall, "toh."   There   she looked that way,

kóskos núwaʔ   okúhsaʔ tho   tyokeʔtoteʔkó· thikʌ́ aʔé· wí· é·nik
pig   this time face   there   it is looking in big that   great   above

if I wanted to drink, a ketchup bottle. (24) She carried that and put it down upstairs.
(25) And we are upstairs again. (26) And that's what happened again, someone was dragging a chair downstairs. (27) Dragging a chair around, someone was dragging it. (28) Just
like this (Verland makes a knocking-dragging sound on the table), it made a noise. (29) So
we spent the night like that, we were scared, and then he [Kirby] said, "seems like it's taking
a long time for it to become daylight, it's so scary." (30) So the next night, I'm alone again
with my mother, Kirby went home. (31) The two of us were alone again now. (32) But it
was right after it got dark again. (33) We were sitting there, we didn't even have a dog.
(34) There was a noise at the window, "toh." (35) She looked over that way, this time it was
a pig face showing through great big way above

newspaper kwí· yako?lholú,   átste kwí· ná·wati. (36) Nále?
newspaper   she has covered it, outside   that side.   Then again

wa?akoná·khwʌ? ki?wáh. (37) Wa?í·lu?, "la?nikuhláksʌ?, nihaya?tó·tʌ   núwa?
she got mad   right.   She said, "his mind is bad,   what kind of body this time

thotké·tote?."   (38) Wa?elihwanela?ákhu? kwí· nʌ? né·. (39) Tho?nʌ́   tho
he is looking in."   She swore repeatedly   that one.   And then there

tahasteliste?kó· lake?níha. (40) Nʌ kwí· né· tahatáwyahte?, onísta? tsi?
he laughed big   my father.   So then it's he came in,   oh boy   how

na?akoná·khwʌ?. (41) "Nisʌ?tahetkʌ?tó·tʌ,   ni·yót tho   tisa·té·,
she got mad.   "You are such a darn ugly kind, look'it there you are holding it up,

tho   ya?tekaye·lí· tyótkut kʌ?   yukyatyanlúhsluhe?   kanúsku."
there it is enough   always   right here we two are being haunted in the house."

(42) "Ni·yót núwa?   tho   tisa·té·   kóskos okúhsa?." (43) Wahʌ́·lu?,
      "Look'it this time there you are holding it up pig face."   He said,

"yah kʌ   te?satshanuní   kóskos okúhsa? ʌ́hseke?   ʌyólhʌne?."
"not   question you are not happy pig face   you will eat tomorrow."

(44) "Head cheese ʌhsatu·ní·   ʌyólhʌne?." (45) Né· tho   thyeyawʌ́·u.
      "Head cheese   you will make tomorrow."   It's that's just what happened.

where she had covered it with newspaper, [showing in from] the outside. (36) Did she ever get mad then. (37) She said, "the devil! what's looking in the window now." (38) Did she ever swear, her. (39) And then my father started to laugh really hard. (40) So then he came in, oh boy did she get mad. (41) "What a terrible person you are, just look'it that thing you are holding up, it's enough that we are always being haunted here in the house." (42) "Now look'it, this time you're holding up a pig face." (43) He said, "you're not happy? you can eat the pig face tomorrow." (44) "You can make head cheese tomorrow." (45) That's just what happened.

An Unusual Spittoon

(Told by Mercy Doxtator to Karin Michelson on August 20, 1998)

(1) Né· ka?ikʌ tsi? niwakkaló·tʌ.　　(2) Kwahotokʌ́·u tho niyawʌ́·u.
It's this　　what kind of story I have.　　Just for real thus it has happened.

(3) Né· kwí· ka?ikʌ tsi? ka·yʌ́· yukhlolí,　　Kwahawʌ́·se　　yutátyats,
So it's this　　the one that she has told me, They Carry Things for Her is her name,

khále? lo·néhkwe?　　Tá·wet Sumas né· luwa·yátskwe?. (4) Né· kati? wí· ka?ikʌ
and　　spouse used to be Dave Summers it's was his name.　　Well it's　　this

tsi? niyakokaló·tʌ.　　(5) Né· wí· n ka?ikʌ úska útlatste? wa?khékwahte?
what kind of story she has.　　So it's　　this　　one time　　I invited them

utahninatá·la?　　kʌ́·, khále? né· wí· ka?ikʌ yukyenhúsa?. (6) Né· kati? wí· ka?ikʌ
the two should visit see, and　　so it's this　　my in-laws.　　Well it's　　this

tsi? na?a·wʌ́ne?, wa?khékwahte? utahninatá·la?,　　né·n,　　wa?kí·lu?, nʌ kwí·
how it happened, I invited them　　the two should visit, it's that, I said,　　so then

tsha?katnaktahslísane?,　　wa?kí·lu?, "kʌh kwí· nú· nʌtsyanú·wete?　　nʌ
when I finished fixing the bed, I said,　　"over here　　you two will sleep overnight when

ʌsnislʌ́htalawe?."　　(7) Wa?í·lu?, "wé·ne kwí· nok ʌwa·tú· ʌyakya·láte?,
you two will get sleepy."　　She said, "evidently　　it has to be　　we two will lie down,

nʌ se? wí· né· wahu·níse? ákte?　　tsi? kanuhwétsta?,　　né· wí· tsi?
so then too it's a long time different at I sleep somewhere, because

nihakyelá·se,"　　wa?í·lu?, "úska útlatste? kʌ́·　　wa?akyanuhwétha?,
what he has done to me," she said, "one time　　y'know we two went to bed,

né·n,　　né· ní· ukeslʌhto·lí· thikʌ́ tsi? kwa?nyóh thok náhte? yahu·táne?
it's that, it's me it woke me up that　　that seems like something　　it landed

(1) This is the story I have. (2) It really happened this way. (3) The one who told it to me, her name is They Carry Things for Her, and her husband's name was Dave Summers. (4) So anyway this is her story. (5) So this one time I invited them to visit, and these were my in-laws. (6) Well the way it happened, I invited them to visit, so I said, when I finished making up the bed, I said, "over here is where the two of you will sleep over when you get sleepy." (7) She said, "I suppose the two of us will have to lie down [together], it's been a long time now that I've been sleeping apart, because of what he did to me," she said, "one time we went to bed and then, I got woken up because it seemed like something landed

kahúhtaku." (8) Nʌ kwíꞏ néꞏ tayutkétskwahte? kʌ́ꞏ,   neꞏné kaʔikʌ́ tho
in my ear."   So then it's she arose quickly y'know, it's that this   there

nihonitsklúti oyuʔkwákli?, néꞏ s wíꞏ tsi? latyuʔkwanhútaʔas. (9) Néꞏ s kwíꞏ thikʌ́
he has spit tobacco juice, because   he chews tobacco.   So it's   that

tyótkut loyuʔkwánhute?   kʌ́ꞏ,   tahnúꞏ kyuhte wíꞏ tho   niꞏyót kaʔikʌ́
always he has a mouthful of tobacco y'know, and   supposedly that's how it is this

tshahotáꞏwha?   loyuʔkwánhute?.   (10) Néꞏ kwíꞏ néꞏ tsi? naʔaꞏwʌ́ne?
when he went to bed he has a mouthful of tobacco.   It's that   how it happened

laꞏtéꞏ   loslʌhtaksʌ́hsluhe?, tho   néꞏ niꞏyót tsi? wahoslʌhtáksʌ? kaʔikʌ́ tsi?
he says he is dreaming,   that's it's how it is that he dreamed   this   that

kátsha? ok núꞏ yahanitskluꞏtí kaʔikʌ́ n oyuʔkwákeli?. (11) Néꞏ kwíꞏ néꞏ kaʔikʌ́
somewhere   he spit that way this   tobacco juice.   It's that   this

tho   niꞏyót tsi? loslʌhtaksʌ́hsluhe? tsi? yahanitskluꞏtí   thikʌ́ s wíꞏ spittoon
that's how it is that he is dreaming   that he spit that way that   spittoon

kʌs kwíꞏ latinaʔtúkhwa? kʌ́ꞏ   tshiwahuꞏníse?. (12) Tho núꞏ   kaʔikʌ́
customarily what they call it y'know a long time ago.   That's where this

nahoslʌhtáksʌ?, tho núꞏ   nyahanitskluꞏtí. (13) Néꞏn   nʌ kwíꞏ néꞏ túꞏske?
he dreamed,   that's where he spit that way.   It's that so then it's truly

waʔakonáꞏkhwʌ? kaʔikʌ́ n loꞏnéꞏ   Kwahawʌ́ꞏse, néꞏ wíꞏ tsi? yuhúhtaku néꞏ nukwáꞏ
she got mad   this   spouse Kwahawʌ́ꞏse, because   in her ear it's where

yahanitskluꞏtí, tho   uhte wíꞏ néꞏ niꞏyót   kaʔikʌ́ tsi? loslʌhtaksʌ́hsluhe?,
he spit that way, that's supposedly it's how it is this   that he is dreaming,

nʌ kwíꞏ wahanitskluꞏtí, nók tsi? néꞏ wahoslʌhtáksʌ? spittoon se? nukwáꞏ
so then he spit,   but   it's he dreamed   spittoon too where

in my ear." (8) So then she jumped up, he had spit tobacco juice, because he chewed tobacco. (9) He always had a mouthful of tobacco, and I guess that's how it was when he went to bed, he had tobacco in his mouth. (10) How it happened is he said he was dreaming, the way he dreamed it was that he spit the tobacco juice somewhere. (11) The way he was dreaming was that he spit into what they called a spittoon a long time ago. (12) That's where in his dream he spit. (13) So then his wife Kwahawʌ́ꞏse got really mad, because he spit into her ear, I guess that's how he was dreaming, so then he spit, but he dreamed he spit into a spittoon.

yahanitsklu·tí·.   (14) Né·n   wa?í·lu?, kwáh wa?í·lu? "ne? thó·ne? tetyotá·u
he spit that way.   It's that she said, just   she said "at that time   it stopped again

thikʌ́ a·yakya·láte?   kahúhtaku tshyahanitsklu·tí·."   (15) Né· kyale? wí·
that   that we two lie down in my ear   when he spit that way."   So again

né· nikú   wa?ukwayéshu? tshiyeka·látuhe?   kʌ́·,   né· s wí· tsi?
it's how much we laughed   when she is telling a story y'know, because

nihotiste·líst   kʌ́·   a·hnika·látu?,   tahnú· s lotikalaká·te?,
how they are amusing y'know for the two to tell stories, and   they have many stories,

swake?nikulhʌ́hslu? s kwí· ní· thikʌ́ náhte? nihotikaló·tʌhse?.   (16) Nók tsi?
I have forgotten many   me   that   what   kind of stories they have.   But

né· kati? wí· ka?ikʌ́ tho   nikakaló·tʌ   ka?ikʌ́ wa?kuhlo·lí· kʌ́·,   tho   kati?
it's anyway   this   that's the kind of story this   I told you   y'know, that's then

ok wí· núwa?   niwakka·lés   ka?i·kʌ́.
only   this time how long is my story this.

(14) So she said, she said "at that time we stopped sleeping together when he spit into my
ear." (15) We laughed a lot when she was telling her story, because they were really amusing telling their stories, and they had a lot of stories, I've forgotten many of the stories they
had. (16) But anyway, I told you this story, that's only how long my story is this time.

Worms in the Soup

(Told by Norma Kennedy to Karin Michelson on June 30, 2009)

(1) Shekólih.   (2) Norma ní· yúkyats   o?sluni?ké·ne.   (3) Thiwé·sa?
      Hello.   Norma   me   is my name   white man's way.   She Wanders

yukna?túkhwa?   Ukwehuwehnéha?.   (4) Wá·kelhe? kwí· a·kwaka·látuhse?
what they call me   in the Native way.   I thought   I would tell you all a story

(1) Hello. (2) Norma is my English name. (3) She Wanders is what I'm called in Indian.
(4) I thought I would tell you a story,

ka?ikʌ́, tsi? nikakaló·tʌ   ka?ikʌ́ aknulhá·   khále? lake?níha yah thye?yawʌ́·u
this,   what kind of story it is this   my mother and   my father   it had to be

tsi? Otstʌhlonú·ke   wá·nehte?,   yah kwí· tehonanúhte?   tó· náhe?
that at the United States the two went there, not   they don't know   how long

ʌhonahtʌtyúhake?,   kwʌ?táti? ʌhonahtʌtyúhake?,   tá·thuni? tá·t núwa?
they will be gone away,   all day   they will be gone away,   or   maybe

yʌtsyólhʌne? nʌ   elhúwa? áshne<u>we</u>?.   (5) Wísk kyuhte wí· tá·tkʌ
the next day   then   right then   the two will get home.   Five   supposedly or maybe

yá·ya?k tsha?tewakohsliyá·ku   ne? thó·ne?, nók tsi? tsi? niyo·lé· wakanúhte?
six   when I have crossed over winters   at that time, but   as far as   I know

yah nuwʌtú tehonahtʌ́ti   tho náhe? aknulhá·   khále? lake?n<u>íha</u>.
not   never   they have not gone away that long   my mother and   my father.

(6) Tyótkut kʌs   teyakwayás<u>he</u>. (7) Yawʌtúnya?t kwí· tsi? náhe?
      Always   habitually we are together.   It is lonely   while

lonahtʌ́ti.   (8) Yah kwí· te?waklʌ?nhá·u   yah kánike?
they have gone away.   Not   I haven't gotten used to not   anywhere

tha·hné·she<u>ke</u>?.   (9) Rita yutátyats   thikʌ́ yakonatahlenʌ́, né· kwí·
the two won't be around.   Rita is her name   that   she is visiting,   so it's

tyekwanʌ́   yuke?kʌ́ha   tsha?teyonohsliyá·ku   kyuhte wí· ka?ikʌ́ Rita.
she is biggest my older sister they have crossed winters alike supposedly this   Rita.

(10) Né· kati? wí· thikʌ́ wʌhnisla·té· tshahyahtʌ·tí·   aknulhá·   khále? lake?níha,
       Well then it's   that   a day exists   when the two left my mother and   my father,

né· kwí· thikʌ́ yo?kálashʌ kwí· ʌtsyakwatekhu·ní·,   osahé·ta? kwí·
so it's   that   evening   we will have a meal again, beans

a story about [the time] my mother and father had to go to the States, they didn't know how
long they would be gone, whether they would be gone all day, or maybe they would get
home only the next day. (5) I guess I was five or maybe six years old at that time, but as far
as I know my mother and my father had never been away that long. (6) We were always
together. (7) So it was lonely while they were gone. (8) I wasn't used to the two of them
not being there. (9) This lady was visiting, Rita was her name, she was the same age as my
oldest sister I guess, this Rita. (10) Well anyway that day when my mother and my father
went away, for our supper,

wa?knina?tsiha·lʌ·,   né· kwí·   ʌtsyákwake?   nʌ   ʌtsyakwatekhu·ní·
the two hung a kettle, so it's   again we will eat it when   again we will have a meal

yo?kaláshʌ.   (11) Né· kati? wí· thikʌ́, kwáh nʌ   thóha   tsha·ka·lí·
evening.   Well then it's that,   just   then almost when it would be cooked

ohnekákli?, né· wa?tyuwʌ́li? kwí· thikʌ́ Rita kwí·, ya·wét kwí· Rita
soup,   it's she stirred it   this   Rita,   like   Rita

tsyakokhu·ní.   (12) Né· kwí· thikʌ́ wa?tyuwʌ́li?, wa?i·lu?, "O·ké· satkátho
again she is cooking.   So it's   that   she stirred it,   she said,   "Oh my look

ni·yót."   (13) Nʌ kwí· né· tho   teyakoshlihʌ?uháti?, tho   nyahá·yʌ?
how it is."   So then it's there she is hurrying,   there she went over there

Rina.   (14) Wa?i·lu?, "náhte? ni·yót," wa?í·lu? Rita, "ni·yót kwí· ne? kʌ́
Rina.   She said,   "what   it is so," she said   Rita, "look'it   won't you

otsi?nu·wá· tho   latiyá·tit."   (15) Nʌ kwí· ya?utke?to·tʌ́· oni? né·n   Rina,
worms   there they are in it."   So then she looked in   too   it's that Rina,

wa?í·lu?, "o·ké· yah kwí· né· thau·tú·   thikʌ́ aétwake?   ni·yót."
she said,   "oh my not   it's   it can't be that   that you and we eat it like it is."

(16) "Otsi?nú·wá· tekayéstu."   (17) Tahnú· a?é· kwí· nikaná·tsya?   thikʌ́
      "Worms   it is mixed in."   And   great   is the size of kettle that

yonátstu   yonathnekakli?tslu·ní. (18) Kwáh kyuhte wí· ahsʌnʌ́ niyo·lé·
they have used it they have made soup.   Just   supposedly half   how far

nítkale?   thikʌ́ tsi? niyawe?towanʌ́   osahé·ta? yotina?tsíhale?.
it is in there that   how   it is a large amount beans   they have hung a kettle.

(19) Né·n   akwekú se? wí· thikʌ́ onʌ́ ísi?   ya?ona·tí·.   (20) Né· tsi?
      It's that all   too   that   now   yonder they threw it away.   Because

the two of them [Rina and Rita] boiled beans [for soup], that's what we would eat when we
have our supper. (11) Well, when the soup was almost done, Rita stirred it, Rita was like the
one cooking. (12) So she stirred it and she said, "Oh my gosh, look at this." (13) So then
Rina rushed right over there. (14) She said, "what's wrong?," Rita said, "would you look at
that, there's worms in it." (15) So then Rina looked in it too, she said, "oh my, we can't eat
this the way it is." (16) "There's worms mixed in." (17) And it was a great big kettle that
they used to make soup. (18) I guess half of it was filled [because] it was a large amount of
beans they were boiling. (19) So they threw it all out. (20) Because

tekatsiʔnuwayéstu kiʔwáh. (21) Né· tsiʔ yaʔkato·kʌ́neʔ   ne·né· thikʌ́
worms are mixed in   right.   Because it became apparent that's it that

kok ni·wá·seʔ kʌ́·   kwaʔnyóh kanikwʌhtalawísklaʔ niwahsohkó·tʌhseʔ
just little things y'know seems like   red-white   is their colour

tho   yoʔklúnyuheʔ,   tho   kiʔ   nityawenú   thikʌ́ osahé·taʔ, né·n
there   things are floating,   there actually it has come from that   beans,   it's that

wá·knelheʔ   né· otsiʔnu·wá· kʌ́h. (22) Tho   kiʔ   nikú   thikʌ́ átste
the two thought it's worms   see.   That's actually the amount that   outside

yaʔknikalhate·ní·   né· tsiʔ tekatsiʔnuwayéstu. (23) Né·n,   né· seʔ né·
over there the two emptied it   because worms are mixed in.   It's that, it's too it's

thikʌ́ kwahotokʌ́·u tsiʔ tho   ni·yót   thikʌ́ a·hsnaʔtsiha·lʌ́·   osahé·taʔ,
that   just for real   that that's how it is that   you should hang a kettle beans,

yah kiʔ   ní· teʔwakanúhteʔ thikʌ́ kátshaʔ nú· nítwehseʔ   thikʌ́ kok ni·wá·seʔ
not   actually me I don't know   that   where   it comes from that   just little things

kʌ́·tho yoʔklúnyuheʔ.   (24) Nók tsiʔ né· kiʔ   thikʌ́ tho   niyawʌ́·u
here   things are floating.   But   it's actually that   thus   it has happened

neʔ thó·neʔ, yah kiʔ   teʔské·yaleʔ   náhteʔ katiʔ waʔákwakeʔ thikʌ́
at that time,   not   actually I don't remember anymore what   then   we ate   that

tshusayakwatekhu·ní·   yoʔkaláshʌ. (25) Kháleʔ yah teʔské·yaleʔ
when we had a meal again evening.   And   not   I don't remember anymore

sá·neweʔ   kʌ n   lakeʔníha kháleʔ aknulhá· neʔ thó·neʔ. (26) Tá·tkʌ
the two got home question my father and   my mother at that time.   Or maybe

tshusayólhʌneʔ   nʌ elhúwaʔ sá·neweʔ.   (27) Né· kiʔ   ok   thikʌ́
when the next morning then right then the two got home.   It's actually only that

there were worms in it, right. (21) Because they came to realize that these little things, these kind of pink things that were floating around there, it was from the beans, they thought it was worms. (22) They dumped the whole amount outside because of the worms that were mixed in. (23) So that's really the way it is when you boil beans, I don't know where they come from, those little things that float around. (24) But that's what happened at that time, I don't remember anymore what we ate for supper. (25) And I don't remember anymore whether my father and mother come home at that time [that night]. (26) Or maybe it was the very next morning before they got home. (27) All

ké·yale?   tsi? niyawe?towaná   osahé·ta? ísi?   ya?ona·tí·.
I remember that it is a large amount beans   yonder they threw it away.

(28) Thok ki?   ok   ní· niwakka·lés   ka?i·ká.   (29) Nʌ ki?wáh.
     That's actually only me   how long is my story this.   So long.

I remember is that they got rid of a lot of beans. (28) That's the extent of my story. (29) So
long.

My First Christmas Tree

(Told by Mercy Doxtator on January 16, 1999)

(1) Thó·nʌ   oyá·   náhte? ʌsekka·látu?,   né·n   né· kwí· né· ka?iká
     And then   another   what   I will tell a story again, it's that so it's   it's this

ya·wét   kyuhte wí· kwáh tyotyeláhtu ukwanúhtʌne? tsi? Christmas.
kind of like supposedly just   first   I found out about that Christmas.

(2) Nók tsi? kwáh ké·yale?   thiká aknulhá·   wa?uhtʌ·tí·,   akwatauntieha kwí·
     But   just   I remember that   my mother she went away, my auntie

lóna?   tho   wahyate?sléhtayʌ? tho   wa?utítane?, St. Thomas wahʌ·néhte?.
man and wife there the two parked a car   there she got in,   St. Thomas they went there.

(3) Kwáh kwí· a?nyóh wa?thuttsyaptá·na? tsi?   nʌ wí· thóha Christmas.
     Just   seems   they went shopping   because then   almost Christmas.

(4) Né·n,   wahá·lu?, wahá·lu? lake?níha, "wé·ne kwí· tá·t núwa?," wahá·lu?,
     It's that, he said,   he said   my father, "evidently   maybe,"   he said,

"aetyatluto·tá·   Christmas tree."   (5) Nʌ kwí· náhte? wa?kanuhtunyu·kó·
"you and I should put up a tree Christmas tree."   So then   what   I thought about

(1) And then I'll tell another story, so it's kind of like I guess the very first time I found out
about Christmas. (2) I remember my mother went away, my auntie and her husband parked
their car and she got in, they went to St. Thomas. (3) It seems they went shopping, because
it was almost Christmas time. (4) So he said, my father said, "I suppose maybe," he said,
"you and I should put up a Christmas tree." (5) So then what I was thinking was

kátsha? kati?   né· nú·   ʌtyakníhawe?   ka?ikʌ́, wahili?wanu·tú·se?
where   anyway   it's where   we two will bring it from this,   I asked him

wa?kí·lu?, "kátsha? né· nú·   ʌtitnilutáhawe?   kʌ́·, íhselhe?
I said,   "where   it's where you and I will bring a tree from eh,   you want

aetwatluto·tʌ́."   (6) Wahʌ́·lu? "ísi? nukwá·" wahʌ́·lu?
you and we would put up a tree."   He said   "yonder"   he said

"tyotuní   kʌ́·, kwah nók tʌtyahahi·yá·ke?   kʌ́·, né· thikʌ́ skalu·tát
"it is growing see, just   you and I will cross a road see, it's that   one tree

yʌhʌ́kko?."   (7) Ya·wét kwí· né· kwí· nyʌyakni·kó·   kʌ́·,
over there I will pick it."   Kind of like   so it's   over there we two will pick it see,

nʌ kwí· né· kwáh kati? wí· kʌ? náhe? thikʌ́ nʌ   wahʌ́·lu?, "nʌ kʌ
so then   it's just   well   some while that   then   he said,   "now question

salha·lé·   aetnilutakó·na?."   (8) Wa?kí·lu? "hʌ́· o·nʌ́."
you are ready   for you and me to go and get a tree." I said   "yes now."

(9) Nʌ kwí· né· átste   ya?áknewe?,   wahʌ́·lu?, "ʌhsaté·sle? ki?wáh,
     So then   it's outside we two got over there, he said,   "you will crawl right,

yah wí·" wahʌ́·lu? "téhselhe?   úhka? náhte? a·yukhikʌ́   ka?ikʌ́ tsi?
not"   he said   "you don't want anyone   one would see us this   that

wetnilutanʌskó·na?."   (10) LaotiDanford, tho nú·   thonahtʌ́ti,
you and I are on our way to steal a tree."   The Danford's,   that's where   their home,

tahnú· kwáh s tho   ohʌtú   tho   kaluto·tú·   thikʌ́, ohnéhta? kwí·
and   just   there in front there   there are trees around that,   evergreen

na?kalutó·tʌ?.   (11) Nʌ kwí· né· wahʌ́·lu?, "yah wí·" wahʌ́·lu? "téhselhe?
what species of tree.   So then   it's he said,   "not"   he said   "you don't want

where were we going to get it, I asked him, I said, "where are we going to get a tree? [if]
you want us to put up a tree." (6) He said "there's some growing right over there, all we
have to do is cross the road, I'll get one of the trees over there." (7) So it was kind of like
we would get it over there, so then in just a while he said, "are you ready now for us to get a
tree?" (8) I said "yes now." (9) So then we got outside, he said, "you crawl, right," he said
"you don't want anyone to see that we are on our way there to steal a tree." (10) That's
where the Danford's home was, and right out front there were these trees, evergreen trees.
(11) So then he said, "you don't want

úhkaʔ náhteʔ a·yukhikʌ́   kaʔikʌ́, ʌhsaté·sleʔ   kiʔwáh, yah katiʔ né·
anyone   one would see us this,   you will crawl right,   not   then   it's

úhkaʔ   tha·yukhi·kʌ́·."   (12) Nʌ kwí· né·, nʌ kwí· tho kwí· to·kʌ́skeʔ
anyone   one won't see us."   So then   it's,   so then   there   truly

waʔtkatutshotúniʔ,   nʌ sok wí· kwahotokʌ́·u waʔkaté·sleʔ kʌ́h.   (13) Tho kwí·
I got down on my knees, so then too just for real   I crawled   y'know.   That's

ni·yót   kaʔikʌ́ katé·sleʔ   onyʌhtakúshuʔ wí· neʔ kʌ́h, nyaʔákneʔ   kʌ́h.
how it is   this   I am crawling   through the snow it's that,   we two went over there see.

(14) Né·n,   tho kwí· yohatátiʔ   thikʌ́ tho   waʔtyakyahahi·yá·keʔ kʌ́h.
      It's that, there   a road extends that   there   we two crossed a road   see.

(15) Ato·kʌ́· kwí· laha·wí·   lakeʔníha, kháleʔ wé·ne kwí· á·shaleʔ sʌ́·,
      Axe   he is carrying it my father,   and   evidently   blade   also,

wé·ne   laha·wí·   kʌ́·,   nók tsiʔ né· kiʔ   thikʌ́ á·shaleʔ wá·latsteʔ
evidently he is carrying it y'know, but   it's   actually that   blade   he used it

waʔthalútyahkeʔ kʌ́h.   (16) Nʌ kwí· tutahá·sleʔ   kʌ́·,
he cut a tree   y'know.   So then   he dragged it back this way see,

nʌ kyaleʔ wí· wahakhlo·lí·, wahʌ́·luʔ, "hányo" wahʌ́·luʔ, "sasaté·sle kaʔikʌ́,
so again   he told me,   he said,   "come on" he said,   "crawl again   this,

ni·yót   thikʌ́ tá·t núwaʔ úhkaʔ ok a·yukhi·kʌ́·."   (17) Tho s kwí·
watch it   that   maybe   someone   someone would see us."   That's

thok nikú   wakanúhteʔ tho kwí· ná·kyeleʔ tsiʔ náhteʔ lakhlo·líheʔ lakeʔníha,
only how much   I know   thus   I did   that   what   he tells me   my father,

kwáh sʌ́· aʔnyóh aúkwʌkeʔ,   "náhteʔ katiʔ aolí·waʔ?   tsiʔ yah nisé·
just   also   seems   I should have said, "what   well   the reason   that   not   you

anyone to see us, so you will crawl, right, then no one will see us." (12) So then, so then truly I got down on my knees, and so then I was really crawling. (13) That's how come I was crawling through the snow I mean, we were on our way over there. (14) So we crossed the road that went along there. (15) My father was carrying an axe, and he must have been carrying a saw too, he used the saw to cut down a tree. (16) So then he dragged it back this way, so again he told me, he said, "come on," he said "crawl again, and watch it, maybe someone might see us." (17) That's how little I knew, I did what my father told me, seems like also I should have said, "well how come YOU're not

thaʔhsaté·sleʔ   kʌ́·, yuknilutanʌskohátiʔ   seʔ kaʔi·<u>kʌ́</u>."   (18) Nók tsiʔ
you won't crawl eh,   we two are stealing a tree too this."   But

kwáh s   uhte wí·   né·, nók tsiʔ ya·wét   kyuhte wí· lakwatnutolyá·thaʔ
just   supposedly it's, but   kind of like supposedly he is teasing me

kyuhte wí· thikʌ́ lakeʔníha, né· aolí·waʔ   kwáh ní· wahakhlo·lí· a·katé·se<u>le</u>ʔ.
supposedly that   my father,   it's the reason just   me   he told me   I should crawl.

(19) Né·n,   nʌ kwí· né· thikʌ́ tho   naʔa·wʌ́neʔ waʔaknilutanʌ́skoʔ, kháleʔ nʌ kwí·
      It's that, so then it's   that   thus it happened   we two stole a tree,   and   so then

sayákneweʔ,   nʌ kwí· yaha·yʌ́·teʔ,   tho kiʔ ok náhteʔ thikʌ́ wahatu·ní· tsiʔ nú·
we two got home,   so then he brought it in, something   that   he made it   where

naʔtʌka·táneʔ ka·lúteʔ kʌ́·,   kwáh tho   corner tho   yahatluto·tʌ́·
it will stand up tree   y'know, just   there corner there over there he stood up a tree

kʌ́h.   (20) Tahnú· yah s kwí· né· nuwʌtú teʔwakatkáthu uhte i·kélheʔ
y'know.   And   not   it's   never   I have not seen   I think

Christmas tree, yah katiʔ wí· ní· náhteʔ   teʔwakanúhteʔ náhteʔ katiʔ
Christmas tree, not then   me   anything I don't know   what   then

nʌkayelʌ́ha<u>ke</u>ʔ. (21) Tahnú· kwáh s ké·yaleʔ   thikʌ́ tsiʔ kwah nók yukni·yʌ́·
it will be done.   And   just   I remember that   that just   we two have

crepe paper, né· thikʌ́ waʔthahlihtániʔ   kʌ́·,   nʌ sok wí· né· thikʌ́
crepe paper, it's that   he broke it into pieces y'know, so then too it's   that

waʔákyatsteʔ waʔakniyaʔtahslu·ní· yukyatlu·tó<u>te</u>ʔ.   (22) Kháleʔ
we two used it we two dressed it up   we two have a tree put up.   And

kanúsku   sʌ́· waʔakniyaʔtahslu·ní·, né· kiʔ   ok   thikʌ́ onikwʌ́htalaʔ
inside the house also we two dressed it up,   it's actually only that   red

crawling, it's the two of us stealing a tree." (18) But I suppose, I guess it was kind of like
my father was teasing me, that's why he told me I should crawl. (19) So then that's how it
happened that we stole a tree, and so then we got home, he brought it in, he made something
where the tree would stand up, he put the tree right in a corner. (20) And I think I had never
seen a Christmas tree, so I didn't know anything about how it's done. (21) And I remember
that we just had crepe paper, he broke it up into little pieces, and so then we used that to
decorate our tree. (22) And also inside the house we decorated, red

khále? awʌ·lá· niwahsohkó·tʌ crepe paper, né· thikʌ́ wa?ákyatste?
and   green   is the colour   crepe paper, it's that   we two used it

wa?akniya?tahslu·ní· kanúsku.   (23) Khále? wí· n yukyatlu·tóte?,
we two dressed it up   inside the house.   And   we two have a tree put up,

né· kwí· sʌ́· wa?akniya?tahslu·ní·. (24) Né·n,   nʌ kwí· tú·ske? teyukyatohtálhu
so it's also we two dressed it up.   It's that, so then truly   we two have tidied up

khále? kwa?nyóh kwáh sʌ́· yukyatlu·tóte?,   yukniya?tahsluní   sʌ́·
and   seems like just also we two have a tree put up, we two have dressed it up also

kanúsku,   nʌ né· tshyusa·yúwe?   aknulháh. (25) Tsi? kwí· né·
inside the house, then it's when she got home my mother.   How   it's

na?akonehla·kó· tsi? niyuknilutiyó   kʌ́,   khále? kwáh sʌ́·
she got surprised how we two have a nice tree y'know, and   just   also

kaya?tahsluní ki?wáh. (26) Tho   kati? wí· ní· nú·   a·kí·lu? kwáh tyotyelʌ́htu
it is decorated right.   That's well   me where I'd say   just   first

wakanuhtʌ́·u   Christmas. (27) Khále? ké·yale?   thikʌ́ tsi? kwáh
I have found out about Christmas.   And   I remember that   that just

tsyo?k náhte?   tyakoka?táti?   aknulhá· tshyusa·yúwe?   kʌ́·,   wa?í·lu?
all kinds of things she has lots along my mother when she got home y'know, she said

yah kwí· náhte?   kʌ? thya·kyéle?   kʌ́·, yah ní· thau·tú·   a·kátkʌhse? náhte?
not   anything I should not touch it eh, not me it's can't be that I examine what

tsyehawinúti?   kʌ́·,   wa?í·lu? kwí· wa?úhsehte?. (28) Yah kwí·
she is bringing things back y'know, she said   she hid it.   Not

te?wakanúhte? kátsha? nú· na?úhsehte?, nók tsi? né· kwí· onʌ́ n yah kwí·
I don't know   where   she hid it,   but   so it's   then   not

and green crepe paper, we used that to decorate inside the house. (23) And our tree, we decorated it also. (24) So then we had everything all tidied up, and like we had our tree up also, we had the house decorated also, when my mother got home. (25) She was so surprised that we had such a nice tree, and it was decorated, right. (26) Well I'd say that was the very first time I found out about Christmas. (27) And I remember that my mother had all kinds of things with her when she got back home, she said I shouldn't touch anything, I couldn't look to find out what she was bringing back, she said she hid it. (28) I don't know where she hid it, but

tha·yukwanúhtʌneʔ náhteʔ thikʌ tsyehawinútiʔ   tsiʔ niyo·lé· yʌkáheweʔ
we won't find out   what   that   she is bringing things back   until   it will come time

Christmas. (29) Tho   katiʔ wí· nikú   thikʌ ní· ké·yaleʔ   Christmas
Christmas.   That's   well   how much that   me   I remember Christmas

tsiʔ   niyawʌ́·u,   kwáh tyotyelʌ́htu kyuhte wí· tshukeʔnikú·lohteʔ   tsiʔ
what   has happened,   just   first   supposedly   when I became aware   that

tʌyakwatcelebrate Christmas.
we will celebrate   Christmas.

we didn't find out what she brought until it was Christmas time. (29) Well that's how much
I remember about Christmas and what happened, I guess the very first time I became aware
that we celebrate Christmas.

A Steamy Story

(Told by Norma Kennedy to Karin Michelson on April 22, 2008)

(1) I·kélheʔ a·kuka·látus   kaʔikʌ, né· kwí· n ukyatʌ·ló·,   Anne yutátyats,
       I want   I would tell you a story this,   so it's   we two friends, Anne   is her name,

waʔukka·látuhseʔ kaʔikʌ, nʌ kwí· isé· kwí· ʌskuka·látuhseʔ.   (2) Tsiʔ
she told me a story this,   so then   you   I will tell you a story.   How

niyawʌ́·u   kaʔikʌ oyú·kwaʔ yukwayo·té·,   oskánhe kwí· yukwayo·té·
it has happened   this   tobacco   we are working,   together   we are working

kaʔikʌ, Só·s   yutátyats,   Só·s   lónaʔ   oskánhe yukwayo·té·.   (3) Tahnú·
this,   Susan is her name, Susan man and wife   together   we are working.   And

kʌs kwí· né· tsiʔ kʌs   nihonuʔwéskwaniheʔ ta·hyatparty.   (4) Nʌ kyaleʔ wí·
habitually it's how   usually they enjoy   that the two party.   So again

(1) I want to tell you a story, and it's my friend, Anne is her name, she told me this story, so
then I'll tell YOU the story. (2) The way it happened was we were working in tobacco, we
were working together, Susan was her name, we were working together with Susan and her
husband. (3) And the two of them really liked to party. (4) So

wé·ne   ka?ikʌ́ kwa?ahsu·té· wé·ne   tehonatparty   ka?ikʌ́ Só·s   lóna?.
evidently this   last night   evidently they have partied this   Susan man and wife.

(5) Né· tsi? yah akwáh   te?yakota?kali·té· tshutayakoyo?tʌ́hsa? ka?ikʌ́
     Because not especially she is not healthy   when she came to work this

wʌhnisla·té·. (6) Wé·ne   tsi? thok   niyutyélhahkwe? kwa?ahsu·té·.
a day exists.   Evidently that something she was doing   last night.

(7) Né·n   áhsok   né· nʌ tayakotutáhkwʌ? ka?ikʌ́ Só·s   átste
     It's that all of a sudden it's then she had the urge   this   Susan outside

yʌhtákhwa?   yaa·yʌ́·.   (8) Tahnú· wa?í·lu? só·tsi?   inú
one goes there for it that she goes over there.   And   she said too much far

kanuhsákta? wí· yusa·yʌ́·,   tho kwí· nú· tkanúhsote?
near the house   for her to go over there again, that's where there is a house

átste   yʌhtákhwa?.   (9) Wa?í·lu?, "tsi? na?tewakeshlíhʌhse? ka?ikʌ́
outside one goes there for it.   She said, "how I am in a hurry   this

átste   yʌhtákhwa?   yaa·ké·,   tahnú· niwinú tkanúhsote?
outside one goes there for it that I go over there, and   so far   there is a house

tho   yusa·ké·   átste   yʌhtákhwa?."   (10) Né·n   wa?í·lu?,
there for me to go over there again outside one goes there for it."   It's that she said,

wa?í·lu? Anne, wa?í·lu?, "ísi? kwí· ne? kʌ́ nukwá·, a?é· na?kahu·wáti."
she said Anne, she said, "yonder   is it   where,   far   side of the boat."

(11) "Tho nukwá· ya?sahkwatasé,   ʌwa·tú· átste   ʌ́hsehte?   ne·tho."
      "That's where you go around that way, it can be outside you will go there that place."

(12) Né· kʌs wí· thikʌ́ kahuwaké·lu?   kʌs wí·, kahuwe·yá· latina?túkhwa?
      It's habitually that   there are boats strewn habitually, boat   what they call it

the night before they must have partied again, Susan and her husband. (5) Because she
wasn't too healthy when she came to work this day. (6) She must have done something the
night before. (7) So all of a sudden Susan felt the urge to go to the bathroom. (8) And she
said it was too far, close to the house, for her to go back there, that's where the outhouse
was. (9) She said, "I'm in such a hurry to go to the bathroom, and the outhouse is so far for
me to go back there to the bathroom." (10) So she said, Anne said, she said, "right over
there, okay, on the far side of the boats." (11) "There, go around that way, you can go to the
bathroom there." (12) There were all these boats lying around, boat is what it's called,

thikʌ́,   oyú·kwaʔ wí· tho   lʌnetaʔásta̱ʔ.   (13) Né· kwí· n   oʔsluniʔkéhaʔ
that,   tobacco   there they use it to put things in.   So it's   white man's way

boats latinaʔtúkh<u>wa</u>ʔ.   (14) Ok neʔn Ukwehuwé, kahuwe·yá· kwí· né·
boats what they call it.   But as for Native,   boat   it's

latinaʔtúkh<u>wa</u>ʔ.   (15) Né· katiʔ wí· thikʌ́ kwáh kʌʔ nikú   tho   ka·yʌ́·
what they call it.   So anyway it's that   just   some amount there it is lying

kahuwe·yá·, yah kwí· náhteʔ áhsu   teʔkanláhtit,   elhúwaʔ seʔ
boat,   not   anything not yet there are no leaves in it, just then   too

tyakwatahsawá·neʔ kaʔikʌ́ astéhtsiʔ wí· kaʔi·<u>kʌ́</u>.   (16) Nʌ kwí· né· waʔí·luʔ Anne,
we are going to begin   this   morning   this.   So then   it's   she said   Anne,

"tho kwí· neʔ kʌ yaʔsahkwatasé   thikʌ́ ísiʔ nukwá· tsiʔ tkahu·wáyʌʔ,
"there   is it   you go around that way that   yonder   at   there is a boat there,

yah né· úhkaʔ tha·yesa·<u>kʌ́·</u>."   (17) Nʌ kiʔ ok wí· né· yetákheʔ   kaʔikʌ́
not   it's   anyone one won't see you."   Right away   it's   she is running this

Só·s,   tho   yaʔuhkwata·sé·,   tho   yaʔtyutnuso·tʌ́·   kaʔikʌ́ aʔé·
Susan,   there   she went around that way,   there   she squatted over there this   far

naʔkahu·wáti.   (18) Yakotahséhtu kwí· né· tsiʔ yakonúhteʔ, thusayakwatye·lʌ́·
side of the boat.   She has hidden   it's   as   she knows,   suddenly to our surprise

ní· yaʔakwatkáthoʔ,   yah né· teʔwé·ni niyotsha·tóteʔ   thikʌ́ aʔé· naʔkahu·wá<u>ti</u>.
us   we looked that way,   it's incredible   how steam is rising that   far   side of the boat.

(19) Né· wí· né· tsiʔ   niyauhwʌtsyawísto tsiʔ nú· yaʔtyutnuso·tʌ́·,   tho kwí·
      So it's   because how the ground is cold where   she squatted over there,   there

né· kwah nók tsiʔ tyotsha·tóteʔ tsiʔ átste   wá·yʌ<u>hteʔ</u>.   (20) Né·n   i·yʌ́lheʔ
it's   just   steam is rising at   outside   she went there.   It's that   she thinks

they put tobacco in them. (13) In English they are called 'boats.' (14) But in Indian, *ka-huwe·yá·* is what they are called. (15) So anyway there were a few boats there, there weren't any [tobacco] leaves in them yet, we were just about to get started that morning. (16) So then Anne said, "there, okay, go around over there right where the boat is, nobody will see you." (17) Right away Susan ran and she went around over there, she squatted over there on the other side of the boat. (18) She was hidden she thought, and we, we were suddenly astounded as we looked over that way, it was incredible the steam coming up on the other side of the boat. (19) It was because the ground was so cold where she squatted, it was just steaming there where she went to the bathroom. (20) She thought

né· yakotahséhtu   kʌ́h, tsiléhkwaʔ né· tho   ya·hohkwata·sékeʔ
it's she has hidden eh,   almost   it's there he would have gone around that way

kaʔikʌ́ lukwé tsiʔ   wahatkáthoʔ tsiʔ ni·yót   tyotsha·tóteʔ ísiʔ nukwá·,
this   man   because he saw   that how it is steam is rising yonder,

wahonehla·kó· né· onʌ́ náhteʔ né· thi·kʌ́. (21) Nʌ kwí· né· úhkaʔ ok
he wondered   it's now   what   it's that.   So then   it's someone

waʔthuwa·tʌ́steʔ   waʔí·luʔ, "tákʌʔ tho   yʌhʌ́hse   thikʌ́,
someone stopped him she said, "don't   there you go over there that,

aʔtsyók   ʌkuhlo·lí·   náhteʔ aolí·waʔ thikʌ́ tsiʔ tyotsha·tóteʔ." (22) Né·
after a while I will tell you what   the reason that   that steam is rising."   It's

thahatye·lʌ́·   né· úhkaʔ ok tho   tutaye·táneʔ   yahatkáthoʔ,
he suddenly noticed it's someone there someone stood up again he looked that way,

Só·s   né· tho   tayakoké·tohteʔ. (23) Ne·né· aolí·waʔ   tyotsha·tóteʔ né· tsiʔ
Susan   it's there she appeared.   That's it the reason steam is rising   because

tho   yaʔtyutnuso·tʌ́·.   (24) Né· kiʔ   thikʌ́ thok   nikaka·lés.
there she squatted over there.   It's actually that   that's only how long is the story.

(25) Thok   ni·kú.
       That's only how much.

she was hidden, and this man almost would have gone around that way because he saw how
it was steaming right over there, he wondered what that was. (21) So then someone stopped
him, she said "don't go over there, after a while I will tell you why it's steaming." (22) Suddenly he noticed that someone stood up and he looked over that way, and Susan rose up.
(23) That's the reason it was steaming, because she squatted [to pee] there. (24) That's only
how long the story is. (25) That's all.

How I Learned to Swear

(Told by Norma Kennedy to Karin Michelson on April 22, 2008)

(1) I·kélheʔ   a·kuka·látus   tsiʔ   nikakaló·tʌ   kaʔikʌ́, kwáh kwí·
     I want   I would tell you a story   what   kind of story it is   this,   just

to·kʌ́skeʔ tho   niyawʌ́·u.   (2) Úska wʌhnisla·té· kaʔikʌ́ átste   nukwá·
truly   thus   it has happened.   One   a day exists   this   outside   where

thoyo·té·   likstʌ·ha.   (3) Kwí·tel luwa·yáts   likstʌ·ha.   (4) Tho s kwí·
he is working   my husband.   Peter   is his name   my husband.   There

thikʌ́   kʌʔ nikanuhsá·   tkanúhsoteʔ   ohná·kʌʔ   tsiʔ yukninúhsoteʔ.
that   it is a small house   there is a house   in the back   at   we two have a house.

(5) Ohná·kʌʔ   nukwá· tkanúhsoteʔ   kʌʔ nikanuhsá·, tho s nú·   thikʌ́
     In the back   where   there is a house   it is small house,   that's where   that

thoyoʔtʌ́staʔ, tsyoʔk wí· náhteʔ latu·níheʔ kʌs,   a·kí·luʔ   kyuhte wí·
he works,   different things   he makes   habitually,   I would say   supposedly

layʌtu·níheʔ.   (6) O·yʌ́teʔ s kwí· látstaʔ?   tsyoʔk náhteʔ a·hatu·ní·,
he does woodwork.   Wood   he uses it   different things   for him to make,

kohsa·tʌ́s kʌs   sʌ́· wahatu·ní· thikʌ́, o·yʌ́teʔ wí· yunyá·tu.
horse   habitually   also   he made   that,   wood   it is made out of.

(7) Kohsa·tʌ́s wí· tehutkalʌhlúkhwaʔ latiksaʔshúha. (8) Kwáh kʌs kwí·
     Horse   rocking chair   children.   Just   habitually

tsyoʔk náhteʔ   thikʌ́ latu·níheʔ, tho s kwí· nú· thoyoʔtʌ́staʔ thikʌ́ kʌʔ nikanuhsá·
all kinds of things   that   he makes,   that's where   he works   that   it is a small house

tkanúhsoteʔ.   (9) Né· katiʔ wí· kaʔikʌ́ wʌhnisla·té· náleʔ tho   wá·lehteʔ
there is a house.   Well then it's   this   a day exists   again   there   he went there

(1) I want to tell you a story and the way the story goes, it really happened this way. (2) One day my husband was working outside. (3) Peter was my husband's name. (4) There was this small building, a shed, at the back of our house. (5) In the back there was this shed, that's where he worked, he made different things, I guess I would say he was doing woodwork. (6) He would use wood to make different things, he made horses also, made out of wood. (7) Rocking horses for children. (8) He made all kinds of things, and that's where he would work, in that shed. (9) Well this one day he went

tsi? tkanúhsote?,   nʌ kyale? wí· latelha·láts   utahatáhsawʌ? thok náhte?
at   there is a house, so again   he is getting ready that he starts   something

a·hatu·ní·.   (10) Kwáh kati? wí· thikʌ nʌ   tshyahá·lawe?   tsi?
he should make.   Just   well then   that   when when he got over there at

tyonhoká·lute? wá·lelhe? a·hanhotukó,   né·n   yahatkátho?   ohutsyá·ke,
door   he wanted he would open a door, it's that he looked that way on the ground,

thahatye·lʌ́·   né· kʌ?   waté·sle?   ótku?.   (11) Tahnú· yah kʌs kwí·
suddenly he is surprised it's right there it is crawling snake.   And   not   usually

né· te?shakotshá·nihse? ótku?, né· uhte i·kélhe? thikʌ garter snake kuwana?túkhwa?
it's he is not afraid of   snake, it's I think   that   garter snake what they call it

ka?ikʌ́ ótku?.   (12) Nʌ sok wí· wa?thayá·tahkwe? thikʌ ótku?, né· s wí· tsi?
this   snake.   So then too he picked it up   that   snake, because

nihayélha?   thikʌ nʌ   wa?teshakoyá·tahkwe? s thikʌ ótku?, nʌ sok wí· oska·wáku
what he does that   when he picked them up   that   snake, so then too in the bush

kʌs   nya?teshakoya?tóya?ake?.   (13) Né· kyale? wí· wá·lelhe? ka?ikʌ́
habitually he threw them straight over there.   It's so again   he thought this

tho na·ha·yéle?, né· kyale? wí· wa?thayá·tahkwe? thikʌ ótku?, né·n   tho   né·
thus he would do, it's so again   he picked it up   that   snake, it's that there   it's

wahoka·lí· thikʌ, tsi? né· niyoshno·lé· ísi?   ya?tusahaya?tóya?ake?   thikʌ,
it bit him   that,   how   it's it is fast   away   he threw it straight over there again that,

wahʌ́·lu?, "the damn thing bit me."   (14) Kwáh kwí· tsyo?k náhte? tutahʌhlúni?,
he said,   "the damn thing bit me."   Just all kinds of things   he said things again,

o?sluni?kéha? kwí· né· ka?ikʌ́ wahalihwanela?ákhu?.   (15) Tsi?   wahoka·lí· wáh.
white man's way   it's this   he swore repeatedly.   Because it bit him   right.

to the shed again, he was getting ready again to start making something. (10) Well right
when he got to the door he wanted to open the door, he looked on the ground, and suddenly
he was taken aback, right there was crawling a snake. (11) And he wasn't afraid of snakes, I
think they call this snake a garter snake. (12) So then he picked up the snake, because what
he does when he picks up snakes, he flings them into the bush. (13) So he thought that's
what he would do, so he picked up the snake, and there it bit him, real quick he flung it
away, he said, "the damn thing bit me." (14) He said all kinds of things, he was swearing
away in English. (15) Because it bit him.

(16) Né·n,   waʔkí·luʔ kwí· "tá·t núwaʔ latetsyʌ́ʔthne né· yaáhseʔ,
     It's that, I said   "maybe   at the doctor's it's you should go over there,

ni·yót ótkuʔ wesaka·lí·, tá·t núwaʔ sʌ́haʔ ʌhsatahalu·ní· n," lasnú·ke wí· wahoka·lí·.
look'it snake it bit you,   maybe   more   you will get worse," his hand   it bit him.

 (17) Né·n   yah tehothutatú   latetsyʌ́ʔthne yaá·leʔ,   tho kwí·
      It's that not   he did not consent at the doctor's he should go over there, that's

thye·yót   thikʌ́ kwʌʔtátiʔ kwí·, yaháhsaneʔ kwí· wahoyo·tʌ́· kwáh kwʌʔtátiʔ.
just how it is that   all day,   he finished out   he worked   just   all day.

 (18) Nʌ   kiʔ   né· kwáh kʌʔ náheʔ kaʔikʌ́ tóhkaʔ niyohslaké
      Then actually it's just   some while this   a few   years amount to

tho   niyawʌ́·u   kaʔikʌ́ n ótkuʔ wahoka·lí·.   (19) Tó·, tá·t núwaʔ wísk
thus it has happened this   snake it bit him.   Oh,   maybe   five

niyohslaké   utu·kó·teʔ thikʌ́, nʌ   kiʔ   né· shotukóhtu   likstʌ·ha.
years amount to it went by   that,   then actually it's he has passed on my husband.

(20) Nʌ   kiʔ   swakulhaʔtsíwaʔ.   (21) Takanakla·kó·   tho nukwá·,
     Then actually I am all by myself again.   I moved from there that's where,

kʌh nukwá· sakanáklateʔ, a·sé· kwí· waʔuknuhsúniʔ.   (22) Né·n,
over this way I settled again, new one they built a house for me.   It's that,

tsyohslatkʌ́ uhte i·kélheʔ kaʔikʌ́, né· kyuhte wí· yá·yaʔk niwʌhní·take   onʌ́
one year ago I think   this,   it's probably   six   months amount to then

kaʔikʌ́ tho nityawʌ́·u,   ukeslʌhtáksʌʔ, úska útlatsteʔ ukeslʌhtáksʌʔ kaʔikʌ́,
this   thus it has happened, I dreamed,   one time   I dreamed   this,

kátshaʔ ok nú· yehe·ké·seʔ,   tahnú· nʌ kwí· wakelha·lé· usakahtʌ·tí·,   né·n
somewhere   I am over there, and   so then   I am ready   that I leave again, it's that

(16) So I said "maybe you should go to the doctor's, look'it, a snake bit you, maybe you will get worse," it bit him on his hand. (17) He refused to go to the doctor's, so it was left like that all day, and he finished working the whole day. (18) Then it was a while, not too long, a few years that this happened, that a snake bit him. (19) Oh, maybe five years went by, by then my husband had died. (20) I was all alone again. (21) I moved away from there, I moved in over here, they built me a new house. (22) It was one year ago I think, I guess it's been six months that this happened, I dreamed, one time I dreamed, I was somewhere, and so then I was ready to leave, so

ya?kya·kʌ́ne?,   yah   né·   kánike?   te?ska?sléhtayʌ?   aké·slet.   (23)   Nʌ kwí·
I went out,   not   it's anywhere   there's no car anymore my car.   So then

kwáh tsyo?k úhka?   wa?kheli?wanu·tú·se?,   "yah   kʌ   te?satkáthu n   aké·slet,
all kinds of people   I asked them,   "not   question you have not seen my car,

uke?slehtu·tí·   aké·slet."   (24)   Wa?kí·lu?   "kʌh nú·   niwakate?slehtayʌ·táhkwe?,
I lost   my car."   I said   "over here I have parked my car,

né·n   yah   kánike?   te?ka?sléhtayʌ?."   (25)   Yah   ki?   né·   úhka? náhte?
it's that not   anywhere   there is no car."   Not   actually   it's   anyone

te?yakotkáthu n   aké·slet.   (26)   Nʌ kwí·   kwáh   kʌ? niyo·lé·   kʌ́·   nyahá·ke?
one has not seen   my car.   So then   just   some distance   y'know   I went over there

thikʌ́,   kwáh tsyo?k úhka?   yesekheli?wanu·tú·se<u>he</u>?.   (27)   "Yah   kʌ
that,   all kinds of people   over there I am asking them again.   "Not   question

te?satkáthu n   aké·slet."   (28)   Yah kwí·   úhka?   te?yakotkáthu.   (29)   Né·n,
you have not seen   my car."   Not   anyone   one has not seen it.   It's that,

shayá·tat   thikʌ́   wa?tyakyátlane?,   wahʌ́·lu?,   "kwáh   tsi? wakanúhte?   né·   thikʌ́
one person   that   we two met,   he said,   "just   I think   it's   that

ísi? nukwá·   íthnete?   tehnukwé,   lonanúhte?   uhte i·kélhe?   kátsha? n
right over there   the two are standing   two men,   they know   I think   where

sá·slet."   (30)   Nʌ kwí·   né·   tho   nyahá·ke?   tsi? nú·   íthnete?   ka?ikʌ́
your car."   So then   it's   there   I went over there   where   the two are standing   this

tehnukwé,   wa?kheli?wanu·tú·se?,   wa?kí·lu?,   "tsyanúhte?   kʌ   kátsha? né·n
two men,   I asked them,   I said,   "you two know   question   where   it's that

aké·slet."   (31)   Wahʌ́·lu?   thikʌ́   shayá·tat,   "kʌ́·slet wí·   aowʌshúha   tho   kaké·lu?
my car."   He said   that   one man,   "car   its belongings   there   it is strewn

I went out, my car wasn't anywhere. (23) So then I asked all kinds of people, "you haven't seen my car? I lost my car." (24) I said "I had my car parked over here, and now there's no car anywhere." (25) No one had seen my car. (26) So then I went on a ways, I was asking all kinds of people there again. (27) "You haven't seen my car?" (28) No one had seen it. (29) And so I met this one man, he said, "I think there's two men standing right over there, I think they know where your car is." (30) So then I went over there where these two men were standing, I asked them, I said, "do you two know where my car is?" (31) The one man said, "there's car parts spread all

ka?ikʌ́ ohutsyá·<u>ke</u>."   (32) Tho kwí· ni·yót   thikʌ́ tho   tshyahá·kewe?, kwáh
this   on the ground."   That's   how it is that   there when I got there, just

tsyo?k nú· nikaké·lu? ka?slethokúha wí· watestákhwa?, nʌ kwí· wahili?wanu·tú·se?,
all over   it is strewn cars   it gets used for, so then I asked him,

"tsyanúhte? kʌ   kátsha? né·n   aké·slet."   (33) Nʌ kwí· wahʌ́·lu?
"you two know question where   it's that my car."   So then he said

"hʌ́·, kʌ? nukwá· kaké·lu?,"   wahʌ́·lu?, "wa?tyaknikhahsyu·kó· sá·slet,
"yes, right here   it is strewn," he said,   "we two took it apart   your car,

tsyakyatewyʌ́·tuhe?." (34) Né·n   ya?katkátho?   ohutsyá·ke,   tho   né·
we two are fixing it."   It's that I looked that way on the ground, there it's

kaké·lu? tekakhahsyúkwʌ aké·slet.   (35) Nʌ kwí· né· tú·ske? wa?khená·khwahse?
it is strewn it is all taken apart my car.   So then it's truly   I got mad at them

ka?ikʌ́ tehnukwé tsi?   tehotikhahsyúkwʌ   aké·slet, kwáh kwí· tsyo?k náhte?
this   two men   because they have taken apart my car,   all kinds of things

tutakheyʌ́hahse?, wa?kí·lu? "la?nikuhláksʌ úhte,   úhka? né· náhte?
I belittled them,   I said   "the devil   supposedly, who   it's what

yesalihwawí   ta·hsekhahsyu·kó· aké·slet." (36) O·ké· kwí· tsi?
one has given you permission that you take apart my car."   Oh my   how

niwaklʌ?nhá·u a·klihwanela?ákhu? o?sluni?ké·<u>ne</u>.   (37) Né·n   tshá·ki?   thikʌ́
I know how   that I swear   white man's way.   It's that when I woke up that

tsha?ólhʌne?,   nʌ   né· kanuhtunyúkwas thikʌ́ tsi? nikaslʌhtó·tʌ,
when it became morning, then it's I am wondering   that   what kind of dream it is,

takanuhtunyu·kó·, kátsha? né· nú· twakewyʌtehtʌ́·u tho   ni·yót   tsi?
I started to think,   where is it   I have learned   that's how it is that

on the ground." (32) And that's how it was when I got there, strewn all over the place were car parts, so then I asked him, "do you two know where my car is?" (33) So then he said, "yes, it's spread out right here," he said, "we took your car apart, we're fixing it again." (34) So I looked on the ground, and there spread out, all taken apart was my car. (35) So then I got really mad at these two men because they had taken apart my car, I said all kinds of things to tell them off, I said, "the devil, who gave you permission to take apart my car?" (36) Oh my gosh, did I know how to swear in English. (37) So when I woke up in the morning, I was wondering about the dream, I started to think way back, where had I learned

a·klihwanela?ákhu?. (38) Ne·né· yusakehyá·lane? thikʌ́ ne? thó·ne? a?é· nukwá·
that I swear.   It's that I remembered again that   at that time   way over there

tshiteknákle? thikʌ́ ótku? wí· tshahoka·lí· likstʌ·ha.   (39) Wé·ne   ne? thó·ne?
when I reside   that   snake   when it bit him my husband.   Evidently at that time

né· twakathu·té· thikʌ́ tho nikawʌnó·tʌ,   nók tsi? o?slu·ní· kwí· né·
it's I hear   that   that's the kind of words, but   white man   it's

wahatwʌnu·táhkwe?   khále? tshiwakeslʌhtaksʌ́hsluhe?, né· kyuni? wí· tho
he spoke in a language and   when I am dreaming,   it's also   that's

nikawʌnó·tʌ   wá·katste? o?slu·ní· wa?katwʌnu·táhkwe?, onísta? uhte
the kind of words I used   white man I spoke in a language,   gosh   supposedly

tsi? nikwaklʌ?nhá·u a·klihwanela?ákhu?. (40) Né· ki?   ní· tho   niyo·lé· tsi?
how I know how   that I swear.   It's actually me that's how far that

wa?kanuhtúni? tsi? wé·ne   tsi? tho nú·   takewyʌtéhtane? a·klihwanela?ákhu?.
I thought   that evidently that that's where I learned   that I swear.

(41) Nók tsi? ne? thó·ne? ki?   ok   waklʌ?nhá·u a·klihwanéla?ake? nʌ
        But   at that time actually only I know how   that I swear   when

wakeslʌhtaksʌ́hsluhe?. (42) Né· ki?   thikʌ́ tho   niwakkaló·tʌ,   tho   ki?
I am dreaming.   It's actually that   that's my kind of story, that's actually

niyo·lé·   thikʌ́, nók tsi? ʌkkwe·ní·   ki?   a·klihwanela?ákhu? tá·t waki·tá·s.
the extent that,   but   I will be able actually I would swear   if   I am sleeping.

(43) Tá·t ukeslʌhtaksʌ́hslu?. (44) Né· ki?   tho   nikaka·lés   ka?i·kʌ́.
        If   I dreamed.   It's actually that's how long the story is this.

to swear like that? (38) Then I remembered again back then when I lived way over there, when a snake bit my husband. (39) It must have been at that time I heard those kinds of words, but he was speaking English and when I was dreaming, those were the words I was using too, I was speaking in English, gosh I guess I really knew how to swear. (40) As far as I can tell, that's where I must have learned to swear. (41) But the only time I know how to swear is when I'm dreaming. (42) So that's my story, that's it, but I can only swear if I am sleeping. (43) If I am dreaming. (44) That's how long this story is.

More Favourite Memories

Here are six more stories that are about some favourite memories from when the storytellers were young.

The story *A Hairy Adventure* was told by Mercy Doxtator in 1999. Ten years later, when Norma Kennedy and I were reviewing my transcription and translation of this story, Norma recalled that she was there with Mercy, and so in 2009 Norma recorded her recollection of what happened that day in *A Scary Hairy Adventure*. On the back cover of this book is a picture of Mercy and Norma as little girls.

A Wish Comes True

(Told by Norma Kennedy to Karin Michelson on November 3, 1994)

(1) Tshiwahu·níse? a?é·   kʌs   tyakwanákle? kalhakú,
     A long time ago far away habitually we reside   in the woods,

tho kwí· nú· yehoyo·té·   lake?níha layʌtákwas.   (2) Yah ki?
that's where he is working over there my father   he cuts wood.   Not   actually

te?ské·yale?   tó·   tsha?tewakohsliyá·ku,   nók tsi?
I don't remember anymore how many when I have crossed over winters, but

kwáh tsi? wakanúhte? kayé uhte   tá·tkʌ   wísk, yah ki?   kwahotokʌ́·u
just   I think   four supposedly or maybe five, not   actually just for real

te?ské·yale?   tó·   tsha?tewakohsliyá·ku.   (3) Nók tsi?
I don't remember anymore how many when I have crossed over winters.   But

elhúwa?   ki?   tho   ya?akwanáklate?,   tahnú· s tsi? nikʌtu·níhe? né· tsi?
just recently actually there we settled over there, and   how   I am lonely   because

yah   thau·tú· oskánhe usayakyatnutólyahte? Mercy.   (4) Né·n   lau?wéskwanihe? s
not   it can't be together that we two play again   Mercy.   It's that he enjoys

thikʌ́ lake?níha a·hatolátha?,   né· kwí· nʌ   ʌtákta?   khále? yawʌtatokʌ́htu
that   my father   that he goes hunting, so it's   when Saturday and   Sunday

yah kwí· tehoyo·té·   nʌ s kyale? wí· wahatolátha?.   (5) Né·n   sá·lawe?
not   he is not working so again   he went hunting.   It's that he got home

thikʌ́ kwa?yʌ́ha kwí· shakoya?taha·wí·, áhsʌ uhte i·kélhe? nikutí   kwa?yʌ́ha.
that   rabbit   he is carrying them, three I think   how many rabbit.

(6) Nʌ kyale? wí· wahiyatló·loke? thikʌ́ wa?shakoyʌ·séle? kwa?yʌ́ha. (7) Tahnú·
     So again   I watched him   that   he skinned them   rabbit.   And

(1) A long time ago we lived way over in the woods, that's where my father was working
cutting wood. (2) I don't remember anymore how old I was, but I think four or maybe five,
I don't really remember anymore how old I was. (3) But we had just moved there, and I was
so lonely because Mercy and I couldn't play together anymore. (4) My father liked to go
hunting, so on Saturdays and Sundays when he wasn't working he would go hunting. (5) So
[one time] he got home and he was carrying rabbits, three rabbits I think. (6) So I watched
him skin the rabbits. (7) And then

waha·kú· kwí·   thikʌ́ kwaʔyʌ́ha ohsí·ta?.   (8) Wahʌ́·luʔ, "watlaʔswiyó yakʌʔ
he gave it to me   that   rabbit foot.   He said,   "it is good luck   reportedly

thikʌ́, kwáh tsiʔ náhteʔ ʌhsatlʌ́nhahteʔ tho   kiʔ   nʌya·wʌ́neʔ." (9) Nʌ kwí·
that,   whatever   you will wish for   thus   actually it will happen."   So then

né· thikʌ́ waʔkatla·kó·, wahʌ́·luʔ, "nók tsiʔ nok ʌwa·tú· tʌsteníhʌʔ   thikʌ́
it's that   I claimed it,   he said,   "but   it has to be   you will shake it that

kwaʔyʌ́ha ohsí·taʔ, nʌ   ʌwa·tú·   tho   nʌya·wʌ́neʔ náhteʔ ʌhsatlʌ́nhahteʔ."
rabbit foot,   then   it can be thus   it will happen   what   you will wish for."

(10) Nʌ kwí· né· yahá·khaweʔ thikʌ́, nʌ kwí· né· kanuhtunyúkwas kʌs,
        So then   it's   I took it away   that,   so then   it's   I am wondering   habitually,

náhteʔ uhte   a·katlʌ́nhahteʔ.   (11) Yah kiʔ   né· teʔwahu·níseʔ, shekú né·
what   possibly I should wish for.   Not   actually it's   not a long time,   still   it's

tá·t núwaʔ tókhaʔ ok   minit,   ókhnaʔ   né· ukwanúhtʌneʔ náhteʔ a·katlʌ́nhahteʔ.
maybe   a few   only   minute, and then   it's I came to know   what   I should wish for.

(12) Nʌ sok wí· yaʔkatkeʔto·tʌ́· tsiʔ yohsuhtaká·luteʔ, nʌ   waʔtekteníhʌʔ
        So then too   I looked out   at   window,   then   I shook it

kwaʔyʌ́ha ohsí·taʔ, nʌ sok wí· waʔkí·luʔ, "waʔkatlʌ́nhahteʔ Mercy uta·yʌ́·
rabbit foot,   so then too   I said,   "I wish for   Mercy   that she comes

utayenatá·laʔ."   (13) Kwáh kiʔ   né· kwáh olihwiyó   tsiʔ wísk minit
that she comes to visit."   Just   actually it's   just   a sure thing   that   five   minute

utu·kó·teʔ tsiʔ náheʔ   né· wakʌ́   ókhnaʔ   yaʔkatkeʔto·tʌ́· tsiʔ yohsuhtaká·luteʔ
it went by   how long since it's   I have said   and then   I looked out   at   window

ókhnaʔ   né· aʔé·   úhkaʔ ok ta·yʌ́·,   yah kiʔ   kwahotokʌ́·u
and then   it's   far away   someone   someone is coming,   not   actually just for real

he gave me a rabbit foot. (8) He said, "it's good luck they say, whatever you wish for, that's
what will happen." (9) So then I kept it, he said, "but you have to shake the rabbit foot, then
what you wish for can happen." (10) So then I took it, and so then I'm wondering, what
could I wish for. (11) It wasn't long, maybe only a few minutes, and then it came to me
what I should wish for. (12) So then I looked out of the window, then I shook the rabbit
foot, and so then I said "I wish that Mercy would come to visit." (13) For sure just five
minutes went by since I said it and then I looked out of the window and then far away someone was coming, I couldn't really

óksaʔ ok   teʔyotú·u   a·kheyʌ·télene?   úhkaʔ náhoh<u>teʔ</u>.   (14) Né·
right away it couldn't be that I recognize them who.   It's

yaʔkhená·tuʔ   aknulhá·   waʔkí·luʔ,   "úhkaʔ ok   ta·yʌ·,   nók tsiʔ
I called out to her my mother   I said,   "someone   someone is coming,   but

yah teʔwakanúhteʔ, só·tsiʔ   inú, yah tha·kkwe·ní· a·kathlo·lí· úhkaʔ náhoh<u>teʔ</u>.
not   I don't know,   too much far,   not   I am not able that I tell   who.

(15) Nʌ kwí· né· yaʔutkeʔto·tʌ́· waʔí·luʔ,   "ó· Clifford khále? Sophia khále?
      So then   it's she looked out   she said,   "oh   Clifford   and   Sophia   and

Mercy." (16) O·ké· tsiʔ né· naʔkatshanu·ní· tsiʔ   tayenatá·laʔ   né· tsiʔ
Mercy."   Gee   how   it's I got happy   because   she came to visit because

nikheyaʔti·sáks.   (17) Wé·ne kwí· to·kʌ́skeʔ náhteʔ wahʌ́·luʔ lakeʔníha tsiʔ
I am missing her so.   Evidently   it's true   what   he said   my father   that

watlaʔswiyó thikʌ́ kwaʔyʌ́ha ohsí·taʔ né· tsiʔ   tho   naʔa·wʌ́neʔ náhteʔ
it is good luck that   rabbit foot   because thus   it happened   what

waʔkatlʌ́nhah<u>teʔ</u>.
I wished for.

make out right away who. (14) I called out to my mother, I said, "someone is coming, but I
don't know, it's too far, I can't tell who." (15) So then she looked out, she said, "Oh, Clifford and Sophia and Mercy." (16) Gee, I was so happy that she came to visit because I was
missing her so. (17) It must be true what my father said, that a rabbit foot is good luck because what I wished for happened.

My Dog Blackie

(Told by Mercy Doxtator in August 1995)

(1) Né· kwí· núwaʔ   kaʔikʌ́ tsiʔ náhteʔ i·kélheʔ a·kathlolí,   né· s wí· n
     So it's   this time   this   that   what   I want   I would tell about, so it's

(1) So this time what I want to tell about,

tshiwahu·níse?, ya·wét   kyuhte wí· kʌ? tshitwakyʌ́ha kʌ́·,   tehniyáshe s
a long time ago, kind of like supposedly when I was young y'know, two

waknʌskwayʌ·táhkwe? é·lhal. (2) Shayá·tat kʌs   o?swʌ?tósku? nihaya?tó·tʌ
I used to have a pet   dog.   He is one habitually all black   how he looks

khále? shayá·tat owískla? né· nihaya?tó·tʌ, nók tsi? lottsistohkwa·lú· s athéhsa?
and   he is one white   it's how he looks, but   he has spots all over brown

niwahsohkó·tʌ.   (3) Né· kati? wí· ka?ikʌ́, lotiste·líst kʌs   ka?ikʌ́
is the kind of colour.   Well then it's this,   they are funny habitually this

akitshenʌ?shúha kʌ́·,   úska útlatste? thikʌ́, aknulhá·   wahuwattéhtʌ? akitshe·nʌ́·
my pet animals   y'know, one time   that,   my mother she scolded him my pet

tsi? ka·yʌ́· o?swʌ́·ta? nihaya?tó·tʌ, Blackie s kwí· shakwana?túkhwa?. (4) Né·n,
the one that black   how he looks, Blackie   what we call him.   It's that,

yah kwí· thikʌ́ tehau?weskwaní·u tsi? wahuwattéhtʌ? kʌ́·,   nʌ sok wí·
not   that   he is not enjoying   that she scolded him y'know, so then too

wahathahítane?   thikʌ́, ya·wét   tsi? yótte?   laneway, tho   thikʌ́
he went down the road that,   kind of like at   the end of it laneway,   there   that

yaháti?   kʌ́·,   kwáh s nók tethaká·nle?   kʌ́·,   lolha·lé· kwí·
over there he sat down y'know, just   he is looking this way y'know, he is ready

yusahuwáhʌle?   aknulháh. (5) Tahnú· kwí· yah thye?shuwahʌlú,
for her to call him again my mother.   And   not   she didn't call him again,

nʌ kyale? wí· wahatu·kóhte? kʌ́·, a?é·   wá·le? thikʌ́, áhsok   nále?
so again   he continued on see,   over there he went that,   suddenly then again

tutahatkalhate·ní·   kʌ́·,   yakwatto·kás kʌ   tsi? niyo·lé· nʌ   wá·le? kʌ́h.
he turned around again y'know, we notice   question how far   then he went eh.

a long time ago, like I guess when I was young, I had two pet dogs. (2) One was all black
and one was white, but he had brown spots. (3) Well anyway my pets were funny, this one
time, my mother gave my dog heck, the one that was black, Blackie is what we called him.
(4) So he didn't like it that she scolded him, so then he started walking down the road, and
kind of at the end of the laneway he sat down, he just was looking back, he was ready for
my mother to call him back. (5) And she didn't call him back, so he went on again, he went
way further, then suddenly he turned around, do we notice how far he went?

(6) Né·n,   yah kwí· náhte?   úhka?   te?yakawʌ́   kʌ́·,   nʌ kyale? wí·
    It's that,   not   anything anyone   one hasn't said   see,   so again

wahatu·kóhte?.   (7) A?é· nukwá· tyoháhute?,   nále?   ya?tha·táne?,
he continued on.   Over there   there is a path,   again   over there he stopped,

nále?   tethaká·nle?   kʌ́·,   tó· kati? náhe? ka?ikʌ́ nʌ   úhka? ok
then again   he is looking this way   y'know,   how long then   this   then   someone

yʌshuwáhʌle?.   (8) Tahnú· kyale? wí· yah tho   te?yawʌ́·u,
someone will call him again.   And   again   not   thus   it didn't happen,

nʌ kyale? wí· wahatu·kóhte?.   (9) Kwáh kʌ? niyo·lé· nále?   ya?tusaha·táne?.
so again   he continued on.   Just   some ways   then again   over there he stopped.

(10) Nále? tethaká·nele?.   (11) Né· s kwí· ka?ikʌ́ lolha·lé·   tsi?
    Again   he is looking this way.   So it's   this   he is anticipating   that

a?tsyók kwí· onʌ́ úhka? ok yʌshuwáhʌle?,   tahnú· kwí· yah úhka?
after a while   then   someone   someone will call him again,   and   not   anyone

thye?shuwahʌlú,   nʌ kyale? wí· wahatu·kóhte?.   (12) Tho   ni·yót   thikʌ́
one didn't call him,   so again   he continued on.   That's   how it is   that

wa?otukohtuháti? kʌ́h,   né·n,   khále? kwí· onʌ́ wa?shakni·tʌ́le?   kʌ́·,
it was going along   y'know,   it's that,   and   then   we two took pity on him   y'know,

í·   khále? aknulhá·,   nʌ kwí· ya?tyakohʌ·léhte?,   yusahuwaná·tu?
me   and   my mother,   so then   she hollered over there,   she called out to him again

Blackie. (13) Kwáh kwí· né· óksa?   tutahatákhe?   kʌ́·, nahatshanu·ní·
Blackie.   Just   it's   right away   he ran back this way   see,   he got so happy

tsi? yusahuwáhʌle?   kʌ́· úhka? ok, nʌ kwí· wa?wé·nene? kwí· tsi?
that   someone called him again   y'know   someone,   so then   it became evident   that

(6) No one said anything, so again he went on. (7) Way over there was another lane, over
there he stopped again, again he looked back, how long before somebody would call him?
(8) And again that didn't happen, so again he went on. (9) Not too far and he stopped again.
(10) Again he was looking back. (11) He was anticipating that after a while someone would
call him, and nobody called him, so he kept on going. (12) And that's the way it was going,
and then we took pity on him, my mother and I, so then she hollered, and she called Blackie.
(13) Right away he came running back, he was so happy that someone called him back, so
then it showed that

shakwanolúkhwaʔ seʔ akitshe·nʌ́· é·lhal.   (14) Kwáh kwí· né· tóhkaʔ ok   minit
we love him   too my pet   dog.   Just   it's several only minute

ókhnaʔ tho sá·laweʔ,   tsiʔ nishotshanunihátiʔ?   tsiʔ   úhkaʔ ok
and then there he got home, how he is going along happy because someone

yusahuwáhʌleʔ.   (15) Tho   kiʔ   nikú   thikʌ́ wá·kelheʔ
someone called him again.   That's actually how much that   I thought

a·kathlolí   kʌ́h.
I would tell eh.

we loved my dog. (14) It was only a few minutes, he got home and he was going along so
happy because someone called him. (15) That's all I thought I would tell.

A Hairy Adventure

(Told by Mercy Doxtator on January 16, 1999)

(1) Shekólih. (2) Ú·waʔ ʌtáktaʔ yoʔkalá·u, January 16th, 1999. (3) Tsiʔ
      Hello.   Now   Saturday night,   January 16th, 1999.   That

náhteʔ i·kélheʔ a·kka·látu   kaʔikʌ́ kwahotokʌ́·u tho niyawʌ́·u
what   I want   I would tell a story this   just for real   thus it has happened

tshikeksáh.   (4) Elhúwaʔ kʌʔ nahéhaʔ kʌ́·,   tho   tshiyakwanákleʔ tsiʔ nú·
when I was a child.   Right then a little while y'know, there when we reside   where

tyukwanuhso·táhkweʔ kʌ́·, yukwatsyalʌ́·u kwí·, né· aolí·waʔ   yah tho
we had a house   see, we had a fire,   it's the reason not there

teʔskanúhsoteʔ.   (5) Né· katiʔ wí· kaʔikʌ́, elhúwaʔ tho   tshaʔakwanáklateʔ
there is no longer a house.   Well then it's this,   right then there when we settled in

kaʔikʌ́ tsiʔ nú· tyukwahtʌtyú·neʔ, aʔé·   naʔoháhati   kʌ́·,   tho
this   where our home used to be, over there that side of the road y'know, there

(1) Hello. (2) Now it's Saturday night, January 16th, 1999. (3) The story I want to tell
really happened when I was child. (4) We were living there just a little while where we used
to have a house, we had a fire, that's why the house isn't there anymore. (5) Well it was
right after we moved to where our home used to be, over on the other side of the road,

tkanúhsote?, onuhsaka·yú. (6) Yah úhka? te?yé·tlu?, wé·ne tsi?,
there is a house, an old house. Not anyone one doesn't dwell, evidently that,

i·kélhe? s kwí· ní· wé·ne tsi? kanuhsiyo·hné· tshiwahu·níse? kʌ́·, yah
I thought me evidently that it was a nice house a long time ago y'know, not

náhte? te?skawi·sát, yah oni? te?tsyonhokahlu·tú·, yonhoká·lute?
anything there is no glass anymore, not too there are no doors anymore, there is a door

kyuhte wí· né· nók tsi? yah kwí· te?kanho·tú·. (7) Né·n úska útlatste?
supposedly it's but not the door is not closed. It's that one time

thikʌ́ kanuhsanúnhe? kʌ́·, wá·kelhe?, "tó· kati? sʌ́· katkʌ?sé·na
that I am home by myself y'know, I thought, "how much then also let me go see

ka?ikʌ́," ka·té· wí· tho tkanúhsote?, yah úhka? te?yé·telu?.
this," I am saying there there's a house, not anyone one doesn't dwell.

(8) Né· s kwí· thikʌ́ lu·té· John Danford yakʌ? tho nú· nihanáklehkwe?
So it's that they say John Danford reportedly that's where he used to reside

kʌ́·, né· kyuhte wí· n laotihwa·tsíle? tho nú· nihonahtʌtyú·ne?. (9) Nók tsi?
see, it's supposedly their family that's where their home used to be. But

nʌ kwí· ka?ikʌ́ wa?twakatuhútsyohse? a·katkʌ?sé·na? náhte? nítyot
so then this I wanted I would go and see what it is like there

ne·tú. (10) Nʌ kwí· né· tho yahá·kewe? kʌ́·, kwáh kwí· nók
that place. So then it's there I got over there see, just

wa?tkahahi·yá·ke? ókhna? tho yahá·kewe? ya?katáyahte?. (11) Né·n,
I crossed the road and then there I got over there I went in. It's that,

wa?tkatkahtúni? thikʌ́ kanúsku, né· ki? wá·kelhe? kwa?nyóh uhte wí·
I looked around that in the house, it's actually I thought seems like supposedly

there was a house, an old house. (6) Nobody lived there, I thought that it must have been a nice house a long time ago, there wasn't any glass anymore, there weren't any doors either, there was a door I guess, but the door wasn't closed. (7) So this one time I was by myself minding the house, I thought, "how about I go and see about this," this house that I am saying was there, no one was living there. (8) They say John Danford used to live there, I guess that's where they had their family home. (9) But then I wanted to go and see what it was like there. (10) So then I got there, I just crossed the road and then I got there, I went in. (11) So I looked all around inside the house, I thought it seemed like maybe

kanuhsiyo·hné·   tshiwahu·níseʔ tsiʔ s náheʔ tho   latinákleʔ kʌ́·   kaʔikʌ́ n
it was a nice house a long time ago while   there they reside y'know this

laotiDanford.   (12) Tho   sʌ́·   kalistakhwá·tsloteʔ, nʌ kwí· waʔkláthʌʔ thikʌ́,
the Danfords.   There also a staircase,   so then I climbed up that,

é·nik   niyawe·nú.   (13) Né· kwí· thikʌ́ tho   ni·yót   yonuhsu·tú·,
upstairs where it has gone.   So it's   that   that's how it is there are rooms,

wé·ne   tsiʔ tho s nú·   nihunuhwetstákhwaʔ. (14) Nók tsiʔ né· thikʌ́ úska
evidently at   that's where where they sleep.   But   it's that one

yonúhsuteʔ,   tho   tká·nyoteʔ kwaʔnyóh yeksayʌtákhwaʔ. (15) Yonutoʔtslu·tú·.
there's a room, there it is standing seems like a cupboard.   It has drawers.

(16) Tho   katiʔ wí· thikʌ́, né· s kwí· né·n   yeksá· tsiʔ naʔteyakoʔnyalhá·teʔ,
      There well   that, so it's   it's that a child how she snoops and is nosey,

kháleʔ tsyoʔk náhteʔ i·yʌ́lheʔ   a·yakoto·kʌ́·seʔ   náhteʔ ni·yót.
and   different things one wants one would find out what   it is like.

(17) Taknutoʔtslatilu·tʌ́· katiʔ wí· thikʌ́, wakatkʌʔséniʔ náhteʔ tho   i·wát.
      I pulled out a drawer so then   that,   I have examined what   there it is inside.

(18) Kwáh ki?   né· nók kahyatuhsliʔshúha aʔnyóh tho   watáliʔ.
      Just   actually it's only papers   seems there they are inside.

(19) Nók tsiʔ tho kwí· thikʌ́ tekahkókwas. (20) Yah s kwí· teʔwakanúhteʔ?
      But   there   that I am snooping.   Not   I don't know

náhteʔ kéhsaks,   kwáh kyuhte wí· nók tsiʔ i·kélheʔ ta·kahko·kó.
what   I am looking for, just   supposedly but   I want I would snoop.

(21) Né·n   kwáh ok   ní· thaʔkatye·lʌ́·   kháleʔ thok náhteʔ thikʌ́
      It's that all of a sudden me I suddenly noticed and   something   that

it was a nice house a long time ago while the Danfords were living there. (12) There was a staircase also, so then I climbed up it, where it went upstairs. (13) And there were these rooms, it must have been that's where they slept. (14) But this one room, in it there was this kind of cupboard. (15) It had drawers. (16) Well there's a child for you, she snoops and has to touch everything, and she wants to find out about things and what they're like. (17) Well I pulled out a drawer, I looked around to see what was inside. (18) All that was inside were like these papers. (19) But I kept snooping. (20) I didn't know what I was looking for, I guess I just wanted to snoop. (21) All of a sudden I noticed it and

yaʔkye·ná·, takatihʌ́thoʔ, onúhkwis né· tho kwaʔnyóh, aʔé· kiʔ
I felt it,   I jerked it,   hair   it's there seems like, great actually

nikanuhkwísles   thikʌ́ waʔketshʌ·líʔ.   (22) Onístaʔ kwí· né· tsiʔ nʌ
how long is the hair   that   I found it.   Gosh   it's that then

takatú·nekeʔ, tho   yaʔkatkʌhlá·tahkweʔ thikʌ́, nʌ sok wí· sektákheʔ   kʌ́·,
I got startled,   there quickly I let go of it   that,   so then too   again I am running y'know,

nyusakahkwé·nʌhteʔ, sakahtʌ·tí·   kʌ́·,   wá·kelheʔ, kwáh yah nuwʌtú shekú tho
I went down again,   I went home y'know, I thought,   just   not   never   even   there

thyusa·ké·   kʌ́·, né· kwí· ní· wá·kelheʔ tá·t núwaʔ yakotyanlutstákhwaʔ.
I won't go back over there eh,   so it's   me   I thought   maybe   someone is haunting it.

(23) Nók tsiʔ yah s kiʔ   né· náhteʔ teʔyakwatkáthos kʌ́·,   tsiʔ náheʔ thikʌ́
       But   not   actually it's anything we don't see   y'know, while   that

tho   kanúhsoteʔ.   (24) Tahnú· né·n,   nʌ kwí· ní· tshaʔakwanakla·kó·
there there is a house.   And   it's that, so then   us   when we moved away

ati tsiʔ   tho s kwí· yukwahtʌ́ti, nók tsiʔ waʔakwanakla·kó·, né· s wí· tsiʔ
even though there   our home,   but   we moved away,   because

niyotho·lé·   kohslaʔké·ne. (25) Nʌ kwí· kháleʔ e·só· sʌ́· tkanye·yʌ́·,
how it is cold wintertime.   So then   and   lots   also   there's snow on the ground,

yah s kwí· thau·tú·   a·hoyoʔtʌ́hsaʔ   lakeʔníha, kanatá·ke wí· yehoyó·tʌhseʔ,
not   it can't be that he goes to work my father,   in town   he works over there,

só·tsiʔ   e·só· kanye·yʌ́·.   (26) Nʌ kwí· kanatá·ke nyaʔakwanáklateʔ.
too much lots   there's snow on the ground.   So then   in town   we settled over there.

(27) Né·n   sayákwaweʔ thikʌ́, wé·ne kwí· né· tshaʔtyokʌnhu·tí·   náleʔ?
       It's that we got home   that,   evidently it's   when it became summer   then again

I felt something, I yanked it towards me, hair seems like, I found a really long hank of hair. (22) Gee, did I ever get startled, I let go of it real quick, and so then I was running, I went back downstairs, I went home, I thought I would never ever go back there again, I thought maybe it was haunted. (23) But we didn't see anything while the house was there. (24) And so then we moved away even though it was our home, but we moved away, because it was so cold in the wintertime. (25) And then there was so much snow too, my father couldn't go to work, he was working in town, there was too much snow. (26) So then we moved into town. (27) So we came home, it must have been summertime when

tho   sayákwaweʔ tsiʔ tyukwahtʌ́ti, yah né· kátshaʔ   teʔskanúhsoteʔ.
there we got home at   our home,   not it's anywhere there is no house anymore.

(28) Wé·ne kwí· úhkaʔ ok lotiká·tshi.   (29) Kwáh kiʔ   yah kátshaʔ
       Evidently   someone they have taken it apart.   Just   actually   not   anywhere

teʔskayeluní   tsiʔ tho   kanuhso·táhkweʔ.   (30) Né· katiʔ wí· thikʌ́ tho
there is no trace at   there there used to be a house.   Well then it's   that   that's

niwakkaló·tʌ.   (31) Ukwatetshahníhtʌʔ kwí· thikʌ́ tsiʔ onúhkwis waʔketshʌ·lí·
my kind of story.   It scared me   that   that hair   I found it

kʌ́h.   (32) Tho   kiʔ   ok wí· né· niwakka·lés   kaʔi·kʌ́.
y'know.   That's actually only   it's how long is my story this.

we got to our home again, the house wasn't there anymore. (28) Someone must have torn it
down. (29) There was no trace that there used to be a house there. (30) Well that's my
story. (31) It scared me, finding that hair. (32) That's the extent of my story.

A Scary Hairy Adventure
(Told by Norma Kennedy to Karin Michelson on June 30, 2009)

(1) Shekólih. (2) Norma yúkyats   oʔsluniʔké·ne. (3) Thiwé·saʔ
       Hello.   Norma is my name   in English.   She Wanders

niwaksʌnó·tʌ   Ukwehuwehnéhaʔ. (4) Wá·kelheʔ a·kwaka·látus
is my kind of name   in the Native way.   I thought   I would tell you all a story

tsiʔ   niyawʌ́·u   tshikeksáh.   (5) Né· kwí· n Mercy kwí· yutátyats
what   has happened when I was a child.   So it's   Mercy   is her name

kheyuhwatʌ́ha. (6) Tsyóhslat uhte i·kélheʔ sʌ́haʔ e·só· tewakohsliyá·ku
my niece.   One year   I think   more   lots   I have crossed over winters

tsiʔ né· ni·yót   akau·lhá·. (7) Nók tsiʔ tyótkut kʌs   kiʔ   thikʌ́
as   it's how it is as for her.   But   always   habitually actually that

(1) Hello. (2) Norma is my English name. (3) She Wanders is my Indian name. (4) I
thought I would tell you a story about what happened when I was a child. (5) So Mercy was
the name of my niece. (6) I think I was one year older than her. (7) But

yuknu?wéskwanihe? nále?   wa?akwanatahle·náwe?, oskánhe kwí·
we two enjoy   then again we visited,   together

wa?akyatnutólyah<u>te</u>?.   (8) Kwáh yah nuwʌtú tha?teyukyatlihotálhu,
we two played.   Just   not   never   we two have not quarrelled,

tyótkut ukyatʌ·ló·,   tyótkut yukyatshanuní   nʌ   oskánhe wa?ukyata·t<u>ʌ</u>le?.
always   we two friends, always   we two are happy when   together we two were left.

(9) Né· kati? wí· ka?ikʌ́ úska útlatste? yukwanatahlenʌ́ kyale? wáh.
     Well then it's this   one time   we are visiting   again   right.

(10) Nʌ kyale? wí· thikʌ́ átste kwí· yeyukyatnutolyá·tu.   (11) Tahnú·
      So again   that   outside   we two are playing over there.   And

uknulha?tsíwa?   uhte i·kélhe? thikʌ́ nále?   yakyanuhsanúnhe?,
we two are all alone   I think   that   then again   we two are home by ourselves,

wé·ne kwí· tsi? tá·t núwa? tyutʌhni·núhe? lonéhtu   yukhiyʌ?ok<u>úha</u>.
evidently   at   maybe   they sell   they have gone there our parents.

(12) Nók tsi? uknulha?tsíwa?   ki?   ka?ikʌ́, Mercy kwí· yutátyats,
      But   we two are all alone   actually   this,   Mercy   is her name,

uknulha?tsíwa?   ki?   ka?ikʌ́ Mercy khále? í·,   tahnú· nʌ kwí·
we two are all alone   actually   this   Mercy   and   me, and   so then

wa?uknino·lú·se? yukyatnutolyá·tu.   (13) Wa?í·lu?, "náhte? kati?   núwa?
we two tired of it   we two are playing.   She said,   "what   anyway   this time

nʌtsityátye<u>le</u>?."   (14) Tahnú· tho kwí· tkanúhsote?   thikʌ́ elʌ́
again you and I will do."   And   there   there is a house there   that   other

na?oháhati   tsi? nú· nihatinákle? Mercy. (15) Elʌ́   na?oháhati   thikʌ́
side of a road   where   they reside   Mercy.   Other   side of a road   that

the two of us always enjoyed it when we visited, we two would play together. (8) We never
ever quarreled, we were always friends, we were always happy when we were left to be together. (9) Well this one time we were visiting again, right. (10) So the two of us were
playing outside again. (11) And we were all alone, I think we were by ourselves minding
the house, I guess maybe our parents were gone to the store. (12) But we two were all
alone, Mercy's her name, Mercy and I were all alone, and so then we got bored playing.
(13) She said, "what will you and I do next?" (14) And there was a house across the road
from where Mercy lived. (15) Across the road

tkanúhsote?,   yah kwí· úhka?   te?yé·tlu?   ne-<u>tho</u>.   (16) Yah oni?
there is a house, not   anyone   one doesn't dwell that place.   Not   even

te?kawisatáli?   thikʌ́ yohsuhtakahlu·<u>tú</u>·.   (17) Khále? tsi? yonhokahlu·tú·,
there is no glass   that   openings in the wall.   And   at   openings for doors,

yonhoká·lute?   ki?   né·, nók tsi? yah kwí· te?kanho·<u>tú</u>·.
there's a door opening actually it is, but   not   the door isn't closed.

(18) Nʌ kwí· wa?kí·lu?, "tyatkʌ?sé·na   thikʌ́ náhte? akwáh
       So then   I said,   "let's you and I go and see that   what   exactly

nikanuhsó·tʌ   thikʌ́ tkanúhsote?."   (19) Nʌ kyale? wí· wa?í·lu?,
kind of house it is   that   there is a house there."   So again   she said,

"háo? ki?wáh."   (20) Nʌ kwí· wa?tyakyahahi·yá·ke?   ókhna? ya?áknewe?
"sure okay."   So then   we two crossed the road   and then   we two got there

tsi? tkanúhsote?.   (21) Nʌ kwí· wa?akyate?nyʌ·tʌ́· thikʌ́ ya?akní·leke?
at   there is a house there.   So then   we two tried   that   we two pushed

kánhohe?, utenhotu·kó·   ki?   nʌ? né·. (22) Nʌ kwí· ya?akyatáwyahte?
door,   the door opened actually that one.   So then   we two entered

wa?tyakyatkahtúni<u>?</u>.   (23) Kwáh ki?   né· tóhka? niyonúhsute? thikʌ́
we two looked all around.   Just   actually it's   a few   there are rooms   that

ehtá·ke nukwá·, wa?akní·lu? kwí· kwa?nyóh uhte   kanuhsiyo·hné·   thikʌ́
downstairs,   we two said   seems like   probably   it was a nice house   that

tho   tshihatinákle?,   né· kwí· n John Danford laohwa·tsíle? tho nú·
there   when they reside, so it's   John Danford   his family   that's where

nihati?tlu·táh<u>kwe</u>?.   (24) Né· kwí· lotinúhsote?   ka?ikʌ́ tsi? nú· yeyákneh<u>se</u>?.
they used to dwell.   So it's   it's their house   this   where   we two are over there.

was a house, no one lived there. (16) There wasn't even any glass in the windows.
(17) And the doors, there was a door, but it wasn't locked. (18) So then I said, "let's you
and I go and see what exactly that house is like." (19) So she said, "sure okay." (20) So
then we crossed the road and we got to the house. (21) So then we tried to push the door,
and it opened. (22) So then we went in and we looked all around. (23) There were a few
rooms downstairs, we said it seemed like it was probably a nice house when they were living
there, it was John Danford's family that used to live there. (24) So it was their house where
we were.

(25) Nʌ   waʔakyatkáthoʔ,   tho   sʌ́·   kalistakhwá·tsloteʔ,   nʌ sok wí·
     Then   we two looked,   there also   staircase,   so then too

waʔakniláthʌʔ,   é·nike   yaʔákneweʔ   thikʌ́,   yaʔtyakyatkahtúniʔ
we two climbed up,   upstairs   we two got over there   that,   we two looked around over there

kyuniʔ wí· ne·<u>tho</u>.   (26) Tóhkaʔ   kyuniʔ né·   nityonúhsuteʔ   thikʌ́,   wé·ne   tsiʔ
even   that place.   A few   too   it's   there are rooms   that,   evidently   that

tho nú·   ʌthunuhwetstákhwahkweʔ tsiʔ náheʔ   tho   latinákele<u>ʔ</u>.   (27) Né· katiʔ wí·
that's where   they will use it as bedrooms   while   there   they reside.   Well it's

kaʔikʌ́ úska yonúhsuteʔ,   kwaʔnyóh yeksayʌtákhwaʔ   tá·tkʌ
this   one   there is a room,   seems like   it is used to store dishes   or maybe

yutslunyahkwahlákhwaʔ   tho   tká·nyoteʔ   thikʌ́,   yonuʔtotslu·tú· kih.
it is used to set clothes inside   there   it is standing   that,   it has drawers   actually.

(28) Nʌ kyaleʔ wí· thikʌ́ tsiʔ   naʔteyukniʔnyalhá·teʔ,   tsyoʔk náhteʔ
     So again   that   how   we two are nosey and touch everything,   everything

yáknelheʔ   kʌʔ nya·yakniyél.   (29) Tayakyatilu·tʌ́·   thikʌ́ yonutoʔtslu·tú·, kwáh
we two want   we two would touch it.   We two pulled it   that   drawers,   just

né· nók kahyatuhsliʔshúha tho   i·wát,   nʌ kyaleʔ wí· waʔakyatkʌʔséniʔ thikʌ́
it's only papers   there it is inside, so again   we two examined   that

náhteʔ nikahyatuhsló·tʌ, yah kwí· tha·yaknikwe·ní· a·yakniwʌnahno·tʌ́· neʔ thó·neʔ,
what   kind of paper it is,   not   we two aren't able   that we two read   at that time,

só·tsiʔ   kʌʔ naʔteyaknáh. (30) Né·n,   né· thikʌ́ oyá·   yonutó·tsluteʔ
too much   we two are little.   It's that, it's that   another drawer

tutayakyatilu·tʌ́·,   tho kiʔ ok nahté·shuʔ i·wát,   yah teʔyukyanúhteʔ
again we two pulled it, all kinds of things   it is inside, not we two don't know

(25) Then we looked, there was a staircase also, so then we climbed up it, we got upstairs, we looked all around up there even. (26) There were a few rooms, it must have been that that's where they had their bedrooms while they were living there. (27) Well there was this one room, there was like this cupboard or maybe a dresser standing there, and it had drawers. (28) So we were so nosey we just wanted to touch everything. (29) We pulled out the drawers, there were just all these papers inside, so we looked through them to see what kind of papers, we weren't able to read at that time, we were too little. (30) So there was another drawer and we pulled it, all kinds of things were inside, we didn't know

oh náho<u>hte?</u>. (31) Nʌ kwí· kʌ? nutaye·yéle? thikʌ́ Mercy. (32) Onúhkwis né·
what.   So then   she did like this   that   Mercy.   Hair   it's

tho   wa?etshʌ·lí· thikʌ́, a?é· nikanuhkwísles,   tahnú· kalatskʌ?túni? ki?wáh.
there she found   that,   great how the hair is long, and   it is braided   right.

(33) Tahnú· wé·ne   tsi? akokstʌ́ha akonúhkwis, né· tsi? tekayéstu   thikʌ́
       And   evidently that   old lady   her hair,   because it is mixed in   that

ata?kʌ́·la? khále? ostúha o?swʌ́·ta? niwahsohkó·tʌ,   wé·ne   tsi? yakonhlá·tu?
grey   and   a little black   is the kind of colour, evidently that   she has grey hair

ka?ikʌ́ tsi? ka·yʌ́·   akonuhkwish<u>kʌ́h</u>.   (34) Né· na?ukyatétshʌ?,   né· thikʌ́
this   the one that her hair no longer.   It's   how we two got scared, it's that

wa?áknelhe?,   wé·ne   tsi? awélu?uske? aonúhkwis, nʌ sok wí· a?é·
we two thought, evidently that   a witch   her hair,   so then too   far away

ya?tyakóya?ake? thikʌ́ onúhkwis Mercy, né· tsi?   na?ukyatétshʌ?,
she flung it   that   hair   Mercy,   because   how we two got scared,

kwáh né· nók a?é·   nya?kanuhkwislúti<u>?</u>.   (35) Nʌ sok wí· tutayakyahkwé·nʌhte?,
just   far away the hair flew over there.   So then too   we two descended again,

kwahikʌ́ tsi? yoshnoláti?   tsi? tutayakyahkwé·nʌhte?, tusayakyaláhtate? thikʌ́,
just really that   it's going along fast that   we two descended again,   we two ran again   that,

tutayakniyakʌhtá·tsyahte?   thikʌ́ tkanúhsote<u>?</u>.   (36) Nʌ sok wí·
we two went out real quick again   that   there's a house there.   So then too

tusayakyaláhtate?, tusayakyahahi·yá·ke?,   tho kwí· nyusayáknewe?
we two ran again,   we two crossed the road again,   there   we two got over there again

tsi? nú· thotinúhsote?   Mercy. (37) Yah ki?   nuwʌtú tho
where   they have a house Mercy.   Not   actually never   there

what. (31) So then Mercy did like this (Norma demonstrates feeling around in something).
(32) She found hair, really long hair, and it was braided. (33) It must have been an old person's hair, because it was mixed grey and a little bit of black, she must have gone grey, the
one whose hair it was. (34) We got so scared, we thought, it must be a witch's hair, and so
then Mercy flung that hair far away, because we got really scared, the hair just went flying.
(35) And so then we went back down again, we went down really really fast, we ran, we
went out of that house so quick. (36) And so then we ran, we crossed the road, and we got
back to where Mercy's house was. (37) We never ever

tshye?tsyuknenú   né· tsi?   na?ukyatétsh^?.   (38) Yakotyanlustákhwa? kwí·
we two haven't gone because how we two got scared.   Someone is haunting it

yaknina?túkhwahkwe?   thik^ tkanuhso·táhkwe?.   (39) Né· ki?   thik^
we two used to call it that   that   there used to be a house there.   It's   actually   that

tho nikú   wá·kelhe? a·kwaka·látus.   (40) N^ ki?wáh.
that much   I thought   I would tell you all.   So long now.

went back there again because we got so scared. (38) We used to call that house the haunted
house. (39) That's all I thought I would tell you. (40) So long now.

Friday Nights

(Told by Olive Elm to Karin Michelson in October 2005)

(1) Wé·ni kwí· utakatáhsaw^? a·kka·látu?.   (2) Né· k^s   ka?ik^ tsi?
     Evidently   I should begin   that I tell a story.   It's   habitually this   how

nityohtú·ne? ní· tshikeksá·,   ya·wét wí· tsha?katótyake?. (3) Ó· tá·t núwa?
it was so   me   when I was a child,   kind of like   when I grew up.   Oh   maybe

nineteen fifty-four tshiyohslashe·tás.   (4) Né· k^s   thik^ wískhatut yo?kalá·u,
nineteen fifty-four   when it counts years.   It's   habitually that   Friday   night,

nále?   twenty-five cents wa?ukhwístu?   aknulhá·,   tsi? tyut^hni·núhe?
then again   twenty-five cents   she gave me money my mother, at   there they sell

wa?ákwehte? k^? nityukway^·sa?. (5) Né· thik^ tho   nikú   wakhwístay^?
we went there   we young people.   It's   that   that's   how much   I have money

u·tú·   k^s   potato chips wa?khni·nú· khále? pop ókhale? elhúwa?
it ould be   habitually potato chips   I bought   and   pop   and   right then

(1) I guess I should begin to tell the story. (2) How it was when I was a young girl, like
when I was growing up. (3) Oh, maybe about the year 1954. (4) Friday nights my mother
would give me twenty-five cents, us young people would go to the store. (5) I had enough
money that I could buy potato chips, and pop, and at that time

tsha?kaya·kʌ́ne? thikʌ́ popsicle, né· kʌs thikʌ́ wa?khni·nú· khále?
when it came out that popsicle, it's usually that I bought it and

sukwathwistata·tʌ́le? kʌs ʌwa·tú· thikʌ́ Nickelodeon kʌs tho yahukwatí,
I had money left over usually it can be that Nickelodeon habitually there I threw it in,

five cents áhsʌ nikalʌ·náke ʌwatlʌno·tʌ́·. (6) Né· s kati? wí· thikʌ́
five cents three the songs amount to it will play songs. Well it's that

tho ni·yót, tho nikú yukwahwístayʌ? kʌ? nityukwayʌ́·sa?, tho né·
that's how it is, that's how much we have money we young people, that's it's

nikú ʌkahni·nú· ne? thó·ne? nú· tshiwathawinúti?. (7) Tahnú·
how much it will buy at that time when the era is going along. And

ya?weskwa?tú·ne? nʌ s kwí· né· tsi? akwekú kʌs kwí· né· Ukwehuwehné·ke
it was enjoyable then because all habitually it's in the Native way

yukwatwʌnutáhkwʌ kʌ? nityukwayʌ́·sa?, teyukwatha·lú·, yukwayéshuhe?,
we are speaking in a language we young people, we are talking, we are laughing,

yah né· úhka? o?slu·ní· te?yutwʌnutákhwa? tho nú· tshikaha·wí·.
not it's anyone white man one does not speak in a language that's when is the era.

(8) Kwáh né· shekú Onʌyote?a·ká· yakwatwʌnutákhwa?
     Just it's still People of the Standing Stone we speak in a language

kʌ? nityukwayʌ́·sa?. (9) Né·n, tho s kwí· a?é· nú· ya?teyakwatlásta?
we young people. It's that, there way over there over there we meet

thikʌ́ tyutʌhni·núhe?, Sandy kʌs yakwana?túkhwa?, wískhatut yo?kalá·u,
that there they sell, Sandy habitually what we call it, Friday night,

tho s nikʌtyohkwanʌ́ kʌ? nityukwayʌ́·sa? tho ya?tyakwátlane? thikʌ́
that's how big a crowd we young people there over there we met that

the popsicle had just come out, so I would buy that, and I would have money left over and I could put that in the Nickelodeon, for five cents it played three songs. (6) Well that's the way it was, that's how much money us young people had, it would buy all that stuff back in those times. (7) And it used to be nice because us young people all spoke in Indian, we would be talking, laughing, nobody spoke in English in those days. (8) Us young people still spoke Oneida. (9) So we used to meet over there at this store, Sandy we called it, on Friday nights, a lot of us young people would meet over there

waʔakwatlʌnotúnyuʔ,   five cents   tho   yʌyakwahwístʌhteʔ   thikʌ́   Nickelodeon.
we played music,   five cents   there   over there we will drop money   that   Nickelodeon.

(10)   Áhsʌ   nikalʌ·náke   ʌwatlʌno·tʌ́·,   thoʔnʌ́   átste   kʌs   nukwá·
        Three   the songs amount to   it will play songs,   and then   outside   habitually   where

tetyukwátkwʌ   sʌ́·,   yaʔwéskwaʔt   kih.   (11)   Né·n,   núwaʔ   kʌh nú·
we are dancing   also,   it's enjoyable   indeed.   It's that,   this time   over here

niwathawinútiʔ   yah   núwaʔ   tho   té·tsyot,   latiksaʔshúha
an era is going along   not   this time   that's   it is not so anymore,   children

kʌʔ nithotiyʌ́·saʔ   ʌhatiya·kʌ́neʔ,   yah   kiʔ   né·   thya·ya·wʌ́·   tsiʔ   tóhkaʔ
young people   they will go out,   not   actually   it's   it has to be   that   a few

nikahwístake   elhúwaʔ   ʌwa·tú·   thok náhteʔ   ʌhatihni·nú·.   (12)   Kháleʔ
dollars amounts to   just then   it can be   something   they will buy it.   And

neʔ thó·neʔ   yah   né·   e·só·   teʔkaʔslehtanákleʔ,   tyótkut   né·   owahaʔkéshuʔ   ehtaʔkéshuʔ
at that time   not   it's   lots   cars are not plentiful,   always   it's   on all the roads   on foot

yukwathahitákheʔ   kátshaʔ nú·   waʔukwehtuháti‿ʔ.   (13)   Né·   núwaʔ
we travel in the path   where   we are on our way there.   It's   this time

kʌh nú·   niwatha·wí·   yah   thya·ya·wʌ́·   tsiʔ   ʌhseʔnikú·lalakeʔ   owahaʔkéshuʔ
over here   is the era   not   it has to be   that   you will be careful   on all the roads

nyʌhʌ́hseʔ,   só·tsiʔ   yoshno·lé·   tsiʔ   lotí·slehseʔ,   neʔ thó·neʔ   yah   né·
you will go over there,   too much   it is fast   as   they are driving,   at that time   not   it's

náhteʔ,   kwáh s   né·   nók   bicycle   yukwaʔslenútiʔ,   yah   kiʔ   né·   kánikeʔ
anything,   just   it's   only   bicycle   we are going along riding,   not   indeed   it's   nowhere

ká·slet.   (14)   Yah   oniʔ   nuwʌtú   tha·she·kʌ́·   kʌʔ nithotiyʌ́·saʔ   kátshaʔ nú·
car.   Not   too   never   you won't see them   young people   where

and we would play music, we would drop five cents in the Nickelodeon. (10) It would play three songs, and then outside also we would be dancing, it was so nice. (11) Nowadays it's not like that anymore, the young people, teenagers, they'll go out, and they've got [to have] a few dollars before they can buy something. (12) And at that time there weren't many cars, we always walked on the roads to wherever we were going. (13) Nowadays you have to be careful walking on the roads, because they are driving so fast, at that time there weren't any [cars], we were just riding bicycles, there were no cars anywhere. (14) And too you never saw any young people where

na·hotihnekihlʌ́hake?   a·hotinahalahtu?úhake?.   (15) Né· kʌs
they would have been drinking   they would have been getting drunk.   It's habitually

kwáh tho   niyukwatu?weskwá·tu tsi? núwa? ni·yót.   (16) Nʌ?ú·wa? kwa?nyóh
just   that's how we had fun   as   this time how it is.   Now   seems like

né· se? ok ʌwa·tú· lotihnekí·lʌ   né· elhúwa? ʌhutu?wéskwahte?.   (17) Yah
it's   too only it can be they have drunk it's just then they will have fun.   Not

ki?   né·n   tho nú·   tshiwathawinúti?.
actually it's that that's when the era is going along.

they would have been drinking, getting drunk. (15) We had as much fun [without drinking]
as how it is now. (16) Nowadays it seems like they have to be drinking before they have a
good time. (17) Not in those times.

Wintertime

(Told by Barbara Schuyler to Karin Michelson and Norma Kennedy on July 16, 2008)

(1) Oyá· tshityó·kalas wa?kahtʌ·tí· kʌ́·,   tahnú· wa?tyakwátlane? kʌ́·
     Other night   I set out   y'know, and   we met up   y'know

akwatʌlo?sla?shúha. (2) Tahnú· ne? thó·ne? kʌ́·   yah kʌs kwí· né· úhka?
my friends.   And   at that time y'know not habitually it's anyone

te?yako?sléhtayʌ?.   (3) Ehta?késhu? kʌs   yah thya·ya·wʌ́· nya?ákwe?
one doesn't have a car.   On foot   habitually it has to be   we went over there

kʌ́·, tyótkut kwí· owaha?késhu? teyukwatawʌ́li? kwa?ahsuté·ke. (4) Né·n   ka?ikʌ́
see, always   on the roads we are travelling at night.   It's that this

wahsuta·té· kʌ́·,   ohna·kwáli? núwa?   tekahna·kwálake wa?tyakwátsha?ahte?.
a night exists y'know, tire   this time two tires   we burned it up.

(1) The other night I went out, and I met up with my friends. (2) And at that time no one
had a car. (3) We had to walk to where we were going, we were always travelling the roads
at night. (4) So this one night, we burned up two tires.

(5) Ka?ikʌ kaná·tslaku kʌ·,   tahnú· s thikʌ Hilda tyonúhsote?.
     This   in the ditch y'know,   and   that   Hilda there she has a house.

(6) Tahnú· thikʌ s a?é· nikalu·tá·   tkalu·tóte?   ne·tú. (7) Tho kwí· nú·
     And   that   great is the size of tree there is a tree there there.   That's where

thikʌ ná·ku tho   tayakwate·ká·te? ka?ikʌ ohnakwala?shúha. (8) Tho   kʌs kwí·
that   under there we set fire to it   this   several tires.   There habitually

thikʌ tyakwakʌ́nyate?   kʌ·,   teyukwatha·lú·   yukwayeshúnyuhe? kʌ·,
that   we are standing around y'know,   we are conversing   we are laughing   y'know,

tsi? niyo·lé· yahútsha?ahte? ka?ikʌ yotékha?   kʌ·,   nʌ kyale? wí·
until   it burned up   this   it is in flames y'know,   so again

sayakwahtʌtyu·kó·.   (9) Tahnú· ka?ikʌ elhúwa?   wakyʌtá·u   ka?ikʌ
we all went home again.   And   this   just recently I have obtained this

kohsla?kékha? atyá·tawiht. (10) Né· kwí· wakátstu.   (11) Nén,   né· thikʌ
winter type   coat.   So it's   I am wearing it.   It's that, it's that

wahsuta·té·   yah kwí· te?wakatkáthu tsi?   niwahsohkó·tʌ.   (12) Sayólhʌne?
a night exists not   I didn't see   what   kind of colour it is.   The next day

astéhtsi? kʌ·   aknulhá·   wa?í·lu?, "kátsha? nú· níhseskwe?."   (13) "Ni·yót,
morning   y'know my mother   she said, "where   you were around."   "Look'it,

ni·yót satyá·tawi?t." (14) "Kwáh o?swʌ?tósku?." (15) Tahnú· yah kwí·
look'it your coat."   "Just   it's all black."   And   not

tho   te?wahsohkó·tʌ ka?ikʌ n akwatyá·tawi?t tshukyʌ·táne?.   (16) Tho
thus is not the colour this   my coat   when I obtained it.   Thus

niwahsohko?tʌ·hné·   tsi? ni·yót o?nehsalúhkwa?. (17) Nén,   núwa? o?swʌ́·ta?
is the colour it was once as   how it is sand.   It's that, now   black

(5) In the ditch, and by Hilda's house. (6) And there used to be a great big tree there. (7) So under that we set fire to the tires. (8) A bunch of us were standing around there, talking and laughing, until the fire burned out, and then we all headed home again. (9) And I just recently got a [new] winter coat. (10) And so I was wearing it. (11) So, that night I didn't see what colour it was. (12) The next morning my mother said, "where were you?" (13) "Look at your coat." (14) "It's all black." (15) And that wasn't the colour of my coat when I got it. (16) It was like the colour of sand [tan]. (17) Now it was black.

niwahsohkó·tʌ. (18) Nʌ   naʔakyahkwíshluʔ   sayakninóhaleʔ   akwatyá·tawiʔt,
is the colour.   Then   we two did it intensely   we two washed it again   my coat,

yah teʔyotú·u tho   nusuhsohkó·tʌneʔ   tsiʔ   niwahsohkoʔtʌ·hné·   tshukyʌ·táneʔ.
not   it couldn't   thus   become the colour again   as   the colour it was once   when I obtained it.

(19) Niwahu·níseʔ   waʔotye·náwasteʔ   kʌ·   usustáthʌʔ.   (20) Só·tsiʔ
       A long time   it took time to do it   y'know   for it to dry again.   Too much

ka·tʌ́s.   (21) Tho   kiʔ   ok   uhte wí·   ni·kú.   (22) Nʌ   kyuhte
it is thick.   That's   actually   only   supposedly   how much.   Now   supposedly

i·kélheʔ   wá·ksaneʔ.
I think   I finished.

(18) Then we tried really hard to wash my coat, but it couldn't get to be the same colour as when I got it. (19) It took a long time for it to dry. (20) Because it was so thick. (21) I guess that's all. (22) I think I'm finished now.

Customs

In the recordings in this section we learn about some Oneida customs. The first three stories are about the ability of some people, called *dreamers* or *seers* or *fortune-tellers*, to determine what is afflicting someone and what medicine will help, or in some cases to foresee the future. *The Dreamer* is a conversation between Olive Elm and Mercy Doxtator that took place immediately after Olive recorded the story *Visits to My Auntie's* in the 'Pranks and Mishaps' section, and Mercy's speech is given in italics.

Some traditions are not like they used to be, and Hazel Cornelius talks about this in her story about getting married and starting life together. A tradition that is not exactly like it used to be, but is still ongoing, is what happens when someone in the Oneida community passes on, something that Mercy Doxtator describes in *After a Loss*. (Mercy was a member of a choir directed by her late husband Dayton Doxtator and she sang [all night] at countless wakes.)

Mercy Doxtator recorded two other customs, which are practiced by children. One is the well-established tradition of going out to get *hoyan* on New Year's Day. *Hoyan* refers to a homemade donut. On New Year's Day, children visit their relatives and receive hoyan. Aunts make a special donut doll for their nieces. The word **hoyan** is believed to come from the Dutch word for New Year (*nieuwjaar*). The other children's custom that Mercy talks about is the Oneida version of the tooth fairy.

Mercy usually asked people to begin their recordings by giving their name and the names of their parents and siblings. As a result we can learn a lot from these recordings about how to refer to and talk about kin relations.

The Spoiled Child

(Told by Mercy Doxtator to Karin Michelson on February 11, 1994)

(1) Shekólih. (2) Né· ka?ikʌ́ i·kélhe? a·kka·látu   ka?ikʌ́, to·kʌ́ske?
      Greetings.   It's this   I want   I would tell a story this,   truly

tho   niyawʌ́·u   nʌ   wahu·níse?.   (3) Né· kati? wí· ka?ikʌ́ lotikstʌ́ha
thus   it has happened   when   a long time ago.   Well it's   this   old persons

lóna?,   kátsha? ok wí· nú· kʌ́·tho Ukwehuwé·ne   né· nihninʌ́klehkwe?,
man and wife,   somewhere   here   at the Native people's it's   the two used to reside,

lonatlé·slayʌ?   yeksá·, né· kati? wí· ka?ikʌ́ teshakotíshnyehe?   kʌ́·,
they have a grandchild a girl,   well it's   this   they are looking after her   see,

tahnú· uhte wí·   ka?ikʌ́ tsi? na?a·wʌ́ne?, kwahikʌ́ tsi? wa?shakotiksa?táksahte?
and   supposedly this   what   happened,   just really that   they made a bad child of her

kʌ́h.   (4) Í·nelhe? kwí· só·tsi?   lotiwilanʌ́ste?   kʌ́·,   né· aolí·wa?
y'know.   The two thought so much   they treasure a child y'know, it's   the reason

wa?shakotiksa?táksahte?.   (5) Úska kati? wí· útlatste? thikʌ́ wa?akonuhwáktʌ?
they made a bad child of her.   One   well   time   that   she got sick

thikʌ́ yeksáh. (6) Tho   niyo·lé· na?akonuhwáktʌ? thikʌ́, kwáh se? nok u·tú·
that   girl.   Thus   so far   she got sick   that,   just   too it had to be

wa?u·láte?.   (7) Tahnú· s kwí· né·n   tsi? né· ni·yót yeksa?shúha, kwáh kwí· ikʌ́
she lay down.   And   it's that how it's   it is so children,   just really

tsi? yakonuhwáktanihe? nʌ   elhúwa? wa?u·láte?.   (8) Né· kati? wí· ka?ikʌ́
that   she is sick   then   right then she lay down.   Well it's   this

tho kwí· na?a·wʌ́ne? kʌ́h. (9) Nʌ kati? wí· tóhka? niwʌhnislaké   thikʌ́,
thus   it happened   see.   Then anyway a few   days amount to   that,

(1) Greetings. (2) This story I want to tell you, it really happened a long time ago. (3) Well there was this old couple, they lived somewhere here on the Reserve, they had a grand-daughter, well they were looking after her, and I guess what happened was that they spoiled her bad. (4) They thought they loved her so much, that's why they spoiled her. (5) Well one day the little girl got sick. (6) She got so sick, she just had to lie down. (7) And [you know] how it is with children, she had to be really sick to lie down right away. (8) Well that's what happened. (9) Then anyway it was a few days,

né·   oni?   kwáh ok oná   niyakonuhwáktanihe?,   tahnú· yah   tehonanúhte?   ka?iká
it's   too   still the same   how she is sick,   and   not   they don't know   this

náhte?   akwáh   niyakoyá·tawʌhse?.   (10) Tahnú· s   a?nyóh   sayólhʌne?   nʌ   sʌ́ha?
what   exactly   it is happening to her.   And   seems   the next day   then   more

yakotahalʌní·u   yakonuhwáktanihe?.   (11) Nʌ   ki? wí·   wa?í·lu?   thiká
her condition has worsened   she is sick.   Then   actually   she said   that

akokstʌ́ha,   "tá·t núwa?   tho   nyaetyáhkete?   thiká   tsi?   thonúhsote?   thiká
old lady,   "maybe   there   you and I should go visit   that   at   he has a house   that

shakotkʌ́·sehe?,   tá·t núwa?   a·shakótkʌhse?   ka?iká   yeksá·,   tá·t núwa?
he sees into them,   maybe   he would see into her   this   girl,   maybe

a·hatkátho?   náhte?   onúhkwa?t   a·yútste?."   (12) Nʌ kati? wí·   né·   ka?iká
he would see   what   medicine   she should use."   Well then   it's   this

tho kwí·   ni·yót   tsi?   wa?thotilihwayʌ·tá·se?   kʌ́·,   khále?   ya?éhawe?   sʌ́·
that's   how it is   that   they came to an agreement   y'know,   and   she took along   also

akotyá·tawi?t   ka?iká   yeksá·,   né· wí· né·   tho   ni·yót   tá·t   yah thau·tú·   tho
her dress   this   girl,   it's that   that's   how it is   if   it can't be   there

yaa·yʌ́·   tsi? ka·yʌ́·   yakonuhwáktanihe?,   tho ki? ok wí· náhte?
that one goes over there   the one that   someone is sick,   something

akowʌ́   nyʌhʌ́shawe?.   (13) Nʌ kati? wí·   wahyahtʌ·tí·,   tho
one's belonging   you will take it along.   Well then   the two set out,   there

wá·nehte?   kʌ́·,   ehta?késhu? kwí· nyahá·ne?   kʌ́h.   (14) Tho
the two went there   see,   on foot   the two went over there   y'know.   There

nyahá·newe?   thiká tsi?   thohtʌ́ti   shakotkʌ́·sehe?   kʌ́·,   nʌ kwí· tho kwí·
the two got over there   that   at   his home   he sees into them   y'know,   so then   there

it was just the same, she was still sick, and they didn't know what on earth was ailing her.
(10) And it seemed as though the next day her sickness was worse. (11) Then the old lady
said, "maybe we should go to that fortune-teller's house, maybe he can tell the girl's fortune,
maybe he can see what medicine she should use." (12) Well then that's how they came to a
decision, and also she took along the girl's dress, that's how it is if the person that's sick
can't go there, you take something along that belongs to them. (13) So then they set out,
they went there, and they walked. (14) They got to the home of the dreamer, and so then

yahyatáyah<u>te</u>ʔ.   (15) Nʌ kwíʔ wahathlo·lí·   kaʔikʌ́ lokstʌ́ha tsiʔ náhteʔ
the two entered.   So then   he told about it this   old man   that what

nihyatyelá·<u>ne</u>ʔ.   (16) Nʌ kwíʔ wahʌ́·luʔ yakʌʔ   thikʌ́ shakotkʌ́·seheʔ,
the two are here to do. So then   he said   reportedly that   he sees into them,

"sniha·wíʔ   katiʔ kʌ   thok náhteʔ akowʌ́ yeksáh."   (17) Waʔíʔ·luʔ kwíʔ n
"you two are bringing then   question something of hers girl."   She said

akokstʌ́ha, "hʌ́· akotyá·tawiʔt kwíʔ kha·wíʔ   kʌ́h."   (18) Nʌ kwíʔ né·
old lady,   "yes her dress   I am bringing see."   So then   it's

wahʌ́·luʔ kwíʔ, né· kwíʔ wahʌ́·luʔ kaʔikʌ́, "nok ʌwa·tú· né· ʌkatkú·slahkweʔ,
he said,   so it's he said   this,   "it has to be it's I will use it for a pillow,

akeslʌ́htaku tho   nʌ́tweʔ,   tsiʔ náhteʔ ʌwakeslʌ́htáksʌʔ náhteʔ
in my dream there it will come, that what   I will dream   what

ʌyakoyaʔtakén<u>ha</u>ʔ."   (19) Nʌ kwíʔ né· wahʌ́·luʔ yakʌʔ   thikʌ́ shakotkʌ́·seheʔ,
it will help her."   So then   it's he said   reportedly that   he sees into them,

"tewʌhnislaké tʌtísneʔ   kʌ́·, nʌ   uhte   ʌwakanúhtekeʔ."
"two days   you two will come back eh, then supposedly I will know."

(20) Nʌ kwíʔ né· sahyahtʌ·<u>tí</u>·.   (21) Né·n   to·kʌ́skeʔ tewʌhnislaké ókhnaʔ
     So then   it's the two went home.   It's that truly   two days   and then

tho   íshneʔ   kʌ́h.   (22) Nʌ kwíʔ né· kaʔikʌ́ wahʌ́·luʔ yakʌʔ
there the two are walking again y'know.   So then   it's this   he said   reportedly

thikʌ́ n shakotkʌ́·seheʔ,   "tsiʔ náhteʔ waʔkatkátho? akeslʌ́htaku kʌ́·   kaʔikʌ́
that   he sees into them, "that what   I saw   in my dream   y'know this

akolihwá·ke yetshiyatléha   kʌ́·, né· wíʔ tho   nikayélhaʔ tsiʔ yakonuhwáktaniheʔ
about her   your granddaughter see, so it's thus it is doing   that she is sick

they went in. (15) So then the old man told what it was they were there for. (16) So then the fortune-teller said, "did you bring some belonging of the little girl's?" (17) The old lady said, "yes, I brought her dress." (18) So then he said, so he said, "I must use this for my pillow, it will come to me in my dream, what I will dream is what will help her." (19) So then the dreamer said, "come back in a couple of days, I should know by then." (20) So then the two went home. (21) In two days they walked there again. (22) So then the dreamer said, "what I saw in my dream concerning your granddaughter, it's occurring that she is sick

tsiʔ   sóʔtsiʔ   yeksaʔtáksʌ.”   (23) “Tahnú· isé· sniV·waʔ   tsiʔ tho
because   so much   she is a bad child."   "And   you   you two, your fault   that   thus

niyawʌ́·u,   sóʔtsiʔ   waʔetshiksaʔtáksahteʔ kʌ́·, nʌ   núwaʔ   yah náhteʔ
it has happened,   too much   you spoiled her   see,   then   this time   not   anything

thusayutwʌ·nálahkweʔ   náhteʔ   a·yetshihlo·lí·.”   (24) “Tsiʔ katiʔ náhteʔ
she doesn't obey anymore   anything   you would tell her."   "That   then   what

ʌyakoyaʔtakénhaʔ kʌ́·, nʌ   kʌ́·tho yʌtsitsyahtʌ·tí·   ʌtsyatkwílyahkeʔ
it will help her   see,   when   here   you two will leave again   you two will sever twigs

thikʌ́ áhsʌ nikakwi·láke   thikʌ́ onikwʌ́htalaʔ nikakwiló·tʌ.”   (25) “Né· thikʌ́
that   three   twigs amount to   that   red   kind of twig."   "It's   that

ʌ́tsyatsteʔ   kʌ́·, nʌ   yʌtsísneweʔ   ʌyetshiʔtanuwʌhsláli?.” (26) “Né·
you two will use it   see,   when   you two will get home   you will whip her."   "It's

thikʌ́ ʌkakwe·ní· ʌkatáhkoʔ   wahétkʌʔ kʌ́h.”   (27) Nʌ kwí· né· to·kʌ́skeʔ kwí·
that   it will be able   it will take out   it is bad   y'know."   So then   it's   truly

nʌ   sahyahtʌ·tí·,   kháleʔ to·kʌ́skeʔ kwí· wahyatkwílyahkeʔ   thikʌ́ áhsʌ
then   the two went home,   and   truly   the two severed twigs   that   three

nikakwi·láke   onikwʌ́htalaʔ nikakwiló·tʌ.   (28) Nʌ kyaleʔ wí· wahyatu·kóhteʔ.
twigs amount to   red   kind of twig.   So again   the two continued on.

(29) Wahʌ́·luʔ yakʌʔ   thikʌ́ lokstʌ́ha, “olihwiyó kwí· kaʔikʌ́ tsiʔ yah
       He said   reportedly   that   old man,   "a sure thing   this   that   not

teʔwakuʔwéskwaniheʔ tsiʔ náhteʔ nok ʌwa·tú· nʌ́kyeleʔ, nok ʌwa·tú·
I don't enjoy   that   what   it has to be   I will do,   it has to be

ʌkheʔtanuwʌhsláliʔ yethiyatléha.”   (30) Waʔí·luʔ kwí· thikʌ́ akokstʌ́ha,
I will whip her   our granddaughter."   She said   that   old lady,

because she is really badly-behaved.” (23) “And you two, it's YOUR fault what has happened, you spoiled her too much, so now she doesn't obey and do anything you tell her.”
(24) “What will help her then is that when you leave here, you will pick three red [willow]
whips.” (25) “You will use those, when you get home you will whip her.” (26) “That can
take out the badness.” (27) So then they went home, and they picked three red [willow]
whips. (28) And so they continued on. (29) The old man said, “I sure don't feel good about
what I have to do, having to give our granddaughter a whipping.” (30) The old lady said,

"nók tsiʔ   sanúhteʔ   kwíˑ   tsiʔ   náhteʔ   wahʌ́ˑluʔ,   néˑ   sók   ʌyakoyaʔtakénhaʔ   kʌ́ˑ
"but   you know   that   what   he said,   it's   only   it will help her   y'know

néˑ   akonúhkwaʔt,   kaʔikʌ́   oˑkwíleʔ."   (31)   Nʌ kwíˑ   néˑ   nʌ   tshyusáˑneweʔ,
it's   her medicine,   this   twig."   So then   it's   then   when the two got home,

kháleʔ   kwíˑ   tho   kwíˑ   sʌ́ˑ   niˑyót   tsiʔ   luwatihlolí   tsiʔ   nok sʌ́ˑ   ʌwaˑtúˑ
and   that's   also   how it is   that   someone has told them   that   it has to be also

aˑhayuʔkúthoʔ   thikʌ́,   tsiʔ niyoˑléˑ   nʌ   ʌ́ˑlatsteʔ   thikʌ́ n   áhsʌ   nikakwiˑláke
he should burn tobacco   that,   until   then   he will use   that   three   twigs amount to

onikwʌ́htalaʔ   nikakwilóˑtʌ.   (32)   Néˑ   onúhkwaʔt   ʌyakoˑtúˑseʔ   thikʌ́
red   kind of twig.   It's   medicine   it will have an affect on her   that

yeksáˑ   táˑt   ʌhayuʔkúthoʔ   nyaˑléhkweʔ.   (33)   Tho   katiʔ wíˑ   naʔaˑwʌ́ˑ.
girl   if   he will burn tobacco   prior.   That's   anyway   what happened.

(34)   Néˑn   tho   nyahatáyahteʔ   tsiʔ   tyetaˑkéleʔ   kʌ́ˑ,   nʌ kwíˑ   tahatáhsawʌʔ   kwíˑ
         It's that   there   he went in   at   she is lying   see,   so then   he started

thikʌ́   waʔshakóliʔ   kʌ́h.   (35)   Thikʌ́   tutyeˑlʌ́hteʔ   oˑkwíleʔ,   kwáh   yah   náhteʔ
that   he beat her   y'know.   That   first   whip,   just   not   anything

thyeʔyakottokʌ́   tsiʔ   waʔshakoyʌhtániʔ,   yah   kiʔ   náhteʔ   thyeʔyuttoˑkás.
she didn't perceive   that   he struck her with it,   not   actually   anything   she doesn't feel.

(36)   Nʌ kwíˑ   nén   teknihatúˑthne   kʌ́h.   (37)   Néˑ   kiʔ   kwáh   néˑ   tsháˑkat,
         So then   it's that   second   see.   It's   actually   quite   it's   it's the same,

yah   náhteʔ   thyeʔyuttoˑkás.   (38)   Tsiʔ niyoˑléˑ   ahsʌhatúˑthne   aʔnyóh,   nʌ
not   anything   she doesn't feel.   Until   third   seems like,   then

ostúha   waʔuttsíˑtʌhteʔ.   (39)   Kháleʔ   onʌ   kwahotokʌ́ˑu   waʔtyushʌ́thoʔ   kʌ́h.
a little   she whimpered.   And   now   just for real   she cried   y'know.

"but you know what he said, it will only help her, her medicine, this whip." (31) So then
they got back home, and also how they were told was that he had to burn tobacco before he
used those three red [willow] whips. (32) The medicine would be effective for the little girl
only if he burned tobacco beforehand. (33) Anyway that's what happened. (34) So he went
in to where she was lying, and then he started to punish [beat] her. (35) At the first whip,
she didn't feel him striking her with it at all, she didn't feel a thing. (36) So then the second
one. (37) It was the same, she didn't feel anything. (38) Until the third one it seems, then
she started to whimper a little. (39) And then she really started crying.

(40) Neʔ thóˑneʔ katiʔ wíˑ thikʌ́ nʌ   wahatkʌ́ˑlahteʔ tsiʔ waʔshakoʔtanuwʌhsláliʔ
      At that time   well   that   then   he quit   that   he whipped her

shakotléha,   tsiʔ   nʌ   seʔ lonúhteʔ   nʌ   kwahotokʌ́ˑu waʔtyushʌ́thoʔ,
his granddaughter,   because   then   too   he knows   when   just for real   she cried,

nʌ katiʔ   uttáhkoʔ   tsiʔ náhteʔ n wahétkʌʔ.   (41) Neʔ thóˑneʔ katiʔ wíˑ thikʌ́
well then   it got taken out   that   what   it is bad.   At that time   well   that

nʌ   wahatkʌ́ˑlahteʔ tsiʔ waʔshakóliʔ.   (42) Néˑn,   sayólhʌneʔ   néˑ thikʌ́ ókhnaʔ
then   he quit   that   he beat her.   It's that,   the next day   it's   that   and then

elók   ítsyʌʔ   tsiʔ   nitsyakotaʔkaliˑtéˑ kʌ́h.   (43) Néˑ s katiʔ wíˑ luˑtéˑ
all over   she is walking   how   she feels well again   y'know.   It's anyway   they say

kaʔikʌ́   lotikstʌhokúha   tsiʔ   akwekú kʌ́ˑtho loyʌ́thu   Shukwayaʔtísuʔ,   íˑ
this   old people   that   all   here   he has planted   Our Creator,   us

ukwanúhkwaht; shekú yeksaʔshúha,   néˑ kiʔ   akonúhkwaʔt   thikʌ́ onikwʌ́htalaʔ
our medicine;   even   all the children,   it's   actually   one's medicine   that   red

nikakwilóˑtʌ. (44) Teyotuhutsyóhu katiʔ tyótkut aˑyukwayʌˑtákeʔ kʌ́ˑ,
kind of twig.   It is essential   then   always   we should have it   y'know,

nók tsiʔ yah kwíˑ náhteʔ   tho   téˑtsyot   nʌʔúˑwaʔ tsiʔ niyohtúˑneʔ
but   not   anything   that's   not how it is anymore   this time   as   how it was

tshiwahuˑníseʔ. (45) Nʌ kwíˑ núwaʔ kwáh kwíˑ n íˑ,   yukwatotyákhuʔ,
a long time ago.   So then   now   just   we,   we are grown-ups,

yah kwíˑ teʔtsitwatwʌnalákhwaʔ   náhteʔ yukhihloˑlíheʔ.   (46) Tho
not   you and we don't obey anymore   what   they tell us.   Thus

niyoˑléˑ nyaháˑweʔ   shekú n yeksaʔshúha,   kwahotokʌ́ˑu yah náhteʔ
how far   it is going over there   even   all the children,   just for real   not   anything

(40) At that time then he quit whipping his granddaughter, because then he knew that when she really cried, all that was bad got taken out. (41) At that time then he quit beating her. (42) So the next day she was walking around, she was feeling so well again. (43) Anyway the old people say that Our Creator has provided everything here, our medicine; even the children, their medicine [which is] the red [willow] whip. (44) It's essential that we have it always, but nothing is the same anymore like it was a long time ago. (45) So then even us, we grown-ups, we don't always do what we are told. (46) As far as that goes, even the children, they really don't

te?tsyutwʌnalákhwa?   náhte?   a·sheyá·liste?   kʌ·,
one doesn't obey anymore   anything   you would forbid her from doing   y'know,

a·hetshá·liste?   sʌ·.   (47)   Kwáh   kati? wí·   akwekú   tsha?teyukwa?nutánhʌ
you would forbid him   also.   Just   anyway   all   we are to blame

kyuhte wí·,   só·tsi?   akwekú   yukwatkʌhlá·tu   tsi?   niyukwaliho?tʌ·hné·.
supposedly,   too much   all   we have quit   what   kind of traditions we had.

(48)   Né·   tetsyukwáhkwʌ   la?slu·ní·   tsi?   né·   náhte?   shukwahlo·líhe?   kʌ·,   nʌ kwí·
        It's   we have picked up   white man   that   it's   what   he tells us   see,   so then

núwa?   ni·yót kwí· n   ukwaksa?ta?shúha   kʌ·,   kwáh kwí· ikʌ   tsi?   yah   te?yoyánle?
now   how it is   all our children   eh,   just really   that   not   it is not good

tsi?   núwa?   nihatiksa?tó·tʌhse?.   (49)   Tahnú·   í·   ukwalí·wa?   tho   ni·yót
how   this time   how all the children are.   And   us   our fault   that's   how it is

yethiyʌ?okúha   khále?   yethiyatle?okúha,   tahnú· kwáh kwí· akwekú
you and we, our children   and   you and we, our grandchildren,   and   just   all

nʌ   tho   ni·yót.   (50)   Yah   kati?   thya·ya·wʌ́   tsi?   tʌtsitwate·ní·
now   that's   how it is.   Not   well   it has to be   that   you and we will change it again

thikʌ,   a·kí·lu?   né·   sʌ́·   aetwatkʌ́·lahte?   tsi?   náhte?   shukwahlolí   la?slu·ní·,
that,   I'd say   it's   also   you and we should quit   that   what   he has told us   white man,

né·   ki?   tusétwahkwe?   tsi?   náhte?   teshukwawí
it's   actually   you and we should pick it up again   that   what   he has given it to us

Shukwaya?tísu?.   (51)   Tho   kati? wí·   né·   ka?ikʌ   niwakkaló·tʌ.   (52)   Tá·t núwa?
Our Creator.   Thus   anyway   it's   this   how my story is.   Maybe

úhka? ok   kánhke ok   ʌyakothu·táne?   kʌ·,   ʌyutwʌ·nálahkwe?   tsi?   náhte?
someone   some time   someone will hear   y'know,   someone will value   that   what

obey anything you are forbidding them [her], forbidding him also. (47) Anyway all of us are to blame because I guess all of us have quit following our ways. (48) We have picked up what the white man has told us, so then look at our children now, it sure isn't nice the way they are nowadays. (49) And it's OUR fault that's how it is with our children and our grandchildren, and they are all like that. (50) Well we have to change [things], I'd say also we should quit what the white man tells us, we should begin again with what Our Creator has given us. (51) So that's my story. (52) Maybe someone sometime will hear this, they will value

wa?kihlúni? kʌ·,   khále? tá·t núwa? kánhke ok   thok   nʌya·wʌ́ne? kʌ·,
I all said   y'know,   and   maybe   sometime   something   will happen   y'know,

kwáh akwekú tʌswatte·ní·   ʌtsyoyánlʌne?.   (53) Aya·wʌ́· s kwí·
just   all   again it will change again it will become good.   I hope so

né· tho nu·saya·wʌ́·.   (54) Tho   kati?   ok wí· na?katkwe·ní· ka?ikʌ́
it's   thus again it should happen.   That's anyway only   I am best able this

tsi?   niwakkaló·tʌ.
what   kind of story I have.

all that I say, and maybe sometime something will happen, everything will change again and
be right again. (53) I hope so, it's going to happen again. (54) So that's the best I can do
with my story.

The Dreamer

(Olive Elm talking to Mercy Doxtator and Karin Michelson, 1993)

(1) *Úhka? kati? né· náhte? ka?ikʌ́ Rose sheyathlolí*   *kʌ́h.* (2) Rose,
     Who   then   it's   what   this   Rose you are telling about her   eh.   Rose,

né· kwí· né·n   aknulhá· tekyatahnútlahkwe?. (3) Úska ok   yako·yʌ́· wí· n
so it's   it's that   my mother   the two were siblings.   One   only   she has

teyutahnútlahkwe? kwahotokʌ́·u *hmm,* nók tsi? nʌ   núwa?   Myrtle khále?—
she had a sibling   for real   *hmm,* but   then   this time   Myrtle   and—

(4) *Ne? kʌ   thikʌ́, náhte? akwáh, Calvin lo·(né·).*   (5) Hʌ́· Calvin
     It   question that,   what   exactly, Calvin (spouse).   Yes Calvin

lone?kʌ́,   Myrtle ókhale? Herman, Heman kʌs kwí· luwana?túkhwa?.
late spouse, Myrtle   and   Herman, Heman habitually   what they call him.

(1) *So who is this Rose you're talking about?* (2) Rose, that was my mother's sister. (3) She
had only one real sister, *hmm,* but then there was Myrtle and— (unfinished) (4) *That's—
what the heck—Calvin's (wife) (interrupted)?* (5) Yes, Calvin's late wife, Myrtle and Herman, Heman they used to call him.

(6) Khále? Elijah Katkat, khále?, né· kwí· áhsʌ nihatí   thikʌ́, nók
    And   Elijah Cutcut, and,   so it's three how many they are that, but

né·n   tsha?tewahsʌnʌ́ ok,   ok ne?n   aknulhá·,   kwáh né· nók Rose ókhale?
it's that half   only, and as for my mother, just it's only Rose and

Bill luwa·yátskwe?, úska yonatʌno?sʌtshʌ·táh<u>kwe?</u>. (7) Tahnú· aknulhá·
Bill was his name, one they used to have a brother.   And   my mother

onulha?kʌ́,   tshahanáklate?   Bill, ne? thó·ne? né· tyakawʌhe·yú.   (8) Tahnú·
her late mother, when he was born Bill, at that time it's then she has died.   And

yah ki?   ní· te?wakanúhte? tsyʌteli·hné·   kʌ   Tsyohsa?áh<u>tu</u>.
not actually me I don't know you used to know her question She Has Taken it All.

(9) *KsʌnahlukÚ   kih.*   (10) Ne·né· yahoya?táhawe?, né· wí·
    I've heard of her name actually.   It's   she took him,   it's

aonatauntiehkʌ́, Tsyohsa?áh<u>tu</u>;   Rose khále? aknulháh.   (11) Ne·né·
their late aunt, She Has Taken it All; Rose and   my mother.   It's

yahoya?táhawe?, ne·né· wahaótya<u>ke?</u>.   (12) Tho s thatináklehkwe?   thikʌ́,
she took him,   it's   she brought him up.   There they used to reside that,

a?é·,   náhte? akwáh, Sowátis ki?   lohni·núh<u>kwe?</u>. (13) Sé·yale?
over there, what   exactly, Hiram actually he had bought it.   You remember

kʌ   thikʌ́ Sowátis tsi? nú· tyotyelʌ́htu thohni·núh<u>kwe?</u>. (14) Kwáh
question that   Hiram   where first   he had bought it.   Just

kʌ? niyo·lé·   tkanuhso·táhkwe?,   ya·wét   tsi? niyo·lé· tyohatáti?,
some distance there used to be a house, kind of like as far as a road extends,

kwáh kʌ? niyo·lé· tkanúhso<u>te?</u>.   (15) *Kátsha? nú· ya·wét.* (16) Tho   ki?
just some distance there is a house.   *Where   like.*   There actually

(6) And Elijah Cutcut, and, the three of them, but they were only half [brothers and sisters to my mother], as for my mother, there was just Rose and Bill was his name, they [my mother and Rose] had only the one brother. (7) And my mother's mother, when Bill was born, at that time she died. (8) And I don't know whether you used to know Tsyohsa'ahtu? (9) *I've heard of her.* (10) She's the one that took him, their late auntie, Tsyohsa'ahtu; Rose and my mother's [auntie]. (11) She's the one that took him, she brought him up. (12) They used to live over there—what the heck—Hiram, [where] he had bought a place. (13) Do you remember Hiram, where he bought his first place? (14) Quite far away there used to be a house there, kind of as far as the road goes [from here to the road], there's a house so far [from the road]. (15) *Like where?* (16) There,

núwaʔ   thikʌ́,   áktaʔ   tsiʔ   tyenákleʔ   Joanne,   Joanne Ireland,   tho   ya·wét.
this time   that,   near   at   she resides   Joanne,   Joanne Ireland,   there   kind of like.

(17) Sanúhteʔ   wí· n   Elizabeth   tsiʔ nú·   tyonúhsoteʔ.   (18) *Hmm.* (19) Tho
       You know   Elizabeth   where   she has a house.   *Hmm.*   There

kiʔ   kʌʔ nukwá·,   ostúha   aʔé· nukwá·   ná·wati,   tho   tkanuhso·táhkweʔ.
actually   a ways towards,   a little bit   over there   that side,   there   there used to be a house.

(20) Tho s nú·   thatináklehkweʔ   thikʌ́   Tsyohsaʔáhtu   kháleʔ   Hsiʔtakéhteʔ
       That's where   they used to reside   that   She Has Taken it All   and   Hsi'takehte'

kʌs   luwa·yáts   loneʔkʌ́.   (21) *Hmm.* Ne·né·   wahuwayótyakeʔ   Bill   nʌ
habitually   is his name   late spouse.   *Hmm.* It's   they brought him up   Bill   when

tshaʔyaíheyeʔ   lotinulháh.   (22) Thoʔnʌ́   loʔníha   oyá·   sahónyakeʔ.
when she died   their mother.   And then   her father   another   he married again.

(23) Né· kwí·   né· onʌ́ n   Myrtle   ókhaleʔ   Elijah   ókhaleʔ   Herman   tho
       So it's   it's   then   Myrtle   and   Elijah   and   Herman   there

yaʔthati·táneʔ.   (24) Tahnú· kʌs   laksotkʌ́,   aknulhá·
over there they stood up.   And   customarily   my late grandfather,   my mother

loʔnihkʌ́,   nʌ s thikʌ́   luwanaʔtúkhwaʔ   "The Dreamer,"   né· wí· n
her late father,   then   that   what they call him   "The Dreamer,"   it's

shakotkʌ́·seheʔ.   (25) *Hmm.* (26) *Náhteʔ katiʔ luwa·yátskweʔ Ukwehuwehné·ke.*
he sees into them.   *Hmm.*   *What   then   was his name   Indian way.*

(27) Neʔ kʌ n.   (28) *Yahsotkʌ́.*   (29) Yah   kiʔ   ní· teʔwakanúhteʔ
       It   question.   *Your late grandfather.*   Not   actually   me   I don't know

nók tsiʔ Bill kiʔ   luwa·yáts   ya·wét wí· n   oʔsluniʔké·ne.   (30) *Hmm.*
but   Bill   actually   is his name   like   white man's way.   *Hmm.*

near where Joanne lives, Joanne Ireland, kind of like there. (17) You know Elizabeth, where
her house is? (18) *Hmm.* (19) A ways from there, a little bit over on the other side, there
used to be a house there. (20) That's where they used to live, Tsyohsa'ahtu and her late husband, Hsi'takehte' was his name. (21) *Hmm.* They were the ones that brought Bill up when
their mother died. (22) And then her [my mother's] father married again. (23) So that's
when Myrtle and Elijah and Herman were born. (24) And my late grandfather, my mother's
late father, they called him "The Dreamer," he was a fortune-teller. (25) *Hmm.* (26) *What
was his Indian name?* (27) You mean? (28) *Your late grandfather.* (29) I don't know but
Bill was like his English name. (30) *Hmm.*

(31) Yah ki?   ní· te?wakanúhte? náhte? luwa·yátskwe?   Ukwehuwehné·<u>ke</u>.
     Not actually me   I don't know   what   used to be his name Indian way.

(32) *Náhte? s uhte   né· ni·yót   thikʌ́ tsi? latiyʌteli·hné·   tshiwahu·níse?*
     What   supposedly it's how it is that   that they used to know a long time ago

a·kí·lu? a·huwʌnátkʌhse?.   (33) Yah ki?   ní· te?wakanúhte?, né· s ki?
I'd say one would see into them.   Not actually me   I don't know,   it's   actually

núwa? né·n aknulhá·   yuthlolyányuhe? wí· n lo?nihkʌ́,   tahnú· Rose
then   it's that my mother she tells about it   her late father, and   Rose

ya?shakotʌ́nyehte? yakʌ?   né· wa?utawya?tá·na?, wé·ni kwí· Mt. Elgin kyuhte wí·
he sent her away   reportedly it's she went to school, evidently   Mt. Elgin   supposedly

nú·   tshyeyutawyá·tha?,   ya·wét wí· Residential School.   (34) *Mhm.*
where   when she goes away to school, kind of like   Residential School.   *Mhm.*

(35) Tho   yakʌ?   né· nú·   yaha·<u>yʌ́·</u>.   (36) Tahnú· n aknulhá·
     That's reportedly it's where she went over there.   And   my mother

yah né· tehothutatú   a·yutawya?tá·<u>na?</u>.   (37) Né· se? aolí·wa? yah né·
not it's he didn't consent that she goes to school.   It's   too the reason   not   it's

náhte? te?yehyatuhslayʌte·<u>lí</u>.   (38) Nʌ kwí· lonulha?tsíwa?   kʌs
anything she doesn't have an education.   So then   they are by themselves   habitually

yakʌ?,   né·n   né· s yakʌ?   thikʌ́ nʌ   wahotitá·wha?, swatyelʌ́ s yakʌ?,
reportedly,   it's that it's reportedly that   when they went to bed, sometimes reportedly,

e·só· kyuni? wé·ni   yah te?yakehya·lú·,   wa?í·lu? "kwáh s ké·yale?
lots   too   evidently not she doesn't remember, she said "just   I remember

thikʌ́ swatyelʌ́   úhka? ok wí· náhte? tho   wahʌ·néwe? wí·, lʌ·nélhe? wí·
that   sometimes   someone   there they arrived,   they want

(31) I don't know what his Indian name was.
  (32) *I wonder how a long time ago they would know about telling people's fortunes.*
(33) I don't actually know, my mother used to tell that her late father, and he sent Rose away
to go to school, I guess it must have been Mt. Elgin where she went away to school, it was
kind of like a Residential School. (34) *Mhm.* (35) That's where she went. (36) And he
didn't let my mother go to school. (37) That's why she really doesn't have any education.
(38) So then they were home by themselves usually, and when they went to bed, sometimes—there's lots I guess she didn't remember—she said "I just remember sometimes people would get there, they wanted

a·shakótkʌh<u>se</u>ʔ."   (39) *Hmm.* (40) Thok kʌs   yakʌʔ   náhteʔ
he would see into them."   *Hmm.*   Some habitually reportedly anything

atslunyákhwaʔ tho   wahona·tíˑ, né·kwíˑ thikʌ́ kháleʔ kwíˑ oyuʔkwaʔu·w<u>ę́</u>.
clothing   there they left it, so it's   that   and   native tobacco.

(41) Né·kwíˑ thikʌ́ ʌ́·latsteʔ,   né·s yakʌʔ   thikʌ́ nʌ   wahotá·whaʔ,
     So it's   that   he will use it, it's reportedly that   when he went to bed,

tho s yakʌʔ   wahahweʔnu·níˑ oyuʔkwaʔuwé, ya·wét kwíˑ né·kwíˑ
there reportedly he wrapped it up native tobacco, kind of like so it's

wahatkʌ́·slah<u>kwe</u>ʔ.   (42) Wahʌ́·luʔ yakʌʔ   úska útlatsteʔ, "tá·t yah
he supported himself with it.   He said   reportedly one time,   "if   not

tha·kiʔtlu·tákeʔ, tá·t yah kʌʔ   tha·kitáklakeʔ nʌ   ʌséhsyeʔ
I won't be home,   if   not right here I won't be lying when you will wake up again

tákʌʔ ʌsatétsh<u>ʌ</u>."   (43) Wahʌ́·luʔ, "aʔtsyók ok   ʌswakúhakeʔ   kaló·
don't   you get afraid."   He said,   "after a while only I will have gotten home before

tsiʔ niyo·léˑ nʌ   ʌyólhʌneʔ."   (44) Nʌ s yakʌʔ   wíˑ thikʌ́ tá·t thok náhteʔ
until   when it will be daylight."   Then reportedly that if   something

wahoslʌhtáksʌʔ, swatyelʌ́ s yakʌʔ   óksaʔ ok   thikʌ́ wahoslʌhtáksʌʔ tsiʔ
he dreamed,   sometimes reportedly right away that   he dreamed   what

nikanuhkwaʔtslóˑtʌ wíˑ a·yútsteʔ n   a·yakoyaʔtakén<u>haʔ</u>.   (45) *Hmm.*
kind of medicine it is   one should use that it should help one.   *Hmm.*

(46) Óksaʔ ok   kʌs   yakʌʔ   wahakó·naʔ   ati n   kwaʔahsuté·<u>ke</u>.
     Right away habitually reportedly he went to go get it even though night-time.

(47) Né· kyuhte wíˑ thikʌ́ waʔshakohlo·líˑ tákʌʔ a·yakotétsh<u>ʌ</u>.
     It's supposedly that   he told her   don't she shouldn't be afraid.

to have their fortune told." (39) *Hmm.* (40) They would leave a piece of clothing, that and some Indian tobacco. (41) He would use that, when he went to bed, he would wrap up the Indian tobacco [in the clothing], he would kind of like use it as a pillow. (42) He said one time, "if I'm not home, if I'm not lying right here when you wake up, don't be alarmed." (43) He said, "after a while I'll be back, before daylight." (44) They say if he dreamed something, sometimes right away he would dream what kind of medicine someone should use to help them. (45) *Hmm.* (46) Right way he would go and get it even though it was night-time. (47) He told her she shouldn't become afraid.

(48) Kʰále? wa?í·lu?, "swatyelʌ́ s," wa?í·lu?, "kwáh wakathu·té· tehohʌlétha?."
And   she said, "sometimes,"   she said, "just   I hear   he is hollering."

(49) Ya·wét kwí·   loslʌhtaksʌ́hsluhe?   ki?wáh.   (50) Né· s   kyuhte wí·   né·   tá·t
Kind of like   he is dreaming things   right.   It's   supposedly   it's   if

yóhtlut   tsi?   náhte?   na?akoyá·tawʌ?   wí·   ka?ikʌ́   uhka? wí· náhte?   shakotkʌ́·sehe?.
it is scary   that   what   happened to someone   this   anyone   he sees into them.

(51) Swatyelʌ́ s   yakʌ?   thikʌ́   tá·t núwa?   tewʌhnislaké   tá·thuni?   áhsʌ
Sometimes   reportedly   that   maybe   two days   or   three

niwahsu·táke   nʌ   elhúwa?   ʌhakwe·ní·   ʌhathlo·lí·   náhte?   wí·
the nights amount to   then   right then   he will be able   he will tell   what

tehonatuhutsyoní   wí·   a·honanúhtʌne?.   *Hmm.*
they want   that they find out.   *Hmm.*

> (52) *Yah   kati?   tehsé·yale?   wahetshatkátho?   kʌ   ni?i·sé.*
> *Not   then   you don't remember   you saw him   question   as for you.*

(53) Táh, táh.   (54) Oliverha   uhte i·kélhe?   yu·té·   kʌ? tshihlá·   tshahlʌ́heye?.
No,   no.   Oliver dear   I think   she says   when he is little   when he died.

(55) Tahnú·   yu·té·   lattókhahkwe?   yaʌkʌ?.   (56) Tahnú·   yu·té·   né·
And   she says   he was knowledgeable   so they say.   And   she says   it's

yakʌ?   thikʌ́,   sé·yale?   kʌ   nisé·   thikʌ́   Southwold   kʌs
reportedly   that,   you remember   question   you   that   Southwold   habitually

thatʌhninúhahkwe?   Derbyshire.   (57) *Uhuh.*   (58) Tho s   yakʌ?   nú·
he used to sell there   Derbyshire.   *Uhuh.*   That's   reportedly   where

yehótyehse?   laohwísta?,   la·té·   latewyʌ́·tuhe?.   (59) Ya·wét   tsi? wí·
he leaves it over there   his money,   he says   he is saving it.   Kind of like   how

(48) And she said, "sometimes," she said, "I heard him hollering." (49) He was like dreaming, right. (50) I suppose if it was scary what was happening to whosoever's fortune he was telling. (51) Sometimes it was maybe two days or three nights before he was able to tell what they want to know. *Hmm.*

(52) *So you don't remember whether you saw him?* (53) No, no. (54) I think she [my mother] said Oliver was little when he died. (55) And she said he was knowledgeable so they say. (56) And she said—do you remember [in] Southwold, the man that ran the store there, Derbyshire? (57) *Uhuh.* (58) That's where he left his money, he said he was saving it. (59) It's like how

núwaʔ   niˑyót   bank   néˑ wíˑ   nyaesaˑtíˑ,   *hmm,* tho s   yakʌʔ
now   so it is bank   it's   you would leave it over there,   *hmm,*   that's   reportedly

núˑ   nyehótyehseʔ   thiˑ<u>kʌ́</u>.   (60) Tahnúˑ   tshihonuhwáktaniheʔ   thikʌ́ n
where   he leaves it over there that.   And   when he is sick   that

loʔnihkʌ́,   lakeʔníha s   yakʌʔ   loyoʔtʌ́hslehseʔ   thikʌ́,   tho
her late father,   my father   reportedly   he goes to work   that,   there

yahatuˑkóˑteʔ   Southwold,   kwáh   seʔ   kʌs   yakʌʔ   tahayakʌhtáˑtsiʔ
over there he passed by   Southwold,   just   too   habitually   reportedly   he rushed out

thikʌ́   Derbyshire.   (61)   Yah thyaˑyaˑwʌ́ˑ   tsiʔ   every day   ʌholiʔwanuˑtʌ́ˑ   thikʌ́
that   Derbyshire.   It has to be   that   every day   he will ask about him   that

lokstʌ́ha   náhteʔ   niyohtuháti<u>ʔ</u>.   (62)   Tahnúˑ   yakʌʔ   nʌ   tshahlʌ́heyeʔ   nʌ
old man   what   how it is going.   And   reportedly   then   when he died   then

tho   wáˑlehteʔ   lakeʔníha,   waʔíˑluʔ   yakʌʔ   aknulháˑ   tho núˑ   tkaˑyʌ́ˑ
there   he went there   my father,   she said   reportedly   my mother   that's where   it is there

laohwísta<u>ʔ</u>.   (63)   Néˑn,   tho   tshyaháˑlaweʔ   lakeʔníha   wahaliʔwanuˑtʌ́ˑ,
his money.   It's that,   there   when he got there   my father   he asked about it,

wahʌ́ˑluʔ   yakʌʔ   néˑ   thikʌ́   Derbyshire,   "yah   néˑ   náhteʔ   teʔkaˑyʌ́ˑ   ne<u>tú</u>."
he said   reportedly   it's   that   Derbyshire,   "not   it's   anything   it is not there   that place."

(64) Yuˑtéˑ   aknulháˑ   néˑ   kyuhte wíˑ   néˑ   aolíˑwaʔ   sóˑtsi?   waʔthoʔnikulhaˑlʌ́ˑ
      She says   my mother   it's   supposedly   it's   the reason   so much   it concerned him

nʌ   tsiʔ   nihonuhwáktaniheʔ   tsiʔ   lonúhteʔ   kʌʔ   láhaweʔ   laohwístaʔ
when   how   he is sick   because   he knows   right here   he holds   his money

kʌ́ˑ,   tahnúˑ   waʔíˑluʔ,   tyótkut   yakʌʔ   loyoˑtéˑ,   wéˑni kwíˑ   tsiʔ   kwáh
y'know,   and   she said,   always   reportedly   he is working,   evidently   that   quite

nowadays you leave it in the bank, *hmm,* that's where he was leaving it. (60) And when her late father was sick, my father would go to work, he would stop there on his way through Southwold, that Derbyshire would come rushing out. (61) Every day he had to ask about the old man and how he was doing. (62) And then when he died, my father went there, my mother said that's where his money was. (63) So when my father got there and he asked about it, Derbyshire said, "there's nothing there." (64) My mother said supposedly that's why he was so concerned when he [the old man] was so sick, because he knew that right there he was holding his money, and she said, he was always working, so there must have been quite

kʌʔ nikú   ohwístaʔ tho tkayʌ·táhkweʔ,   thousand utahotkʌhlá·<u>tu</u>keʔ.
some amount money   there it used to be there, thousand would he have released it.

(65) Yah né· náhteʔ   thaʔtethotkʌhlá·<u>tu</u>. (66) Né· s wí· né· yah náhteʔ
      Not it's anything he didn't release it.   It's that   not   anything

tehatihyatúhahkweʔ *hmm* tho nú·   nikaha·<u>wí</u>·. (67) *Wahohwistákhwaʔ.*
they didn't used to write *hmm* that's where is the era.   *He took money from him.*

(68) Tahnú· yakonúhteʔ nén   aknulhá· tsiʔ shakohlo·líheʔ seʔ tsiʔ tho wí· nú·
      And   she knows   it's that my mother that   he tells her   too   that that's where

nika·yʌ́· laohwístaʔ, tá·t kánhke náhteʔ   na·hoyá·tawʌʔ   tho kwí· nú·
it is there his money,   if   when   anything should happen to him that's where

nyʌye·kó·   wáh. (69) Yah kiʔ   thaʔtethotkʌhlá·<u>tu</u>. (70) Tahnú·
over there she will pick it up right.   Not actually he didn't give it out.   And

yah kwí· náhteʔ   tha·yekwe·ní· náhteʔ   a·yaí·luʔ,   yah seʔ kánikeʔ
not   anything she is not able anything she could say, not   too   nowhere

teʔkahyatúhslayʌʔ.
there is no paper.

(71) *Kánhke katiʔ né· ákteʔ   nihawenú   thikʌ́ latʌhninúhahkweʔ.*
      When   then   it's different he has gone away that   he used to sell.

(72) Neʔ kʌ n   Derbyshire. (73) *Hmm.* (74) Liyʌtéluʔ kiʔ   niʔí·,
      The   question Derbyshire.   *Hmm.*   I knew him actually me,

wé·ni kwí· tsiʔ tá·t núwaʔ forty kwí· twakanaklatú, wé·ni   tsiʔ tá·t núwaʔ
evidently   that maybe   forty   I was born then, evidently that maybe

né· kwí· teshonatahsu·téleʔ thikʌ́ n Stand Even. (75) Wé·ni   katiʔ
so it's   they are connected that   Stand Even.   Evidently then

a lot of money there, a thousand dollars had he let go of it. (65) But he gave out nothing.
(66) They didn't used to write anything down in those days. (67) *He took his money away
from him.* (68) And my mother knew that he was telling her that's where his money was, if
ever anything happened to him she could get it over there. (69) But he didn't let go of it.
(70) And she couldn't very well say anything, there was no paper anywhere.

   (71) *So when did that storekeeper go away from there for some place else?* (72) You
mean Derbyshire? (73) *Hmm.* (74) I knew him, it must have been maybe—I was born in
1940, so I guess maybe Stand Even took it over from him. (75) It must have been

tsi? kátsha? ok nú· tá·t núwa? fifty, nineteen fifty fifty-one kátsha? ok nú·
that somewhere maybe fifty, nineteen fifty fifty-one somewhere

tshanakla·kó· thikʌ́ Derbyshire, Stand Even núwa? tho saháti?̲.
when he moved away that Derbyshire, Stand Even this time there again he moved.

(76) Ké·yale? ní· thikʌ́ tsi? né· laulhá· laowʌhkʌ́ thikʌ́ yutʌhni·núhe?̲.
I remember me that that it's him his former belonging that one sells.

(77) Ké·yale? sʌ́· s ní· kʌ? tshiká· kʌ́·, kwáh s nya?tewʌhnislaké kʌ́·
I remember also me when I am little y'know, just every day y'know

tho kétha? kʌ́·, nʌ s ké·yale? thikʌ́ aknulhá· wa?ukhwístu?,
there I go there y'know, then I remember that my mother she gave me money,

yah kwí· te?wakanúhte? tó· ni·kú. (78) Nók khninú·nehse? thikʌ́
not I don't know how much amount. Just I go to buy that

Crackerjacks. (79) Mmm, Crackerjack tá·thuni? Lucky Elephant. (80) Hʌ́·.
Crackerjacks. Mmm, Crackerjack or Lucky Elephant. Yes.

(81) Kwáh tsi? wakanúhte? wísk kʌs uhte i·kélhe? kwénis nikano·lú· thikʌ́
I think five habitually I think pennies it costs that

elhúwa? tsha?kutiya·kʌ́ne?̲. (82) Tahnú· né· s aolí·wa? tyótkut khninú·nehse?,
right then when they came out. And it's the reason always I go to buy it,

né· thikʌ́ tsi? anisnuhsohlókta? kʌs tho i·wát, né· tewakatuhutsyo·ní̲.
it's that because ring habitually there it is in it, it's I want it.

around 1950, 1951 about, when Derbyshire moved away, then Stand Even moved there. (76) *I remember he used to own that store.* (77) *I remember also when I was little, I would go there everyday, I remember my mother would give me money, I don't know how much.* (78) *Only I would go and buy Crackerjacks.* (79) Mmm, Crackerjack or Lucky Elephant. (80) *Yes.* (81) I think five cents is how much it cost right when they came out. (82) *And the reason I would always go to buy them is because there was a ring inside, and I wanted it.*

Forecasting Things to Come

(Told by Margaret Antone to Mercy Doxtator on July 24, 1995)

(1) Né· kwí· ka?ikʌ aknulhá·   Lizzie yutátyats,   khále? lake?níha Jake.
     So it's   this   my mother Lizzie is her name, and   my father   Jake.

(2) Tsi? nikú   lotihwatsi·láyʌ?,   tsya·ták niyáki?.   (3) Tommyha
     What amount they have a family, seven   we amount to.   Tommy dear

thakwa·nʌ́.   (4) Tehaluwálya?ks.   (5) Thó·nʌ   Ní·ki.   (6) Helen   né·
he is the oldest.   He Breaks Nails.   And then Nellie.   Helen   it's

kuwa·yáts   o?sluni?ké·ne.   (7) Thó·nʌ   Ná·mʌn, yah né· te?wakanúhte?
is her name   white man's way.   And then Norman,   not   it's   I don't know

náhte? luwa·yáts   Ukwehuwehnéha?.   (8) Tho ne? nʌ Enoch, yah oni? né·
what   is his name in the Native way.   And then   Enoch,   not   too   it's

te?wakanúhte? náhte? luwa·yáts   Ukwehuwehnéha?.   (9) Thó·nʌ   í·,   Kuwáklit.
I don't know   what   is his name in the Native way.   And then   me, Margaret.

(10) Khále? Kate, yah oni? né· te?wakanúhte? náhte? yutátyats.   (11) Khále?
      And   Kate, not   too   it's   I don't know   what   is her name.   And

Evelyn. (12) Tsya·ták niyáki?.   (13) Kʌ? tshiyakwá·sa?   né· s thikʌ́
Evelyn.   Seven   we amount to.   When we were small   it's   that

lake?níha, lake?nihkʌ́,   nʌ wí· lawʌheyú, tashukwáhʌle?   tahnú· yah e·só·
my father,   my late father,   then   he has died, he called us to him   and   not   lots

tehatatíhahkwe?.   (14) Kwahikʌ́ tsi? tehoto·té· kʌs.   (15) Nók tsi?
he didn't used to speak.   Just really   that   he is still   customarily.   But

ka?ikʌ́ wahsuta·té·   nʌ s tashukwáhʌle?   yakwaksa?shúha kok tshiyakwá·sa?.
this   a night exists   then   he called us to him   all of us children   when we were just small.

(1) So my mother's name is Lizzie, and my father's is Jake. (2) We were seven, that's how many children they had. (3) Tommy is the oldest. (4) He Breaks Nails. (5) And then Nellie. (6) Helen is her name in English. (7) And then Norman, I don't know his Indian name. (8) And then Enoch, I don't know his Indian name either. (9) Then me, Margaret. (10) And Kate, I also don't know her [Indian] name. (11) And Evelyn. (12) There were seven of us. (13) When we were small my father, my late father, he's passed on now, he called us to him and he didn't used to talk a lot. (14) He was really quiet. (15) But this one night he called all of us children to him when we were just small.

(16) Wahʌ·luʔ "kʌh swatyʌ·tú." (17) Nʌ kwí· tho kwí· waʔtyakwahwánhakeʔ,
He said, "over here sit down." So then there we made a circle,

oshuʔkalá·ke waʔakwatyʌ·tú·, waʔakwatahúhsatateʔ náhteʔ ok ʌshukwahlo·lí.
on the floor we sat here and there, we listened whatever he will tell us.

(18) Né· s né· washukwahlo·lí kaʔikʌ tsiʔ niyawʌ́hsleʔ ohʌtú nukwá·,
It's that he told us this what is going to happen ahead where,

tó· kiʔ ok kwí· náheʔ. (19) Tahnú· nʌ wahu·níseʔ kaʔikʌ nyeswakathlo·lí.
some while. And then a long time ago this there I am telling about.

(20) Né· thikʌ s wahʌ́·luʔ, "ʌswatkáthoʔ thikʌ uhkaʔ ok owahaʔkéshuʔ
It's that he said, "you all will see that someone on the roads

ʌhatákheʔ yah thyahalatátiʔ." (21) Nʌ s kwí· ní·
he will be running not his feet won't be along the ground." So then us

yukwanehlakwʌ́·u náhteʔ katiʔ né· lʌ·té· thi·kʌ́. (22) Né·n tsiʔ nʌ
we are amazed what then it's he means that. It's that then

ʌshukwahlo·lí náhteʔ né· lʌ·té· thikʌ tsiʔ né· né·n bicycle. (23) Bicycle
he will tell us what it's he means that that it's it's the bicycle. Bicycle

núwaʔ ʌhotí·sleʔ owahaʔkéshuʔ yah kwí· thyahatilatátiʔ. _Mhm._
now they will ride on the roads not their feet won't be along the ground. _Mhm._

(24) Kháleʔ yah teʔské·yaleʔ náhteʔ s né· wahʌ́·luʔ thikʌ n
And not I don't remember anymore what it's he said that

automobile kiʔ sʌ́·, tahnú· yah teʔkanákleʔ neʔ thó·neʔ. (25) Wahʌ́·luʔ
automobile actually also, and not it is not plentiful at that time. He said

"né· sʌ́· thikʌ, tho ʌkatákheʔ tho ʌhatiyaʔtitakhenútyeʔ ʌhonatunhahlátiʔ."
"it's also that, there it will run there they will be riding in it they will be going joyfully."

(16) He said, "sit down over here." (17) So then we sat around [him] in a circle on the floor, we listened to whatever he had to tell us. (18) He told us about what was going to happen in the future, for quite a while [he talked]. (19) And this was a long time ago that I'm talking about. (20) He said, "you will see someone running on the roads without his feet touching the ground." (21) So then we were amazed, what does he mean? (22) Then he tells us what he means and that's the bicycle. (23) A bicycle they will be riding on the roads without their feet on the ground. _Mhm._ (24) And I don't remember anymore what he said about the automobile also, and there weren't many at that time. (25) He said, "also, it will be going by, people will be riding in it and going along joyfully."

(26) "Khále? énik nʌwatu·kóhte? thok náhte? tʌyawʌhale·lé·."   (27) Í· s kwí·
      "And   above it will go by   something it will go by noisy."   Us

tho   yukwanehlakwʌ́·u, náhte? kati? né· lʌ·té·   ka?i·kʌ́. (28) Né·n
there we are amazed,   what   then it's he means this.   It's that

né· kwí· né·n airplane. (29) Khále? wahʌ́·lu? "ʌtwʌhnisla·téke? sʌ́·
so it's it's the airplane.   And   he said "there will be a day also

tʌyauhutsishuhkwáni?."   (30) "ʌtwatahaluní·sele?." (31) Tahnú·
it will earthquake here and there."   "It's going to get worse."   And

núwa? né· núwa? kwáh tho niyohtuháti?.   (32) Khále? kawelu·té·se?.
this time it's this time just that's what is going on.   And   it gets windy.

(33) ʌtkawelaha·wí· kawela?shátste?, né· kyuni? wí· né· nʌ   kwáh tho
      Wind will come   strong wind,   it's too   it's now just   that's

ni·yót.   (34) Tahnú· ne? thó·ne? twʌhnisla·téhkwe?   yah né· tho   té·yot.
how it is.   And   at that time there used to be a day not it's that's not how it is.

Mhm.   (35) Nók tsi? nʌ ki? ok tshihutkáthos náhte? niyawʌ́hsle?   ohʌ·tú.
Mhm.   But   already   then they see what   is going to happen ahead.

(36) Khále? ʌwahno·tú·. (37) ʌtwʌhnisla·téke? nʌ   né· núwa?   ʌwahno·tú·
      And   it will flood.   There will be a day when it's this time it will flood

kwáh tsyo?k nú·, nʌ ki? ok oni? wí· né· tho   ni·yót.   (38) Kʌtyohkwanʌ́
everywhere,   already   too   it's that's the way it is.   A lot of people

ʌyakólyo? oni? né· ʌtkalihu·ní·.   *Mhm.* (39) A·lé·   wa?twatslide
it will kill them too it's it will be the reason. *Mhm.*   Sometimes it did slide

yahú·sʌne?. (40) Nʌ kwí· tó·k nihatí   tho wahʌníheye?. (41) Nʌ s kwí·
it fell in.   So then so many of them there they died.   So then

(26) "And high up something will be going by, something noisy." (27) Us, we were
amazed, what does he mean by this? (28) It's the airplane. (29) And he said, "come a day
there will be earthquakes too." (30) "It's going to get worse." (31) And that's just what's
happening now. (32) And it will get windy. (33) Winds will come, strong winds, that's just
how it is now. (34) And back in those days that's not how it was. *Mhm.* (35) But already
they could see what was going to happen in the future. (36) And it will flood. (37) There
will be a day when there will be floods everywhere, it's already that way. (38) A lot of people will be killed because of it too. *Mhm.* (39) At times there was a landslide. (40) So then
so many people died there. (41) So then

thikʌ   tho   ni·yót   shukwahlo·líheʔ, tá·t núwaʔ kwáh akwekú ókhnaʔ
that   that's   the way it is   he tells us,   maybe   just   all   and then

tho   niyohtuhátiʔ.   (42) Kháleʔ né· s kiʔ   sʌ· ní· kaʔikʌ, onʌ́ e·só·
that's   what is happening.   And   it's   actually also me   this,   now   lots

waʔkanuhtunyu·kó· kaʔikʌ núwaʔ naʔukwahle·wáhteʔ,   uʔtalihaʔtániʔ.
I thought about it   this   now   it seriously impacted us, it got hot repeatedly.

(43) Tahnú· lu·té·   o·tsísteʔ núwaʔ tʌ́tw" eʔ n   oyá·   né· núwaʔ
     And   they say fire   this time   it will come another it's this time

ʌtsyuhutsyóhaleʔ.   (44) Né· s ní· thikʌ tho nú·   kwáh s otokʌ́u tsiʔ
it will cleanse the earth again.   It's   me   that   that's where just for real   that

swatyelʌ́   ukwanuhtunyukwáhtʌʔ. Uhuh. (45) Nʌ   kiʔ   núwaʔ   niyoʔtalíhʌ.
sometimes   it makes me think.   Uhuh.   Then in fact   this time   how it is hot.

Mhm.   (46) Tá·t núwaʔ thʌtwatye·lʌ́·   waʔtyoʔtúhkwahkweʔ.
Mhm.   Maybe   you and we will be surprised suddenly   it sparked a fire.

(47) Yah úhkaʔ teʔyakonúhteʔ.   (48) Kwahotokʌ́·u tsiʔ yah teʔyukwanúhteʔ
     Not   anyone one doesn't know.   Just for real   that   not   we don't know

oh   niyawʌ́hsleʔ.   (49) Tahnú· núwaʔ lu·té·   kʌs   né· kiʔ
how it is going to happen.   And   this time   they say habitually it's   actually

né·n   watlʌ·náyʌʔ ya·satáyahteʔ, lu·té·,   "satelha·lát." (50) Yah seʔ
it's that   church service   you should enter, they say, "get ready."   Not   too

teʔyukwanúhteʔ kánhke. (51) Tahnú· tutetwaya·kʌ́neʔ   ókhnaʔ?
we don't know   when.   And   you and we came out again   and then

sayukwaʔnikúlhʌʔ. Mhm. (52) Sayukwaʔnikúlhʌʔ náhteʔ ni·yót   tsiʔ
again we forgot.   Mhm.   Again we forgot   what   is the way   that

that's the way he was telling us, maybe just all of it is already happening. (42) And also me, I think a lot about it, that we get punished, it gets hot all the time. (43) And they say a fire will be the next to come and it will cleanse the earth again. (44) That's where it really makes me wonder sometimes. *Uhuh.* (45) It's so hot now. *Mhm.* (46) Maybe we will be surprised suddenly as a fire sparks up. (47) No one knows. (48) Really we don't know what's going to happen. (49) And they say you should go into a church, they say, "get ready." (50) We don't know at all when. (51) And we come out [of church] again and already we forget. *Mhm.* (52) We forget again the way

tayukhihlo·lí·   yukwatlʌnayʌhnu·<u>hné·</u>.   (53)   Kwáh s otokʌ́·u   tsiʔ
there they told us   we have gone to church.   Just for real   that

a·yakonuhtunyukwáhtʌʔ   kwíˑ,   kwáh   ʌtkaye·líkeʔ   a·yunuhtunyu·kó·   né·
it should make one think,   just   it will be right   one should think about   it's

náho<u>hteʔ</u>.   (54)   Tho   kiʔ   ok   niyo·lé·   thikʌ́   ʌkkwe·ní·   kwáh   nʌʔú·<u>waʔ</u>.
what.   That's   actually   only   how far   that   I will be able   just   now.

(55)   Tá·t núwaʔ   waʔtsyók   niya·lé<u>hkweʔ</u>.
       Maybe   later   after a while.

we were told in church. (53) It really makes a person think, the right way to think about
things. (54) That's as much as I can for now. (55) Maybe after a while [I can go on].

Starting Life Together

(Told by Mercy Doxtator to Hazel Cornelius on August 23, 1995)

(1)   Né· kwíˑ níˑ kaʔikʌ́,   Tewatnatukóthaʔ   niwaksʌnó·tʌ
       So it's   me this,   She Passes Through the Village   my name is so

Ukwehuwehnéhaʔ.   (2)   Aknulhá·,   Katsí·tsyawaks   né·   yutátyats.
in the Native way.   My mother,   She Shakes the Flowers   it's   is her name.

(3)   Lakeʔníha   yah   né·   teʔwakanúhteʔ   náhteʔ   né·   luwa·yáts,   swakeʔnikulhʌ́·u
       My father   not   it's   I don't know   what   it's   is his name,   I have forgotten

náhteʔ   luwa·yáts   Ukwehuwehnéhaʔ,   Joe   kwíˑ   né·   luwa·yáts.   (4)   Thoʔnʌ́
what   is his name   in the Native way,   Joe   it's   is his name.   And then

tékni   tewakeʔkʌ·shʌ́·   tehnukwé,   shayá·tat   Latákheʔ   luwa·yáts   ókhaleʔ
two   I have two siblings   two male persons,   he is one   He is Running   is his name   and

(1) So it's me, She Passes Through the Village is my Indian name. (2) My mother's name is
She Shakes the Flowers. (3) I don't know what my father's name is, I've forgotten what his
Indian name is, Joe is his [English] name. (4) And then I have two brothers, one is named
He is Running and

shayá·tat swake?nikulhʌ́·u náhte? luwa·yáts,   yah tha·kkwe·ní· usakehyá·lane?,
he is one   I have forgotten   what   is his name,   not   I am not able   that I remember,

nók tsi? Ken ki?   luwa·yáts.   (5) Né· kati? wí· ka?ikʌ́ tsi? s ni·yót   tsi?
but   Ken   actually   is his name.   So then it's   this   how   is the way   that

yukhlolí   aksótha   tsi? Oshwe·kʌ́· né· nukwá· nityakothwatsilinú
she has told me   my grandmother that Ohsweken   it's   where   her family comes from

akaulhá·, tho   Irish takahwatsilatáti?   nahatiya?tó·tʌ?   tsi? nityakawe·nú.
her,   there   Irish   family extends from   they are that kind   at   she has come from there.

(6) Tho s nú·   thatinákle? thikʌ́ Oshwe·kʌ́·, tho s ki?   yakwanatá·le? se?
      That's where   they reside   that   Ohsweken,   there   actually   we visit   too

tshiwahu·níse? tsi? nú· thatinákle?, kwáh s onikwʌ́htala? nihotinutsistó·tʌ.
a long time ago   where   they reside,   just   red   their heads are that kind.

(7) Né· kʌs kwí· thikʌ́ yu·té·   aksótha   né· tsi?   Irish se? nahatiya?tó·tʌ?,
      So it's   that   she says   my grandmother because   Irish   too   they are that kind,

tho kwí· nú· nityakothwatsilinú n aksótha   onulhá·,   tho?nʌ́ kʌh
that's where   her family comes from   my grandmother her mother,   and then   over here

né· nukwá· yakonyáku?   aksótha.   (8) Nʌ kati? wí· e·só· s kwí· kwáh
it's   where   she has married   my grandmother.   Well then   lots   just

tsyo?k náhte?   niyawʌ́·u,   nʌ tayawʌ?uháti? onʌ́ tsi? twanákele?.
all kinds of things   it has happened,   now   it's happening   now   at   you and we reside.

(9) Ostúha ok   kʌs   tsi? s kehya·lú·   tsyo?k náhte?, né· kʌs kwí·
      A little   only   habitually   that   I remember things   different things,   it's   habitually

núwa?   oni? wʌhnislaténi? waknehlákwas tsi? na?teyottenyuháti?
this time   too   day after day   I am surprised   how   it's going along changing

one, I've forgotten what his name is, I can't remember, but Ken is his [English] name.
(5) So the way that my grandmother used to tell me is that her family is from Ohsweken, her
descendants were Irish, that's the kind of people she is from. (6) That's where they lived, in
Ohsweken, we used to visit there a long time ago where they lived, they had red hair.
(7) My grandmother said it's because they are Irish, that's where my grandmother's
mother's family is from, and then my grandmother married over here. (8) So a lot, all kinds
of things have happened, are happening now where we live. (9) Only a little bit I remember
about different things, every day I'm surprised how all kinds of things are changing.

kwáh tsyoʔk náho<u>hteʔ</u>.   (10) Yotlatstú·neʔ   kʌs   watʌ́·nyoteʔ,   úhkaʔ ok
all kinds of things.   It used to happen   customarily   a ceremony,   someone

waʔakónyakeʔ,   né· s thikʌ́ wahutatyanyu·kó·   tsyoʔk náhteʔ,   washakotihlo·lí·
someone got married, it's   that   they spoke about things different things, they told them

tsiʔ   na·hotiliho?tʌ́hakeʔ   nʌ   wahotínyakeʔ,   aʔé·   niyo·lé· yaʔthatiníhalaneʔ,
what   their lifestyle should be when   they got married,   great   extent   they covered,

wahuthlolyányuʔ   tsyoʔk náhteʔ   na·hotiliho?tʌ́hakeʔ,   kʌh wʌhnislaténiʔ   yah
they told about things different things   how their lifestyle should be, these days   not

tho   té·tsyot.   (11) Kwáh   núwaʔ   nók úhkaʔ   a·yutatliʔwanu·tú·seʔ
that's   not how it is anymore.   Just   this time only anyone   one would ask one

a·yuta·tí·,   kwáh kiʔ nók "tʌkheyatcongratulate kiʔ   ok   niʔí·."
that one speaks,   just only   "I will congratulate them actually only   me."

(12) Yah kwí· náhteʔ   sʌ́haʔ ísiʔ nú·.   (13) Ok wí· n   tho nú·
       Not   anything more   yonder.   And as for that's when

twʌhnisla·téhkweʔ, ohná·kʌʔ twʌhnisla·téhkweʔ, akwekú s nʌ   wahuwatihlo·lí·
it used to be a day,   back   it used to be a day,   everything then   they told them

tsiʔ   na·hotiliho?tʌ́hakeʔ   tsiʔ   a·hutataskénhaʔ,   a·hotiyo·tʌ́·,
what   their lifestyle should be that   they should apply themselves, they should work,

ta·huthwatsiláshnyeʔ,   tá·t kánhke nʌhuthwatsilu·ní·   ta·shakotíshnyeʔ
they should look after a family, if   when   they will make a family they should look after them

kiʔ wí·, a·hotiyo?tʌ́hsekeʔ   sʌ́·, a·hatiyʌthóhsekeʔ,   né· ta·hotíshnyeʔ
actually, they should be working also, they should be planting, it's it should nurture them

nʌ   a·yóhslateʔ,   kwáh kiʔ tsyoʔk náhteʔ a·hotinʌskwayʌ·tákeʔ   sʌ́·
when   it would be winter, just   all kinds of   they should have animals   also

(10) Once there was a ceremony, someone got married, and they would talk [make a speech] about different things, they would tell them what their life should be like when they got married, they covered a wide range of things, they talked about different things, all about the way their life should be, these days that's not how it is anymore. (11) Now it's just they ask anyone to speak, it's only "me, I'm just going to congratulate them." (12) Nothing more. (13) But in those days, back in those days, they were all told about what their lifestyle should be, that they should apply themselves, they should work, they should look after their families, when they have a family they should look after them, they should work also, they should farm, it should nurture them come winter, they should have all kinds of animals too,

tsyo?k   na?kutiya?tó·tʌ?,   né· kwí· a·honunhehkwʌ́hake?   nʌ
different   what kind they are,   so it's   they should use it to keep them alive   when

a·yóhslate?,   ókhna?   yah kwí· te?tsitwayʌtelí   tho
it would be winter,   and then   not   you and we don't know about it anymore   thus

nusayohtúhake?   shekú n, kítkit   ok   oni?   usayukwayʌ·táke?   yah oni?
it should be that way again   still,   chicken   only too   we should have again   not too

né· te?tsyukwa·yʌ́·.   (14) Kwah nók   lonʌtyohkwanʌ́ tsi? ka·yʌ́·   yah
it's   we do not have it anymore.   Just   they are a lot of   the one that   not

thau·tú·   aetwa?wá·lake?.   (15) Yah kati? s ní·   te?wakanúhte? náhte?,
it can't be   that you and we eat meat.   Not   then   me   I don't know   what,

yah ní· te?waklʌ?nhá·u a·kka·látu?   náhte?, yah tho té·yot   tsi?
not   me   I don't know how   I should tell stories   what,   not   thus it is not so   that

te?wakatatlihunyʌ·ní.   (16) Ókhale? tsi? nikú   yukkalatuní,
I have not taught myself.   And   how many   one has told me a story,

swake?nikulhʌ́·u, swake?nikulhʌ́·tskwʌ,   yah tha·kkwe·ní· a·kehyá·lake?   kʌs.
I have forgotten,   it's easy for me to forget,   not   I am not able   that I remember   habitually.

(17) Né· kati?   ní· áhsʌ ki?   ok wí· nitsyákyu?   ní· tsyukwatatʌlʌ́
       So anyway it's   us   three actually only   we are that many   us   we are left

khe?kʌ?okúha. (18) Tsyeyá·tat kwí· kwáh kʌ? nityakáskwa?,   Kennyha
all my siblings.   She is one   quite   she was the youngest,   Kenny

shako?kʌ́ha,   wísk niyohslaké   na?tehyátle?   sʌ́ha? kʌ? nityakoyʌ?ʌ́skwa?,
his younger sister,   five   years amount to   the two are apart   more   she was the younger child,

wá·tlu? né· niwʌhní·take   nityakawenú   ókhna?   né· sayaíheye?,   ne·né·
nine   it's   months amount to   she has come from   and then   it's   again she died,   it's that

different kinds, it should see them through the winter, and now we don't know anything
about that way anymore, we should have chickens too, we don't have them anymore either.
(14) There's just a whole lot of [animals, wild game] that we can't eat. (15) I don't know
what (unfinished), I don't know how to tell stories (unfinished), that's not the way I taught
myself [to tell stories]. (16) And so many stories they told me, I've forgotten, I forget easily, I can't remember (tape too quiet to make out). (17) So anyway there are only three of us
brothers and sisters left. (18) The youngest one, Kenny's younger sister, they were five
years apart and she was the younger child, she was nine months old and already she died,

thikʌ́ waʔakólyoʔ yaʔteyakaulislakútha?   waʔúhsahkeʔ, ne·né·   yaʔtyakoku·tʌ́·.
that   it killed her   it takes one's breath away one coughed,   it's that it overcame her.

(19)   Kwáh katiʔ ní· nók úska teyakyatahnútlahkweʔ   kháleʔ tékni
       Just   then   me   only one   we two used to be sisters   and   two

tewakatʌnoʔsʌ·shʌ́·. (20) Tho   kiʔ   ok   uhte i·kélheʔ ni·kú.
I have two brothers.   That's   actually only I think   how much.

what killed her was the whooping cough, that's what took her. (19) Then I had just one sister and two brothers. (20) That's enough I think.

After a Loss

(Told by Mercy Doxtator to Karin Michelson on June 30, 2000)

(1) Shekólih. (2) Ú·waʔ wískhatut áhsʌ niwáshʌ tshiskaha·wí· awʌ́hihteʔ.
     Hello.   Now   Friday   three tens   is the date   strawberry.

(3) Tahnú· tewáshʌ tewʌʔnyáweluʔ yohslashe·tás.   (4) Tsiʔ náhteʔ i·kélheʔ
     And   two tens   hundred   it counts years.   That   what   I want

a·kathlolí kaʔikʌ́ wʌhnisla·té·, né· kyuhte wí· aolí·waʔ   né· i·kélheʔ a·kathlolí,
I would tell this   a day exists,   it's   supposedly   the reason it's   I want   I would tell,

né· tsiʔ   kaʔikʌ́ wahlʌ́heyeʔ tshutayolhʌʔuhátiʔ   oskánhe yukniyó·tehkweʔ,
because this   he died   when it was becoming daylight together   we two used to work,

ya·wét kyuhte wí· waʔtwakeʔnikulha·lʌ́· tshaʔklihwá·lukeʔ tsiʔ wahatu·kóhteʔ.
it's like supposedly   it disturbed me   when I heard news   that   he passed on.

(5) Nók tsiʔ tsiʔ kwí· náhteʔ i·kélheʔ a·kathlolí tsiʔ ní· niyukwalihó·tʌ
     But   that   what   I want   I would tell what we   customs we have

(1) Hello. (2) Today it's Friday, the thirtieth of the time of the strawberry [June]. (3) And
it's the year 2000. (4) What I want to tell about today—I guess the reason I want to tell
about it is because someone I used to work with died early this morning, it's like I guess it
disturbed [saddened] me when I heard the news that he had passed on. (5) But what I want
to talk about is the customs we have

kʌh nú·   niyakwanákle?   Yakyukwehuwé, tshiwahu·níse? s kwí· ní·   aknulhá·
over here   where we reside   we Native people,   a long time ago   me   my mother

e·só· yukhlolí   tsi?   naesaliho?tʌ́hake?   nʌ   tho   ni·yót   tsi?
lots   she has told me   what   customs you should have   when   that's   how it is   that

satla?swaksá·tu.   (6) Né· s tho   ni·yót   tsi?   yukhlo·líhe? kʌ́·,   nʌ
you have had bad fortune.   It's   that's   how it is   that   she tells me   y'know,   when

náhte?   wesatla?swáksahte?   ya?tʌhsato·táte?   ki?,   tákʌ? náhte?,
anything   bad fortune affected you   over there you will keep still   actually,   don't   anything,

tá·t   ʌwa·tú·   yah náhte?   tha·hsátyele?   tho   náhe? tsi?   na?tekyátle? nʌ
if   it's possible   not   anything   you should not do   that   time   that   is between   when

wesatla?swáksahte?   tsi? niyo·lé· ya?káhewe? n Skana?tsíhale? kʌs,   yu·té·
bad fortune affected you   until   it's that time   Ten Day Feast   customarily,   she says

kʌs   ʌhsate?nyʌ·tʌ́· ʌsali?wiyóhake?   thikʌ́ tho   náhe?.   (7) Tákʌ?
customarily   you will try   you will have a good disposition   that   that   time.   Don't

sʌ́·   kátsha?   tʌhsatlihotálho khále? sali?wiyóhak.   (8) Né· ki?   né·
also   anywhere   you will quarrel   and   you have a good nature.   It's   actually   it's

akwáh   thikʌ́ yu·té·,   tákʌ? ʌsa?nikúlhʌ tsi?   tho   nʌyohtúhake?,   khále?
above all   that   she says,   don't   you forget   that   that's   the way it will be,   and

ati   yah isé· te?satla?swaksá·tu,   tá·t núwa? né· né·n   úhka? ok tho
no matter   not   you   you have not had bad fortune,   maybe   it's   it's that   someone   there

yenákle?   kʌ́·tho Ukwehuwé·ne,   kwáh ki?   tho   nʌsayelʌ́hake?
someone resides   here   at the Native people's,   just   actually   thus   you will be doing

tsi?   ni·yót   tá·t se? núwa?   isé· satla?swaksá·tu.   (9) Né· kyuhte wí·
as   how it is   if   too   this time   you   you have had bad fortune.   It's   supposedly

here where we Indians live, a long time ago my mother told me a lot about what customs you should have when you have had bad fortune like that. (6) That's the way she used to tell me, when such bad fortune affected you, you should keep still, not anything, if you could go without doing anything during the time between when you had the bad fortune until the time of the Ten Day Feast, she said you should try to have a good disposition for that time. (7) Also, don't quarrel anywhere and be good-natured. (8) And the most important thing she said is, don't forget the way it should be, and even if it wasn't you who had the bad fortune, maybe it's someone living here on the Reserve, you will do just as if you were the one with the bad fortune. (9) I guess

aolí·waʔ   kwáh   kʌ́·tho   waʔkáheweʔ,   kwáh s   yakʌʔ   yah   náhteʔ
the reason   just   here   it came time,   just   they say   not   anything

thahútyeleʔ   wí· n   kʌ́·tho   tsiʔ   yakwanákleʔ   kʌ́·,   nʌ kwí·   núwaʔ   tá·t
they won't do   here   at   we reside   y'know,   so then   this time   if

thok náhteʔ   lonatkʌnísuʔ,   óksaʔ   kiʔ   waʔthati·tʌ́steʔ   kʌ́·,   yah   náhteʔ
something   they are meeting,   immediately   actually   they stopped   see,   not   anything

thusahutkʌnísaneʔ   tsiʔ niyo·lé·   ʌwatu·kóhteʔ,   tsiʔ niyo·lé·   ʌhuwayaʔtátaneʔ,
they won't meet again   until   it will pass,   until   they will bury him,

tá·thuniʔ   ʌyutatyaʔtátaneʔ.   (10)   Tahnú·   tho s kwí·   nutayohtuhátiʔ
or   they will bury her.   And   thus   the way it has been going on

kaʔikʌ́   nʌ   tshiwahu·níseʔ,   né· s   thikʌ́   nʌ   yakotlaʔswaksá·tu,   ókhnaʔ   tho kwí·
this   now   a long time,   it's   that   when   one is grieving,   and then   there

wáhsehteʔ   waʔsheʔnikuhkétskoʔ   kwáh   tsiʔ   nʌskwe·ní·   kʌ́·,   tá·t núwaʔ
you went there   you raised their spirits   just   how   you will be able   see,   maybe

kwah nók tsiʔ   waʔtesnithalúniʔ   tá·thuniʔ   thok wí· náhteʔ,   tá·t núwaʔ   sʌ́·   thok náhteʔ
just   you two conversed   or else   something,   maybe   also   something

sha·wí·   kahwa·tsíleʔ   a·huteku·ní·,   kwáh   kʌs   katiʔ wí·   tsiʔ   a·kí·luʔ   kwí·
you are bringing   family   they should eat,   just   usually   well then   that   I'd say

lotilihowanáhtu   tsiʔ   niyukwalihoʔtʌ·hné·   teyukwatatyaʔtakénhʌ,
they are enlarging a matter   what   custom we used to have   we are helping one another,

sʌ́haʔ kwí·   thikʌ́   tho nú·   nikaha·wí·   kʌ́h.   (11)   Né· s katiʔ wí·   sʌ́·   thikʌ́
more   that   that's when   is the era   y'know.   Well then it's   also   that

nʌ   yaʔkáheweʔ   ya·wét kwí·   nʌ   ʌhatinú·nawʌʔ,   né· s kwí·   thikʌ́   tyoyanáhʌ
then   it's that time   it's like   then   they will have a Wake,   so it's   that   it follows

it's why even up to now, they won't do anything here where we live, so then if they have
some kind of meeting, immediately they stop, they won't have any kind of meeting again
until after they bury him or they bury her. (10) And that's the way it has been all along,
since long ago, when someone is grieving, then you go there to raise their spirits as much as
you can, or maybe the two of you just talk or else something (unfinished), maybe too you
bring something for the family to eat, well I would say they make a big deal about the custom we used to have of helping one another, more so at that time. (11) Well it's at that time
also when they will have like a Wake, and it's done following

náhte?   niholiho?tʌ·hné·   ka?ikʌ   wahatu·kóhte?,   tá·t   lolihwiyostú·ne?,   nʌ kwí·   né·
what   custom he had   this   he passed on,   if   he was Christian,   so then   it's

úhka? ki? ok wí·   né·   tho   wá·lewe?   thikʌ   ʌhatlihwahno·tʌ·   kʌh.   (12)   Khále?
someone   it's   there he arrived   that   he will give a sermon see.   And

tá·t   lonúhses,   lonuhsesú·ne?,   nʌ kwí·   né·   ya·wét kwí·   ne·né·   tshá·kat,
if   he is Longhouse, he was Longhouse,   then   it's   kind of like   it's that   it is the same,

úhka? ok   tho   ʌ́·lawe?   ʌhata·tí·   tsi?   niholiho?tʌ·hné·   lotukóhtu.
someone   there he will arrive   he will speak   what   custom he had   he has passed on.

    (13)   Né· kati? wí·   ní·   ka?ikʌ   ʌkathlo·lí·   tsi? s   né·   nihatiyélhahkwe?,   tsi? s
            Well then it's   me   this   I will tell   what   it's   they used to do,   what

nihatiyélha?   tá·t   lolihwiyostú·ne?   kʌ́·,   né· kwí·   né·   onʌ́   ka?ikʌ   nʌ
they do   if   he was Christian   y'know,   so it's   it's   then   this   when

ʌhatinú·nawʌ?   ókhna?   wahuwatínhane?   tehatilihwákhwa?,   tho
they will have a Wake   and then they hired them   they sing,   there

ʌhúti?   tʌhatilí·wahkwe?,   khále?   tsi? s   niyohtú·ne?   tshiwahu·níse?
they will sit down   they will sing,   and   how   the way it was   a long time ago

kwáh   kwa?ahsutáti?   tʌhatilí·wahkwe?   kwáh   tsi? niyo·lé·   ʌtkaké·to?,   nʌ
just   all night long   they will sing   just   until   the sun will rise,   then

elhúwa?   ʌhutkʌ́·lahte?   tsi?   tehotilihwáhkwʌ.   (14)   Tahnú·   skalʌ·nát   kʌs
just then   they will quit   that   they are singing.   And   one song   customarily

wa?thatilí·wahkwe?   nʌ   thutahsawá·ne?,   kwáh   akwekú   thikʌ   tho   wathlo·líhe?
they sang   when   they are going to start, just   all   that   thus   it tells

náhte?   aolí·wa?   tsi?   nʌ   wahutyʌ·tú·   nʌ kwí·   tʌhatilí·wahkwe?,   né·   kʌ·té·
what   the reason   that   then   they sat around   so then   they will sing,   it's   it means

the tradition of the one who passed on, if he was Christian, then someone arrives there to give a sermon. (12) And if he is Longhouse, if he was Longhouse, then it's kind of like the same, someone will come to speak according to the tradition of the one who has passed on.

(13) Well I'm going to talk about what they used to do, what they do if he was Christian, so when it's time for them to have a Wake, then they hire singers, they will sit down and sing, and the way it used to be a long time ago they would sing all night long until the sun comes up, only then did they stop singing. (14) And they sing this one song when they are about to start, it tells everything about why they sit down and they sing, it means

tsi? kwa?ahsutáti? kwí· tʌhatilí·wahkwe?, khále? nʌ   astéhtsi?   nʌ
that all night long   they will sing,   and   then in the morning when

takaké·to?,   nʌ   wahutkʌ́·lahte? khále? katokʌ́ tsi? nikalʌnó·tʌ thikʌ́
the sun rose, then they quit   and   certain what kind of song that

tʌshatilí·wahkwe?, né· kwí· né· onʌ́ thikʌ́ n astéhtsi?   tehatilihwákhwa?.
they will sing again, so it's   it's then that   in the morning they sing.

(15) Né· s kati? wí· thikʌ́ tho niyohtú·ne? tshiwahu·níse? kʌtyohkwaké·lu?
      Well then it's   that   thus how it was a long time ago several groups

sʌ́·   tehatilihwákhwa?, swatyelʌ́ s tóhka? nikʌtyóhkwayʌ? wí· né·n
also they sing,   sometimes a few   there are groups   it's that

Ukwehuwé·ne,   katokʌ́ kwí· tsi? ka·yʌ́· ʌhuwatínhane?   tsi? ka·yʌ́·
at the Native people's, certain   the one that they will hire them the one that

tehonatuhutsyoní a·hatinú·nawʌ?.   (16) Tahnú· s oni? né· thikʌ́ nʌ
they want   they would hold a Wake.   And   too it's that   then

wahutyʌ·tú·   tehatilihwákhwa?, ókhna? skalʌnát   tʌhatilí·wahkwe? thikʌ́
they sat down they sing,   and then it is one song they will sing   that

ókhna?   shayá·tat wa?tha·táne?, ne·né· onʌ́ thikʌ́ wa?tha·táne?, wahatá·liste?
and then he is one he stood up,   it's that then that   he stood up,   he forbade

tákʌ? úhka? a·yehlotʌ́   tho   kanúsku   né· tsi? tʌhoti?nikulha·lʌ́·
don't anyone one should smoke there in the house because it will bother them

tehatlihwákhwa?. (17) Khále? ʌshakothálhahse? sʌ́· tsi? ka·yʌ́· yakotló·lu,
they sing.   And   he will advise them also the one that one is watching,

tákʌ? kwí· só·tsi?   ta·hutlakalé·last.   (18) Khále? tákʌ? sʌ́· átste sʌ́·
don't   too much they should make noise.   And   don't also outside also

that they will sing all night long, and then in the morning when the sun comes up, then they
stop and they sing a certain song again, one that they sing in the morning. (15) So that's the
way it was a long time ago, there were several groups of singers, sometimes there were a
few groups on the Reserve, they hired the certain ones that they wanted to have do the
Wake. (16) And then the singers sit down, and they start to sing this one song, then a person
stands up, he stands up and he tells people no one should smoke in the house because it will
bother the singers. (17) And he also advises those who are watching not to make too much
noise. (18) And also, they shouldn't

náhte?   ta·hoti?nikulhalʌ́,   tákʌ? náhte?   a·hutste·líst   náhte?   loti·yʌ́·
anything it should bother them,   don't anything they should take over   what   they have

lonatla?swaksá·tu.   (19) Kwáh kʌs   ki?   akwekú thikʌ́
they have undergone bad fortune.   Just   usually actually all   that

wa?shakothálhahse? shekú latiksa?shúha, wa?shakothálhahse? tsi? nʌyohtúhake?
he advised them   even   all the children, he advised them   how   it will be the way

thikʌ́   tsi? náhe? tho   ʌhʌné·sheke?.   (20) Né· kati? wí·   nʌ   tahutáhsawʌ?
that   while   there they will be around.   Well anyway it's   then   they started

wa?thatilí·wahkwe? kʌ́·,   thó·nʌ   oni? nya?káhewe? ahsúthʌ,   ókhna?
they sang   y'know, and then   too   it's that time   midnight,   and then

wahutkʌ́·lahte?, ne·né· onʌ́ thikʌ́ nʌ   né· wahutekhu·ní·, tahnú· né· kwí·
they quit,   it's   then   that   when   it's   they ate,   and   so it's

nya·lé· ʌhutekhu·ní· tsi? ka·yʌ́·   tehatilihwákhwa?. (21) Thó·nʌ   tsi? ka·yʌ́·
first   they will eat   the one that they sing.   And then   the one that

lonatla?swaksá·tu né· núwa?   ʌshúti?,   né· núwa?   ʌshutekhu·ní·.
they are bereaved   it's   this time they will sit down again, it's   this time they will eat again.

(22) Thó·nʌ   thikʌ́ nʌ   akwekú ʌhutekhu·ní· n kahwa·tsíle?, né· nʌ   tsi? ka·yʌ́·
       And then   that   then   all   they will eat   family,   it's   then   the one that

yakotló·lu   ʌwa·tú· né·n   núwa?   ʌshutekhu·ní·,   kwáh tsi? niyo·lé·
they are watching   it can be it's that this time they will eat again, just   until

akwekú ʌhonáhtane?,   nʌ   elhúwa?   tʌthutáhsawʌ? tʌshatilí·wahkwe?.
all   they will eat their fill, then   right then   they will start   they will sing again.

(23) Ne·né· onʌ́ kwáh kwí· nʌ   kwa?ahsutáti?. (24) Nʌ kwí· ka?ikʌ́ tsi? kʌ́·tho
       It's that   then   just   then   all night long.   So then   this   that   here

be bothered by anything outside (e.g. car radios), they shouldn't take over [touch] anything
that belongs to the bereaved. (19) He advised everyone, even the children, he advised them
about the way it should be while they are there. (20) Well anyway then they would start to
sing, and then when it's midnight, then they quit, and it's then that they eat, and the first
ones to eat are the singers. (21) And then the bereaved sit down, they eat next. (22) And
then all the family eat, then those who are looking on can eat next, until everyone has had
enough to eat, then they'll start to sing again. (23) All night long. (24) So now here

waʔkáheweʔ,   skʌtyóhkwat   ok   tsyukwa·yʌ́·   Ukwehuwéne   tehatilihwákhwaʔ,
it came time,   one group   only   we have one   at the Native people's   they sing,

kháleʔ yah   onʌ́   tho   té·tsyot   thikʌ́ kwaʔahsutáti?   yaʔtahatílhʌhteʔ
and   not   now   that's   not how it is anymore   that   all night long   they should stay up

ta·hatilí·wahkweʔ,   tho s   núwaʔ   thikʌ́   akwáh   ahsúthʌ   ok   niyo·lé·   ókhnaʔ
that they sing,   there   this time   that   mostly   midnight   only   as far as   and then

wahutkʌ́·lahteʔ,   tá·t núwaʔ   wahuwatikhwánuteʔ,   ókhnaʔ   né·   sahuhtʌ·tí· n
they quit,   maybe   they feed them food,   and then   it's   they went home

tehatilihwákh<u>wa</u>ʔ.   (25) Né· s kwí· né·n   kahwa·tsíleʔ, nʌ ki? ok wí· né·
they sing.   So it's   it's that   family,   already   it's

yaʔtusahotiyá·tisteʔ,   tá·t núwaʔ   shekú   tho   lʌ·né·seʔ   laonukwé·taʔ,
again they are left alone, maybe   still   there   they are around   their relatives,

tho kwí·   ʌhʌné·shekeʔ   tsiʔ niyo·lé·   waʔólhʌneʔ.   (26)   Tho kati? wí·
there   they will be around   until   it became daylight.   So that's

ní·   ni·yót   kaʔikʌ́   tsiʔ   klihwayʌtelí   kaʔikʌ́   yakotlaʔswaksá·tu.
me   how it is   this   that   I know about a matter   this   one is bereaved.

(27) Tho s nihatiyélhaʔ kʌ́·,   kháleʔ nʌ   oye·lí· niwʌhnislaké   thikʌ́
         That's   what they do see,   and   then   ten   days amount to   that

ʌhutnúhtuhteʔ nʌ   yaʔkáheweʔ Skanaʔtsíha<u>le</u>ʔ.   (28)   Neʔ thó·neʔ   né· onʌ́
they will wait   when   it's that time   Ten Day Feast.   At that time   it's   then

thikʌ́ akwekú kwí· yakoló·lu   tsiʔ náhteʔ loyʌ·táhkweʔ   tá·thuniʔ
that   all   one has gathered that   what   he used to have   or

yakoyʌ·táhkweʔ n   tsyakotukóhtu.   (29) Kwáh akwekú thikʌ́ wahatiló·lokeʔ,
she used to have   one has passed on.   Just   all   that   they gathered it,

the time has come, we have only one group of singers on the Reserve, and that's not how it
is anymore, that they stay up all night to sing, mostly until midnight only and then they quit,
maybe they feed them, and then the singers go home. (25) So the family are left by themselves again already, maybe their relatives are still there, they will be there until it becomes
daylight. (26) So me, that's what I know about being bereaved. (27) That's what they do,
and then they wait ten days when it's time for the Ten Day Feast. (28) At that time everything is gathered up that used to belong to him or to her, to the one who has passed on.
(29) They gather everything together,

ókhnaʔ   wahatihweʔnu·ní· s thikʌ́,   ahsli·yé· thikʌ́   waʔtyehwánhakeʔ   kʌ́·,   né· kwí·
and then they wrapped it up   that,   string   that   one tied it up   see,   so it's

né· kaʔikʌ́ akowʌ́,   tá·t núwaʔ   úhkaʔ ok   laonukwé·taʔ   tá·thuniʔ   akotʌló·slaʔ
it's this   one's belongings, maybe   someone   their relatives   or maybe   her friend

tá·thuni laotʌló·slaʔ,   né· kwí· ʌyeye·ná·   kaʔikʌ́   atslunyákhwaʔ   tá·thuniʔ
or   his friend,   so it's   one will receive this   clothing   or

thok wí· náhteʔ   a·huwʌnehyahlákhwakeʔ   tsiʔ ka·yʌ́· n shonatukóhtu.
something   that one keeps remembering them with it the one that   they have passed on.

(30) Kwáh   akwekú thikʌ́ yʌhatíhsaʔahteʔ   kanúsku   náhteʔ   kayʌ·táhkweʔ n
        Just   all   that   they will take all   in the house   what   it used to lie

laonawʌshúha   oniʔ né· ya·wét kyuhte wí· né· laonatslunyákhwaʔ   kʌ́h.
all their belongings   even it's   like   supposedly it's   their clothing   see.

(31) Thó·nʌ   thikʌ́   neʔ thó·neʔ   sʌ́·   né· luté· s kwí· né· yeskʌhá
        And then   that   at that time   also   it's they say   it's   last

tusahu·túteʔ   kʌ́·,   thikʌ́ n oye·lí· niwʌhnislaké   yaʔkáheweʔ   kakhwáheleʔ
they ate together again   see,   that   ten   days amount to   it's that time   a meal is set

kiʔwáh. (32) Tho   oniʔ né· kaksáheleʔ,   nʌ   né· akwekú   tho   káheleʔ tsiʔ
right.   There   too   it's   a dish is set,   then   it's all   there   it is set   that

náhteʔ kalákwʌ,   akwekú   tho   i·wát   káksaku   tsiʔ náhteʔ,   tahnú·
what   it is selected,   everything   there   it is inside   in the dish   that   what,   and

né· s kwí· né· waʔkutikhu·ní·   tsiʔ náhteʔ akwáh   thawe·ká·skweʔ
so it's   it's   they prepared a meal   that   what   above all   he most found tasty

tá·thuniʔ tyakawe·ká·skweʔ   tsiʔ náheʔ? yakúnheʔ,   né· kwí· thikʌ́ akwekú né·
or else   she most found tasty   while   one is living,   so it's   that   all   it's

and then they wrap it up, they tie it up with string, so these belongings of theirs, maybe some relative or her friend or his friend will get some clothing or something for them to remember those who have passed on. (30) They take everything in the house that used to belong to them, even like I guess their clothing. (31) And then at that time also they say it's the last time they would eat together, on the tenth day a dinner is put on. (32) A dish is set out, and everything is put out that is selected, everything is there in the dish what (unfinished), and they prepare whatever he or she most liked to eat while they were living, and all that

ʌkakhuníhake?.   (33) Thó·nʌ   akwekú thikʌ́ tho   wa?étane? káksaku.
food will be prepared.   And then   all   that   there one put it in in the dish.

(34) Nʌ   né· tho kwí· né· s kwí· yeskʌhá   tusahu·túte?,   ʌyólhʌne? né·
      Then it's there   so it's   the last time they ate together again, the next day it's

onʌ́   ʌyuhtʌ·tí·   tá·thuni? ʌhahtʌ·tí·   shotukóhtu.   (35) Tho s ki? wí· nú·
then   she will leave   or else   he will leave   he has passed on.   That's   actually   where

yahá·le?   tsi? thotuhutsya·té· Shukwaya?tísu?. (36) Khále?   thikʌ́ n kákhwa?
he went there   at   there is his land   Our Creator.   And   that   food

káksaku   lonétʌ?,   wahutsha·tú· s né· thikʌ́, wahú·kwate? kátsha? ok nú·,
in the dish   they have put it in,   they bury it   it's   that,   they dug   somewhere,

tsi? né· s kwí· lu·té   tsi? nú· yah úhka?   tha?teyutawʌlyé·tha?,   tho   thikʌ́
that   so it's   they say   where   not   anyone   one won't travel,   there   that

ʌhú·kwate?, ʌhutsha·tú·   thikʌ́ kákhwa?, lu·té· s kwí· né· thikʌ́ kákhwa?, ne·né·
they will dig,   they will bury   that   food,   they say   it's   that   food,   that's it

wahutekhu·ní· n tsi? ka·yʌ́·   nʌ   shonatukóhtu.   (37) Tho kati? wí· nikú
they ate   the one that   when they have passed on.   Well that's   how much

ka?ikʌ́ wá·kelhe? a·kwahlo·lí·   kʌ́·,   tsi?   niyukwalihó·tʌ tsi? s ní·
this   I wanted   I would tell you all y'know, what   are our customs   what   we

niyakwayélha? úhka? náhte? wahatu·kóhte? tá·thuni? wa?utu·kóhte?, nʌ kyale? wí·
we do   anyone   he passed on   or else   she passed on,   so again

oyá·   sashukwatukóhtʌ?   a·kí·lu?   kʌ? nithoyʌ́ha kʌ́·,   tahnú·
another   he has passed on before us   I would say   a young man   y'know,   and

lahlúkhahkwe?   nʌ ki? ok ale? wí· oyá·,   úska sayukwa·tí·   tsi? ka·yʌ́·
he used to be a speaker   already   another, one   we have lost again   the one that

food is prepared. (33) And then everything is put in the dish. (34) So then that's the last
time they eat together, the next day she will start her journey or he will start his journey, the
one who has passed on. (35) He is going to the land of Our Creator. (36) And they bury the
food they've put in the dish, they dig somewhere, they say where no one will travel (so the
buried food won't be disturbed by anyone walking there), they dig there, they bury the food,
they say it's that food they will eat, those who have passed on. (37) Well that's how much I
wanted to tell you, what our customs are, what we do about someone's passing, his passing
or her passing, and again another person has passed before us, I'd say a young man, and he
was a speaker and already another one, we have lost one again who

lahlúkhahkwe? tsi? niyakwawʌnó·tʌ. (38) Tho kati? wí· nikú   ka?ikʌ́
he used to speak such is our language.   So that's   how much this

wá·kelhe? a·kwahlo·lí·.
I wanted   I would tell you all.

spoke our language. (38) That's all I wanted to tell you.

Getting Hoyan

(Told by Mercy Doxtator on January 16, 1999)

(1) Né· kyuhte wí· sʌ́· a·kathlo·lí·   hoyá·n, kwáh ní· tyotyelʌ́htu ké·yale?
     It's supposedly also I should tell about hoyan, just me first   I remember

wa?tkathoyanhtá·na?,   tho kwí· nú· thikʌ́ ka·té·   tsi? tyukwanuhso·táhkwe?,
I am going to get hoyan, that's where that I am saying that we used to have a house,

nʌ wí· tho nukwá· tshiyakwanákle? thikʌ́, astéhtsi?   wa?úkyehte? aknulhá·,
then   that's where when we reside   that,   in the morning she woke me my mother,

wa?í·lu?, "háo?   kwahikʌ́" wa?í·lu? "satkétsko, yah thya·ya·wʌ́· tsi?
she said, "come on really"   she said "get up,   it has to be   that

wa?tehsathoyanhtá·<u>na?</u>."   (2) "Tahnú· satauntie,   né· nya·lé· yʌhsáhkete?
you are going to get hoyan."   "And   your auntie,   it's first   you will go to

yʌhsya?tuníhslako?,   nʌ yakʌ?   tyolha·lé· kʌ́·   saya?tu·ní."
over there you will pick up a doll, now reportedly it is ready y'know your doll."

(3) Nʌ kwí· né· thikʌ́ wa?katslu·ní, kwáh kyuhte wí· tsi? kwahikʌ́ yohtá·nawʌ?
     So then it's that I got dressed, just supposedly that just really it is warm

(1) I guess I should talk also about hoyan, the very first time I remember going to get hoyan,
I'm talking about where our house used to be, when we were living there, early in the morning my mother woke me up, she said "come on," she said "get up, you have to go get
hoyan." (2) "And first you have to go over to your auntie's to get a doll, your doll is ready."
(3) So then I got dressed, I guess I dressed real warm

tsiʔ   waʔkatslu·ní· tsiʔ   kwáh seʔ yah teʔwé·ne tó· náheʔ   Áskeweʔ
how   I got dressed because   just too it's incredible how long   I will get home

waʔtkathoyanhtá·<u>naʔ</u>.   (4) NA kwí· né· yaʔtkaláhtateʔ, kwáh s ké·yaleʔ   thikʌ́
I am going to get hoyan.   So then it's I ran over there, just   I remember   that

waʔtkaláhtateʔ, kwáh tsiʔ niyo·lé· aʔnyóh   yaʔktákheʔ   kʌ́·,
I ran,   just how far it is seems like I went that way running y'know,

naʔtewakeshlíhʌhseʔ thikʌ́ yaa·kéweʔ   akwatauntiehné·<u>ke</u>.   (5) Kwáh s kwí·
how I am in a hurry that   I should get over there   at my auntie's place.   Just

yah só·tsiʔ   teʔwinú,   núwaʔ   quarter of a mile uhte wí·   naʔteyakwáte<u>leʔ</u>.
not too much it is not far, this time quarter of a mile   supposedly   we are far apart.

(6) Né·n   tho   tshyahá·keweʔ   thikʌ́, kwáh kwí· tewakhʌlehtá·neʔ,
     It's that there when I got over there that,   just   I am going to holler,

"hoyá·n hoyá·n."   (7) NA kiʔ ok wí· né· tutenhotu·kó·,   né· né·n   lo·né·,
"hoyan hoyan."   Right then   it's again the door opened, it's it's that spouse,

tho   íthlateʔ?   Katsya, Katsya luwanaʔtúkhwaʔ kʌs,   nʌ kwí·
there   he is standing   Katsya, Katsya what they call him customarily, so then

yaʔkatáyah<u>teʔ</u>.   (8) NA kiʔ ok wí· né· yolha·lé· akyaʔtuní, tayu·kú·
I went in.   Right then   it's it is ready my doll,   she gave it to me

akyaʔtuní, ókhnaʔ wí· tutakya·kʌ́neʔ   kʌ́·,   niswakatshanunihátiʔ   tsiʔ
my doll,   and then   I came out again y'know,   I am going along so happy again because

ukyaʔtunihslayʌ·tá<u>neʔ</u>.   (9) Né· s kwí· aʔnyóh   tho   ni·yót   tsiʔ thonehtáhkwʌ
I received a doll.   So it's   seems like that's how it is that   they believe

tshiwahu·níseʔ, tsiʔ nú· tyenákleʔ   satauntieha, né· kiʔ   tho nú·
a long time ago, where   she resides your auntie,   it's actually that's where

because there was no telling how long before I would get home from going to get hoyan.
(4) So then I ran over there, I remember I ran, seems like I ran all the way, I was in such a
hurry to get to my auntie's. (5) It wasn't too far, I guess a quarter of a mile we [lived] apart.
(6) So when I got there, I was hollering "hoyan hoyan." (7) Right away the door opened,
her husband, Katsya was standing there, Katsya they used to call him, so then I went in.
(8) Already my doll was ready, she gave me my doll, and then I came out again, I was going
along so happy because I had gotten a doll. (9) Seems like that's what they believed a long
time ago, where your auntie lives is where

ʌhsyaʔtunihslakó·naʔ   ká·, ʌyesayúniʔ   ká·   kayaʔtu·ní. (10) Né·n
you will go and get a doll   see,   she will make for you   y'know   doll.   It's that

tshyusa·kéweʔ   thikʌ́, nʌ kwí· waʔkhenaʔtu·há·seʔ aknulhá·   akyaʔtuní kʌ́h.
when I got home   that,   so then   I showed it to her   my mother   my doll   y'know.

(11) Waʔí·luʔ, "nʌ katiʔ kʌ́"   waʔí·luʔ "salha·lé·   ta·hsathoyanhtá<u>na</u>ʔ."
       She said,   "well then   question"   she said   "you are ready   that you go and get hoyan."

(12) Nʌ kwí· né· waʔkahtʌ·tí·, né·n   tahnú· seʔ s wí· né· naʔtekutlúni?
       So then   it's   I set out,   it's that   and   too   it's   they are far apart

tsiʔ yukwanuhso·tú·, né·n   yah s kiʔ   aʔnyóh   teʔwé·ne   tsiʔ
at   we have houses,   it's that   not   actually   seems like   it's incredible   how

niswakkaʔtátiʔ   thikʌ́ hoyá·n nʌ   sa·kéweʔ.   (13) Kʌ́haleʔ kwáh s kyuhte wí·
I have lots going along   that   hoyan   when   I got home.   And   just   supposedly

ukwatlaʔswi·yósteʔ yah tho   teʔkanye·yʌ́·   owahaʔkéshuʔ,   u·tú· kwí·
I became lucky   not   there   there isn't snow on the ground   all over the roads,   it could be

kwáh ok skʌ·nʌ́· waʔkahtʌ·tí·, yah kwí· kátshaʔ   só·tsiʔ teʔkanye·yʌ́·
just   in peace   I set out,   not   anywhere   much   there isn't snow on the ground

kʌ́h.   (14) Tho   kiʔ   ní· ni·yót   thikʌ́ tsiʔ ké·yaleʔ   hoyá·n, kháleʔ
y'know.   That's   actually   me   how it is   that   that   I remember   hoyan,   and

oyá·   né· né·n   kaló· nukwá· tyakohtʌ́ti, sʌ́haʔ kiʔ   né· kʌʔ nityakoyʌ́ha
another   it's   it's that   on this side   her home,   more   actually   it's   she is young

tsiʔ ní· ni·yót,   Annabelle kʌs   yutátyats.   (15) Né· né·n   thikʌ́
as   me   how it is,   Annabelle   customarily   is her name.   It's   it's that   that

kwáh ké·yaleʔ   tsiʔ waʔkheyatnúhtuhteʔ, wé·ne kwí· tho   ni·yót   tsiʔ
just   I remember   that   I waited for her,   evidently   that's   how it is   that

you get a doll, she makes a [donut] doll for you. (10) So when I got back home I showed
my mother my doll. (11) She said, "well then" she said "are you ready to get hoyan?"
(12) So then I left, so our houses were far apart, [yet] it seemed like I really had a lot of
hoyan when I got home. (13) And I guess I was lucky that there wasn't snow on the roads,
so without any trouble I could get going, because there wasn't much snow anywhere.
(14) That's the way I remember hoyan, and another time, her home was over here [close to
here], she was younger than me, Annabelle was her name. (15) So I remember I waited for
her, it must have been that's the way

wa?tyuknilihwayʌ·tá·se? tsi? né· ʌyákne?   kʌh.   (16) Nʌ kwí· né·
we two planned the matter that it's we two will go y'know.   So then it's

to·kʌ́ske? kwí· né· wa?ákne?   wa?tyakyathoyanhtá·<u>na</u>?.   (17) Kwáh s kwí· né·
truly   it's we two went we two went to get hoyan.   Just   it's

kok náhe? kaló· se? né· ʌ́tye ni·kále?, kwáh akwekú yeyukwáktu
a little while before too it's noon,   just   all   we have gone up to

tsi? nikú   kanuhso·tú· wí· tho   ákta?   lotinuhso·<u>tú·</u>.   (18) Yu·té·
as many as there are houses there close by they have houses.   She says

se? s wí· aknulhá·,   kwáh né·, kwah nók astéhtsi? "ʌhsatkétsko? ókhna?
too   my mother,   just   it's, as soon as morning   "you will get up and then

tʌhsathoyanhtá·<u>na</u>?."   (19) "Nʌ   né· ʌtsisúhake?   ʌ́tye ni·ká<u>le</u>?."
you will go and get hoyan."   "Then   it's you will have gotten home noon."

(20) Né· s kwí· né· tho   nitsyohtú·ne? tshiwahu·ní<u>se</u>?. (21) Né· núwa?
       So it's   it's that's how it was   a long time ago.   It's this time

kʌ́·tho wa?káhewe?, né· ki?   né· kʌ́·tho nʌ   tshiyotuhkóhtu   oye·lí·
here   time has come, it's actually it's here   then   when it has passed ten

nʌ   tshutahutáhsawʌ? wa?thuthoyá·n ka?ikʌ́ oyá· tsi? nitwʌtesú·<u>ne</u>?.
then   when they started   they did hoyan   this   other as   the week was long.

(22) Kwáh kati? wí· teyottenyuháti? kʌ́·,   yah náhte? tho té·tsyot
       Just   anyway it is changing   y'know, not   anything   thus it is not so anymore

tsi? s niyohtú·ne?, akwekú s né· ehta?késhu? yákwe?   kʌ́·
as   how it was,   all   it's on foot   we are going y'know

teyukwathoyanhtuháti?,   né· núwa? kʌh wa?káhewe?, kwáh
we are going along getting hoyan,   it's this time here time has come, just

we planned it, that the two of us would go together. (16) So then we went to get hoyan.
(17) It was just a little while before noon, we had gone to all the houses that belonged to
people close by. (18) My mother would say, early in the morning, "you should get up and
then go get hoyan." (19) "Then you will be home by noon." (20) So that's how it was a
long time ago. (21) Now the time has come, here it is past 10 o'clock when they started to
go out for hoyan the week before last. (22) Things are changing, nothing is the way it used
to be, we all walked to get hoyan, the time has come now,

loti?slenúti?   tho   wahutitahkoha·tú· latiksa?shúha tahatitakhenúti?,   shekú
they are riding along   there   they all got out   children   they come running,   even

né· ótya?k yah tha?tahotihʌ·léhte? "hoyá·n."   (23) Né· ki?   né·n   thikʌ́
it's   some   not   they won't holler   "hoyan."   It's   actually it's that that

kʌ? wa?úhkete? yeksá·, tayenhohaya?ákhu?   nʌ? né·.   (24) Nʌ   úhka?
here   she came by   girl,   she knocked on the door   that one.   When   anyone

tsha?enhotu·kó·,   nále?   elhúwa? wa?tyakohʌ·léhte? "hoyá·n."
when anyone opened the door,   then again   right then   she hollered   "hoyan."

(25) Tho   kyuhte wí· nikú   ka?ikʌ́ wá·kelhe? a·kwahlo·lí·   tsi? náhte?
        That's   supposedly how much this   I wanted   I should tell you all that what

kehya·lú·   hoyá·n. (26) Tho   ki?   ni·kú.
I remember   hoyan.   That's   actually how much.

they ride [in cars], the children all get out and come running, some of them won't even holler "hoyan." (23) A girl came by here, she knocked on the door. (24) When someone
opened the door, then only she hollered "hoyan." (You're supposed to yell "hoyan" outside
the house before you knock on the door, and not, like at Halloween, after someone opens the
door.) (25) I guess that's all I wanted to tell you about what I remember of hoyan.
(26) That's all.

Beaver, Let's Trade Teeth!

(Told by Mercy Doxtator to Karin Michelson on March 9, 2000)

(1) Tsi? náhte? ʌkka·látu?   kwahotokʌ́·u tho   niyawʌ́·u.
       That   what   I will tell a story   just for real   thus   it has happened.

(2) Tshiwahu·níse? kʌ́·   tshikeksá·   ké·yale? s thikʌ́ nále?
       A long time ago   y'know   when I was a child I remember   that   then again

wa?o?nétskane? knawí·ke, nʌ   thóha   a·katnawilota·kó·,   khále? aknulhá·
it became loose   my tooth,   then   almost   I would lose a tooth, and   my mother

(1) The story I will tell really happened. (2) A long time ago when I was a child I remember
my tooth got loose, I was about to lose a tooth, and my mother

ya?utáthʌle?   akwatauntie.   (3) Né· s thikʌ́ tho   wá·yuwe? kʌ́·,
she called over to her   my auntie.   It's   that   there she arrived y'know,

wa?utathlo·lí· kʌ́·   nále?   yo?nétskʌ knawí·ke, nʌ   thóha   a·katnawilota·kó·.
she told her   y'know then again it is loose my tooth,   now   almost   I would lose a tooth.

(4) Nʌ ki? ok wí· thikʌ́ tayúkhʌle?,   wa?í·lu?, "ká·ts"   wa?í·lu? "kátkʌs
    Right then   that   she called me over, she said,   "come here" she said "let me look

thikʌ́, nʌ   kʌ   tú·ske? yo?nétskʌ tsi? snawi·lóte?."   (5) Wa?kí·lu?
that,   now question it's true it is loose   at   you have a tooth."   I said

"hʌ́· o·nʌ́."   (6) Tahnú· s yah té·kelhe?   a·yuknawilotakó,   wá·kelhe? né· tsi?
"yes   now."   And   not   I don't want one would pull my tooth, I thought   because

yonuhwákte?, yah s kati? wí· óksa?   té·kelhe?   tho   ya?taáktan
it hurts,   not   so then   right away   I don't want there   I would stand over there

tsi? tyé·tlu?   kʌ́h,   khále? kwí· onʌ́ tho   ya?téktane?.   (7) Nʌ kwí·
at   she is sitting y'know, and   then there I stood over there.   So then

wa?tkátskalawe? thikʌ́, ókhna?   wa?í·lu?, "tó·   kátkʌs   ka?ikʌ́,
I opened my mouth that,   and then she said,   "how   let me take a look   this,

né· kʌ   ka?ikʌ́ tsi? ka·yʌ́· yo?nétskʌ," wa?kí·lu? "né· wáh."   (8) Ókhna?
it's question this   the one that it is loose," I said   "it is indeed."   And then

né· wa?ehnyota·kó·, yah náhte? só·tsi?   thye?wakattokʌ́, ókhna? né· tho
it's she pulled it out, not   anything too much   I didn't perceive,   and then it's   there

tyéhawe?   aknawi·lá·, nʌ kwí· tayu·kú·   kʌ́h. (9) Wa?í·lu?,
she is holding my tooth,   so then   she handed it to me see.   She said,

"ʌhsya·kʌ́ne?," wa?í·lu?, "nʌ   átste   ya?tʌ́stane?,   ʌ́ti nukwá·
"you will go out," she said,   "then   outside   over there you will stand, south

summoned my auntie. (3) So she got there, and she [my mother] told her that my tooth was
loose, I was about to lose a tooth. (4) Right away she called me over to her, she said, "come
here," she said, "let me take a look, is it true you have a loose tooth?" (5) I said, "Yes."
(6) And I didn't want my tooth to be pulled, I thought because it hurts, so I didn't want to
stand over there right away, where she was sitting, but then I did go stand over there. (7) So
then I opened my mouth, and then she said, "how about I take a look, is this the one that's
loose?," I said "it's the one." (8) And then she pulled it out, I didn't notice too much of anything, and then she was holding my tooth, so then she handed it to me. (9) She said, "go
out," she said, "stand outside,

nʌhsatye·lá<u>·te</u>ʔ.”   (10) “Thoʔnʌ́   ʌhsí·luʔ,   'tsyoní·tuʔ   tetyatatnawi·lú·.”
you will face."   "And then   you will say,   'beaver   let's you and I trade teeth '."

(11) “Ókhnaʔ” waʔí·luʔ, “ohná·kʌʔ nukwá· yʌsa·tí·   thikʌ́ n onawi·lá· kʌ́h.”
       "And then" she said,   "behind   you will throw that   tooth   see."

(12) Nʌ kwí· né· tho   ná·kye<u>le</u>ʔ.   (13) Tho kwí· thikʌ́ wakyenawá·ku,   tho
       So then   it's thus   I did.   There   that   I am holding onto it,   there

íkhaweʔ n   onawi·lá·, ókhnaʔ   waʔkí·luʔ, “tsyoní·tuʔ   tetyatatnawi·lú.”
I am holding   tooth,   and then   I said,   "beaver   let's you and I trade teeth."

(14) Ókhnaʔ   ohná·kʌʔ nukwá· yahukwa·tí· kʌ́h.   (15) Né· s aolí·waʔ   tho
       And then   behind   I threw it   see.   It's   the reason that's

ni·yót   tsiʔ yukhihlo·líheʔ, né· wí· tsiʔ tsyoní·tuʔ, yah kwí· teʔwé·ne tsiʔ
the way it is   that   they tell us,   because   beaver,   it's incredible   what

naʔtehanawili·yó·seʔ kʌ́·,   tahnú· kwahikʌ́ tsiʔ owísklaʔ ni·yót,   kháleʔ
nice teeth he has   y'know,   and   just really that   white   how it is,   and

kwahotokʌ́·u tsiʔ lanawili·yó·seʔ   kiʔwáh.   (16) Né· s kwí· aolí·waʔ   thikʌ́
just for real   that   he has nice teeth right.   So it's   the reason   that

yu·té·   akwatauntie kʌ́·, né· thikʌ́ tʌtsyatatnawi·lú·,   tho   katiʔ   ni·yót
she says   my auntie   see,   it's   that   you two will trade teeth,   that's   so then   how it is

nʌ   ʌsehsnawilo·táneʔ,   kwáh tshikʌ́ kanawiliyó   kʌ́h.   (17) Né· katiʔ wí·
then   you will get a tooth   just   for real   it is a nice tooth y'know.   So anyway it's
       again,

ní· thikʌ́ tho   niwakkaló·tʌ.   (18) Yah só·tsiʔ   teʔkaka·lés,
me   that   that's   the kind of story I have.   Not   too much   it is not a long story,

nók tsiʔ né· kiʔ   kwahotokʌ́·u tho   niyawʌ́·u.   (19) Tho   katiʔ wí·
but   it's actually   just for real   thus   it has happened.   That's   so anyway

face south." (10) "And then you will say 'beaver, let's trade teeth!'" (11) "And then," she
said, "throw the tooth behind you [over your shoulder]." (12) So then that's what I did.
(13) I held onto it, I held the tooth, and then I said, "beaver, let's trade teeth!" (14) And then
I threw it behind me. (15) The reason that's the way they tell us, is because it's incredible
what nice teeth the beaver has, and they are really white, and he has just really nice teeth.
(16) It's why my auntie said, you two will trade teeth, that way you will get another tooth, a
really nice tooth. (17) So anyway that's the story I have. (18) It's not too long a story but it
really happened. (19) That's

nikú   ka?ikʌ   wá·kelhe?   a·kka·látu?   kʌh.
how much   this   I wanted   I should tell a story   eh.

all I wanted to tell.

How to Divert a Storm

(Told by Mercy Doxtator to Karin Michelson on July 9, 2002)

(1)   Ú·wa?   tekníhatut,   wá·tlu?   tshusakaha·wí·   ohyótshe_li?_.   (2)   Tsi?   náhte?
      This time Tuesday,   nine   when again is the era string bean.   That   what

kathlolyá·ne?   ka?ikʌ   wʌhnisla·té· tsi? s náhte?   thonehtáhkwʌ   Ukwehuwé,
I am going to tell about   this   a day exists   that   what   they believe   Native people,

tá·t kʌs   yakʌ?   thikʌ   kwahikʌ   wʌhnisláksʌ,   tahnú· takawelaha·wí·,
if   customarily reportedly that   just really it is bad weather, and   wind is coming,

tsi? s nahati·yéle?   kʌ·   kwa?nyóh ok   uhkwata·sé·   ya·wét wʌhnisláksʌ;   tsi? s
what   they did   see   just seems like it went around like   it is bad weather; how

ni·yót tsi? thonehtáhkwʌ wahu?slo·tʌ·   kʌs.   (3)   Wakanúhte? kati? wí·
it is so that   they believe   they stood up an axe customarily.   I know   then

ka?ikʌ tsi? tho   ni·yót.   (4) Né· kwí· né·n   liyʌha   núwa?, tá·t kwa?nyóh
this   that   that's how it is.   It's   it's that my son   then,   if   seems like

kwahikʌ   i·wélhe? a·wʌhnisláksat,   tá·t núwa? kwahikʌ   tutayó·kalawe?,
just really it wants   it would be bad weather, maybe   just really it got dark again,

(1) Today it's Tuesday, the ninth of July, when again it's the time of the string bean.
(2) What I'm going to tell about today is what the Native people believe; they say if there is
really bad weather, and it is getting windy, what they do so that the bad weather kind of like
goes around [is diverted], the way they believe is that they drive an axe into the ground.
(3) I know that's how it is. (4) So my son, if it seems like the weather is going to get real
bad, maybe it's getting really dark,

takawelaha·wí· sÁ·,   nʌ sok wí· wahaya·kʌ́ne?, yaha?slo·tʌ́·;   né·n
wind came   also, so then too he went out,   over there he stood up an axe; it's that

to·kʌ́ske?, to·kʌ́ske? kʌs   ki?   thikʌ́ uhkwata·sé· n wʌhnisláksʌ,   yah
truly,   truly   customarily actually that   it went around it is bad weather, not

ní· tha?tayukwáhkwah<u>te</u>?. (5) Tho   kati? wí· ni·yót   ka?ikʌ́ tsi? thonehtáhkwʌ n
us   it won't strike us.   That's well then how it is this   that   they believe

Ukwehuwé   tsi? tho niyawʌ́·u.   (6) Tho   ki?   ok   ní· nikú
Native people that thus it has happened.   That's actually only me   how much

ka?ikʌ́ tsi?   ni·yót tsi? wakanúhte? thikʌ́ né· náhoh<u>te</u>?.
this   how   it is so that I know   that   it's   what it is.

it's getting windy too, so then he goes out, he plants an axe in the ground; so truly the bad
weather goes around [the axe and the weather is diverted], it doesn't strike us. (5) That's
then the way the Native people believe it happens. (6) That's how much how I know about
it.

Growing Up and Working

In the five narratives in this section the theme is working. As is evident from some of the stories in previous sections, Oneidas used to work at various jobs that required them to move from place to place, such as cutting wood or picking berries. This aspect of Oneida life was maintained from earlier generations. According to Campisi (1979, p. 488), during the early and mid-twentieth century many Oneidas depended on farming for subsistence, with people also working at woodcutting, making and selling baskets and husk rugs, picking fruit, and working in the tobacco and flax fields. The stories here talk about such seasonal work, how children learned to work and what kind of responsibilities they had, some of the hardships, and some of the good memories too.

When Georgina Nicholas recorded her story about what her life was like growing up, she intended her story to impress upon the young people of today that it was hard work at the time; her story gives lots of details about day-to-day life for those whose parents had their own farms on the Reserve. Her story takes us through fall, winter, spring, and summer. (Thanks to Olive Elm for help with translating Georgina Nicholas's story.) Clifford Cornelius chose also to deliver a message in his story, namely how important an education is nowadays; but he also relates some pretty hilarious episodes from his life.

Harvesting and preparing tobacco, at the time that Olive Elm, Mercy Doxtator, and Norma Kennedy are talking about, was quite a process. The leaves were picked and loaded into "boats" that were brought to the teams of workers. Two people would alternate handing three leaves to a "tier." The tier tied each bundle of three leaves handed to him or her with string that was located on a spool standing beneath a "horse." The horse was a set of two crossed poles, across which a stick was placed (so it looked much like a sawhorse). The tier would hang the tied bundle of three leaves on the stick. He or she would tie the next bundle without breaking the string and hang that bundle on the other side of the stick; the string was broken only when the stick was filled with thirty-two bundles, sixteen bundles on each side of the stick. All of this work was done while the tiers and handers were standing. The stick was then removed by one of the leaf-handers and placed on a pile. The pile of sticks was removed to the kill (kiln) for drying.

An Oneida Childhood

(Told by Georgina Nicholas in 1981)

(1) E·só· nʌ   waʔkanuhtunyu·kó· tsiʔ náheʔ nʌ   tyukliʔwanutú·se   a·kka·látuʔ
Lots   now   I thought it over   while   then   they have asked me   that I tell a story

tsiʔ ni·yót tsiʔ twakatotyáku.   (2) Náhteʔ uhte   kwáh tyoka·láyʌʔ
how   it is so   that   I have grown up.   What   supposedly   just   is the most value

a·kathlolyániʔ.   (3) Áhsok   thikʌ́ núwaʔ   waʔwʌ·téne̲ʔ.   (4) Yotká·teʔ
for me to tell about.   All of a sudden   that   this time   it became bright.   Often

kʌs wí·   né· wakathlolí úhkaʔ ok a·huwatika·látuhseʔ   latiksaʔshúha, tsiʔ né·
habitually   it's   I am telling   someone   one should tell them stories   children,   how   it's

nikayoʔtʌhslowanʌ́·neʔ? tsiʔ ní· nikaha·wí· tshiyakwaksaʔshúha.   (5) E·só· seʔ wí·
it was a big job   at   us   is the era   when we were children.   Lots   too

núwaʔ teyottenyá·u,   e·só· oʔsluniʔkéhaʔ?   tsiʔ   nitsyukwalihó·tʌ. (6) A·kí·luʔ
now   it has changed,   lots   white man's way what   our lifestyle is like.   I'd say

uhte wí·   tá·t núwaʔ áhsʌ niwáshʌ tá·thuniʔ áhsʌ niwáshʌ wísk niyohslaké
supposedly   maybe   three   tens   or else   three   tens   five   years amount to

onʌ́, kwahikʌ́ tsiʔ waʔoshno·láneʔ tsiʔ waʔtwatte·ní· tsiʔ ni·yót tsiʔ tyúnhe̲ʔ.
now,   just really   that   it accelerated   that   it changed   how   it is so   that   we live.

(7) Loti·kwáts   latiksaʔshúha. (8) Akwekú kakwatákwʌ nʌ   tsyoʔk náhteʔ,
They are well-off   children.   All   it is prepared   now   different things,

yah kwí· tho   teʔyoyoʔtʌhsláksteʔ tsiʔ né· niyohtú·neʔ   tshiwahu·níse̲ʔ.
not   thus   it is not heavy work   as   it's   how it was so   a long time ago.

(9) Kanúsku   yohne·kóteʔ,   kakwatákwʌ oniʔ kanúsku   tó·k ni·wá·
In the house   there is water,   it is prepared   also   in the house   a certain size

(1) I've thought a lot since I've been asked to tell the story about the way it was when I was growing up. (2) What is most important for me to tell about. (3) All of a sudden it dawned on me. (4) Often I'm saying people should tell stories to the children, there was such a lot of work at the time we were children. (5) A lot has changed, our ways are a lot like the white people's ways. (6) I'd say it's maybe thirty or thirty-five years now that it really has begun to change fast in the way we live. (7) The children are well-off. (8) Everything now is prepared [for them], the work is not so heavy as it was a long time ago. (9) In the house there's water, and also it's fixed inside the house something of a certain size

watnuhsataliha?tákhwa?, tyóktut kwí· ostúha yotékha?.   (10) Kwah nók
it is used to heat the house, always   a little   it is in flames.   Just

yʌyehwata·sé· tsi? niyo?talíhʌ teyakotuhutsyoní, ókhna? kok náhe? tayo?talíhʌ?.
one will turn it   how   it is warm   one wants,   and then   a little while   it warmed up.

(11) Lonanúhte? s lutyenahni·núhe? tó· ki? ok kwí· na?teka·lú·,   átste   tho
      They know   they sell oil   just so much   are the intervals, outside there

ʌthate?sléhtayʌ?,   tho kwí· tka?nahko·tú· ʌhayenátane?,   né· kwí· wateká·tha?
he will set his vehicle, there   there are drums   he will fill with oil, so it's   what it burns

kanuhsatalihá·tha?.   (12) Loti?slehtayʌ·tú· sʌ́·,   ʌhunúhtu? kwí· tsi? nú·
it heats the house.   They have cars   also,   they will decide   where

nyʌhʌ·né·,   ʌwa·tú· oni? kanatá·ke ʌhutʌna?tslahninú·na?,   né· oni?
over there they will go, it can be too   in town   they will go and buy groceries, it's too

né· tkanuhsowa·nʌ́·se?   tsyo?k nú· nikanuhso·tú·,   kwáh tsyo?k nahté·shu?
it's   there are large buildings all over   there are buildings, all kinds of things

lutʌhninúnyuhe?.   (13) Kwáh kwí· nók ʌhsé·sle?,   nʌ   tsyo?k náhte?
they sell things.   Just   you will drag it,   then all kinds of things

tho   ʌhsetáli?   tsi? náhte? tesatuhutsyo·ní. (14) Kʌ? s nukwá·
there you will put them in that   what   you want.   Right there

tho   tkakwatákwʌ, tho kwí· nú· yʌhʌ́hsewe?   nʌ   ʌsano·lú·se?
there it is prepared,   that's where you will arrive over there when you will tire of

shninúnyuhe?.   (15) Tho kwí· nú· ʌtyúshete?   tsi?   niyoka·lá·   náhte?
you are buying things.   That's where one will add up what   size is the cost   what

shninú·ne?.   (16) Kaluwalahlúni?   sʌ́· yuttsistótha?.   (17) Tsyo?k wí·
you intend to buy.   There are wires set up also one puts on lights.   All kinds of

to heat the house with [a furnace], and there's always a bit of a fire going. (10) All one has to do is turn [a knob] to however warm one wants, in a little while it will warm up. (11) The people who sell the oil know just how long between times, someone will park outside with a truck, there are drums there and he will fill them with oil, that's what is used for fuel and to heat the house with. (12) People have cars too, they can go where they want, they can even go to town to buy groceries, and there are big buildings all over, they sell all kinds of things. (13) All you have to do is push [a cart], you put all the things in there that you want. (14) Right there [a place] is set up, that's where you go when you get tired of shopping. (15) This is where someone will add up how much it costs what you are going to buy. (16) Also there are wires put up for lights.

nahté·shuʔ   ʌwa·tú·   tho   yaʔtʌyuhsútlʌʔ,   kanohalenyuʔtákhwaʔ
things   it can be   there   one will connect it over there,   it is used for washing

kastathá·thaʔ,   yuthnekalihaʔtákhwaʔ   yekhunyaʔtákhwaʔ,   kawistótha<u>ʔ</u>.
it dries it,   it is used for heating water   it is used for preparing food,   it cools it.

(18) Kwáh kiʔ tsyoʔk nahté·<u>shuʔ</u>.   (19) Yukwatluwalahlúniʔ sʌ́·
      Just all kinds of things.   We have wires set up   also

yutwʌnataʔá<u>staʔ</u>.   (20) ʌwa·tú· kwíʔ tʌyetha·lʌ́·   yáhtet
it is used for inserting one's voice.   It can be   one will converse   without

kwáh a·yenatá·laʔ   kátshaʔ ok nú·. (21) Kwáh kiʔ   yah náhteʔ
just   that one goes to visit   somewhere.   Just   actually   not   anything

teʔyoyoʔtʌhsláksteʔ kaʔikʌ́ nikaha·wí·, yah kwíʔ tehatiyʌtelí n   latiksaʔshúha
it is not heavy work   this   era,   not   they don't know about   children

tsiʔ   niyohtú·neʔ tshiwahu·ní<u>seʔ</u>. (22) Shekú né· ʌhutayaʔtá·naʔ   tho   oniʔ
what   it was like   a long time ago.   Even   it's   they will go to school   there   too

né· átste   kanuhsáktaʔ   ʌtwateʔsléhtayʌʔ,   ʌhutitáliʔ   ʌhutayaʔtá·<u>na</u>ʔ.
it's   outside   near the house   a vehicle will park,   they all will get in   they will go to school.

(23) Tho kwíʔ yʌwateʔsléhtayʌʔ   ʌhutitahkoha·tú·. (24) Né· oniʔ né· tsiʔ
      There   over there a vehicle will park   they all will get out.   It's   too   it's   how

nithotinuhsiyó   tsiʔ nú· yehutayá·<u>tha</u>ʔ.   (25) Elhúwaʔ kʌʔ nahéhaʔ
theirs is a nice building   where   over there they go to school.   Recently   a little while

tkanuhsísu<u>ʔ</u>.   (26) Yo·yʌ́· sʌ́· kawistóthaʔ, yah kwíʔ teʔyoʔtalíhʌ
then the building was finished.   It has   also   it cools it,   not   it is not hot

kwaʔkʌnhé·ke   lutayá·<u>tha</u>ʔ.   (27) Tsyoʔk sʌ́· náhteʔ   tho   kaké·luʔ   náhteʔ
in the summertime   they go to school.   All kinds of things also   there   it is strewn   what

(17) You can plug in all kinds of things, a washer and a dryer, a tea kettle and pots to cook
with, a refrigerator. (18) Just all kinds of things. (19) We also have wires put up to make
telephone calls. (20) You can talk without having to go and visit somewhere. (21) There's
nothing hard about the work nowadays, children don't know what it was like a long time
ago. (22) Even to go to school, there's a bus that parks right outside the house, they all get
in and they go to school. (23) The bus stops there and they all get out. (24) They have such
a nice building too where they go to school. (25) It was just a little while ago the building
was finished. (26) It has air conditioning too, so it's not hot in the summertime for those
that go to school. (27) There are also all kinds of things around

a·hʌ·nútsteʔ,   tsyoʔk wí·   naʔkayoʔtʌhsló·tʌʔ   a·hatiyʌtéhtaneʔ.   (28) Nʌ   kiʔ
for them to use, different   kinds of work   for them to learn.   Now   actually

ʌtkatáhsawʌʔ   ʌkka·látuʔ,   tsiʔ nahté·shuʔ ké·yaleʔ?   tshikeksáh.
I will start   I will tell a story, that   what all   I remember when I was a child.

(29) Atsyá·ktaʔ   tkanúhsoteʔ,   kanuhso·táhkweʔ   kiʔwáh, tekalu·tátuʔ.
      Near the river there is a house, there used to be a house I mean,   a log structure.

(30) Elhúwaʔ kiʔ   kʌʔ nahéhaʔ thotinuhsaká·tshi.   (31) Tho nú·
      Recently actually a little while they have dismantled a building.   That's where

ní· twakatotyáku.   (32) Lonulhá· kwí· Ukwehuwé   lonatnuhsu·ní.
me   I have grown up.   Them   Native people they have made a house.

(33) Kʌh nú·   tshahutnato·lʌ́neʔ.   (34) E·só· kyuhte wí· kalhayʌtú·
      Over here when they found a village.   Lots   supposedly there is a forest

tho nú·   tshikaha·wí·. (35) Nʌ kwí· wahatilutyá·khuʔ thikʌ́ wahutlutahslu·ní·,
that's when is the era.   So then they cut trees   that   they trimmed trees,

waʔthatilutaʔslúniʔ wahutshuhtúnyahteʔ.   (36) Wahatinawaʔtstálhoʔ kwí· tsiʔ
they stacked logs   they made a wall out of it.   They smeared mud   at

naʔtekutlúniʔ   tsiʔ naʔtekalutaʔslúniʔ.   (37) Tetsyalú kanúsku   nukwá·
there are intervals at   there are logs stacked.   Both   inside a house where

kháleʔ átste   nukwá·, tákʌʔ kwí· ta·kawelu·kót,   kháleʔ nʌ   ʌwataʔklo·kó·
and   outside where, so as not   air won't penetrate, and   when   it will snow

kháleʔ nʌ   ʌyokʌ·nóleʔ yah kwí· thaʔta·yu·kóhteʔ.   (38) Úska kiʔ ok kwí·
and   when   it will rain   not   it won't penetrate.   One   actually only

yonúhsuteʔ,   thok   nikanúhsaʔ   tsiʔ nikalute·sú·seʔ.
there is a room, thus only is the size of a house as   how long are the logs.

for them to use, for them to learn different kinds of work [trades]. (28) Now I will begin to
tell the story about all the things I remember when I was a child.

(29) Near the river is a house, there used to be a house I mean, a log house. (30) It was
just a little while ago they tore down this building. (31) That's where I grew up. (32) The
Indians were the ones who built the house. (33) When they first came to this place.
(34) There was a lot of forest here at that time. (35) So then they cut the trees and they
trimmed them, they stacked the logs and made walls out of them. (36) They smeared mud
between the layers of logs. (37) Both on the inside of the house and on the outside, so that
the draft wouldn't come through, and when it snows and when it rains, it won't come
through. (38) There was only one room, it was only as big as how long the logs were.

(39) É·nike kwí· yuní,   tho kwí· né· nú·   tyukwatnaktahlúni?   tsi? nú·
Upstairs   it is made, that's   it's where   we have beds put around   where

niyukwʌtá·sta?.   (40) Lotnaktunyáni?   thikʌ́ lake?níha o·yʌ́te? náhte?,
where we sleep.   He has made beds   that   my father   wood   what,

kwa?nyóh ok thihotnuto?tslunyáni? thikʌ́; yakotyalunyáni? aknulhá· thikʌ́,
seems just like   he has just made boxes   that;   she has made bags   my mother   that,

ʌnékli? s kwí· kanánhu?   ka?ikʌ́, tho nú·   niyakwanuhwétsta?.   (41) Né· s
straw   it is filled with   this,   that's where   we go to bed.   It's

thikʌ́ kohsla?ké·ne nʌ   tá·t só·tsi?   wa?tkanyo?kwata·sé·, wa?akwa·yé· s
that   wintertime   then if   too much   snow swirled,   we woke up

astéhtsi?,   kanye·yʌ́·   tsi? yakwana?skwaké·lu?.   (42) Yohtá·nawʌ s kwí· tsi?
in the morning,   snow is lying   at   we are nestled in bed.   It is warm   at

yukwʌ·tá·s   tsi?   yakau?wéskwanihe? aksótha   a·yutkʌhu·ní·,
we are sleeping   because   she enjoys   my grandmother   that she makes quilts,

né· s thikʌ́ yokʌhákste?,   tsyo?k náhte? atya?tawi?tho·kú·, wa?utkʌhúnyahte?.
it's   that   it is heavy cloth,   all kinds of   a bunch of coats,   she made quilts from it.

(43) Kwáh kwí· ikʌ́ yohtá·nawʌ?.
     Just really   it is warm.

   (44) Kanʌna?ké·ne kʌs   thikʌ́ lake?níha twa?kanhá·ke   nukwá·
      In the fall   habitually   that   my father   at the Chippewa's   where

yahahni·nú·,   tó· ki? ok kwí· nikálha?.   (45) Né· s thikʌ́ kohsla?ké·ne
over there he bought,   how only   big is the woods.   It's   that   wintertime

nʌ   wahayʌ·táko?, né· s kwí· wahatʌhni·nú·, nʌ kwí· tho   ni·yót   tsi? yakyúnhe?.
then   he cut wood,   so it's   he sold it,   so then   that's   how it is   that   we live.

(39) There was an upstairs, and that's where we had our beds and where we slept. (40) My father made the beds out of wood, it's kind of like boxes he made; my mother made ticks, they were filled with straw, that's where we slept. (41) In the wintertime if there was a bad snowstorm, we would wake up in the morning, there would be snow covering us where we lay nestled in our beds. (42) It was warm where we slept because my grandmother liked to make quilts, heavy cloth, from all kinds of old coats, that's what she used to make quilts. (43) It was really warm.

   (44) In the fall my father would go to the Chippewa side and buy [wood], however big the area with trees was. (45) In the wintertime he would cut the wood, he would sell it, and so then that's how we lived.

(46) Astéhtsiʔ s   thikʌ́ wahatkétskoʔ wahattsisti·yósteʔ,   wahaya·kʌ́neʔ,
     In the morning that   he got up   he made a good fire, he went out,

washakonutú·naʔ   laotshenʌ́ʔshúha kohsa·tʌ́s. (47) Tsiʔ s nihonʌskwi·yó·seʔ,
he went and fed them his animals   horse.   How   he has nice animals,

lolʌ́ʔnhá·u   ta·shakóshniʔ.   (48) Nʌ   ʌyutkétskoʔ   aknulhá·   nʌ
he knows how   he should care for them.   When she will get up my mother   then

ʌhuwakhúniʔ.   (49) Kwáh   kʌs   otokʌ́·u   waʔekhu·ní· thikʌ́,
she will cook for him.   Just   habitually for real she cooked   that,

waʔuteʔwahlu·tʌ́·, tayuthnʌnaʔtatalíhahteʔ,   waʔuteʔnhuhsu·tʌ́·, tayutnaʔtalu·tʌ́· s
she fried meat,   she warmed up potatoes also, she fried eggs,   she baked bread also

katsíhkoteʔ. (50) Kwáh s kwí· nʌ   waʔekhwísaneʔ,   nʌ   tutahatáyahteʔ,
a fist stands.   Just   then   she finished making a meal, then he came back in,

nʌ kwí· wahatekhu·ní·. (51) Tsiʔ náheʔ latekhu·níheʔ nʌ   ʌshuwatʌnaʔtslúniʔ
so then   he ate.   While   he is eating   then she will fix lunch for him

nʌʔú·waʔ. (52) Kwáh s kwí· kwahikʌ́   waʔtyehaʔúweʔekeʔ laotʌná·tsliʔ, aʔáhslaku
this time.   Just   just really she wrapped it up   his lunch,   in a basket

waʔakétaneʔ, ʌwa·tú· kwí· né· ostúha shekú ʌyoʔtalihʌ́hakeʔ nʌ   ʌhatekhu·ní·
she put it in, it can be   it's a little still   it will be warm   when he will eat a meal

ʌ́tye ni·kʌ́leʔ. (53) Shekú s tshaʔtetyó·kalas thikʌ́ ókhnaʔ né· wahathahítaneʔ.
noon time.   Still   when it is dark   that   already it's   he took to the road.

(54) Wahó·sleʔ waté·slehseʔ, wahayʌtakó·naʔ.   (55) Kwʌʔtáti? s lohtʌ́ti.
      He rode   cutter,   he went to cut wood.   All day   he has gone.

(56) Swatyelʌ́ s kiʔ   úhkaʔ ok wahónhaneʔ a·hoyaʔtakénhaʔ tá·t kwí· só·tsiʔ
      Sometimes   actually someone   he hired him   that he helps him   if   too much

(46) He would get up early in the morning and make a real good fire, he would go out, and
go feed his horses. (47) He had really nice horses, he knew how to take care of them.
(48) When my mother got up she would make him something to eat. (49) She would make a
whole meal, she fried meat, warmed up potatoes also, she fried eggs, also she made some
ovenbread. (50) She would just get done fixing his meal, then he came back in, and so then
he would eat. (51) While he was eating she would make his lunch. (52) She would wrap his
lunch up real good, she put it inside a basket, so it could still be a bit warm when he ate at
noon. (53) It was still dark and already he would be on the road. (54) He would ride on a
cutter, he would go to cut wood. (55) All day he was gone. (56) Sometimes he would hire
someone to help him if the logs were too big.

kalutowa·n<u>ʌ·se</u>ʔ.   (57) Nók tsiʔ né· kiʔ   né·n yotká·teʔ laulhaʔtsíwaʔ?
there are large trees.   But   it's actually it's often   by himself

ʌhayʌtá<u>ko</u>ʔ.   (58) Né· s nʌ   ʌ́shlaweʔ   shoyʌtakaʔtátiʔ,
he will cut wood.   It's   when   he will get home   again he has a lot of wood with him,

oniʔ aʔé· nihohlé·naʔ   thikʌ́; swatyelʌ́   yʌhatukóhtahkweʔ   kátshaʔ ok nú·
too   great is the size of pack that;   sometimes   he will go right on with it   somewhere

ʌhayʌtayʌ·hná·,   swatyelʌ́   tho   ʌhayʌtitáh<u>ko</u>ʔ.   (59) Né· s kwí· thikʌ́ nʌ
he will deliver wood, sometimes   there he will unload wood.   So it's   that   when

ʌ́shlaweʔ   nʌ   tʌhayʌtá·li<u>hte</u>ʔ.   (60) Tʌhayʌto·tʌ́·;   yá·yaʔk
he will get home   then   he will cut up wood.   There he will stack wood;   six

niyohsí·take   ni·yús   khále? áhsʌ niyohsí·take   nityótteʔ thikʌ́, skayʌ·tát
feet amount to it is long   and   three   feet amount to   it is high   that,   one cord

latinaʔtúkhwaʔ tsiʔ ni·yót   tsiʔ lutʌhni·nú<u>he</u>ʔ.
what they call it   how   is the way   that   they sell it.

   (61) Lakeʔníhaᴤ lohsótha   teyakwayás<u>he</u>.   (62) Né· s kwí· yakolʌʔnhá·u
           My father   his grandmother we stay together.   So it's   she knows how

a·yutaʔahslu·<u>ní</u>.   (63) Né· s kwí· nʌ   wahatluto·lʌ́neʔ kalutiyó   oʔnu·ná·,
that she makes baskets.   So it's   when   he found a tree   it is a nice tree   splints,

né· s kwí· tashakolutahawíhtʌ? lohsó<u>tha</u>.   (64) Shekú kwí· tshiyakotshá·nit
so it's   he brought her a tree   his grandmother.   Still   then she is industrious

lohsótha,   akaulhá· kʌᴤ   waʔehwá·e<u>ke</u>ʔ.   (65) Tó· kiʔ ok kwí· niwaʔslátiʔ
his grandmother,   her   habitually   she pounded it.   So much   it is wide

thikʌ́ ʌtwatlaʔnʌtáhsiʔ tsiʔ yakohwaʔehá<u>ti</u>ʔ.   (66) Waʔtyuhkwata·sé·,
that   it will peel off   as   she is pounding along.   She went all the way around,

(57) But most of the time he would be by himself cutting wood. (58) When he got home he
had a lot of wood with him, a great big pile of it; sometimes he would keep right on going to
deliver the wood somewhere, sometimes he would unload it [at home]. (59) When he got
home he would cut the wood up. (60) He would pile the wood; six feet long and six feet
high, they call this one cord and that's how they used to sell it.

   (61) My father's grandmother lived with us. (62) She really knew how to make baskets.
(63) So when he found a good tree for splints, he would bring it to his grandmother.
(64) His grandmother still could work hard, she would pound [the logs] herself.
(65) [Strips] just a certain width would come off as she kept pounding. (66) She went all the
way around [the log],

né· s thikʌ́ nʌ   waʔutyé·nihteʔ   né· núwaʔ sayútyʌʔ   thikʌ́;
it's   that   when   she accumulated enough   it's   then   she sat down again   that;

o·wíseʔ s thikʌ́ wá·yutsteʔ waʔe·kéteʔ,   kwáh kwí· ikʌ́ waʔtyostalátheneʔ
glass   that   she used   she scraped it,   just really   it got shiny

kaló·   tsiʔ niyo·lé· tayutáhsawʌʔ waʔutaʔahslu·ní·.   (67) Tho s kwí·
before   until   she started   she made a basket.   That's

wakhlʌʔtú·nehseʔ thikʌ́ tsiʔ yakoyoʔtátyehseʔ.   (68) Nók tsiʔ yah kiʔ
I am tagging along   that   as   she goes around working.   But   not   actually

nuwʌtú teʔyukwateʔkwáhtu,   a·yaí·luʔ   "wáhs, kʌʔ nukwá· nyahá·se,
never   she didn't chase me away,   for her to say   "go,   right here   go over there,

tákʌʔ tʌskeʔnikulha·lʌ́." (69) Tho s kwí· né· ni·yót   tsiʔ waʔakwayʌtéhtaneʔ
don't   you will bother me."   That's   it's   how it is that we learned

oh náhteʔ a·yukwayo·tʌ́· tshiyakwaksaʔshúha.   (70) Kwah nók yukwatló·lu.
anything   that we work   when we were children.   Just   we are watching.

(71) Swatyelʌ́ s thikʌ́ waʔkheyaʔtakénhaʔ, kʌʔ kiʔ ok kwí· ni·ká·,
      Sometimes   that   I helped her,   little only   size I am,

yah kiʔ   tha·yaí·luʔ,   "tákʌʔ kʌʔ nyʌhʌ́hsyel." (72) Né· thikʌ́ tó·k nikú
not   actually she won't say,   "don't   you will touch it."   It's   that   some amount

waʔutaʔahslu·ní· thikʌ́, tho   áktaʔ   watukóthaʔ tyoʔslehtá·kat, kwáh kanuhsáktaʔ s
she made baskets   that,   there   nearby it passes by train,   quite   near the house

tho   tkalistatátiʔ.   (73) Yah kwí· teʔwinú   tkanúhsoteʔ   tsiʔ nú· ʌwa·tú·
there tracks extend.   Not   it is not far   there is a house where   it can be

ʌyutítaneʔ.   (74) Tsiʔ nú· naʔteka·tá·seʔ. (75) Ké·yaleʔ   thikʌ́, ó· tá·t núwaʔ
one will get on.   Where   it stops.   I remember   that,   oh maybe

when she had enough [strips] she would sit down; she would use a piece of glass to scrape
them, they would get really smooth before she started to make a basket. (67) I would be
following her around as she was working. (68) But she never chased me away, for her to
say "go, get away from here, don't bother me." (69) This is how we learned to work at
things when we were children. (70) Just from watching. (71) Sometimes I would help her, I
was just a little person, but she wouldn't say, "don't touch that." (72) She would make several baskets, the train used to go nearby there, right near the house was where the tracks used
to go. (73) Not too far away there was a building where you could get on [the train].
(74) Where it stops. (75) I remember, oh, maybe

áhsʌ   tshaʔtewakohsliyá·ku   thikʌ́,   waʔukékwahteʔ   waʔákneʔ
three   when I have crossed over winters   that,   she invited me   we two went

waʔakyataʔahslahninú·naʔ   Sʌhtamís.   (76) Waʔakyathleʔnítaneʔ   kiʔwáh.
we two went and sold baskets   St. Thomas.   We two put our packs in   right.

(77) Wé·ni kwí· yaʔakyanú·weteʔ.   (78) Yusayólhʌneʔ   tutayakyatítaneʔ
        Evidently   over there we two slept over.   The next day   we two got on again

thikʌ́; kwáh tho   nitsyakohleʔnakaʔtátiʔ   tsiʔ ni·yót   tshaʔakyahtʌ·tí·,
that;   just   thus   again she has along a lot of packs   as   how it is   when we two went away,

né· yotká·teʔ kwah nók tʌyenu·wáyʌhteʔ náhteʔ ʌyutaʔahslahni·nú·.   (79) Swatyelʌ́ s
it's   often   just   she will trade   what   she will sell baskets.   Sometimes

kiʔ   né· ohwístaʔ tayuta·tú·.
actually it's   money   one gave it to her.

  (80) Nʌ kwí· né· tshiyutayá·thaʔ   yukeʔkʌ́ha.   (81) Wísk
          So then   it's   when she goes to school   my older sister.   Five

niyohslaké   naʔteyakyátleʔ;   kwáh s kʌʔ niyo·lé·   tkanúhsoteʔ
years amount to   we two are apart;   quite   some distance   there is a house

tyutatlihunyʌní·thaʔ.   (82) Kwáh kwí· tshaʔtewahsʌnʌ́ tsiʔ ni·wá·   Ukwehuwé·ne.
there they teach them.   Just   half   as   is the size   the Reserve.

(83) Shekú kiʔ   núwaʔ tho   tkanúhsoteʔ.   (84) Kalistaʔkéshuʔ s kwí·
        Still   actually   now   there   there is a house.   Along the railway tracks

nyahá·yʌʔ   thikʌ́ waʔutayaʔtá·naʔ.   (85) Úska katiʔ wí· útlatste?
she went over there   that   she went to school.   One   well   time

thikʌ́ astéhtsiʔ   waʔukeslʌhto·lí· waʔí·luʔ, "ʌ́tneʔ   kʌ́h."
that   in the morning she woke me up   she said, "you and I will go   question."

I was three years old, she invited me to go with her to sell baskets in St. Thomas. (76) We would put our bundles [on the train]. (77) We must have stayed there overnight. (78) The next day we would get back on [the train]; she would have just as many bundles with her as she had when we went away, [because] often she would just make trades with the baskets she had for sale. (79) Sometimes though they gave her money.

  (80) My older sister was already going to school. (81) We were five years apart; it was quite a ways to where the school was. (82) It was right in the middle of the Reserve. (83) That building is still there. (84) She would walk along the railroad tracks to go to school. (85) One time she woke me up early in the morning and she said, "do you want to come with me?"

(86) Tsi? kwí· náhe? wa?katslu·ní· thikʌ wa?ukhiyatʌna?tslúni? ki? wí·, khále?
    While   I got dressed that   she fixed lunch for us   actually, and

wa?ekwata·kó· a·yakyatekhu·ní·   astéhtsi?.   (87) Shekú kwí· né·
she prepared it for us two to eat a meal in the morning.   Still   it's

loti·tá·s   lake?níha khále? aknulháh.   (88) Wé·ni kwí· wahyáttoke?
they are sleeping my father and   my mother.   Evidently   the two noticed

aknulhá·   khále? lake?níha tsi? wa?kataya?tá·na?, yah ki?
my mother and   my father that I went to school,   not   actually

te?tyukihnúksu.   (89) Tóhka? kwí· niwʌhnislaké   thikʌ wa?ákne? s
they did not come after me.   A few   days amount to that   we two went

wa?akyataya?tá·na?.   (90) Kʌkwité·ne kwí· ka?ikʌ tshutakatáhsawʌ?. (91) Wísk
we two went to school.   Springtime   this   when I started.   Five

uhte wí·   tsha?tewakohsliyá·ku.   (92) Áhsok   thikʌ nʌ ukno·lú·se?
supposedly when I have crossed over winters.   All of a sudden that   now I tired of it

tsi? katayá·tha?, yah té·kelhe? a·katkétsko?. (93) Wahʌ·lu? lake?níha, "hányo
that I go to school, not I don't want that I get up.   He said   my father, "come on

ka?ikʌ" wahʌ·lu? "satkétsko." (94) "Isé· wí· íhselhe? a·hsataya?tá·na?,
this"   he said   "get up."   "You   you want that you go to school,

tasku·ták kwí· nʌ satáyaht."   (95) Nʌ kwí· yah thye?wakyelʌ   yahá·ksane?
persist   now go to school."   So then   not   I could not help it I finished

wa?katáyahte?. (96) Kanʌna?ké·ne kwí· thikʌ nále?   tutayakyatáhsawʌ?
I went to school.   In the fall   that   then again again we two began

sayakyatáyahte?.   (97) Nʌ kwí· tho na?tewakohsliyá·ku   tsi?
again we two went to school.   So then thus I have crossed over winters as

(86) So while I was getting dressed she made lunch for the two of us, and she fixed us something to eat for breakfast. (87) My father and mother were still sleeping. (88) My mother and father must have noticed that I went to school, but they didn't come after me. (89) A few days I went to school with her. (90) This was springtime when I started. (91) I guess I was five years old. (92) All of a sudden I got tired of going to school, I didn't want to get up. (93) My father said, "come on," he said "get up." (94) "You're the one who wanted to go to school, so you keep going to school." (95) So then I had no choice but to finish going to school. (96) In the fall we started to go to school again. (97) So then I was at that age

nityutahsáwhaʔ aʔyutáyahte̱ʔ.   (98) Tsiʔ s niyotho·lé· thikʌ́ kohslaʔké·ne,
how one starts   that one goes to school.   How   it is cold   that   wintertime,

nók tsiʔ yah kwí· thya·ya·wʌ́· tsiʔ waʔakyatayaʔtá·naʔ,   astéhtsiʔ s   thikʌ́
but   it has to be   that   we two are going to school,   in the morning   that

waʔakyahtʌ·tí·, tho s kwí· yukyatnutolyaʔtuháti̱ʔ,   swatyelʌ́ s tho   onyʌhtá·ke
we two left,   there   we two are going along playing,   sometimes   there   on the snow

tho   waʔakyataʔáhslayʌʔ   ukyatʌná·tsliʔ   tsiʔ náheʔ waʔakyatnutólyahteʔ
there   we two set down our baskets we two, our lunch   while   we two played

kʌʔ nahéhaʔ, waʔakyatu·kóhte̱ʔ.   (99) Né· yaʔákneweʔ kwí·   yutatlihunyʌní·thaʔ,
a short while,   we two continued on.   It's   we two got over there   they teach them,

ostúha né· tyonuhsatho·lé· wí·   tsiʔ nú· niyakwayʌtákhwaʔ ukwatʌná·tsheli̱ʔ.
a little   it's   it is a very cold building where   we store   our lunch.

(100) Tho s kwí· thikʌ́ ʌ́tye ni·káleʔ thikʌ́ nʌ   yaʔkáheweʔ a·yakwatekhu·ní·,
          There   that   noon   time   that   then   it came time   that we eat a meal,

yowislátuʔ né·n   akwatʌná·tsliʔ, aʔé· s kwí· ni·wá·   thikʌ́ yenʌstalihaʔtákhwaʔ
it has frozen   it's that   my lunch,   great   is the size   that   stove

tho   ká·nyoteʔ,   tho s kwí· yotékhaʔ   thikʌ́, tho kwí· wá·khlʌʔ akná·talok,
there   it is standing, there   a flame burns   that,   there   I set   my bread,

sakawistana·wʌ́· nʌ   waʔkatekhu·ní̱·.
it thawed again   then   I ate a meal.

   (101) Kháleʔ kwí· nʌ   tho   ni·ká·   ʌwa·tú· s ostúha ʌwakyo·tʌ́·.
              And   then   thus   I am so big   it can be   a little   I will work.

   (102) Kanúsku s kwí· né· nukwá· yakoyo·té· n   yukeʔkʌ́ha.
              Inside the house   it's   where   she is working   my older sister.

when they start to go to school. (98) It would be so cold in the wintertime, but we had to go
to school, in the morning we would leave, and we would play along the way, sometimes we
would put our baskets with our lunch in them down on the snow while we played for a short
while, and then we would go on. (99) We would arrive at the school, and it would be quite
cold in this room where we kept our lunch. (100) At noon when it was time for us to eat, my
lunch would be frozen, there was a great big stove, it had a fire going in it, so put my bread
on it, it would thaw out and then I'd eat.

   (101) And then I was old enough that I could work a little. (102) My older sister was
working inside.

(103) Sayáknewe? s   thikʌ́ yukyataya?tahnu·hné·,   né· kwí· né· ʌkkwe·ní·
       We two got home that   we two have gone to school, it's   it's I will be able

ʌkyʌtínyuhte?   ki?wáh.   (104) A?é· s nikanutó·tsla?   thikʌ́ tsi? ká·nyote?
I will bring in wood right.   Great   is the size of box that   at   it is standing

yenʌstaliha?tákhwa?, ohná·kʌ? tho   tka·yʌ́·,   yah kwí· thya·ya·wʌ́ne? tsi? kwáh
stove,   behind   there it is there, it has to be   that just

ʌ́knane? thikʌ́ kaló·   tsi? niyo·lé· tʌtyó·kalawe?. (105) Yah s sʌ́·   thya·ya·wʌ́· tsi?
I will fill it that   before until   it will get dark.   Not   also   it has to be that

wa?ketsyʌ́·na?,   waté·slehse? s kwí· thikʌ́ wa?ké·sle? ohná·kʌ? tsi? tyakwanákle?,
I went after water, sleigh   that   I dragged it behind   at   we reside,

tho   tka?náhkote?   thikʌ́ yohnáwelote?, tyótkut kwí· yonathnekahtʌtyuháti?.
there there is a barrel that   a spring,   always   water is travelling.

(106) Tho s kwí· nú· ya?kétsyʌhte?,   kwahikʌ́ kahneki·yó.   (107) Khále?
       That's where   over there I drew water, just really it is good water.   And

kwí· onʌ́ thikʌ́ kanuhsákta?   wahathneku·ní· lake?níha. (108) Wa?thatinʌ·yátu?.
then   that   near the house he built a well   my father.   They erected stones.

(109) Nʌ kwí· yah te?swinú   yusayétsyʌhte?.
       So then   not it is not far anymore for one to draw water over there again.

   (110) Kʌkwité·ne thikʌ́ nʌ   né· núwa?   yusakáhewe?   usayakwayʌthóhslu?.
           Springtime that   then it's this time it came time again that again we plant.

(111) Tsi? s nikaha·wí· tehati?nhúhsya?ks thikʌ́, nʌ   tahatáhsawʌ?
       At   is the era   they break eggs   that,   then he started

wahathʌtahslunyáni?. (112) Wa?thahnʌna?tá·lihte? thikʌ́ a·yakwayʌ́tho?.
he prepared fields.   He cut up potatoes   that   for us to plant.

(103) We would get home from school, it would be up to me to bring wood inside.
(104) There was a great big box where the stove was, it was behind [the stove], I would have
to fill this right up before it got dark. (105) Also I would have to go and get water, so I
would pull this sleigh and in the back of where we lived, there was a barrel and a spring, and
it was always running with water. (106) That's where I used to get the water, really good
water. (107) And then my father built a well near the house. (108) They put stones around
it. (109) Then it wasn't too far to get water.
   (110) In the springtime it was time for us to do the planting. (11) At Easter he would start
preparing the fields. (112) He would cut up potatoes for us to plant.

(113) Né· s   thikʌ́   wahakalhátho?,   tetsyalúhkwʌ   nukwá·   wa?thathʌto·tʌ́·   ki?wáh.
      It's   that   he ploughed,   both sides   where   he piled the field   right.

(114) Kwáh   ki?   kʌ? niyáki?,   né·   sʌ́·   latiksa?shúha   tho   ákta?
      Quite   actually   some number of us,   it's   also   children   there   close by

latinákle?   washakónhane?,   wa?ukwahnʌna?tu·tí·   kwí·   tó·k na?teka·lú·,
they reside   he hired them,   we dropped potatoes   some intervals,

tsyohsi?tátshu?   kwí·   na?teka·lú·,   nʌ   wa?ukwahnʌna?tu·tí·.   (115) Thó·ne? nʌ
one foot each   intervals,   then   we dropped potatoes.   And then

tahakalhátho?.   (116) Tóhka?   kwí·   na?tʌhahkwata·sé·   ʌshakalhátho?,
he ploughed.   Several   he will go all the way around   again he will plough,

nále?   ʌtsyonʌhlo·tʌ́·   ʌtsyukwahnʌna?tu·tí·.   (117) Tóhka? s kwí·
then again   again a gang will form   again we will drop potatoes.   A few

nikaya·láke   wa?akwayʌ́tho?.   (118) Ʌyakwáhsane?   thikʌ́   nʌ   ʌtsyólhʌne?
sacks amount to   we planted.   We will finish   that   then   the next day

tʌha?kʌhlá·lihte?.   (119) Tóhka?   niwʌ·táke   thikʌ́   tʌsha?kʌhlá·lihte?
he will break up earth.   A few   weeks amount to   that   he will break up earth again

thikʌ́   tsi? nú·   nʌyakwayʌ́tho?   kʌ? nikanʌhá·sa?.   (120) Né· s   thikʌ́   ahsli·yé·
that   where   we will plant   small seeds.   It's   that   string

atahslá·ke   kahwanhákhu?,   né· kwí·   ʌtyakwayanáhawe?   ʌyottakwalihsyúhake?
on a stick   it is tied all around,   so it's   we will follow the track   it will be straight

tsi?   ʌyakwayʌ́tho?.   (121) Thó·ne? nʌ   thikʌ́   tho   ále?   tʌtyakwa?kʌhlá·lihte?,
at   we will plant.   And then   that   there   again   we will break up earth,

yuneklalohlókta?   ʌyákwatste?   thikʌ́;   kwáh kwí· ikʌ́   wa?kʌhliyó,   né·   núwa?
rake   we will use   that;   just really   it is good earth,   it's   then

(113) He would start to plough, piling up [the earth] on both sides. (114) There was quite a
few of us, and also he would hire the children who lived close by, we would drop the potatoes in rows, rows that were one foot apart, we dropped the potatoes. (115) And then he
would plough some more. (116) Several times he would go around ploughing, then a bunch
of us would start dropping potatoes again. (117) We planted a few bags. (118) We would
finish and then the next day he would disk [break up the earth]. (119) In a few weeks he
disked again where we would plant small seeds. (120) Strings were tied to sticks, this is
what we would go by so that [the rows] would be straight where we plant. (121) And then
we would break up more ground, we used a rake; it was really good earth, then

kanʌhékliʔ ʌyákwatsteʔ thikʌ́ ʌyakwáhatatsteʔ.   (122) Neʔ thó·neʔ nʌ
seeder (?) we will use   that   we will make a straight path.   And then

ʌyukwanʌhu·tí·,   tutayukwaʔkʌhlu·tí·. (123) Yah kwí· só·tsiʔ?   thaʔteyóhses.
we will drop seeds, again we threw earth.   Not   too much   it is not deep.

(124) Kwáh kwí· tsyoʔk nahté·shuʔ yukwayʌ́thu,   kwáh tsyoʔk naʔkahtehló·tʌhseʔ.
       All kinds of things   we have planted, all kinds of   roots.

(125) OnuʔuslaʔshúHa. (126) O·nʌ́steʔ, osahé·taʔ. (127) Kwáh s kwí· aʔé·
       Pumpkins.   Corn,   beans.   Just   great

niyukwahʌ·tá·   thikʌ́; tóhkaʔ s kwí· niwʌhnislaké thikʌ́ waʔukwatye·náwasteʔ
is the size of our field that; a few   days amount to that   we used up time to do it

waʔakwayʌ́tho. (128) Á·nuk, waʔakwaʔnukslotúni? s nʌʔ né·,   tó· kiʔ ok kwí· né·
we planted.   Onions, we stood up onions   the ones, so much only   it's

naʔteka·lú·. (129) O·nʌ́steʔ kháleʔ osahé·taʔ, né· né·n atshó·ktaʔ kwí· né·
intervals.   Corn   and   beans,   it's that hoe   it's

ʌyákwatsteʔ ʌyakwakahlu·táteʔ tsiʔ nú· né· nʌ   ʌyukwasaheʔtu·tí· kháleʔ
we will use   we will make holes   where   it's when   we will drop beans   and

ʌyukwanʌstu·tí·. (130) Onuʔúsliʔ kwáh s né· aʔnyóh waʔakwatunyáni?
we will drop corn.   Melons   just   it's seems   we made here and there

thikʌ́ teyothweʔnuní thikʌ́ kwaʔnyóh é·nike tyótteʔ, tho   waʔakwakahlu·táteʔ,
that   it is a round pile that   just seems up   it is high, there   we made holes,

yakwasnú·ke s kwí· waʔákwatsteʔ, tho nú·   naʔukwanʌhu·tí·. (131) Nʌ kwí·
our fingers   we used,   that's where   we dropped seeds.   So then

núwaʔ   né· ʌtyakwatnúhtuhteʔ a·yotiké·tohteʔ.   (132) Tóhkaʔ s kwí·
this time it's we will wait   for them to appear.   A few

we used a seeder (?) to make straight rows. (122) We dropped the seeds in there, and we
threw earth on them. (123) Not too deep. (124) We planted all kinds of things, all kinds of
roots. (125) Pumpkins. (126) Corn, beans. (127) We used to have a big garden, so it would
take us a few days to plant. (128) Onions, we stood those, just so far apart. (129) For the
corn and the beans, we would use a hoe to make holes where we would drop in the beans
and the corn. (130) For the melons we would make mounds kind of high, we made holes
using our fingers, that's where we would drop in the seeds. (131) So then we would wait for
them to come up. (132) After a few

niwʌ·táke   thikʌ́ nʌ   tayotiké·toht<u>e</u>ʔ. (133) Nʌ kwí· né· onʌ́   yah thya·ya·wʌ́·
weeks amount to   that   then they appeared.   So then it's   then it has to be

tsiʔ ʌyakwatʌneklóskaluʔ;   tho s kwí· né· naʔteka·lú· thikʌ́ yohaténiʔ,   ʌwa·tú·
that   we will hoe;   thus   it's far apart   that   there are rows, it can be

tʌhanaʔkʌshlo·lʌ́·; tsiʔ kwí· naʔtekutlúniʔ ʌyakwaneklóskaluʔ tá·thuniʔ ʌyakwaté·sleʔ
he will harrow;   at   intervals   we will hoe   or else   we will crawl

ʌyakwaneklota·kó· tá·t só·tsiʔ   áktaʔ yotanekluní tsiʔ nú· niyukwayʌthóhs<u>lu</u>ʔ.
we will pick weeds   if   too much   close   weeds grow   where   we have planted things.

(134) Náleʔ   yusakáheweʔ usayakwahnʌnaʔtayʌ́thoʔ,   né· kwí· né·n
       Then again   it's time again for us to plant potatoes again, so it's   it's that

kohslaʔké·ne ʌyakwahnʌná·tak<u>e</u>ʔ. (135) Kháleʔ o·nʌ́steʔ kháleʔ osahé·taʔ, né· kwí·
wintertime   we will eat potatoes.   And   corn   and   beans,   so it's

né· onʌ́ ʌwatunísaneʔ.   (136) Ukwehuwehnéhaʔ kwí· o·nʌ́steʔ kháleʔ
it's   then it will finish growing.   Native   corn   and

Ukwehuwehnéhaʔ osahé·taʔ. (137) Tóhkaʔ kʌs kwí· niyotityóhkwake osahé·<u>ta</u>ʔ.
Native   beans.   A few   habitually groups amount to   beans.

(138) First of July kʌs   thikʌ́ ókhnaʔ né· yaʔkáheweʔ au·tú·
       First of July   habitually that   already   it's it's that time   it could be

a·yakwahnʌná·tak<u>o</u>ʔ. (139) Kháleʔ o·nʌ́steʔ sʌ́h. (140) Nʌ kwí· nʌ
that we pick potatoes.   And   corn   also.   So then   then

ʌtsyakwahnʌná·takoʔ   thikʌ́; tsiʔ s tyoháhuteʔ   thikʌ́ tho
we will pick potatoes again that;   at   there's a laneway   that   there

tayakwathyatuhslo·tʌ́·, náleʔ   yaʔkáheweʔ a·yakwathnʌnaʔtahni·nú· kháleʔ
we put up a paper,   then again   it's that time   for us to sell potatoes   and

weeks they would come up. (133) So then we would have to hoe; the rows were far enough
apart, so that he could harrow; we would hoe between the rows or else we would crawl and
take out the weeds if the weeds were growing too close to where we planted. (134) And
then it was time for us to plant potatoes again, and we would eat these potatoes in the wintertime. (135) And the corn and beans would be ripe. (136) Indian corn and Indian beans.
(137) There would be a few varieties of beans. (138) First of July it was already time for us
to pick the potatoes. (139) And the corn too. (140) So then we would pick potatoes again;
at the end of the laneway we put up a sign, it was time for us to sell potatoes and

a·yakwatnʌstahni·<u>nú</u>·. (141) Kwáh kwí· tsyoʔk náhteʔ shekú ohyótsliʔ, né· kwí·
for us to sell corn. All kinds of things even string beans, so it's

núwaʔ ʌtsyukwayo·tʌ́· ʌtsyakwatʌhni·nú·; swatyelʌ́ s tsiʔ naʔteyukwayenhalá·u
this time we will work again we will sell again; sometimes how we have been busy

thikʌ́ yukwatʌhni·<u>nú</u>·. (142) Swatyelʌ́ s waʔakwathnʌnaʔtó·ktʌʔ,
that we have been selling. Sometimes we ran out of potatoes,

yah kwí· thya·ya·wʌ́· tsiʔ sakhnʌnaʔtakó·naʔ, náleʔ kok náheʔ oyá·
it has to be that again I went and got potatoes, then again a little while other

tho sayuteʔsléhtayʌʔ.
there again someone parked their car.

for us to sell corn. (141) All kinds of things, even butter beans, so we would work to sell these; sometimes we would be really busy selling. (142) Sometimes we ran out of potatoes, so I had to go and get more potatoes, [because] in a little while someone else would stop.

A Lifetime Working
(Told by Clifford Cornelius to Mercy Doxtator in 1994)

(1) Shekóli swakwe·<u>kú</u>. (2) Kaluhyʌtí ní· yúkyats kaʔikʌ́ tahnú·
Greetings all of you. Blue Sky Going By me is my name this and

Ukwehuwé·ne knáke<u>le</u>ʔ. (3) Tahnú· yá·yaʔk niwáshʌ yá·yaʔk
at the Native people's I reside. And six tens six

tewakohsliyá·ku. (4) Yah akwáh só·tsiʔ teʔkehya·lú·
I have crossed over winters. Not quite too much I don't remember things

tsiʔ nú· tshikaha·wí· kwahikʌ́ tsiʔ tshikeksá·, yah katiʔ akwáh só·tsiʔ
where is the era just really when I was a child, not well then quite too much

(1) Greetings to all of you. (2) Blue Sky Going By is my name and I live on the settlement. (3) And I'm sixty-six years old. (4) I don't really remember too much around the time I was a child, so I don't really

te?wakkalaká·te?   a·kwahlolyányu?,   nók tsi? ké·yale?   ki? n   lake?nihkʌ́
I don't have many stories for me to tell you all,   but   I remember actually my late father

wahu·níse?   Dorchester s nú·   yeyakwanaklátyehse?,   latiyʌtákwas
a long time ago   Dorchester   where   over there we reside all around,   they cut wood

khále?   teyakwatʌhnu·téle?   tehniyáshʌ.   (5) Nʌ   né·   kwáh s   tsha?tehnikwanʌ́
and   we are siblings   two.   Then   it's   just   the two are big

thikʌ́ ne? thó·ne?, nʌ   kʌs   né· lotiyo·té·   lake?níha oskánhʌ,
that   at that time,   then habitually it's they are working   my father   together,

ya·wét   kyuhte wí· a·kí·lu? luwaya?takénhas tsi?   tehatʌ́·tsha?as ne? thó·ne?.
kind of like supposedly I'd say   they help him   as   he earns   at that time.

(6) Kwáh kʌs ikʌ́ tsi? wʌtoláti?   tsi? tyakyúnhe?, nók tsi? shekú ki?
     Just really   it is going along hard as   we live,   but   still   actually

lotiyo·té·   kwahikʌ́ tsi? watyesʌ́,   tóhka? ok   kwénis   tehutʌ́·tsha?as.
they are working   just really   it is cheap, a few   only   pennies   they earn.

(7) Nók tsi? lotiyo·té·   kʌs   kih.   (8) Né· kati? wí·   a?é·
     But   they are working habitually indeed.   Well anyway it's   way over

Dorchester nú·   yeyakwanákle?,   nʌ   tho   tsha?tewakohsliyá·ku wí·
Dorchester   where we reside over there,   then   that's   when I have crossed over winters

a·kataya?tá·na?,   tho   kati? nú·   ostúha yewakatayá·tu.
I could go to school, that's   well   where   a bit   over there I have gone to school.

(9) Tóhka? niwʌhní·take   u·tú·   wa?katáyahte? tahnú·   nok u·tú·
     A few   months amount to it could be I went to school and then   it had to be

wa?akwanakla·kó·, wahuthwehnota·kó·   tsi? nú· nihatiyʌtákwas, ákte?
we moved away,   they finished working the area where   they cut wood,   different

have too many stories to tell you, but I do remember my late father and us, a long time ago
we lived all around Dorchester, they were cutting wood, and my two brothers. (5) They
were both already pretty big at that time, so they were working together with my father then,
I guess I could say they were helping him earn [money] at that time. (6) Those were hard
times just to survive, but still they worked though [labour] was really cheap, they made only
a few pennies. (7) But they worked. (8) Well anyway we were living over in Dorchester,
that's when I was old enough I could go to school, so that's where I got a bit of schooling.
(9) I could go to school for a few months and then we had to move away, they got done
working the area where they were cutting wood,

núwaʔ   nú·   nyusayákoh.   (10) Né·   aolí·waʔ   só·tsiʔ   yah
this time   where   again we went over there.   It's   the reason   too much   not

teʔwakhyatuhslayʌtelé·u tsiʔ   tyótkut nók yukwanaklakwʌhátiʔ tshikeksá·,
I didn't get book learning   because   always   only   we are going moving   when I was a child,

kwáh kʌs   kok náheʔ   kátshaʔ ok nú· yeyakwanákleʔ   ókhaleʔ   wahatíhsaneʔ
just   habitually   a little while   somewhere   we reside over there   and   they finished

latiyʌtákwas ókhaleʔ ákteʔ   núwaʔ   nú·   yusayukwanaklakwʌhátiʔ.
they cut wood   and   different   this time   where   again we are on our way moving over there.

(11) Yah katiʔ wí· náhteʔ teʔyotú·u   tá·tkʌ   a·kataya?tá·naʔ,   kháleʔ onʌ́
Not   well then   any   it couldn't be   or maybe   that I go to school,   and   then

tho   nitwakenú   nʌ   oniʔ ní· yah thya·ya·wʌ́·neʔ tsiʔ ukyo·tʌ́·, nʌ
that's   where I have come from   then   too   me   it has to be   that   I worked,   then

oniʔ waʔkheyaʔtakénhaʔ latiyʌtákwas.   (12) Nʌ   takatáhsawʌʔ wa?tkatʌ́·tshaneʔ
too   I helped them   they cut wood.   Then   I started   I earned

oniʔ niʔí·,   nók tsiʔ kwáh kiʔ kʌʔ nikú a·kí·luʔ kehya·lú·   thikʌ́ tsiʔ
too   as for me,   but   some amount just   I'd say   I remember   that   that

yukwʌtʌhtá·u lakeʔnihkʌ́   oskánhʌ teyakwatʌhnutlúnyuʔ, ukwatʌnoʔsʌ́ha nʌ
we are poor   my late father   together   we siblings,   we siblings   then

né· tetsyalú yotinyákuʔ,   nʌ   né· yah oskánhʌ teʔtsyakwʌ́·tluʔ   thikʌ́
it's   both   they are married,   then   it's   not   together   we don't dwell anymore   that

neʔ thó·neʔ, ké·yaleʔ   aʔé·   sʌ́·   Dutton né· yehatinolótshyus,
at that time,   I remember   way over   also   Dutton   it's   they husk corn over there,

katsyapslanákleʔ s latinolótshyus olihwakayú, tahnú·   kʌs   three cents a bushel
jobs are plentiful   they husk corn   old times,   and   habitually   three cents a bushel

and we went some place else. (10) The reason why I never got much education is because
we were always moving around when I was a child, we would live somewhere for a little
while and they would finish cutting wood and we would be on our way moving to some
place else. (11) Well then there wasn't any possibility that maybe I could go to school, and
then I was old enough that I had to work too, then I helped them at cutting wood. (12) Then
I started to earn [a living] too, but I remember a few things, that we were poor, my late father and my brothers and me, my sisters were both married by then, they weren't living together with us anymore at that time, I remember they were husking corn over in Dutton,
there were a lot of jobs husking corn in the old days, and three cents a bushel

tá·tkʌ   né· two,   one cents a bushel   lonatkalyaʔkʌ·níheʔ   neʔ thó·<u>neʔ</u>.
or maybe   it's   two,   one cents a bushel   they get paid   at that time.

(13) Kwahikʌ́ tsiʔ wʌtolátiʔ̲.
       Just really   it is going along hard.

  (14) Tahnú· yukwanʌ́skwayʌʔ kʌs   thikʌ́ é·lhal, lakwanʌ́ police dog.
         And   we have a pet   customarily that   dog,   he is big   police dog.

(15) Né· thikʌ́ teyakwatʌhnutlúnyuʔ Tsyo kháleʔ Walte, yawʌtatokʌ́htu
       It's   that   we siblings   Joe   and   Walter, Sunday

wʌhnisla·té· thikʌ́ yah tehotiyoʔtényuʔ,   wahyatoláthaʔ   né· thikʌ́
a day exists   that   not   they are not working, the two went hunting   it's   that

kalhakú   yahá·neʔ,   é·lhal nyahyatnʌskwáhaweʔ, né·n   tho
in the woods the two went over there,   dog   the two took a pet,   it's that   there

né· yahuwayaʔto·lʌ́·neʔ   ʌtilú   kalhakú   thikʌ́, tho   tahyatli·yó·
it's   they found him over there   raccoon in the woods that,   there   the two fought there

thikʌ́ é·lhal. (16) Wahatikwe·ní· wahuwályoʔ thikʌ́ ʌtilú,   nʌ kwí·
that   dog.   They were able   they killed him that   raccoon,   so then

tutahuwayaʔtáha<u>weʔ</u>. (17) Kháleʔ lakeʔníha wahoyʌ·séleʔ thikʌ́ ʌtilú,
they brought him back.   And   my father   he skinned him   that   raccoon,

wahatnehwahninú·<u>naʔ</u>. (18) Tho   nikú   yaʔthawe·ná·seʔ   thikʌ́ lakeʔnihkʌ́
he went and sold a pelt.   That's   how much   he received in profit   that   my late father

neʔ thó·neʔ, kwahikʌ́ wakahtahkwáksʌhseʔ kʌs,   tewakahyakwilakeʔto·tú· tsiʔ
at that time,   just really   I have awful shoes   customarily,   my toes are sticking out   what

niwakahtahkó·tʌhseʔ, wahakwe·ní· thikʌ́ tho   nikú   tahuwa·yú·   kané·waʔ,
kind of shoes I have,   he was able   that   that's   how much   they gave him   pelt,

or maybe it was two, one cents a bushel they got paid at that time. (13) Those were really hard times.

(14) And we used to have this dog, a big police dog. (15) My brothers Joe and Walter, that one Sunday they weren't working, the two of them went hunting and they went into the bush, they took the dog, and then they found this raccoon in the woods, and it fought with the dog. (16) They were able to kill the raccoon, so then they brought it back. (17) And my father skinned the raccoon, and he went and sold the pelt. (18) My late father got that much for it at that time, I had these really awful shoes, my toes were sticking out of my shoes, he was able to have them give him that much for the pelt,

wahatnehwahni·nú·, oyá· sukwahtahkwayʌ·tá·ne? thikʌ́ kwáh ase?shúha.
he sold a pelt,   other again I got shoes   that   just   new ones.

(19) Onísta? tsi? niya?wéskwa?t thikʌ́ oyá·   tusakaláhtane?,
      Gee   how   it is pleasant   that   another   I put on shoes again,

yah te?waklʌ?nhá·u   ohtáhkwase? ta·kaláhtane?.   (20) Tho s
not I don't know about new shoes   I would put on shoes.   That's

niwʌtoláti?   thikʌ́ ne? thó·ne?, yah tha·hakalakwe·ní· lake?nihkʌ́   oyá·
how it is going along hard that   at that time,   not   he couldn't afford   my late father another

usahahtahkwahni·nú· tsi?   loyo·té·   tsyo?k nikú   lotkalya?kʌ·níhe?.
that again he buys shoes because   he is working   how much only he is getting paid.

(21) Kwah nók tsi? tyakyunhéti?   ki?wáh, kwáh thok   ni·kú.
      Just   that   we go on living   right,   just   that's only   how much.

(22) Ne? thó·ne? nʌ   kaló·   takaha·wíhte?   a·kí·lu?   kalhakú   núwa?
      At that time   then forward   it brought it along   I would say   in the bush   this time

sahatiyʌtakó·na?   thikʌ́ s, tho kwí· elók kwí· tsyukwanaklakwʌháti? thi·kʌ́.
they went to cut wood again that,   there   all over   we are moving around   that.

(23) Tyótkut tsi? yukwʌ·tʌ́t   tshiwakatehyá·lu?.
      Always   how   we are poor when I was growing up.

(24) Úska sʌ́· útlatste? ké·yale? a?é·   Belmont né· ákta? tkálhayʌ?,
      One   also time   I remember way over   Belmont it's   near   there is a forest,

tho   ále? yahotiyo·tʌ́·   Ukwehuwé s latiyʌtákwas.   (25) Tahnú·
there again they worked over there Native people they are cutting wood.   And

frame house ní· kanúhsote?   tsi? yakwʌ́·tlu?   thikʌ́, tahnú· ka?ikʌ́ nʌ
frame house us   there is a house   at   we are are staying   that,   and   this   then

he sold it, and I got new shoes. (19) Gee, it was so nice to put on other shoes, I wasn't used
to putting on new shoes. (20) Times were that hard back then, my late father couldn't afford
to buy another [pair of] shoes because he was working, and he was getting paid only so
much. (21) We were just surviving, right, that's all. (22) At that time, from that time on I'd
say, they were cutting wood in the bush, so we were moving all over. (23) We were always
poor when I was growing up.

(24) One time too I remember way over near Belmont was a forest, the Indians were
working cutting wood there. (25) And we were living in a frame house, and

kohslaʔké·ne   kiʔwáh,   kwahiká tsiʔ   kanyeyʌ·tú·   thiká   neʔ thó·neʔ,
wintertime   right,   just really   there's snow on the ground   that   at that time,

tahnú·   tyukwanuhsáksʌ   kaʔiká   tsiʔ nú·   niyakwʌ́·tluʔ,   nʌ   waʔó·kalaweʔ
and   we have the worst house   this   where   we are staying,   when   it got dark

thiká,   ké·yaleʔ   waʔukwʌtá·whaʔ,   tahnú·   yohsuhtaká·luteʔ   áktaʔ   thiká
that,   I remember   we went to bed,   and   opening in the wall   near   that

tho   yukwatnáktayʌʔ,   né·n   só·tsiʔ   yukwʌtyohkwaná,   kayé kwí·   niyáki?,
there   we have put a bed,   it's that   too much   we are a big crowd,   four   we total,

Walte   khále?   Tsyo   khále?   í·   khále?   lakeʔní̱ha.   (26) Akwáh   thiká   tho kwí·
Walter   and   Joe   and   me   and   my father.   Quite   that   thus

nikanákta?   tho   yakwʌta·kéleʔ   kanaktá·ke,   tsiʔ niwahsu·tés   oná
is the size of the bed   there   we are lying   on the bed,   during the night   then

waʔukwanáktʌ̱neʔ.   (27)   Tahnú·   tsiʔ nukwá·   yeyakwaku·há·   tho nukwá·
a bed fell through on us.   And   where   we rest our heads   that's where

yahú·sʌ̱neʔ.   (28)   Tahnú·   tyukwanuhsatho·lé·   sá·,   yah teʔyotékhaʔ   stove,
it fell down.   And   our house is very cold   also,   not   there's no fire burning   stove,

tsiʔ   niyotho·lé·,   nʌ   lakeʔnihká   wahá·luʔ   "yekʌʔtahetká·tayʌ kwí·   kaʔiká,
how   it is cold,   then   my late father   he said   "let the ugliness lie over there   this,

só·tsiʔ   yotho·lé· a·katkétsko?   usetwatnaktu·ní·,   tho   niyohtúhak."
too much   it is cold   for me to get up   that you and we fix a bed,   thus   let it be so."

(29)   Nʌ kwí·   tho   yakwaluʔto·tú·   kwaʔahsutátiʔ   tho   yukwʌ·tá·s.
       So then   there   we are standing on our heads   all night   there   we are sleeping.

(30)   Tahnú·   tsiʔ niwahsu·tés   nʌ   né·   tutaʔklo·kó·   sá·,   kwahiká   tsiʔ
       And   during the night   then   it's   again it snowed   also,   just really   that

it was wintertime, there was a lot of snow that time, and it was a really awful house where
we were living, one night I remember we went to bed, and we had our bed close to the window, so we were too many, there were four of us, Walter and Joe and me and my father.
(26) The bed was that big, all of us were lying there on the bed, then during the night the bed
fell through on us. (27) And it's [the end] where we had our heads that fell. (28) And our
house was very cold too, there was no fire burning in the stove, it was so cold, then my late
father said "to the heck with it, it's too cold for me to get up so that we can fix the bed, just
let it be." (29) So then we slept upside down all night. (30) And during the night it snowed
too,

waʔtwatstorm thikʌ́, tsiʔ yohsuhtaká·luteʔ kátshaʔ ok nú· niyoká·luteʔ tho
it did storm   that, at   opening in the wall somewhere   an opening   there

takanyʌhtínyuhteʔ, né·n   sayólhʌneʔ   astéhtsiʔ aʔé· nikanyʌ́htatʌs
snow came in,   it's that it became the next day morning great how the snow is thick

yakwanaʔskwá·ke   yukwataʔklokwʌ́·u, kwah nók tusutenyʌhto·kó·
on our nestled bodies it has snowed on us, just   again snow dispersed

waʔakwatkétskoʔ astéhtsiʔ.   (31) Á· nʌ   elhúwaʔ nʌ   wahate·ká·teʔ stove,
we got up   in the morning.   Oh then   right then then he made a fire stove,

kwáh kʌʔ náheʔ nʌ   waʔonuhsatalíhʌʔ,   nʌ kwí· waʔakwatekhu·ní· breakfast.
just   some while then the house warmed up,   so then   we ate a meal   breakfast.

     (32) Tahnú· kʌs   tsyoʔk wí· náhteʔ kateʔnyʌ́thaʔ a·kheyaʔtakénhaʔ wí· n
            And   usually all kinds of things I am trying   for me to help them

lotiyo·té·   tsiʔ   yah seʔ ní· teʔwakyo·té·   shekú neʔ thó·neʔ, nʌ kwí·
they are working because not   too me I am not working still   at that time, so then

úska útlatsteʔ thikʌ́ Tsyo kháleʔ í· yakní·tluʔ,   wahʌ́·luʔ, "í· kwí· núwaʔ
one   time   that   Joe   and   I   we two are at home, he said,   "us   this time

tyateyʌ́·tu   breakfast, ʌtwatekhu·ní·   astéhtsiʔ."   (33) Nʌ kwí·
let's you and I fix breakfast,   you and we will eat a meal in the morning."   So then

waʔakyatkétskoʔ waʔakyatu·ní·, porridge waʔakyatu·ní· thikʌ́, tahnú· yah kwí·
we two got up   we two made it,   porridge we two made it that,   and   not

ní· teʔyuknilʌ́ʔnhá·u,   aʔé· nikuhkó· yaʔuknihneku·tí·   thikʌ́ thoʔnʌ́,
us   we two don't know how,   great big amount we two poured water that   and then,

tahnú· porridge núwaʔ yaʔukya·tí·,   tahnú· né· tsiʔ nʌ   tayolíhʌʔ
and   porridge this time we two added it,   and   because then it came to a boil

there was a bad storm, in the window somewhere there was an opening and the snow came
in there, so the next morning there was a thick layer of snow [where] it had snowed on us as
we lay nestled in bed, the snow was just flying [when] we got up in the morning. (31) Ah
well then he made a fire in the stove, in a while the house warmed up, so then we ate breakfast.

(32) And then I was trying to do all kinds of things to help the workers, because I wasn't
working yet at that time, so then this one time Joe and I were at home, he said, "let's you
and I fix breakfast, we'll all eat it in the morning." (33) So then the two of us got up to
make it, we made porridge, and we didn't know how, we poured in a huge amount of water,
and then we added the porridge, and because then the porridge came to a boil,

thikʌ porridge, tayaweʔtowanháhsleʔ né· thi·<u>kʌ</u>. (34) Kháleʔ onʌ́ waʔka·ná·neʔ
that porridge, it grew larger   it's that.   And   then it filled up

yukyateksáheleʔ,   wahʌ́·luʔ "nok ʌwa·tú· ʌtnikalhate·ní·,   oyá· pan
we two have set down a dish, he said   "it has to be   you and I will empty it, other pan

tho nukwá· ʌtsitnétane<u>ʔ</u>."   (35) Nʌ kyaleʔ wí· waʔaknikalhate·ní· úska.
that's where again you and I will put it in."   So again   we two emptied it   one.

(36) Shekú sʌ́haʔ ok   só·tsiʔ e·só· waʔka·ná·neʔ oniʔ né· thikʌ́, kháleʔ onʌ́
     Still   nevertheless too much lots it filled up   too it's that,   and   then

tóhkaʔ niyukyateksáheleʔ,   akwekú tayonahnuhátiʔ. (37) Yah teʔwé·ne
a few   we two have set down dishes, all   it was filling up.   It's incredible

naʔukniká·tʌneʔ   porridge thikʌ́ neʔ thó·neʔ, nók tsiʔ waʔakníhsaneʔ kiʔ,
how we two got a lot of porridge   that   at that time, but   we two finished   actually,

kháleʔ nʌ kwí· astéhtsiʔ   nʌ tú·skeʔ lotinehlakwʌ́·u   yukwaká·teʔ porridge
and   so then in the morning then truly   they are surprised we have a lot porridge

waʔakwatekhu·<u>ní</u>·.
we ate a meal.

(38) Kháleʔ oyá·   sʌ́· né· né·n kʌ́·tho   né· Ukwehuwé·ne   yakwanákleʔ
     And   another also it's that right here it's   at the Native people's we reside

thikʌ́, lakeʔníha né· lotiyo·té·,   nʌ kwí· tetsyalú Walte kháleʔ Tsyo,
that,   my father   it's they are working, so then both   Walter and   Joe,

nʌ   akwekú lotiyo·té·   o·nʌ́. (39) Akulhaʔtsíwaʔ onʌ́ s kí·tluʔ
then all   they are working then.   All by myself   then   I am at home

kaʔikʌ́ wʌhnislaténi. (40) Né· thikʌ́ núwaʔ   kanuhtunyúkwas   kaʔikʌ́
this   days exist.   It's that   this time I am thinking it over this

there got to be more and more of it. (34) And soon our dish got filled up, he said, "we have to empty some, we'll put some into another pan." (35) So we emptied [some out of] one. (36) Nevertheless there was still too much, and it filled up that one too, and soon we had a few containers, all filling up. (37) It's incredible what a lot of porridge we got at that time, but we finally finished, and in the morning they were truly surprised we had a lot of porridge for us to eat.

   (38) And another [time], we were living here on the Reserve, my father and them were working, so both Walter and Joe, they were all working then. (39) I was home all by myself these days. (40) So I was wondering,

náhteʔ akwáh naákyeleʔ aˑkheyaʔtakénhaʔ, nók oniʔ n usukekhuníhakeʔ
what   quite I might do that I help them,   if only   again I would be cooking

nʌ   usahotikéˑtohteʔ.   (41) Nʌ kwíˑ waʔkatʌʔnikuhloˑlʌ́ˑneʔ thikʌ́,
when   again they would appear.   So then   I found my mind   that,

ʌskatnaʔtaluˑtʌ́ˑ   kʌs kwíˑ kaʔikʌ́, lakeʔnihkʌ́ s waʔkatkáthoʔ tsiʔ nihayélhaʔ
again I will bake bread habitually this,   my late father I saw   how he does it

wahanaʔtaluˑníˑ, katsihkoˑtúˑ latinaʔtúkhwaʔ.   (42) Nʌ sok wíˑ thikʌ́
he made bread,   fists standing is what they call it.   So then too   that

waʔkateʔskutakhwaʔtsláˑlʌʔ   kháleʔ othéˑtsliʔ waʔkkóˑnaʔ,   tahnúˑ kwáh
I set down what one uses for frying and   flour   I went and got it,   and   just

kok nikú   skaˑyʌ́ˑ thikʌ́ othéˑtsliʔ, kwah nók tsiʔ úska ʌkatsheʔlhuˑníˑ
a small amount it is left   that   flour,   just only   one   I will make dough

tsyoʔk nikú   skaˑyʌ́ˑ. (43) Nʌ kwíˑ waʔkateksáˑlʌʔ,   nʌ sók   waʔtekyestányuʔ
only how much it is left.   So then   I set down a dish, and then   I mixed things

thikʌ́, néˑn   tsiʔ kwíˑ niwakatshanuní kwáh klʌnotátyehseʔ   thikʌ́, tsiʔ
that,   it's that how   I am happy   just   I am going around singing that,   what

niyolihowanʌ́ tsiʔ   nikatyélhaʔ kaʔiˑkʌ́. (44) Waʔkatnaʔtaluˑníˑ thikʌ́, nʌ   kwáh
a big deed   what I am doing   this.   I made bread   that,   then   just

takateyʌ́ˑtuʔ, kwáh waʔktsihkotúniʔ   kwáh kʌʔ naʔkyelániʔ   thikʌ́,
I took care,   just   I patted it all over with my fists just   I did it all over this way that,

waʔtektakwʌ́htʌhteʔ oshéˑlhaʔ. (45) Nʌ sók   oven yaʔkétaneʔ,   takateˑkáˑteʔ,
I flattened it   dough.   And then   oven I put it in there, I made a fire,

takattsistiˑyósteʔ.   (46) Kwáh kʌʔ náheʔ   nʌ   wáˑkelheʔ nʌ   uhte wíˑ
I made good flames.   Just   a little while then   I thought   then   supposedly

what the heck could I do to help them, if only I could have dinner on when they showed up
again. (41) So then I got an idea, I would bake some bread, I saw how my late father made
bread, what they call ovenbread. (42) So then I set down the frying pan and I went and got
the flour, and there was just a small amount of flour left, I could make just one dough [loaf],
only so much was left. (43) So then I set down my bowl, and I started to mix everything
together, I was so happy I was singing away, because I was doing something worthwhile.
(44) I started to make the bread, I took such care, I kneaded it doing it just like this (demon-
strating how), flattening the dough. (45) Then I put it in the oven, I made a really good fire.
(46) In a little while I thought

yona?tala·lí.   (47) Nʌ kwí· yusakatke?to·tʌ́·, nʌ   ki?   né· tú·ske?,
bread is cooked.   So then   again I looked in,   then   actually it's truly,

nók tsi? kwahikʌ́ kawiskliyó, yah brown te?yawʌ́·u.   (48) Nók tsi?
only   just really a nice white, not brown it hasn't happened.   But

nʌ ki? yona?talahnilhá·u   oni? ka?ikʌ́, nʌ kwí· wé·ni   wa?ka·lí·.
already it has become hard bread too   this,   so then evidently it got cooked.

(49) Atnʌyálho?, tho   né· niyohnilhá·u   thikʌ́ akná·talok, kwáh oni?
     Giant,   there it's how it has become hard that   my bread,   just   too

né· a?nyóh   cement waktáhkwʌ   thikʌ́, niyolakalé·ni
it's seems like cement I have taken out that,   there is such a loud noise

atekhwahlakhwá·ke wa?ká·lane?. (50) Né·n,   yah né· kaná·talok te?yotú·u,
on the table   it landed.   It's that, not it's bread   it hasn't become,

kwáh né· nók tsi? wa?ka·lí· kwí·, nók tsi? wa?ona?talahnílhʌ? nʌ? né·.
just   it's but   it got cooked, but   it became hard bread   that one.

(51) Né· kati? wí· lake?nihkʌ́   sá·lawe?   thikʌ́, wahʌ́·lu? "náhte?," wa?kí·lu?
     Well then   my late father he got home that,   he said   "what,"   I said

"nʌ ki? núwa?   né· swakatna?talísu?."   (52) Wahʌ́·lu? "kátsha?," "ísi? nukwá·
"already this time it's I have finished bread."   He said   "where,"   "right over there

káhele?."   (53) Nʌ kwí· yahahla·kó·,   "ot ohnáhte?" né· tsi?
it is sitting."   So then   he picked it up over there, "what the—"   because

nihona?khwʌ́·u thikʌ́ lake?nihkʌ́, yah kwí· né· shekú né·n   é·lhal yah
he is so mad   that   my late father, not   it's even   it's that dog   not

tha·hakwe·ní· aá·lake?   ni·yót.   (54) Wahʌ́·lu? "náhte? náhsyele?."
he is not able   he could eat it how it is.   He said   "what   you did."

the bread must be done. (47) So then I looked in, then it was [cooked], but it was really
white, it didn't get brown. (48) But it had become hard too, so then it must have gotten
cooked. (49) By golly, my bread had become so hard, it was just like cement [what] I took
out, it landed on the table with a loud noise. (50) It didn't turn into bread, but it got cooked,
it had become hard, that. (51) Well then my late father got home, he said "what (unfinished)," I said, "I've made bread already." (52) He said "where?" [I said] "it's right over
there." (53) So then he picked it up, "what the—?," because my late father was so mad, not
even a dog could eat it, how it was. (54) He said "what did you do?"

(55) Wa?kí·lu? "kwáh ki? nók tsi? ohne·kánus nyuhukwa·tí· khále?
I said "just actually but cold water I added and

othé·tshel*i?*." (56) Wahʌ́·lu? "teyotuhutsyóhu baking powder sʌ́·
flour." He said "it needs to be baking powder also

yaesátyuke? khále? tyohyó·tsis, né· thikʌ́ a·yokwényuke?
you should have added and salt, it's that it would have been able to

a·yottu?kwʌ́·uke? a·hsatna?talu·*tʌ́·*." (57) Né· oni? wahʌ́·lu? "kwáh
it would have risen should you bake bread." It's too he said "just

ya?shetkʌ?táhsa?ahte? n othé·tsli?, yah thau·tú· usakatna?talu·tʌ́· oyá·,
you used it all the heck up flour, not it can't be that again I bake bread another,

nok ʌwa·tú· tyutʌhni·núhe? ale? yʌhʌ́ske? ʌskna?talahninú·na?
it has to be there one sells again again I will go over there again I will go and buy bread

a·yakwatekhu·ní· yo?kaláshʌ, niyakwatuhkálya?ks onʌ́." (58) Á· ot ohnáhte?
for us to eat a meal in the evening, we are so hungry now." Oh what

né· nahoná·khwʌ? thikʌ́, nʌ sok wí· né· wa?katé·ko? ní· thikʌ́, khále? oska·wáku
it's he got so mad that, and so then it's I fled me that, and in the bush

ní· nyahá·ke?, tsi? niyo·lé· sá·lawe?, kwáh kʌ? náhe? nále? tuta·ké·,
me I went over there, until he got home, just some while again I came back,

nʌ ki? né· shona?kwʌtá·u, nʌ kwí· sayakwatekhu·ní· yo?kalásh*ʌ*.
already it's he was over his anger, so then we ate a meal again in the evening.

(59) Ok wí· n akná·talok, yah ní· te?wakanúhte? kátsha? né· nyehóti,
And as for my bread, not me I don't know where it's he has thrown it,

wé·ne kwí· ísi? nyehóti. (60) Kwáh né· nók wahina?ku·ní·
evidently yonder he has thrown it away. Just it's only I made him mad

(55) I said "I just added water and flour." (56) He said "you were supposed to put in baking powder too, and salt, that's what would have made it rise for you to bake it." (57) He said too "you used up all the darn flour, so I can't bake another bread, I have to go to the store to buy bread for us to eat for supper, and we're so hungry now." (58) Oh boy did he ever get mad, and so then I took off, and I went into the bush, until he came home, a little while later I came back, already he was over being mad, so then we ate supper. (59) And as for my bread, I don't know where he got rid of it, he must have thrown it away. (60) All I did was make him mad

wa?kate?nyʌ·tʌ· a·hiya?takénha? thok náhohte?.
I tried   I would help him   something.

(61) Khále? kati? wí· né· onʌ́ thikʌ́, nʌ oni? ní·, tho ní· nitwakenú
      And   anyway it's then that,   then even me, there me I have come from

nʌ wa?ktsyapslisákha?, tahnú· yah kwí· te?kahlúkha? o?slu·ní·, olihwiyó tsi?
then I went to look for a job, and   not   I don't speak   white man, a sure thing that

wʌto·lé·. (62) Kwahikʌ́ tsi? wʌto·lé·, shekú n a·ktsyapslisákha?   tsi?
it is hard.   Just really that it is hard, still   for me to go look for a job because

yah te?kahlúkha? o?slu·ní·   kwahotokʌ́·u, kwáh kwí· náhte?   a·yukli?wanu·tú·se?
not   I don't speak white man just for real,   just   anything for them to ask me

khále? kwáh kwí· nók "I s'pose," wé·ni ki?wáh "I s'pose."   (63) Kwáh kwí·
and   just   "I s'pose,"   I suppose   "I s'pose."   Just

náhte?,   khále? "yes, no," kwáh kwí· tsyo?k náhte? ka?ikʌ́, thok ní· nikú
anything, and   "yes, no,"   all kinds of things   this,   that's me how much

wakanúhte?. (64) Nók tsi? wa?kattsyapslo·lʌ́·ne? ki?   construction work,
I know.   But   I found a job   actually construction work,

kátsha? ok nú· wísk yawʌ·lé· tsha?tewakohsliyá·ku   tshutakatáhsawʌ?
somewhere   five   teen   when I have crossed over winters when I started

ukyo·tʌ́·. (65) Nʌ kwí· u·tú·   ukyo·tʌ́· thikʌ́, sixty cents an hour,
I worked.   So then   it could be I worked that,   sixty cents an hour,

forty cents an hour wakatkalya?kʌ·níhe? kwáh tshutakatáhsawʌ? construction.
forty cents an hour   I am getting paid   just   when I started   construction.

(66) Tahnú· wa?tkatatéshnye? thikʌ́ tutáhsawʌ? ne? thó·ne?. (67) Khále? onʌ́
      And   I looked after myself that   it began   at that time.   And   then

trying to help him with something.

(61) And then well, then even me, I was old enough then to go look for a job, and I didn't speak English, it sure was hard. (62) It was really hard, even for me to go and look for a job because I didn't really speak any English, anything at all they would ask me, and just "I s'pose," I suppose "I s'pose." (63) Anything at all, and "yes, no," all these things [they would ask me], that's all I knew. (64) But I found a job in construction, I was about fifteen years old when I started to work. (65) So then I could work, I was getting paid sixty cents an hour, forty cents an hour right when I got started in construction. (66) And I looked after myself starting at that time. (67) And then

tayawe?towanháhsle?, oyú·kwa? sʌ́· ukyo?tʌ́hsa? onʌ́, nʌ se? kwáh
it became a bigger pile, tobacco also I went to work now, then too just

akulha?tsíwa? o·nʌ́. (68) Lake?nihkʌ́, nʌ né· wahokstʌ·há·ne?, yah né·
all by myself now. My late father, then it's he became old, not it's

te?shoyó·tʌhse? tsi? s nʌ tayohtuháti?. (69) Nʌ akulha?tsíwa? kwí·
he doesn't work anymore how then the way it's going. Then all by myself

onʌ́, ya?tewakya?tístu. (70) Elók swakyo?táti? London khále? St. Thomas,
now, I am all alone. All over I am working around London and St. Thomas,

construction wakyo·té·, 85 cents an hour khále? onʌ́ ukwatkályahkse?.
construction I am working, 85 cents an hour and now I got paid.

(71) Uknehla·kó· tsi? e·só· thikʌ́ tho ni·kú. (72) Ne? thó·ne? nʌ oyú·kwa?
I got surprised that lots that that's how much. At that time tobacco

ukyo?tʌ́hsa?. (73) Nʌ né· sʌ́ha? yeswe·só· wa?kathwistu·ní·, nók tsi?
I went to work. Then it's more it is lots again I made money, but

akwekú kwí· swakatyesáhtu, yah te?kattókhahkwe? ne? thó·ne? ohwísta?,
all I have wasted, not I didn't have sense at that time money,

shekú kwí· né·n núwa? tho ki? ni·yót, yah te?kattókha?.
still it's that this time that's actually how it is, not I don't have sense.

(74) Nók tsi? sʌ́ha? ki? yah te?kattókhahkwe? kwí· utahséhtahkwe?
But more actually not I didn't have sense you may believe

ok oni? n yáhtʌ?, nók tsi? sʌ́ha? ki? yah te?kattókhahkwe? tshiwahu·níse?.
and or not, but more actually not I didn't have sense long time ago.

(75) A?é· akwáh oyú·kwa? yeyukwayo·té· Percy Ireland khále?
Far away mostly tobacco we are working over there Percy Ireland and

[jobs] became more numerous, I went to work in tobacco too, and I was by myself now. (68) My late father had gotten old, he wasn't working anymore the way it used to be. (69) Then I was all by myself, all alone now. (70) I was working all over in London and St. Thomas, working in construction, and I was paid 85 cents an hour now. (71) I was surprised that it was so much. (72) At that time then I went to work in tobacco. (73) Then I made even more money, but I wasted it all, I didn't have any sense about money at that time, and it's still that way now, I don't have any sense. (74) But even more I had no sense, you can believe it or not, but even more I didn't have any sense a long time ago.

(75) We were working in tobacco way over there with Percy Ireland and

Simpson Ireland, oyú·kwaʔ yukwayo·té·   aʔé·   Simcoe ákta<u>ʔ</u>.   (76) Tho nú·
Simpson Ireland,   tobacco   we are working far away Simcoe near.   That's where

thikʌ́ yukwayo·té·,   tahnú· kwáh né· tutye·lʌ́·teʔ oyú·kwaʔ ukyo·tʌ́·, yah
that   we are working, and   just it's first   tobacco   I worked, not

teʔwaklʌʔnhá·u né· kwahotokʌ́·u, nók tsiʔ Simpson ókhaleʔ Percy waʔuklihúniʔ
I don't know how it's just for real,   but   Simpson and   Percy they taught me

ta·yakwatprime oyú·<u>kwaʔ</u>.   (77) Nók tsiʔ né· kʌs   ní· tetwakeʔkashayʌ́,
for us to prime   tobacco.   But   it's habitually me   I am the slowest,

tho kwí· thikʌ́ lotinaʔkhwʌʔuhátiʔ,   yukwattehtanyuní·<u>neʔ</u>.   (78) Kháleʔ
there   that   they are going along mad, they are scolding me all along.   And

katiʔ   oniʔ wí· onʌ́ thikʌ́ ukeshwá·tʌʔ   tsiʔ tho   ni·yót,   tahnú·
well then too   now   that   I became disgusted that that's how it is, and

waʔklihwá·lukeʔ tsiʔ lakeʔníha, aʔé·   né· Leamington loyoʔtʌ́hsu,
I heard news   that my father,   way over there it's Leamington   he has gone to work,

factory Heinz shakoyoʔtʌ́hseheʔ ne·<u>tú</u>.   (79) Tahnú· waʔklihwá·lukeʔ tsiʔ
factory Heinz   he works for them   that place.   And   I heard news   that

thutʌ́nhahseʔ   canning factory a·hotiyo·tʌ́·,   úhkaʔ   tho   yaá·laweʔ
they are hiring there   canning factory   that they work, anyone there he would get over there

ʌhuwánhaneʔ   kih.   (80) Nʌ kwí· wahihlo·lí· Simpson, waʔkí·luʔ, Percy
they will hire him actually.   So then I told him   Simpson,   I said,   Percy

kiʔ,   nʌ   kiʔ   wahihlo·lí·, waʔkí·luʔ, "ʌkahtʌ·tí·, ní· ʌkatkʌ́·lahteʔ ní· onʌ́
actually, then actually I told him,   I said,   "I will leave, me   I will quit   me   then

oyú·kwaʔ wakyo·té·,   ʌkahtʌ·tí· ʌtáktaʔ,   Leamington ní· yʌhʌ·ké·."
tobacco   I am working, I will leave Saturday, Leamington   me   I will go over there."

Simpson Ireland, we were working in tobacco way over near Simcoe. (76) That's where we
were working, and it was the first time I worked in tobacco, I didn't know how really, but
Simpson and Percy taught me for us to prime tobacco. (77) But I was very slow, they would
be cross, giving me heck all along. (78) And well finally I got disgusted with the way it
was, and I heard that my father had gone to work over in Leamington, he was working for
them at the Heinz factory there. (79) And I heard that they were hiring people to work at the
canning factory, anybody who went there would get hired. (80) So then I told Simpson, I
said, it was Percy actually, I told him, I said, "I'm leaving, I will quit working in tobacco,
I'm leaving on Saturday, I'm going to Leamington."

(81) "Kanyó· onʌ́ ʌwakatkályah<u>kseʔ</u>."   (82) Nʌ kwí· né· ukwatkályaʔkseʔ,
    "As soon as   I will get paid."   So then   it's I got paid,

nʌ kiʔ ok wí· né· waʔkathleʔnu·ní·, bus waʔkatítaneʔ, Leamington nyaha·ké·.
right then   it's   I packed up,   bus I got on,   Leamington   I went over there.

(83) Tho yahá·keweʔ, tú·skeʔ né· kwáh óksaʔ ok wahiyaʔto·lʌ́·neʔ lakeʔníha
    There I got over there, truly   it's just   right away   I found him   my father

tsiʔ nú· nihanákleʔ, tho yahá·<u>keweʔ</u>.   (84) Nʌ kwí· Monday, Monday tho
where he resides,   there I got over there.   So then   Monday, Monday there

yaʔkáheweʔ, nʌ Shatyelhaʔkó· kʌs laboss thikʌ́ neʔ thó·neʔ, tahnú·
it's that time, then Big Wellington Sickles habitually the boss that   at that time, and

yah tho thaʔtewakohsliyá·ku shekú neʔ thó·neʔ au·tú· aukyo·tʌ́·
not thus I haven't crossed over winters still   at that time   it could be   I could work

factory, yah thya·ya·wʌ́· tsiʔ sixteen naʔtʌsohsliyaʔkúhakeʔ, tahnú· elhúwaʔ
factory,   it has to be   that sixteen   you will have crossed over winters, and   just then

ní·, kwah nók nʌ kiʔ né· thóha sixteen, nók tsiʔ áhsu kiʔ sixteen
me, just   then actually it's almost sixteen, but   not yet actually sixteen

té·kʌ.   (85) Nʌ kwí· Shatyélhaʔ wahʌ́·luʔ, kwáh kwí· nók wahʌ́·luʔ, "í·
it is not.   So then W.S.   he said,   just only   he said,   "me

tʌketha·lʌ́· akwekú, ʌkhehlo·lí· tsiʔ sixteen tesohsliyá·ku,
I will talk   all,   I will tell them that sixteen you have crossed over winters,

tákʌʔ náhteʔ ʌhsí·<u>lu</u>."   (86) Nʌ kwí· laulhá· waʔákneʔ office, tho
don't   anything you will say."   So then   him   we two went office,   there

yaʔákneʔ, tho laulhá· waʔthatha·lʌ́· akwe·<u>kú</u>.   (87) Né· a·kí·luʔ,
we two went over there, there him   he talked   all.   It's I'd say,

(81) "As soon as I get paid." (82) So then I got paid, right away I packed up, I got on the bus, I went to Leamington. (83) I got there, immediately I found my father where he was staying, and I went there. (84) So then Monday, it was Monday, Big Wellington Sickles was boss at that time, and I still wasn't old enough at that time that I could work in a factory, you had to be sixteen years old, and just then me, I was almost sixteen, but not sixteen yet. (85) So then Wellington Sickles said, all he said was, "I'll do all the talking, I'll tell them that you are sixteen, you don't say anything." (86) So then I went to the office with him, the two of us went there, he was the one that did all the talking. (87) I'd say,

kwáh   nʌ   óksaʔ   tsiʔ   wahuthu·táteʔ   waʔukénha<u>ne</u>ʔ.   (88) Nʌ kwí· tho
just   then right away that they consented   they hired me.   So then   there

kiʔ   oniʔ wí· ní·   ukyo·tʌ́· thikʌ́, kwáh   yaʔtkó·ktʌʔ   tsiʔ náheʔ tho   ukyo·tʌ́·
actually   too   me   I worked that,   just   there I ended it   while   there I worked

tomato season kiʔwáh,   nʌ   waʔakwáhsaneʔ,   nʌ kyaleʔ wí· tutayakwahtʌ·<u>tí</u>·.
tomato season   right,   then we finished,   so again   we left there to come home.

(89) Nʌ kyaleʔ   kanatá·ke   sukyoʔtʌ́hsaʔ   thi·<u>kʌ́</u>.
       Again   in town   again I went to work   that.

   (90) Tsiʔ   katiʔ wí· niyawʌ́·u   tsiʔ   ostúha wakyʌtéluʔ   a·khya·tú· kháleʔ
         How   so then   it has happened that   a little   I have learned that I write and

oʔslu·ní·   a·katwʌnu·táhkweʔ,   London waʔktsyapslisákhaʔ   thikʌ́, tho
white man   that I speak in a language, London   I went to look for a job that,   there

yahá·keweʔ   employment office, wahʌ́·luʔ thikʌ́ shakotsyapslatshʌlyá·se, wahʌ́·luʔ
I got over there   employment office,   he said   that   he finds jobs for them,   he said

"yah   náhteʔ   teʔka·yʌ́·,"   kwáh núwaʔ   nók tsiʔ wahʌ́·luʔ, "tá·t" wahʌ́·luʔ
"not   anything is not there," just   this time   but   he said,   "if"   he said

"sanúhteʔ   kʌ   úhkaʔ ok náhteʔ sʌ́haʔ kʌʔ nikúha   lo·yʌ́· Grade 6 education,"
"you know   question someone   more   a small amount he has   Grade 6 education,"

né· kiʔ   wahʌ́·luʔ "teyukwatuhutsyoní, ya·shakwatʌ́nyehteʔ kátshaʔ ok nú·
it's   actually he said   "we need it,   we would send him   somewhere

a·hatayaʔtá·naʔ   to upgrade his education." (91) Waʔkí·luʔ "í·   kiʔ   úska
that he goes to school   to upgrade his education."   I said,   "me   actually one

tewakatuhutsyo·ní," tahnú· kwáh né· ʌtyukkályaʔkseʔ   sʌ́h.   (92) Nʌ kwí·
I want it,"   and   just   it's they will pay me for it there also.   So then

right away they agreed to hire me. (88) So then I worked there too, I worked there through
the tomato season to the end, then we finished, so we came home again. (89) And I went
back to work in town.

(90) So then the way it happened that I learned a bit to write and speak English, I went to
look for a job in London, I got to the employment office, the person who finds jobs for people said, he said "there's nothing available," but then he said, "if" he said "you know of
someone who has less than a Grade 6 education," he said "we need [someone], we would
send him somewhere to go to school to upgrade his education." (91) I said, "I'm one that
wants it," and they would pay me for it too. (92) So then

waʔkatatshʌnínyuhteʔ kiʔwáh, kháleʔ waʔknánhuʔ information tsyoʔk náhohte̱ʔ.
I put my name in   right,   and   I filled out   information   all kinds.

(93) Waʔkatayaʔtá·naʔ, tsyóhslat tsiʔ náheʔ wakatayaʔtahnu·hné· Petrolia,
      I went to school,   one year   while   I have gone to school   Petrolia,

tho nú·   Grade 7 yaʔukwatkʎ·lahteʔ   tsiʔ náheʔ waʔkatáyahte̱ʔ. (94) Tahnú·
that's where Grade 7 they left me over there while   I went to school.   And

nʌ kwí· né· tshiwakhwatsi·láyʌʔ ní· thikʎ neʔ thó·neʔ, kʎ·tho katiʔ né· latí·tluʔ
so then   it's when I have a family me   that   at that time,   here   well   it's   they dwell

Ukwehuwé·ne,   Petrolia né· ní· yekí·tluʔ   tho náheʔ thi·kʎ.
at the Native people's, Petrolia it's me   I dwell over there that while   that.

(95) Neʔ thó·neʔ nʌ   wá·ksaneʔ katayá·thaʔ,   nʌ   kalístatsiʔ núwaʔ
      At that time then I finished   I go to school, then iron   this time

sukyoʔtʎhsaʔ   ísiʔ   Ford plant tshutahutnuhsu·ní·,   tho
again I went to work yonder Ford plant   when they built a house, there

yewakyoʔtʎ·u   ostúha   ne·tú.   (96) Neʔ thó·neʔ nʌ   Detroit núwaʔ
I have worked over there a little bit that place.   At that time then Detroit   this time

nukwá· nyusa·ké·,   tho   núwaʔ   nukwá· nyusukyo·tʎ·,
where   again I went over there, that's this time where   again I worked over there,

kalístatsiʔ né· ukyo·tʎ· né· tho   kʌʔ náheʔ, tsiʔ niyo·lé· nʌ   fruit products
iron   it's I worked   it's there some while, until   then fruit products

yahukyo·tʎ·,   five years tsiʔ náheʔ tho   wakyoʔtʎ·u   fruit products Detroit.
I worked over there,   five years   while   there I have worked   fruit products   Detroit.

(97) Tho s yakwanáklehkweʔ thikʎ akwa·tsíleʔ, Marina kháleʔ Foster
      There we used to reside   that   my family,   Marina   and   Foster

I put my name in, I filled out information, all kinds. (93) I went to school, one whole year I was in school in Petrolia, Grade 7 was where they put me while I went to school. (94) And so then I already had a family at that time, they were living here on the Reserve, I lived over there in Petrolia all that while. (95) At that time then I finished going to school, then I went to work in iron over at the Ford plant when they were building it, I worked there for a bit. (96) Then I went to Detroit, that's where I worked next, I did ironwork there for a while, until I worked in fruit products, five years I worked in fruit products there in Detroit. (97) I lived there with my family, when Marina and Foster

kʌʔ tshaʔtehnáh.   (98) 1955, 1957 kátshaʔ ok nú· yohslashe·tás né·
when the two were small.   1955, 1957 somewhere   it counts years it's

tho nú·   yeyakwanáklehkweʔ.
that's where   we used to reside over there.

(99) Né· katiʔ wí· wʌto·lé· lukwé yah tehahyatuhslayʌtelí,   kwáh ok
      Well then it's it is hard man   not he doesn't have an education, just

tsiʔ ka·yʌ́·   náhteʔ   a·hatsyapslatshʌ·lí· wʌto·lé·.   (100) Nok ʌwa·tú·
the one that   anything   he should find a job it is hard.   It has to be

a·hahyatuhslayʌtelíhakeʔ. (101) Né· katiʔ ní·   aolí·waʔ   só·tsiʔ   wʌto·lé· tsiʔ
that he has an education.   Well then me   the reason too much   it is hard that

waʔtkatukohtányuʔ tsyoʔk náhteʔ tsiʔ   yah teʔkhyatuhslayʌtelí,   shekú n
I went through things   different things   because not I don't have an education, even

tsiʔ náheʔ Detroit tshiwakyo·té·,   e·só· shekú yah teʔkhyatuhslayʌtelí
while   Detroit when I am working, lots   still   not I don't have an education

neʔ thó·neʔ, nók tsiʔ nʌ   kiʔ   né· ostúha   ísiʔ nú· ní· wakanúhteʔ tsiʔ
at that time, but   then actually it's a little bit further me   I know   as

ni·yót   kwáh tshututáhsawʌʔ, nók tsiʔ shekú kiʔ   sʌ́haʔ ok nók aolí·waʔ
how it is just   when it began,   but   still   actually anyway   only the reason

wakyo·té·   tho nukwá· tsiʔ   ati   úhkaʔ ʌhakwe·ní·   kiʔ   ʌhoyo·tʌ́·
I am working there   because no matter anyone he will be able actually he will work

tsiʔ náhteʔ wakyó·tʌhseʔ. (102) Kháleʔ nʌ   kalístatsiʔ ukyo·tʌ́·, yah kiʔ
that what   I work.   And   then iron   I worked,   not actually

nok thau·tú·   kwahikʌ́ a·hahyatuhslayʌtelíhakeʔ neʔ thó·neʔ. (103) Tekyattíhʌ
it did not have to be just really that he has an education   at that time.   It is different

were small. (98) Somewhere around the year 1955, 1957 is when we lived over there.

(99) Well it was hard for a man with no education, to find any kind of job at all was hard. (100) He had to have an education. (101) It's why it was so hard, I went through all kinds of things because I wasn't educated, even while I was working in Detroit, I still didn't have much education at that time, but I knew a bit more than I did at the very beginning, but the only reason I even worked there anyway [without an education] was because anybody could do the work that I worked at. (102) And then I did ironwork, you didn't really need to have an education [to do ironwork] at that time. (103) It's different

ale?   né· kalístatsi? today a·hoyo?tʌ́hsa?,   lu·té·   yukhlo·líhe? today
again   it's iron   today for him to go to work, they say   they tell me today

nok ʌwa·tú·   Grade 12 education   ʌsayʌ·táke?   kalístatsi?   ʌsayo·tʌ́·.
it has to be   Grade 12 education   you will have it iron   you will work.

(104) Ne? thó·ne? yah né· nok thau·tú·.   (105) Né· kati?   aolí·wa?
        At that time not   it's it does not have to be.   Well anyway   the reason

tyso?k náhte? wakyo?tʌ́·u   tsi?   ʌwa·tú·   se? né· tsyo?k nahté·shu?
different things I have worked because it can be   too   it's   all kinds of things

yesalihúni?   right on the job, yah tho té·yot   tsi? núwa?   ni·yót.
one is teaching you   right on the job,   not   thus it is not so as   this time how it is.

(106) Nok ʌwa·tú· ʌsalʌ?nha?úhake?   ʌsayo·tʌ́·   tsi? niyo·lé· nʌ   ʌyesánhane?,
        It has to be   you will know how   you will work   until   then   one will hire you,

tahnú· tá·t yah tha·yesate?shʌ·nʌ́·   aesayo·tʌ́·   oh   né· kati? nʌya·wʌ́·ne?
and   if   not   one won't give you a chance for you to work how it's   then   it will happen

ʌhseyʌtéhtane?   aseayo·tʌ́·.
you will get practice   for you to work.

(107) A·kí·lu? ní· tá·t úhka? ok náhte? satahúhsate?   náhte? wakathlolí, tahnú·
        I'd say   me   if   someone   you are listening what   I am telling,   and

tákʌ? núwa? ʌsashwá·tʌ? tsi? satayá·tha?,   né· ki?   a·kuhletsya·lú·
don't   this time you will resent that you go to school,   it's   actually   I would encourage you

tákʌ? kwí· aesashwá·tʌ,   yahá·tshan, yahá·tshan, tsi? nikú   ʌwa·tú·
don't   you would resent it,   finish,   finish,   how much   it can be

ʌhsatáyahte?,   né· tsi? ʌtwʌhnisla·téke? tʌsatuhútsyohse?. (108) Tá·t núwa?
you will go to school, because it will come a day   you will need it.   Maybe

again to do ironwork today they say, they tell me that today you have to have a Grade 12
education to do ironwork. (104) Not at that time. (105) Anyway, that's why I worked at so
many different [jobs] because they could teach you everything right on the job, that's not
how it is nowadays. (106) You have to know how to do the work before you get hired, and
if they won't give you a chance to work how will you get the experience to work?

(107) I'd say if someone is listening to what I am talking about, don't resent going to
school, I would encourage you to not let it get to you, finish, finish, go to school as much as
you can, because a day will come you will need it. (108) Maybe

kʌ·tho waʔkáheweʔ tsiʔ kahwistá·eks, kwahikʌ́ tsiʔ wʌto·lé·. (109) Tákʌʔ
here   time has come   at   it strikes metal, just really that it is hard.   Don't

katiʔ   tho   ni·yót tsiʔ tʌhsatʌ́·nukeʔ tsiʔ ní· ni·yót   tsiʔ tewakatʌ́·nu kwáh
well then thus so it is that you will err   as me how it is that I have erred just

í·,   katsyapslanáklehkweʔ olihwakayú, kʌʔ nikatsyapslá·saʔ a·hoyo·tʌ́·,   né· kwí·
me, jobs used to be plentiful old times,   small jobs   he could work,   so it's

ní· thikʌ́ kenyahe·sʌ́.   (110) ʌwa·tú· yah tha·katáyahteʔ,   don't have no
me that   I depend on it.   It can be not I won't go to school, don't have no

education, ʌwa·tú· kiʔ   ʌwakyo·tʌ́· sʌ́haʔ ok.   (111) Latiyʌtákwas   sʌ́·
education,   it can be actually I will work nevertheless.   They cut wood also

ʌwa·tú· kwí· né· yah tehahyatuhslayʌtelí   a·hataʔshaloʔthi·yó·.
it can be   it's not he doesn't have an education for him to sharpen a saw.

(112) Ótyahkeʔ kʌs   lu·té·,   yukhlo·líheʔ s olihwakayú, lu·té·,   tsiʔ náheʔ
       Some   habitually they say, they tell me   old times,   they say,   while

ʌhakwe·ní·   Lukwehuwé ʌhataʔshaloʔthi·yó· kháleʔ ʌhahyoʔthi·yáteʔ laoto·kʌ́·,
he will be able Native man   he will sharpen a saw and   he will sharpen   his axe,

tho   kiʔ   náheʔ   kwáh yah náhteʔ thaʔtahotworry,   tyótkut tsiʔ
that's actually how long just   not anything he should not worry, always because

ʌhotsyapslayʌ·tákeʔ.   (113) Nók tsiʔ yaʔkáheweʔ né· tsiʔ kahwistá·eks nʌ   né·
he will have a job.   But   it's that time it's at   it strikes metal now it's

wahutstáhsiʔ   crosscut saw, chain saw núwaʔ né· lútstaʔ   latiyʌtákwas,
they finished using crosscut saw,   chain saw this time it's they use they cut wood,

kháleʔ yah tho té·tsyot   tsiʔ latiyʌtákwas tsiʔ ni·yót   olihwaka·yú.
and   not that's not how it is anymore that they cut wood as   how it is old times.

the time has come now, it's really hard. (109) Don't make the kind of mistakes I made, there used to be a lot of jobs in the old days, small jobs that a man might do, and me, I counted on that. (110) It was possible for me not to go to school, don't have no education, I could work nevertheless. (111) Cutting wood also, it doesn't take an education to sharpen a saw. (112) Some say, they tell me that in the old days, they used to say, as long as an Indian could sharpen a saw and sharpen his axe, he had nothing to worry about, because he would always have a job. (113) But there came a time when they were done using the crosscut saw, now they use a chain saw for cutting wood, and cutting wood is not like it was in the old times.

(114) Né· núwaʔ   tsyoʔk náhteʔ   kwahotokʌ́·u tsiʔ nok ʌwa·tú·
      And   this time all kinds of things just for real   that it has to be

ʌhsyatuhslayʌtelíha<u>keʔ</u>.   (115) Shekú a·hsyʌtakó·naʔ   nok ʌwa·tú·
you will have an education.   Even   for you to go cut wood it has to be

ʌhsyatuhslayʌtelíha<u>keʔ</u>.
you will have an education.

  (116) Ok neʔ thó·neʔ yah nʌʔ né·, né· katiʔ ní· kenyahesʌ́,   tahnú· utó·ktʌʔ,
        But at that time not that's it, well it's me I depend on it, and   it ended,

ukwató·ktahseʔ kiʔwáh, kwahikʌ́ tsiʔ wʌto·<u>lé</u>·.   (117) Tá·t núwaʔ né· tsiʔ
it ended for me right,   just really that it is hard.   Maybe   it's at

nitwakenú   shekú tsyoʔk náhteʔ   a·kkwe·ní·   toká·t kwí·
where I have come from still   all kinds of things I would be able if

a·khyatuhslayʌtelíha<u>keʔ</u>.   (118) Ok neʔ tsiʔ   yah teʔkhyatuhslayʌtelí
I would have an education.   But   because not   I don't have an education

yah kwí· thau·tú·   náhteʔ   na·kátyeleʔ, shekú n tá·t a·khyatuhslayʌtelíhakeʔ
not   it can't be anything that I do,   still   if   I would have an education

office kwí· wé·ne   aukyó·tekeʔ,   au·tú·   tsiʔ nitwakenú   she·<u>kú</u>.
office   evidently I may be working, it could be at   where I have come from still.

(119) Wakataʔkali·té· ó<u>ni</u>ʔ.   (120) Nók tsiʔ yah kiʔ   thau·tú·   né· tsiʔ
      I am healthy   too.   But   not   actually it can't be because

yah teʔwákyʌʔ education tsiʔ ni·yót   tsiʔ latiliʔwanú<u>tha</u>ʔ.   (121) Né· katiʔ wí·
not   I don't have education as   how it is that   they are asking.   Well then

a·kwahletsya·lú·   tsiʔ ka·yʌ́· swatahúhsateʔ   tsiʔ náhteʔ wakathlolí, tákʌʔ
I would encourage you all the one that you all are listening that what   I am telling,   don't

(114) Nowadays for all kinds of things you really have to have an education. (115) Even to cut wood you have to have an education.

   (116) But as for that time it wasn't the case, I depended on that, and that has ended, it ended for me right, it's really hard. (117) Maybe at my age I could still do things if I had an education. (118) But because I don't have an education I can't do anything, still if I had an education I would be working in an office, I could still [do it] at my age. (119) I'm healthy after all. (120) But I can't because I don't have the education like they are asking for. (121) So I would encourage all you who are listening to what I'm talking about, don't

ʌswatkʌ·lat   tá·t   swatayá·thaʔ,   toká·t   shekú   tsyóhslat   satayaʔtá·nehseʔ,
you all quit   if   you all go to school,   if   still   one year   you are going to school,

yahá·tshan,   akwekú   yahá·tshan   tsiʔ nikú   teyotuhutsyóhu   a·hsatáyahteʔ,
finish,   all   finish   how much   it should be   for you to go to school,

shekú   seyʌtéhtan   thok náhohteʔ.   (122)   Yah   tho   té·yot   tsiʔ   ta·hsatunhuka·lí·
still   learn   something.   Not   that's   not how it is   that   you should suffer

tsiʔ   ni·yót   tsiʔ   wakatatʌlʌ́   nʌʔú·wa,   tho   katiʔ   nikú   wá·kelheʔ   náhteʔ
as   how it is   that   I am left   now,   that's   anyway   how much   I thought   what

a·kí·luʔ,   kwah nók   a·knihletsya·lú·   tsyatataskénhʌ
I would say,   just   I would encourage you two   you two are trying your best

kʌʔ   nitisniyʌ́·saʔ,   sniyʌ·télen,   kwáh s   tsiʔ nikú   ʌwa·tú·.   (123)   Tákʌʔ   kwáh ok
you two young ones,   you two learn,   just   how much   it can be.   Don't   just

thʌtsyatye·sát   tsiʔ   tesnúnheʔ,   né·   aolí·waʔ   tsiʔ   ʌtwʌhnisla·tékeʔ
you two will waste it   at   you two are alive,   it's   the reason   because   there will come a day

tʌtehsatatlihwástʌʔ   tá·t   ʌhsatye·sáhteʔ.   (124)   Wakatleʔslaká·teʔ   kwáh
you will regret it   if   you will waste it.   I have many grandchildren   just

waʔkáheweʔ   tsiʔ   kahwistá·eks,   ótyahkeʔ   kwáh ok   thyehonatyesahtuhátyeʔ
time has come   at   it strikes metal,   some   just   they are going along just wasting

tsiʔ   náhteʔ   nihutyélhaʔ,   kwáh   yah   náhteʔ   thaʔtehotitíhʌ,   nók tsiʔ
that   what   they are doing,   just   not   anything   they do not care,   but

ʌtwʌhnisla·tékeʔ   kiʔ   ta·wé·   tʌthutatlihwástʌʔ,   khehlo·líheʔ   oniʔ
it will come a day   actually   it is coming   they will regret it,   I tell them   too

ʌshʌnehyá·laneʔ   oniʔ   náhteʔ   khehlo·líheʔ,   ʌtwʌhnisla·tékeʔ   ʌhotitʌ́htaneʔ
they will remember   too   what   I tell them,   it will come a day   they will become poor

quit if you're going to school, if you have one year left to go to school, finish, finish as much as you need to go to school, learn something more. (122) That way you won't suffer the way that I am left now, that's all I thought I would say, just that I would encourage you young people to try your best, learn, as much as you can. (123) Don't waste your life, the reason is because there will come a day you will regret if you waste it. (124) I have a lot of grandchildren and this very hour some of them are just wasting their time at what they're doing, they don't care about anything, but a day will come, it is coming, they will be sorry, I tell them too and they will remember too what I tell them, come a day they will lose out

né· ʌkalihu·ní.   (125) Snitsyakʌ́   kati? kʌ? nitisniyʌ́·sa?,
it's   it will be the reason.   You two try your best   then   you two young people,

tsyatunhahni·lát   khále? tsyatʌ?nikuhkátstat. (126) Tho   nikú   wá·kelhe?
you two persevere   and   you two endure.   That's   how much I wanted

náhte? a·kí·lu?.
what   I would say.

because of it. (125) So do your best you young people, stick it out and don't give up.
(126) That's all what I wanted to say.

Learning to Work in Tobacco

(Told by Olive Elm to Karin Michelson on January 29, 1998)

(1) Shekólih. (2) Wé·ni kwí· a·kwaka·látuhse?   tsi? ni·yót tsi? twakatáhsawʌ?
     Hello.   So I guess   I may tell you all a story   how   it is so   that   I have started

oyu?kwá·ke wakyo·hté·.   (3) Áhsʌ   yawʌ·lé· tsha?tewakohsliyá·ku
tobacco   I am working.   Three   teen   when I have crossed over winters

tshutakatáhsawʌ?.   (4) Tahnú· né· ki? n   laknulhá· Jake luwa·yáts   wahaklihúni? n
when I started.   And   it's actually my uncle   Jake is his name   he taught me

aukyo·tʌ́·   utakhenláhtu?.   (5) Tahnú· s tsi?   nihakwattéhtanihe?, nále?
that I work   that I hand leaves to someone.   And   how   he scolds me,   then

só·tsi?   wakya?takʌheyú tshutakatáhsawʌ?. (6) Né· s nʌ   tahinláhtu?,
too much   my body has died   when I started.   It's   when   I handed leaves to him,

"hányo   tesashlíhʌ." (7) "Só·tsi?   nʌ   ki?   saya?takʌhe·yú." (8) Tá·thuni?,
"come on   hurry up."   "Too much   now   actually   your body has died."   Or,

(1) Hello. (2) So I guess I'll tell you the story about how it was that I got started working in
tobacco. (3) I was thirteen when I started. (4) And it was my uncle Jake that taught me how
to hand [tobacco] leaves. (5) And he used to really get after me, because I was so slow
when I started. (6) When I would hand him leaves [he'd say], "come on, hurry up!"
(7) "You're too slow." (8) Or,

"tékni ok, ka·té· se? áhsʌ ni·kú."   (9) "Áhsʌ nikanláhtake
"two   only,   I am saying   too   three   how much."   "Three   the leaves amount to

ʌtésku?."   (10) Nʌ kyale? wí· sʌ́ha? wa?katya?tashno·láte?.   (11) Tahnú· s
you will hand it to me."   So again   more   I did it quickly.   And

né· nʌ wa?katya?tashno·láte?, nʌ kʌs né· sʌ́ha? yah tha·kkwe·ní·
it's   when   I did it quickly,   then   habitually   it's   more   not   I am not able

áhsʌ nikú a·khla·kó· ónlahte?.   (12) Tá·thuni? ʌwaká·sʌhse?.
three   how much   I would pick it up   leaf.   Or   I will drop it.

(13) Nʌ kyale? wí· tho sahatli?wáksahte?.   (14) Né· s nʌ wa?ó·kalawe?,
So again   there   again he got in a rage.   It's   when   it got dark,

nʌ wa?akwatolíshʌ?, nʌ kʌ? nú· nahahnyo·tʌ́· khilslákta? oshú·kale?,
when   we rested,   then   right there   he stood it up   near the kill   board,

tho wahateshwá·lʌ?.   (15) Né· wí· wahʌ́·lu?, "nʌ ukeshwanú·wake? tsi?
there   he set his back on it.   So it's   he said,   "now   I got a sore back   because

yah te?salʌ?nhá·u utashenláhtu?,"   nʌ kyale? wí· wahakhlo·lí·
not   you don't know how   you should hand leaves to someone,"   so again   he told me

tsi? naákyele?.   (16) Wahʌ́·lu? "yah ki? thya·ya·wʌ́· tsi? katokʌ́ tsi? niyo·lé·
how   I should do it.   He said   "it has to be   that   certain   how far

ʌtéstate?, né· aolí·wa? tsi? ka·yʌ́· lahwánhaks tá·thuni? yehwánhaks
you will extend it,   it's   the reason   the one that   he ties   or   she ties

yah kwí· tha·yakoshwanú·wake?."   (17) "Tsi? tá·t só·tsi? ehtá·ke
not   one won't get a sore back."   "Because   if   too much   below

ʌ́state? yah thya·ya·wʌ́· tsi? ya?tʌyutnʌ́tshatate? yʌyeye·ná·
you will extend it   it has to be   that   one will extend one's arm   way over one will grasp

"two only, I said three." (9) "You're to hand me three leaves." (10) So then I would start to go faster. (11) And then I would rush, and even more I couldn't pick up three leaves. (12) Or I would drop them. (13) So then he would start ranting again. (14) At night, when we would rest [get done for the day], he would put a board right up against the kill, and he would put his back up against [this board]. (15) And he'd say, "I've got a sore back because you don't know how to hand leaves," so he would tell me again how to do it. (16) He said "you have to hand them at a certain level, that way whosoever is tying won't get a sore back." (17) "Because if you hand them too low, the person has to reach over to grasp

oyú·kwaʔ tsiʔ niyo·lé· nʌ a·yehwánhakeʔ tá·thuniʔ a·hahwánhake<u>ʔ</u>.”   (18) Kwáh kwí·
tobacco   before   she would tie it   or   he would tie it.”   Just

nyaʔtewʌhnislaké thok náhteʔ wahaklihúnyʌʔ tsiʔ naákye<u>le</u>ʔ.   (19) Né·n,   áhsʌ
every day   something   he taught me   how   I should do it.   It's that, three

kyuhte wí· niwʌ·táke   thikʌ́ tsiʔ náheʔ núwaʔ tshyahutéhsaneʔ yukwayo·té·
supposedly weeks amount to that   while   then   when it got done   we are working

oyú·kwaʔ, nʌ   wahʌ́·luʔ, “nʌ   kiʔ   ostúha sayʌtehtaʔuhátiʔ,” wahʌ́·luʔ
tobacco,   then   he said,   “now   actually   a little you are learning,”   he said

“nʌ   kiʔ   ʌwa·tú· a·stsyapslisákhaʔ,   tá·t núwaʔ nʌ   kátshaʔ ok nú·
“now   actually   it can be that you go look for a job, maybe   now   somewhere

utayesánhan<u>eʔ</u>.”   (20) Tahnú· tsiʔ   nuknehla·kó·   e·só· ukwatkályah<u>kse</u>ʔ.
someone would hire you.”   And   how   I was surprised   a lot   I got paid.

(21) Wé·ni tsiʔ tá·t núwaʔ tsya·ták nikahwístake   swʌhníslat ukwatkályah<u>kse</u>ʔ.
      Evidently   maybe   seven   dollars amount to one day   I got paid.

(22) Nʌ   kyuhte wí· kátshaʔ ok nú· kaʔikʌ́ kayé niwáshʌ wísk niyohslaké
      Then   supposedly somewhere   this   four   tens   five   years amount to

tsiʔ náheʔ onʌ́ kaʔi·<u>kʌ́</u>. (23) Tsiʔ náheʔ niswakathlo·lí.   (24) Né·n,   nʌ kwí·
since   now   this.   Since   I am telling about.   It's that, so then

tusayokʌnhu·tí·   nʌ sók   waʔktsyapslisákhaʔ   aukyoʔtʌ́hsaʔ   úhkaʔ ok
it came summer again and so then   I went in search of a job that I go and work   someone

utakhenláh<u>tu</u>ʔ.   (25) Né·n,   kwáh kiʔ   né· kok náheʔ   ókhnaʔ
that I hand leaves to someone.   It's that, just   actually it's a little while   and then

waʔkenhaʔtslo·lʌ́neʔ waʔktsyapslo·lʌ́neʔ, né·n   Nellieha ʌtyakninláhtuʔ,
I found hired work   I found a job,   it's that Nellie   we two will hand leaves to her,

the tobacco before she or he can tie it.” (18) Every day he taught me something [different]
about how I should do it. (19) So I guess it was three weeks before we got through working
the tobacco, then he said, “now you are getting to know a little,” he said “now you can go
and look for a job, maybe now you will get hired somewhere.” (20) And I was really surprised I got paid so much. (21) I guess I got paid maybe seven dollars a day. (22) I think it
was about forty-five years since this was. (23) Since the time I'm talking about. (24) So
come next summer I went and looked for a job working to hand leaves to somebody.
(25) So in a little while I found work, I found a job, we would hand leaves to Nellie,

í· khále? Annabelle wa?tyakniye·ná·.   (26) Tahnú· né· tsi? na?ukniyanlʌ́hsle?
me and Annabelle we two pulled together.   And it's how it's going well for us

tsi? wa?tyakniye·ná·,   kwahotokʌ́·u wa?akniyʌtéhtane?, elhúwa? kyuhte wí·
at we two pulled together, just for real we two learned,   recently supposedly

né· kuwalihunyʌní   aulhá· Annabelle utayakonláhtu?.   (27) Tsi?
it's one has taught her her Annabelle that she hands leaves to someone.   How

na?ukniyanlʌ́hsele?. (28) Wa?tyakniye·ná·   wa?akniyʌtéhtane?, nók tsi? né·
it's going well for us.   We two pulled together we two learned,   but it's

kyuni? wí· né· tsi? onulhá·   Nellieha, nále?   yah thutayakniye·líte? s
too   because her mother Nellie,   then again not we two won't do it right

ʌyuknihlo·lí·   kyuni? wí· nʌ? né·, tsi?   né· sok ʌwa·tú·   ʌyesahlo·lí·
she will tell us two too   that one, because it's it has to be too one will tell you

tsi? niyo·lé· ʌhseyʌtéhtane? náhte? nihsatyélha?. (29) Wa?uknihlo·lí· s kyuhte wí·
until   you will learn what you are doing.   She told us two supposedly

né· nále?   yah te?tyakniye·líts.   (30) Tá·thuni? só·tsi?   e·só·
it's then again not we two do not do it right.   Or   too much a lot

tʌyaknitha·lʌ́·,   kwah nók yukniyéshuhe?   wa?uknihlo·lí· kʌs,   "hányo
we two will converse, just   we two are laughing she told us two habitually, "come on

tsyatwá·nik   sniyotʌ́   ka?i·kʌ́." (31) "Yah né· thau·tú· aetwáhsane?,
you two shut up you two work this."   "It can't be   that you and we finish,

kwah nók kʌ? tesníthale?   khále? kʌ? tesnihʌlétha?
just   here you two are conversing and here you two are hollering

sniyéshuhe?."   (32) Nʌ kyale? wí· wa?akyatwá·nike? kʌ? náhe? nále?
you two are laughing."   So again we two got quiet a while then again

me and Annabelle would work as a team (Nellie was Annabelle's mother and the "tier").
(26) And the two of us made a good team, we learned a lot, I guess Annabelle herself was
just recently taught to hand leaves. (27) It was going well for us. (28) We worked together
and we learned, but also it's because her mother Nellie, when we weren't doing it right she
would tell us, because you have to be told until you get to know what you are doing. (29) I
guess she would tell us when we weren't doing it right. (30) Or we would talk a whole lot,
we were just laughing and she would tell us, "come on, be quiet and get to work." (31) "We
can't get done with the two of you here just talking and hollering here and you two laughing." (32) So then we would be quiet again for a while but then

tayakyatáhsawʌʔ   sayakyata·tí·.
we two started   we two spoke again.

(33)   Yaʔwéskwaʔt   kʌs   kiʔ   tsiʔ   naʔukwayo·tʌ́·,   áhsok   nále?
        It is nice   usually   actually   that   we worked,   suddenly   then again

waʔokʌ·nóleʔ,   yah teʔwé·ni   naʔakwayaʔtana·wʌ́·,   tho   kiʔ   yukwayo·hté·.
it rained,   it's incredible   how we got wet,   there   actually   we are working.

(34)   Né· s wí· tsiʔ   neʔ thó·neʔ   nʌ   wahʌ́·luʔ   kʌs   laboss,   nʌ sók
        Because   at that time   then   he said   habitually   the boss,   and so then

nʌ   ʌtyakwatáhsawʌʔ   a·yukwayo·tʌ́·,   yah kiʔ thya·ya·wʌ́·   tsiʔ   ʌyakwatnúhsikeʔ
then   we will start   that we work,   it has to be   that   we will fill the house

tsiʔ niyo·lé·   nʌ   ʌyakwatkʌ́·lahteʔ.   (35)   Né· katiʔ   aolí·waʔ   ati   yokʌnolú,
until   then   we will quit.   Well it's   the reason   no matter   it is raining,

yah kiʔ thya·ya·wʌ́·   tsiʔ   waʔukwayo·tʌ́·   tsiʔ niyo·lé·   waʔakwatnúhsikeʔ   nʌ
it has to be   that   we worked   until   we filled the house   then

waʔakwatkʌ́·lahteʔ.   (36)   Wahʌ́·luʔ   kʌs,   tá·t yah   thaútnaneʔ n   skanúhsat,
we quit.   He said   habitually,   if   not   it won't get filled   one house,

yah kiʔ thau·tú·   a·hate·ká·teʔ   óksaʔ ok,   tá·t núwaʔ   ʌwahétkʌneʔ n   oyú·kwaʔ.
it can't be   that he fires it up   right away,   maybe   it will spoil   tobacco.

(37)   Né· kiʔ   aolí·waʔ   lu·té·   kʌs   nok ʌwa·tú·   ʌyakwatnúhsikeʔ
        It's   actually   the reason   they are saying   habitually   it has to be   we will fill the house

tsiʔ niyo·lé·   nʌ   ʌyakwatkʌ́·lahteʔ.   (38)   Wakyoʔtʌ́·u   oniʔ,   shekú   nʌ   tetyó·kalas,
until   then   we will quit.   I have worked   too,   still   when   it gets dark,

shekú   tho   yukwayo·té·,   né· s wí·   nále?   watéhsaʔas,   wʌto·lé· kwí·
still   there   we are working,   it's   then again   it gets finished,   it is difficult

we would start to talk again.
   (33) It was nice us working, but then all of a sudden it would rain, and we would get soak-
ing wet, yet we'd be working. (34) Because at that time the boss used to say, once we get
started working, we have to fill the kill before we quit. (35) That is why no matter if it's
raining, we have to work until we fill the kill and then we quit. (36) He said, if the whole
kill didn't get filled, he couldn't fire it up right away, and the tobacco might spoil. (37) This
is the reason why they say we have to fill the kill before we quit. (38) I've worked too, even
when it's dark, still we're working there, this is when it's finishing up,

utakutáyahteʔ   oyú·kwaʔ,   oskanʌ́ha   tsiʔ   tayonatayaʔtuhátiʔ,   swatyelʌ́ s   tá·t núwaʔ
for them to come in   tobacco,   slowly   that   they are coming in,   sometimes   maybe

a·kí·luʔ   tékni   waʔtkahwistá·ekeʔ   waʔakwatnúhtuhteʔ,   tahnú·   oyá·   tekahu·wáke
I'd say   two   metal struck   we waited for it,   and   another   two boats

tututáyahteʔ,   nʌ kyaleʔ wí·   sayakwahwánha<u>ke</u>ʔ.   (39) Nʌ katiʔ   aolí·waʔ   thikʌ́
it came in,   so again   we tied again.   Well then   the reason   that

waʔukwayo·tʌ́·,   nʌ   tetyó·kalas   kwáh sók   wahuttsistotúnyuʔ   laotí·slet,
we worked,   then   it gets dark   just too   they put on lights   their cars,

kaʔslehtaké·luʔ,   waʔukwayo·tʌ́·   kanyó· ok   au·tú·   a·yakwatnúhsi<u>ke</u>ʔ.
there's cars strewn around,   we worked   so that   it could be   that we fill the house.

(40) Wahatiyuʔkwiha·lʌ́·   sʌ́·,   né· kiʔ ok u·tú·   ká·slet   wahʌ·nútsteʔ   wahuttsistotúni<u>ʔ</u>.
        They hung tobacco   also,   it had to be   car   they used   they put on lights.

(41) Nʌ   sa·kéweʔ   wakyoʔtʌhsu·hné· n   tetyó·kalas,   kwáh   olihwiyó   tsiʔ   nʌ
        Then   I got home   I have gone to work   it gets dark,   just   a sure thing   that   then

tá·t núwaʔ   thóha   wá·tluʔ   niyohwistá·e,   nʌ   sa·kéweʔ   wakyoʔtʌhsu·hné·,
maybe   almost   nine   metal has struck,   then   I got home   I have gone to work,

aknulhá·   yutwilanúnha<u>ʔ</u>.   (42) Yah   né·   teʔwé·ni   naʔakoná·khwʌʔ
my mother   she is minding a child.   Not   it's   it's incredible   how she got mad

aknulhá·   niwakeʔniskwʌʔuháti<u>ʔ</u>.   (43) Waʔí·luʔ,   "kátshaʔ   né·   nú·
my mother   how I am coming along late.   She said,   "where   it's   where

tisatkáthu   nʌ   tetyó·kalas   shekú   swayo·h<u>té</u>·."   (44) Waʔí·luʔ   yah
you have seen   then   it gets dark   still   you all are working."   She said   not

né·   thutayakéhtahkweʔ   tsiʔ   yukwayo·té·   nʌ   tetyó·kalas,   yu·té·   "ákteʔ
it's   she didn't believe it   that   we are working   then   it gets dark,   she says   "different

the tobacco is hard to get in, [the tobacco] are slow coming in, sometimes I'd say we waited maybe two hours, and then another two boats would come in, so we would start tying again. (39) Well that's why we worked, when it was dark people just put the lights on their cars, the cars that were all around, we worked so that we could fill the kill. (40) Also [when] they hung the tobacco, they had to use the cars for lights. (41) When I got home from work it was dark, I'm sure it was almost nine o'clock, when I got home from work, my mother was babysitting. (42) My mother got really upset at my being so late. (43) She said, "where did you ever see when it's dark and you people are still working?" (44) She said she didn't believe that we were working and it's dark, she says

uhte   ale? nú·   nyehéhsehse?,   sa·té·   sayo?tʌhsu·hné·."
supposedly again where over there you are around, you say you have gone to work."

(45) Tahnú· nʌ   wa?kí·lu?, "tá·t kwí· tákʌ? utaséhtak   onʌ́, né· ki?
      And   then I said,   "if   don't you would believe it now,   it's actually

ok wí· ʌwa·tú· Nellieha yʌhsatwʌnáta?ahse?, ʌyesahlo·lí·   tsi? tú·ske? nʌ kíh."
it has to be   Nellie   you will telephone her, she will tell you that   it's true   indeed."

(46) Kwah nók sayeste·líste?, wa?í·lu?, "wé·ni   ki? wí· tá·t sa·yʌ́·   úhka? ok
      Just   she laughed,   she said, "evidently actually if   you have someone

utayesashwanétane?   tsi? tkaye·lí· náhte? skhlolí,   wé·ni   kati? wí·
for someone to back you up that it is right what   you are telling me, evidently well

to·kʌ́ske?." (47) E·só· ki?   thikʌ́ tho niyawʌ́·u,   nʌ   kʌs
it's true."   A lot actually that   thus it has happened, then habitually

tutayo?kala?uháti?,   nʌ   elhúwa? wa?akwatnúhsike?.   (48) Nʌ   sʌ́ha? tá·t
it is getting dark again, then just then we filled the house.   Then   more   if

lotiya?takʌheyú   tsi? ka·yʌ́· latiyu?kwákwas.   (49) Tá·t latiya?tashno·lé·,
their bodies have died the one that they pick tobacco.   If   they are fast,

kwáh kʌs   ki?   né· swatyelʌ́ s tékni teyohwistá·e   ókhna?
just   habitually actually it's sometimes two   metal has struck and then

yukwáhsu?.   (50) Tá·t ki?   kʌtyohkwi·yǫ́.   (51) Nók tsi? ki?
we have finished.   If   actually   it's a good group.   But   actually

yah thya·ya·wʌ́· tsi? kʌtyohkwiyó,   nʌ   elhúwa? yoshno·lé· ʌwatéhsane?.
it has to be   that it's a good group, then just then it is fast   it will get finished.

(52) Yah thau·tú· thikʌ́ kwah nók kok náhe? khále? useswatolishʌ·táke?.
      It can't be   that   just   a little while and   again you all would be resting.

"you must have been some place else, and you said you were at work." (45) And then I
said, "if you don't believe it, you just have to telephone Nellie, she'll tell you that it's true,
so there." (46) She just laughed, she said, "I guess if you have somebody to back you up
that it's right what you're telling me, well then I guess it's true." (47) A lot of times this
happened, it is getting dark and then only we filled our kill. (48) More so if the ones who
were picking the tobacco were slow. (49) If they were fast, then sometimes by two o'clock
we were done. (50) If it was a good group. (51) But it had to be a good group, only then it
would get done fast. (52) You couldn't be resting every little while.

(53) Né· s ki?   ní· nʌ   wa?ukwayo·tʌ́·, kwáh wa?ukwayo·tʌ́· kwáh
     It's   actually us   when   we worked,   just   we worked   quite

tsi? niyo·lé· ʌ́tye ni·kále?, a·lé·   kʌs   ókhna?   yukwanuhsatasé
until   noon time,   at times usually and then we have gone around the house

tsi? niyo·lé· nʌ   ʌ́tye ni·ká<u>le</u>?. (54) Ókhna? né·n   oyá·   elʌ́ nukwá· ná·wati
until   then noon time.   And then it's that another across   side

tetyukwatáhsaw<u>ʌ</u>?.   (55) Nʌ kati? né· tá·t tho   na·ya·wʌ́ne?,   yoshno·lé· kwí·
we have started again.   So then it's if   thus it would happen, it is fast

ókhna?   ʌyakwatnúhsi<u>ke</u>?.   (56) Nʌ s nʌ   ʌtákta? kwáh kʌs   tsya·ták
and then we will fill the house.   Then then Saturday just   habitually seven

niyohwistá·e   astéhtsi?   ókhna?   tayakwatáhsawʌ?, né· wí· niyoshno·lé·
metal has struck in the morning and then we started,   so it's   it is so fast

teyukwatuhutsyoní a·yakwáhsane? tsi?   ʌtákta?,   au·tú· kwí· né· kanatá·ke
we want   we should finish because Saturday, it could be it's   town

ya·yákowe?.   (57) Nʌ   tayakwatáhsawʌ? uhte   kwáh kʌs kwí· shekú
that we go over there.   Then we started   supposedly just   habitually still

yoshno·lé·, kwáh se? s wa?kʌ́·lu?, "hányo   tesnishlíhʌ,   hányo   hányo   tákʌ?
it is fast,   just   too   she said,   "come on   you two hurry, come on come on, don't

ʌtsyatya?takʌhe·yát   tá·t ísnelhe?   yoshno·lé· aetsyatatwʌni·yó<u>ne</u>?."
you two let your bodies die if   you two want it is fast   for you two to free yourselves."

(58) Nʌ kyale? wí· wa?tyuknishlíh<u>ʌ</u>?. (59) Ya?wéskwa?t kʌs   ki?   tsi?
     So again   we two hurried.   It is nice   habitually actually because

niyukwe?tiyó   tsi? ka·yʌ́· tyakninlahta·wí<u>he</u>?.   (60) Ati tsi?   áhsok
she is a nice person the one that we two hand leaves to her.   Even though suddenly

(53) So then we worked, we worked right until noon, there were times we moved around the kill before noon. (54) And then we got started on the other side. (55) So then if that happened, we filled our kill real quick. (56) Then on Saturdays we started right at seven o'clock in the morning, we wanted to finish fast because it's Saturday, so we could go to town. (57) Then we would start to go faster still, she said, "come on, hurry, come on, come on, don't slow up if you want to get away early." (58) So then we rushed. (59) It was nice because she was really good [to us], this person that we were handing leaves to. (60) Even though suddenly

náleʔ   waʔukyattéhtʌʔ,   nók tsiʔ yukwanúhteʔ kwí· né· tsiʔ,   nók tsiʔ a·kí·luʔ
then again   she scolded us two,   but   we know   because, but only   I'd say

yowʌnolehtányuheʔ oniʔ nʌʔ né·.
she is kidding   too   that one.

she would get after us, but we know it's because she's only kidding.

All about Tobacco

(Told by Mercy Doxtator to Karin Michelson on January 30, 1998)

(1) Ú·waʔ wískhatut, áhsʌ niwáshʌ tshískaleʔ   teyakohúhtyaʔks,   1998.
     Now   Friday,   three tens   it's that time again one's ears are freezing, 1998.

(2) Né· kyuhte wí· a·kathlo·lí·   tsiʔ ní· náhteʔ kehya·lú·   ya·wét
     It's supposedly I should tell about that me   what   I remember things kind of like

a·kí·luʔ oyú·kwaʔ aolihwá<u>ke</u>.   (3) Tsiʔ s wí· niyohtú·neʔ   tshiwahu·níseʔ,
I'd say tobacco concerning.   How   the way it was a long time ago,

lotitshahnihtú·neʔ   yukhiyʌʔokúha, tyótkut elók   shʌ·né· lotiyoʔtʌ́hslehseʔ,
they used to be industrious   our parents,   always all over they go   they go to work,

kwáh tsiʔ uhte náhteʔ utahsanuhtúniʔ   né· kiʔ   núwaʔ   sahotiyoʔtʌ́<u>hsa</u>ʔ.
whatever probably   you might think of it's actually this time again they went to work.

(4) Luhyákwas,   latiyʌ́thos, nʌ   sʌ́· nyaʔkáheweʔ wahatiyuʔkwayʌthóhsluʔ
     They pick berries, they plant,   then also it came time   they went planting tobacco

sʌ́·,   nʌ kiʔ ok aleʔ wí· wahutaténhaneʔ,   kátshaʔ ok nú· tahuwatínhaneʔ,
also,   and then again   they hired themselves out,   somewhere   someone hired them,

(1) Today it's Friday, the thirtieth of January, the time when one's ears are freezing, 1998.
(2) I guess I should talk about what I remember, like I'd say, concerning tobacco. (3) The
way it was a long time ago, our parents used to be industrious, they were always going all
over to work, whatever you might think of, they went to work at. (4) They picked berries,
they planted, and then also it would be the time for them to go planting tobacco, and then
again they would hire themselves out, they would get hired somewhere,

swatyelʌ́ s kwahotokʌ́·u tho   yahúti<u>ʔ</u>.   (5) Tho   akwekú kwáh tsiʔ
sometimes   just for real   there they moved over there.   There all   just   how

nikahwatsi·lá·,   tho   yahúti?   kʌ́·,   nʌ   wahotiyo·<u>tʌ́·</u>.   (6) Tahnú· s kwí·
big is the family, there they moved over there   see,   then they worked.   And

né· neʔ thó·neʔ kok   né· nihʌ·ná·seʔ   latiksaʔshúha ókhnaʔ   wahuwatilihúniʔ
it's at that time   small only it's   the size they are   children   and then   they taught them

a·hotiyo·<u>tʌ́·</u>.   (7) Né· katiʔ   aolí·waʔ   nʌ   ʌhutótyakeʔ   ʌhotitshahnihtʌ́hakeʔ
that they work.   So then it's   the reason   when   they will grow up   they will be industrious

kiʔwáh.   (8) Khále? s wí· né· ne? thó·ne? tshiwathawinúti?,   yah   né·
right.   And   it's   at that time   when it was those times,   not   it's

te?kanáklehkwe? n welfare núwa?   latina?túkhwa? kʌ́·,   yah kati?   thya·ya·wʌ́·
it wasn't present   welfare   this time   what they call it   y'know,   not   well then   it has to be

tsi? wahotiyo·tʌ́· kʌ́h.   (9) Né· s kati? wí·   ní· tsi? náhte? kehya·lú·
that   they worked   see.   So then anyway me   that   what   I remember things

a·kí·lu?   oyú·kwa? a·kathlo·lí·,   kwáh s tsyo?k nú·   niyakwʌ́·tlu?,
I would say   tobacco   for me to talk about, just   all over the place we dwell,

úska útlatste? ké·yale?   a?é·   né· Walsingham tho   kuwa·yáts tho nú·
one time   I remember way over   it's Walsingham   there   it is named that's where

thikʌ́ ya?akwáti?   kʌ́·,   wahotiyo·tʌ́· aknulhá·   khále? lake?níha, tahnú·
that   we moved over there y'know,   they worked   my mother   and   my father,   and

lake?níha lahwánhaks kʌs   né·n   oyú·<u>kwa?</u>. (10) Ok wí· n   aknulhá·,
my father   he is tying   habitually it's that   tobacco.   And as for my mother,

ne·né· thuwanlahta·wíhe?   lake?<u>níha</u>. (11) Né· kati? thikʌ́ tho   ni·yót kwí·
it's that she is handing leaves to him   my father.   Well then   that   that's how it is

sometimes they moved there. (5) The whole family moved there, then they worked.
(6) And at that time the children would be just small and already they were taught to work.
(7) That's why when they grew up they would be industrious, right. (8) And at that time, in
those days, what today they call welfare wasn't around, so they had to work. (9) So then
anyway what I remember, I'd say, about tobacco to talk about, we lived all over, one time I
remember way over in Walsingham, so it's called there, that's where we moved to, my
mother and father worked, and my father was tying tobacco. (10) And my mother, she was
handing leaves to my father. (11) Well that's how it was,

elók   shotiyoʔtátiʔ   kʌ·, né· kaʔikʌ́ waʔthútlaneʔ kaʔikʌ́ shayá·tat
all over   they are going along working   see, it's this   they met   this   he is one

Polish nahayaʔtó·tʌ́ʔ.   (12) Elhúwaʔ uhte wí· tho   nithawenú   Poland
Polish what kind he is.   Recently   supposedly there he has come from Poland

kʌʔ wá·laweʔ, waʔthyátlaneʔ lakeʔníha, waʔthyatatyʌ·téleneʔ   kiʔ wí·
here he arrived, the two met   my father,   the two got to know each other actually

kaʔikʌ́ wí· n laPolish.   (13) Wahʌ́·luʔ, "yah" wahʌ́·luʔ? "náhteʔ teʔwakhwístayʌʔ
this   Polish man.   He said,   "not"   he said   "anything I don't have money

nók tsiʔ tsiʔ na·katshanu·ní· a·skyó·tʌhseʔ   kʌ́h."   (14) "Yah thau·tú·
but   how I would get happy you would work for me y'know."   "Not   it can't be

a·kukályaʔkseʔ tsiʔ niyo·lé· tá·t núwaʔ kanʌná·ke tá·thuniʔ ʌyóhslateʔ."
I would pay you   until   maybe   fall   or   it will be winter."

(15) "Nók tsiʔ ʌkukályahkseʔ." (16) "Kwáh thok   nikú   énik   nukwá·
     "But   I will pay you."   "Just   that's only how much upstairs where

ʌswátiʔ   kháleʔ tʌkwakhwáshniʔ,   e·só· yukwayʌthóhsluʔ,
you all will move and   I will have you all as boarders, lots   we have planted things,

kwáh tsiʔ náhteʔ teswatuhutsyoní ʌwa·tú· kwí· ʌ́swakeʔ."   (17) Nʌ katiʔ wí·
just   that what   you all want   it can be   you all will eat."   Well then

né·n   lakeʔníha wahathu·táteʔ kaʔikʌ́ ʌhoyó·tʌhseʔ.   (18) Né·n   to·kʌ́skeʔ
it's that my father   he consented   this   he will work for him.   It's that truly

tshaʔkáheweʔ,   né· kwí· nʌ   tshahatyuʔkwahni·nú· wahokályahkseʔ.
when it came time, so it's   when   when he sold tobacco   he paid him.

(19) Tsiʔ kwí· né· nahatshanu·ní· kʌ́,   kwáh kwí· ya·wét   a·kí·luʔ tsiʔ
     How   it's he got happy   y'know, just   kind of like I'd say   as

they were going working all over, then they met this person, he was Polish. (12) I guess he
had recently come from Poland and got here, he met my father, he and this Polish man got to
know one another. (13) He said, "I don't have any money but I would be so happy if you
worked for me." (14) "I can't pay you until maybe the fall or winter." (15) "But I will pay
you." (16) "The only [thing I can do] is you will live upstairs and I will give you room and
board, we have planted lots, whatever you want you can have to eat." (17) Well then my
father consented to work for him. (18) So truly when it came time, when he sold his tobacco
he paid him. (19) He was so happy, I'd say

niyóhsles   yukwahwístayʌʔ kʌ· tsiʔ nikú   wahokályah<u>kseʔ</u>. (20) Tóhkaʔ
the winter is long   we have money   see   how much   he paid him.   Several

niyohslaké   thikʌ́ wahoyó·tʌhseʔ,   kháleʔ onʌ́ tahanakla·kó·   thikʌ́
years amount to   that   he worked for him,   and   then   he moved this way   that

tho nukwá·,   kʌ́·tho   sʌ́haʔ áktaʔ wahátiʔ,   wahatnatahni·nú·, tsiʔ uhte wí·
that direction,   over here   more   near   he moved,   he sold his place,   at   supposedly

naʔtekyátleʔ   Mount Brydges kháleʔ Strathroy tho   thikʌ́ wahanatahni·nú·,
the two are apart   Mount Brydges   and   Strathroy   there   that   he bought a place,

tho   núwaʔ   nú·   thikʌ́ yusahoyó·tʌhseʔ   lakeʔní<u>ha</u>.
that's   this time   where   that   he worked for him over there again   my father.

(21) Nók tsiʔ kaʔikʌ́ akté·shuʔ sʌ́·   nú· s   lotiyoʔtʌ́hslehseʔ, kwáh s kwí·
     But   this   different   also   where   they go working,   just

ké·yaleʔ   thikʌ́, kʌʔ s ok tshi·ká· kʌ́·   waʔukslu·ní· s   thikʌ́ aknulhá·   kháleʔ
I remember   that,   when I was small y'know   she dressed me   that   my mother   and

yaʔekʌháhaweʔ.   (22) Tahnú· s wí· swatyelʌ́ s nʌ   yotholéniʔ
she took along a blanket.   And   sometimes   then   it was cold now and again

kaʔikʌ́, né· s kyuhte wí· aolí·waʔ   kehya·lú· tsiʔ   nikwístoh<u>seʔ</u>. (23) Tho
this,   it's   supposedly the reason   I remember because I am so cold.   There

thikʌ́ tsiʔ yaʔakoyo·tʌ́·,   tho kwí· watekhwahlaʔtslatátiʔ, tho nú·
that   at   she worked over there,   there   a table extends,   that's where

nikáheleʔ   oyú·kwaʔ kʌ́·, tho   atekhwahlaʔtslokú tho s thikʌ́ ya·wét
it is sitting on top   tobacco   see,   there   under the table   there   that   kind of like

waʔuknaktúniʔ,   tho kwí· ní· nú·   nʌka·láteʔ   kʌ́·, tá·t shekú i·kélheʔ
she made a bed for me,   that's   me   where   I will lie down   see,   if   still   I want

we had money through the winter with how much he paid him. (20) Several years he
worked for him, and then he moved away from there, he moved closer to here, he sold his
place, I guess between Mount Brydges and Strathroy he bought some property, that's where
my father worked for him again.

(21) But they also used to work in some different places, I remember, I was just small, my
mother would dress me and she would take along a blanket. (22) And sometimes it was cold
by then, it's probably the reason I remember, because I was so cold. (23) There where she
was working was a long table, that's where the tobacco was, underneath the table she made
kind of like a bed for me, that's where I would lie down, if I still wanted

usuki·táweʔ,   nók tsiʔ yah kwíʔ thau·tú·   kaʔikʌ́ só·tsiʔ   waknehlakwʌ́·u tsiʔ
I would sleep again,   but   not   it can't be   this   so much   I am amazed   what

niyotye·lʌ̲́. (24) Tehniyáshe nihwánhaks, tahnú· kaʔikʌ́ tsiʔ náhteʔ nihwánhaks
it is doing.   Two   two are tying, and   this   what   two are tying

atahslá·ke thikʌ́, yah teʔské·yaleʔ   tá·tkʌ áhsʌ niwáshʌ tékni tsiʔ nikú
on a stick   that,   not   I don't remember anymore maybe three tens   two   how much

oyú·kwaʔ? tsiʔ kwíʔ nikʌthóhkwake   kʌ́h.   (25) Áhsʌ nikanláhtake
tobacco   what   the bundles amount to   y'know.   Three   the leaves amount to

thikʌ́ skʌthóhkwat wahahwánhakeʔ, ya·wét kwíʔ yá·yaʔk yawʌ·lé· uskatí nukwá·
that   one bundle   he tied,   like   six   teen   one side

wahahalúniʔ kwíʔ ya·wét thikʌ́ oyú·kwaʔ kʌ́h. (26) Thó·nʌ   aknulhá·   ne
he hung several like   that   tobacco   see.   And then   my mother   it's

né·n   thuwanlahta·wíhe̲ʔ.   (27) Thó·nʌ   kaʔikʌ́ nʌ   ʌhátnaneʔ thikʌ́ áhsʌ
it's that   she hands leaves to him.   And then   this   then   he will fill it that   three

niwáshʌ tékni nikʌtstótslake   ókhnaʔ   waʔtha·yá·keʔ thi·k̲ʌ́. (28) Ókhnaʔ
tens   two   the bundles amount to   and then   he broke it   that.   And then

waʔutahslahla·kó· aknulhá·, aʔé· nukwá·   naʔtyeyʌto·tʌ́· khále̲ʔ s onʌ́ aʔé·
she took a stick off   my mother, way over there   she piled it   and   then great

naʔtekayʌ·tés,   a·kí·luʔ kyuhte wíʔ tá·t núwaʔ ísiʔ   kyuhte wíʔ né· nú·
how high is the pile,   I'd say   supposedly maybe   further   supposedly it's where

five feet naʔtekayʌ·tés   thikʌ́ oyú·kwaʔ kʌ́h. (29) Tahnú· kaʔikʌ́ kwáh
five feet   how high is the pile that   tobacco   see.   And   this   just

kʌs   tewatkʌ́ni, úhkaʔ náhteʔ tyeyaʔtashno·lé· a·yehwánhakeʔ tá·thuniʔ
habitually competition, who   someone is fastest that she ties   or

to sleep, but I couldn't because I was too amazed at what was going on. (24) Two people
were tying, and what they were tying to a stick, I don't remember anymore if it was thirty-
two, how many bundles of tobacco there were. (25) He would tie three leaves to one bundle, and he would hang the tobacco [on the stick] so there were like sixteen [bundles] on one
[each] side. (26) And then my mother was handing leaves to him. (27) And then he would
fill [the stick] with the thirty-two bundles and then he would break [the string]. (28) And
then my mother would take off the stick, she would pile it over to the side and soon there
was a really high pile, I'd say maybe over five feet is how high the pile of tobacco would be.
(29) And it was a competition, who was the fastest at tying,

a·hahwánhake?, né· wí· tsi? ka·té·   tehniyáshe nihwánhaks khále? kayé
that he ties,   because   I am saying two   two tie   and   four

nikutí   tá·thuni? nihatí   teshakotinlahta·wíhe?.
so many females   or   so many males they hand leaves to someone.

(30) Teyukwé·take ʌthuwanláhtu?   lake?níha. (31) Khále? teyukwé·take
      Two persons   they will hand leaves to him my father.   And   two persons

ʌthuwanláhtu?   shayá·tat.   (32) Tahnú· ka?ikʌ tsi? nú· nahutahslá·lʌ?,
they will hand leaves to him one person.   And   this   where   they set sticks,

kohsa·tʌs latina?túkhwa? thi·kʌ. (33) A?é· s ehtá·ke thikʌ tho   ká·nyote?
horse   what they call it that.   Way   below   that   there it is standing

ahsli·yé·, tho nú·   ʌtkaláthʌ? thikʌ, tsi? kwí· naha·yéle? thikʌ ʌhahwánhake?
string,   that's where it climbs up that, how   he did it   that   he will tie

tsi? nú· ʌthatáhsawʌ?. (34) Ókhna? nʌ   ʌtwatye·lʌhte? ʌthuwanláhtu?,
where   he will start.   And then then it will be first   one will hand leaves to him,

a?é· nukwá·   ná·wati nyʌho·tí·   kʌ·, thó·nʌ né·n   tsyeyá·tat
way over that way that side he will throw it see, and then it's that one person

tʌthuwanláhtu?   kʌh né· nukwá· ná·wati. (35) Tho kwí·
again one will hand leaves to him over this way   that side.   Thus

niyohtuháti?.   (36) Tahnú· yoshno·lé·, nok ʌwa·tú· ʌknishno·léke?   tsi? ka·yʌ·
it is going along.   And   it is fast,   it has to be the two will be fast the one that

thuwanlahta·wíhe?.   (37) Tho   kati? ni·yót thikʌ ka·té·   kwáh s tewatkʌni
they hand leaves to him.   Thus   then   it is so that   I am saying just   competition

úhka? náhte? nya·lé· ʌyéhsane?   kʌh. (38) Tahnú· astéhtsi?
who   first   someone will finish y'know.   And   in the morning

because I was saying two were tying and four were handing leaves. (30) Two people would
hand leaves to my father. (31) And two people would hand leaves to one person. (32) And
where they set the sticks on, it's called a horse. (33) Standing below it was the [cone of]
string, that's where it [the string] came up, how he did it was he would tie it [the string to the
stick] where he would start. (34) And then someone handed him the first [bunch of] leaves,
he would [tie them and] flip [them] over to the far side [of the stick], and then the other person would hand him leaves on this side next. (35) And that's how it was going along.
(36) And fast, the two would have to be fast who were handing leaves to him. (37) That's
how, I'm saying, there was a competition who would finish first. (38) And in the morning

tsi? niyo·lé·   nʌ   ʌthutáhsawʌ?   yah thya·ya·wʌ́·   ka?ikʌ́   tsi?   wahatikó·na?   thikʌ́
before   then   they will start   it has to be   this   that   they went and got   that

tóhka?   kwí·   nikú,   yá·ya?k   kʌs   uhte i·kélhe?   nikʌtstótslake
several   how many,   six   habitually   I think   the bundles amount to

thikʌ́   atahsli?shúha.   (39)   Tahnú·   yah thya·ya·wʌ́·   tsi?   akwekú   ʌhúshete?.
that   sticks.   And   it has to be   that   all   they will count it.

(40)   Teyotuhutsyóhu   wísk   niwáshʌ   wí· n   skʌthóhkwat.   (41)   Swatyelʌ́ s   tá·t nú·wa?
          It needs to be   five   tens   one bundle.   Sometimes   maybe

ísi? nú·   kwí·   yah thya·ya·wʌ́·   tsi?   ʌhsóthsi?   ki?wáh.   (42)   Yah thya·ya·wʌ́·
further   it has to be   that   you will take it out   right.   It has to be

tsi?   wísk   niwáshʌ   niwatáhslake.   (43)   Tho   thikʌ́   tsi?   tyotekhwahlá·tslate?
that   five   tens   the sticks amount to.   There   that   at   the end of the table

tho   wahatihnyotúni?   thikʌ́,   ya·wét   kwí·   yá·ya?k   kyuhte wí·   nikʌtstótslake
there   they stood them up   that,   like   six   supposedly   the bundles amount to

thikʌ́   atáhsli?,   tho   nikú   thikʌ́   ʌhatihwánhake?,   ya·wét   kwí·   wé·ne tsi?
that   stick,   that's   how many   that   they will tie,   like   evidently

áhsʌ   tewʌ?nyáwelu?   wí· n   tsyukwé·tat   lahwánhaks.   (44)   Kwáh   ok
three   hundred   one person   he ties.   Just   only

thiwakwekú   wé·ne   kwí·   tsi?   twelve hundred sticks,   wé·ne   tsi?   tho náhe?
just the whole amount   evidently   that   twelve hundred sticks,   evidently   that   that long

thikʌ́,   kwáh kwí·   swʌhníslat   thikʌ́   nahonatye·náwaste?.   (45)   Kwáh   kati?
that,   just   one day   that   it took them to do it.   Just   then

swatyelʌ́ s   thikʌ́   tho   nihatiya?tashno·lé·   latihwánhaks,   tá·t núwa?   a·kí·lu?
sometimes   that   that's   how fast they are   they tie,   maybe   I'd say

before they started they had to get several, I think six bundles of sticks. (39) And they had to count them all. (40) There had to be fifty [sticks] to one bundle. (41) Sometimes if there were more you had to take that out. (42) There had to be fifty sticks. (43) At the end of the table is where they put the sticks, like I guess six bundles of sticks, that's how many they would tie, it must have been three hundred that each person was tying. (44) Altogether there must have been twelve hundred sticks, it would take them, I'd say, one whole day to do it. (45) Sometimes the tiers were that fast, maybe I'd say,

swatyelʌ́ s   né· s   kyuhte wí·   né·   tyoshno·lé·   two-thirty   ókhnaʔ   lotíhsu̱ʔ.
sometimes   it's   supposedly   it's   it is quickest   two-thirty   and then   they have finished.

(46)   Tahnú·   tá·t   lotiyaʔtakʌheyú,   nʌ   kiʔ   né·   tá·t núwaʔ   wísk
And   if   they are slow,   then   actually   it's   maybe   five

nitsyohwistá·e   tá·thuniʔ   yá·yaʔk   nitsyohwistá·e,   kháleʔ
metal has struck again   or   six   metal has struck again,   and

waʔkatkathóhsluʔ,   kháleʔ   onʌ́   kwáh   lonattsístoteʔ   tsiʔ   niwahu·níseʔ
I saw repeatedly,   and   then   just   they have put lights on   because   such a long time

lotiyo·hté·.   (47)   Kháleʔ   tsiʔ   ka·yʌ́   kahʌtá·ke   nukwá·   thotiyoʔtʌ́staʔ,
they are working.   And   the one that   in the field   where   they are working,

yah   oniʔ   né·   thya·ya·wʌ́·   tsiʔ   ʌhonanúhtekeʔ   kátshaʔ   ka·yʌ́   ʌhatiyú·kwako̱ʔ.
not   too   it's   it has to be   that   they will know   which one   they will pick tobacco.

(48)   Tahnú·   ehtá·ke   ʌthutáhsaw̱ʌʔ.   (49)   Tá·t núwaʔ   tekanláhtake   wí· n   úska   plant
And   below   they will start.   Maybe   two leaves   one   plant

thikʌ́   tá·t núwaʔ   tekanláhtake   ʌha·yá·keʔ   kʌ́h.   (50)   Tho   kwí·   niyohtuháti?
that   maybe   two leaves   he will detach   y'know.   That's   how it is going

thi·ḵʌ́.   (51)   Tahnú·   kwáh   ok   thihʌ·né·   kaʔikʌ́,   tahnú·   shayá·tat   kʌ́·,
that.   And   just   only   they are just walking   this,   and   one man   y'know,

ne·né·   onʌ́   kahuwe·yá·   tahó·sleʔ   kʌs,   kahʌtá·ke   kwí·   tsiʔ
it's that   then   boat   he is driving this way   habitually,   in the field   at

naʔtekutlúniʔ   tsiʔ   kayʌthóhsluʔ,   tho kwí·   thikʌ́   ʌwatu·kóhteʔ
where are spaces   where   it is planted all around,   there   that   it will pass by

kahuwe·yá·,   tahnú·   kohsa·tʌ́s   kwí·   twatilútha̱ʔ.   (52)   Tahnú·   thikʌ́   nʌ
boat,   and   horse   it is pulling it.   And   that   then

sometimes I guess the soonest they would finish is two-thirty. (46) And if they were slow, then maybe it was five o'clock or six o'clock, and I saw many times, and they would have lights on because they were working so long. (47) And the ones who were working in the field, they had to know which tobacco [leaves] to pick. (48) And they would start [picking] from the bottom. (49) Maybe two leaves per plant, maybe he cut off two leaves. (50) That's the way it was. (51) And they just would be walking, and this one man, he would be driving the boat, in the field between the rows of plants, that's where the boat would pass, and a horse would be pulling it. (52) And when

wahutyé·nihteʔ   oyú·kwaʔ ókhnaʔ   tsiʔ tkahu·wáyʌʔ
they accumulated enough   tobacco   and then   at   there's a boat there

nyehʌ·né·,   tho nú·   nʌhatinlahtítane<u>ʔ</u>   (53) Tho s katiʔ
they are walking over there,   that's where   they will put the leaves in.   That's   well

thikʌ́ niyohtuháti<u>ʔ</u>,   tahnú· yah oniʔ   né· thya·ya·wʌ́· tsiʔ ʌhuteshno·láteʔ   kʌ́·,
that   how it is going,   and   not   too   it's it has to be   that   they will be fast at it y'know,

né· tsiʔ   tá·t lʌnélheʔ niyoshno·lé· a·hatíhsaʔn,   yah thya·ya·wʌ́· tsiʔ
because if   they want it is fast   for them to finish, it has to be   that

ʌhuteshno·láteʔ,   tahnú· kwáh kwí· né· tshá·kat   tsiʔ ka·yʌ́·   tsiʔ
they will be fast at it,   and   just   it's   the same   the one that   at

twatekhwahlá·tsloteʔ   thotiyo·té·,   kwáh kwí· tsiʔ niyoshno·lé· akwekú
there's a table standing there   they are working, just   how   it is fast   all

wahʌnetáhkoʔ kahu·wáku khále? nyusahutʌ́nyehteʔ,   khále? kahʌtá·ke
they took it out   in the boat   and   they sent it back that way,   and   in the field

nyusahó·sleʔ   tsiʔ ka·yʌ́· ya·wét kwí· kahuwe·yá· latólyehs<u>e</u>ʔ.
he rode it back over there   the one that kind of like   boat   he drives.

(54) Né· katiʔ wí· thikʌ́ tho   ni·yót   kwáh s wahatíhsaneʔ kʌ́·, tá·t núwaʔ
      Well then   that   that's how it is   just   they finished   see,   maybe

a·kí·luʔ núwaʔ   September náleʔ   elhúwaʔ wahatíhsaneʔ lotiyo·té·,
I'd say   this time September then again right then they finished   they are working,

nʌ kwí· tú·skeʔ lotshanuní tsiʔ ka·yʌ́·   shakónhahseʔ tsiʔ   u·tú· kwí· tho náheʔ
so then   truly   he is happy the one that he hires them   because it could be   that long

wahotiyo·tʌ́·, yah úska só·tsiʔ   te?yotholatú   — náhteʔ akwáh i·kélheʔ
they worked,   not   one   too much it has not gotten cold   — what   exactly I want

they had accumulated enough tobacco, they went over to where the boat was, that's where
they put the leaves in. (53) So that's the way it was, and too they had to be fast, because if
they wanted to finish early, they had to go fast, and it's the same with the ones that were
working at the table, they had to take everything out of the boat really fast and send it back,
and he would ride it back to the field, the one who was like driving the boat. (54) Well
that's how it was, they finished, I'd say maybe it was September before they finished working, so then the boss would be so happy because they could work all that time, not once did
it get real cold—what is it I'm trying

a·kí·lu.   (55) U·tú·   tho náhe? wahotiyo·tʌ́· yah ki?   te?yohsa?kʌsla·yʌ́·.
I would say.   It could be that long they worked   not   actually there is no frost.

(56) Kwáh s kwí· tsi? nihotshanuní thikʌ n shakónhahse? tashakokhwahélhahse?
     Just   how he is happy   that   he hires them   he put on a dinner for them

kʌ́·, né· nʌ   ya·wét kwí· wa?thutcelebrate kwí· tsi? u·tú·   wahatíhsane?.
see, it's then kind of like   they celebrated   that it could be they finished.

   (57) Tahnú· s kwí· né·n   thikʌ́ ne? thó·ne? yah kwí· te?we·só·   tehatikályahks.
        And   it's that that   at that time   not   it is not a lot they pay.

(58) E·só· kyuhte wí· né·n   ne? thó·ne? tsi?   yah se? né· te?kano·lú·se?
     Lots   supposedly it's that at that time because   not   too   it's things are not costly

náhte?   a·yekhwahni·nú·.   (59) Kwáh s ké·yale?   úska sʌ́· útlatste?
anything   for one to buy food.   Just   I remember one   also time

Port Stanley núwa?   ákta? thikʌ́ wahnitsyapslo·lʌ́ne? aknulhá·   khále? lake?níha,
Port Stanley   this time near   that   the two found a job   my mother and   my father,

tho ki?   thikʌ́ tahotiyo·tʌ́·, tahnú· wé·ne s kwí· ka?ikʌ́ kwahikʌ́ tsi?
there actually that   they worked,   and   evidently   this   just really that

lonatkanuní   ka?ikʌ́ tsi? ka·yʌ́· wahuwatiyó·tʌhse?, kwáh s ké·yale?   tsi?
they are well-off   this   the one that they worked for them, just   I remember that

lotiwi·láyʌ?,   né· s kwí· oskánhe yukwatnutolyá·tu. (60) Né·n   loti·yʌ́· oni?
they have children, so it's   together we are playing.   It's that they have too

né· thikʌ́ kohsa·tás kok nityótte? kʌ́·,   tho s oni? niyukwayo·té· kʌ́h.
it's that   horse   only it is so high y'know, there too   we are working y'know.

(61) Í· kwí· tekhenlahta·wíhe?,   úhka? ki? ok wí· oyá·   yehwánhaks,
     Me   I hand leaves to someone, someone   other someone ties,

to say? (Mercy tripped over her words and says this to herself.) (55) They could work that
long without it freezing. (56) The boss was really happy and he put on a dinner for them,
it's kind of like they celebrated that they could get finished.

   (57) And at that time they didn't pay a lot. (58) I guess it was a lot at that time because it
didn't cost a lot to buy groceries. (59) I remember one time my mother and father found a
job near Port Stanley, they worked there, and the people they worked for must have been
really well-off, I remember they had children, and we were playing together. (60) And they
had a horse too [to tie tobacco], only so high [a short one], and we would be working too.
(61) I would hand leaves to someone, and someone else would be tying,

yakwaksaʔshúha kwí· kaʔi·kʌ́. (62) Tho   katiʔ wí· yukwayoʔtátyehseʔ kaʔikʌ́,
all of us children   this.   There so then we are working along this,

kwáh kwí· tsiʔ nihonatyelʌ́ lonatotyákhuʔ,   tho kyuniʔ wí· ní·.
just   what they are doing they are grown-ups, thus too   us.

(63) Wé·ne kwí· yoshno·lé· waʔakwayʌtéhtaneʔ a·yukwayo·tʌ́·, tahnú· yah
      Evidently   it is fast   we learned   we should work, and   not

teʔwakanúhteʔ tó·   naʔtewakohsliyá·ku   neʔ thó·neʔ. (64) Kwah nók
I don't know   how many   I have crossed over winters at that time.   Just only

ké·yaleʔ   tsiʔ kok niyo·lé·   tyutatlihunyʌní·thaʔ, tho   seʔ wí· thikʌ́
I remember that a short distance school,   there too   that

nyaʔukwatʌ́nyehteʔ aknulhá·   nʌ   tshutahutáhsawʌʔ sahutáyahteʔ.
she sent me   my mother   when   when they started   they went to school again.

(65) Kwáh ké·yaleʔ   neʔ thó·ne tsiʔ yah teʔwakuʔweskwaní·u, né· tsiʔ
      Just   I remember at that time that not   I was not happy,   because

yah ní· teʔkahlúkhaʔ   kʌ́·   náhteʔ né· nʌ́kyeleʔ, yah seʔ ní·
not   me I don't know a language y'know what   it's I will do,   not   too   me

teʔkahlúkhaʔ oʔsluniʔké·ne   a·kwʌnanu·táhkweʔ.   (66) Nók tsiʔ sʌ́haʔ ok
I don't know   white man's way that I speak in a language.   But   anyway

yaʔukwatʌ́nyehteʔ. (67) Tho s kwí· thikʌ́ katayaʔtá·nehseʔ   kʌ́·,   yah s kwí·
she sent me.   There   that I am going to school y'know, not

teʔwakanúhteʔ náhteʔ akwáh niyotyelʌ́, yah seʔ náhteʔ   teʔwakanúhteʔ.
I don't know   what   mostly it is doing, not too anything I don't know.

(68) Nók tsiʔ khále? onʌ́ wahyatsyapslísaneʔ,   nʌ kyaleʔ wí· tutayakwahtʌ·tí·,
      But   and   then the two finished the job, so again   we left to come home,

and we were all of us children. (62) So then we were working there, whatever the grown-ups were doing, we [did it] too. (63) We must have learned fast how to work, and I don't know how old I was at that time. (64) All I remember is that there was a school close by, my mother sent me there when they started back to school again. (65) I just remember at that time I was not happy, because I didn't know the language and what would I do? I didn't know how to speak English. (66) But she sent me anyways. (67) I was going to school there, and I didn't know much what was going on, I didn't know anything. (68) But they finished the job, and so we left to come home again,

nʌ kwí· ákteʔ   núwaʔ   nú·   sahoyoʔtʌ́h<u>sa</u>ʔ.   (69) Kwáh tsiʔ niyo·lé·
so then different this time where he went to work again.   Right   until

a·kí·luʔ kwáh kʌʔ tshi·ká·,   né· kyuhte wí· tá·t núwaʔ tsya·ták
I'd say   just   when I was such a size, it's supposedly maybe   seven

tshaʔtewakohsliyá·ku,   nále?   thikʌ́ s kehya·lú·,   tho   áleʔ
when I have crossed over winters, then again that   I remember things, there again

thikʌ́ Walsingham ákta? yaʔakwanáklate<u>ʔ</u>.   (70) Kwáh né· kwahotokʌ́·u
that   Walsingham near   we settled over there.   Just   it's just for real

kanúhsoteʔ   tsiʔ nú· naʔakwáti<u>ʔ</u>. (71) Tekahwatsi·láke katiʔ thikʌ́ tho
there's a house   where   we moved.   Two families   then   that   there

waʔakwátiʔ, kaʔikʌ́ skahwatsi·lát tékni né· tehotiwi·láyʌʔ   teknukwé
we moved,   this   one family   two   it's they have two children two female persons

khále? shayá·tat   lu·<u>kwé</u>.   (72) Né· kati?   tsiʔ ka·yʌ́·   tshaʔtetyuknenú,
and   one person male person.   Well then it's the one that we two are the same age,

só·tsiʔ kwí· oni? kʌʔ naʔteyakná· a·yukniyo·tʌ́·,   kwáh s kwí· nók tho kwí·
too much too   we two are small for us two to work, just   there

yaʔteyakniʔnikúlhaleʔ   tsiʔ thotiyoʔténi<u>ʔ</u>.   (73) Kaʔikʌ́ lutʌnoʔsʌ́ha
over there we two are a bother at   they are around working.   This   they siblings

kʌ́·,   khále? tho   né· wahotiyo·tʌ́·, ne·né· tyotyelʌ́htu wahotiyo·tʌ́· oyú·kwaʔ,
y'know, and   there it's they worked,   it's that first   they worked   tobacco,

wahninlahtitáhkoʔ kwí· thikʌ́ kahuwe·<u>yá</u>·. (74) Tho s kwí· thikʌ́ wahní·lʌʔ
the two unloaded leaves that   boat.   There   that   the two set it

atekhwahlakhwá·<u>ke</u>. (75) Né·n   kwáh s né· kyaleʔ wí· yah thya·ya·wʌ́· tsiʔ
on the table.   It's that just   it's so again it has to be   that

then he went to work some place else. (69) Right until I'd say I was so big [a bit older],
maybe when I was seven years old, and then I remember, we moved near Walsingham.
(70) It was a real house where we moved to. (71) We were two families that moved in there,
this one family had two girls and one boy. (72) The one that was the same age as me, she
and I were too small to work, we would just be a bother where they were working. (73) Her
sister and brother, they worked, that was the first they worked in tobacco, they unloaded
leaves from the boats. (74) They would set them on the table. (75) And so again I had

tho kwí· waʔkheyatló·lokeʔ.   (76) Kwáh kwí· tsiʔ náhteʔ tehonatuhutsyoní
there   I watched them.   Just   that   what   they want

nʌ kiʔ ok aleʔ wí· teyaknitákheʔ,   í· kwí·, tá·t núwaʔ yah tho té·ku   tehoti·yʌ́·
right then   we two are running,   us,   maybe   not it is not enough   they have

atáhsliʔ, nʌ kiʔ ok aleʔ wí· sayaknikó·naʔ,   tá·thuniʔ waʔtwátyahkeʔ kwí·,
stick,   right then   again we two went to get it, or   it broke,

yah thya·ya·wʌ́· tsiʔ í· kwí· oyá·   ʌtsyaknikó·naʔ.   (77) Tá·thuniʔ
it has to be   that us   another again we two will go get it.   Or

waʔaknitsyʌ́·naʔ   núwaʔ   lʌ·nélheʔ a·hatihnekí·la.   (78) Tá·thuniʔ
we two went after water   this time they want   they would drink.   Or

ʌhutukályahkeʔ?   yah kwí· thya·ya·wʌ́· tsiʔ waʔakyatu·ní kwí· sandwiches, nʌ
they will get hungry   it has to be   that   we two made   sandwiches,   then

tho   tayakníhaweʔ   waʔakhi·núteʔ.   (79) Kháleʔ nʌ   thóha ʌtye ni·káleʔ
there   we two brought it we two fed it to them.   And   then   almost noon   time

kháleʔ aknulhá·   waʔí·luʔ, "wá·s onʌ́, wá·s onʌ́ satsyahtʌtí   kʌ́·,
and   my mother she said, "go   now, go   now you two go back home   eh,

sasnikhunyá·na."   (80) Tahnú· s tsiʔ niyoʔtalíhʌ thikʌ́ neʔ thó·neʔ, kwáh s
you two go cook again."   And   how   it is hot   that   at that time,   just

ké·yaleʔ   kʌ́·   saʔakyahtʌ·tí   kiʔwáh.   (81) Yah thya·ya·wʌ́· tsiʔ í·
I remember y'know we two went home   right.   It has to be   that me

sakate·ká·teʔ   né· tsiʔ í·   sʌ́haʔ kyuhte wí· kkwanʌ́ tsiʔ ni·yót
I made the fire again because me   more   supposedly I am big   as   how it is

tsyeyá·tat.   (82) Yah thya·ya·wʌ́· tsiʔ ʌskate·ká·teʔ   tahnú· tsiʔ
one female person.   It has to be   that   I will make a fire again   and   how

to watch them. (76) Whatever they wanted we would run right away, maybe they didn't have enough sticks, so right away we would go and get them, or else [one] would break, so we had to get another one. (77) Or else we would get water [if] they wanted to drink. (78) Or they got hungry, so the two of us would have to make sandwiches, then we brought them there and gave them [the sandwiches] to eat. (79) And then when it was almost noon my mother would say, "go on now, go on back home now, you two go and cook." (80) And it was so hot at that time, I remember we went home. (81) I was the one that had to make the fire because I guess I was bigger than the other girl. (82) I had to make a fire and

niyoʔtálihʌ,   nók tsiʔ   yah thyaʔyaʔwʌ́·   tsiʔ   ʌskate·ká·teʔ,   yah seʔ thyaʔyaʔwʌ́·
it is hot,   but   it has to be   that   I will make a fire again,   it has to be too

tsiʔ   ʌtsyaknikhuʔ<u>ní</u>·.   (83)   Ké·yaleʔ s   thikʌ́   kwah nók
that   again we two will make a meal.   I remember   that   just

waʔaknihnʌnaʔtóhaleʔ,   tho   thyeyolaʔwístaleʔ   ókhnaʔ   sayaknihnʌná·<u>to</u>ʔ.
we two washed potatoes,   there   it just has the peel on   and then   again we two boiled potatoes.

(84)   Waʔakyateʔwahlu·tʌ́·   sʌ́h.   (85)   Yah kwí·   teʔwé·ne   tsiʔ   niyoʔtalíhʌ,
       We two fried meat   also.   Not   it's incredible   how   it is hot,

tho kwí·   yuknikhuní   kʌ́h.   (86)   Tahnú·   naʔteyáknaʔ   ok,
there   we two are cooking   y'know.   And   how big we two are   only,

né·n   nʌ kiʔ ok   thikʌ́   tsyoʔk náhteʔ   yukyanúhteʔ   náhteʔ   na·yakni·yéleʔ
it's that   already   that   all kinds of things   we two know   what   we two should do

a·yukniyo·<u>tʌ́</u>·.   (87)   Nʌ   sahotiyoʔtʌ́hsaʔ,   nʌ kyaleʔ wí·
we two should work.   Then   again they went to work,   so again

sayakniksoholéniʔ   niʔí·,   sayakyatuhewániʔ,   thó·nʌ   náleʔ
we two washed dishes again   us,   we two swept again,   and then   then again

ʌwa·tú·   a·yakyatnutolyaʔtá·naʔ,   tá·thuniʔ   náleʔ   a·kakwe·ní·   tho
it's possible   that we two go and play,   or   then again   it could be   there

nyusayákneʔ   tsiʔ   thotiyo·<u>hté</u>·.   (88)   Né· s kwí·   thikʌ́
that we two walk back over there   at   they are working.   So it's   that

yuknuʔwéskwani<u>he</u>ʔ.
we two enjoy it.

(89)   Né·n   kh, áleʔ onʌ́,   nʌ   nyaʔkáheweʔ,   nʌ   oniʔ   ní·   tho   ni·ká·
       It's that   and   then,   then   it came time,   then   too   me   thus   I am so big

it was so hot, but I had to make a fire, the two of us had to cook dinner. (83) I remember we used to just wash the potatoes, and then we boiled them with the peels still left on. (84) We fried meat also. (85) It was really, really hot, [but] we did the cooking. (86) And we were only small, and already we knew about all kinds of things, what to do, how to work. (87) Then they went back to work, and we washed the dishes again, we swept, and then we could go and play, or it might be that we went back to where they were working. (88) So we had a good time.

(89) And then, then the time came, then I too was big [old] enough

au·tú·   aukyo?tʌ́hsa?.   (90) Nʌ kyale? wí· kwáh tyotyelʌ́htu uhte i·kélhe?
it could be   that I go to work.   So again   just   first   I think

ukyo·tʌ́ laksótha   wa?áko?. (91) Cultus kuwa·yáts tsi? nú· thikʌ́ tho
I worked   my grandfather we went.   Cultus   it is named where   that   there

ya?akwáti?   kʌ́·, bunkhouse kʌs   latina?túkhwa?, tho   thikʌ́
we moved over there see,   bunkhouse   customarily what they call it,   there   that

wa?akwáti?. (92) Kwáh s tsyo?k nú·   nikanaktaké·lu?   kʌ́·,
we moved.   Just   all over the place there are beds strewn around y'know,

isé· kwí· yʌhsatatlákwahse?   kátsha? nú· ʌhsanú·wete?.
you   over there you will choose for yourself where   you will stay overnight.

(93) Khále? kwáh akwekú yakwahawinúti?   ukwakʌha?shúha kʌ́·,   tho kwí·
      And   just   all   we are taking along   our blankets   y'know,   there

thikʌ́ wa?akwáti? bunkhouse. (94) Né·n   nʌ kwí· né· ʌtwatye·lʌ́hte? ukyo?tʌ́hsa?.
that   we moved   bunkhouse.   It's that   so then   it's   it will be first   I went to work.

(95) Nʌ kwí· waklʌ?nhá·u, nʌ   se? e·só· niyohslaké   onʌ́ wa?kheyatló·loke?
      So then   I know how,   then   too   a lot   years amount to   then   I watched her

aknulhá·   thuwatinlahta·wíhe?.   (96) Nʌ kati? wí· núwa?   u·tú·   í·
my mother   she hands leaves to them.   Well then it's this time it could be   me

usukyo·tʌ́·   kʌ́h. (97) Kwáh ké·yale?   thikʌ́ ne? thó·ne? téklu?
that again I work y'know.   Just   I remember that   at that time   eight

nikahwístake   swʌhníslat ukwatkályahkse?. (98) Onísta? kwí· né· tsi? s
the money amounts to one day   I got paid.   Gosh   it's   how

niwaknehlákwas tsi?   niwe·só·   tekatʌ́·tsha?as kʌ́h.   (99) Tahnú· yah s
I am surprised   how   it is so much I am earning   y'know.   And   not

that I could go to work. (90) I think the first time I worked we went with my grandfather.
(91) Cultus was the name of the place where we lived, a bunkhouse was what they called it,
that's where we moved. (92) There were beds all around, you choose your own bed where
you were going to sleep. (93) And we would have all our blankets with us, and we lived
there in the bunkhouse. (94) So then that's the first time I went to work. (95) So then I
knew how, many years I had watched my mother handing leaves. (96) Well now I could
work. (97) I remember at that time I got paid eight dollars a day. (98) Gosh, I was so surprised I was making so much money. (99) And

tha·yukwatkályaʔkse? tsiʔ niyo·lé· ʌtáktaʔ,   né· tsiʔ   shekú n ʌtáktaʔ   ʌyukwayo·tʌ́·
we won't get paid   until   Saturday, because still   Saturday we will work

kih.   (100) Tahnú· í· s kwí· né· onʌ́, tó· katiʔ náheʔ ʌyukwayo·tʌ́· tó·
actually.   And   we   it's then, how long then   we will work   how

niyakwayaʔtashno·lé·. (101) Né· s kwí· a·kí·luʔ   kwahikʌ́ tsiʔ
we are fast.   So it's   I would say just really that

waʔakwatyaʔtashno·láteʔ, two-thirty ókhnaʔ   waʔakwáhsaneʔ. (102) Tahnú· kwí·
we did it fast,   two-thirty   and then we finished.   And

yah thau·tú· kátshaʔ nú· a·yakwatawʌ́·naʔ, kwah nók tho   thikʌ́ greenhouse tho s
it can't be   anywhere   that we go bathe, just   there that   greenhouse there

tyo·yʌ́·   shower. (103) Nʌ kwí· waʔtyukwashlíhʌʔ, yakyukweshúha kwí· nya·lé·
there it has shower.   So then   we hurried,   all of us people   first

tho   ya·yákweʔ,   waʔtyakwatatníhahteʔ thikʌ́ waʔtyakwatshower.
there we could walk over there, we took turns   that   we showered.

(104) Thó·nʌ   né· núwaʔ   onʌ́ lʌnu·kwé. (105) Nʌ kwí· tutayakwaya·kʌ́neʔ,
     And then it's this time then men.   So then   again we came out,

nʌ kwí· yukwatslunyá·tu,   nʌ kwí· yukwalha·lé· a·yukwatkályaʔkse?
so then   we have gotten dressed, so then   we are ready that we get paid

kanatá·ke nya·yákoʔ.
in town   that we go over there.

    (106) Tho s ni·yót   thikʌ́ e·só· kwí· niyohslaké   thikʌ́ oyú·kwaʔ
         That's how it is that   lots   is the amount of years that   tobacco

ukyo·tʌ́·, tahnú· tetyonú·yanit. (107) Né· thikʌ́ yoshéstaleʔ aʔnyóh   thikʌ́ n
I worked, and   it is the dirtiest.   It's   that   it is gummy   seems like that

we wouldn't get paid until Saturday, because we even worked on Saturdays. (100) And it
was up to us, how long we would work and how fast. (101) So I would say we really
worked fast, by two-thirty we finished. (102) And there was no place we could go and
bathe, just the greenhouse had a shower. (103) So then we would hurry, all of us [ladies]
would go there first, we took turns showering. (104) And then it was the men. (105) So
then we would come out again, and then we were dressed, and then we were ready to get
paid and go to town.

(106) That's how it was, a lot of years I worked in tobacco, and it was very dirty. (107) It
seems like

oyú·kwaʔ,   né· katiʔ   nʌ   ʌsayo·tʌ́·,   kwáh s   aʔé·   naʔtekashéstaʔ   thikʌ́,
tobacco,   so it's   when   you will work, just   great is the size of the gum that,

tahnú·   kwáh   oʔswʌ́·taʔ   nikashestó·tʌ   sesnú·<u>ke</u>.   (108)   Yah katiʔ thya·ya·wʌ́·
and then just   black   what kind of gum   your hand.   It has to be

tsiʔ   thikʌ́ kwáh s   kanohalé·tslayʌʔ   thikʌ́,   nók   yoyánleʔ   thikʌ́   né·   ʌ́hsatsteʔ
that   that   just   there is a soap   that,   only   it is good   that   it's   you will use it

nʌ   ʌhsahtsyóha<u>leʔ</u>.   (109)   ʌskala·kéweʔ   thikʌ́   óshes.   (110)   Kháleʔ
when   you will wash your hands.   It will wipe off   that   gum.   And

nʌ   ʌ́tshaneʔ,   ati   nʌ   ʌsehsahtsyóhaleʔ   shekú   kiʔ
then   you will finish,   no matter   then   you will wash your hands again   still   actually

aʔnyóh   otsí·nkwal   naʔtehsesnuhsó·tʌh<u>seʔ</u>.   (111)   Kháleʔ   yah sʌ́· teʔwé·ne
seems like   yellow   what kind of hands you have.   And   it's incredible also

ni·yót   kʌs   stsyeʔelakú,   kwahotokʌ́·u   yotayá·tu   thikʌ́   oyú·kwaʔ
how it is   habitually   your nails,   just for real   it has come in   that   tobacco

oʔswʌ́·taʔ   ni·yót.   (112)   Yaʔwéskwaʔt kʌs   neʔ thó·neʔ   tshiyukwayó·tʌhseʔ,
black   how it is.   It is nice   habitually   at that time   when we are working,

né·   kyuhte wí·   tsiʔ   kʌʔ nityukwayʌ́·saʔ,   kwáh s kwí·   tewatkʌ́ni   úhkaʔ náhteʔ
it's   supposedly   because   we young people,   just   competition   who

tyeyaʔtashno·<u>lé</u>·.   (113)   Tho   katiʔ   ni·yót   thikʌ́,   kháleʔ   onʌ́,   nʌ   oniʔ   ní·
one does it fastest.   That's   then   how it is   that,   and   then,   then   too   me

ukényakeʔ   nʌ   ukhwatsilayʌ·táneʔ   kʌ́·,   nʌ s kwí·   sʌ́haʔ   wʌto·lé·   kʌ́·,   nók tsiʔ
I got married   then   I had a family   see,   so then   more   it is hard   y'know,   but

nʌ   kiʔ   sʌ́haʔ   teyotuhutsyóhu   aukyo·tʌ́·   tsiʔ   wakwi·láyʌʔ   kwí·   o·nʌ́.
then   actually   more   it is needed   I should work   because   I have a child   now.

the tobacco was gummy, so when you worked, there would be a huge amount of gum, and it
was black, on your hands. (108) There was a certain soap, it was the only one good to use
for washing your hands. (109) It got rid of the gum. (110) And when you were finished,
even after you washed your hands again, it seemed like your hands were still all yellow.
(111) And your nails looked really awful, the tobacco got right into them so they were black.
(112) It was nice working at that time, I guess because we were young, it was just a competition who was fastest. (113) That's how it was, and then, then I got married and I had a
family, so then it was harder, but it was more important for me to work because I had a child
now.

(114) Nʌ kwí· ukyoʔtʌ́hsaʔ kiʔwáh.   (115) Tho kwí· wʌto·lé· kwí· thikʌ́
      So then   I went to work right.   There   it is hard   that

yah thya·ya·wʌ́· tsiʔ waʔkatʌ́nhaneʔ úhkaʔ ok wahuwatʌʔnikú·lalʌʔ?   liyʌ́ha.
it has to be   that I hire   someone   someone looked after him my son.

(116) Kháleʔ onʌ́ tehniyáshe.   (117) Tho kwí· ni·yót   thikʌ́ tyótkut
      And   then two.   That's   how it is that   always

kenhaʔtsli·sáks   úhkaʔ náhteʔ a·huwʌnatʌʔnikú·lalʌʔ   kheyʌʔokúha.
I look for a hired person anyone   one should look after them my children.

(118) Tahnú· nʌ   kyuhte wí· nʌ   a·kí·luʔ sʌ́haʔ e·só· tshihatikálya?ks neʔ thó·neʔ.
      And   then supposedly then I'd say   more   lots   when they pay   at that time.

(119) Né·n   kháleʔ onʌ́ thikʌ́ tutáhsawʌʔ,   kwáh s nók takatáhsawʌʔ ukyo·tá·
      It's that and   then that   it started again, just   I started   I worked

kháleʔ waʔkatnʌ́tshoʔ kʌ́h.   (120) Né· thikʌ́ tho s niyo·lé· kaʔikʌ́
and   my arm swelled y'know.   It's   that   that's how far   this

nuknʌtshanú·wakeʔ, wá·kelheʔ seʔ s, "nʌ   kiʔ   yah tho   thyusa·ké·
my arm got sore,   I thought   too,   "now actually not there I won't go back over there

ʌyólhʌneʔ, só·tsiʔ   waknʌtshanú·waks." (121) Nʌ   seʔ oniʔ kwáh aʔé·
tomorrow,   too much   my arm is sore."   Then too too   just   great

naʔteknʌ́tshaʔ   tsiʔ niyo·tó·   kʌ́h.   (122) Né·n   sayólhʌneʔ sʌ́haʔ kiʔ ok
is the size of my arm how   it is swollen y'know.   It's that the next day nevertheless

tho   sá·kehteʔ   sukyoʔtʌ́hsaʔ.   (123) Tho   katiʔ wí· thikʌ́
there I went back there I went to work again.   That's well then that

naʔohtuhátiʔ   kʌ́·,   tóhkaʔ niyohslaké   ukyo·tá· n oyú·kwaʔ,
how it is going along y'know, several is the amount of years I worked   tobacco,

(114) So then I went to work, right. (115) It was hard, I had to hire out for someone to look after my son. (116) And soon there were two. (117) That's the way it was, I was always looking to hire somebody to mind my children. (118) And I guess they paid more at that time. (119) And then it started, I would just start working and my arm would start to swell. (120) That's how much my arm got sore, I thought, "I won't go back [to work] tomorrow, my arm is too sore." (121) My arm was really big, it was so swollen. (122) But the next day anyway I would go back there to work again. (123) Well that's the way it was, several years I worked in tobacco,

kwáh s kwí· ya?tkó·ktʌ?   thikʌ́ ukyo·tʌ́·, tho s kwí· né· nihatiyélha? kʌ́·,
just   I went to the end   that   I worked,   thus   it's   they do it   y'know,

tho kwí· nahatshanu·ní·   shukwánhahse?, kwáh kwí· wa?shakokhwánute?   ki?wáh.
there   how he got happy he hires us,   just   he gave them food to eat   right.

(124) Tho kati? wí· thikʌ́ niyawʌ́·u,   shekú s né· swatyelʌ́ tá·t wa?ákwelhe?
       Thus well then that   it has happened, still   it's   sometimes if   we wanted

oyá· náhte? a·yukwayotʌ́,   né· thikʌ́ s lu·té· s kwí· wa?tyakwatsucker.
other   what   we should work, it's   that   they say   we suckered.

(125) Tá·t núwa? né· thikʌ́ kʌ? nikanlahtá·sa?, yah thya·ya·wʌ́· tsi? né·
       Maybe   it's   that   small leaves,   it has to be   that   it's

wa?akwayá·khu?, sʌ́ha? ʌyoyánlʌne? thikʌ́ oyú·<u>kwa?</u>. (126) Né· kwí· sʌ́· thikʌ́
we cut them,   more   it will be good that   tobacco.   So it's   also   that

wakyo?tʌ́·u   oni? nʌ? né·, tahnú· s i·kélhe? inú s uhte   nya?ákwe?
I have worked   too that,   and   I think   far   supposedly over there we walked

thikʌ́; khále? onʌ́ nʌ   wahniyʌtéhtane? n kheyʌ?okúha, tehniyáshe s
that;   and   then then the two learned   my children,   two

yekhéhas wí· n a·hniyʌtéhtane? ki?   a·hotiyo·<u>tʌ́·</u>.
I take them   that the two learn   actually that they work.

(127) Khále? kwí· né· onʌ́, yah tho   te?yo·lé· onʌ́ ka?ikʌ́ a·kí·lu? kwáh
       And   it's   now, not   that's not so far now   this   I'd say   just

kʌ? wa?káhewe?,   yah kyuhte i·kélhe? thusutetshʌ·lí·   úhka? náhte?
here   time has come,   not   I think   it won't be found anymore anyone

ya·yakoyo·tʌ́·   oyú·<u>kwa?</u>. (128) Tahnú· s kwí· nén   ne? thó·ne? ʌwa·tú·
that one works over there   tobacco.   And   it's that   at that time   it can be

I would finish working right to the end [of the season], that's how they used to do it, and the
person who hired us would be so happy, he would feed them [put on a dinner]. (124) Well
that's how it happened, still sometimes maybe we thought we'd do something else, sucker-
ing they say. (125) Maybe those small leaves, we have to cut them off, and the tobacco
would turn out better. (126) So I worked at that too, and it seems to me like we walked far;
and my children learned, I would take the two of them so they would learn how to work.

   (127) And now, as far as that goes I would say that the time has come, I guess you can't
find anyone to work in tobacco anymore. (128) And at that time

ʌhsyuʔkwayʌ́thoʔ,   thó·neʔ nʌ   ʌhsatʌneklóskaluʔ,   thó·nʌ   ʌhsyuʔkwakó·naʔ.
you will plant tobacco, and then   you will hoe,   and then you will go pick tobacco.

(129) Thó·nʌ   tsiʔ yeskʌhá né· núwaʔ   onʌ́ n, yah s kiʔ   né· onʌ́
       And then at   last   it's this time then,   not   actually it's then

teʔské·yaleʔ   náhteʔ né· latinaʔtúkhwaʔ thikʌ́, ya·wét tshiyolha·lé·
I don't remember anymore what   it's what they call it that,   like   when it is ready

oyú·kwaʔ, né· kyuhte wí· onʌ́ ʌhutelha·láteʔ   ʌhutyuʔkwahni·nú· kiʔwáh.
tobacco,   it's supposedly then they will get ready they will sell tobacco right.

(130) Tho   katiʔ wí· ní· nikú   thikʌ́ ké·yaleʔ   oyú·kwaʔ, oyú·kwaku
       That's anyway me how much that   I remember tobacco,   in tobacco

wakyó·tehkweʔ kʌ́·,   a·kí·luʔ yaʔwéskwaʔt tá·t kʌʔ nityakoyʌ́ha, nók tsiʔ né·
I used to work   y'know, I'd say   it is fun   if   a young person,   but   it's

ké·yaleʔ wí· né· yah teʔwʌto·lé·.   (131) Nʌ   núwaʔ   tsiʔ ka·yʌ́·   latinlahtákwas,
I remember it's not   it is not hard.   Then   this time the one that they pick leaves,

primers kwí· latinaʔtúkhwaʔ,   kwáh s né· onʌ́ latiyaʔtitákheʔ.   (132) Né·n
primers   what they call them, just   it's now   they are riding in it.   It's that

tshiwahu·níseʔ né· yah thya·ya·wʌ́· tsiʔ ehtaʔkéshuʔ? lʌ·né·   kʌ́h.
a long time ago it's it has to be   that on foot   they are walking y'know.

(133) Latiyaʔtitákheʔ   kʌ́·   thikʌ́, kháleʔ kwáh tho   áktaʔ   kahuwí·sleʔ,
       They are riding in it y'know that,   and   just   there close by a boat is going by,

tho kwí· wahutiyuʔkwítaneʔ. (134) Yah katiʔ náhteʔ   tho   té·tsyot,
there   they put tobacco in it.   Not   then   anything thus   it is not so anymore,

shekú né· onʌ́ yo·yʌ́· núwaʔ elevators. (135) Nʌ   ʌhsatahslahla·kó·   ókhnaʔ
even   it's now   it has this time elevators.   When   you will remove sticks and then

you could plant tobacco, and then you would hoe, and then you would go and pick the tobacco. (129) And then the last thing, I don't remember anymore what they call it, like when the tobacco is ready, I guess when they get ready to sell their tobacco, right. (130) So anyway that's how much I remember about tobacco, I used to work in tobacco, I'd say it was fun if someone was young, but I remember it wasn't hard. (131) Nowadays those who pick the leaves, primers they're called, now they ride in something. (132) A long time ago they had to walk. (133) They ride, and there's a boat going close by, they put the tobacco in it. (134) So nothing is like that anymore, now they even have elevators. (135) When you take the stick off

tho   ʌhsatahslá·lʌʔ   ókhnaʔ   né· waʔkaláthʌʔ,   kwah nók úhkaʔ ok é·nik
there   you will set sticks on it   and then   it's   it will climb up,   just   someone   above

íthlateʔ,   né·   ʌhayuʔkwiha·lʌ́·.   (136) Tshiwahu·níseʔ né· yah thya·ya·wʌ́· tsiʔ
he is standing,   it's   he will hang tobacco.   A long time ago   it's   it has to be   that

tshusahʌ·néweʔ   latiprimers, ókhnaʔ sahatiha·lʌ́·   nʌʔú·waʔ.   (137) E·só·
when they came back   the primers,   and then   they hung it again   this time.   Lots

katiʔ wí· tsiʔ teyottenyá·u.   (138) Yah kwí· náhteʔ   tho té·yot   tsiʔ s
anyway   that   it has changed.   Not   anything   thus   it is not so   as

niyohtú·neʔ tshiwahu·níseʔ.   (139) Kháleʔ né· kwí· ka·té·   yah seʔ né·
it was so   a long time ago.   And   so it's   I am saying   not   too   it's

tha·huthu·táteʔ   kaʔikʌ́   kʌ́ʔ nithotiyʌ́·saʔ a·hotiyo·tʌ́·,   só·tsiʔ   teyonú·yanit.
they won't consent   this   young people   that they work,   too much   it is dirty.

(140) Tho   katiʔ wí· nikú   wá·kelheʔ ní· a·kathlo·lí· kʌ́h.
       That's   anyway   how much   I thought   me   I would tell   eh.

you put it on [the elevator] and it goes up, someone is just standing at the top, he hangs the
tobacco. (136) A long time ago when the primers came back, next they hung [the tobacco].
(137) A lot has changed. (138) Nothing is the way it was a long time ago. (139) And I'm
saying that the young people won't agree to work [in tobacco], it's too dirty. (140) So that's
anyway how much I thought I would tell.

My First Job in Tobacco

(Told by Norma Kennedy to Karin Michelson on April 15, 2012)

(1) Shekólih. (2) Thiwé·saʔ   ní· yúkyats   Ukwehuwehnéhaʔ.   (3) Kháleʔ
     Greetings.   She Wanders   me   is my name   Native way.   And

Norma yúkyats   oʔsluniʔké·ne.   (4) Ohkwalí niwakiʔtaló·tʌ.   (5) Kháleʔ
Norma   is my name   white man's way.   Bear   is my clan.   And

(1) Greetings. (2) She Wanders is my Indian name. (3) And Norma is my English name.
(4) I am Bear clan. (5) And

Onʌyoteʔa·ká·   niwakuhutsyóʔtʌ.   (6) Yawʌtatokʌ́htu wʌhnisla·té·,
People of the Standing Stone   is my nation.   Monday   a day exists,

kayé   yawʌ·lé· tshiskaha·wí·   wahsakayu·té·seʔ wʌhniʔta·té·.   (7) Tewáshʌ
four   teen   when again is the era   it is thundering   a month exists.   Twenty

tewʌʔnyáweluʔ tékni yawʌ·lé· yohslashe·tás.   (8) I·kélheʔ a·kwahlolí   tsiʔ
hundred   two   teen   it counts years.   I want   I would tell you all that

náhteʔ kehya·lú·   tshikeksáh.   (9) Né· kwí· thikʌ́ yaʔteyohslaké oyú·kwaʔ
what   I remember when I was a child.   So it's   that   every year   tobacco

lotiyo·té·   aknulhá· kháleʔ lakeʔníha.   (10) Kháleʔ tekniyáshe
they are working   my mother and   my father.   And   two

tekatʌhnu·téleʔ, nʌ   oniʔ né· yotiyó·tʌhseʔ.   (11) Knihwánhaks kwí· oyú·kwaʔ
I have sisters,   then   too   it's   they work.   Two tie   tobacco

kaʔikʌ́ tekniyáshe.   (12) Kháleʔ lakeʔníha oyú·kwaʔ né· layuʔkwákwas nʌʔ né·.
this   two.   And   my father   tobacco   it's   he picks tobacco that one.

(13) Ok neʔn   aknulhá· thuwatinlahta·wíheʔ   nʌʔ né·.   (14) Ok wí· neʔn í·
        And as for my mother she hands leaves to them that one.   And as for   me

só·tsiʔ   ní· shekú kʌʔ niká· aukyo·tʌ́·,   nók tsiʔ swatyelʌ́ kʌs   tho
too much   me   still   I am small for me to work, but   sometimes habitually there

wá·kehteʔ   tsiʔ thotiyoʔtʌ́staʔ,   waʔkheyaʔtakénhaʔ aknulhá·,   í· kwí·
I went there   at   where they work,   I helped her   my mother, me

takhenláhtuʔ   tsiʔ náheʔ ostúha waʔutolíshʌʔ.   (15) Né· ké·yaleʔ   thikʌ́
I handed leaves to them   while   a little she rested.   It's   I remember that

kwáh tyotyelʌ́htu luwayoʔtʌ́hseheʔ kaʔikʌ́, tho   kiʔ   thikʌ́ a·kí·luʔ kyuhte wí·
just   first   they work for him   this,   there actually that   I'd say   supposedly

I am of the Oneida Nation. (6) It's Monday, the fourteenth of the month of April, 'it thun-
ders.' (7) The year is 2012. (8) I want to tell you what I remember about when I was a
child. (9) Every year my mother and my father worked in tobacco. (10) And I have two
sisters, and they worked too. (11) They were tying tobacco, these two. (12) And my father
was picking tobacco. (13) And my mother, she was handing leaves. (14) And me, I was
still too small to work, but sometimes I went to where they were working, I helped my
mother, I handed leaves while she rested a little. (15) I remember the very first person they
worked for, I guess

Port Burwell ákta?. (16) Tho ki? thikʌ́ kanyatalaktúti? nú·
Port Burwell near. There actually that along the lake where

nihoyu?kwayʌ́thu ka?ikʌ́ tsi? ka·yʌ́· luwayo?tʌ́hsehe?. (17) Ne? thó·ne? ki?
he has planted tobacco this the one that they work for him. At that time actually

thikʌ́ twakatáhsawʌ? tho s wá·kehte? tsi? thotiyo·té· wa?kheya?takénha?.
that I have started there I went there at they are working I helped them.

(18) Tho?nʌ́ ákte? núwa? nú· sahotiyo?tʌ́hsa?, tho ki? núwa? né·
And then different this time where they went to work, there actually this time it's

thikʌ́ Cultus nukwá· ákta?, Cultus kuwa·yáts. (19) Kʌ? ki? ok ni·wá· kʌ́·
that Cultus where near, Cultus is its name. It is just small y'know

thikʌ́ yutʌhni·núhe? nók tsi? tho ki? nú· thikʌ́ yahotiyo·tʌ́·,
that store but that's actually where that they worked over there,

tho uhte i·kélhe? nú· yehotíhsu? yeskʌhá
that's I think where they have finished over there last

yeshotiyó·tehkwe?. (20) Tho ki? né· thikʌ́ Tilsonburg ákta?.
they used to work over there. There actually it's that Tilsonburg near.

(21) Wahotiyo?tʌ́hsa? kwí· ka?ikʌ́ wʌhnisla·té·, né·n yah
They went to work this a day exists, it's that not

kyuhte wí· tehonha?tslolʌ́·u ka?ikʌ́ shakónhahse? tsyeyá·tat wí·
supposedly he has not found a worker this he hires them one person

utayutatenláhtu?. (22) Tahnú· s kwí· lakwatló·lu thikʌ́
for one to hand leaves to someone. And he is watching me that

nále? wa?kheya?takénha? aknulhá·, lonúhte? kwí· tsi? ʌkkwe·ní·
when again I helped her my mother, he knows that I will be able

near Port Burwell. (16) The person they were working for had planted tobacco along the lake. (17) It was at that time I started to go to where they were working and help them. (18) And then they went to work some place else, near Cultus, Cultus was the name of it. (19) There was just a small store there but that's where they worked, I think that's where they finished, the last place they worked. (20) It was near Tilsonburg.

(21) They went to work this one day, I guess the boss didn't find one person to hand leaves (normally there are two people handing leaves). (22) And he used to watch me when I helped my mother, so he knew that I was able

ʌtekhenláhtuʔ.
I will hand leaves to someone.

(23) Nʌ kwíˑ néˑ wahakliʔwanuˑtúˑseʔ aˑkathuˑtáteʔ
      So then it's he asked me   I would consent

kʌ   aukyoʔtʌ́hsaʔ,   táˑt núwaʔ tshaʔtewʌhnisliyó tsiʔ náheʔ, wahʌ́ˑluʔ,
question   that I go to work, maybe   half a day   how long,   he said,

wahanhaʔtslisákhaʔ   úhkaʔ ok aˑshakónhaneʔ   utayakoyoʔtʌ́hsaʔ.
he is going to look for a worker someone   he would hire someone that someone come to work.

(24) Nʌ kwíˑ néˑ waʔkíˑluʔ ʌkateʔnyʌ́ˑtʌ́ˑ kiʔwáh.   (25) Nʌ kwíˑ tho   wáˑkehteʔ,
      So then it's I said   I will try   right.   So then there I went there,

wakuʔwéskwaniheʔ s kwíˑ kaʔikʌ́ kheyaʔtakénhas   tekhenlahtaˑwíheʔ.
I enjoy   this   I am helping them I am handing leaves to someone.

(26) Néˑn   túˑskeʔ kwíˑ néˑ thikʌ́ tshaʔtewʌhnisliyó ukyoˑtʌ́ˑ, nʌ kwíˑ
      It's that truly   it's that   half a day   I worked,   so then

yaʔkáheweʔ   ʌ́tye niˑkáleʔ, náleʔ   waʔakwatolíshʌʔ,   waʔakwatekhunyáˑnaʔ
it was that time noon time,   then again we rested,   we went to eat a meal

ʌ́tye niˑkáleʔ. (27) Néˑn   tho   sáˑlaweʔ   thikʌ́ shukwánhahseʔ, wahʌ́ˑluʔ,
noon time.   It's that there he got there again that   he hires us,   he said,

"yah" wahʌ́ˑluʔ "teʔwaketshʌ́li   úhkaʔ náhteʔ utayakoyoʔtʌ́hsaʔ,   ʌhsathuˑtáteʔ
"not" he said   "I have not found anyone   one would come to work, you will consent

kʌ́h,   ʌskweˑníˑ   kʌ   yaʔtʌhsʌhnislóˑktʌʔ.   (28) Nʌ kwíˑ waʔkíˑluʔ,
question, you will be able question you will finish out the day.   So then   I said,

"hʌ́ˑ kyuhte iˑkélheʔ, ʌkateʔnyʌ́ˑtʌ́ˑ kih."   (29) Nʌ kyaleʔ wíˑ sukyoʔtʌ́hsaʔ
"yes I think so,   I will try   actually."   So again   I went to work again

thikʌ́ utuˑkóˑteʔ ʌ́ti.   (30) Néˑn   waʔkkweˑníˑ kiʔ   waʔkʌhnislóˑktʌʔ.
that   it passed   noon.   It's that I was able   actually I finished out the day.

to hand leaves. (23) So then he asked me would I agree to go to work maybe half a day, he
said, he was going to look for a worker, someone he could hire to come to work. (24) So
then I said I would try, right. (25) So then I went there, I enjoyed helping them, handing
leaves to someone. (26) And so really I did work half a day, so then it was noon, then we
took a break, we went to eat lunch. (27) And so the boss got there again, he said, "I did not
find anyone to come to work, would you agree to it, are you able to finish out the day?"
(28) So then I said, "yes, I think so, I'll try." (29) So I went back to work that afternoon.
(30) I was able to finish out the day.

(31) Né·n   sayólhʌneʔ astéhtsiʔ elhúwaʔ yakwatekhu·níheʔ   astéhtsiʔ kaló·
     It's that the next day morning   just then we are eating a meal morning   before

tsiʔ niyo·lé· a·hotiyoʔtʌ́hsaʔ.   (32) Né·n   tho   áleʔ   sá·laweʔ   thikʌ́
until   they should go to work.   It's that there again he got there again that

shukwánhahseʔ, wahʌ́·luʔ, "yah" wahʌ́·luʔ "teʔwaketshʌ́li úhkaʔ náhteʔ
he hires us,   he said,   not   he said   "I have not found anyone

a·yakoyo·tʌ́·,   ʌskwe·ní·   kʌ   shekú   tshaʔtewʌhnisliyó aesayo·tʌ́·."
one would work, you will be able question still   half a day   that you work."

(33) "Tá·t núwaʔ"   wahʌ́·luʔ "úhkaʔ ok náhteʔ ʌkatetshʌ·lí· utayakoyoʔtʌ́hsaʔ."
     "Maybe"   he said   "someone   I will find   one would come to work."

(34) Nʌ kyaleʔ wí· waʔkí·luʔ, "hʌ́·, ʌkateʔnyʌ·tʌ́· kiʔwáh."   (35) Kwáh kʌs kwí·
     So again   I said,   "yes, I will try   right."   Just   habitually

né· nók tsiʔ twakuʔwéskwaniheʔ ukyoʔtʌ́hsaʔ.   (36) Né·n   waʔkʌhnisló·ktʌʔ
it's only that I most enjoy   I went to work.   It's that I finished out the day

aleʔ,   né· thikʌ́ kwʌʔtátiʔ ukyo·tʌ́·, né·n   tho   sá·laweʔ   shukwánhahseʔ,
again, it's that all day   I worked, it's that there he got there again he hires us,

wahʌ́·luʔ, "yah thau·tú·" wahʌ́·luʔ "a·ketshʌ·lí· úhkaʔ   utayakoyoʔtʌ́hsaʔ,"
he said,   "it can't be"   he said   "that I find   anyone   one would come to work,"

wahʌ́·luʔ, "tá·t tesatuhutsyoní isé· tho   aesayo·tʌ́·   kwáh tsiʔ
he said,   "if   you want   you   there you would work   just as

niwakʌ́nhes,   ʌwa·tú· kiʔ   isé· kwí· ʌkúnhaneʔ."   (37) Nʌ kwí· né·
how long is the season, it can be actually you   I will hire you."   So then   it's

waʔkheliʔwanu·tú·seʔ aknulhá·   a·yuthu·táteʔ   kʌ   aukyo·tʌ́·.   (38) Waʔí·luʔ
I asked her   my mother she would consent question that I work.   She said

(31) So the next morning we were eating breakfast just before they went to work. (32) So
the boss got there again, he said, "I did not find anyone to work, are you able to work half a
day still?" (33) "Maybe" he said "I will find someone who would come to work." (34) So
again I said, "yes, I will try, right." (35) I was just so happy to go to work. (36) So I finished out the day again, I worked the whole day, so the boss got there again, he said, "I
couldn't" he said "find anyone who would come to work," he said, "if you want to work the
whole season I could hire YOU." (37) So then I asked my mother would she allow me to
work. (38) She said

"isé· kwí· né· onʌ́ n tá·t íhselhe? ʌskwe·ní·   kʌ́h, ʌsayo·tʌ́·   kih."
"you   it's up to   if   you think you will be able eh,   you will work actually."

(39) Nʌ kwí· né· kwahikʌ́ tsi? wa?katshanu·ní· né· tsi? waku?wéskwanihe? se?
       So then   it's just really that   I became happy   because   I enjoy   too

ní· aukyo·tʌ́· utakhenláhtu?.   (40) Né·n   wa?kkwe·ní· ki?   né·
me   that I work   that I hand leaves to someone.   It's that   I was able   actually   it's

thikʌ́ wa?kkʌnhi·yá·ke?   tsi? náhe? lotiyó·tʌhse? oyú·kwa?, kwáh ki?
that   I crossed over the season while   they work   tobacco,   just   actually

ya?kó·ktʌ?   tsi? niyo·lé· wahatíhsane? ukyo·tʌ́·.
I finished out   until   they finished   I worked.

   (41) Né· kwí· né· onʌ́ tutye·lʌ́hte? ukwatkálya?kse?, onísta? uhte   tsi?
          So it's   it's   then it was first   I got paid,   gosh   supposedly how

nuknehla·kó·   wakhwistaká·te?.   (42) Yah te?ské·yale?   tó· nikú
I was surprised   I have a lot of money.   Not   I don't remember anymore how much

latikálya?ks ne? thó·ne?, nók tsi? uknehla·kó·   ki?   tsi? e·só· ukwatkályahkse?.
they pay   at that time,   but   I was surprised   actually that a lot   I got paid.

(43) Wísk kwí· niwʌhnislaké   thikʌ́ tsi? nikú   ukyo·tʌ́·, kwáh a?nyóh
       Five   days amount to   that   how many I worked, just   seems like

sakehyá·lane? tékni yawʌ·lé· nikahwístake   uhte i·kélhe? thikʌ́ swʌhníslat
I remember   two   teen   dollars amount to I think   that   one day

ne? thó·ne?. (44) Tahnú· wísk kwí· niwʌhnislaké   ukyo·tʌ́·, tahnú· tékni yawʌ·lé·
at that time.   And   five   days amount to I worked, and   two   teen

nikahwístake   swʌhníslat. (45) Tho kwí· nikú   thikʌ́ ukwatkályahkse?.
dollars amount to one day.   That's   how much that   I got paid.

"it's up to you, if you think you can, you can work." (39) So then I was really happy because I enjoyed working at handing leaves. (40) So I was able to the spend the whole season
as long as they were working in tobacco, I worked right to the end until they finished.
   (41) So then was the first time I got paid, gosh I was really surprised I had a lot of money.
(42) I don't remember how much they paid at that time, but I was surprised that I got paid a
lot. (43) I worked for five days, I seem to remember it was like twelve dollars per day I
think at that time. (44) And I worked five days, and twelve dollars a day. (45) So that's
how much I got paid.

(46) Né·n,   né· ki?   thikʌ́ teknihatú·thne ukwatkálya?kse?,   nʌ   kanatá·ke
     It's that, it's actually   that   second   I got paid,   then uptown

wá·nehte?   aknulhá·   khále? lake?níha, tho kwí· wa?uke·kwáhte?,   wahʌ́·lu?
the two went there my mother and   my father, there   they invited me,   he said

lake?níha, "kʌ? nukwá· n sahwísta?," wahʌ́·lu?, "í· kwí· ʌkha·wáke?,   nók
my father, "here   your money," he said,   "me   I will hold onto it, just

ʌskhlo·lí·   nʌ   náhte? ʌhsla·kó·   ʌhsatathni·nú·se?."   (47) Tahnú· s kwí·
you will tell me then what   you will choose you will buy for yourself."   And

yuknu?wéskwanihe? lake?níha a·yakyatahúhsatate? thikʌ́ Cleveland Indians
we two enjoy   my father that we two listen to that   Cleveland Indians

tehuttsihkwá·eks, né· s thikʌ́ tekhénhes, né· kwí· ukyatteam.   (48) Tahnú·
they play ball,   it's that I back them, so it's we two, our team.   And

yah kwí· né· te?yonu?wéskwanihe? aknulhá·   khále? n teyakwatʌhnu·téle?
not   it's they don't enjoy   my mother and   we are siblings

a·kutahúhsatate?. (49) Tahnú· kʌ? ok kʌs ni·wá· thikʌ́ yukni·yʌ́·   watlʌnótha?,
that they listen.   And   it is just small   that   we two have it plays music,

tahnú· yah kwí· akwáh   te?yoyánele?. (50) Né· kati? wí· wahili?wanu·tú·se?,
and   not   especially it is not good.   Well it's   I asked him,

wa?kí·lu?, "ʌwa·tú·   kʌ n oyá·   usakhni·nú·   watlʌnótha?."
I said,   "it can be question another I would buy again it plays music."

(51) Wahʌ́·lu?, "kano·lú·   ki?   thikʌ́, ʌwa·tú· kwí·" wahʌ́·lu?
     He said,   "it is expensive actually that,   it can be"   he said

"tʌtyátyeste?   ki?wáh." (52) Nʌ ki? ok wi· né· tho   wahakya?taha·wíhte?
"you and I will add it right."   Right away   it's there he took me along

(46) So, then the second time I got paid, my mother and father went uptown, they invited me
along, my father said, "here is your money," he said, "I will hang onto it, you just tell me
what you choose that you will buy for yourself." (47) And my father and I used to enjoy
listening to the Cleveland Indians baseball games, I used to root for them, it was our team.
(48) And my mother and my sisters didn't like to listen [to ball games]. (49) And we had
just a small radio, and it wasn't very good. (50) Well then I asked him, I said, "can I buy
another radio?" (51) He said, "it's expensive," he said "you and I can chip in, right."
(52) So right away he took me

tsiʔ nú·   thutʌhni·núheʔ   watlʌnótha<u>ʔ</u>.   (53) Laulhá·   kwí·   wahala·kó·   tsiʔ ka·yʌ́·
where   they sell   it plays music.   Him   he chose it   the one that

tyoyánel<u>eʔ</u>.   (54) Kháleʔ   neʔ thó·neʔ   battery   kʌs kwí·   né·   wátstaʔ   watlʌnót<u>ha</u>ʔ.
it is best.   And   at that time   battery   habitually   it's   it uses   it plays music.

(55) Nʌ kwí·   né·   wahakályahkeʔ   kiʔwáh.   (56) Kwáh kwí·   né· nók   sayákwaweʔ,
So then   it's   he paid   right.   Just   it's   we got back,

nʌ kiʔ ok wi·   né·   waʔthanahsu·tʌ́·   kaʔikʌ́   watlʌnóthaʔ,   ókhnaʔ   tho nú·
right away   it's   he hitched it   this   it plays music,   and then   that's where

yahlotálhoʔ   tsiʔ nú·   naʔtehuttsihkwá·eks.   (57) Tehuttsihkwá·eks   kwí·
he snagged it over there   where   they play ball.   They play ball

neʔ thó·neʔ   yoʔkalásh<u>ʌ</u>.   (58) Nʌ kiʔ ok wi·   né·   tho   waʔakyátiʔ
at that time   evening.   Right away   it's   there   we two sat down

waʔakyatahúhsatat<u>eʔ</u>.   (59) Ok neʔn   aknulhá·   kháleʔ n   teyakwatʌhnu·téleʔ,
we two listened.   And as for   my mother   and   we are siblings,

oyá· kwí·   né·   náhteʔ   waʔtyotiʔnikulha·lʌ́·,   yah   seʔ   né·   teʔyonuʔwéskwaniheʔ
other   it's   what   they bothered with,   not   too   it's   they don't enjoy

a·kutahúhsatateʔ   tehuttsihkwá·eks.
that they listen   they play ball.

(60) Né· katiʔ wí·   ké·yaleʔ   thikʌ́   né·   ní·   tyotyelʌ́htu   waʔkhni·nú·   tsiʔ nikú
Well then it's   I remember   that   it's   me   first   I bought it   how much

tewakatʌ́·tshuʔ   tshututye·lʌ́hteʔ   ukyo·tʌ́·   kháleʔ   ukwatkályah<u>kse</u>ʔ.   (61) Tékni
I have earned   when it was first   I worked   and   I got paid.   Two

yawʌ·lé·   tshaʔtewakohsliyá·ku   neʔ thó·neʔ   tshukyoʔtʌ́hsaʔ.   (62) Né·n,
teen   when I have crossed over winters   at that time   when I went to work.   It's,

to where they sold radios. (53) He was the one who chose the one that was the best.
(54) And at that time radios used batteries. (55) So then he paid for it. (56) Just as soon as
we got back again, right away he hooked up the radio, and then he turned it to [the station]
where they were playing ball. (57) They were playing ball that evening. (58) Right away
the two of us sat down and we listened. (59) And my mother and my sisters, they got into
something else, they didn't like to listen to ball games.

(60) Well I remember the first thing I bought with how much I made the first time I
worked and I got paid. (61) I was twelve years old when I went to work. (62) So

nʌ   tshusayákwaweʔ,   nʌ kwíˑ tshutuˑkóˑteʔ   thikʌ́ latiyuʔkwákwas.   (63) Náleʔ
when   when we got home,   so then   when it passed   that   they pick tobacco.   Then

kanatáˑke   sayákwehteʔ   kaʔikʌ́, néˑ kwíˑ néˑ onʌ́ n aknulháˑ   yaʔukyaʔtáhaweʔ,
uptown   again we went there   this,   so it's   it's   then   my mother   she took me,

waʔíˑluʔ, "yah thyaˑyaˑwʌ́ˑ tsiʔ ʌtnihniˑnúˑ   oyáˑ ʌsehsatslúnyahteʔ   néˑ tsiʔ
she said, "it has to be   that   you and I will buy   other   you will dress with again   because

nok ʌwaˑtúˑ ʌhsatawyaʔtáˑnaʔ."   (64) Nʌ kwíˑ néˑ yaʔukyaʔtáhaweʔ,   tóhkaʔ kiʔ
it has to be   you will go to school."   So then   it's   she took me,   a few   actually

nikú   atyáˑtawiʔt ukyʌˑtáneʔ kháleʔ kohslaʔkékhaʔ? atyáˑtawiʔt kháleʔ aˑséˑ
how many   dress   I obtained   and   winter kind   coat   and   new

áhtaʔ, teyoyaˑnáke uhte iˑkélheʔ áhtaʔ   ukyʌˑtáneʔ kháleʔ teyulahtahkwanetaʔásta?
shoes, two pairs   I think   shoes   I obtained   and   overshoes

kohslaʔkékhaʔ. (65) Kwáh kiʔ tsyoʔk nahtéˑshuʔ thikʌ́ ukyʌˑtáneʔ neʔ thóˑneʔ.
winter kind.   Just   all kinds of things   that   I obtained   at that time.

(66) Tahnúˑ wíˑ kwahikʌ́ tsiʔ wakatshanuní néˑ tsiʔ íˑ   akhwístaʔ wáˑkatsteʔ
      And   just really that   I am happy   because   me   my money   I used

waʔkatathninúnyuhseʔ   tsyoʔk nahtéˑshuʔ, nʌ kiʔ ok wíˑ néˑ waʔakníhsaneʔ
I bought things for myself   all kinds of things,   right then   it's   we two finished

waʔaknihninúniʔ   tsiʔ náhteʔ teyotuhutsyóhu, néˑ sʌ́ˑ n atláhtiʔ sʌ́ˑ ukyʌˑtáneʔ
we two bought things   that   what   it is needed,   it's   also   socks   also   I obtained

kháleʔ naʔkúkhaʔ. (67) Kwáh kiʔ tsiʔ náhteʔ teyotuhutsyóhu aˑyutslúnyahteʔ
and   underwear.   Just   whatever   it is needed   for one to wear

néˑ kiʔ   ukyʌˑtáneʔ. (68) Néˑ kiʔ   thikʌ́ tho   nikú   kéˑyaleʔ
it's   actually I obtained.   It's   actually that   that's how much   I remember

when we got home, it [the season] was over for picking tobacco. (63) We went uptown again, my mother took me along, she said, "you and I have to buy some other clothes for you to wear because you have to go to school." (64) So then she took me, and I got a few dresses and a winter coat and new shoes, I got two pairs of shoes I think and winter boots. (65) I just got all kinds of things at that time. (66) And I was really happy because I used my money to buy all these things for myself, then we finished buying what was needed, also I got socks and underwear. (67) Everything that was needed for you to wear, that's what I got. (68) So that's how much I remember about

tshututye·lʌ́hte? tshukyo·tʌ́·   wa?tkatʌ́·tshane?, nʌ   ki?   né· kaló·
when it was first   when I worked   I earned,   then   actually   it's   this way

takaha·wíhte? ya?teyohslaké ki?   ókhna? wakelha·lé· aukyo?tʌ́hsa?.
it went forward   every year   actually   and then   I am ready   that I go to work.

(69) Ne? thó·ne? ki?   ní· tyotáhsawʌ? tyótkut wakyo·té·   khále? kʌh
      At that time   actually   me   it has begun   always   I am working   and   here

wa?káhewe?   shekú ki?   wakyo·hté·.   (70) Ati tsi?   nʌ   teyotuhutsyóhu
the time has come   still   actually   I am working.   Even though   now   it should be

aukwatolishʌ·táke? tsi? na?tewakohsliyá·ku o·nʌ́.   (71) Nók tsi?   waku?wéskwanihe?
I should be resting   at   the age I am   now.   But   I enjoy it

ki?   ní· aukyo·tʌ́·, sʌ́ha? kwí· tsi?   oyá· náhte? swakyo·té·,   né·
actually   me   that I work,   more   because   another   what   again I am working,   it's

núwa? swakyo·té·   a·khelihúni?   Ukwehuwé usahutwʌnu·táhkwe?
this time   again I am working   I should teach them   Native   that they speak in a language

kʌ? nithotiyʌ́·sa?.   (72) Nʌ   ki?   tóhka? niyohslaké   né· tshiwakyo·té·,
young people.   Then   actually   a few   years amount to   it's   when I am working,

nʌ   ki?   né· teyotuhutsyóhu ka?ikʌ́ aukwatolishʌ·táke?, nók tsi? shekú ki?
then   actually   it's   it should be   this   I should be resting,   but   still   actually

wakyo·hté·.   (73) Né· tsi?   waku?wéskwanihe?.   (74) Né· ki?   tho   nikú
I am working.   Because   I enjoy it.   It's   actually   that's   how much

tsi? náhte? kehya·lú·   khále? tsi? núwa?   náhte? nikatyélha? kʌh wʌhnisla·té·.
that   what   I remember   and   that   this time   what   I am doing   here   a day exists.

(75) Wé·ne kwí· tsi? nʌ   thok   ni·kú.   (76) Nʌ ki?wáh.
      Evidently   that   then   that's only   how much.   So long.

the first time I worked and made money, then from that time forward, every year I was ready to go to work. (69) Starting at that time I always worked and up to now I'm still working. (70) Even though I should be retired now, for how old I am now. (71) But I enjoy working, the more so because I'm working at something else, this time I'm working to teach young people to speak the Native language. (72) It's a few years since I've been working at that, I should be retired, but I'm still working. (73) Because I enjoy it. (74) That's all I remember and what I'm doing today. (75) I guess that's all. (76) So long.

Reflections

The last three recordings are about growing up, about the kinds of jobs people worked at, the foods the storytellers enjoyed (or didn't enjoy so much), the way food was prepared, getting together with friends, the positive influence of resourceful parents, loving and generous grandparents, and generally memories about good times as well as times of hardship.

The recording by Pearl Cornelius is more conversational (see also *The Dreamer* recorded with Olive Elm in the 'Customs' section), and Mercy's speech is given in italics to set it apart from Pearl's.

As is already evident from many of the stories in earlier sections, people used to move around a lot in pursuit of making a living. So it is interesting to compile an inventory of verb stems that are used for the equivalent of English 'live' or 'reside.' There are at least five groups of stems. The first is the stem **-nakle-** 'reside, dwell, live' (and in some contexts 'be plentiful'), and two other stems built on this stem, **-anaklat-** 'relocate, settle, be born,' and **-anaklakw-** 'move away, pick up one's things and move away.' (The composition of the derived stems is given in the entries for these stems in the 2002 dictionary by Michelson and Doxtator.) The second of these, **-anaklakw-**, has a derived stem **-anaklakwʌhatye-** 'move around from place to place.'

The second stem, or set of stems, is based on **-ahtʌty-** 'leave, set out, go away, get underway.' With the s- REPETITIVE prefix, this stem is used for 'go home.' And with the t- CISLOCATIVE prefix and the particle **tsiʔ**, it is the usual expression for 'someone's home' (for example, **tsiʔ twakahtʌ́ti** 'my home,' literally 'where I have left from'). The derived stem **-ahtʌtyuhatye-**, usually with the tet- or tuta- DUALIC plus CISLOCATIVE prefixes, is used for 'be on one's way home from somewhere' (for example, **tutahonahtʌtyuháti?** 'they are on their way home again').

Third, the stem **-atyʌ-**, which otherwise means 'sit down,' can also mean 'move, move in, stay, live' (usually temporarily somewhere). An example from Mercy's story in this section is **yaʔakwáti?** 'we moved over there.'

Fourth, the stem **-iʔtlu-** means 'be sitting, be at home, dwell.' An example, again from Mercy's story, is **yakwʌ́·tlu?** 'we dwell.'

And finally, the verb stem **-w-/-ew-/-aw-/u-** 'arrive,' with the s- REPETITIVE prefix, is used for 'go, get home' (for example, **sá·laweʔ** 'he got back home').

My Childhood

(Told by Mercy Doxtator on May 12, 1998)

(1) Ostúha ka?ikʌ́ yʌkatu·kóhte? oyá· núwa? náhte? ʌskathlo·lí·, né·
A little this I will go on other this time what I will tell again, it's

kyuhte wí· núwa? usakathlo·lí· tsi? ní· náhte? kehya·lú· tshikeksáh.
supposedly this time I should tell again that me what I remember when I was a child.

(2) Kwáh s ikʌ́ tsi? a·kí·lu? kwáh ya?weskwa?tú·ne? Ukwehuwé·ne. (3) Tyótkut
Just really that I'd say just it used to be pleasant on the Reserve. Always

elók tsyákwe? yakwanatá·lehse? kʌ́·, tá·thuni? tkutinatá·lehse? tsi? tyukwahtʌ́ti.
all over we go we go visiting see, or they come visiting at our home.

(4) Né· s kati? wí· thikʌ́ ya?wéskwa?t, nále? wakanúhte? úhka? ok
Well then it's that it is fun, when again I know someone

taku·né·, tá·t yotiwi·láyʌ? nʌ kyale? wí· ʌwa·tú· úhka? ok oskánhe
they are coming, maybe if they have a child so again it can be someone together

ʌyakwatnutólyahte?. (5) Tahnú· s kwí· né· tsi? s né· niyotilihó·tʌ yukhinulhá·
we will play. And it's how it's the way they are our mothers

thikʌ́ ne? thó·ne? tshiyakwaksa?shúha, yah se? s wí· né· te?yukwalí·wayʌ? thikʌ́
that at that time when we were children, not too it's we have no business that

a·yakwatahúhsatate? náhte? yonathlo·lí. (6) Kwáh s né· onʌ́ óksa?,
we should listen anything they are telling about. Just it's then right away,

"wá·s, wá·s átste, wá·s tsya·kʌ́n, átste satnutolya?tá·na." (7) Tho né·
"go, go outside, go go out, outside go play." That's it's

ni·yót thikʌ́ tsi? ʌyukhihlo·lí· né· tsi? yah te?yukwanáktote? náhte?
how it is that that they will tell us because not it is not our place anything

(1) I'll go on a little bit and tell you something else, I guess I should talk about what I remember from when I was a child. (2) I'd say it really used to be pleasant on the Reserve. (3) We were always going all over the place visiting, or people would come to visit at our home. (4) So it was fun, when I knew people were coming, maybe if they had children then I could play with someone. (5) And the way our mothers used to be at that time, when we were children, we had no business listening to anything they were talking about. (6) Right away it's "go, go outside, go out, go play outside!" (7) That's how they would tell us because we didn't have the chance

a·yakwatlihwatahúhsatate? náhte? yonathlo·lí.   (8) Yah tho té·yot
for us to listen to the business what they are telling about.   Not that's not how it is

tsi? núwa? ni·yót kʌ́·tho wa?káhewe?, kwáh né· akwekú nihonatahúhsate?
as this time how it is right here time has come, just it's all they are listening

latiksa?shúha náhte? niyotye·lʌ́. (9) Kwáh akwekú nihonanúhte? náhte? niyotye·lʌ́.
children what is doing. Just all they know what is doing.

(10) Oyá· sʌ́· náhte? sakehyá·lane?, né· s né· thikʌ́ tsi? náhe? watliyó
Another also what I remember, it's it's that during war

kʌ́·, a?é· s tkanuhso·táhkwe?, kwáh s ikʌ́ tsi? kanuhsiyó
y'know, way over there there used to be a house, just really that it is a nice house

kʌ́·, tho s yakʌ? nú· nihutyʌtákhwa? shakotilihunyʌ·níhe? tá·t yah
y'know, that's reportedly where they use it to stay they teach them if not

tehotinúhsote? ákte? nú·. (11) Nók tsi? yah kwí· te?watésta? ka?ikʌ́,
they don't have a house else where. But not it is not used this,

nʌ kwí· tho s nú· ya?tekútlahse? ka?ikʌ́ yukhinulhá·, kwáh kwʌ?táti? thikʌ́
so then that's where they meet over there this our mothers, just all day that

tho ʌtkuné·sheke? ahsʌ́hatut wʌhnisla·té· wa?kuti?nikhúni?. (12) Tahnú·
there they will be around Wednesday a day exists they sewed things. And

kʌs thikʌ́ ka·té· tsi? náhe? watliyó, né· s thikʌ́ latisotá·l laonatuniforms,
habitually that I am saying during war, it's that soldiers their uniforms,

né· thikʌ́ tho ka·yʌ́·, tho kwáh s thikʌ́ niyotstenye·sú·se?
it's that there it is lying, there just that there are piles here and there

laonatuniforms tá·thuni? overcoats, shekú laonaná·lole? kʌ́h. (13) Né· sʌ́·
their uniforms or overcoats, even their hats y'know. It's also

to listen in on any of their business, what they were talking about. (8) It wasn't the way it is
now at this time, all the children are listening to what's occurring. (9) They all know what's
happening.

(10) Another thing I remember, it was during the war, there used to be a house over there,
a really nice house, that's where the teachers used to stay if they didn't have a residence
some place else. (11) But it wasn't being used, so then that's where our mothers would
meet, all day on Wednesdays they would be there sewing things. (12) And I'm talking during the war, the uniforms from the soldiers were kept there, there were piles of their uniforms or overcoats, even their hats. (13) Also

thikʌ́ latiairforce laonatslunyákhwaʔ tho kwí· ka·yʌ́· kʌ́·, né· thikʌ́ ʌwa·tú·
that air force their clothes there it is lying y'know, it's that it can be

a·ku·nútsteʔ yukhinulhá· a·kutiʔnikhúni̱ʔ. (14) Waʔkutkʌ́hatuʔ sʌ́·, tá·t núwaʔ
that they use it our mothers that they sew things. They made quilts also, maybe

a·kí·luʔ tóhkaʔ kwí· nikú ʌwa·tú· ʌkutíhsaneʔ swʌhníslat, niyotityohkwanʌ́
I'd say a few how many it can be they will finish one day, they are a big group

seʔ s waʔkutkʌ́ha̱tu̱ʔ. (15) Kháleʔ kwáh s ké·yaleʔ kʌ́·, né· s kiʔ né·n
too they made quilts. And just I remember y'know, it's actually it's that

aknulhá· tsiʔ s niyoyánleʔ a skirt waʔukúniʔ kʌ́·, né· wí· thikʌ́
my mother how it is nice a skirt she made for me y'know, it's that

wá·yutsteʔ thikʌ́ tá·t núwaʔ laairforce laotuniform. (16) Tsiʔ s kwí· niyotilʌʔnhá·u
she used that maybe air force his uniform. How they know how

thikʌ́ kutiʔníkhuheʔ, né· s sʌ́· thikʌ́ ukyalá·seʔ, George kwí· luwa·yátskweʔ,
that they sew, it's also that we two cousins, George was his name,

ne·né· thikʌ́ akwatauntieha kʌ́· wahuwayúniʔ uniform, waʔústohteʔ thikʌ́,
it's that that my auntie y'know she made for him uniform, she reduced it that,

kwáh kwí· nók weʔthóhtsiʔ laksá· wí· á·latsteʔ uniform, shekú
just only it is the right size a boy he should wear it uniform, even

overcoat waʔústohteʔ oniʔ nʌʔ né·. (17) Tsiʔ s kwí· né· niyotsinaʔtolʌ́ kʌ́·,
overcoat she reduced it too that one. How it's it is a dapper one y'know,

kwaʔnyóh laairforce, shekú né· kwáh lonaʔalo·lú̱. (18) Waʔústohteʔ oniʔ
seems like the air force, even it's just he has on a hat. She reduced it even

né·n aná·lo̱leʔ. (19) Né· s kwí· thikʌ́ tho ni·yót kʌ́·, kwáh akwekú
it's that hat. So it's that that's how it is y'know, just all

clothes from the air force were kept there, our mothers could use them to sew things.
(14) They made quilts too, I'd say maybe they could finish a few in one day, there were a lot
of them making quilts. (15) And I remember, my mother made a really nice skirt for me,
she used an air force uniform maybe. (16) They really knew how to sew, also my cousin,
George was his name, my auntie made a uniform for him, she took it in, it was just the right
size that a boy could wear the uniform, she even took in the overcoat, that too. (17) He
looked really sharp, just like the air force, he was even wearing the hat. (18) She even took
in the hat. (19) So that's the way it was,

tsyoʔk ni·yót   tsiʔ   waʔukhiyúniʔ   yukhinulháh.   (20) Kwáh s ké·yaleʔ   thikʌ́
different kinds   that   they made for us   our mothers.   Just   I remember   that

náleʔ   ahsʌ́hatut   tsiʔ s niwakatshanuní tsiʔ   nʌ kyaleʔ wí· kaʔikʌ́
when again Wednesday   how   I am happy   because   so again   this

ʌyukwʌtyohkwánhʌʔ   yakwaksaʔshúha, sayakwaya·kʌ́neʔ yakwatayá·thaʔ,
we will get to be a big crowd   we children,   we went out again   we go to school,

nʌ sok wí·   né· tewalelútiʔ,   úhkaʔ náhteʔ   nya·lé· nyaa·yúweʔ
and so then   it's   the race is on,   who   first   someone would get over there

tsiʔ nú·   tku·né·seʔ   yukhinulháh.   (21) Nʌ kwí· né·   tho   yaʔákwaweʔ
where   they are around   our mothers.   So then   it's   there   we got over there

kʌ́·,   nʌ kwí· waʔukhinaʔtu·há·seʔ kwí· náhteʔ waʔukhiyúni̲ʔ.   (22) Kwáh s kwí·
y'know,   so then   they showed it to us   what   they made for us.   Just

né· tsyoʔk náhteʔ   kutu·níheʔ, kutkʌhu·níheʔ   sʌ́·,   kutkʌ́hatuheʔ, kwáh kwí·
it's   all kinds of things   they make,   they make blankets   also,   they quilt,   just

tsiʔ niyóhsles   thikʌ́ yotiyo·té·   kʌ́·, kwáh tsyoʔk nikutyélhaʔ,   né· nʌ
during the winter   that   they are working see,   different things they are doing, it's   then

tho s kayʌ·táyʌʔ   thikʌ́ ʌwa·tú· kwʌʔtátiʔ tho   ʌtkuné·shekeʔ,   yah s kwí·
there   there is wood   that   it can be all day   there   they will be around,   not

né· teʔwakanúhteʔ kátshaʔ né· nú·   nityawenú   o·yʌ́teʔ, nók tsiʔ tho
it's   I don't know   where   it's   where it has come from wood,   but   there

kiʔ   tekayʌ·tóteʔ, ʌwa·tú· ʌkute·ká·teʔ,   ʌwa·tú· oniʔ tho   ʌkutikhu·ní̲·.
actually wood is piled,   it can be they will make fire, it can be even   there   they will cook.

(23) Neʔ thó·neʔ kwáh tyotyelʌ́htu wakatkáthu kanúsku   kahne·kó̲·.   (24) Ó·
        At that time   just   first   I have seen   in the house   a well.   Oh

our mothers made every kind of thing for us all. (20) I remember on Wednesdays I was so
happy because there would be a lot of us kids, we got out of school and then the race was
on, who would get there first where our mothers were. (21) So then we got there, and then
they showed us what they made for us. (22) They were making all kinds of things, they
were making blankets too, they were quilting, all winter long they were working, they were
doing all kinds of things, there was wood there and they could be there all day, I don't know
where the wood came from, but there was wood piled up there, they could make a fire, and
they could cook even. (23) At that time it was the first time I saw water [come] in the
house. (24) Oh,

tsi? nuknehla·kó·   thikʌ́ tho   kapámpslote? kanúsku,   né· kwí· thikʌ́
how I was surprised that   there there's a pump in the house, so it's   that

tho kwí· nú· nʌhsétsyʌhte?   tá·t íhselhe? a·shnekí·la.   (25) Ó· tsi? s
that's where you will draw water if   you want you would drink.   Oh how

niwaku?wéskwanihe? thikʌ́ tho nú·   só·tsi? kanuhsiyó   kʌ́·,   shekú s
I enjoy it   that   that's where so much it is a nice house y'know, still

né· thikʌ́ oshu?kalá·ke, kwahikʌ́ tsi? teyostaláthe? tsi?   né· s kyuhte wí· onʌ́
it's that   floor,   just really that it is shiny   because it's   supposedly then

tá·t núwa? tewatwax. (26) Tsi? s ki?   nikanuhsiyó   thi·kʌ́. (27) Tho
maybe   it is waxed.   How   actually it is a nice house that.   That's

kati? wí· nú·   thikʌ́ s ka·té·   yakwétha? ahsʌ́hatut.   (28) Kwáh tho
anyway where that   I am saying we go there Wednesday.   Just   there

ya·wét   ya?tyokʌnhu·tí·, tho   ki?   thikʌ́ yakwétha? kwáh tsi? nikú ahsʌ́hatut.
kind of like it became spring, there in fact that   we go there every   Wednesday.

   (29) Né· núwa?   thikʌ́ ya·wét   tsi? nú· a·kí·lu? nyeswakathlolí,
        It's this time that   kind of like where   I'd say   I am going on telling about

kwáh s kwí· né· ótya?k kʌs   kyuhte wí· loti?sléhtayʌ?, nók tsi? né· kyuhte wí·
just   it's some habitually supposedly they have cars, but   it's supposedly

tsi? akwekú tewatration ne? thó·ne?, yah kwí· te?yakó·slehse?, yah kyuhte wí·
that all   it is rationed at that time, not   one doesn't drive, not supposedly

sʌ́· tha·hatikalakwe·ní· a·hoti?slehtayʌ·táne? ótyahk. (30) Ké·yale? s né·n
also they could not afford that they obtain a car some.   I remember it's that

akwatauntieha tsi? loti?sléhtayʌ? Model T, nók tsi? yako·yʌ́· s buggy, né· s kwí·
my auntie   that they have a car Model T, but   she has   buggy, so it's

I was so amazed there was a pump inside the house, that's where you would draw water if
you wanted to drink. (25) Oh I really enjoyed it there, such a nice place, even the floors,
they were really shiny because I guess maybe they were waxed. (26) It was a really nice
house. (27) That's were I'm saying we went on Wednesdays. (28) Kind of like in the
spring, we went there every Wednesday.

   (29) Like the time and place I'd say I'm talking about, some people I guess had cars, but I
guess everything was rationed at that time, people didn't drive, I guess also some couldn't
afford to have a car. (30) I remember my auntie, they had a car, a Model T, but she had a
buggy,

thikʌ́ waʔkuwashaluˑtʌ́ˑ akotsheˑnʌ́ˑ kohsaˑtʌ́s. (31) Kwáh s kéˑyaleʔ tsiʔ
that they harnessed her pet animal horse. Just I remember that

Molly uhte iˑkélheʔ s kuwanaʔtúkhwaʔ thikʌ́ akotsheˑ<u>nʌ́</u>ˑ. (32) Néˑ kwíˑ thikʌ́
Molly I think what they called it that her pet animal. So it's that

waʔukwáˑsleʔ náleʔ waʔtyakwatawʌlyéhsaʔ kátshaʔ ok núˑ, táˑthuniʔ Southwold
we rode when again we travelled somewhere, or Southwold

waʔákwehteʔ, néˑ kwíˑ waʔukwáˑsleʔ thikʌ́ horse and buggy. (33) Tsiʔ s
we went there, so it's we rode that horse and buggy. How

niyaʔwéskwaht. (34) Yah kwíˑ néˑ kátshaʔ thaˑhsatkáthoʔ aˑkatákheʔ káˑslet,
it is enjoyable. Not it's anywhere you won't see that it runs car,

néˑ ok thikʌ́ táˑt taˑyakwátlaneʔ úhkaʔ ok oyáˑ, táˑt lotiˑyʌ́ oniʔ néˑ
it's only that maybe should we meet someone other, maybe they have too it's

buggy kháleʔ kohsaˑtʌ́s kwíˑ ʌtwatiluˑ<u>tʌ́</u>ˑ. (35) Néˑ s wíˑ tsiʔ yaˑwét kʌs
buggy and horse it will pull it. So it's that kind of like habitually

néˑ kwáh uhte tsiʔ nikú kanúhsoteʔ latifarmer kwíˑ neʔ thóˑ<u>neʔ</u>.
it's just supposedly as many there is a house farmers at that time.

(36) Kwáh tsyoʔk nihotinʌskóˑtʌ kʌ́ˑ, tyonhúskwalut, kohsaˑtʌ́s,
     All different they have kinds of animals y'know, cow, horse,

kítkit, kóskos, kwáh kiʔ tsyoʔk náhteʔ lotinʌ́skwayʌʔ, shekú nén yah kwíˑ
chicken, pig, just all kinds of they have animals, even it's that not

néˑ thaˑhsatkáthoʔ tractor, néˑ kiʔ ok wíˑ thikʌ́ team, néˑ kwíˑ thikʌ́
it's you won't see tractor, it's actually only that team, so it's that

ʌhotiyoˑtʌ́ˑ kahʌtáˑ<u>ke</u>. (37) ʌhotiyʌthóhsluʔ sʌ́ˑ, kwáh s kéˑyaleʔ oniʔ
they will work on the field. They will plant things also, just I remember too

and they harnessed her horse to it. (31) I remember her horse was called Mollie I think.
(32) We rode in that when we travelled somewhere, or we went to Southwold, so we rode in
that horse and buggy. (33) It used to be so nice. (34) You wouldn't see a car anywhere, but
maybe we met someone else, maybe they had a buggy too and a horse would be pulling it.
(35) It was like I guess every house was farmers at that time. (36) They had all kinds of
animals, cows, horses, chickens, pigs, they had all kinds of animals, you wouldn't even see a
tractor, only a team [of horses], they were working in the fields. (37) They would plant
things also, I remember too

né·n   tsiʔ s niwakuʔwéskwaniheʔ thikʌ́ ya·wét   tho   kiʔ   tsiʔ
it's that how   I enjoy it   that   kind of like there actually at

tkawyhuhatátiʔ áktaʔ, tho s niyo·lé·   thikʌ́ tkahʌtaké·luʔ   kʌ́·
river   near,   that's as far as that   there are fields around y'know

akwatauntieha wí· lo·né·,   Katsya kʌs   luwanaʔtúkhwaʔ.   (38) Tho s thikʌ́
my auntie   spouse, Katsya habitually what they call him.   There   that

waʔakwatitáliʔ wagon, wagonslá·ke waʔakwatitáliʔ, kháleʔ atshó·ktaʔ wí·
we got in   wagon,   on the wagon we got in,   and   hoe

yaʔakwaháwhuʔ kʌ́·,   kwáh s ké·yaleʔ   tsiʔ kwáh oniʔ ní· yukni·yʌ́· n
we took   y'know, just   I remember that just   too   us   we two have

í·   kháleʔ George thikʌ́ kok   ni·yús   atshó·ktaʔ, né· kwí· aolí·waʔ
me   and   George that   just short how long it is hoe,   so it's   the reason

nʌ   ʌthutáhsawʌʔ ʌhutaneklóskaluʔ, yah oniʔ ní· thya·ya·wʌ́· tsiʔ tho
when   they will start   they will hoe,   not   too   us   it has to be   that   there

waʔukniyo·tʌ́· kʌ́h.   (39) Tsiʔ s kwí· niyaʔwéskwaʔt thikʌ́, né· thikʌ́ nʌ
we two worked y'know.   How   it is fun   that,   it's   that   when

ʌyakwáhsaneʔ, nʌ   kiʔ   ʌwa·tú· tsiʔ tkawyhuhatátiʔ yʌyákweʔ
we will finish,   then   actually   it can be at   river   we will go over there

ʌyakwata·wʌ́·,   kwáh s kyuhte wí· nók tsiʔ sayakwatyaʔtóhaleʔ kʌ́·   tá·t
we will take a bath, just   supposedly only   we washed again   y'know if

tsiʔ nikú   waʔtyukwateʔtukhwa·lʌ́·, kháleʔ sayakwatekhunyá·naʔ tsiʔ tkanúhsoteʔ,
how much we sweated,   and   we went to eat again   at   there is a house,

tahnú· kwáh s kiʔ   aʔnyóh inú thikʌ́ nyaʔukwá·sleʔ   kʌ́h.
and   just   actually seems   far   that   we drove over there y'know.

how much I used to enjoy it, like near the river, that's how far the [his?] fields went, my
auntie's husband, Katsya was his name. (38) We would get into the wagon, and we took
hoes, I remember we even had one, George and I, it was just a short hoe, and that's why
when they started to hoe, the two of us would have to work too. (39) It was so much fun,
when we would finish, we could go to the river to take a bath, I guess we just washed ourselves if we sweat a lot, and we would go to eat again at the house, and it seemed like we
drove really far.

(40) Kwáh s kati? wí· ya?wéskwa?t, né· oná n ohwa?ektá·ke sá· thiká,
      Well then   it's fun,   it's then   barn   also that,

ké·yale?   tho nú·   niyuknu?wéskwanihe? thiká George a·yakyanutolya?tá·na?,
I remember that's where we two enjoy it   that   George that we two go and play,

a?é· kwí· thiká wa?akniláthʌ?   kʌs,   onékli? kwí· thiká, tho kwí·
far away   that   we two climbed up habitually, hay   that,   there

wa?tyakyanitskwahkwáni? kʌ́·   yukyatnutolyá·tu.   (41) Né· nʌ n, né· s sʌ́·
we two jumped around   y'know we two are playing.   It's when, it's   also

thiká nále?,   a·kí·lu?   né· kyuhte wí· nále?   wahatiyʌtho·kó·, kwáh s
that   when again, I would say it's supposedly when again they harvested,   just

ké·yale?   thiká elók   shʌ·né·   latifarmers, kwáh s ki?   né· kyale?
I remember that   all over they are going farmers,   just   actually it's again

thiká nále?   akwatauntiehne tahotiyo?tʌ́hsa?, tsi? s niwaku?wéskwanihe?,
that   then again at my auntie's   they came to work, how   I enjoy it,

né· wí· tsi? wakanúhte? tsi? niyakokhwaká·te?   akwatauntieha, kwáh s kwʌ?táti?
because   I know   that she has a lot of food my auntie,   just   all day

wa?knikhu·ní· thiká aknulhá· khále? akwatauntieha kʌ́·,   nʌ   wahʌ·néwe? wí· n
the two cooked that   my mother and   my auntie   y'know, then they got there

lotiyó·tʌhse? lutekhunyá·ne?   kʌ́·, ʌtye ni·kále? wí· thiká ʌhuwatikhwánute?.
they work   they are here to eat see, noon time   that   they will feed them.

(42) Tahnú· s a?é· niyakotekhwahlá·tsles. (43) Kwáh s kwí· né· thiká wahati·náne?
      And   great how long her table is.   Just   it's that   they filled it

latifarmers wahutyʌ·tú·,   nʌ kwí· wahutekhuni?kó·.   (44) Kwáh s ké·yale
farmers   they sat around, so then they ate a huge meal.   Just   I remember

(40) Well, it was fun, also the barn, I remember that's where George and I liked to go and
play, we would climb way up, there was hay, and we would jump around there playing.
(41) And when, also when I'd say they harvested, I remember the farmers went all over [to
the different farms], they came to work at my auntie's, I really enjoyed it, because I knew
that my auntie had a lot of food, all day my mother and my auntie would cook, then the
workers would get there to eat, so they would feed them lunch. (42) And she had a great
long table. (43) The farmers filled up [all the spaces] sitting [at the table], and then they ate
a huge meal. (44) I remember

tsiʔ nikú   waʔutnaʔtalutúniʔ, wá·yat khále? katsihko·tú· sʌ́·   waʔutnaʔtalutúniʔ,
how much   she baked several,   pie   and   ovenbread   also   she baked several,

né·   sʌ́·   thikʌ́ ké·yaleʔ s   butter beans, né· thikʌ́ ya·wét kwí· mustard beans
it's   also   that   I remember   butter beans,   it's   that   kind of like   mustard beans

kʌs   latinaʔtúkhwaʔ, ó· tsiʔ s thikʌ́ wake·ká·seʔ   thi·kʌ́.   (45) Kwáh kwí· ikʌ́
customarily   what they call it,   oh how   that   I like the taste   that.   Just really

tsiʔ ya·wét   kyuhte wí· s né· s thoti·kwáts   kʌh Ukwehuwé·ne kaʔikʌ́
that   kind of like   supposedly   it's   they are most well-off here   on the Reserve   this

akwatauntieha tsiʔ   nihotinʌskwaká·teʔ,   né· oniʔ n thonatʌnaʔtslaká·teʔ,
my auntie   because   they have many animals,   it's   too   they have the most provisions,

e·só· s kwí· sʌ́·   náleʔ latiyʌ́thos tshiwahu·níseʔ.   (46) Akwekú s kyuhte wí· né·
a lot   also   again   they plant   a long time ago.   All   supposedly   it's

tho   ni·yót.   (47) Ok wí· n   í·,   ya·wét kʌs   kyuhte wí· ní· yukwʌ·tʌ́t
that's   the way it is.   But as for   us,   like   habitually supposedly us   we are poor

tsiʔ   yah wí· ní· teʔyukwanʌ́skwayʌʔ,   khále? ohwaʔektá·ke, yah kwí· kátshaʔ
because   not   us   we don't have animals,   and   barn,   not   anywhere

teʔkahwaʔektá·tsloteʔ.   (48) Kháleʔ né· s kwí· thikʌ́ náleʔ   wahatíhsaneʔ,
there is no barn.   And   so it's   that   then again they finished,

tá·t núwaʔ tewʌhnislaké, tá·t núwaʔ áhsʌ niwʌhnislaké   thikʌ́, ʌhatíhsaneʔ
maybe   two days,   maybe   three how many days that,   they will finish

latihwá·eks, ókhnaʔ tá·t núwaʔ né· núwaʔ n oyá·   a farmer tethonúhsoteʔ,
they thrash,   and then   maybe   it's   this time   another   farmer   again at his house,

né· núwaʔ ʌshuwayaʔtakénhaʔ   thi·kʌ́. (49) Kwáh aleʔ   né· tshá·kat kwí·
it's   this time   again they will help him that.   Just   again it's   the same

she baked everything, she baked pie and also ovenbread, I remember also butter beans, like
mustard beans they called it (because they pickled butter beans with mustard), oh, I found
them so tasty. (45) I guess my auntie [and uncle] were like the most well-off here on the
Reserve because they had so many animals, so they had the most food, and also they planted
a lot a long time ago. (46) I guess it was like that for everyone [planting]. (47) But us, I
guess we were kind of poor because we didn't have animals, and as for a barn, there was no
barn [in our family]. (48) And when they finished, maybe [in] two days, maybe three days,
they would finish thrashing, and then maybe at another farmer's house, they would help him
out next. (49) It was the same again,

yah thya·ya·wʌ́· tsiʔ onulhá· kwí· núwaʔ   ʌtkutikhuniʔkó·,   né· kwí·
it has to be   that   them   this time   they will cook a big meal there, so it's

núwaʔ   ʌshuwatikhúniʔ   lotiyó·tʌhseʔ. (50) Olihwiyó   kʌs kwí·
this time   again they will cook for them   they work.   A sure thing   habitually

tsiʔ   yaʔweskwaʔtú·neʔ.
how   it used to be fun.

  (51) Thó·nʌ   né· sʌ́·   kehya·lú·   nʌ   ka·té·   akwekú tewatration, né·
         And then   it's also I remember then I'm saying all   it is rationed, it's

aolí·waʔ   yah kátshaʔ   teʔyukwá·slehseʔ automobil. (52) Né· kiʔ ok wí· ʌwa·tú·
the reason   not   anywhere we don't drive   car.   It's   actually has to be

kaʔikʌ́ horse and buggy waʔukwaʔsléhsuʔ   tá·t yákwelheʔ kátshaʔ ok nú·
this   horse and buggy   we drove here and there if   we want   somewhere

ya·yákoh.   (53) Né· kyuniʔ wí· né·n   akwekú tewatration, onutákliʔ
we would go over there.   It's   too   it's that all   it is rationed,   sugar

tewatration, kháleʔ gas, motor oil, ohna·kwál, owistóhseliʔ. (54) Há·,   shekú n
it is rationed, and   gas, motor oil,   tires,   butter.   Oh yeah,   even

oʔwá·luʔ. (55) Kwáh s akwekú ration books yukwa·yʌ́· uskátshuʔ, í·   úska wáki?
meat.   Just   all   ration books   we have   each one,   me   one   I have

aknulhá·   kháleʔ lakeʔníha. (56) Né· kwí· thikʌ́ náhteʔ   ʌyakwahninú·naʔ, úska
my mother   and   my father.   So it's   that   anything we will go and buy,   one

thikʌ́ stamp ʌhatiye·ná· kʌ́·, nʌ   kiʔ   né· wesató·ktahseʔ, yah thau·tú· shekú
that   stamp they will take see, then   actually it's you ran out of it,   it can't be   still

tsiʔ niyo·lé· next week né· elhúwaʔ ʌwa·tú·   thok náhteʔ usashni·nú·.
until   next week   it's   only then   it can be   something   you would buy again.

they had to cook a big meal, they cooked for the workers this time. (50) It sure used to be
fun.
   (51) And then also I remember, I'm saying everything was rationed, that's why we didn't
drive cars anywhere. (52) We had to ride a horse and buggy if we wanted to go somewhere.
(53) Everything was rationed, sugar was rationed, and gas, motor oil, tires, butter. (54) Oh
yeah, even meat. (55) Everyone, we each of us had a ration book, I had one, my mother and
my father. (56) So anything we go and buy they would take one stamp, then if you ran out
of [something], it couldn't be until the next week before you could buy something.

(57) Tho s kwí· niyohtuháti? thikʌ́, khále? ké·yale? nʌ tshutliyohslʌ·táne?,
That's how it is going along that, and I remember when when the war ended,

nʌ né· London nukwá· tshyeyakwanákle? kʌ́·, kwáh ké·yale? kwáh
then it's London where when we reside over there y'know, just I remember just

ale? né· elhúwa? sakya·kʌ́ne? wakataya?tahnu·hné·, swakahtʌtyuháti? thikʌ́,
again it's right then I went out again I have gone to school, I am on my way home that,

né·n áhsok nʌ wakathu·té· wa?tyohʌ·léhte? kʌ́, tahnú· tsi? niyokalé·ni.
it's that suddenly then I hear it screamed eh, and how it is a loud noise.

(58) Yah s kwí· te?wakanúhte? náhte? aolí·wa? ka?ikʌ́ tho na?a·wʌ́ne?, né·n
Not I don't know what the reason this thus it happened, it's that

tshyusa·kéwe? wa?kheli?wanu·tú·se? aknulhá·, wa?kí·lu? "náhte? né· thikʌ́
when I got home I asked her my mother, I said "what it's that

wa?tyohʌ·léhte?." (59) Wa?í·lu?, né· kwí· né· kʌ·té· tsi? nʌ utliyohslʌ·táne?.
it screamed." She said, it's it's it means that now the war ended.

(60) Né· kwí· né· thikʌ́ tsha?ó·kalawe? ké·yale? lake?níha kanatá·ke
So it's it's that when it got dark I remember my father uptown

wá·lehte?, tho yakʌ? nikú ukwé streetslá·ke tehonatkwʌháti?,
he went there, that's reportedly how many person on the street they are dancing along,

né· nʌ tehotilihwáhkwʌ tsi? niyo·lé· nahutshanu·ní· tsi? nʌ kwí·
it's then they are singing to that extent they got happy because so then

utliyohslʌ·táne?, nʌ kwí· ʌshʌnéwhu? latisotá·l. (61) Tho kati? wí· ní·
the war ended, so then they will come home soldiers. That's well then me

nikú thikʌ́ ké·yale? tshikeksá·, tsi? náhte? niyotyelʌ́ kʌs.
how much that I remember when I was a child, that what it is doing habitually.

(57) That's how it was, and I remember when the war ended, we were living in London then, I remember I had just got out of school, I was on my way home, suddenly I heard a screaming noise, and it was really loud. (58) I didn't know why that was happening, so when I got home I asked my mother, I said "what is that screaming?" (59) She said it means the war is over. (It was a siren.) (60) Then in the evening I remember my father went uptown, there were so many people in the streets dancing, they were singing, that's how happy they got because the war ended, so then the soldiers would come home. (61) Well that's how much I remember about when I was a child, what occurred.

(62) Né· sʌ́· waʔkehyahlá·sluʔ thikʌ́ tsiʔ elók kʌs
It's also I remember things that that all over habitually

tsyukwanaklakwʌháti?, né· s kyuhte wí· né·n aknulhá· khále? lakeʔníha,
we are moving around, it's supposedly it's that my mother and my father,

kwáh kwí· tsyoʔk náhteʔ lonatatenhá·u náhteʔ na·hni·yéleʔ
all kinds of things they have hired themselves out anything for the two to do

ta·hyatʌ́·tshane?. (63) Ké·yaleʔ s waʔakwanakla·kó· kátsha? ok nú· kalhakú
that the two earn. I remember we moved away somewhere in the woods

yaʔakwáti?, kwáh tsi? niyóhsles tho kwí· kaʔikʌ́ yakwʌ́·tlu?
we moved over there, just as the winter is long there this we dwell

kalhakú latiyʌtákwas. (64) Kwáh s tsyoʔk nú· nikanúhsoteʔ, tho kwí· nú· thikʌ́
in the woods they cut wood. All over there is a house, that's where that

nihatí·tlu?, tá·thuni? né· s ki? ní· ké·yale? tsi? nú· niyakwʌ?tlu·táhkwe?
they dwell, or it's actually us I remember where we used to dwell

tóhka? nʌ ki? nihatí tho latí·tlu?, aknulhá·
a few then actually they are that many there they dwell, my mother

tehuwatikhwáshnyehe?. (65) Né· kwí· thikʌ́ ʌhuwatikhúni? kʌ́·,
she looks after them with food. So it's that she will cook for them y'know,

kakhuní kwí· nʌ shʌ·néwe? lotiyoʔtʌhsu·hné·. (66) Né·n
food is cooked when they got back again they have gone to work. It's that

kʌkwité·ne thikʌ́ khále? sayákwawe? Ukwehuwé·ne. (67) Tá·t núwa? kwah nók
springtime that and we got home on the Reserve. Maybe just

ostúha sayenohalényu? aknulhá· khále? sayuthleʔnu·ní·, khále?
a little she washed things again my mother and she packed up again, and

(62) I also remember us moving all over the place, I guess my mother and my father would hire themselves out to do all kinds of things to make money. (63) I remember we moved away, and we moved to somewhere in the woods, all winter we stayed in the woods while they were cutting wood. (64) There were shacks everywhere, that's where they lived, or I remember where we used to live there were a few of them already living there, my mother provided meals for them. (65) So she would cook for them, the meal was cooked when they got back from working. (66) In the springtime we got back to the Reserve. (67) Maybe my mother did a bit of laundry and she packed up again, and

ákteʔ   núwaʔ   nú·   yusayákweʔ,   né· s núwaʔ   onʌ́   aʔé·
different this time where we went over there again,   it's   this time then   far away

tho   áktaʔ Toronto yaʔákweʔ,   kwáh s ké·yaleʔ   Clarkstown kuwa·yáts.
there near   Toronto we went over there,   just   I remember Clarkstown it is named.

(68) Waklihwahlukú   tsiʔ tho   núwaʔ   nú·   Mississauga latinaʔtúkhwaʔ.
     I have heard news that that's this time where Mississauga what they call it.

(69) Tho   áleʔ   né· thikʌ́ yaʔakwátiʔ,   akwatauntieha né· tho nú·
     There again   it's that   we moved over there,   my auntie   it's that's where

tyenákleʔ   thikʌ́, tyótkut fruit farm lotiyo·té·   thikʌ́ lónaʔ.
she resides that,   always fruit farm they are working that   man and wife.

(70) Tho nú·   thikʌ́ yaʔákwaweʔ,   wahyá·yakoʔ   núwaʔ   aknulhá·
     That's where that   we got over there, the two picked fruit this time my mother

kháleʔ lakeʔníha, kwáh s ké·yaleʔ   thikʌ́ tsiʔ í·   sʌ́·   waʔukúniʔ   waʔká·yakoʔ
and   my father, just   I remember that   that me   also she made me I picked fruit

kʌ́h.   (71) Yah kʌs kwí· teʔwakanúhteʔ tó·   tshi·ká·,   nók tsiʔ
y'know.   Not habitually I don't know   how much I am big then,   but

tshitwaknolú·seheʔ a·ká·yakoʔ,   tahnú· s waʔí·luʔ s aknulhá·,   "kwah nók
I am most lazy then for me to pick fruit, and   she said   my mother, "just

kaʔikʌ́ skanutó·tslat ʌhsátnaneʔ ókhnaʔ   ʌwa·tú· ʌhsatnutolyaʔtá·naʔ."
this   one box   you will fill it and then it can be you will go and play."

(72) Nʌ kyaleʔ wí· waʔkahkwíshluʔ thikʌ́ waʔká·yakoʔ, skanutó·tslat kwí·
     So again   I exerted myself that   I picked fruit,   one box

nʌ   waʔkátnaneʔ ókhnaʔ   tho   wá·kiʔ,   tho   waʔkatnutó·tslayʌʔ tsiʔ
then I filled it   and then there I put it down, there I put down a box   at

we went some place else, one time we went way near Toronto, I remember it was called
Clarkstown. (68) I hear that place is called Mississauga now. (69) We moved there, that's
where my auntie lived, she and her husband always worked on a fruit farm. (70) We got
there, my mother and father picked fruit [berries] then, I just remember that she made me
pick berries too. (71) I don't know how big I was then, but I was really really lazy to pick
berries, and my mother said, "you just fill one box and then you can go and play." (72) So I
really worked hard picking berries, then I filled one box and then I put it down, I put the box
down

yukwathahatáti̱ʔ.   (73) Nʌ kwíˑ níˑ wáˑkelheʔ kaʔikʌ́ nʌ katiʔ wíˑ ʌwaˑtúˑ
our path going along.   So then me I thought   this   well then   it can be

ʌkatnutolyaʔtáˑna̱ʔ. (74) Waʔíˑluʔ aknulháˑ,   "shekú skanutóˑtslat ʌsehsátnaneʔ
I will go and play.   She said   my mother, "still   one box   again you will fill it

nʌ   ʌwaˑtúˑ ʌhsatnutolyaʔtáˑna̱ʔ." (75) Nʌ kyaleʔ wíˑ sakáˑyakoʔ   kʌ́h.
then it can be   you will go and play."   So again   I picked fruit again y'know.

(76) Néˑn   tho   néˑ thikʌ́ naʔohtuhátiʔ, kháleʔ néˑ onʌ́ kwʌʔtátiʔ kwaʔnyóh s
      It's that that's it's that   how it is going, and   it's soon all day   seems like

kwah nók skanutóˑtslat ʌskátnaneʔ,   nʌ   ʌwaˑtúˑ ʌkatnutolyaʔtáˑna̱ʔ. (77) Kháleʔ
just   one box   I will fill it again, then it can be I will go and play.   And

néˑ onʌ́ kwáh kwʌʔtátiʔ waʔkáˑyako̱ʔ. (78) Néˑn   tho s kwíˑ thikʌ́ niˑyót
it's then just   all day   I picked fruit.   It's that that's   that   how it is

nyaʔtewʌhnislaké kʌ́ˑ   yakwahyákwas.   (79) Kháleʔ nʌ   waʔkatlihoˑlʌ́neʔ,
every day   y'know we are picking fruit.   And   then I got an idea,

néˑ kiʔ   ok wíˑ kaʔikʌ́ néˑ s wíˑ tsiʔ nihashnoˑléˑ néˑ lakeʔníha aˑháˑyako̱ʔ,
it's actually only   this   because   he is so fast it's my father for him to pick fruit,

yah s kwíˑ néˑ náhteʔ   tehauní   tékni tewʌʔnyáweluʔ nikanutóˑtslake
not   it's anything he has not made two   hundred   is the amount of boxes

aˑhátnaneʔ n swʌhníslat. (80) Wáˑkelheʔ yah kwíˑ náhteʔ   thaˑháttokeʔ   kaʔikʌ́
that he fills   one day.   I thought   not   anything he won't notice this

aˑhinutoʔtslanʌ́skoʔ,   nʌ katiʔ néˑ ʌwaˑtúˑ aˑkatnutolyaʔtáˑna̱ʔ. (81) Nʌ kwíˑ
were I to steal a box from him, well then it's   it can be that I go and play.   So then

tho   náˑkyeleʔ kʌ́ˑ, nʌ kwíˑ kwáh sekhaˑwíˑ   thikʌ́ carrier, kwáh kanáˑnu
that's what I did see, so then just   again I am carrying that   carrier, quite it is full

in our row. (73) So then I thought well, I could go and play. (74) My mother said, "fill one
more box, then you can go and play." (75) So again I picked berries. (76) So that's how it
was going, and then all day it was like I have to fill just one box, then I can go and play.
(77) And then I picked berries the whole day. (78) So that's how it was, every day we were
picking berries. (79) And then I got an idea, it was just because my father was so fast at
picking berries, he had no problem filling two hundred boxes in one day. (80) I thought he
would not notice anything if I stole a box from him, then I could go and play. (81) So then
that's what I did, so then I'm carrying the carrier again, it was filled with

tsi? nikú   wa?ká·ya<u>ko</u>?. (82) Né·n   nʌ kwí· wá·kelhe? nʌ kwí· ʌwa·tú·
how much   I picked fruit.   It's that so then   I thought   so then   it can be

a·katnutolya?tá·<u>na</u>?. (83) Né·n   tho   né· waháttoke? ka?ikʌ́ lake?níha,
that I go and play.   It's that there it's he noticed   this   my father,

tho   uhte wí·   né· lohsetuháti?   né· tó· nikú   nʌ   wahátnane?
there supposedly it's he is going along counting it's how many then   he filled

kʌ́·,   tahotó·ktahse?,   né· yah tho   té·ku   tehotnutó·tslayʌ?
y'know, he came up short, it's not   that's not how many   he does not have boxes

tsi? ná·le<u>lhe</u>?.   (84) Nʌ kwí· né· waháttoke? wé·ne   tsi? í·
as   so he thought.   So then   it's he noticed   evidently   that me

linuto?tslanʌ́skwas   lohyákwʌ,   nʌ kyale? wí· né· ukwatye·lú·<u>se</u>?.
I am stealing boxes from him   he has picked fruit, so again   it's   I got thwarted.

  (85) Kwáh s kati? wí· thikʌ́ tsyo?k náhte?   nishonatliholʌ́   náhte?
        Just   well   that   all kind of things   they are finding ways   what

na·hútyele?   tshiwahu·níse? ta·hutatéshni?,   né· wí· tsi? yah né·
they should do   a long time ago   they should support themselves,   because   not   it's

nuwʌtú tehotilihwahlukú   náhte? né·n   welfare. (86) Kwáh kwí· elók
never   they have not heard of   what   it's that   welfare.   Just   all over

shʌ·né· kʌ́·,   shekú s né· ké·yale?   né· thikʌ́ wa?kayu?kwʌ·táne?,   né· tsi?
they go y'know, even   it's I remember it's that   tobacco came to an end, because

oyú·kwa? kʌs   sʌ́· wahotiyo?tʌ́hsa?   aknulhá·   khále? lake?níha kʌ́·,
tobacco   habitually also they went there to work   my mother and   my father   see,

ókhna? Leamington núwa?   nyusayákwe?   kʌ́h.   (87) Né· ale? né·
and then Leamington   this time   we went over there again   y'know.   It's   again   it's

all the berries I picked. (82) So then I thought then I could go and play. (83) And so my
father noticed, I guess he was counting how many [boxes] he filled, he was short, he didn't
have as many boxes as he thought. (84) So then he must have noticed that I was stealing
from him boxes of berries he had picked, so I lost out again.

(85) Well they found all kinds of things to do a long time ago to support themselves, because they never heard of what welfare was. (86) They would go all over, I even remember
the tobacco [season] ending, because my mother and father went to work also in tobacco,
and then we went to Leamington next. (87) So for

thikʌ́   tó· kiʔ ok kwí· náheʔ   tho   yakwʌ́·tluʔ,   lotiyo·té·   thikʌ́   Heinz factory,
that   some only   while   there   we dwell,   they are working   that   Heinz factory,

aknulhá· s teyuhyakʌ́slus   né· tomatoes, kháleʔ lakeʔníha   yah s kwí· né·
my mother   she peels fruit   it's tomatoes,   and   my father   not   it's

teʔwakanúhteʔ náhteʔ né· nihatyélhaʔ,   nók tsiʔ kwáh s nók ké·yaleʔ   tsiʔ
I don't know   what   it's   he is occupied doing,   but   just   I remember   that

kwaʔahsu·té·ke né· loyó·tʌhseʔ.   (88) Tho s katiʔ wí· thikʌ́ tsiʔ niwʌhnísles
at night-time   it's   he works.   There so then   that   during the day

lakeʔníha kyuhte wí· né· wé·ne   lakeʔnikú·laleʔ   kháleʔ nʌ   ʌyó·kalaweʔ
my father   supposedly it's   evidently he is looking after me   and   then   it will get dark

nʌ kwí· né· aknulhá·   teyakniyáshe   kʌ́·, nʌ   né·n   lakeʔníha núwaʔ
so then   it's   my mother we two are together see,   then   it's that my father   this time

shoyoʔtʌhsu·hné·.
he has gone to work again.

   (89) Né· s katiʔ wí· tho   naʔohtuháti?,   kháleʔ kanʌnaʔké·ne nʌ kyaleʔ wí·
         Well then it's   that's how it is going along,   and   in the fall   so again

sayákwaweʔ Ukwehuwé·ne, tó· kiʔ ok kwí· náheʔ wé·ne   u·tú·   yah
we got home   at the Reserve,   some while only   evidently   it could be   not

teʔshoyoʔtʌ́·u   tsiʔ   wé·ne s kwí· tsiʔ wahyathwístayʌʔ   tsiʔ nikú
he did not work anymore   because evidently   that the two put by money how much

waʔthyatʌ́·tshaneʔ tsiʔ niwakʌ́nhes.   (90) Né·n   kháleʔ onʌ́ London
the two earned   during the season.   And It's   and   then London

yaʔakwanáklateʔ.   (91) Tho kʌs   ké·yaleʔ   thikʌ́ kók   nikanúhsaʔ
we settled over there.   There habitually I remember that   small is the size of house

some time we lived there, they were working at the Heinz factory, my mother was peeling
tomatoes, and I don't know what my father was doing, all I remember was that he was working nights. (88) So during the day I guess my father must have been the one looking after
me and then in the evening my mother and I were together, then my father went to work.

   (89) Well that's the way it was, and in the fall we came back to the Reserve, I guess for a
while it was possible for him not to work because the two of them must have saved whatever
they earned during the season. (90) And then we moved to London. (91) I remember it was
a really small house there,

kʌ·,   kwáh s thok   nikanúhsaʔ   skanáktat tho   ka·yʌ́·   tho nú·
y'know,   just   thus only   is the size of house   one bed   there   it is lying   that's where

niyakwanuhwétstaʔ khále? kok   niwatekhwahlá·tslaʔ tho   ká·nyoteʔ khále?
we sleep   and   just small   is the size of table   there   it stands   and

wé·ne   tsi? áhsʌ   niwanitskwahlá·tsla<u>ke</u>.   (92) Thok   nikú   thikʌ́ khále?
evidently   that   three   is the amount of chairs.   That's only   how much   that   and

wé·ne s kwí· tá·t núwa? yenʌstaliha?tákhwa? kyuhte wí· sʌ́·   wé·ne   tho
evidently   maybe   stove   supposedly   also   evidently   there

ká·nyoteʔ tsi? yekhunyá·tha?   aknulhá·,   yah s ki?   te?kanuhsowanʌ́   thikʌ́
it stands   at   she uses it to cook   my mother,   not   actually   it is not a big house   that

tsi? nú· niyakwʌ́·tlu?, tahnú· kʌ? nukwá· tyonúhsute?,   né· né·n   washroom,
where   we dwell,   and   right there   there is a room,   it's   it's that   washroom,

oyá· s né· ya·wét   oskánhe yakwátsta?   washroom, oyá· wí· sʌ́·   tho
other   it's   kind of like   together   we are using   washroom,   other   also   there

lonatnuhsaníhʌ.   (93) Né· kyale? thikʌ́ tsi? niyóhsles   tho   yakwʌ́·tlu? kʌ́·,
they are renting.   It's   again   that   during the winter   there   we dwell   y'know,

né· s uhte wí·   tsi?   niyukwanuhsatho·lé· né·n   Ukwehuwé·<u>ne</u>.   (94) Tahnú· thikʌ́
it's   supposedly   how   our house is cold   it's that   on the Reserve.   And   that

tsi? náhe? tho   yakwʌ́·tlu? kanatá·ke, kwáh ok tho   sakatye·lʌ́·   aknulhá·
while   there   we dwell   in town,   just   there   I suddenly noticed   my mother

yah te?yé·tlu?   sa·kéwe?   tho   wakataya?tahnu·<u>hné·</u>. (95) Tahnú· kwáh
not   she is not home   I got home   there   I have gone to school.   And   just

akulha?tsíwa? sa·kéwe?, yah kwí· úhka? té·yʌhse?   kʌ́·,   né·n
all by myself   I got home,   not   anyone   one is not around   y'know,   it's that

just big enough for there to be one bed and that's were we slept, and there was just a small
table and I guess three chairs. (92) That's all and maybe there was a stove also where my
mother cooked, it wasn't a big house where we lived, and right over there was a room, a
washroom, we were like using the washroom together with other people, there were others
renting too. (93) We lived there all winter, I guess our house was really cold on the Reserve.
(94) And while we were living in town, I suddenly became aware that my mother was not at
home when I got home from school. (95) And I was all by myself when I got home, there
was no one there, so

kwáh né· kok náhe?   tho   wá·yuwe?   akwatauntieha yukihnúk<u>se</u>?.
just   it's   only a little while   there   she got there   my auntie   she is here to get me.

(96) Wa?í·lu?, "tho nukwá· nʌtéhse?   tsi? nukwá· tyukwahtʌ́ti."   (97) Tahnú· s
    She said,   "that's where   you will come   where   our home is."   And

yah kwí· só·tsi?   te?winú   tha?teyakwátle? kʌ́·,   nʌ kwí· tho nukwá·
not   too much   it is not far   we are not apart   y'know, so then   that's where

nyahá·ke?   kʌ́h.   (98) Nʌ kwí· wa?ukhlo·lí· tsi? hospital né· yakotayá·tu
I went over there   y'know.   So then   she told me   at   hospital   it's   she has entered

aknulhá·,   wa?akowilayʌ·táne? né· lukwé,   né· kwí· núwa?   onʌ́ li?kʌ́ha   Ira.
my mother, she got a child   it's   male being, so it's   this time   then   my brother   Ira.

(99) Tsi? nuknehla·kó·   thikʌ́ tsi?   na?a·wʌ́ne?, yah kwí· náhte?   te?wakanúhte?
     How   I was surprised   that   what happened,   not   anything   I don't know

tsi? yakowilayʌtá·sle?   kʌ́h.   (100) Né·n   tsi?   na?katshanu·ní· thikʌ́
that   she is going to get a child   y'know.   It's that how   I got happy   that

tsi? wake?kʌ·shʌ́·   lukwé.   (101) Nʌ kwí· né· tho kwí· wahakya?taha·wíhte?
that   I have a sibling   male person.   So then   it's   that   he took me along

lake?níha wahiyatkʌ?sé·na? li?kʌ·<u>ha</u>.   (102) Né·n   sayákwawe?   thikʌ́ tsi?
my father   I went to see him   my brother.   It's that   we arrived again   that   at

tyukwatnuhsaníhʌ,   kʌ? ki? ok kwí· ní·la?   kʌ́·,   nʌ   kyuni? wí· né·
we are renting a house,   small only   is his size y'know, then   too   it's

yah s kwí· te?wakanúhte? náhte? akwáh niyakwayélha? tsi?   niyukwanúhsa?
not   I don't know   what   quite   we are doing   what   is the size of our house

se? ok,   kwáh se? nók kok ni·wá·   thikʌ́ room tsi? nú· niyukwatnuhsaníhʌ.
too   only,   just   too   only small   is the size that   room   where   we are renting a house.

in a little while my auntie got there to come get me. (96) She said, "you will come to our
place." (97) And we weren't too far apart, so then that's where I went. (98) So then she told
me that my mother had gone to the hospital, she had a baby boy, it was my brother Ira.
(99) I was really surprised at what happened, I didn't know anything about her having a
baby. (100) I was really happy that I had a brother. (101) So then my father took me to see
my brother. (102) So we got back to where we were renting, he was just so small, I don't
know how we managed with the size of our house, the room where we were renting was just
so small.

(103) Tahnú· kwáh sʌ́· nʌ baby sʌ́· nʌ tho wahanáklate?, né· kwí·
       And   just   also then baby also then there he settled in,   so it's

sʌ́ha? wa?ukwʌtyohkwánhʌ?. (104) Nók tsi? tho s né· ni·yót thikʌ́ aknulhá·
more   we got to be more of us.   But   that's it's how it is that   my mother

yukénhahse?, í· né· nok ʌwa·tú· ʌknohaléni? thikʌ́ o?tsyú·khale?.
she hires me, me it's it has to be I will wash   that   diaper.

  (105) Né· s kati? wí· thikʌ́ nále? kʌkwi·té·, né· s kyuhte wí· nʌ wá·ksane?
      Well it's   that   then again spring,   it's   supposedly then I finished

tsi? katayá·tha?, nʌ kyale? wí· tsyukwanaklakwʌháti? Ukwehuwé·ne sayakwáti?.
at   I go to school, so again   we are moving again   on the Reserve we moved again.

(106) Tsi? niyo·lé· thikʌ́ nále? sayóhslate?, nʌ kyale? wí·
      Until   that   then again it became winter again, so again

tsyukwanaklakwʌháti? kanatá·ke né· sayakwanáklate?, né· s wí· nʌ só·tsi?
we are moving again   in town   it's we settled again,   it's   then too much

yukwanuhsatho·lé· wí· n Ukwehuwé·ne. (107) Né·n khále? onʌ́ tóhka?
our house is cold   on the Reserve.   It's that and   then a few

niyohslaké thikʌ́ kanatá·ke niyakwanákle?, né· s kwí· ní· onʌ́ ya·wét
the years amount to that   in town   we reside,   so it's   me then kind of like

kyuhte wí· teenager kyuhte wí· tsha?ka·tú·, nók tsi? kwáh s ní· ké·yale?
supposedly teenager supposedly when I became, but   just   me I remember

thikʌ́ tsi? kwáh tsyo?k nihatiya?tó·tʌ oskánhe yakwatayá·tha? kʌ́·,
that   that just   all different kinds of people together we go to school y'know,

Greek, Jew, Japanese, kwáh tsyo?k nahonahutsyó·tʌ? tho lutayá·tha?.
Greek, Jew, Japanese, just   all different kinds of nations   there they go to school.

(103) And now there was a baby living there too, so there were even more of us. (104) But the way it was is my mother got me to do it, I was the one who had to wash the diapers.

  (105) So in the spring, I guess I finished going to school, and we moved to the Reserve again. (106) Until it was winter again, so we moved into town again, because our house was too cold on the Reserve. (107) And so for a few years we lived in town, I guess it's kind of like when I became a teenager, but I remember I went to school together with all different kinds of people, Greek, Jew, Japanese, all different nationalities went to school there.

(108) Yah   nuwʌtú   teʔke·yáleʔ   thikʌ́   úkhaʔ náhteʔ   a·yukwʌ́hahseʔ   tsiʔ
      Not   never   I don't remember   that   anyone   that one belittles me   that

kukwehu·wé̱.   (109) Né· s   kyuhte wí·   né· tsiʔ   kwáh   seʔ   tsyoʔk
I am Native.   It's   supposedly   because   just   too   different

nitsyukwenú   kʌ́,   tsiʔ niyo·lé·   sa·kéweʔ   Ukwehuwé·ne   nʌ s   ní·   waʔkáttokeʔ
we have come from   y'now,   until   I got back   at the Reserve   then   me   I noticed

tsiʔ né· s kyuhte   né· onʌ́ discrimination latinaʔtúkhwaʔ, yah   úhkaʔ   só·tsiʔ
that   it's   supposedly   it's   then   discrimination   what they call it,   not   anyone   too much

teʔtyukwatʌ·ló·   kutiksaʔshúha   tshaʔtetyukwe·nú·seʔ,   shekú   né·   nʌ   né·   yah
we are not friends   girls   we are the same age,   even   it's   then   it's   not

teʔskuhlúkhaʔ   Ukwehuwehné·<u>ke</u>.   (110) Yah   né·   thusakutwʌnu·táhkweʔ
they aren't fluent anymore   in the Native way.   Not   it's   they won't speak anymore

tsiʔ niyakwawʌnó·tʌ.   (111) Nʌ   né·   tyótkut   oʔsluniʔké·ne   yonatwʌnanutáhkwʌ.
what is our language.   Then   it's   always   white man's way   they are speaking.

(112) Neʔ thó·neʔ   katiʔ wí·   ní·   thikʌ́   nʌ   a·kí·luʔ   wakyʌtéluʔ   yah
     At that time   well   me   that   then   I would say   I have recognized   not

náhteʔ   só·tsiʔ   tha·yukwatste·lísteʔ,   kwáh kwí· nók   tsiʔ   naʔtekutí kwí· né·
anything   too much   they won't bother with me,   just only   how   many they are   it's

onatʌ·ló·   kʌ́h.   (113) Né·   a·yakonehla·kó· s kwí·   tsiʔ   naʔukye·lá·seʔ   kʌ́h.
they are friends   y'know.   It's   one would be surprised   what   they did to me   y'know.

  (114) Nʌ s kwí·   núwaʔ   kʌ́·tho   waʔkáheweʔ   kanuhtunyúkwas   tsiʔ
      So then   this time   here   time has come   I am wondering   what

niyawʌʔuhátiʔ   tsiʔ   niyakwawʌnó·tʌ.   (115) Tsiʔ s   niyawʌtúnyaʔt   a·kanuhtunyu·kó·
is happening   as   is our language.   How   it is lonely   for me to think about

(108) Never do I remember anyone say anything to me to put me down because I'm Native.
(109) I guess it was because we came from all different places, until I got back to the Reserve, then I noticed what they call discrimination, I wasn't friends with many girls the same
age, they didn't even speak Indian anymore. (110) They didn't speak our language anymore. (111) They were always speaking English. (112) At that time I would say I learned
that they didn't want to have anything to do with me, all of them were just friends among
themselves. (113) One would be surprised at what they did to me.

  (114) So now the time has come when I'm wondering what is happening with our language. (115) It's so lonely to think about

só·tsiʔ   nʌ   tú·skeʔ   kʌtyohkwaná   wahuʔwʌ·táneʔ   tsiʔ ka·yʌ́·   luhlúkhah<u>seʔ</u>.
too much   then   truly   many people   they perished   the one that   they are fluent.

(116)   Aknulhá·   né· s kwí· né·n   tyótkut   Ukwehuwehné·ke   ʌyakyatwʌnu·táhkweʔ
        My mother so it's   it's that always   in the Native way   we two will speak

nʌ   waʔknatá·laʔ   kʌ́h.   (117)   Kháleʔ nʌ kwí· kʌtyohkwaná   akwatauntiehokúha
when   I went to visit   y'know.   And   so then   many people   my aunties

nʌ   yah   kátshaʔ   teʔsku·né·<u>seʔ</u>.   (118)   Kʌtyohkwaná   sʌ́·   tsiʔ ka·yʌ́·
then   not   anywhere   they are not around anymore.   Many people   also   the one that

luhlúkhahseʔ,   nʌ kati ʔ wí·   né·   shonatukóhtu.   (119)   Kwáh s kati ʔ wí·
they are fluent,   well then   it's   they have passed on.   Just   well

swatyelʌ́   waʔkʌtu·ní·, kanuhtunyúkwas   kháleʔ   kyuhte wí· onʌ́   yah
sometimes   I got lonely,   I am thinking   and   supposedly   soon   not

thusayukwathu·tékeʔ   uhkaʔ náhteʔ   a·yakotha·láke<u>ʔ</u>.   (120)   Shekú s kwí·
we would not be hearing anymore   anyone   one would be talking.   Still

núwaʔ n teyakwalihwákhwaʔ   kʌ́·,   yotlatstú·neʔ   nʌ   waʔakwalʌnó·ktʌʔ
this time   we are singers   see,   there was a time   when   we came to the end of a song

kháleʔ   kwah nók   tetyukwatha·lú·,   aóskuʔ kwí·   nók   Ukwehuwehné·ke
and   just   we are conversing again,   purely   only   in the Native way

yukwatwʌnutáhkwʌ.   (121)   Né·   núwaʔ   onʌ́   waʔakwalʌnó·ktʌʔ
we are speaking in a language.   It's   this time   now   we came to the end of a song

tusayakwatha·lú·,   akwekú   né·   oʔsluniʔké·ne   luhlúkhaʔ,
we conversed again,   all   it's   white man's way   they are speaking fluently,

ukweʔtasé·shuʔ   latiyá·taleʔ,   kwáh s   kati ʔ wí· onʌ́   kwahotokʌ́·u   tsiʔ
all new people   they are members,   just   well   now   just for real   that

so many who are fluent dying. (116) My mother and I would always speak the Oneida language when I went to visit. (117) And all my aunties aren't around anymore. (118) A lot of
them who are fluent, they have passed on. (119) Sometimes I get lonely, I'm thinking and
soon I guess we won't be hearing anyone speak anymore. (120) Those of us who sing still,
there was a time when we came to the end of a hymn and we were just talking, all in Indian
we were talking. (121) Now we come to the end of a hymn and we are talking again, everyone is speaking in English, all the new ones who are members [in our choir], it just really

yawʌtúnyaʔt swatyelʌ́   né· a·yunuhtúniʔ.   (122) Kháleʔ kyuhte wí·
it is lonely   sometimes it's   should one think about things.   And   supposedly

nʌ   yah   thusayukwathu·tékeʔ   ta·katha·lákeʔ? kʌ́h.   (123) Ótyaʔk   sʌ́·,
then   not   we won't be hearing anymore   that it is spoken y'know.   Some   also,

ati   yuhlúkhaʔ   yah   kiʔ   tha·yutwʌnu·táhkweʔ.   (124) Tsiʔ s
although   one knows a language   not   actually   they won't speak in a language.   How

niwakateʔshʌnáksʌ thikʌ́ tá·t tho   ni·yót   wakanúhteʔ yuhlúkhaʔ
I feel uncomfortable   that   if   that's   how it is   I know   one knows a language

né·n   oʔsluniʔké·ne   kiʔ   yakotwʌnutáhkwʌ.   (125) Né· kyuhte wí·
it's that   white man's way   actually   one is speaking in a language.   It's   supposedly

tho   yaʔta·kaye·lí·   kaʔikʌ́ tsiʔ nikú   onʌ́   waʔkata·tí·. (126) Tho kwí·
that's   it should be enough   this   how much   now   I spoke.   That's

nʌkúhakeʔ   nʌʔú·waʔ.
it will be all   this time.

makes one lonely sometimes to think about it. (122) And I guess then really we won't be
hearing it spoken anymore. (123) Some also, although they understand they won't speak.
(124) I feel really uncomfortable if how it is, is that I know someone understands, yet they
are speaking English. (125) I guess that will be enough how much I've talked. (126) That
will be all this time.

Family and Friends

(Told by Pearl Cornelius to Mercy Doxtator on September 11, 1993)

(1) Pearl ní· yúkyats.   (2) Tsyo Kaníles   lakyʌ́ha.   (3) Kháleʔ Libéki
       Pearl me is my name.   Joe   Cornelius   my father.   And   Rebecca

aknulháh.   (4) Kháleʔ teyakwatʌhnutlúniʔ kʌ́·,   Tsim né· luwa·yáts.
my mother.   And   all of us siblings   y'know, Jim   it's   is his name.

(1) Pearl is my name. (2) Joe Cornelius is my father. (3) And Rebecca is my mother.
(4) And my sisters and brothers, Jim is his name.

(5) Khále? Lillian, khále? Shirley, Edna, Mary, Ida.   (6) Tho?nʌ
     And   Lillian,   and   Shirley, Edna, Mary, Ida.   And then

yakwatʌno?sʌ?okúha.   (7) Alec, khále? Frank, khále? Shako·wíhe?.   (8) Ókhale?
all of us siblings.   Alec, and   Frank, and   The Giver.   And

Mike, Edward.   (9) Tho   né· nihatí   teyakwatʌhnu·téle?.   (10) Ó·
Mike, Edward.   That's it's how many they are   us siblings.   Oh

kʌ? tshitwakyʌha kʌ·,   aksótha   ní· ya?ukya?táhawe?, só·tsi? s
when I was young y'know,   my grandmother me   she took me,   too much

yukwʌtyohkwanʌ́ tsi? nú· niyukwanúhsote?.   (11) Né· ní· oskánhe wa?akwáti?
we are a big crowd where   we have a house.   It's us   together we lived

aksótha   Aggieha khále? laksótha   Amos, Tsya?tí·lu s kwí· luwa·yáts,
my grandmother Aggie   and   my grandfather Amos, Tsya'tí·lu   is his name,

tsi? Amos kʌs kwí·   sʌ́h.   (12) Né· ní· wa?tyakwayáshene?.   (13) Tho s nú·
but Amos customarily also.   It's us   we came to be together.   That's where

ya?kahtʌ·tí·   nʌ   wa?kataya?tá·na?.   (14) Kátsha? nú· nisatayá·tu.
I left for there when   I went to school.   *Where   you have gone to school.*

(15) Mount Elgin, nále? yah   tha·ke?nya·kʌ́·ne?.   (16) *Se?nya·kʌ́·se?*   *kʌ.*
      Mount Elgin,   when not   I won't run away.   *You are running away question.*

(17) Ó· swatye·lʌ́.   (18) Khále? onʌ́   nʌ   wa?katkʌ́·lahte? kataya?tá·nehse?,
      Oh sometimes.   And   soon then   I quit   I am going to school,

tho?nʌ́   in the spring thikʌ́ nʌ   latiyu?kwayʌ́thos, a?é· s   Kinglake
and then in the spring that   then   they plant tobacco, way over Kinglake

ukyo?tʌ́hsa?.   (19) All summer tho   yekí·telu?.
I went to work.   All summer   there I dwell over there.

(5) And Lillian, and Shirley, Edna, Mary, Ida. (6) And then my brothers. (7) Alec, and Frank, and Shako·wíhe'. (8) And Mike, Edward. (9) That's how many brothers and sisters I have. (10) Oh when I was young my grandma took me, because there were too many of us at our house. (11) I lived together with my grandma, Aggie, and my grandfather, Amos, Tsya'tí·lu was his [Indian] name, but [he was called] Amos too. (12) That's who I [lived] together with. (13) That's where I left from when I went to school. (14) *Where did you go to school?* (15) Mount Elgin, when I didn't run away. (16) *Did you run away?* (17) Oh, sometimes. (18) And soon I quit going to school, and then in the spring when they were planting tobacco, I went to work way over at Kinglake. (19) All summer I lived there.

(20) Waʔakwathwehnotaˑkóˑ   nʌ kyaleʔ wíˑ saˑkéweʔ.   (21) *Tóˑ s néˑ nikú*
We finished working the area   so again   I came home.   *How much*

latikályaʔks neʔ thóˑneʔ. (22) Oˑkéˑ,   50 cents an hour. (23) Nók tsiʔ eˑsóˑ s kwíˑ
they pay   at that time.   Oh my,   50 cents an hour.   But   a lot

néˑ thikʌ́ tshiwahuˑníseʔ, 50 cents an hour. (24) Néˑ nʌʔúˑwaʔ 50 cents an hour
it's   that   a long time ago, 50 cents an hour.   It's   now   50 cents an hour

yah kiʔ   thaˑskalakweˑníˑ skanáˑtalat. *Mhm* (25) Thoʔnʌ́ kohslaʔkéˑne nʌ
not   actually you won't afford one bread.   *Mhm*   And then wintertime   then

túˑskeʔ wahatikalatúniʔ thikʌ́ lotikstʌhokúha. (26) Néˑ s thikʌ́ John Laets kháleʔ
truly   they told stories that   old people.   It's   that   John Elijah and

Simon Laets tho   wahotikéˑtohteʔ. (27) *Néˑ kʌ   thikʌ́ tehutʌhnutlúniʔ*
Simon Elijah there   they showed up.   *It's question that   they are siblings*

yahsotkʌ́.   (28) Hʌ́ˑ, neˑéˑ.   (29) Tóˑk náheʔ thikʌ́ 4 o'clock
your late grandfather.   Yes,   that's it.   Some time   that   4 o'clock

5 o'clock thikʌ́ náleʔ yetsistalákhwaʔ s kwíˑ néˑ latihaˑwíˑ   thikʌ́,
5 o'clock   that   then   lantern   it's   they are carrying that,

néˑ s kwíˑ níˑ thikʌ́ náleʔ ukitáˑwhaʔ, kwáh s áhsok   kʌs   náleʔ
so it's   me   that   then   I went to bed, just   all of a sudden habitually then

sákiʔ   náleʔ wakathuˑtéˑ náleʔ, "ihéh." (30) Nʌ   uhte   aleʔ wíˑ
again I woke up then   I hear   then,   "ihéh."   Then supposedly again

tahotikaliˑyóˑseʔ.   (31) Yah kwíˑ níˑ teʔwakanúhteʔ, waʔkatkétskoʔ
they got most entertained by stories.   Not   me   I don't know,   I got up

astéhtsiʔ,   nʌ kyaleʔ wíˑ akwekú shonahtʌtyúkwʌ.   (32) Kohslaʔkéˑne
in the morning, so again   all   they have gone home.   Wintertime

(20) We finished up working, so I came home again. (21) *How much did they pay at that
time?* (22) Oh my, 50 cents an hour. (23) But that was a lot a long time ago, 50 cents an
hour. (24) Nowadays 50 cents an hour won't get you one loaf of bread. *Mhm* (25) And then
in the wintertime the old people really told stories. (26) John Elijah and Simon Elijah would
show up. (27) *Were they brothers to your late grandpa?* (28) Yes, that's it. (29) Some time
about 4 o'clock, 5 o'clock they used to carry a lantern, so me, I would go to bed, then all of
a sudden I would wake up again and then I would hear, "ihéh." (30) I guess they were really
being entertained by their stories. (31) I don't know, in the morning I would get up, they all
would be gone home again. (32) It was wintertime,

yah s te?wé·ne   niyotho·lé·,   tho kwí· né· latikalatúnyu<u>he?</u>.   (33) Kwa?k∧nhé·ke
it's incredible   how cold it is,   there   it's they tell stories.   Summertime

yah né· tehatika·látu<u>he?</u>.   (34) *Náhte? s yak∧?   né· aolí·wa?   yah*
not   it's   they don't tell stories.   *What   reportedly it's   the reason not*

tehatika·látu<u>he?</u>.   (35) Yah ní· thik∧ te?wakanúhte? náhte? uhte   né·
they don't tell stories.   Not   me   that   I don't know   what   maybe it's

aolí·wa?   tsi? yah tehatika·látu<u>he?</u>.   (36) Kwáh thik∧ December
the reason   that   not   they don't tell stories.   Just   that   December

niw∧hní·tes,   uhte i·kélhe? nále? ∧thutáhsaw∧? ka?ik∧, tho kwí· nú· thik∧
during the month,   I think   then   they will start   this,   that's where that

ya?t∧hútlane?,   *[hmm]* ∧hatikalatúni?,   kwa?ahsutáti?   kháfi tá·thuni?
over there they will meet, *[hmm]*   they will tell stories,   through the night coffee or else

tí· lotihnekí·lu.   (37) Yah ki?   nuw∧tú náhte?   thik∧ a?nyóh wí· oyá·
tea   they have drunk.   Not   actually never   anything that   seems like   other

a·honatstúhake? wí· tsi? latikalatúnyu<u>he?</u>.   (38) Áhsok   k∧s   oni?
they would be using   as   they are telling stories.   All of sudden habitually too

thik∧ nále? social dance Kanuhséshne,   tho kwí· nú· ny∧yákne?
that   then   social dance   at the Longhouse,   that's where   we two will go over there

aksó<u>tha</u>.   (39) Tá·t yah tha?ta·knúnyahkwe? n∧ ki? ok ale?,
my grandmother.   If   not   I wouldn't dance   right then again,

"hányo   thi·<u>k∧</u>. (40) "Tehsnúnyak."   (41) N∧ ki? ok ale? wí· tutakt∧stá·tsyahte?,
"come on   that."   "Dance."   Right then again   I jumped up,

tewakatkw∧háti<u>?</u>.
I am going along dancing.

was it ever cold, there they were telling stories. (33) In the summertime they didn't tell stories. (34) *Why didn't they tell stories [then]?* (35) I don't know why they didn't tell stories.
(36) During the month of December, I think then they would start, there they would meet,
[hmm] and tell stories, all night long they drank coffee or tea. (37) Seems it was never for
them to use anything else as they were telling stories. (38) Then occasionally there would
be a social at the Longhouse, I would go there with my grandmother. (39) If I didn't dance
then right away, "come on!" (40) "Dance!" (41) Right away then I would jump up, I would
go dancing.

(42) Khále? tsi? náhe? lake?níha, Tsim kʌs   né· tshiyákwehse?, né· s nén
      And   at a time my father, Jim habitually it's when we go,   it's it's

latlʌnayʌ·hné·se? s nʌ? né·, tahnú· nʌ kwí· né· ka?ikʌ́ kyuhte wí· tshihatchief
he goes to church   that one, and   so then it's this   supposedly when he is chief

wé·ne,   nʌ kwí· né· wahatkʌ́·lahte? tsi? latlʌnayʌ·hné·se?, nʌ   né· nén úska
evidently, so then it's he quit   that he goes to church, then it's it's one

sʌ́ha? wa?tháshni?.   (43) Né· ki?   nén thikʌ́ laksotkʌ́,   tsi? wí·
more   he looked after it.   It's actually it's that   my late grandfather, at

tyutlʌnayʌtákhwa? thikʌ́ elʌ́   na?oháhati,   náhte? akwáh luwa·yáts, Tsya?tí·lu,
church   that   other side of the road, what   exactly is his name, Tsya'tí·lu,

Nikalas kʌs wí·   luwa·yáts wí· laksótha.   (44) Né· s kwí· né· wa?ákwe?
Nicholas customarily is his name   my grandfather.   So it's   it's we went

thikʌ́ wa?akwatlʌnayʌ·hná· í·   khále? Tsim khále? lake?níha. (45) Kwáh
that   we went to church   me and   Jim and   my father.   Just

kʌs kwí· né· nók wa?tyakwahahi·yá·ke?. (46) Né· kati? wí· thikʌ́ nále?
habitually it's only we crossed the road.   Well then it's   that   then

tshutu·kó·te?   yukwatlʌnayʌhnu·hné·, tho   tutayakwa·tá·ne? laksothné·ke,
when it passed   we have gone to church, there we stopped again at my grandfather's,

né· kwí· né· thikʌ́ tyótkut swahyo·wáne? ʌshukwá·yanute?.   (47) Né· kati? wí·
so it's   it's that   always   apple   he will give us fruit to eat.   Well then it's

thikʌ́ nále? tshusayukwayakʌ?uháti?   lake?níha khále? í·,   né· nʌ n Tsim.
that   then   when we are going out again   my father and   me, it's then Jim.

(48) Wahʌ́·lu? Tsim, "wa?tsyók wa?tsyók." (49) Tusahatkalhate·ní·,   tho
      He said   Jim, "wait   wait."   He turned around again,   there

(42) And there was a time my father,—Jim used to come with us, he [my father] was going to church, and then I guess when he was chief, then he quit going to church, then he
looked more after [the other] one [his Longhouse belief]. (43) So my late grandfather, it
was across the road from the church, what the heck was his name, Tsya'tí·lu, Nicholas was
my grandfather's name. (44) So we used to go to church, me and Jim and my father.
(45) We just had to cross the road. (46) Well when church was over, we would stop at my
grandfather's, and he always gave us apples to eat. (47) Well one time we were on our way
out again [from my grandfather's], my father and me, and then Jim. (48) Jim said, "wait,
wait." (49) He turned around again,

yahá·lawe?   tho   tkaya·lóte?,   thok náhte?   yahatáhko?
he went over there   there   there's a bag standing there,   something   over there he took it out

nʌ sók   laohna?tátslaku   waháta<u>ne</u>?.   (50) Wá·lelhe?   né·   kʌ n   swahyo·wáne?,
then too   in his pocket   he put it in.   He thought   it's   question   apple,

ohnʌná·ta?   nʌ? né·.   (51) *Ohnʌná·ta?.*   (52) Hʌ́·,   ohnʌná·ta?   né·   lonʌskwʌháti?.
potato   that one.   *Potato.*   Yes,   potato   it's   he is stealing.

(53) Á·,   tsi? nikú   washakwaste·líste? s.   (54) Kwáh   kyuhte wí·   ne? thó·ne?
      Oh,   how much   we laughed at him.   Just   supposedly   at that time

yeskʌhá   shotlʌnayʌhnu·hné· n Tsim,   nʌ wí·   né· Kanuhséshne   né·   nukwá·
last time   he has gone to church   Jim,   then   it's   at the Longhouse   it's   where

nyahá·le?   wí· n   lake?níha.   (55) Tho kwí·   né·   nukwá·   ya?tháshni?.
he went over there   my father.   That's   it's   where   over there he nurtured it.

   (56) Ó·ts,   kwáh   se? s   tsyo?k   na?tetyukwaya?tawʌ́·u,   shekú s   núwa?
       Gee,   just   too   all kinds of   things have happened to us,   still   this time

né·n   thikʌ́ ké·yale?   thikʌ́   tshiyonuhsakayú   tsi? nú·   niyakwʌ́·te<u>lu</u>?.
it's that   that   I remember   that   when it is an old house   where   we dwell.

(57) Kwáh   se? s   ya·wét   thikʌ́   kʌ? nikanúhsa?,   bedroom   kyuhte wí·   ya·wét.
      Just   too   like   that   the room is so big,   bedroom   supposedly   like.

(58) Kwáh tsyo?k nú·   nikanaktaké·lu?   thikʌ́   yakwʌ?tsyuhkwaké·<u>lu</u>?.
      Everywhere   there are beds all over   that   we are nestled all over.

(59) Kwáh s   nʌ   ki?   né· a·hsatkátho?   thikʌ́   roof,   nʌ   ʌkanye·yʌ́·
      Just   then   actually   it's   you should look at   that   roof,   when   it will snow

tá·thuni?   ʌyokʌ·nóle?   tho s   ki?   thikʌ́ takuhkwé·nʌhte?.   (60) Né·   nále?   yah
or else   it will rain   there   actually   that   they came down.   It's   then   not

he went to where there was a bag there, he took something out and then he put it in his
pocket. (50) He thought it was an apple, it was a potato. (51) *A potato?* (52) Yes, he was
stealing a potato. (53) Oh, how much we laughed at him. (54) I guess that was the last time
Jim went to church, then my father went to the Longhouse. (55) And he looked after it over
there.

    (56) Gee, all kinds of things happened to us, I still remember it was an old house where
we lived. (57) There was a room kind of just so big, I guess a bedroom like. (58) There
were beds everywhere and we would be all nestled in them. (59) You looked at the roof,
when it would snow or rain it would come down there. (60) Also back then

sʌ́· teʔtyukwakʌhaká·teʔ,   né· thikʌ́ khotho·kú·   yukwahlúniʔ.
also we don't have many blankets back then,   it's   that   a bunch of coats   it is covering us.

(61) Tsiʔ s uhte wí·   niyukwʌ·tʌ́t tshiwahu·níseʔ.   (62) Shekú kiʔ   núwaʔ
      How   supposedly we are poor   a long time ago.   Still   actually   this time

né· waki·tʌ́t, nók tsiʔ yah kwí· tho   teʔyo·lé·   tsiʔ s niyohtú·neʔ.   (63) *Nók tsiʔ*
it's   I am poor,   but   not   that's   not how far   how   it was.   *But*

thikʌ́ neʔ thó·neʔ tshiwathawinútiʔ, yah kiʔ   nuwʌtú aʔnyóh   né·
that   at that time   during those times,   not   actually   never   seems like   it's

teʔtwanuhtúnyuheʔ   tsiʔ niyukwʌ·tʌ́t. (64) Tá·im. (65) Kwáh tsiʔ náheʔ
you and we don't think   how   we are poor.   Oh no.   While

twatekhu·níheʔ,   [mmm] né· kiʔ   né· akwáh tyukwalihowanáhtu.
you and we are eating,   [mmm] it's   actually it's   mostly   we consider it very important.

(66) Ne·é·. (67) Né· sʌ́· né· thikʌ́ waʔkhe·kʌ́· aksotkʌ́   waʔutnaʔtalu·tʌ́·
       It is.   It's   also it's that   I saw her   my late grandmother she baked bread

thikʌ́, né· s kwí· né· tsiʔ tyótkut ati   tó·   niyoʔtalíhʌ yakokhuní   kiʔ,
that,   so it's   it's   that   always   no matter   how   it is hot   she is cooking   actually,

átste s tyakóthnyoteʔ   thikʌ́ stove, tho kwí· yakokhu·ní.   (68) Kwaʔakʌnhéꞏke
outside she has standing   that   stove,   there   she is cooking.   Summertime

yah teʔwé·ne naʔteyakoteʔtúkhwaleʔ, tho   kiʔ   né· yakokhu·ní.
it's incredible   how she is sweating,   there   actually   it's   she is cooking.

(69) Né· katiʔ wí· thikʌ́ úska útlatsteʔ waʔkhe·kʌ́· thikʌ́ waʔutnaʔtalu·tʌ́·, ne·né·
      Well then   that   one   time   I saw her   that   she baked bread,   it's that

thikʌ́ ashes ohutsyá·ke   waʔe·yʌ́·, yah kiʔ   ní· teʔské·yaleʔ
that   ashes   on the ground   she put it,   not   actually   me   I don't remember anymore

we didn't have many blankets, we had a bunch of coats covering us. (61) I guess we were
really poor a long time ago. (62) I'm still poor, but not as bad as back then. (63) *But back
in those times, we never seemed to think that we were that poor.* (64) Oh no. (65) *While we
had food to eat, [mmm] that was the most important thing.* (66) It was. (67) Also I saw my
late grandmother bake bread, because always no matter how hot it was she was cooking, she
had her stove outside, she was cooking there. (68) In the summertime she would be really
sweating, there she was cooking. (69) Well this one time I saw her bake bread, she put
ashes on the ground, I don't remember anymore

kwahotokʌ·u náhteʔ naʔe·yéleʔ thikʌ́ tsiʔ tá·tkʌ oyá· énik tutayako·tí·
just for real what she did it that but or maybe another above again she threw

ashes. (70) Né·n tho seʔ wí· waʔkanaʔtala·lí·. *Mmm* (71) Né· oniʔ tsiʔ
ashes. So it's there too bread became cooked. *Mmm* It's even how

seʔ wí· niyawéku̲ʔ. (72) Kwáh úska ok waʔkatkáthoʔ thikʌ́ tho naʔe·yéleʔ
too it is tasty. Just one only I saw that thus she did it

waʔutnaʔtalu·tʌ̲́·. (73) Wé·ne s kwí· tho nihatiyélhaʔ thikʌ́ tshiwahu·níseʔ s
she baked bread. Evidently thus they do it that a long time ago

lutnaʔtalútha̲ʔ. (74) Né· s kyaleʔ ní· kanuhtúnyuheʔ thikʌ́ swatyelʌ́ tho
they bake bread. It's again me I am thinking that sometimes thus

naákyeleʔ a·katnaʔtalu·tʌ́· a·kato·kʌ́·neʔ, tó· niyawékuʔ í·
I should do it I should bake bread it would be known, how it is tasty me

a·katnaʔtalu·tʌ̲́·. (75) *Né· s kwí· né· yu·té· aknulhá· tsiʔ sʌ́haʔ s kwí·*
should I bake bread. *So it's it's she says my mother that more*

thikʌ́ náleʔ latiskalákwas [hʌ́·] *tshiwahu·níseʔ, yah kwí· teʔwé·ne kátshaʔ nú·*
that when they are harvesting flax [yes] *a long time ago, it's incredible where*

nihatí·tluʔ kʌ́·, né· kiʔ tho ni·yót thikʌ́ tho kahʌtá·ke ya·wét tho
they dwell y'know, it's actually that's how it is that there in the field kind of like there

ʌkutikhu·ní kʌ́·, né· kiʔ né· yu·té·, tho ni·yót tsiʔ waʔkutnaʔtalu·tʌ́·,
they will cook y'know, it's actually it's she says, that's how it is that they baked bread,

[hmm] *tahnú· s yu·té· s tsiʔ niyawéku̲ʔ.* Mmm
[hmm] *and she says how it is tasty.* Mmm

(76) Ó·ts, yukwʌ·tʌ́t seʔ s wí· wé·ne thikʌ́, né· s kiʔ núwaʔ ní·
Gee, we are poor too apparently that, it's actually this time me

how she did it but maybe she put more ashes on top. (70) So the bread got cooked. (71) Did it ever taste good too. (72) I saw her bake bread that way only the one time. (73) It must be that's how they used to make bread a long time ago. (74) I'm thinking some time I should make bread that way to see how good it would turn out, how tasty it would be were I to bake bread. (75) *It's what my mother used to say, especially when they were picking flax a long time ago, they lived any place and every place, that's how they would kind of cook out there in the field, that's what she used to say, that's how they would cook bread, and she said it was so good.*

(76) Gee we must have been poor,

ké·yale?   thikʌ́ tyótkut thikʌ́ né· yakotná·talute?   aknulháh.   (77) Swatyelʌ́ s
I remember   that   always   that   it's she is baking bread my mother.   Sometimes

nók thikʌ́ katsihko·tú· ʌyákwake? khále? ohnʌná·<u>ta?</u>.   (78) O?wá·lu? swatye·lʌ́.
only that   ovenbread   we will eat and   potatoes.   Meat   sometimes.

(79) Tho   ki?   ok   nikú   thi·<u>kʌ́</u>.   (80) *Né· s kati? kʌ   tsi?*
      That's actually only how much that.   *It's   then   question because*

a·kí·lu? kati? kʌ   só·tsi?   swʌtyohkwa·<u>nʌ́</u>.   (81) Yah kwí· ní·
I'd say   then   question too much   you all are a big crowd.   Not   me

te?wakanúhte? wé·ne ki?wáh.   (82) Né· s kwí· né· kyuhte wí· aolí·wa?,
I don't know   I suppose so.   So it's   it's supposedly the reason,

aksótha kwí·   nyeyukya?táhʌ,   né· tsi? só·tsi?   yukwʌtyohkwanʌ́, tahnú·
my grandmother she has taken me, because too much   we are a big crowd, and

niyukwanuhsáksʌ s sʌ́· tsi? nú· niyakwʌ́·te<u>lu</u>?.   (83) Tho   sʌ́· nítyot
our house is so bad   also where   we are living.   That's also how it is there

thikʌ́ n aksothné·ke   né· tshyahá·kewe?,   sʌ́ha? kwí· tsi?   énik
that   at my grandmother's it's when I got over there, more   because upstairs

nʌ? né·.   (84) Né· s thikʌ́ nʌ   wa?káwelute? kwáh kyuhte   elók   ní·
that one.   It's   that   when   it got windy   just   supposedly all over me

swaknaktí·se<u>le</u>?.   (85) Nále? wí· tú·ske? yowelu·<u>tú</u>. (86) Ó·, tsi? s niyóhtlut.
I am in the bed riding.   So when   truly   it is windy.   Oh, how   it is scary.

(87) Nók tsi? yah ki?   nuwʌtú thye?wakya?táhʌ yowelu·<u>tú</u>. (88) Sáki?
      But   not actually never   it didn't take me   it is windy.   I woke up again

katokʌ́   kih.   (89) Né· sʌ́· s oni? thikʌ́ tá·t só·tsi?   wa?kwístoske?, né· s né·
the same actually.   It's also   too   that   if   too much   I got cold,   it's that

I remember my mother was always making bread. (77) Sometimes all we had to eat was ovenbread, and potatoes. (78) Meat sometimes. (79) That's all. (80) *Was it because there were too many of you?* (81) I don't know, I suppose so. (82) I guess that's the reason, so my grandmother took me, because there were too many of us, and we had such an awful house where we lived. (Mercy says something we can't make out.) (83) That's the way it was also when I got to my grandmother's, more so because there was an upstairs. (84) It would get windy, and I was in the bed riding all over the place. (85) When it was really windy. (86) Oh, it was so scary. (87) But the wind never took me. (Mercy says something we can't make out.) (88) I woke up and it [everything] was the same. (89) Also if I got too cold,

thikʌ   kítkit   ostó·sliʔ ya·wét né· yakotunyá·tu   okʌ́haʔ.   (90) Ó·ts,
that   chicken   feather   like   it's she has made it out of blanket.   Gee,

yoʔtalíhʌ s kwí· né· thi·kʌ́.   (91) Kítkit   ostó·sliʔ kaná·nu.   (92) Kastoʔslaná·nu,
it is warm   it's that.   Chicken   feather   it is full of.   It is full of feathers,

né· s ki?   ní· waʔkáhkwase?.   (93) Harvey kʌs kwí· né· akwáh
it's   actually me   I covered up with.   Harvey   habitually it's mostly

teyakyatatnʌ́skwas,   wahawístoske? tsi? niwahsu·tés ókhale? tho
we two steal from each other,   he got cold   during the night   and   there

tehahyakwilotáti?   wahakkʌhanʌ́sko?.   (94) Sákye? s   ní· thikʌ́
he is going along on tiptoes   he stole a blanket from me.   I woke up again   me   that

yah te?wé·ne nikwístohse?, tahnú· kwí· ya·wét   tho s kwí· tekanuhsakháhsi   thi·kʌ́.
it's incredible   how I am cold,   and   kind of like   there   the room is divided   that.

(95) Né· né·n laulhá· tho nukwá· thanuhwétsta? ok ne?n   í·   kʌh nukwá·,
     It's that   him   over there   where he sleeps   and as for   me   over here,

nʌ   ukkʌhu·tí·   nʌ sók   í·   núwa?   sektákhe?   í·   núwa?
then   I lost a blanket   then too   me   this time   I am running again   me   this time

sahikʌhanʌ́sko?.   (96) Úhka? né·n   Harvey. (97) Harvey,
I stole a blanket from him again.   Who   it's that Harvey.   Harvey,

Harvey Elijah. Mhm (98) Né· kwí· né·n, né·n   aksótha
Harvey Elijah. Mhm   So it's   it's,   it's that my grandmother

tehuwashnyé·u.   (99) Luwatléha   kati? kʌ.   (100) Wé·ne ki?wáh,
she has cared for him.   Her grandson   then   question.   I suppose so,

hʌ́·, kʌ? ki? ok kwí· né· a?nyóh tshikapepísla?   tsha?yaíheye? lonulha?kʌ́.
yes,   just little   it's seems   when he is a little baby   when she died   his late mother.

she made kind of like a blanket out of chicken feathers. (90) Gee it was warm. (Can't make out what Mercy says.) (91) It was filled with chicken feathers. (92) Full of feathers, that's what I would cover up with. (93) Harvey and I sort of used to steal it from each other, during the night he would get cold and he'd come tiptoeing and steal the blanket from me. (94) I would wake up and I would be really cold, and the room was kind of like divided. (95) So he slept over there, and me over here, then I would lose my blanket and this time it's me that's running, this time I would steal the blanket from him. (96) *Who is this Harvey?* (97) Harvey, Harvey Elijah. (98) My grandmother looked after him. (99) *Her grandson then?* (100) I suppose so, yes, he was kind of just a little baby when his mother died.

(101) Yah kwí· ní· te?kheyʌtélu?   úhka? né· náhohte?.   (102) Úhka? né·n
      Not   me   I don't know of her   who it is.   Who   it's that

lonulháh.   (103) Yu·té· s kwí· aknulhá·   luwa?kʌ·ha.   (104) Né· s kwí· né·
his mother.   She says   my mother   her younger brother.   So it's   it's

tho ni·yót tyótkut "ní·" yu·té·   "li?kʌ·ha."   (105) Ne? kʌ n
that's how it is always "me" she says "my younger brother."   The question

Harvey.   (106) Hʌ́·.   (107) Wé·ne kwí· tsi? tá·t núwa? né·n   tekyatʌhnútlahkwe?
Harvey.   Yes.   Evidently   that maybe   it's the the two were sisters

kyuhte wí· wé·ne.   *Hmm*
supposedly.   Hmm

  (108) *Náhte? kati?   sʌ́· oyá· a·kí·lu? sehya·lú·   náhte? nisaya?tawʌ́·u,*
        What   anyway also other I'd say you remember what   has happened to you,

tho s kʌ   né· ni·yót ne? thó·ne? kanákle?   a·yehnekílhake?   kati? náhte?
thus   question it's it is so at that time it is present one would be drinking or   what

né· ni·yót.   (109) Táh, yah kwí· né· nuwʌtú te?yukwahnekí·lu thikʌ́ tho
it's that way.   No, not   it's never   we didn't drink   that   there

tshityukwe·nú·se?.   (110) Tsi? núwa?   ni·yót a·she·kʌ́·
when we have come from there.   How this time it is so you would see them

kwáh olihwiyó   tsi? oye·lí· tá·thuni? úska yawʌ·lé· ókhna?   a·she·kʌ́·
just   a sure thing that ten   or   eleven   and already you would see them

lotinahalahtú·u, tshiwahu·níse? yah né· tho   té·yot.   (111) Shekú núwa?
they are drunk,   a long time ago not   it's that's not how it is.   Even   this time

né· thikʌ́ a·hatihlo·tʌ́·,   yah kyuni? ní· te?yukwatkáthu. (112) Nók kʌs
it's that   for them to smoke, not   too   us   we didn't see it.   Only habitually

(101) I didn't know her, who it was. (102) Who his mother was. (103) My mother used to
say her younger brother. (104) That's how it was, she always said "my brother." (105) You
mean Harvey? (106) Yes. (107) Maybe it was her sister, I suppose.

  (108) *What else I'd say do you remember happening to you, how about people drinking at
that time, was it around then or how was it?* (109) No, we never drank when we were that
age. (110) The way you see them now they must be ten or eleven and already you see them
drunk, a long time ago it wasn't like that. (111) Even for them to smoke, we didn't see that
either. (112) It used to be just

thikʌ́ Jake khále? Enoch, Gordon, nʌ kyuni? wí· né· akwekú yah kánike?
that   Jake and   Enoch, Gordon, now too   it's all   not anywhere

te?shʌ·né·se?.   (113) Né· s né· thikʌ́ tsi? kwí· né· náhe? Sandyha
they are not around anymore.   It's   it's that   while   dear Sandy

tshitho·yʌ́·   store, tho s nʌ tahʌ·néwe?   thikʌ́ nʌ?ú·wa? wahatihnekahni·nú·.
when there he has store, there then they got there that then   they bought liquid.

(114) Kátsha? ok nú· nyahʌ·né·   thikʌ́, a?é· nukwá·   nyahʌ·né·,
       Somewhere   they went over there that,   way over there they went over there,

kaná·tslaku tho s né· thikʌ́ yahutyʌ·tú·.   (115) Tho   kyuni? ní·
in the ditch there it's that   they sat down over there.   There too   us

niyakniyá·tale?,   í·   khále? Gladys. (116) Ya·wét   kʌs   kyuhte wí·
we two are among, me   and   Gladys.   Kind of like habitually supposedly

yakhi?nikú·lale?   tsi? lotihnekí·lu.   (117) Nók tsi? nʌ kwí· né· kwáh
we are looking after them   as   they are drinking.   But   so then   it's quite

kʌ? nithonenú o·nʌ́. Mhm   (118) Yah kwí· né· thikʌ́ tsi? núwa?   ni·yót.
they are older then. Mhm   Not   it's that   as   this time how it is.

(119) Ó·, né· s kyuni? né· thikʌ́ áhsok   nále? wahatika·látu?,
       Oh,   it's   too   it's that   all of a sudden then   they told stories,

wahotiyéshu?, áhsok   nʌ   wahuthnekó·ktʌ?,   áhsok
they laughed,   all of a sudden then they ran out of liquid, all of a sudden

sayakwahtʌtyu·kó· s. Mhm (120) Tho s ki?   akwáh thikʌ́ kátsha? ok nú·
we left to go home.   Mhm   There actually mostly that   somewhere

ahsúthʌ thikʌ́, nále? tusayakwale·ní·   kaná·tslaku   tyakwʌtskwahlúni?.
midnight that,   then   again we dispersed   in a ditch   we are sitting around.

Jake and Enoch, Gordon, they're all not around anymore. (113) While Sandy (Sandy Elijah, Pearl's uncle) had a store, they would come there and buy a drink. (114) They'd go somewhere, they would go far away and sit in the ditch over there. (115) And we were with them, me and Gladys. (116) It was kind of like we were looking after them as they were drinking. (117) But they were quite a bit older. *Mhm* (118) Not like it is today. (119) Oh, then all of a sudden they started telling stories too, they would laugh, then all of a sudden they would run out of drinks and we up and left to go home. *Mhm.* (120) It was, what, around midnight, then we each of us went on our way after sitting around in the ditch.

(121) Khále? onʌ́ Clara, uhte i·kélhe? sʌ́· thikʌ́ nʌ wa?ukwatya?tálhahse?.
And soon Clara, I think also that then she joined us.

(122) Tóhka? kyuhte i·kélhe? niyotlátstu uhte i·kélhe?. (123) *Ne? kʌ n*
A few I think times I think. *The question*

Clarabelle. (124) Hʌ́·. (125) *Né· kʌ tsha?tetisnenú thi·kʌ́.*
Clarabelle. Yes. *It's question you two have come from the same that.*

(126) Né· kyuhte i·kélhe?, hʌ́·. (127) Khále? Betty Lou, Betty Lou s kwí· ní·
It's I think, yes. And Betty Lou, Betty Lou us

akwáh oskánhe tsha?teyakyatawʌ́lyehe?. (128) Nók tsi? sʌ́ha? kwí· né·
mostly together when we two travel around. But more it's

okstʌ·ha. (129) Kwáh olihwiyó tsi? two years thikʌ́ nʌ sʌ́ha?
female old person. Just a sure thing that two years that now more

okstʌ́ha tsi? ní· ni·yót. (130) Né· s kwí· ya·wét wake?nikú·lale?,
female old person as me how it is. So it's kind of like she watches over me,

tákʌ? a·knahko·lʌ́n kyuhte wáh. (131) *Tahnú· sʌ́ha ok.* (132) Hʌ́·,
so as not I should find a mate supposedly right. *And anyway.* Yes,

sʌ́ha? ok, hʌ́·. (133) Né· kwí· aolí·wa? nʌ kayé niwakwi·láyʌ?. (134) *Náhte?*
anyway, yes. So it's the reason now four I have children. *What*

kati? nisé· núwa? ni·yót tsi? teskánle? ka?ikʌ́ tsi? niyohtuháti? tsi?
so then you this time how it is that you are looking this how it is going at

tninákle? kwáh s a?nyóh yoyánle? kʌ náhte? nisa?nikuhló·tʌ.
you and I reside just it seems it is good question what is your opinion.

(135) Yoyánle? kih. (136) Tsi? ní· niyo·lé· nikatkáthos, yah náhte?
It is good actually. How me as far as I see, not anything

(121) And then Clara, I think she joined us then too. (122) A few times I think. (123) *You mean Clarabelle?* (124) Yes. (125) *Are you two the same age?* (126) I think so, yes. (127) And Betty Lou, Betty Lou and I sort of went around together. (128) But she was older. (129) She must be two years older than me. (130) It's kind of like she watched over me, so I wouldn't get a man supposedly. (131) *But [it happened] anyway.* (132) Yes anyway, yes. (133) That's why now I've got four children. (134) *How do you view the way things are going where we live [on the Reserve], is it good? what's your opinion of things?* (135) It's good. (136) As far as I see, there's nothing

aʔnyóh   teʔwahétk˄ʔ.   *Mhm*   (137) Akwekú kiʔ   tayoyanlátiʔ.
seems like   it is not bad.   *Mhm*   All   actually   is going along well.

(138) Tá·   n˄   kyuhte wí· tho   nikú   kaʔik˄, tsiʔ nikú   waʔklí·wakuʔ,
       Well   now supposedly that's how much this,   how much   I know information,

tho   kiʔ   nikú   ké·yaleʔ   kaʔi·k˄.
that's actually how much I remember   this.

that seems bad. (137) Everything is going along well. (138) Well that's about it, that's all
the information I have, that's how much I remember.

A Lifetime of Memories
(Told by Verland Cornelius to Mercy Doxtator in 1995)

(1)   Verland kaʔik˄ yúkyats,   Verland Cornelius tahnú· ohkwalí nukiʔtaló·t˄ʔ.
      Verland   this   is my name, Verland Cornelius   and   bear   such is my clan.

(2)   Né· katiʔ ok   uhte wí·   ní· a·kathlo·lí·   tsiʔ kwáh tsiʔ nú·
      It's   well   only supposedly me   I could tell about that   right   where

tshututáhsaw˄ʔ ké·yaleʔ   tshikúnheʔ,   aʔé·   aksothné·ke
when it began   I remember   when I am alive,   way over there   at my grandmother's

lakeʔníha lonulhaʔké·ne tyakwanákeleʔ.   (3) Tahnú· s   neʔ thó·neʔ   kwah nók
my father   at his mother's   we reside.   And   at that time   just

cook stove yakóthnyoteʔ   aksótha.   (4) Aʔé· niwaʔkó·.   (5) Kwáh ok
cook stove   she has it standing   my grandmother.   Great   it is real big.   Only

thiyakwatnuhsatalihá·thaʔ.   (6) Tahnú· né· yah né· tha·hutnuhsatalíhahteʔ
we just used it to warm the house.   And   it's   not   it's   they won't heat up the house

(1) Verland is my name, Verland Cornelius and I am Bear Clan. (2) I guess all I could tell
about is what I remember of the very beginning of my life, we lived over at my grandmother's, my father's mother's. (3) And at that time my grandmother just had a cook stove.
(4) A great big huge one. (5) It was all we used to warm the house. (6) And they wouldn't
heat the house

nʌ   ʌyó·kalawe̲ʔ.   (7) Kwáh s yowisa·lú·   yukwatnaʔtsyahlúniʔ
when   it will get dark.   Quite   it has turned to ice   we have buckets set around

ohne·kánus, tsiʔ niyotho·lé· astéh̲tsiʔ.   (8) Tahnú· s aksótha
cold water,   how   it is cold   in the morning.   And   my grandmother

yakotsiʔtsyaká·teʔ   kʌs.   (9) Tsiʔ s né· naʔe·yéleʔ aʔé· niwaʔkó·
she has a lot of flowers habitually.   How   it's   she did it   great   it is real big

yako·yʌ́· cardboard box.   (10) Atekhwahlakhwá·ke waʔé·lʌʔ, thoʔnʌ́   akwekú
she has   cardboard box.   On the table   she set it,   and then   all

tho   waʔetsheʔtitáliʔ.   (11) Thoʔnʌ́   tayekʌho·lóke̲ʔ.   (12) Yah né·
there   she put jars in it.   And then   she covered it with a blanket.   Not   it's

nuwʌtú teʔyotiwistoʔkwanʌ́stu thi·k̲ʌ́.   (13) Thoʔnʌ́   ʌyukwʌtá·whaʔ ní·
never   they did not freeze   that.   And then   we will go to bed   us

é·nik   né· nukwá·.   (14) Tho kwí· né· thikʌ́ ké·yaleʔ   aksótha,
upstairs   it's direction.   There   it's   that   I remember   my grandmother,

yakotetsheʔtaké·luʔ s wí·   tá·t i·yʌ́lheʔ   átste wí· usayu·tú·
she has containers strewn around   if   one wants   one can go to the bathroom

tsiʔ niwahsu·tés. (15) Úska tshaʔtekanuhsiyó, ya·wét   kanuhsowanʌ́,
during the night.   One   half of a house,   kind of like   a big house,

kanáktayʌʔ?   kháleʔ kwáh tsiʔ ʌtehsláthʌʔ   elʌ́ ná·wati, ne·né· kahikho·kú·,
there is a bed   and   just   as   you will climb up other side,   it's that   all the fruit,

né· a·kí·luʔ wí· bushel basket yakotasheʔnutslaké·luʔ.   (16) Né· thikʌ́
it's I'd say   bushel basket   she has baskets strewn around.   It's   that

ehtá·ke s   né· s kiʔ,   yah s teʔské·yaleʔ   kátshaʔ s né· nú·
downstairs   it's   actually, not   I don't remember anymore where   it's   where

at night-time. (7) Our buckets of water had turned to ice, it was so cold in the morning.
(8) And my grandmother had a lot of plants. (9) How she used to do it was she had a great
big cardboard box. (10) She would set it on the table, and then she put all the jars [of plants]
in it. (11) And then she covered it with a blanket. (12) They never froze. (13) And then we
would go to bed upstairs. (14) I remember my grandma had containers all around if a person wanted to go to the bathroom during the night. (15) One half of the house was kind of
bigger, there was a bed and as you climbed up [the stairs] on the other side, all this fruit, she
had I'd say bushel baskets of it all around. (16) And downstairs,—I don't remember where

nihanuhwétsta? laksótha,   nók tsi? wa?akwa·láte? s ní· thikʌ́ aksótha
he sleeps   my grandfather,   but   we lay down   us   that   my grandmother

í·   ahsʌnʌ́ wa?ka·láte?. (17) Tho?nʌ́ aknulháh.   (18) Lake?níha wí· nʌ
me middle I lay down.   And then my mother.   My father   then

tshihawʌhe·yú̲.   (19) Né· thikʌ́ tsi? niwahsu·tés sayutkétsko?.   (20) Né·n,
when he has died.   It's that during the night she got up again.   So it's,

né·n thikʌ́ tho kwí· sayuté?wahte?   ki?wáh. (21) Né·n   astéhtsi? s
so it's that   there   she missed a target right.   It's that in the morning

thikʌ́ ʌyutkétsko?   astéhtsi? s   yeyé·wate? s   thikʌ́ tsi?   akaulhá· s wí·
that   she will get up in the morning she is an early riser that   because   herself

yuteka?tá·ne? s   astéh<u>tsi?</u>.   (22) Kʌ? s nikakwilá·sa? astéhtsi?
she is going to make a fire in the morning.   Small twigs   in the morning

tyutahsawa?tákhwa? ʌyute·ká<u>·te?</u>.   (23) Né· thikʌ́ tho   wa?tyakowísko?.
she uses it to start   she will make a fire.   It's that there she slipped.

(24) Yah kwí· né· náhte? te?yúknʌ   aknulhá· nók tsi? tho kwí·
     Not   it's anything we two didn't say my mother but   there

wa?akyatkʌho·lóke?   tákʌ?   a·yúttok   tsi? wa?akniste·líste?.
we two covered up with a blanket so as not she would notice that we two laughed.

(25) Astéhtsi?   kati? wí· kwáh tsi? nikú wa?katkétsko? khále?, "átskwe
     In the morning well then just   as many I got up   and,   "how about it

náhte? wesaslʌhtáksʌ?," 'skabé·bis' kwí· yukna?túkhwa?.   (26) "Né· ki?   ok
what   you dreamed,"   'skababys'   what she called me.   "It's actually only

ukeslʌhtáksʌ? tsi? úhka? ok náhte? wa?tyutá·khetste? astéh<u>tsi?</u>."   (27) Ókhna?
I dreamed   that someone   someone skated   in the morning."   And then

my grandfather slept, but we lay down with my grandmother and I lay down in the middle.
(17) And then my mother. (18) My father had died by then. (19) During the night she
would get up again. (20) So that [night] she missed [the pot], right. (21) So she would get
up early in the morning, she was an early riser because she was the one who was going to
make the fire in the morning. (22) She would use small twigs to start the fire in the morning. (23) There she slipped. (24) My mother and I didn't say anything but we covered [our
heads] with a blanket so she wouldn't notice that we were laughing. (25) Well every morning I got up and, "how about it, what did you dream?," 'skabé·bis' she called me. (26) "I
only dreamed that someone was skating in the morning." (27) And then

né· aksótha   waʔí·luʔ "a·hsnuwʌ́hslayʌʔ uhte wáh."   (28) Né· kwí· né· thikʌ́
it's my grandmother she said   "you should be quiet better be."   So it's   it's   that

kwáh kwí· né· otokʌ́·u tsiʔ yuknolúkhwaʔ thikʌ́ aksótha   tho nukwá·.
just   it's for real   that she loves me   that   my grandmother that direction.

(29) Yah né· thya·ya·wʌ́·neʔ tsiʔ tʌkhetsiʔkwániʔ tsiʔ niyo·lé· nʌ   ʌwakitá·whaʔ.
       It has to be   that I will kiss her   until   then I will go to bed.

(30) Tahnú· wé·ni kwí· kátshaʔ ok nú· yá·yaʔk tshaʔtewakohsliyá·ku   thikʌ́,
       And   evidently somewhere   six   when I have crossed over winters that,

ohʌtú kwí· nukwá· kaʔikʌ́ yewakathloliháti̱ʔ,   lakeʔníha wí· shekú tshihlúnheʔ
ahead   direction this   I am going on telling, my father   still   when he is alive

né· núwaʔ ʌskathlo·lí̱·.
it's this time I will tell.

   (31) Né· thikʌ́ tsiʔ niyawʌ́·u   lakeʔníha wahonuhwáktʌʔ, ká·lahseʔ wí·
          It's   that   how it has happened my father   he got sick,   lacrosse

tehuttsihkwá·eks. (32) Laulhá· s lamanager   thikʌ́ kháleʔ oyá·   kiʔ   sʌ́·
they play ball.   Him   he is manager that   and   another actually also

laʔslu·ní·,   kʌh   Ukwehuwé·ne waʔthuttsihkwá·ekeʔ, tahnú· úhkaʔ ok náhteʔ
a white man, over here on the Reserve   they played ball,   and   someone

Ukwehuwé, Onʌyoteʔa·ká· yah tehokeʔtóhtu.   (33) Nʌ kwí· laulhá·
Native person, Oneida   not   he didn't show up.   So then   him

wahatyá·talʌʔ, tahnú· né· kaʔikʌ́ shayá·tat lashwekaʔa·ká·, kwáh ne·né·
he joined in,   and   it's   this   one man   he is Six Nations, just   it's that

tshaʔtehokahlátiʔ,   lanaʔahté·ne waʔkahnyo·tá·neʔ thikʌ́ ká·nhi̱ʔ.
when he is going after him, in his ribs   it stuck him   that   stick.

my grandma said "you'd better be quiet." (28) So she really loved me, my grandma on that
side [my father's side]. (29) I had to kiss her before I went to bed. (30) And I must have
been about six years old, but I'm getting ahead of myself, I'll talk about when my father was
still alive.

   (31) The way it happened my father got sick, they were playing lacrosse. (32) He was the
manager and this other man was too, he was a white man, they played over here on the Reserve, and some Native man, an Oneida, didn't show up. (33) So then he [my father] joined
in, and this one Six Nations [Mohawk] man, he was after him, and the [lacrosse] stick got
him in the ribs.

(34) Tahnú· kátsha? ok nú· thikʌ́ October tho na?a·wʌ́·ne?, né·n February
    And   somewhere   that   October   thus   it happened,   it's that February

twenty-fifth ókhna? né· wahlʌ́he<u>ye</u>?. (35) Tahnú· ne? thó·ne? yah né·
twenty-fifth   and then   it's he died.   And   at that time   not it's

teyutateshnyé·tha? tehuwatiya?tahawítha? ne? thó·ne?. (36) Tho kwí· né·
where one takes care of one they do not carry them off to at that time.   There   it's

thikʌ́ tsyo?k náhte? onúhkwa?t lute?nyʌ́tha?, lu·té· "né· ka?ikʌ́ ʌsaya?takén<u>ha?</u>."
that   all kinds of   medicine   they try,   they say "it's   this   it will help you."

(37) Tsyo?k wí· náhte? Ukwehuwehné·<u>ke</u>. (38) Yah né· tehoya?takenhá·u.
    All kinds of   in the Native way.   Not   it's it didn't help him.

(39) Khále? nya?kʌníhalane? úhka? ok náhte? wahʌ́·lu?, otsi?nuwahé·ta? se?
    And   it got to the point someone   he said,   fishing worm   too

ʌ́·lake? ka?ikʌ́ né· ʌhoya?takén<u>ha?</u>. (40) Nʌ kyale? wí· né· laksótha,
he will eat it this   it's it will help him.   So again   it's my grandfather,

tsi? ka·yʌ́· kʌ? nihʌná·sa? wáh. (41) Kwah nók akwekú wahatáhko? thikʌ́
the one that they are small   right.   Just   all   he took out   that

tho i·wát layá·t<u>aku</u>. (42) Nʌ sók wa?thahsaktáni? thikʌ́ kwáh kwí·
there it is inside in his body.   And then too he folded it up   that   just

kʌ? ok niswahta?nawʌ́·tsla? "hányo thi·<u>kʌ́</u>." (43) Nʌ sók lolha·lé·
it is only a small ball again "come on   that."   And then too he is ready

ohne·kánus sʌ́· tahowi·sú·, "kwah nók tehsátskalaw," óksa? a?é·
cold water also he gave him a glass,   "just   open your mouth," right away over there

ya?thlóya?ake? lahsa·<u>kú</u>. (44) Né· kwí· thikʌ́ wá·lake?, né· kwí· a?nyóh
he threw it straight at in his mouth.   So it's   that   he ate it, so it's   seems like

(34) And it was around October this happened, and on February 25th he died. (35) And at that time they didn't take them to the hospital. (36) They tried all kinds of medicine, they said "it will help you." (37) All kinds of Indian [medicine]. (38) It didn't help him. (39) And it got to the point that someone said, he should eat a fishing [dew] worm, it would help him. (40) So then my grandfather, [he took] ones that were small, right. (41) He took out the insides of the body. (42) And then he folded it up so it was just a little ball, "come on." (43) Then he was ready and he handed him a glass of water, "just open your mouth," right away he threw it straight into his mouth. (44) So he ate it,

ʌ·wáke? wí· thikʌ́ wa?thotT.B. ki?wáh.   (45) Wahsa?ka?tsláksʌ wahonuhwáktʌ?.
it will eat it   that   he got T.B.   right.   The bad cough   he got sick.

(46) Yah kati? wí· né· tehoya?takenhá·u thi·kʌ́.   (47) Thika·té· n   Ukwehuwehné·ke
       Not   well then   it's   it didn't help him   that.   It is different the Native way

wahatstáni?.
he used several.

    (48) Tahnú· s ka?ikʌ́ núwa?   yah kwí· né· tehotiyó·tʌskwe?   tsi?
          And   this   this time   not   it's   they didn't used to work   as

núwa?   ni·yót.   (49) Aksótha   nók né· thikʌ́ yutya?tawi?tslu·níhe? wí·,
this time   how it is.   My grandmother just   it's   that   she makes dresses,

tsyo?k náhte?   yutaténhahse?   luwʌnatslunyahkunyʌ·níhe? ta·yutʌ́·tshane?.
all kinds of things   she hires herself out   she makes clothes for them   for her to earn money.

(50) Ok ne?n   aknulhá·,   ne·né· thikʌ́ tho s yeyé·tlu?   thikʌ́
       And as for   my mother,   it's that that   there   she dwells over there   that

Akobatí·s   shakotina?túkhwahkwe?.   (51) Yutashe?nutslu·níhe?.   (52) Tho nú·
Mrs. Bodice   what they used to call her.   She makes baskets.   That's where

na?ewyʌtéhtane? thikʌ́ aknulhá· a·yuta?ahslu·ní·,   Akobatí·s
she learned   that   my mother that she makes baskets, Mrs. Bodice

yutashe?nutslu·níhe?. (53) Né·n   tho   lʌta·kéle? s ké·yale? s lake?níha
she makes baskets.   It's that   there   he is lying   I remember   my father

lonuhwáktanihe?, shakotló·lu   yuta?ahslu·níhe?.   (54) Wé·ni s kwí· tá·t núwa?
he is sick,   he is watching her she is making baskets.   Evidently   maybe

ya·wét kwí· a·kí·lu? weekend, nále? wa?akyata?ahslahninú·na?.   (55) Tahnú·
kind of like   I'd say   weekend,   then   we two went and sold baskets.   And

it would sort of eat his T.B., right. (45) He got sick with the bad cough. (46) Well it didn't help him. (47) It's different, the Indian [medicines] that he used.

(48) And then people didn't used to work like it is today. (49) My grandmother made dresses, all kinds of things, she would hire herself out and make clothes for people so as to make money. (50) And my mother, she lived over there, Mrs. Bodice they called her. (51) She was making baskets. (52) That's where my mother learned to make baskets, Mrs. Bodice was making baskets. (53) So I remember my father lying there sick, he was watching as she's making baskets. (54) And I guess maybe kind of like I'd say on weekends, then the two of us would go and sell baskets. (55) And

Model T kʌs kwíˑ lotiʔsléhtayʌʔ,   kok nikahnaˑkwálahseʔ kʌ́h. (56) Yaʔeyaˑkʌ́neʔ
Model T   customarily they have a car, the tires are just small   see.   She went out

thikʌ́, néˑn,   kwáh néˑ thikʌ́ owistóˑkwaʔ néˑ tyoyenʌ́   tsiʔ yokʌnolú
that,   it's that, just   it's   that   frozen thing   it's   it has caught it at   it is raining

rubbertsláˑke wáh.   (57) Tho   néˑ waʔutʌʔnikuhloˑlʌ́neʔ   waʔuthnekatalíhahteʔ
on the tire   right.   There it's she came upon the idea she heated water

thikʌ́, nʌ sók   tho   tayakohnekuˑtíˑ   thikʌ́ ohnakwalaktútiʔ. (58) Kwáh
that,   and then too there she poured water that   along the tire.   Just

thok núˑ   yah s kwíˑ teʔwakanúhteʔ tóˑ náheʔ, nók tsiʔ sayeyaˑkʌ́neʔ
the only thing not   I don't know   how long,   but   she went out again

ókhnaʔ   yowistanawʌ́ˑu, nʌ kiʔ ok wíˑ uˑtúˑ   waʔakyahtʌˑtíˑ. (59) Tahnúˑ
and then   it has thawed,   right then   it could be we two left.   And

neˑnéˑ thikʌ́ wíˑ núwaʔ   nok ʌwaˑtúˑ tʌhsatkrank.   (60) Swatyelʌ́ s thikʌ́
it's that that   this time it has to be you will crank it.   Sometimes that

waʔakolahsʌ́thoʔ wíˑ latinaʔtúkhwaʔ kʌʔ nyaʔtyelatotátiʔ   kʌ́h.
it kicked someone   what they call it   here she is going back on her heels eh.

(61) Sayuteʔnyʌˑtʌ́ˑ kʌs   ok   kiʔwáh, tahnúˑ aˑkíˑluʔ núwaʔ
      She tried again   habitually only right,   and   I'd say   this time

niyukwaʔslehtiˑyóˑseʔ kwíˑ nʌʔúˑwaʔ. (62) Windshield wipers kwíˑ núwaʔ   néˑ
we have such nice cars   now.   Windshield wipers   this time it's

yoˑyʌ́ˑ wíˑ n nʌʔúˑwaʔ. (63) Neʔ thóˑneʔ yah néˑ teʔyoˑyʌ́ˑ.   (64) Tho kwíˑ
it has   now.   At that time not   it's it doesn't have it.   There

néˑ thikʌ́ áhsok   sayuteʔsléhtayʌʔ   kʌs   sayewisakewániʔ.
it's that   suddenly she parked the car again habitually she wiped the glass again.

they had a Model T car, the tires were small. (56) She went out [one time], it was frozen [to the ground] where it had rained on the tires. (57) Then she had a brainstorm, she heated some water, and then she poured the water along the tires. (58) The only thing is I don't know how long, but she went out again and then it had thawed, right away then we could leave. (59) And the thing is you had to crank it. (60) Sometimes it would kick back, as they used to call it, here she would go back on her heels. (61) She kept trying again though, and I'd say nowadays we have such nice cars. (62) They have windshield wipers now. (63) At that time they didn't have them. (64) All of sudden she would park the car and wipe the windshield.

(65) Kwáh aʔnyóh ónhwaleʔ náhteʔ yuknihlátiʔ tákʌʔ
Just seems like fur what we two have it covering us so as not

a·yakniwistó·kwanʌsteʔ yukní·se<u>le</u>ʔ. (66) Tho kʌs Shedden né· s nú·
we two would freeze we two are riding. There habitually Shedden it's where

yaʔutaʔahslahninúniʔ, elók tsyákneʔ, tho s né· nutayeye·lá·teʔ
she sold baskets over there, all over we two are walking, thus it's she managed to do it

a·yakohwistayʌ·tá·<u>ne</u>ʔ. (67) Kháleʔ n aksótha né· thikʌ́ owistóhsliʔ s kwí·
that she obtains money. And my grandmother it's that butter

né· waʔutu·ní·, tyonhúskwalut kʌs kwí· né· lotinʌ́skwayʌʔ, né· s kwí· né·
it's she made, cow habitually it's they have an animal, so it's it's

owistóhsliʔ waʔutu·ní· kháleʔ cheese, cottage cheese. (68) Tahnú· neʔ thó·neʔ n
butter she made and cheese, cottage cheese. And at that time

owistóhsliʔ, wé·ni tsiʔ tékni sílu. (69) Ok neʔn tá·t sʌ́haʔ kʌʔ nikúha,
butter, evidently that twenty-five cents. But if more small amount,

tá·t núwaʔ twenty cents. (70) Kháleʔ n cottage cheese kʌh ni·wá·seʔ,
maybe twenty cents. And cottage cheese it is this size all around

ké·yaleʔ né· tsiʔ oye·lí· né· kwénis. (71) Tho katiʔ ok wí· né· tho
I remember because ten it's pennies. Thus then only it's thus

nithatilihwayelá·thaʔ a·hotihwistayʌ·tá·neʔ neʔ thó·neʔ, yah né· náhteʔ
they manage to do it that they obtain money at that time, not it's anything

tehatihwistatáhkwas tsiʔ núwaʔ ni·yót. (72) Núwaʔ, kwáh núwaʔ
they don't take out money as this time how it is. This time, just this time

yah kwí· teʔwé·ni naʔtehotishlíhʌhseʔ usutʌhniʔtó·ktʌʔ, lonanúhteʔ seʔ
it's incredible how they are in a hurry for the month to end again, they know too

(65) There was this sort of furry thing we had covering us so that we didn't freeze as we were riding. (66) She sold baskets in Shedden, we would walk all over, that's how she managed to do it to get money. (67) And my grandmother made butter, they had a cow, so she made butter, and cheese, cottage cheese. (68) And at that time, butter must have [cost] a quarter. (69) But maybe less, maybe 20 cents. (70) And cottage cheese was this big (motioning how big with the hands), I remember because it was 10 cents. (71) That's the only way they managed to get money at that time, they didn't take out money the way it is now. (72) Now, nowadays, they're in such a big hurry for the month to end, they know

ʌshotihwistayʌ·tá·<u>ne</u>ʔ.   (73) Nók   thikʌ́   wahu·níseʔ   kwáh né· nók tá·t
they will receive money again.   But   that   a long time ago just   it's only if

ʌhatiyʌtakó·naʔ   kohslaʔké<u>ne</u>.   (74) Thok kwí· náhteʔ a·lé·,   nʌ   oniʔ thikʌ́
they will go cut wood   wintertime.   Something   at times, then too   that

e·só· neʔ thó·neʔ, tsyoʔk náhteʔ kutílyoʔ,   a·kí·luʔ kwaʔyʌ́ha tsikwilʌ́·tuʔ, yah
a lot at that time, all kinds of   wild animals, I'd say rabbit   squirrel,   not

thusa·ké<u>ke</u>ʔ.   (75) Né· tsiʔ nikú   nók yakyunhehkwʌ́·neʔ   thikʌ́
I won't eat it anymore.   It's   how much only it used to keep us alive that

neʔ thó·<u>ne</u>ʔ.
at that time.

(76) A·lé·   laksótha   wahatolátha?,   né· kiʔ   thikʌ́ tóhkaʔ
     At times my grandfather he went hunting, it's actually that   a few

nishoyaʔtayʌtátiʔ   tsikwilʌ́·tuʔ, tahnú· aksótha   yakolʌ́ʔnhaʔú·neʔ
he has bodies along with him squirrel,   and   my grandmother she knew how

kyuhte wí· a·yekhu·ní·,   tsiʔ   né· s kwí· thikʌ́ kwahotokʌ́·u wí·
supposedly that she cooks, because it's   that   just for real

tekahsi·núteʔ wí· u·ták waʔutnaʔtsyá·lʌʔ, kwáh s né· nók tsiʔ thikʌ́ núwaʔ   nʌ wí·
it has legs   pot   she set down a pot, just   it's only   that   this time when

washakoyá·theweʔ,   waʔelistahla·kó·   ókhnaʔ   tho   yahuwatiyaʔtitáliʔ thikʌ́ tsiʔ
he brought them there, she took the iron off and then there she put them all in   that   at

yoték<u>ha</u>ʔ.   (77) Wahuwatihuhtsí·tʌhteʔ; … né· kiʔ   thikʌ́ akwekú útshaneʔ
it is in flames.   She singed the hair off them; it's actually that all   it burned

laónhwa<u>le</u>ʔ. (78) Kwáh s nók tsiʔ wahuwʌtáhsyah<u>ke</u>ʔ. (79) Ókhnaʔ nʌ́khleʔ thikʌ́
his fur.   Just   she cut off his tail.   And then then   that

that they will receive money again. (73) But a long time ago the only [way] was if they went to cut wood in the wintertime. (74) Something usually, then there was a lot too at that time, all kinds of wild animals, I'd say rabbits, squirrels, I won't eat it anymore. (75) It's all we used to have to live on at that time.

(76) Sometimes my grandfather went hunting, he would have a few squirrels with him, and I guess my grandmother knew how to cook, because she would set down this pot with legs, and right when he got there with them, she took off the iron [lid from the wood-burning stove] and then she put them in the flames. (77) She singed the hair off them (interrupts herself); she burned off all his fur. (78) And she just cut off his tail. (79) And then

waʔenóhaleʔ ókhnaʔ né· waʔthuwayaʔto·lʌ́· waʔetáhkoʔ kiʔwáh. (80) Ókhnaʔ
she washed it   and then   it's   she split his body   she took it out   right.   And then

né· tho thyehonutsístuteʔ thi·kʌ́. (81) Né· s kwí· né· thikʌ́ nʌ tyolíhʌhseʔ
it's   there   just his head is attached   that.   So it's   it's   that   when   it is boiling

tho kʌs tethutkeʔtotúnyuheʔ thikʌ́ tsikwilʌ́·tuʔ yakonaʔtsíhaleʔ s, yah s kwí·
there   habitually   they are looking out   that   squirrel   she is boiling it,   not

né· tho teʔyo·lé·, núwaʔ n a·katkáthoʔ núwaʔ utukneʔwalá·tʌʔ kiʔwáh.
it's   thus   it is not so far,   this time   I should see it   this time   I should get nauseous   indeed.

(82) Nók tsiʔ neʔ thó·neʔ yah kwí· náhteʔ got no brain. (83) Shekú núwaʔ né·
But   at that time   not   any   got no brain.   Still   this time   it's

yáhtʌʔ. (84) Nók tsiʔ né· kiʔ thikʌ́ tsiʔ ka·yʌ́· onutsí, wahuskenhányuʔ s
not.   But   it's   actually   that   the one that   head,   they fought over it

thikʌ́, yawékuʔ yakʌʔ thikʌ́ onaʔalátslaku i·wát, tho kiʔ ok wí· náhohteʔ,
that,   it is tasty   reportedly   that   in the head   it is inside,   something actually,

yah kiʔ ní· nuwʌtú teʔwake·kú. (85) Né· katiʔ wi· né· thikʌ́
not   actually   me   never   I did not eat it.   Well then it's   it's   that

yakyunhéhkwʌ s kháleʔ ohnʌná·taʔ, akwekú kwí· né· lonulhá· latiyʌ́thos.
it is keeping us alive   and   potato,   all   it's   them   they plant.

(86) Tho né· nikú ʌhatiyʌ́thoʔ lonulhá· kwí· né· ʌhonohsli·yá·keʔ
That's   it's   how much   they will plant it   them   it's   it will last them the winter

sʌ́h. (87) Kwáh s nók thikʌ́ káhik ké·yaleʔ waʔehni·nú·. (88) Kwáh akwekú
also.   Just only   that   fruit   I remember   she bought.   Quite   all

lonulhá· lotiyʌ́thu. (89) Né· s wí· né· thikʌ́ tsiʔ nahati·yéleʔ kákhwaʔ,
them   they have planted it.   So it's   it's   that   what   they did it   food,

she washed it and then she split open his body and took out [the insides]. (80) And then just
his head was attached. (81) So when the water was boiling the squirrels were looking out of
the pot as she was boiling them, it wasn't that much [that bad] then, should I see it now it
would make me sick to my stomach. (82) But back then I didn't have any brains. (83) I still
don't. (84) But the part that was the head, they fought over that, they say it's tasty what's
inside the head, it was something, but I never ate it. (85) Well we lived on that and potatoes,
everyone grew their own. (86) They would plant enough to last the winter also. (87) I remember she just bought fruit. (88) They grew everything themselves. (89) So what they
used to do with food,

wahutsha·tú· kʌs   nʌʔ né·, átste   wáh.   (90) Ké·yaleʔ   né· thikʌ́
they buried it habitually that,   outside   right.   I remember it's that

laksótha   wahatá·kwateʔ aʔé·   niwaʔkó· átste.   (91) Thoʔnʌ́ straw taha·yʌ́·
my grandfather he dug a hole great it's real big outside.   And then straw he laid it

ná·ku.   (92) Thoʔnʌ́ tho   wahahlúniʔ thikʌ́ náhteʔ wí· wahatékhwayʌ́ʔ.
underneath.   And then there he set things that   what   he preserved food.

(93) Thoʔnʌ́ náleʔ straw tutaho·tí·,   thoʔnʌ́ oʔkʌ́·laʔ.   (94) Né· s thikʌ́
      And then again straw he threw it again, and then soil.   It's   that

tho   nihatiyélhaʔ olihwakayú lutékhwayʌheʔ.   (95) Né· katiʔ wí· né· núwaʔ   onʌ́
thus   they do it   old times   they preserve food.   Well then it's   it's this time now

kwaʔyʌ́ha núwaʔ   o·nʌ́. (96) A·lé·   kwaʔyʌ́ha wahuwáliʔ,   né· kyuniʔ né·
rabbit   this time now.   At times rabbit   they killed him, it's too   it's

thikʌ́ tho   naʔe·yéleʔ, waʔeʔwá·loʔ   oniʔ nʌʔ né·.   (97) A·lé·   oniʔ stuffing wí·
that   thus she did it,   she boiled meat also that one.   At times too   stuffing

waʔutu·ní·, kayá·taku waʔétaneʔ.   (98) Tá·t núwaʔ kwah nók special a·kí·luʔ
she made,   in the body she put it in.   Maybe   only   special   I'd say

yukwa·yʌ́· a·yakwaʔwá·lakeʔ, lonulhá· s oniʔ né· yatnʌ́skwayʌʔ   thikʌ́ geese and
we have   for us to eat meat,   them   too   it's   the two keep animals that   geese and

turkey. (99) Né· thikʌ́ a·lé·   turkey, skawilo·wáneʔ né·n   Christmas Day
turkey.   It's   that   at times turkey,   turkey   it's that Christmas Day

kháleʔ onahsakʌ·láteʔ né·n   New Year, ohsla·sé·.
and   goose   it's that New Year,   a new year.

      (100) Né· s katiʔ ok wi· né· tho   ni·yót   tsiʔ lonatlihwahtʌtyé·tu
             Well then it's just   it's   that's   how it is   that   they are conducting their affairs

they buried it, that's what, outside right. (90) I remember my grandfather would dig a great big hole outside. (91) And then he would line the bottom with straw. (92) And then he would put in whatever food he was preserving. (93) And then he threw straw in again, and then soil. (94) That's how they did it the old way to preserve food. (95) Well, the rabbit now. (96) Sometimes they would kill a rabbit, and the way she did it, she boiled that meat too. (97) Sometimes she even made stuffing, and she put it inside the body. (98) Maybe, I'd say, it had to be special for us to eat meat, they also kept their own geese and turkey. (99) Sometimes there was turkey Christmas Day and goose New Year's Day.

   (100) Well that's just how they conducted themselves

olihwakayú, yah tho té·yot núwaʔ, Christmas ta·wé·, yah kwí· teʔwé·ni
old times, not that's not how it is this time, Christmas it is coming, it's incredible

tsiʔ nisahwistaká·teʔ, nʌ seʔ kwáh ok thiyesahwista·wíheʔ.
how you have a lot of money, then too just they just give you money.

(101) Wahsatʌnaʔtslakóꞏnaʔ kwí· kanatáꞏke. (102) Neʔ thóꞏneʔ katiʔ wí· nʌ
You are going for groceries in town. At that time anyway then

a·kí·luʔ yaʔweskwaʔtúꞏneʔ né· neʔ thóꞏneʔ né· tsiʔ tá·t a·kí·luʔ núwaʔ kanatáꞏke
I'd say it was fun it's at that time because if I'd say then town

wahʌꞏnéhteʔ, tyoʔslehtáꞏkat kʌs né· wahutítaneʔ. (103) Ké·yaleʔ thikʌ́
they went there, train habitually it's they got on. I remember that

yotlatstúꞏneʔ aknulhá· tyoʔslehtáꞏkat waʔakyatítaneʔ, Southwold
it was one time my mother train we two got on, Southwold

yaʔakyatitáhkoʔ. (104) Thok kʌs katiʔ wí· né· ni·yót tsiʔ
we two got off over there. That's habitually well then it's how it is that

tehutawʌlyéꞏthaʔ thikʌ́ neʔ thóꞏneʔ. (105) Kháleʔ núwaʔ a·kí·luʔ lutʌnéklyaʔks
they travel that at that time. And this time I'd say they cut grass

núwaʔ, ni·wá·seʔ loti·yʌ́· lawn, lonatnuʔuhliyóstu. (106) Neʔ thóꞏneʔ
this time, big all around they have lawn, they have made sod nice. At that time

né· kwah nók thikʌ́ pushing lawnmower loti·yʌ́·. (107) Yah né· teʔwé·ni tó· náheʔ
it's just that pushing lawnmower they have. It's incredible how long

shataʔshaluꞏníheʔ, sahahyoʔthiyáthuʔ tsiʔ niyo·lé· kʌʔ nyusahohlehátiʔ,
he sharpens a blade again, he sharpened them again until he goes pushing it again,

kʌʔ kiʔ ok aleʔ wí· ni·wá· thikʌ́ kháleʔ kwáh nok ʌwa·tú· ʌshahyoʔthi·yáteʔ.
again only such a size that and just it has to be he will sharpen it again.

traditionally, not like nowadays, Christmas is coming, you have all this money, you just get money given to you. (101) You go and get groceries in town. (102) Back then, I'd say, it was fun at that time because if they went to town, they would get on the train. (103) I remember at one time I would get on the train with my mother, we would get off in Southwold. (104) That's how they travelled at that time. (105) And nowadays I'd say they cut grass, they have huge lawns, they've made their lawns nice. (106) Back then they just had push mowers. (107) It really took some time for him to sharpen the blades, he would sharpen them before he went along pushing it, [he mowed] just a little piece and he had to sharpen them again.

(108) Kwahikʌ́ tsiʔ tekyattíhʌ núwaʔ, tsyoʔk náhteʔ yukwatyánleʔ núwaʔ
        Just really that it is different this time, all kinds of things we have good ones now

aˑkíˑluʔ. (109) Kwáh aˑkíˑluʔ tshaʔteyawʌʔuhátiʔ tsiʔ niˑyót oʔsluˑníˑ tsiʔ
I'd say.   Quite I'd say the same is happening as how it is white people as

niˑyót tsiʔ yukwatlihwahtʌtyeʔtuhátiʔ.   (110) Shekú kiʔ n aˑkíˑluʔ
how it is that we are going along conducting our affairs.   Even actually I'd say

núwaʔ tsiʔ twanakléniʔ,   ótyaʔk néˑ sʌ́haʔ lotinuhsiˑyóˑseʔ
this time at you and we reside here and there, some it's more they have nice houses

Ukwehuwé tsiʔ niˑyót oʔsluˑníˑ.   (111) Oʔsluˑníˑ nʌ lotiˑtʌ́t
Native people as how it is white people.   White people when they are poor

kwahikʌ́ tsiʔ lotiˑtʌ́t.   (112) Tsyoʔk náhteʔ yah tehotiˑyʌ́ˑ.
just really that they are poor.   Different things not they don't have.

(113) Kháleʔ yah oniʔ thaˑhutatewyʌ́ˑtuʔ oʔsluˑníˑ nʌ ostúha
        And not even they don't fix themselves white people when a little bit

lotiˑtʌ́t.   (114) Ókhnaʔ Ukwehuwé ati yakoˑtʌ́t kwáh kiʔ néˑ ikʌ́
they are poor.   But then Native people no matter one is poor just really actually

tsiʔ yakotataskénhʌ aˑyoyánlekeʔ kwíˑ nʌ aˑyuhtʌˑtíˑ.
that one is trying one's best that it is nice   when one should go away.

(115) Kháleʔ nʌ thikʌ́ kaˑtéˑ waʔutaʔahslunyániʔ aknulháˑ, yaʔkáheweʔ
      And then that I'm saying she made baskets my mother, came a time

nʌ waʔíˑluʔ "iséˑ sʌ́ˑ satewyʌˑtét aˑhsataʔahsluˑníˑ."   (116) Wéˑni kwíˑ
when she said "you also practice that you make a basket."   Evidently

tsiʔ aˑkíˑluʔ kátshaʔ ok núˑ tsyaˑták tshaʔtewakohsliyáˑku.
that I'd say somewhere seven when I have crossed over winters.

(108) It's very different now, we have all kinds of better things nowadays I'd say. (109) I'd say it's happening quite the same way as white people the way we are conducting ourselves. (110) Even, I'd say now the places we live, some Native people have better homes than the white people. (111) White people, when they are poor they are really poor. (112) They go without things. (113) White people don't even make themselves presentable when they're a bit poor. (114) But an Indian, no matter if they're poor they will try really hard to [look] nice when they go away.

(115) And then I was saying my mother made baskets, came a time when she said "YOU practice making baskets too." (116) I must have been about seven years old.

(117) Nʌ kwí· né· thikʌ́ kok nika?nune·sú·se? tayu·kú·,   wa?i·lu? "sate?nyʌtʌ́
       So then it's that   just short splints   she gave to me, she said "try

a·hsate?nuhku·ní·."   (118) Kwáh s kwí· né· wa?kate?nuhku·ní· kok náhe?,
that you make a bottom."   Just   it's I made a bottom   a little while,

kwáh nʌ   wakelú·ne? uhte wí· ta·kawʌ́htate?   aktúti?,   khále? né·
just when I thought   probably I should add edging along the side, and   it's

sutká·tshi?.   (119) Nʌ ki? ok ale? wi· né· kutityenúti? o?nu·ná·.
it came apart again.   Right then so again it's they go flying splints.

(120) Nʌ sók ale?   sayaí·lu?,   "sasohlu·kó."   (121) "Sasate?nyʌtʌ́, tá·t núwa?
       Then again too again she said, "pick it up again."   "Try again,   maybe

kánhke ok nók ʌkalihu·ní·   ʌsahwistayʌ·tá·ne?   ʌhsata?ahsluníheke?."
some time only it will the cause of it you will obtain money you will be making baskets."

(122) Nʌ ki? ok ale? wí· né· tho sakate?nowá·lʌ?,   wa?i·lu?, "kʌ? nukwá· sʌ́ha?
       Right then again   it's there again I sat bent over, she said, "here   more

ka?nuniyó   né· íhsatst," nʌ kyale? wí· né· sakate?nyʌ·tʌ́. (123) Tho   thikʌ́
it is a good splint it's use it,"   so again   it's I tried again.   Thus that

ni·yót   tsi? wa?kewyʌtéhtane? a·kata?ahslu·ní·.   (124) Nʌ   núwa? ati
how it is that I learned   that I make baskets.   Then this time no matter

náhte? a·kkwe·ní·   a·katu·ní·. (125) Tahnú· nya?káhewe?   ní·, yah
anything I would be able that I make.   And   there came a time me, not

thusaketshʌ·lí·   o?nu·ná· a·katúnyahte?.   (126) Nʌ kwí· núwa? oyá· náhte?
I won't find anymore splints   that I make with it.   So then   this time other thing

sakatliho·lʌ́·ne?,   kwáh olihwiyó   tsi? 1978 twakatáhsawʌ?, ostaló·kwa?
I thought of means, just   for real sure that 1978 I have started,   beaded necklace

(117) So then she gave me some short splints, she said "try to make the bottom." (118) I
made the bottom for a little while, and just when I thought probably I should add edging,
and it came undone. (119) Right away the splints went flying. (120) So she said again,
"pick them up." (121) "Try again, maybe some day the only way for you to make money
will be to make baskets." (122) So right away again I sat down bent over, she said, "here
are better splints, use them," so I tried again. (123) That's how I learned to make baskets.
(124) Now I am able to make anything, no matter what. (125) And there came a time I
wasn't able to find splints anymore to make them with. (126) So then I thought of other
means [to make money], it had to have been in 1978 I started

katu·ní<u>he</u>ʔ.   (127) Né·n   thikʌ́ sʌ́haʔ waʔkakwe·ní· tsyoʔk náhteʔ   waʔkatunyániʔ,
I make.   It's that that   more   it was able   all kinds of things I made things,

kwáh tho nukhwistayʌ·tá·neʔ   tsiʔ ni·yót   oʔnu·ná· a·kataʔahslu·<u>ní</u>·.
quite   thus how I obtained money as   how it is splints   for me to make baskets.

(128) Kwáh tsyoʔk náhteʔ   aukyʌ·tá·<u>ne</u>ʔ.   (129) Kwáh katiʔ wí· tsyoʔk náhteʔ
       Just   all kinds of things I might obtain.   Just   well then all kinds of

a·yutliho·lʌ́·neʔ   tsyoʔk ni·yót   tsiʔ ta·yutʌ́·tshaneʔ   ati   uhte
one will think of means all kinds of ways that that one earns money no matter supposedly

a·kí·luʔ yah teʔsatawyá·tu.   (130) Ʌskwe·ní·   seʔ tʌhsatʌ́·tshaneʔ
I'd say   not you haven't gone to school.   You will be able too you will earn money

tá·t kiʔ   kwahotokʌ́·u tho nú·   utesaʔnikú·la<u>wʌ</u>ʔ.
if   actually just for real   that's where should you set your mind to it.

   (131) Nʌ   núwaʔ   ótyaʔk núwaʔ a·kí·luʔ núwaʔ   kʌʔ nithotiyʌ́·saʔ,
        Then this time some   this time I'd say   this time young people,

kwahotokʌ́·u tsiʔ yah náhteʔ   tha·hatiwyʌtéhtaneʔ, kwah nók tyótkut watahsatálhaʔ
just for real   that not anything they won't learn,   just   always television

lonatló·lu.   (132) Nʌ   ʌshʌ·néweʔ   lutawyá·thaʔ,   tá·t lutawyá·thaʔ,
they are watching.   When they will get home they go to school, if   they go to school,

nʌ kiʔ ok né· watahsatálhaʔ sahutló·lo<u>ke</u>ʔ.   (133) Né·n   í·   tshikeksá·,
already   it's television   they watched again.   So it's me when I was a child,

kwah ní· nók atnutolyaʔtákhwaʔ wáki<u>ʔ</u>. (134) Kháleʔ a·kya·kʌ́·neʔ
just   me only toy   I have.   And   I should go out

kwaʔkʌnhé·ke kʌs   né· laksotkʌ́   ya·wét kwí· baby buggy wí·
summertime   habitually it's my late grandfather kind of like   baby buggy

making beaded necklaces. (127) So it so happened more that I could make all kinds of things, I got just as much money as I did making splint baskets. (128) I could get [buy] all kinds of things. (129) Well one can think of all kinds of means, all kinds of ways for one to earn money, even if you haven't gone to school. (130) You can earn money if you really set your mind to it.

(131) Nowadays some, I'd say young people, they really won't learn anything, they're just always watching television. (132) When they get home from school, if they go to school, right away they watch television again. (133) When I was a girl, all I had was toys. (134) And I might go out in the summertime, then my late grandfather [took] like

okahkwʌ·ta?.   (135) Tho?nʌ́   kalu·wále?   wa?thahsa?ktáni?,   né· thikʌ́
wheel.   And then   wire   he bent it this way and that, it's that

kʌ? thyahukhleháti?.   (136) Né· thikʌ́ waku?weskwánihe? ohna·kwála? ki?
I went pushing it along.   It's   that   I enjoy   rubber   actually

wa?ké·sele?.   (137) Khále? kohsla?ké·ne laulhá· s né· wahatu·ní· thikʌ́
I dragged it.   And   wintertime   him   it's he made it   that

laksótha,   lake?níha lo?nihkʌ́,   waté·slehse?, tekaya?tanáhsute? s
my grandfather, my father   his late father, sled,   bobsled

latina?túkhwa?.   (138) Akwekú oshú·kale? wí· náhohte?.   (139) Onísta? tho
what they call it.   All   board   is what.   Gee   thus

niwake?slehti·yó.   (140) Nʌ   núwa? kwáh ati   náhte?   nok ʌwa·tú·
it is such a good vehicle.   Then this time just   no matter anything it has to be

ʌshni·nú·.   (141) Waté·slehse? yah te?wé·ni nikano·lú·   (142) Kwáh yah
you will buy it.   Sled   it's incredible it is so expensive.   Just   not

náhte?   tha·hute?nyʌ·tʌ́· lonulhá· a·hutataskénha?.   (143) Kwáh ki?
anything   they won't try   them   that they try their best.   Just   actually

ok ʌwa·tú· "Ma I want this, i·kélhe? a·skhni·nú·s   ka?ikʌ́," nʌ ki? ok ale? wí·
it has to be "Ma I want this,   I want   you would buy it for me this,"   right then again

tá·t yakohwístayʌ?.   (144) Kwahikʌ́ tsi? tekyattíhʌ.   (145) Né· núwa? aolí·wa?
if   she has money.   Just really that   it is different.   It's   now   the reason

só·tsi?   latiksa?táksʌhse?   a·kí·lu? né· tsi? kwáh ok thithuwanawihkó·.
too much   they are bad children I'd say   because just   they just hand it to them big.

(146) Tá·t yáhtʌ? ʌhotiná·khwʌ? ki?,   ʌyesaná·khwahse?   tá·t yah
       If   not   they will get mad actually,   they will get mad at you if   not

the wheel from a baby buggy. (135) And then he bent up a piece of wire [around the wheel], I would go pushing that along. (136) I had fun driving that tire. (137) And in the wintertime, he, my grandfather, my father's late father, made a sled, bobsled is what they called it. (138) [Made] all of wood. (139) Gee, it was such a good vehicle. (140) Nowadays, anything at all, you have to buy it. (141) A sled is really expensive. (142) They won't try hard to strive for things themselves. (143) It has to be "Ma I want this, I want you to buy this for me," so right away [she will] if she has the money. (144) It sure is different. (145) Nowadays the reason the children are so bad, I'd say, is because they just have it royally handed to them. (146) If not, they'll get mad, they will get mad at you if

tha·shni·<u>nú</u>·.   (147) Khále? núwa?   a·kí·lu?, yah tehʌ·nélhe?
you won't buy it.   And   this time I'd say,   not   they don't want

a·hotiyo?tʌ<u>hsa</u>?.   (148) A·hutawya?tá·na?   oni?, wé·ni   tsi? yotká·te?,
that they go to work.   That they go to school even, evidently that often,

nók né· tyutʌhninuhe?kó· yehʌ·né·<u>se</u>?.   (149) Tahnú· se? kwáh tho
only it's at the big store they are around over there.   And   too   just   there

nʌkato·kʌ́·ne?   ʌthutwʌnátane? se? shakotilihunyʌ·níhe? tá·t yah
it will become apparent they will telephone too they teach them   if   not

tha·hutawya?tá·<u>na</u>?.   (150) Nók tsi? yah ki?   náhte?   tha?tehotitíhʌ né· tsi?
they won't go to school.   But   not actually anything they don't care because

yah se? te?yesatshá·ni<u>hse</u>?.   (151) Khále? núwa? nʌ   ʌhutkʌ́·lahte?
not too they are not afraid of you.   And   this time then they will quit

lutawyá·<u>tha</u>?.   (152) Yah ki?   né· náhte? tehotilha·lé·,   "wé·ni kwí·
they go to school.   Not   actually it's anything they are not ready, "evidently

nok ʌwa·tú· ʌknolotshyú·na?   ka?ikʌ́ tá·t i·kélhe? aukhwistayʌ·tá·<u>n</u>."
it has to be   I will go and husk corn this   if   I want   that I obtain money."

(153) "Nok sʌ́· ʌwa·tú· ʌkahyákha? wí· núwa?," luhyákwas   sʌ́·   apple.
      "It has to be also   I will go pick fruit this time," they pick fruit also apple.

(154) Tá·thuni? oyú·kwa? a·hotiyo·tʌ́·   tá·thuni? a·huhyákha?,
      Or else   tobacco   they should work or else   they should go pick berries,

thok wí· náhte? a·hutaneklóskalu?, yah oni? né· kátsha?   te?shoti·yʌ́,
something   they should hoe,   not even it's anywhere they don't have it anymore,

nʌ   núwa? né· a·kí·lu? né· tsi?   ka?ikʌ́ núwa? kwáh ok thihuwʌnatʌna?tsla·wíhe?,
then now   it's I'd say because this   now   just   just they give them groceries,

you won't buy it. (147) And nowadays I'd say, they don't want to go to work. (148) To go to school even, seems often, all they do is hang around the mall. (149) And then it'll come to light and the teachers will telephone if they don't go to school. (150) But they don't care at all because they are not afraid of you. (151) And then they quit going to school. (152) They're not at all anticipating "I have to go and husk corn if I want to get some money." (153) "Also I have to go and pick fruit," they used to pick apples too. (154) Or else they could work in tobacco or they could pick berries, something, they could hoe, they don't even have that [you won't see that] anywhere anymore, I'd say because nowadays groceries are just given to them,

aˑkíˑluʔ nók tsiʔ ohwístaʔ kwíˑ thuwʌnaˑwíheʔ.   (155) Néˑ núwaʔ   thikʌ́ nʌ
I'd say   but   money   they hand it to them.   It's this time that   then

aolíˑwaʔ   sóˑtsiʔ   lotinolúˑseheʔ. (156) Néˑ tsiʔ ʌwaˑtúˑ seʔ yah thaˑhotiyoˑtʌ́ˑ.
the reason too much they are lazy.   Because it can be too   not   they won't work.

(157) ʌhuthwatsiluˑníˑ   oniʔ, yah kwíˑ náhteʔ thaʔtehotitíhʌ nʌ   seʔ,
        They will make a family too,   not   anything they don't care then too,

kwáh tsiʔ nikú sʌ́haʔ lotiwilakáˑteʔ   sʌ́haʔ kwíˑ eˑsóˑ ohwístaʔ
however many   more   they have a lot of children more   a lot   money

wahotiyʌˑtáˑneʔ. (158) Nók tsiʔ kaʔikʌ́ tshiwahuˑníseʔ yah néˑ thyaˑyaˑwʌ́ˑneʔ tsiʔ
they received.   But   this   a long time ago   it has to be   that

wahutataskénhaʔ.   (159) Ok oniʔ wahuˑníseʔ   táˑt yah thaˑhsatawyaʔtáˑnaʔ,
they applied themselves.   And also a long time ago if   not   you won't go to school,

nʌ kiʔ ok néˑ kanuhsoteʔkóˑ   yʌyesatʌ́nyehteʔ.
right then it's boarding school one will send you.

    (160) Néˑ sʌ́ˑ thikʌ́ tshikeksáˑ,   wéˑni   tsiʔ aˑkíˑluʔ kátshaʔ ok núˑ
            It's   also that   when I was a child, evidently that   I'd say   somewhere

tsyaˑták tshyaʔteswahsʌnʌ́ tshaʔtewakohsliyáˑku,   náhteʔ akwáh luwaˑyáts,
seven   and a half   when I have crossed over winters, what   exactly is his name,

Etwet Khaníles   uhte iˑkélheʔ luwaˑyátskweʔ, néˑ tho lotlihuˑtáhkweʔ   thikʌ́,
Edward Cornelius I think   was his name,   it's thus he had an occupation that,

úhkaʔ yah thaˑyutawyaʔtáˑnaʔ,   táˑthuniʔ aʔnyóh waháttokeʔ yah thaˑyekweˑníˑ
anyone not   one won't go to school, or else   seems   he noticed   not   one is not able

taˑyutwiláshniʔ,   ʌshakotiwilákhwaʔ   kiʔ   kanuhsoteʔkóˑ
that one looks after a child, they will take a child away from one actually boarding school

I'd say they're just handing them the money. (155) That's the reason they are so lazy nowadays. (156) Because it's possible for them not to work. (157) They will have a family even, they don't care about anything, the more children they have the more money they will get. (158) But a long time ago they had to do for themselves. (159) And another thing, a long time ago if you didn't go to school, right away you would be sent to boarding school.

(160) Also when I was a child, I must have been about seven and a half years old, what the heck was his name, Edward Cornelius was his name I think, that was his job, anyone wouldn't go to school, or it seems he noticed someone wasn't able to look after their child, their child would be taken away from them and

yʌshakonatkʌ́·lah<u>te?</u>.

they will take and leave one there.

(161) Né· niwakya?tawʌ́·u,   aknulhá· s

It's   it has happened to me,   my mother

yakoyo·té·   thikʌ́ factory.

she is working that   factory.

(162) Kwáh s luwatiya?titályuhe? ki?wáh, yah ki?

Just   they give them rides   right,   not   actually

te?wakanúhte? úhka? kʌs náhte? washakotiya?títane?, nók tsi? wa?uhtʌ·tí· s

I don't know   who habitually   they gave her a ride,   but   she went away

kwáh tsi? nikú astéhtsi?, kwáh s nók sayúhke<u>te?</u>.

however many   morning,   just   she came back.

(163) Tahnú· yako·yʌ́· s kwí·

And   she has

uhka? náhte? a·yukwatʌ?nikú·lalʌ?   akokstʌ·<u>ha</u>.

anyone   that one watches over me   old lady.

(164) Tahnú· yah né·

And   not   it's

te?tyukwatewyʌ?tu·<u>ní</u>.

she didn't do right by me.

(165) Í·   né· wa?ukwatenha?tslunyʌ́ni?,   shekú n

Me   it's   she made me a hired person,   even

waknu?tatáhkwʌ tahnú· yah né· nuwʌtú te?waknu?tatáhkwʌ.

I have milked   and   not   it's   never   I have not milked.

(166) Tahnú· wí·

And

kohsla?ké·ne kwí· ka?ikʌ́ kʌ? kwí· niwʌhnislé<u>sha</u>.

wintertime   this   the day is short.

(167) Yakonehlákwas se? s

She is surprised   too

yakʌ?   thikʌ́ aknulhá· tsi? onú·ta? kok nikú   ítkale? wí·,

reportedly that   my mother that   milk   only a small amount it is in it,

yakotnu?tatewyʌ́·tu kwí· a?nyóh né· ka?ikʌ́ akokstʌ·<u>ha</u>.

she has put milk away   seems   it's   this   old lady.

(168) Né· tsi?   í·   se?

Because me   too

né· wa?knu?tatáhko? tsi? nikú ʌkkwe·<u>ní</u>.

it's   I milked   how much I will be able.

(169) Khále? tsi? náhe? yah né·

And   during   not   it's

nuwʌtú tha·yuthu·táte? í·   a·kétsyʌhte?   tsi? kahne·kó·, né· tsi? né· ki?

never   she won't allow it me   for me to get water at   well,   because   it's   actually

he or she would be taken and left at boarding school. (161) It happened to me, my mother was working at a factory. (162) They used to give them rides, right, I don't know who gave her a ride, but she went away every morning, and she just came back. (163) And she used to have some old lady look after me. (164) And she didn't do right by me. (165) She had me do menial work, even milk [the cow] and I had never milked. (166) And it was wintertime, so the days were short. (167) My mother was surprised there was so little milk in [the container], seems the old lady had been saving the milk. (168) Because I was the one that milked, as much as I could. (169) And all this time she [my mother] would never let ME get water at the well, because

ok kwí· ʌwa·tú· kaná·tsiʔ ʌ·kátsteʔ ya·kétsyʌhte̱ʔ.   (170) Tá·t núwaʔ
has to be   bucket   I will use for me to get water over there.   Maybe

tho yʌkyá·tʌne̱ʔ.   (171) Né· oniʔ né· thikʎ í·,   yah thya·ya·wʎ·neʔ tsiʔ í·
there I will fall that way.   It's too it's that   me, it has to be   that me

waʔketsyʎ·naʔ, yah seʔ náhteʔ tha·yútyeleʔ yukeʔnikú·la̱le̱ʔ.   (172) Tho
I got water,   not too anything she won't do she is watching over me.   There

katiʔ wí· thikʎ yaʔkáheweʔ   thikʎ nʌ   yawʌtatokʎhtu, tho   wahoké·tohteʔ
well then that   there came a time that   then Sunday,   there he showed up

thikʎ Edwet.   (173) Wahʎ·luʔ "né· seʔ katkʌʔsé·neʔ   náhteʔ ni·yót   tsiʔ
that   Edward.   He said   "it's too I've come to see what   the way it is that

tehsatwiláshnyeheʔ   né· kaʔikʎ yeksáh." (174) Waʔuthlo·lí· kwí· tsiʔ
you are caring for a child it's this   girl."   She told   that

yakoyo·té·   tahnú· yako·yʎ· kiʔ   úhkaʔ a·yukeʔnikú·lalakeʔ.
she is working and   she has actually anyone one should be watching over me.

(175) Wahʎ·luʔ "yah kiʔ   tha·kakwe·ní· thi·kʎ." (176) Lawelú·neʔ
       He said   "not actually it won't be able that."   He wanted

a·shakowilákhwaʔ   aʔé·   kanuhsoteʔkó· yʌyukwatkʎ·lahte̱ʔ.
that he takes a child away from her   far away boarding school they will leave me over there.

(177) Né· kiʔ ok wí· né· thikʎ tahnú· nʌ   u·tú·   waʔkhehlo·lí· tsiʔ
       So it's just   it's that   and   then it could be I told her   how

niyukwatenhaʔtslunyʌ·níheʔ   neʔ kʎh. (178) Nʌ sók waʔí·luʔ
she makes me work as a hired person   is it.   Then too she said

"yʌkuyaʔtáhaweʔ kiʔ   nʌ   ʌwakyoʔtʎhsaʔ." (179) Neʔ thó·neʔ katiʔ wí·
"I will take you   actually when I will go to work."   At that time well

I had to use a bucket to get water. (170) Maybe I'd fall in. (171) So it was ME too, I had to
get water, she wouldn't do anything, the one who was watching me. (172) Well the time
came that one Sunday, Edward showed up. (173) He said "I've come to see how you are
looking after this little girl." (174) She told about how she was working and she had someone looking after me. (175) He said "that won't do." (176) He wanted to take her child
away from her and I would be left far away at boarding school. (177) And finally that was
when I could tell her all the menial work she had me do, eh. (178) Then she said "I will take
you when I go to work."

tyotáhsawʌʔ yah nuwʌtú teʔskí·tluʔ, tyótkut tsiʔ yaʔutwiláhaweʔ
it has started not never I don't stay home anymore, always that she took a child

nʌ waʔakoyoʔtʌ́hsaʔ. (180) Né· tsiʔ lʌ·nélheʔ a·shakotiwilákhwa
when she went to work. Because they want that they take a child from her

khále? kʌh nukwá· tayukkʌhlaʔslu·ní· né·n akokstʌ·<u>ha</u>. (181) Tho né· thikʌ́
and over here she mistreated me it's that old lady. There it's that

waʔkkwe·ní· waʔtkahyakʌ·séleʔ, tomatoes kʌs tehuhyakʌ́slus. (182) Kwáh s
I was able I peeled fruit, tomatoes habitually they peel fruit. Just

kanutó·tslayʌʔ, tho waʔtyuktʌ́steʔ nʌ ní· u·tú· waʔtkahyakʌ·sé<u>le</u>ʔ.
there is a box, there they stood me up then me it could be I peeled fruit.

(183) Neʔ thó·neʔ thikʌ́ tyotyelʌ́htu waʔtkatʌ́·tshaneʔ, kwáh tyoteylʌ́htu
At that time that first I earned, quite first

ukwatkályaʔkseʔ ókhnaʔ St. Thomas waʔáknehteʔ waʔkatʌ́nhaneʔ
I got paid and then St. Thomas we two went there I hired

waʔtyuknúhklis<u>te</u>ʔ. (184) Né· ní· thikʌ́ tyotyelʌ́htu teyuknuhklístu
one curled my hair. It's me that first one has curled my hair

thikʌ́ í· waʔkkályah<u>ke</u>ʔ. (185) Tomatoes waʔtkahyakʌ·sé<u>le</u>ʔ. (186) *Tó·*
that me I paid. Tomatoes I peeled. *How*

tshaʔtesohsliyá·ku. (187) Tsya·ták tshyaʔteswahsʌ·n<u>ʌ́</u>. (188) Né· katiʔ wí· thikʌ́
old were you? Seven and a half. Well then it's that

e·só· tsyoʔk náhteʔ waʔuknitʌ́htaneʔ, nók tsiʔ kʌh waʔkáheweʔ yah kiʔ
lots different things we two were poor, but over here the time came not actually

né· úhkaʔ thutahʌnéhtahkweʔ a·shehlo·<u>lí·</u>. (189) Né· tsiʔ náhteʔ
it's anyone they just won't believe it for you to tell them. Because anything

(179) Starting at that time I never stayed home again, she always took [me] when she went to work. (180) Because they wanted to take her child from her and over here the old lady was mistreating me. (181) There I was able to peel fruit, they were peeling tomatoes. (182) There was a box, they stood me up on that and then I could peel fruit. (183) Back then was the first time I earned money, the very first time I got paid and then we [my mother and I] went to St. Thomas and I got someone to give me a perm. (184) It was the first time I got a perm and I paid for it. (185) I peeled tomatoes. (186) *How old were you?* (187) Seven and a half. (188) Well we were poor in a lot of different ways, but to this day no one will believe it were you to tell them. (189) Because [they would say] whatever

ka·té·   kwah nók tsiʔ yakʌʔshúha.   (190) Kwáh ok né· thiyutkalunyányuheʔ.
I am saying just   that fiction.   Just   it's she is just making stories.

(191) Yah tú·skeʔ té·kʌ.
         Not   truly   it is not.

  (192) Né· s katiʔ wí· ní· a·kí·luʔ lonatlaʔswiyó núwaʔ   latiksaʔshúha nʌʔú·waʔ.
         Well then it's   me   I'd say   they are lucky   this time children   now.

(193) Tsiʔ niyo·lé·   naʔtekyattíhʌ tsyoʔk náhteʔ, yah teʔwʌto·lé·; tsiʔ
         To such extent it is different   everything,   not   it is not hard; how

a·hʌnúnhekeʔ.   (194) Kháleʔ wá·tluʔ tshaʔtewakohsliyá·ku   tshututye·lʌ́·teʔ,
for them to live.   And   nine   when I have crossed over winters   when it was first,

né· né·n   yukuhwatʌ́ha né· waʔukénhaneʔ aknulhá· kwí· sʌ́h. (195) Tho
it's it's that my aunt   it's she hired me   my mother   also.   There

waʔáknehteʔ   oyú·kwaʔ wahotiyo·tʌ́·.   (196) Tekhenlahta·wíheʔ nʌʔ né·.
we two went there   tobacco   they worked.   I hand leaves to her is what.

(197) Skahwístat ok   kayé sílu   ukwatkályaʔkseʔ swʌhníslat.   (198) Tahnú·
         One dollar   and   twenty-five cents I got paid   one day.   And

e·só· kwí· né· thikʌ́ tsiʔ wakanúhteʔ.   (199) Wá·tluʔ tshaʔtewakohsliyá·ku
a lot   it's that   I think.   Nine   when I have crossed over winters

tutáhsawʌ́ʔ. (200) Tahnú· kʌs   núwaʔ   aknulhá· kyuhte wí· a·kí·luʔ
it started.   And   habitually this time my mother supposedly I'd say

wʌtoláti?   kyuhte wí· né· tsiʔ yukyatatʌlʌ́ wí· né· yakotataskénhʌ kwí·
it is going along hard   supposedly because we two are left   it's she is trying her best

né· a·yaknúnhekeʔ;   yutunyányuheʔ.   (201) Lakuhwatʌ́ha tsiʔ ka·yʌ́· Detroit
it's   that we two survive; she is making things.   My uncle   the one that Detroit

I'm saying is just fiction. (190) She's just making up stories. (191) It's not true.
   (192) Well then I'd say the children are lucky nowadays. (193) How different everything
is, it's not hard; for them to live. (194) And I was nine years old when it was the first time,
my aunt hired me, my mother also. (195) The two of us went there [where] they were working in tobacco. (196) I was handing leaves to her, is what. (197) I got paid one dollar and
fifty cents a day. (198) And I thought it was a lot. (199) I was nine years old was when it
started. (200) And I guess for my mother it was hard, I'd say, because she and I were left
and she was trying her best for us two to survive, making things. (201) My uncle, the one

thatinákle? s Rol.   (202) Nʌ s né· thikʌ́ washukníkwahte? kohsla?ké·ne nukwá·
they reside   Rol.   Then it's that   he invited us two   wintertime   direction

sʌ́· yotká·te?, ne·né· lahninúhahkwe? tsi? wakatslu·ní; kohsla?kékha?
also often,   it's that he used to buy it   how I am dressed; winter kind

a·katslúnyah<u>te</u>?.   (203) Nʌ oni? Christmas ya?káhewe? tho nukwá·
for me to put on clothes.   Then too Christmas the time came that's where

nyeyáknehse?,   nʌ wahʌ́·lu? "ʌhetshlolyá·na?   kati? kʌ   Santa Claus
we two are over there, then he said   "you will go and tell him then   question Santa Claus

náhte? ʌthyahawíhtʌ?."   (204) "Wé·ni ki?wáh." (205) Nʌ kwí· né· kanatá·ke
what   he will bring for you."   "I suppose."   So then it's uptown

wa?ukya?taha·wíh<u>te</u>?. (206) Tahnu· kwáh olihwiyó tsi? áhsʌ né· nikú
they took me along.   And   just   a sure thing that three it's how many

tsi? nú· ya?káhkete?   tho thʌtskwáhele? Santa Claus. (207) Nʌ kwí· né·
where   I went up to there there he is perching Santa Claus.   So then it's

thusayákwawe? onʌ́, "wahsla·kó· kʌ́h,"   wa?kí·lu? "ʌ́·ʌ". (208) Nók tsi?
we just got back now, "you chose it question," I said   "yes."   But

wahʌ́·lu?, "yah kwí· né· thau·tú· utahatáwyahte? Santa Claus, yah náhte?
he said,   "not   it's it can't be that he comes in Santa Claus,   not   anything

tha·hya·<u>yú</u>·."   (209) Wa?kí·lu? "tó·   né· nʌyesʌ?tanuwʌhsláli?
he won't give it to you."   I said   "oh sure it's how they will beat you up

áhsʌ se? nihatí   wa?khehlo·<u>lí</u>·." (210) "Isé· né· ʌyesʌ?tanuwʌhsláli?,
three too how many they are I told them."   "You   it's they will beat you up,

áhsʌ se? né· nihatí   tahʌ·<u>né</u>·."   (211) Né·n   tú·ske? astéhtsi?
three too it's how many they are they are coming."   It's that truly   in the morning

[where] they lived in Detroit, Rol. (202) He used to invite us in the wintertime often [to stay], he used to buy my clothes; winter things for me to wear. (203) Then at Christmas time that's where we were, then he said "are you going to tell Santa Claus then what he should bring you?" (204) "I suppose." (205) So then they took me uptown. (206) And sure enough there were three places where I went and there was a Santa Claus sitting there [in each place]. (207) So then we got back home, "did you choose?" I said "yes." (208) But he said, "Santa Claus can't come in, he won't give you anything." (209) I said "oh sure, you will get beat up [because] I told three of them." (210) "You will get beat up, there's three of them coming." (211) So in the morning

waʔkatkétskoʔ, buggy né· tho kaʔsléhtayʌʔ kwahotokʌ́·u tsiʔ o·kwíleʔ náhteʔ
I got up, buggy it's there there is a vehicle just for real that sapling what

yunyá·tu. (212) A·kí·luʔ núwaʔ yah kiʔ núwaʔ tehoti·yʌ́· thikʌ́
it is made with. I'd say this time not actually this time they don't have it that

tho ni·yót. (213) Buggy o·kwíleʔ náhteʔ yunyá·tu khále? kayaʔtuní tho
thus how it is. Buggy sapling what it is made with and doll there

kayá·tit kakwa·nʌ́. (214) Onístaʔ uhte wí· né· a·kí·luʔ tsiʔ naʔkatshanu·ní·
it is inside it is big. Gee supposedly it's I'd say how I became happy

niyoyánleʔ ukyʌ·tá·neʔ. (215) "Né· thika·té·, isé· seʔ né·
it is so nice I received it. "It's just as I'm saying, you too it's

ʌyesʌʔtanuwʌhsláliʔ tá·t yah tha·hsathu·táteʔ utahutáwyahteʔ." (216) Kwáh
they will beat you up if not you won't allow that they come in." Just

waʔkí·luʔ yutolishʌtákhwaʔ tho ka·yʌ́· tho né· nú· nʌhanú·weteʔ kanyó· ok
I said couch there it is that's it's where he will sleep so long as

tákʌʔ utahatáwyaht Santa Claus.
so as not he shouldn't come in Santa Claus.

(217) Né· katiʔ wí· thikʌ́ tho ni·yót tsiʔ waʔtyakyatukohtániʔ, e·só·
Well then it's that that's the way it is that we two passed through, lots

tsyoʔk náhteʔ yah teʔyaʔwéskwaht. (218) Kháleʔ útlatsteʔ né· sʌ́·
different things not it is not pleasant. And it happened it's also

waʔewyʌtéhtaneʔ thikʌ́ ono·lá· wí· a·yutu·ní·. (219) Tahnú· nʌ yah
she learned that corn husk mat that she makes. And then not

teʔtsyukniʔsléhtayʌʔ. (220) Nok u·tú· waté·slehseʔ waʔetáliʔ thikʌ́,
we two do not have a car anymore. It has to be sleigh she put them in that,

I got up, there was a buggy made out of wicker. (212) I'd say nowadays they don't have anything like that. (213) The buggy was made out of wicker and there was a big doll in there. (214) Gee I'd say I was so happy, it was really nice what I got. (215) "Like I'm saying, they would beat you up if you wouldn't let them come in." (216) I said there was a couch there and that's where he would sleep so as not to let Santa Claus come in.

(217) Well then that's the way it was that we went through things, lots of different things that were not pleasant. (218) And [one] time too she [my mother] learned to make corn husk mats [rugs]. (219) And we didn't have a car anymore then. (220) She had to put them in a sleigh,

kanutó·tslaku wa?etáli?, kwáh kwí· wa?e·ná·_ne_?. (221) Thiká Shedden nukwá·
in a box   she put them in, just she filled it.   That   Shedden   where

nyeyothahinú   e·só· ʌhsatkátho? yonutahalolʌ́htu. (222) Nʌ kati? wí· tahnú·
the road leads that way lots you will see it is hilly.   Well then   and

yowisakwʌhtálhu. (223) Né· tho né· wa?ako?nya·kʌ́·se? thiká waté·slehse?,
it is covered with ice.   It's there it's it fled from her   that   sleigh,

tahnú· tho kya?titák_he_?. (224) Ukwate?slehtakalhátho? khále? thiká
and   there I was riding in it.   I got turned over in the vehicle and   that

ono·lá·,   kwáh tsyo?k nya?kutitakhenúti_?_. (225) Tó·k wí· né· náhe?
corn husk mat, all over they went running off.   Some   it's while

tho   tyakyaté·slehse?   yaknistelísta?   sʌ́· tsi? niyo·lé· nʌ
there we two are crawling around we two are laughing also until   then

tho   sayuthle?nu·ní·. (226) Nʌ kyale? wí· yukyatukóh_tu_.
there she packed up again.   Then again   we two have gone on.

(227) Ya?áknewe?   tahnú· s né· thiká yukhiyʌte·lí·se? né· onʌ́ tsi?
     We two got over there and   it's that   they know us   it's now that

akaulha?tsíwa?, uknulha?tsíwa?   wáh. (228) Tahnú· wí· nʌ   tshihawʌheyú wí·
she is by herself, we two are by ourselves right.   And   then when he has died

lake?ní_ha_. (229) Yukhiyʌte·lí·se?, né· a·lé· s   yukhiyatʌna?tslunyʌ·níhe?
my father.   They know us,   it's at times they make lunch for us

tho   tutayakníhawe?.   (230) Khále? tsyo?k sʌ́· náhte?   a·lé·
there we two brought it back.   And   also all kinds of things at times

atʌná·tsli? wa?tyuta·tú· khále? ohwísta? sʌ́·, yah kwí· te?wé·ni né· núwa?
groceries   she traded   and   money   also, it's incredible   it's this time

she put them in a box, and she filled it up. (221) That road that goes to Shedden, you'll see a lot of hills. (222) And it was all icy. (223) The sleigh got away on her there, and I was riding in it. (224) The sleigh turned over with me in it and the husk mats went running off [scattered] all over. (225) We were there for some while crawling around and laughing too until she packed up again. (226) Then we went on. (227) We got there and they knew us, that now she was all by herself, we two were by ourselves right. (228) And my father had already died. (229) They knew us, and sometimes they had lunch made for us and we brought it back. (230) And she traded for all kinds of things, groceries sometimes and money also,

tutakanahnuhátiʔ   nʌ   tutayakyahtʌ·tíˑ.   (231) Yah kwíˑ teʔwé·ni tsiʔ
it is going along full again   when   we two left to come home.   It's incredible   how

naʔtetsyuknilihwahkwʌhátiʔ   thikʌ́ tutayakyahtʌ·tíˑ   tsiʔ
we two are going along singing again   that   we two left to come home   how

nitsyuknikhwakaʔtátiʔ.   (232) Né· thikʌ́ tho   ni·yót   a·kí·luʔ
we two have a lot of food again going along.   It's   that   that's   how it is   I'd say

every weekend kháleʔ sayuthleʔnu·níˑ   sayakyahtʌ·tíˑ,   yah s kwíˑ
every weekend   and   she packed up again   we two went away again,   not

teʔwakanúhteʔ náhteʔ naʔe·yéleʔ, nók tsiʔ kháleʔ s kyáleʔ wíˑ onʌ́
I don't know   what   she did it,   but   and   so again   then

sayakoʔslehtayʌ·tá·neʔ.   (233) Nók tsiʔ wʌtolátyeʔ s   kih.
she obtained a vehicle again.   But   it is hard going along   actually.

   (234) Kháleʔ onʌ́, nʌ   tshaʔthyátlaneʔ Lasales. (235) Ne·né· lauʔwéskwaniheʔ
             And   then,   then   when the two met Lazarus.   It's   he enjoys

latiyʌtákwas. (236) Tehonityohkwʌtátyehseʔ.   (237) Tsyoʔk úhkaʔ
they cut wood.   They are a gang going around.   All kinds of people

luwatinhá·u,   lutʌnoʔsʌ́ha   akaulhá· nukwá· kháleʔ laulhá· nukwá·
they have hired them,   they are siblings   her   direction and   him   direction

Victor kwíˑ nʌʔ né·, kháleʔ Dan. (238) Kháleʔ nʌ   ʌyóhslateʔ,   ne·né·
Victor   that's it,   and   Dan.   And   when   it will become winter,   it's that

onʌ́ n kwah nók a·lé·   sayakwáhketeʔ ya·wét tsiʔ nú· nikaha·wíˑ tehutkʌ́nyehseʔ
then   just   at times   we went back   like   where   such time   they compete

Ukwehuwé·ne. (239) Kwah nók nʌ   ʌwatu·kó·teʔ thikʌ́ ókhnaʔ kalhakú   núwaʔ
on the Reserve.   Just as soon as   it will pass   that   and then   in the bush   this time

it [the sleigh] would be really filled up again when we left to come home. (231) We were
singing away as we were on our way home because we had so much food with us.
(232) That's how it was, I'd say, every weekend, she packed up and we went away, I don't
know how she did it, but finally we got another car. (233) But it was hard times.

   (234) And then, then she met Lazarus. (235) He enjoyed cutting wood with them.
(236) He was going all around with a gang [of workers]. (237) All kinds of people hired
them, her brothers from her side [her family] and from his side there was only Victor, and
Dan. (238) And when it got to be winter, that's when we went back, kind of around the time
of the fair on the Reserve. (239) As soon as it [the fair] was over, then it's into the bush,

nukwá·, tho   núwa?   nukwá· sayakyohsli·yá·ke?.   (240) Nʌ   né· thikʌ́
where,   that's this time   where   we spent the winter again.   Then   it's   that

aknulhá·   sʌ́·   wa?eyʌ·táko?   wa?thniye·ná·,   khále?   yuta?ahslu·níhe?   sʌ́h.
my mother   also   she cut wood   the two joined forces,   and   she makes baskets   also.

(241) Tahnú· wa?thuwatikhwáshni?   onʌ́,   khekhunyʌ·níhe? s   ni?í·.
       And   she took them in as boarders   then,   I cook for them   as for me.

(242) Tahnú· s   wa?kí·lu?   ne? thó·ne? tékni ok sílu   taha·kú·   shayá·tat
       And   I said   at that time   only twenty-five cents   he gave it to me   one man

thikʌ́   weekend.   (243) Né·n   yah ki? te?wé·ni   niwakhwistaká·te?
that   weekend.   It's that   it's incredible actually   how I have a lot of money

tsi? wakanúhte?   thikʌ́ tóhka? wí· niha·<u>tí</u>.   (244) Núwa?   a·kí·lu?
I think   that   a few   how many they are.   This time   I'd say

tékni sílu   aesahwistayʌ·tá·ne?,   kwahotokʌ́·u tsi? yah thau·tú· náhte?
twenty-five cents   you should obtain money,   just for real   that   it can't be   anything

a·shni·<u>nú</u>.   (245) Shekú n stamp yah thau·tú· a·shni·<u>nú</u>.   (246) Tsi? niyo·lé·
that you buy.   Even   stamp   it can't be   that you buy.   To what extent

na?tekyattíhʌ nikano·lú·se?   tsyo?k náhohte?.   (247) Ya?wéskwa?t kati? wí· núwa?.
it is different   it is so expensive   everything.   It is nice   well then   now.

    (248) Há·   tho nú·   na?teyukyatlá·u Clifford. (249) Dorchester
           Oh yeah   that's where   we two have met   Clifford.   Dorchester

nú·   yehatiyʌtákwas   tho   yahoké·tohte?,   tahatáwyahte?
where   they are cutting wood over there   there   he showed up over there,   he came in

kwah óksa? ya?katkátho?   nihahnʌ·yés. (250) Tahnú· wa?káttoke? tsi?   ati
instantly   I looked that way   he is so tall.   And   I noticed   that   no matter

that's where we spent the winter. (240) My mother cut wood also working side-by-side with him, and she was making baskets also. (241) And she took in boarders then, I was the one cooking for them. (242) And I said at that time a man would give me only twenty-five cents at the end of the week. (243) So I thought I had really a lot of money with a few of them [paying me]. (244) Nowadays, I'd say if you get twenty-five cents, you really can't buy anything. (245) You can't even buy a stamp. (246) It's so different, everything is so expensive. (247) It's nice nowadays.

(248) Oh yeah, that's where I met Clifford. (249) They were cutting wood over in Dorchester and he showed up there, he came in and instantly I looked over that way, he was so tall. (250) And I could tell that

náhte?   a·hakwe·ní·   a·hoyo·t\A·.   (251) Ati tsi?   wa?káttoke? tsi? yah
anything he would be able   that he works.   Even though I noticed   that not

tehahyatuhslay\Ate·lí. (252) Tahnú· né· a·kí·lu? kyuhte wí· lu·té·   se? e·só·
he is not educated.   And   it's I'd say   supposedly they say too a lot

wa?thatkahtúni? wí· oyá·shu?, tahnú· né· oni? ní· tho   ni·yót, a·kí·lu?
he looked around at   others,   and   it's too   me   that's how it is, I'd say

uknik\Ahtl\A?tslay\A·tá·ne? k\As   khále? aknulhá·   thok náhte? wahuw\Áhahse?,
I got a boyfriend   usually and   my mother something   she belittled him,

"yah né· thaesakálya?kse? thi·k\A."   (253) "Yah né· thaesakálya?kse? thi·k\A."
"not it's it won't pay you   that."   "Not it's it won't pay you   that."

(254) Oyá·   n\A ki? ok ale? né· tsha?olí·wat.   (255) Yah kwí· kátsha?
       Another just again   it's it is the same thing.   Not   anywhere

thutayako?nikuhli·yó·ne?.   (256) N\A kati? wí· wá·kelhe?, "n\A   ki?   yah isé·
she could not find satisfaction.   Well then   I thought,   "now actually not   you

thutahsanúhtu?."   (257) Tahnú· kwáh s a?nyóh né· thihlukwe?ti·yó.
you won't have your way."   And   seems like   it's he is just a nice person.

(258) Tho kwí· ni·yót thik\A lo?níha   loha·wí·   ka?ik\A tho
       Thus   it is so that   his father he is bringing him this   there

tshá·newe?.   (259) Kwáh tshutye·l\Á·te? latiy\Atakó·ne?   kwí· n\A? né·.
when the two arrived.   Just   when it is first they are here to cut wood that's what.

(260) Né· wa?tekhekhwáshni?,   n\A ki? ok k\As kwí· wakekhu·ní. (261) Né·
       It's I looked after them with food, so right then   I am cooking.   It's

thik\A wakekhuní n\A   tutahutawya?táni?,   lo?níha   wah\Á·lu?, "kwa?nyóh ale?
that   I am cooking when they all came in again, his father he said,   "seems like   again

he would be able to work at anything. (251) Even though I noticed that he wasn't educated.
(252) And I'd say I guess they said he looked at a lot of others, and it was like that with me
too, I would get a boyfriend and my mother would say something to put him down, "[he]
won't do for you." (253) "[He] won't do for you." (254) And the next time, right away
again it would be the same thing. (255) There was no satisfying her. (256) Well then I
thought, "you are not going to have your way." (257) And he seemed kind of nice.
(258) The way it was, his father brought him and the two of them got there. (259) When
they came to cut wood the first time, that's what. (260) I was looking after the boarders, so
then I was cooking. (261) I was cooking when they came back in, his father said,

kakhwi·yó.”   (262) “Kwaʔnyóh   úhkaʔ ok náhteʔ   ʌhotlaʔswi·yósteʔ   kaʔikʌ́
it is good food.”   “Seems like   someone   he will become lucky   this

niyekhwayʌ́hu.”   (263) Yah kwí· náhteʔ   teʔwakʌ́   kháleʔ   kwah nók
she is such a good cook.”   Not   anything   I didn't say   and   just

thakwatkáthos   neʔ kʌ́h. (264) Né· s kwí· né·n   waʔó·kalaweʔ nʌ kiʔ ok aleʔ wí·
he is looking at me   is it.   So it's   it's that it got dark   so just again

né· sʌ́· tho   loyo·té·   thikʌ́ nikʌ́·,   náhteʔ akwáh luwa·yáts,   Kastes Bret
it's   also there he is working   that   let's see, what   exactly is his name,   Kastes Bread

kʌs   sʌ́· tho   loyo·té·   kháleʔ Santi Brown, nʌ   waʔó·kalaweʔ kháleʔ
habitually   also there he is working   and   Sandy Brown, then   it got dark   and

waʔakwatyʌ·tú·   waʔtyakwahyatúhslayʌ́ʔ.   (265) Kwáh s tsiʔ niyo·lé·   waʔukwano·lú·seʔ
we sat around   we played cards.   Just   until   we got tired of it

nʌ kyaleʔ wí· waʔukwʌtá·whaʔ? né· wí· thikʌ́ tekanaktanetáliʔ   kiʔ wí· thikʌ́
so again   we went to bed   it's   that   one bed on top of another actually that

tsiʔ yakwanuhwétstaʔ.   (266) Tahnú· s sʌ́·   oyá·   sʌ́·   wakatʌló·slayʌʔ, yah
at   where we go to sleep.   And   also another also I have a friend,   not

teʔwakanúhteʔ náhteʔ nʌya·wʌ́·neʔ kaʔikʌ́ nók tsiʔ yah ki̱ʔ   né· tha·hiná·tuʔ
I don't know   what   will happen   this   but   not actually it's I won't name him

úhkaʔ, só·tsiʔ   yehya·túheʔ kaʔi·kʌ́. (267) Tahnú· kaʔikʌ́ Christmas concert
who,   too much she is writing this.   And   this   Christmas concert

shakotí·skoʔs, wakanúhteʔ tsiʔ tetsyalú tho   yʌhné·sheke̱ʔ.
Baptists,   I know   that both   there   the two will be over there.

(268) Yah teʔwakanúhteʔ náhteʔ nʌya·wʌ́·neʔ, nʌ sok wí· kwáh ok
       Not   I don't know   what   will happen,   so then too just

“what good food.” (262) “Seems like some man is going to be lucky, she is such a good
cook.” (263) I didn't say anything and he was just looking at me, eh. (264) So it got dark
and just then he was also working there, let's see, what the heck was his name, Kastes Bread
was working there and Sandy Brown, it got dark and we sat around and we played cards.
(265) Until we got tired and then we went to sleep, there were bunk beds where we slept.
(266) And also I had another friend, I didn't know what would happen but I won't name
who, because she is recording this. (267) And there was this Baptist Christmas concert, I
knew that they both would be there. (268) I didn't know what would happen, so then

thutakaté·ko?.   (269) A·kí·lu? tsyóhslat tsi? náhe? kwah nók tsi?
just I took off from there.   I'd say   one year   while   just   that

ukyatʌ·ló·   thikʌ́ yáknehse? kwí·   núwa?   wa?tyokʌnhu·tí·   khále?
we two friends   that   we two are going around this time   it became summer   and

St. Thomas sʌ́·   yehoyo·té·,   nʌ kwí· wa?akyatahsatalá·na?   sʌ́·,
St. Thomas   also   he is working over there,   so then   we two are on our way to a show also,

khále? tho   sʌ́·   wahoké·tohte?, tahnú· wa?í·lu? aknulhá·   "tá·t" wa?í·lu?
and   there also   he showed up,   and   she said   my mother "if"   she said

"ìhsélhe? lukwé   aesatʌlo?slayʌ·ták   yah té·kelhe?   kwah nók oskánhe
"you want   a man   that you should have a friend   not   I don't want   just   together

aesné·sheke?,   kwahotokʌ́·u snínyak."   (270) Wa?ukhiyatʌ?nyóthahse?
that you two are going,   just for real   you two marry."   She put on a ceremony for us

ati? wí· né· thi·kʌ́. (271) Yukyatʌ?nyo·táhkwe? ní· tehútkwahkwe?   sʌ́h.
anyway   it's that.   We two had a ceremony   us   they were dancing   also.

I just took off from there. (269) I'd say for one year we were friends going together and
then it was getting summer and he was working in St. Thomas, so then we [my mother and
I] were on our way to a show, and he showed up there also, and my mother said, "if" she
said "you want to have a man friend I don't want the two of you just going together, get
married." (270) She made a big do for us anyway. (271) The two of us had a ceremony and
there was dancing also.

PART III: GRAMMAR

1. Introduction

This part of the volume describes constructions that commonly occur in the stories. Several publications, as well as recent language classes, have concentrated on the structure of *words* and teaching students how to build words. Just as there is structure within words, there are patterns or constructions that involve combining words with other words. Texts, such as the ones here, naturally expose students of the language to the structure of *phrases* and *utterances*, and hopefully lead to a greater understanding about this aspect of the language. The basic word structure of Oneida will be described in section 2 and elsewhere where relevant, but we will assume that students of the language already have explored or soon will explore other sources too: the groundbreaking description of the Oneida verb by Lounsbury (1953), the online teaching grammar by Abbott (2006) (which mentions some phrasal constructions as well), or the monographs by Abbott (2000) and Michelson and Price (2011). In addition, much can be learned about the structure of words from consulting the dictionaries of Abbott, Christjohn, and Hinton (1996) or Michelson and Doxtator (2002). This overview, then, aims to say something more about how the words in these stories occur in larger structures in order to allow the expression of ideas and thoughts that typically are expressed by combining words into syntactic constructions and discourse patterns.

2. Word Structure

2.1 Verbs

Anyone who has had any experience with Iroquoian languages knows that verbs have a complex structure. And, although verbs have the expected function of describing events and states, they are also used in the expression of property concepts (expressed by adjectives in languages like English), in the expression of kinship terms, and as expressions that refer to objects or *entities*. The basic structure of the verb is as in (2.1).

(2.1)   prepronominal prefix—pronominal prefix—base—aspect endings

The *base* is the core of the verb and it can be internally complex, consisting of a *root* plus *prefixes* (REFLEXIVE or SEMI-REFLEXIVE) and/or *suffixes* (BENEFACTIVE, CAUSATIVE, DISLO-CATIVE, DISTRIBUTIVE, INCHOATIVE, INSTRUMENTAL, PROGRESSIVE, REVERSATIVE), and/or an INCORPORATED NOUN. The base is sometimes called *stem*, but note that the term *stem* is used also for the base plus one of the aspect endings described directly below. When a base is structurally complex, its composition is given in Oneida dictionaries.

The description of the other parts of the verb begins here from the end of the verb, with the aspect endings. This is because to some extent the choice of pronominal and prepronominal prefixes depends on which aspect ending occurs with a verb base. From a paradigmatic perspective verb bases belong to one of two basic classes: those that can occur in the three aspectual categories—HABITUAL, STATIVE, and PUNCTUAL—plus an IMPERATIVE form, and those that occur only in the STATIVE aspect. The former are called *active* or *eventive* verbs, or just plain *verb*, in the Iroquoian literature; the latter are called *stative* verbs, or just *state*. Active verbs generally have meanings that involve a change of state or that describe a process or activity. Stative or state verbs generally have meanings that do not involve much motion or change over time (such as being still or holding onto something), including states of being (such as feeling well, being poor) and properties (such as being tall or being rusty).

The different aspect categories specify how the event or situation takes place or unfolds over time, so it concerns the temporal composition of the action. Verbs in the habitual aspect are used for repeated actions, and for the majority of verbs habitual aspect forms are also used for ongoing actions. Habitual verb forms are translated with either the English progressive or the present. For example, **lahwánhaks** is translated either as 'he is tying' or 'he ties.' There are several different forms of each of the aspect suffixes; a habitual verb form can end in **-s**, **-ha?**, **-he?**, **-ehse?**, as well as a few other forms.

The stative aspect form of the majority of active verbs is used for situations that have happened at some time in the past but where the outcome of the event is somehow still relevant after the event has taken place. Stative aspect forms are usually translated with the present perfect; an example is **lotukóhtu** 'he has gone by, he has passed on.' The stative aspect of a minority of active verbs is used for ongoing action, as in **wakatnutolyá·tu** 'I am playing.' (Recall from above that for the majority of active verbs, it is the habitual aspect that is used for ongoing action.) Common stative aspect endings are **-u**, **-ʌ** and **-e?**.

Verbs in the punctual aspect designate the whole event as a single occurrence; for example, **wa?khni·nú·** 'I bought it.' Quite frequently though, there can be multiple occurrences of that event and the punctual aspect can be used for repeated events that take place as part of a routine where in English you might use 'would' ('she would clear the table,' 'she would wash the dishes'). The punctual aspect always occurs with one of three *modal prepronominal* prefixes—FACTUAL, FUTURE, or OPTATIVE—and how a punctual aspect form is used depends to some extent on which of these prefixes occurs. Factual forms are used to assert that an event has happened and are translated with the simple past; for example, **wa?katló·loke?** 'I watched.' Factual forms often begin in **wa?-** or **wa-** or **we-**. Future forms are used to assert that an event will happen and are translated with the future, as in **ʌkatló·loke?** 'I will watch.' The future prefix is **ʌ-**. Optative forms are used to talk about an event that should happen perhaps but has not happened, or an event that won't happen, or one that could happen only under certain conditions; optative forms are usually translated with 'would' or 'should,' thus **a·hatló·loke?** 'he should watch.' Occasionally, when an optative verb follows another verb, the optative verb is translated with 'that' or 'for' ('that he watches' or 'for him to watch'). When there are no other prefixes the optative verb form begins in the long vowel **a·-**. Future forms are the easiest to recognize because the form of the prefix is always **ʌ-**. The factual and optative can each have a number of different forms depending on what other prefixes occur. The best strategy to recognize these prefixes is to study the tables of prepronominal prefixes in Lounsbury (1953) or Michelson and Doxtator (2002).

A subclass of active verbs, *motion verbs*, have an additional aspect form, called PRESENT in this work, which is used for an action taking place 'right now' and to express intention. The present ending is **-e?**. Examples are **yákne?** 'we two are walking' and **latkʌ?sé·ne?** 'he is here to see.'

Active verbs also have an imperative form, which is used for commands, although future forms are also used to make a strong suggestion or give a direction, if not an actual command. Most imperatives have no ending; for example, **teswashlíhʌ** 'Hurry up!' (verb base **-shlihʌ-**). In a few cases, specifically when the punctual aspect ending is **-ne?** or **-ʌ?** or **-a?**, the imperative ends in **-n** or **-ʌ** or **-a**, respectively. An example with **-n** is **tetsitni·tán** 'let's you and I stop again!' This example shows also that commands can include both the addressee ('you') and someone else; such forms are usually translated into English with 'let's' or 'let.'

Stative or state verbs, as mentioned above, occur in only one aspect, the STATIVE aspect. An example of a state verb is **teyostaláthe?** 'it is shiny.' (Some people find the term *stative* confusing, as it refers to both a class of verbs, in which case it is opposed to active verbs, and to an aspectual category, in which case it contrasts with the habitual and punctual aspects.)

Both active and stative verbs can have endings that either follow the (habitual or stative) aspect suffix or, with some verbs, occur suffixed directly to the base. A PAST suffix, **-hkwe?**, **-·ne?**, or **-·hné·**, situates the event or state in a more distant past, as in **waknʌskwayʌ·táhkwe?** 'I used to have a pet.' The so-called CONTINUATIVE suffix, **-k** or **-hak**, is used to talk about states or situations (usually durative situations) that do not exist yet or have not happened yet. The continuative is followed by the punctual aspect ending **-e?** (thus **-ke?** or **-hake?**) and it requires either the future or the optative prepronominal prefix. An example with the optative prefix is **na·hotiliho?tʌ́hake?** 'what their lifestyle should be like.' Finally, some stative (state) verbs, such as **-iyo-** 'good, nice,' can take a PLURAL ending **-·se?**, as in **tsi? nihonʌskwi·yó·se?** 'he has such nice animals.'

Every verb must have a *pronominal prefix*, the function of which is to provide information about the participant(s) that are involved in the situation described by the verb. The pronominal prefixes provide information about the participants in a situation in terms of the categories of *person, number*, and *gender*. The distinctions that are recorded by the pronominals in each of these categories are given in Table 1 on the next page.

First person denotes the speaker(s). EXCLUSIVE denotes the speaker plus someone else (thus *excluding* the addressee—the person who the speaker is addressing or talking to). An example of an exclusive prefix is **yakwa-**, first person exclusive plural ('they and I, we'). INCLUSIVE includes the addressee; an example of an inclusive prefix is **twa-**, first person inclusive plural ('you and I, you and we, we'). Second person is the addressee, and third person is who or what the speaker is talking about.

The gender system is a semantic or "natural" system, which means the gender category is selected according to the natural properties of the referent. The MASCULINE is used for male persons. Animals are also often referenced with masculine prefixes and this is especially so when an animal is personified or given human characteristics. In the plural, the masculine is used also for groups of males and females. The FEMININE and FEMININE-ZOIC genders identify female participants and animals. In the singular, female persons can be referred to with either the feminine or the feminine-zoic (see Abbott, 1984; Michelson, 2015). However, the feminine gender occurs only in the singular, so reference to more than one female person requires the feminine-zoic dual or feminine-zoic plural. The feminine-zoic is also used for animals, although, as mentioned above, animals are often referred to with a masculine prefix. The feminine-zoic has one additional use, and that is as a *default* prefix when the verb has only inanimate, or NEUTER, participants; the default use of the feminine-zoic is described in more detail below. The INDEFINITE category is used for reference to a person or persons when the identity of the referent is not relevant ('one, someone, people, they'). The indefinite always has the same form as the feminine gender and this combination is called FEMININE-INDEFINITE.

Person	Gender	Number
First		Singular
Exclusive		Dual
		Plural
Inclusive		Dual
		Plural
Second		Singular
		Dual
		Plural
Third	Masculine	Singular
		Dual
		Plural
Third	Feminine-zoic	Singular
		Dual
		Plural
Third	Feminine	Singular
Third	Indefinite	

Table 1. Distinctions made by pronominal prefixes

The distribution of pronominal prefixes depends partly also on the meaning of the verb in that every event or state involves a certain number of parties, or sets of participants; in linguistic terms the meaning of verbs includes how many semantic *arguments* a verb has. Examples of verbs that have only one semantic argument (*monadic* verbs) are **-iʔtlu-** 'sit, be at home' or **-nehlakw-** 'become amazed or surprised' or **-yakʌʔ-** 'go out.' Examples of verbs that have two arguments (*dyadic* verbs) are **-hwanhak-** 'tie something' or **-nhaʔ-** 'hire someone' or **-attehtani-/-attehtʌ-** 'scold someone.' One of the arguments of dyadic verbs typically has more agent-like properties (such as being able to bring about a change in the state or condition of the other argument or otherwise affect the other argument), and the other argument has more patient-like properties (such as being more likely to undergo or experience a change of state). Verbs can also have three semantic arguments (*triadic* verbs), in which case the first argument is more agent-like, the second is more patient-like, and the third usually indicates the source or goal or recipient of the action. For example, the verb **-u-** 'give' is a verb where the third argument is the goal (you give something *to* someone), while the verb **-hninu-** 'buy' has a source as the third argument (you buy something *from* someone). In verbs with three arguments the second argument, the more patient-like argument, is usually inanimate. As described below, pronominal prefixes can reference up to two arguments of a verb.

The pronominal prefixes are notorious, probaby because there are so many of them and all of them occur in a single position or slot before the verb stem (Koenig and Michelson [2015]). There are a total of fifty-eight possible combinations of person, number, gender, and agent/patient values. The *form* of each of the fifty-eight prefixes can vary according to the first sound of the stem that the prefix is attached to and whether the prefix occurs at the beginning of a word or not (*initial* versus *medial* or *non-initial*). There are five stem classes in Oneida: C(onsonant) STEMS, a-STEMS, e-/ʌ-STEMS, o-/u-STEMS, and i-STEMS. Tables 2–6 on pages 348–352 give the prefixes that are found with each of these stem classes.

In Tables 2 – 6 the pronominal prefixes are organized into three categories: transitive, agent, and patient. *Transitive* prefixes occur with dyadic verbs and reference two semantic arguments. In the segmented examples here and in the analyzed texts in Appendix 2 the features of the more agent-like argument are given first and those of the more patient-like argument are given second, with the symbol ">" between the two. For example, the transitive prefix **shako-** in the verb form for 'he hires her or them' in (2.2) is identified as 3M.SG>3. The bare number 3 is an abbreviation for prefixes that don't distinguish third person feminine-indefinite, masculine dual and plural, and feminine-zoic dual and plural.

(2.2) **shakónhahse?**
  shako-nha?-se?
  3M.SG>3-hire-HAB
  'he hires her or them'

Intransitive prefixes reference only one argument. Intransitive prefixes fall into two classes: AGENT and PATIENT, respectively abbreviated as A and P. In Tables 2–6, agent (A) prefixes are given in the bolded column and patient (P) prefixes in the bolded row. The verb form in (2.3) has an agent prefix; the one in (2.4) has a patient prefix. These labels correspond to the designations SUBJECTIVE and OBJECTIVE in Lounsbury (1953), Abbott (2000), and the online resources developed by Abbott (2006).

(2.3) **lʌtu·níhe?**
  l-ʌtuni-he?
  3M.SG.A-lonely-HAB
  'he is lonely'

(2.4) **lonú·sehe?**
  lo-nu?se-he?
  3M.SG.P-lazy-HAB
  'he is lazy'

The pronominal prefixes—transitive, agent, patient—reference *animate* arguments. In (2.2) above and in (2.5) below a transitive prefix references two animate arguments, the person doing the hiring or scolding and the person getting hired or scolded. A verb may have a third semantic argument, but then the third argument is *inanimate* and not registered by the pronominal prefix. For example, the verb in (2.6) has a transitive prefix referencing the two animate arguments, the person who is handing leaves and the person who gets the leaves handed to them; the third argument (leaves) is inanimate.

(2.5) **tsi? nihakwattéhtanihe?**
  tsi? ni-hakw-attehtani-he?
  how PART-3M.SG>1SG-scold-HAB
  'he really scolds me, he gives me heck'

	1SG	1DU	1PL	2SG	2DU	2PL	3M.SG	3FZ.SG	A	3FI	3M.DP	3FZ.DP	(3N)
1SG				ku-	kni-	kwa-	li-/-hi-	k(e)-		khe-			
1EX.DU							shakni-	yakni-/-akni-		yakhi-/-akhi-			
1EX.PL							shakwa-	yakwa-/-akwa-					
1IN.DU							ethni-/-hethni-	tni-/-etni-		yethi-/-ethi-			
1IN.PL							ethwa-/-hethwa-	twa-/-etwa-					
2SG	sk(e)-	skni-	skwa-				etsh(e)-/-hetsh(e)-	s(e)-/-hs(e)-/st-		she-			
2DU							etsni-/-hetsni-	sni-/-esni-		yetshi-/-etshi-			
2PL							etswa-/-hetswa-	swa-/-eswa-					
3M.SG	lak(e)-/-hak(e)-	shukni-	shukwa-	ya-/-hya-	etsni-/-hetsni-	etswa-/-hetswa-	lo-/-ho-	la-/-ha-/-hla-		shako-			
3FZ.SG (P)	wak(e)-/uk(e)-	yukni-/-ukni-	yukwa-/-ukwa-	sa-/-esa-	sni-/-esni-	swa-/-eswa-		yo-/-o-	ka-	yako-/ ako-	loti-/-hoti-	yoti-/-oti-	yo-/-o-
3FI	yuk(e)-/-uk(e)-	yukhi-/-ukhi-		yesa-/-esa-	yetshi-/-etshi-		luwa-/-huwa-	kuwa-	ye-/-e-	yutat(e)-/-utat(e)-	luwati-/-huwati-	kuwati-	
3M.DU									ni-/-hni-	shakoti-			
3M.PL									lati-/-hati-				
3FZ.DU									kni-	yakoti-/-akoti-			
3FZ.PL									kuti-				
(3N)									ka-				

Table 2. C-stem pronominal prefixes

Notes:

1 Prefixes with initial **y** have variants without the **y** when the prefix occurs after a **ʔ** that is part of the factual prefix; the **y** is retained after the **ʔ** that is part of the negative prefix **teʔ-**.

2 The inclusive prefixes, the 2nd person dual and plural prefixes, and the 2SG.P prefix, all have variants with an **e** when they are non-initial (e.g. 2nd person dual **sni-** has the medial variant **-esni-**).

3 Prefixes that begin in **e** have variants with **h** before the **e** when they are non-initial (e.g. 1IN.DU>3M.SG **ethni-** has the medial variant **-hethni-**).

4 The 2SG.A **s-**, 3M.DU.A **ni-**, and 3M.SG>2SG **ya-** prefixes have medial variants **-hs-**, **-hni-**, and **-hya-**, respectively.

5 Prefixes that begin in **l** have variants with **h** in place of the **l** when the prefix is non-initial (e.g. 3M.PL.A **lati-** has the medial variant **-hati-**), except that the 3M.SG.A **la-** has the variant **-hla-** when the accent is on the syllable before the prefix (e.g. **ít-hla-teʔ** 'he is standing there').

6 The 1SG.P prefix **wak-** combines with the preceding factual prefix **waʔ-**, so that **waʔ-wak-** comes out as **uk-**.

7 Prefixes that end in a consonant have variants with **e** after the consonant before stems that begin in **kh, sh, sk, sl, st, th, tsh, tsy,** or **ʔ**. These variants are given with **e** in parentheses; e.g. 1SG.A **k(e)-** represents **k-** and **ke-**.

8 The 2SG.A prefix **s-** has the variant **st-** before stems beginning in **s** or **hs**.

	1SG	1DU	1PL	2SG	2DU	2PL	3M.SG	3FZ.SG	A	3FI	3M.DP	3FZ.DP	(3N)
1SG				ku-	kn-	yakwʌ-/-akwʌ-	li-/-hi-		k-	khe-			
1EX.DU							shakn-		yakn-/-akn-	yakhi-/-akhi-			
1EX.PL							shakwʌ-		yakwʌ-/-akwʌ-				
1IN.DU							ethn-/-hethn-		tn-/-etn-	yethi-/-ethi-			
1IN.PL							ethwʌ-/-hethwʌ-		twʌ-/-etwʌ-				
2SG	sk-	skn-	skwʌ-				etsh-/-hetsh-		s-/-hs-	she-			
2DU							etsn-/-hetsn-		sn-/-esn-	yetshi-/etshi-			
2PL							etswʌ-/-hetswʌ-		swʌ-/-eswʌ-				
3M.SG	lak-/-hak-	shukn-	shukwʌ-	yʌ-/-hyʌ-	etsn-/-hetsn-	etswʌ-/-hetswʌ-	lo-/-ho-		lʌ-/-hʌ-	shako-			
3FZ.SG P	wak-/uk-	yukn-/-ukn-	yukwʌ-/-ukwʌ-	sʌ-/-esʌ-	sn-/-esn-	swʌ-/-eswʌ-		yo-/-o-	kʌ-	yako-/-ako-	lot-/-hot-/lon-/-hon-	yot-/-ot-/yon-/-on-	yo-/-o-
3FI	yuk-/-uk-	yukhi-/-ukhi-		yesʌ-/-esʌ-	yetshi-/-etshi-		luwʌ-/-huwʌ-	kuwʌ-	ye-/-e-/ya-/-a-	yutat-/-utat-	luwat-/-huwat-	kuwat-	
3M.DU									n-/-hn-	shakot-			
3M.PL									lat-/-hat-/lʌn-/-hʌn-				
3FZ.DU									kn-	yakot-/-akot-			
3FZ.PL									kut-/kun-				
(3N)									kʌ-				

Table 3. i-stem pronominal prefixes

Notes:

1–6 See Notes 1–6 of Table 2, substituting the appropriate i-stem forms of the prefixes.

7   After prefixes that end in a vowel, the intial **i** of the stem is absent.

8   The verbs **-ihlu-** 'say' and **-ihey-** 'die' have 3FI.A **ya-/-a-** instead of **ye-/-e-**. Also, they are the only two verbs that take the masculine and feminine-zoic variants 3M.PL.A **lʌn-/-hʌn-**, 3FZ.PL.A **kun-**, 3M.DP.P **lon-/-hon-**, and 3FZ.DP.P **yon-/-on-**.

	1SG	1DU	1PL	2SG	2DU	2PL	3M.SG	3FZ.SG	A	3FI	3M.DP	3FZ.DP	(3N)
1SG				kuy-	kn-	ky-	liy-/-hiy-	k-		khey-			
1EX.DU							shakn-/shakniy-	yakn-/-akn-		yakhiy-/-akhiy-			
1EX.PL							shaky-/shakway-	yaky-/-aky-					
1IN.DU							ethn-/-hethn-/ethniy-/-hethniy-	tn-/-etn-		yethiy-/-ethiy-			
1IN.PL							ethy-/-hethy-/ethway-/-hethway-	ty-/ety-					
2SG	sk-	skn-	sky-				etsh-/-hetsh-	s-/-hs-		shey-			
2DU							etsn-/-hetsn-/etsniy-/-hetsniy-	sn-/-esn-		yetshiy-/-etshiy-			
2PL							etsy-/-hetsy-/etsway-/-hetsway-	tsy-/-etsy-					
3M.SG	lak-/-hak-	shukn-/shukniy-	shuky-/shukway-	yay-/-hyay-	etsn-/-hetsn-/etsniy-/-hetsniy-	etsy-/-hetsy-/etsway-/-hetsway-	la-/-ha-/loy-/-hoy-	l-/-hl-/lay-/-hay-		shaka-/shakoy-			
3FZ.SG / P	wak-/uk-	yukn-/-ukn-	yuky-/-uky-	s-/-es-	sn-/-esn-	tsy-/-etsy-		ya-/-a-	y-/ø	yaka-/-aka-/yakay-/-akay-)	lon-/-hon-	yon-/-on-	ya-/-a-
3FI	yuk-/-uk-	yukhiy-/-ukhiy-		yesay-/-esay-	yetshiy-/-etshiy-		luway-/-huway-	kuway-	yak-/-ak-	yutat-/-utat-	luwʌn-/-huwʌn-/luwatiy-/-huwatiy-	kuwʌn-/kuwatiy-	
3M.DU									n-/-hn-	shakon-/shakotiy-			
3M.PL									lʌn-/-hʌn-				
3FZ.DU									kn-	yakon-/-akon-/yakotiy-/-akotiy-			
3FZ.PL									kun-				
(3N)									y-/ø				

Table 4. o- and u-stem pronominal prefixes

Notes:

1–6 See notes 1–6 under Table 2, except note that the 3M.SG.A prefix retains l medially (note 5).

7 Forms of some transitive prefixes appear in the texts, or have been subsequently elicited, that are innovative in that they have developed variants that end in **y**, probably based on prefixes that already have established variants that end in **y**, such as the 3>3M.SG prefix **luway-/-huway-**. Both the variants that are given in Lounsbury (1953, Table 6) and the variants that are attested more recently are given in Table 4.

	1SG	1DU	1PL	2SG	2DU	2PL	3M.SG	3FZ.SG	A	3FI	3M.DP	3FZ.DP	(3N)
1SG				kuy-	kn-	kw-	liy-/-hiy-	k-		khey-			
1EX.DU							shakn-/shakniy-	yakn-/-akn-		yakhiy-/-akhiy-			
1EX.PL							shakw-/shakway-	yakw-/-akw-					
1IN.DU							ethn-/-hethn-/ethniy-/-hethniy-	tn-/-etn-		yethiy-/-ethiy-			
1IN.PL							ethw-/-hethw-/ethway-/-hethway-	tw-/-etw-					
2SG	skw-	skn-	skw-				etsh-/-hetsh-	s-/-hs-		shey-			
2DU							etsn-/-hetsn-/etsniy-/-hetsniy-	sn-/-esn-		yetshiy-/-etshiy-			
2PL							etsw-/-hetsw-/etsway-/-hetsway-	sw-/-esw-					
3M.SG	lakw-/-hakw-	shukn-/-shukniy-	shukw-/-shukway-	yay-/-hyay-	etsn-/-hetsn-/etsniy-/-hetsniy-	etsw-/-hetsw-/etswaw-/-hetsway-	law-/-haw-/lo-/-hoy-	l-/-hl-		shakaw-/shakoy-			
3FZ.SG P	wak-/ukw-	yukn-/-ukn-	yukw-/-ukw-	s-/-es-	sn-/-esn-	sw-/-esw-		yaw-/-aw-	w-	yakaw-/-akaw-	lon-/-hon-	yon-/-on-	yaw-/-aw-
3FI	yukw-/-ukw-	yukhiy-/-ukhiy-		yes-/-es-/yesay-/-esay-	yetshiy-/-etshiy-		luw-/-huw-/luway-/-huway-	kuw-/kuway-	yak-/-ak-/yʌ-	yutat-/-utat-	luwʌn-/-huwʌn-/luwatiy-/-huwatiy-	kuwʌn-/kuwatiy-	
3M.DU									n-/-hn-	shakon-/shakotiy-			
3M.PL									lʌn-/-hʌn-				
3FZ.DU									kn-	yakon-/-akon-/yakotiy-/-akotiy-			
3FZ.PL									kun-				
(3N)									w-				

Table 5. e- and ʌ-stem pronominal prefixes

Notes
1–7 See Notes 1–7 under Table 4.
8   The two verbs **-e-** 'walk' and **-elh-** 'think, want' have 3FI.A **yʌ-** and the initial **e** of the stem is lost.

	1SG	1DU	1PL	2SG	2DU	2PL	3M.SG	3FZ.SG	A	3FI	3M.DP	3FZ.DP	(3N)
1SG				kuy-	ky-	kw-	liy-/-hiy-	k-		khey-			
1EX.DU							shaky-	yaky-/-aky-		yakhiy-/-akhiy-			
1EX.PL							shakw-	yakw-/-akw-					
1IN.DU							ethy-/-hethy-	ty-/-ety-		yethiy-/-ethiy-			
1IN.PL							ethw-/-hethw-	tw-/etw-					
2SG	skw-	sky-	skw-				etsh-/-hetsh-	s-/-hs-		shey-			
2DU							etsy-/-hetsy-	tsy-/-etsy-		yetshiy-/-etshiy-			
2PL							etsw-/-hetsw-	sw-/-esw-					
3M.SG	lakw-/-hakw-	shuky-	shukw-	y-/-hy-	etsy-/-hetsy-	etsw-/-hetsw-	lo-/-ho-	l-/-h-		shako-			
3FZ.SG / P	wak-/ukw-	yuky-/-uky-	yukw-/-ukw-	s-/-es-	tsy-/-etsy-	sw-/-esw-		yo-/-o-	w-/u-	yako-/-ako-	lon-/-hon-	yon-/-on-	yo-/-o-
3FI	yukw-/-ukw-	yukhiy-/-ukhiy-		yes-/-es-	yetshiy-/-etshiy-		luw-/-huw-	kuw-	yu-/-u-	yutat-/-utat-	luwʌn-/-huwʌn-	kuwʌn-	
3M.DU									y-/-hy-	shakon-			
3M.PL									lu/-hu-				
3FZ.DU									ky-	yakon-/-akon-			
3FZ.PL									ku-				
(3N)									w-				

Table 6. a-stem pronominal prefixes

Notes:

1–6 See notes 1–6 under Table 2, substituting the appropriate a-stem forms of the prefixes.

7   The 3FZ.SG.A prefix **w-** combines with the preceding factual prefix **waʔ-** and the following stem-initial vowel so that **waʔ-w-a-** comes out as **u-** (e.g. **waʔ-w-atkʌ́·lahteʔ** → **utkʌ́·lahteʔ** 'she or it quit').

8   Prefixes that end in **u** or **o** absorb the first vowel of the stem (e.g. the stem-vowel **a** is lost after the 3M.PL.A **lu-** or after the 3M.SG.P **lo-**).

(2.6)   **tahinláhtuʔ**
         t-a-hi-nlaht-u-ʔ
         CSL-FACT-1SG>3M.SG-leaf-give-PNC
         'I handed leaves to him'

Likewise, AGENT and PATIENT prefixes reference a single *animate* argument. Some verbs, like the verb for 'laugh' in (2.7), have only one semantic argument. In (2.7) the argument is animate—masculine singular 'he'—and it is referenced with the masculine singular agent prefix. Some verbs have two semantic arguments, one animate and one inanimate. Such verbs also take agent or patient prefixes. For example, the verb 'wrap up' has two semantic arguments, the person doing the wrapping (animate) and the thing being wrapped (inanimate). In (2.8) the animate argument is again the masculine singular and this argument is referenced with the masculine singular agent prefix **-ha-**, the same prefix as in (2.7).

(2.7)   **wahaste·lísteʔ**
         wa-ha-stelist-eʔ
         FACT-3M.SG.A-laugh-PNC
         'he laughed'

(2.8)   **wahahweʔnu·ní·**   **oyuʔkwaʔuwé**
         wa-ha-hweʔnuhi-ʔ   oyuʔkwaʔuwé
         FACT-3M.SG.A-wrap-PNC   Indian tobacco
         'he wrapped up some Indian tobacco'

The choice between agent (A) and patient (P) category for verbs that have one animate argument is sometimes predictable from the meaning of the verb. Active verbs whose meaning suggests that the argument has more agent-like properties will take an agent prefix, while verbs whose meaning suggests that the argument is more patient-like in its properties will take a patient prefix. However, often enough the category is not predictable and whether the verb takes agent or patient prefixes must be learned together with the meaning of the verb. Similarly, state verbs can have either an agent or patient prefix and whether a particular state verb takes agent or patient prefixes must be learned together with the meaning of the verb although, again, in some cases semantic motivations are evident. However, one feature about the distribution of agent and patient prefixes is completely predictable and that is that the STATIVE aspect of *active* verbs requires a PATIENT prefix. The shift from agent prefixes in the habitual and punctual aspects to patient prefixes in the stative aspect holds for all active verbs. Both the verb 'jump up and down' in (2.9) and the verb 'wash dishes' in (2.10) have one animate argument. Examples with agent prefixes in the habitual aspect are given in (2.9a) and (2.10a), and examples with patient prefixes in the stative aspect are given in (2.9b) and (2.10b).

(2.9) a. **tehanitskwákhwaʔ**
 te-h-anitskwahkw-haʔ
DL-3M.SG.A-jump-HAB
'he jumps up and down'

(2.9) b. **tehonitskwáhkwʌ**
te-ho-anitskwahkw-ʌ
DL-3M.SG.P-jump-STV
'he is jumping, he has jumped up and down'

(2.10) a. **keksohalényuheʔ**
ke-ks-ohale-nyu-heʔ
1SG.A-dish-wash-DISTR-HAB
'I am washing dishes'

(2.10) b. **wakeksohaléniʔ**
wake-ks-ohale-nyu-ʔ
1SG.P-dish-wash-DISTR-STV
'I have washed dishes'

All verbs must have a pronominal prefix, so what about verbs that have no animate arguments? Of course verbs can have a single argument that is inanimate, such as a book getting wet or something being heavy. But there are no prefixes that *uniquely* apply to inanimate— or NEUTER—arguments. Verbs with only inanimate or neuter arguments take the feminine-zoic singular prefix as a *default* prefix. By *default* we mean that, just when there are no animate participants, the verb form takes the feminine-zoic singular prefix as a kind of "last resort." Note that the default is the feminine-zoic *singular* prefix even if the verb is used to talk about two or more inanimate objects. We can take as an example verb forms that count two or more objects, such as **tekahu·wáke** 'two boats.' Even though two boats are being counted, the verb form has the feminine-zoic singular agent prefix -ka-. (See section 9 on counting things.) Another example is the verb -**kehlu**-, which in the excerpt in (2.11) is used to talk about all these car parts strewn on the ground; it also has singular prefix -**ka**-.[1] (Note that we use the abbreviation 3Z/N.SG for the default feminine-zoic prefix that occurs on verbs that have only neuter arguments.)

(2.11) **kwáh tsyoʔk nú· nikaké·luʔ kaʔslethokúha wí· watestákhwaʔ,**
kwáh tsyoʔk nú·   ni-ka-kehlu-ʔ   kaʔslet-hokúha   wí·
everywhere   PART-3Z/N.SG.A-strewn-STV   car-PL
w-atest-a-hkw-haʔ
3Z/N.SG.A-get.used-JN-INSTR-HAB
'strewn all over the place were car parts,'

Norma Kennedy, How I Learned to Swear

---

[1] Excerpts are given exactly as they appear in the texts, which means that sometimes the excerpt ends in a comma, sometimes in an utterance-final form and a period, and sometimes without any punctuation (when a clause is followed by another clause without a prosodic break).

Even though there are no neuter prefixes, it is important to recognize the neuter as a *semantic* gender. One reason is that in some cases whether an argument is semantically feminine-zoic or neuter matters when it comes to selecting the correct pronominal prefix. For example, the verb form in (2.12a) with the transitive prefix **kuw-** is used to describe a situation where some people ('they') are talking about a feminine-zoic person (or animal), while the verb form in (2.12b) with the agent prefix **lu-** is used to describe a situation where 'they' are talking about something that is neuter.

(2.12) a. **kuwathlo·líhe?** b. **luthlo·líhe?**
        kuw-at-hloli-he? lu-at-hloli-he?
        3>3FZ.SG-SRF-tell-HAB 3M.PL.A-SRF-tell-HAB
        'they (or she) are talking about her' 'they are talking about it'

The upshot of all this is that from a *semantic* perspective four genders must be recognized (masculine, feminine, feminine-zoic, and neuter), but when we talk about the *form* of the pronominal prefixes there are only three genders (masculine, feminine-indefinite,[2] and feminine-zoic).

As mentioned above in connection with the punctual aspect, verbs can have the FACTUAL (**wa?-**), FUTURE (**ʌ-**), and OPTATIVE (**a·-**) modal prepronominal prefixes. In addition, there are eight other prepronominal prefixes having various functions. They are the **te-** dualic, **s-** repetitive, **t-** cislocative, **y-** translocative, **n-** partitive, **te?-** negative, **th-** contrastive, and **tsh-** coincident. In very general terms, the DUALIC is used with verbs that somehow involve two entities, locations, directions, etc. The CISLOCATIVE indicates direction towards, or location close to, the speaker or some other reference point, while the TRANSLOCATIVE indicates direction away from, or location at a distance from, the speaker or some other reference point. The REPETITIVE expresses repeated action or a return to a previous neutral or "normal" situation. The PARTITIVE is used in verbs of manner, extent, and quantity. The NEGATIVE and CONTRASTIVE are used in negation structures, and the COINCIDENT signals overlap and simultaneity. Often prepronominals must occur with a verb base in order to convey the intended meaning; an example of this is the cislocative in the verb base meaning 'begin, start' (**t-a-k-atáhsawʌ-?** 'I began' CSL-FACT-1SG.A-begin-PNC). Oneida dictionaries make it clear when a particular prepronominal is an essential part of the base. In addition, the prepronominals are a part of a number of constructions including, just as two examples, negation (section 5) and counting (section 9).

2.2 Particles

Just about every sentence or utterance in the texts has at least one particle, and usually several. Very often particles combine and form a kind of "compound" particle; an example is **nʌ kyale? wí·** 'so again.' This complex can be analyzed as four distinct particles: **nʌ** 'then,' **ki?** 'actually, as a matter of fact,' **ale?** 'again,' and **wí·**, a connective particle. Particles can be difficult to translate into English. We feel relatively confident about some translations, like **nʌ kyale? wí·** 'so again,' or **tho nú·** 'that's where,' but in other cases we remain unsure.

---

[2] Recall that the *form* of the feminine singular and the *form* of the indefinite are always the same; thus the term feminine-indefinite.

A good example of this is **kwí·**, which occurs frequently but which we leave untranslated unless it is part of a compound particle such as **nʌ kwí·** 'so then.'

The definition of particle is a word that occurs in one form only, meaning that it is uninflected. This definition generally holds, but it must not be applied literally since there are a few particles that do occasionally occur with an ending. An example is **ákteʔ** 'different,' which can occur with the distributive ending **-shuʔ** in the word **akté·shuʔ** 'different (places).' But **ákteʔ** cannot be identified structurally as a noun or verb and so it is designated a particle. Note that technically, since they occur in only one form, some names for animals (for example, **é·lhal** 'dog') are particles.

The particles of Oneida can be organized into four broad categories: (1) particles that have to do with identification of participants, (2) particles that reflect a speaker's belief about how likely or certain the situation is that s/he is reporting, (3) locational and temporal particles, and (4) connective particles. There are some particles outside of these categories—the negative particle **yah** 'not,' particles that specify degree or quantity (for example, **só·tsiʔ** 'too [much]'), interactional particles such as **hʌ́·** 'yes' and **táh** 'no,' and exclamations such as **yáts** 'Gosh!' Many of the particles mentioned below will be mentioned again in later sections. An alphabetized list of particles, with a reference to any sections that mention the particle, is given in Appendix 1.

2.2.1 Pronouns and Identification of Participants

Since pronominal prefixes provide information about the participants in a situation, and every verb must have a pronominal prefix, independent pronouns are used for contrast and emphasis. The first and second person pronouns are particles: **í·** or **ní·** or **niʔí·** for first person 'I, we, me, us,' and **isé·** or **nisé·** or **niʔi·sé** for second person 'you.' Note that these are used for both singular and non-singular referents.[3]

The particles **náhteʔ** 'what' and **úhkaʔ** or **úhkaʔ náhteʔ** 'who' occur in questions and then function as *interrogative* pronouns. (Oneida also has 'where,' 'when,' 'how,' and 'which' questions. These are described in section 6.) *Indefinite* pronouns consist of the particles that occur in questions plus the particles **thok** or **ok**, thus **thok náhteʔ** 'something' and **úhkaʔ ok** or **úhkaʔ ok náhteʔ** 'someone.'

The particles **kaʔikʌ́** 'this' and **thikʌ́** 'that' often have the meaning of *demonstrative* pronouns. When these occur before a nominal, the demonstrative and the nominal are each independent expressions occurring in apposition. For example, **kaʔikʌ́ yeksá·** is more like 'this-one a-girl' or 'this-one the-girl.' Although **kaʔikʌ́** and **thikʌ́** are consistently translated as 'this' and 'that,' it should be noted that their distribution is more complicated than is suggested by the label "demonstrative pronoun." For example, they can occur after a verb at the end of an utterance, where our understanding of their function is not completely clear at this point.

Overlapping to some extent in function with **kaʔikʌ́** and **thikʌ́** is the particle **né·**, a variant of which occurs in all of the Iroquoian languages; for example, **naʔ** in Onondaga or **né:ʼ**

---

[3] Third person pronouns are built on the stem **-ulhá·** with patient pronominal prefixes: **laulhá·** 'he,' **akaulhá·** 'she,' **aulhá·** 'she, it' (feminine-zoic), **lonulhá·** 'they' (masculine), and **onulhá·** 'they' (feminine-zoic). Patient prefixes that begin in **y**, such as the feminine-zoic plural prefix **yon-**, lack the initial **y**, which is a reflection of the nominal status of these forms. (See section 2.3.)

in Seneca. Most Iroquoianists label this particle "assertion" and translate it as 'it is' or 'it's' or 'it's the case that.' Lounsbury's description of this particle may be helpful: "A particle with meaning similar to that of a generalized third person independent or demonstrative pronoun, *it, he, she, they, him, her, them, this, that, the person, the thing, the one, the way,* etc. It is nearly always a predicative element in a sentence…Such a predication is then usually followed in turn by a descriptive phrase standing in apposition to *né·* and describing it…" (Lounsbury 1953, p. 100). The other Iroquoian languages make frequent use of a particle that is translated as 'the' and that specifies that what follows is a nominal or a noun phrase; for example, **ne?** in Onondaga, **né** or **n** in Mohawk, or **neh** in Seneca.[4] The Oneida equivalent seems to be **ne?n**, but **ne?n** occurs in these texts only in **ok ne?n** (see section 4.3). It does occur in Wisconsin texts edited by Abbott (1982; 1983) but even in those it is not as frequent as, say, **ne?** in Onondaga. There is a similar-sounding particle **né·n**, which is usually shortened and pronounced as if written **nén**. This particle does occur often enough before a nominal and so possibly this particle corresponds to the particles in the other languages mentioned above. However, **né·n** occurs most often at the beginning of an utterance, pronounced with a lowered pitch and frequently followed by a pause, and then it seems to draw attention to what is going to happen next; it alerts the hearer to a shift to a different participant or to a different scene. Also occurring frequently in the recordings is an **n** that occurs all alone, pronounced at the end of a preceding word, and it is possible that this **n** is a short variant of **ne?n**. For example, there is a clear **n** in the expression **ne? kʌ n** 'you mean (so-and-so)?' A problem, though, is that the **n** often occurs after the nasalized vowel ʌ, and in many cases it is unclear whether it is part of the nasalized vowel or really a separate sound. We have left these lone **n**'s untranslated, and we leave their analysis for future study.

Finally, the expression **nʌ? né·** occurs after a verb and usually at the end of an utterance. It focuses attention on a person or object mentioned earlier and is translated, a bit awkwardly, as 'that one, as for that one.'

2.2.2 Certainty and Emphasis

Particles can convey how speakers came about the information they are relating. Expressions that specify source of information are called *evidentials* and a common evidential particle in Oneida is **yakʌ?**, translated 'reportedly' and very likely from the verb root -ʌ- 'say.' Some speakers shorten **yakʌ?** so that it sounds more like **ye?**.

Speakers often indicate how certain they are about the information they are reporting or how likely they believe the situation to be real or true. Expressions that have to do with this kind of knowledge are called *epistemic* and epistemic particles in Oneida include **a?nyóh** or **kwa?nyóh** 'seems, seems like,' **ki?** 'actually,' **ki?wáh** 'indeed, right,' **olihwiyó** 'a sure thing,' **tá·t núwa?** 'maybe' (often reduced to **táthna?** or **tahna?**), **to·káh** 'I don't know,' **to·kʌ́ske?** 'truly,' **uhte** 'supposedly, possibly, probably, I guess,' **wé·ne** or **wé·ni** 'evidently, apparently, it must have been,' **wé·ne ki?wáh** or **wé·ni ki?wáh** 'I suppose, I guess,' and **ya·wét** 'like, kind of like.' The particle **uhte** 'supposedly, probably' combines with the verb form **i·kélhe?** 'think' and the combination comes out sounding like one word, **uhti·kélhe?**.

---

[4] Chafe (1994, p. 153-6) has a good description of **neh** in Seneca. More recently, Chafe (2015) has glossed this particle as 'namely.' Describing the Mohawk particle **né** in recent presentations, Marianne Mithun has captured its meaning with the gloss 'aforementioned.'

In fact, several of these particles represent verb forms that now occur in only one form and no longer function fully as verbs. **Wé·ne** or **wé·ni** is based on a verb root -e?ne- 'evident.' **To·kʌ́ske?** 'truly, it's true,' often shortened to **tú·ske?**, is based on a verb -tokʌ?- 'be found out, become known.' **Olihwiyó** 'a sure thing,' sometimes shortened to **alyó·**, is based on the verb root -iyo- 'good, nice' with the incorporated root -lihw- 'matter, affair, news, business.'

We include here *emphatic* particles. The particle **kwáh**, translated 'just, only,' usually occurs at the beginning of a clause and can have a restrictive force especially in combination with the particle **nok** in **kwáh nok** and **kwah nók tsi?** ('he was *just* sitting there, *all he did* was sit there, he was *only* sitting there'). **Kwáh** is a component also in the expressions **kwahikʌ́** and **kwahotokʌ́·u**, translated 'just really' and 'just for real,' respectively. (Both of these are often followed by the particle **tsi?**.) The particle **se?** 'too' usually occurs after the first word in a clause. Out of context **se?** is translated 'too,' but it seems to be used more as an emphatic than as additive (as in English 'I did TOO!'). It often occurs in negative contexts and then 'no way' is a good English translation. The evidential particle **ki?** 'actually, as a matter of fact' may also have an emphatic component; it typically occurs after another word.

Finally, the expression **ne? kʌ́h** is an *exclamation tag* that occurs at the end of utterances and has an emphatic component; **kʌ́h** is the question particle (**kʌ** when not at the end of an utterance) and the best way we could translate this expression is 'isn't it (so), eh.'

2.2.3 Location and Time

Locational particles are **ákta?** 'near,' **ákte?** '(somewhere) else, different,' **akté·shu?** 'different (places),' **átste** 'outside,' **a?é·** 'way over there, far (away),' **ehtá·ke** 'below, downstairs,' **elók** 'back and forth, side to side,' **é·nik** or **é·nike** 'above, upstairs,' **elʌ́** 'across, other,' **ísi?** 'right there, right over there, yonder,' **kaló·** 'before, this (side),' **kʌh** or **kʌ́·tho** 'over here, this way,' **kʌ?** 'right here, right there,' **ná·ku** 'under,' **ohʌtú** 'in front, ahead of,' **ohná·kʌ?** 'in back, behind,' **ohna?kʌ́·shu?** 'all along behind,' and **tho** 'there, that way.' Most of these can be followed by **nú·** or **nukwá·** 'place, where,' and some can be followed by **ná·wati** 'on (one, this, that) side.' The particles **kʌ?** 'here, right here, right there' and **ísi?** 'right there, right over there' indicate definite locations and these two particles sometimes are accompanied by pointing gestures, with the thumb or finger for **kʌ?** and the lower lip or chin for **ísi?**.

The particles **kʌh** and **tho** have functions in addition to specifying proximal ('over here, this way') and distal ('over there, that way') locations. **Kʌh**, and the longer but less frequent variant **kʌ́·tho**, are used also to indicate relative size or extent, and they must be accompanied by a motion by the hand, or hands, showing how big or how far (see section 10.1). **Tho** is also used anaphorically, 'that's (where, how, when,' etc. See section 8).

The most frequent temporal particle is **nʌ** or **onʌ́** 'then, when.' It can occur in combination with several other particles: **nʌ kwí·** 'so then,' **nʌ sok wí·** 'and so THEN, so then too,' **nále?** 'then again,' and **kanyó· onʌ́** 'when, as soon as.' **Nʌ sok wí·** is actually **nʌ se? ok wí·**, with **se?** providing the emphasis, and **nále?** is composed of **nʌ** plus **ale?** 'again.'

Additional temporal particles are **áhsok** 'suddenly,' **áhsu** 'not yet,' **ahsuhkʌ́** 'before (the time) when,' **a·lé·** 'sometimes, at times,' **astéhtsi?** '(in the) morning,' **a?tsyók** 'after a while,' **ehnók** 'a while ago,' **elhúwa?** 'just then, recently,' **ne? thó·ne?** 'at that time,' **núwa?** or **nʌ?ú·wa?** or **ú·wa?** 'now, this time,' **nuwʌtú** 'never, ever,' **ókhna?** 'and then,' **óksa?** 'right away, immediately,' **shekú** 'still,' **the·tʌ́·** 'yesterday,' **tho ále?** and **thóha** 'almost (time for),' and **tho?nʌ́** or **thó·nʌ** or **thó·ne? nʌ** 'and then.' **Ókhna?** 'and then' is probably composed of a particle **ok** 'only, and' plus a shortened form **naʔ** of **núwaʔ** 'now, this time.' Out of context **shekú** is translated 'still,' suggesting a situation that is continuing, perhaps in spite of some other situation. However in the texts **shekú** occurs more often in negative contexts, where it is translated 'even' or 'not even.' Finally, the particle **kʌs** 'customarily, habitually, usually' specifies the frequency of an event. Very often it is shortened to just **s** and pronounced with the preceding word; in this case we leave it untranslated.

A few temporal expressions are somewhere between verbs and particles in that they are transparently verbal in structure but their meaning and form are relatively fixed. Such temporal expressions include **ahsúthʌ** 'midnight,' **ʌyólhʌneʔ** 'tomorrow,' **sayólhʌneʔ** 'the next day,' **wahu·níseʔ** or **tshiwahu·níseʔ** 'a long time ago,' **(kaʔikʌ́) wʌhnisla·té·** 'today,' **(kaʔikʌ́) wahsuta·té·** 'tonight,' **yoʔkalá·u** or **yoʔkaláshʌ** 'evening, night,' and **kwáh kʌʔ nityoʔkalá·u** 'late at night.'

2.2.4 Connectives

Particles that connect (or *conjoin*) clauses are **ati** 'even though, although,' **kanyó· ok** 'so that, so long as,' **kháleʔ** 'and,' **né· tsiʔ** 'because,' **nók tsiʔ** 'but,' **ok neʔ** 'and as for,' **ókhnaʔ** 'and then' (included also as a temporal particle above), **tahnú·** 'and,' **tákʌʔ** 'so as not,' **tá·t** 'if, maybe,' and **tá·thuniʔ** 'or, or maybe, otherwise.' Both **kháleʔ** and **tahnú·** are translated 'and.' The difference between the two seems to be that **tahnú·** is often used when the event described by a clause is somehow consequent to the event of a preceding clause ('and so'). Only **kháleʔ** can conjoin two nominals.

Most of these particles can be analyzed as combinations of particles. **Kháleʔ** is reduced from **ókhaleʔ**, which also occurs but less often than **kháleʔ**. The longer form **ókhaleʔ** can be analyzed as two particles, **ok** 'only' and **aleʔ** 'again,' with a phonetic **h** joining the two particles. **Nók tsiʔ** 'but' is from **né· ok tsiʔ**, and **ókhnaʔ** 'and then' from **ok núwaʔ**, again with a phonetic **h** joining the two. **Tá·thuniʔ** 'or, or else' is composed of **tá·t** 'if, maybe' plus **uniʔ** 'too, also, even' (once again with the **h**). The particle **uniʔ** has the variant **oniʔ** when it does not occur together with other particles; **uniʔ/oniʔ** is one of two *additive* particles, the other being **sʌ́·** 'also.'

Additional particles that somehow, loosely speaking, link a clause with a previous clause are **kwí·** and **wí·**. These are left untranslated because we just couldn't come up with a satisfying yet accurate translation. In combination with other particles they are translated 'so,' as in **nʌ kwí·** 'so then.' Both **kwí·** and **wí·** are extremely common. The particle **katiʔ** 'then, well, anyway' can also be considered such a connector. It is often used to return to the main topic after the speaker has veered away from the topic to add incidental or background information about the participants or about the situation.

2.3 Nouns

Nouns ordinarily consist of a ROOT, a NOUN SUFFIX (NSF), and a NOUN PREFIX (NPF):

(2.13) **osahé·taʔ**
o-saheʔt-aʔ
NPF-bean-NSF
'bean'

(2.14) **o·wíse?**
o-wis-e?
NPF-ice, glass-NSF
'ice, glass'

(2.15) **kahuwe·yá·**
ka-huwey-a?
NPF-boat-NSF
'boat'

(2.16) **ostó·sli?**
o-sto?sl-i?
NPF-feather-NSF
'feather'

The noun suffix is most often **-a?** or **-e?**. When the vowel of the suffix is accented, the vowel plus **?** is replaced by a long accented vowel. Thus **-á·** is the form of the suffix **-a?** in the word for 'boat' in (2.15). Which suffix occurs must be learned as part of the noun; it is not possible to predict from the last sound of the root or from the meaning of the root whether the suffix is **-a?** or **-e?**. The suffixes **-?** and **-i?** are less common; **-i?** occurs in the word for 'feather' in (2.16) and **-?** occurs below in (2.17) in the word for 'string, thread.' Again, when the vowel before the **-?** is accented the vowel plus **?** is replaced by a long accented vowel, as is the case in (2.17). Some nouns have no suffix; examples are **ohkwalí** 'bear' and **káhik** 'fruit.'

The noun prefix is most often **ka-** or **o-**. These prefixes can be identified with the feminine-zoic/neuter singular agent prefix **ka-** and the feminine-zoic/neuter singular patient prefix **yo-**, the only difference being that the initial glide **y** of **yo-** is absent in nouns. Some roots that begin in vowels don't have any prefix; these are roots that, if they were verb roots, would take the feminine-zoic/neuter agent prefix **w-** (before **a**, **e**, and **ʌ**) or **y** (before **o** and **u**). An example of a noun without a noun prefix is (2.17).

(2.17) **ahsli·yé·**
ahsliye-?
string, thread-NSF
'string, thread'

Nouns that denote objects that can be owned can occur in a *possessive* form. Possessive forms have a POSSESSIVE PREFIX in place of the noun prefix; compare **ohwísta?** 'money' with the noun prefix **o-** and **laohwísta?** 'his money' with the masculine singular possessive prefix **lao-**. Possessive structures are described in some detail in section 3, and Table 8 in that section lists the possessive prefixes.

Some nouns that denote things or beings that commonly occur in numbers larger than one can have a PLURAL ending, **-shuha** or **-okuha**, after the noun suffix. Examples are given in (2.18)–(2.20). Although we use the label PLURAL, this ending is not like the English plural, which is an obligatory inflectional category. In Oneida the plural is not obligatory and it does not form an inflectional paradigm with the singular.

(2.18) **kalute?shúha**
ka-lut-e?-shuha
NPF-tree-NSF-PL
'trees'

(2.19) **okʌha?shúha**
o-kʌh-a?-shuha
NPF-blanket-NSF-PL
'blankets'

(2.20) ukwatʌlo?sla?shúha
ukw-atʌlo-?sl-a?-shuha
1PL.POSS-friend-NMZR-NSF-PL
'my friends, our friends'

Some noun forms have a LOCATIVE ending instead of the noun suffix. The locative endings include **-a?ke** or **-á·ke** 'on, at,' **-aku** 'in,' and **-akta?** 'near.' An example with the locative ending **-á·ke** is given in (2.21). Locative endings can in turn be followed by a DISTRIBUTIVE ending **-shu?**, which adds the meaning that something is distributed along or all over a location. An example with this distributive ending is given in (2.22). Locative forms are often followed by the particle **nú·** or **nukwá·** 'place, where.'

(2.21) **nʌ a?é· niyo·lé· kahʌtá·ke ya?akyatkátho? thikʌ́,**
nʌ   a?é· niyo·lé· ka-hʌt-a?ke   y-a?-yaky-atkatho-?   thikʌ́
then far away   NPF-field-LOC   TRL-FACT-1EX.DU.A-see-PNC   that
'then we looked way off in the field,'

Norma Kennedy, A Scary Light

(2.22) **Kalista?késhu? kwí· nú· tahathahítane?.**
ka-list-a?ke-shu?   kwí· nú·   t-a-h-at-hah-it-a-?-ne?
NPF-metal-LOC-DISTR   where CSL-FACT-3M.SG.A-SRF-path-in-JN-INCH-PNC
'He came along the railway tracks (literally, all along on the metal).'

Norma Kennedy, My Father's Encounter

Finally, verb bases can take a so-called NOMINALIZER suffix and then these derived nouns can occur in all the structures that noun roots occur in. Examples of nominalized verb bases that occur with a noun prefix and noun suffix are given in (2.23) and (2.24).

(2.23) **kahyatúhsli?**
ka-hyatu-hsl-i?
NPF-write-NMZR-NSF
'paper, book'

(2.24) **owistóhsli?**
o-wisto-hsl-i?
NPF-cold-NMZR-NSF
'butter'

The structure consisting of a noun prefix, noun root or stem, and noun suffix is not the only structure used to refer to an object or being. Some words—a large number in fact—have the exact structure of verbs but have acquired a meaning and function so that they, like structural nouns, denote an object or being or *entity*. (These are listed in Michelson and Doxtator [2002] as N or V>N.) These verbs occur in only one aspect form, usually the habitual or stative, and with only one pronominal prefix, most often the feminine-indefinite or the feminine-zoic/neuter singular. An example of a verb that has become an entity expression is **yutolishʌtákhwa?** 'couch' in (2.25). The root of this word is -olishʌ-/-olishʌt- '(be) out of breath.' The **-at-** semi-reflexive derives the stem **-at-olishʌ-/-at-olishʌt-** 'rest.' This word has the feminine-indefinite agent prefix **yu-** and the word ends in **-khwa?**, which is a combination of the **-hkw-** instrumental suffix and habitual aspect suffix **-ha?**. The ending **-khwa?** is found very often in verb forms that have become entity expressions. So more literally the meaning of 'couch' is 'what one uses for resting.'

(2.25) **yutolishʌtákhwa?**
yu-at-olishʌt-a-hkw-ha?
3FI.A-SRF-out.of.breath-JN-INSTR-HAB
'couch'

Some verb forms can both describe a situation and function as an entity expression depending on the context. An example is **lotistó·slote?** 'they have feathers, the feathered ones, birds,' which is used several times in Ruben Cutcut's story about the bat (*Why the Bat Travels at Night*). The structure of this word is given in (2.26). When they refer to an entity such verb forms are examples of what is called an *internally-headed relative clause* (see section 4.2).

(2.26) **lotistó·slote?**
loti-sto?sl-ot-e?
3M.DP.P-feather-stand-STV
'they have feathers, the feathered ones, the birds'

A summary of the structure of non-possessed nouns is given in Table 7.

2.4 Noun Incorporation

Noun incorporation features prominently in Oneida words. It will be mentioned again in other sections and especially in the sections on possession (section 3) and counting (section 9). Noun incorporation is defined as a noun-verb compound where the noun must also be able to occur independently as a free-standing noun (Sapir 1911). The noun stem **-she?lh-** 'dough' is incorporated in (2.27) while in (2.28) it occurs in an external noun form.

Noun prefix o-, ka-	Noun root (e.g. **-kʌh-** 'cloth, blanket')	Noun Suffix -aʔ, -eʔ, -iʔ, -ʔ	
	or Verb base plus nominalizer (e.g. **-hyatuhsl-** 'book, paper' from **-hyatu-** 'write')	Noun Suffix -aʔ, -eʔ, -iʔ, -ʔ	Plural ending -shuha, -okuha
		Locative ending -aʔke/-á·ke 'on, at' -aku 'in' -aktaʔ 'near'	
		Locative ending -aʔke/-á·ke 'on, at' -aku 'in'	Distributive ending -shuʔ

Table 7. Noun structure

(2.27) **ʌkatesheʔlhu·ní·**
ʌ-k-ate-sheʔlh-uni-ʔ
FUT-1SG.A-SRF-dough-make-PNC
'I will make a dough [a loaf]'

Clifford Cornelius, A Lifetime Working

(2.28) **waʔtektakwʌ́htʌhteʔ oshé·lhaʔ.**
waʔ-te-k-takwʌhtʌht-eʔ   o-sheʔlh-aʔ
FACT-DL-1SG.A-flatten-PNC   NPF-dough-NSF
'I flattened the dough.'

Clifford Cornelius, A Lifetime Working

Not every verb can incorporate a noun. An example is the verb **-atst-** 'use,' whose meaning entails a tool or instrument. The noun denoting the tool or instrument cannot be incorporated and must be specified by a separately occurring noun form; in the excerpt in (2.29) **á·shaleʔ** is the noun denoting the instrument.

(2.29) **né· kiʔ thikʌ́ á·shaleʔ wá·latsteʔ waʔthalútyahkeʔ kʌ́h.**
né·   kiʔ   thikʌ́ aʔshal-eʔ   wa-hl-atst-eʔ
it's actually that   blade-NSF FACT-3M.SG.A-use-PNC

waʔ-t-ha-lut-yaʔk-eʔ   kʌ́·
FACT-DL-3M.SG.A-tree-sever-PNC   y'know
'he used the saw to cut down a tree.'

Mercy Doxtator, My First Christmas Tree

Note that the stative aspect of the verb **-atst-** 'use' also has the meaning 'wear.' An example of this use of the verb is the last word in (2.30).

(2.30) **kwaʔnyóh tá·t núwaʔ yakotaʔwástaʔ ahtaʔshúha yakótstu.**
kwaʔnyóh   tá·t núwaʔ   yako-itaʔw-a-st-haʔ   aht-aʔ-shuha yako-atst-u
seems like maybe   3FI.P-sleep-JN-INST-HAB   shoe-NSF-PL   3FI.P-use-STV
'and it seems like maybe she's wearing slippers.'

Rose Antone, A Night Visitor

The verb stem **-unyaʔt-** 'make with' is composed of the root **-uni-/-uny-** 'make' plus the causative suffix **-ʔt-**. It can incorporate the noun that denotes the product but *not* the noun that denotes what is used in the making of the product. In (2.31) the product is a blanket and the noun root **-kʌh-** 'blanket' is incorporated; what the product is made of has to be expressed by the separate noun **ostó·sliʔ** 'feathers.' If you did incorporate the root **-stoʔsl-** 'feather,' as in (2.32), the feather becomes the product.

(2.31) **yakotkʌhunyá·tu kítkit ostó·sliʔ**
        yako-at-kʌh-uny-a-ʔt-u   kítkit   o-stoʔsl-iʔ
        3FI.P-SRF-blanket-make-JN-CAUS-STV   chicken   NPF-feather-NSF
        'she has made a blanket out of chicken feathers'

(2.32) **yakotestoʔslunyá·tu**
        yako-ate-stoʔsl-uny-a-ʔt-u
        3FI.P-SRF-feather-make-JN-CAUS-STV
        'she has made a feather out of it, she has used it as a feather'

Another verb that generally does not incorporate is **-yoʔtʌ-/-yotʌ-** 'work.' The only root that is incorporated into this verb is **-lihw-** 'matter, business, etc.' So when people talk about working, say in tobacco, the noun for tobacco is not incorporated.

(2.33) **oyú·kwaʔ sʌ́· ukyoʔtʌ́hsaʔ onʌ́,**
        o-yuʔkw-aʔ   sʌ́·   waʔ-wak-yoʔtʌ-hs-aʔ   onʌ́
        NPF-tobacco-NSF   also   FACT-1SG.P-work-DISL-PNC   now
        'I went to work in tobacco too,'

Clifford Cornelius, A Lifetime Working

Just as there are verbs that *never* incorporate a noun, there are verbs that *always* incorporate a noun. An example is the state verb **-iyo-** 'good, nice.'

(2.34) **kwáh kwí· ikʌ́ waʔkʌhliyó,**
        kwáh kwí· ikʌ́   w-aʔkʌhl-iyó
        just really   3Z/N.SG.A-soil,earth-good[STV]
        'it was really good earth,'

Georgina Nicholas, An Oneida Childhood

Very often, the noun-verb combination is lexicalized—its meaning cannot be derived or predicted from the meanings that the noun and verb each have outside of incorporation. Nevertheless speakers can produce new combinations of noun plus verb and they use noun incorporation very creatively, sometimes producing words that neither Norma Kennedy nor Mercy Doxtator remember hearing before but whose meaning they immediately understand. An example is the word for toes making a sound, which Rose Antone used in her scary story about what her father heard one night.

(2.35) **Kok náheʔ kháleʔ tutayohyakwilakale·lé· thikʌ́ tho tuta·yʌ́·.**
    kʌʔ ok náheʔ   kháleʔ   t-uta-yo-ahyakwil-a-kalele-ʔ   thikʌ́
    a little while   and   DL-CSL:FACT-3Z/N.SG.P-toe-JN-sound-PNC   that

    tho   t-uta-yʌ-e-ʔ
    there   DL-CSL:FACT-3FI.A-walk-PNC
    'In a little while there was the sound of toes coming again, someone was coming
    again [walking on their toes].'
Rose Antone, A Night Visitor

Given a choice between incorporating a noun and using a separate noun form, more often than not the noun is incorporated. External noun forms seem to be used for contrast or at least when a concept or object is particularly salient. Some stories that have a noun that is incorporated into several different verbs and that is also unincorporated are Mercy Doxtator's story *Beaver, Let's Trade Teeth!* (see also Appendix 1) and Norma Kennedy's story *The Bean Game.*

2.5 Kinship Terms

Kinship terms have some of the structural properties of verbs and some of nouns (Koenig and Michelson, 2010a). For example, kinship terms have transitive pronominal prefixes that otherwise occur on verbs. The kinship term **lakeʔníha** 'my father' in (2.36) has the transitive prefix **lak-/lake-** 3M.SG>1SG. In kinship terms the transitive prefix identifies the older person in the relationship with the more agent-like properties and the younger member with the more patient-like properties; in other words, the prefix **lak-/lake-** in 'my father' otherwise specifies a third person masculine singular agent acting on a first person singular patient, as in the verb form **lakeʔnikú·laleʔ** in (2.36). A property of kinship terms that is associated with noun forms is that some transitive prefixes that occur on kinship terms and that begin in the glides **w** or **y** don't have the glide when the prefix is word-initial. For example, the word **utatyʌ́ha** 'her daughter' has the 3FI>3FI transitive prefix **utat-**, which corresponds to the prefix **yutat-** on verbs.

(2.36) **lakeʔníha kyuhte wí· né· wé·ne lakeʔnikú·laleʔ**
    lake-ʔniha   kyuhte wí·   né·   wé·ne   lake-ʔnikuhlal-eʔ
    3M.SG>1SG-father   supposedly   it's   evidently   3M.SG>1SG-look.after-STV
    'my father must have been the one looking after me'
Mercy Doxtator, My Childhood

Complex kinship expressions consist of two kinship terms. Examples are **aksótha onulhá·** 'my grandmother's mother' ('my grandmother, her mother') or **lakeʔníha lohsótha** 'my father's grandmother' ('my father, his grandmother'). The term that is the index of the expression, namely the person being talked about, is the second term in the expression. For example, **onulhá·** is the index of **aksótha onulhá·**, and **lohsótha** is the index of **lakeʔníha lohsótha**. The other term identifies the member in the kin relation who is related to the term that is the index.

Some kinship terms can take a NOMINALIZER suffix and then be incorporated into the verbs -yʌ-/-yʌt- 'put, lie' and -kaʔte- 'have many.' The verbs take PATIENT prefixes, and in this respect nominalized kinship terms are treated grammatically as if they were alienable nouns (see section 3 on possession). An example with the nominalized root for 'grandchild' is given in (2.37). Some kinship stems can also be incorporated into the verb root -ʌ-, which occurs only with incorporated kinship stems. Again, the stem requires the nominalizer and the verb is inflected with patient prefixes. An example is given in (2.38). (The external nominal **tehnukwé** identifies the siblings as male siblings, i.e. brothers.)

(2.37)   **Wakatleʔslaká·teʔ**
          wak-atle-ʔsl-a-kaʔte-ʔ
          1SG.P-grandchild-NMZR-JN-have.many-STV
          'I have many grandchildren'

Clifford Cornelius, A Lifetime Working

(2.38)   **Thoʔnʌ́ tékni tewakeʔkʌ·shʌ́· tehnukwé,**
          thoʔnʌ́   tékni   te-wake-ʔkʌ-sh-ʌ-ʔ   te-hn-ukwe
          and then two   DL-1SG.P-sibling-NMZR-have-STV   DL-3M.DU.A-person
          'And then I have two brothers,'

Hazel Cornelius, Starting Life Together

3. Possession

Possession involves a relation—a relation between something that is possessed and someone who is the possessor of the possessed item, or a relation of kinship between two persons, which was already described in section 2.5. Some scholars treat part-whole relations, as when talking of a part of an object (say, the legs of a cooking pot), as a kind of possession as well. Oneida expresses possession by two means: with certain verbs or with possessive noun forms. A factor relevant for both verbal and nominal possession is whether the possessed noun is *alienable* or *inalienable*. Inalienable nouns are parts of the body that normally are not separated from the body and so cannot be transferred from one person to another. Alienable nouns are all other nouns, including parts of the body that are more easily separated, such as hair, fur, or feathers. In the sections below, alienable possession is discussed before inalienable. The expression of possession is a good way to review the structure of nouns and verbs.

3.1 Verbal Possession with Alienable Nouns

Possession can be expressed with the stative aspect of verbs that otherwise describe posture. The two postural verbs that occur most often in a possessive function are -yʌ-/ -yʌt- 'put (down), lie' and -ot- 'stand.' The excerpts in (3.1)–(3.3) exemplify the first of these verbs, -yʌ-/-yʌt-, which we gloss as 'have' when it has a possessive function. The pronominal prefixes on the verb identify properties of the possessor and when the possessed noun is alienable the verb requires PATIENT prefixes. Most often the term that is possessed is expressed by an incorporated noun, but sometimes it is expressed by an external nominal, and sometimes by both. In the example in (3.1) the possessed term is incorporated (**-hwist-** 'metal, money'), in (3.2) it is expressed by the external noun **hydro**, and in (3.3) it is expressed both by the incorporated root **-nʌskw-** 'domestic animal' and the noun **é·lhal** 'dog.'

(3.1)   **tho nikú yukwahwístayʌʔ kʌʔ nityukwayʌ́·saʔ.**
  tho nikú   yukwa-hwist-a-yʌ-ʔ kʌʔ nityukwayʌ́·saʔ
  that's how much 1PL.P-money-JN-have-STV we young people
  'that's how much money we young people have.'
Olive Elm, Friday Nights

(3.2)   **Khále? ahsuhkʌ́ tshiyukwa·yʌ́· wí· n hydro.**
  khále? ahsuhkʌ́ tshi-yukwa-yʌ-ʔ   wí· n hydro
  and before when COIN-1PL.P-have-STV   hydro
  'And it was before we had hydro.'
Norma Kennedy, My Father's Encounter

(3.3)   **Tahnú· yukwanʌ́skwayʌʔ kʌs thikʌ́ é·lhal,**
  tahnú· yukwa-nʌskw-a-yʌ-ʔ   kʌs   thikʌ́ é·lhal
  and 1PL.P-animal-JN-have-STV customarily that dog
  'And we used to have this dog,'
Clifford Cornelius, A Lifetime Working

Several state verbs—verbs that occur only in the stative aspect—express alienable possession with PATIENT pronominal prefixes; examples of such state verbs are **-iyo-** 'good, nice,' **-es-/-us-** 'long,' and **-oʔtʌ-** 'kind of.' The state verb **-kaʔte-** 'have many, a lot of' has possession as part of its meaning and this verb also selects PATIENT prefixes. Examples of alienable possession with **-es-/-us-** 'long' and **-kaʔte-** 'have many, have a lot' are given in (3.4) and (3.5). The possessed entity ('skirt') is incorporated into the verb in (3.4).

(3.4)   **Tahnú· kʌʔ ok niyakoʔkha·lés kʌ́h.**
  tahnú· kʌʔ ok ni-yako-ʔkhal-es   kʌ́·
  and this only PART-3FI.P-skirt-long[STV] eh
  'And her skirt is short.'
Verland Cornelius, Ghosts, Flirts, and Scary Beings

(3.5)   **yukwaká·teʔ porridge waʔakwatekhu·ní·.**
  yukwa-kaʔte-ʔ   porridge waʔ-yakw-ate-khw-uni-ʔ
  1PL.P-have.a.lot-STV porridge FACT-1EX.PL.A-SRF-food-make-PNC
  'we have a lot of porridge to eat.'
Clifford Cornelius, A Lifetime Working

3.2 Nominal Possession with Alienable Nouns

The nominal pattern of possession for alienable nouns consists of a POSSESSIVE prefix, the NOUN ROOT (or STEM) and NOUN SUFFIX. The possessive prefixes are given in Table 8. In (3.6) the word for 'metal, money' has the possessive prefix **lao-**.

	a-stem	C-stem	i-stem	e-/ʌ-stem	o-/u-stem
1SG	akw-	ak(e)-	ak-	akw-	ak-
1DU	uky-	ukni-	ukn-	ukn-	ukn-
1PL	ukw-	ukwa-	ukwʌ-	ukw-	uky-
2SG	s-	sa-	sʌ-	s-	s-
2DU	tsy-	sni-	sn-	sn-	sn-
2PL	sw-	swa-	swʌ-	sw-	tsy-
3M.SG	lao-	lao-	lao-	law-	la-
3M.DP	laon-	laoti-	laot-	laon-	laon-
3FZ.SG	ao-	ao-	ao-	aw-	--
3FZ.DP	aon-	aoti-	aot-	aon-	aon-
3FI	ako-	ako-	ako-	akaw-	aka-

Table 8. Possessive prefixes

(3.6) **Tho s yakʌʔ nú· yehótyehseʔ laohwístaʔ,**
tho   kʌs   yakʌʔ   nú·   ye-ho-aty-ehseʔ
that's usually reportedly where TRL-3M.SG.P-drop.off-HAB
lao-hwist-aʔ
3M.SG.POSS-metal,money-NSF
'That's where he leaves his money,'

Olive Elm, The Dreamer

This possessive pattern applies also to the root **-awʌ-** 'belonging.' An example is given in (3.7). The forms of **-awʌ-** are sometimes translated into English with possessive pronouns: 'Did you bring something of *hers*, the little girl's?'

(3.7) **Sniha·wí· katiʔ kʌ thok náhteʔ akowʌ́ yeksáh.**
sni-hawi-ʔ   katiʔ kʌ   thok náhteʔ ako-awʌ   yeksá·
2DU.A-carry-STV then QUESTION something 3FI.POSS-belonging girl
'Did you bring some belonging of the [little] girl's?'

Mercy Doxtator, The Spoiled Child

When the possessed noun and the nominal mentioning the possessor both occur, the more common order is for the possessor to be mentioned first, but the reverse order also occurs. An example of the more common possessor-possessed order is **Suzie Webster akonúhsaʔ** 'Suzie Webster's house.' An example of the opposite order occurs in (3.7), **akowʌ́ yeksáh** 'belonging of the girl's' (her-belonging, girl). Another example is **akotyá·tawiʔt kaʔikʌ́ yeksá·** 'this girl's dress' (her-dress, this, girl) from the same story as (3.7). Examples of both verbal and nominal patterns for an alienable noun come from Mercy Doxtator's story about her dog Blackie. The excerpt in (3.8) has the verbal construction with **-yʌ-/-yʌt-** 'put, have' and the incorporated noun **-nʌskw-** 'domestic animal, pet,' and the excerpt in (3.9) has the nominal construction with the first person singular possessive prefix **ak-**. Note that the root **-nʌskw-** is always incorporated while **-(i)tshenʌ-** is never incorporated, but both mean 'domestic animal, pet.'

(3.8) **tekniyáshe s waknʌskwayʌ·táke? é·lhal,**
       tekniyáshe   kʌs   wak-nʌskw-a-yʌt-ahkwe?   é·lhal
       two   customarily   1SG.P-pet-JN-have-PAST   dog
       'I had two pet dogs,'

Mercy Doxtator, *My Dog Blackie*

(3.9) **shakwanolúkhwa? se? akitshe·nʌ́· é·lhal.**
       shakwa-noluhkw-ha?   se?   ak-itshenʌ-?   é·lhal
       1EX.PL>3M.SG-love-HAB   too   1SG.POSS-pet-NSF   dog
       'we love my pet dog.'

Mercy Doxtator, *My Dog Blackie*

3.3 Verbal Possession with Inalienable Nouns

State verbs—such as **-iyo-** 'good, nice,' **-es-/-us-** 'long,' **-o?tʌ-** 'kind of,' and **-ut-** 'attach'—express inalienable possession by incorporating the noun that denotes the possessed item and selecting AGENT prefixes. (While postural verbs frequently occur in a possessive function with alienable nouns, they occur infrequently with inalienable nouns; an example is given in 3.15.) In (3.10) the inalienable noun **-hsin-** 'tooth' is incorporated into **-es-/-us-** 'long,' and in (3.11) the inalienable noun **-snuhs-** 'finger' is incorporated into **-ut-** 'attach.'

(3.10) **tho wa?katítane? a?é· na?teksine·sú·se?,**
        tho   wa?-k-atita?-ne?   a?é·   na?-te-k-hsin-es-u-?se?
        there   FACT-1SG.A-get.in-PNC   great   PART-DL-1SG.A-leg-long-STV-PL
        'I would get in there [the buggy] with my great long legs,'

Olive Elm, *Visits to My Auntie's*

(3.11) **tsi? thikʌ́ ótku? kwí· tho kutinu?kélha? tsi? yesnuhsu·tú·.**
        tsi?   thikʌ́   ótku?   kwí· tho   kuti-nu?kel-ha?   tsi?
        because   that   snake   there 3FZ.PL.A-suck-HAB   at

        ye-snuhs-ut-u-?
        3FI.A-finger-attach-DISTR-STV
        'because snakes are sucking at her fingers.'

Norma Kennedy, *The Girl with the Bandaged Fingers*

In addition to the state verbs mentioned above with agent prefixes, there are a few state verbs that always select PATIENT prefixes whether the possessed noun is alienable or inalienable. An example of such a verb is **-nuhwak-** 'be sore, hurt, pain.' In the excerpt in (3.12) from the same story as (3.11), the inalienable root **-snuhs-** 'finger' is incorporated into the state verb **-nuhwak-** and the verb has the patient prefix **yako-**.

(3.12) **Né· kati? wí· aolí·wa? yakosnuhsanú·waks,**
        né· kati? wí·   aolí·wa?   yako-snuhs-a-nuhwak-s
        well then it's   the reason   3FI.P-finger-JN-sore-HAB
        'So that's why she has sore fingers,'

Norma Kennedy, *The Girl with the Bandaged Fingers*

The inalienable construction with agent prefixes is used also to describe parts of things. The excerpt in (3.13) describes a pot with legs.

(3.13) **kwahotokʎ·u wí· tekahsi·núteʔ u·ták waʔutnaʔtsyá·lʌʔ,**
kwahotokʎ·u wí· te-ka-hsin-ut-eʔ   u·ták
just for real   DL-3Z/N.SG.A-leg-attach-STV   pot

waʔ-yu-at-naʔtsy-a-hl-ʌʔ
FACT-3FI.A-SRF-kettle-JN-set-PNC
'she would set down this pot with legs [on the stove],'

Verland Cornelius, *A Lifetime of Memories*

3.4 Nominal Possession with Inalienable Nouns

The nominal pattern of possession for nouns that are inalienable body parts consists of AGENT prefixes, the NOUN ROOT, and a LOCATIVE ending. The agent prefix identifies whose body part is being talked about. In (3.14) the possessor of the inalienable noun **-nikwʌʔt-** 'belly' is the first person inclusive dual **tni-**. The LOCATIVE ending has several different forms, including **-é·ne** in (3.14) and **-ʔke/-·ke** in (3.16) below.

(3.14) **í·lelheʔ né· a·hatkátho tninikwʌʔté·ne.**
i-hl-elh-eʔ   né· aa-h-atkatho   tni-nikwʌʔt-é·ne
EPEN-3M.SG.A-want-STV   it's OPT-3M.SG.A-see   1IN.DU.A-belly-LOC
'he wants to see your and my bellies.'

Mercy Doxtator, *Berries and Bellies*

The contrast between patterns that apply to alienable versus inalienable nouns, as well as the difference between verbal and nominal patterns, can be illustrated with teeth, since a tooth can be an inalienable part of the body when still in the mouth or alienable once it has been extracted. The various possibilities are attested in Mercy Doxtator's story about what you are supposed to do when you lose a tooth. In the excerpt in (3.15) the tooth is inalienable; the root **-nawil-/-nawi-** 'tooth' is incorporated into the stative aspect of the postural verb **-ot-** 'stand' and the possessor is identified with agent prefixes. In (3.16) the nominal pattern with agent prefixes and locative ending occurs. Finally, in (3.17) the tooth is no longer in the mouth, and now alienable possession is expressed with a possessive noun prefix. The various possessive patterns are summarized in Table 9.

(3.15) **nʌ kʌ tú·skeʔ yoʔnétskʌ tsiʔ snawi·lóteʔ.**
nʌ   kʌ   to·kʎskeʔ yo-ʔnetskʌ   tsiʔ s-nawil-ot-eʔ
now   QUESTION it's true   3Z/N.SG.P-loose[STV]   at   2SG.A-tooth-stand-STV
'is it true you have a loose tooth?'

Mercy Doxtator, *Beaver, Let's Trade Teeth!*

Verbal Possession		
Alienable	Stative aspect of verbs, **-yʌ-** 'put, lie' or **-ot-** 'stand' Possessed noun is incorporated or an independent nominal	Patient prefixes
	State verbs (such as **-es-/-us-** 'long,' **-iyo-** 'good, nice,' **-oʔtʌ-** 'kind of,' **-kaʔte-** 'have many, have a lot') With **-kaʔte-** 'have many' the possessed noun is incorporated or an independent nominal; otherwise the possessed noun is incorporated into the verb	
Inalienable	State verbs (such as **-es-/-us-** 'long,' **-iyo-** 'good, nice,' **-oʔtʌ-** 'kind of,' **-ut-** 'attach') Possessed body part noun is incorporated	Agent prefixes
Nominal possession		
Alienable	Noun root (or stem) plus noun suffix	Possessive prefixes
Inalienable	Noun root plus locative ending	Agent prefixes

Table 9. Possessive structures

(3.16)   **waʔutathlo·lí· nále? yoʔnétskʌ knawí·ke,**

waʔ-yutat-hloli-ʔ   nʌ   aleʔ   yo-ʔnetskʌ   k-nawi-ʔke

FACT-3FI>3FI-tell-PNC   then   again   3Z/N.SG.P-loose[STV]   1SG.A-tooth-LOC

'she told her that my tooth was loose,'

Mercy Doxtator, Beaver, Let's Trade Teeth!

(3.17)   **ókhna? né· tho tyéhawe? aknawi·lá·,**

ókhna?   né·   tho   t-ye-haw-e?   ak-nawil-a?

and then   it's   there   CSL-3FI.A-hold-STV   1SG.POSS-tooth-NSF

'and then there she was holding my tooth,'

Mercy Doxtator, Beaver, Let's Trade Teeth!

4. Clauses

4.1 Clauses, Utterances, and Constructions

Oneida and other Iroquoian languages are often described as languages in which a verb can also constitute a clause. What is meant by such a statement is that a verb, or clause, can usually stand on its own as a sentence. Because the texts in this work are organized into *utterances*—stretches of discourse that are delimited by utterance-final phonology—the description is not couched in terms of sentences. Verbs can constitute a clause on their own but usually clauses in Oneida include other elements as well, maybe (1) one or more particles that link the situation expressed by the verb to a previously mentioned situation, (2) one or more particles that add emphasis or degree of certainty about the actuality of the situation,

(3) a locative or temporal expression, (4) a noun or other referring expression. These possibilities are illustrated in the excerpts in (4.1) – (4.3). The excerpt in (4.1) below has one clause and it begins with a particle sequence, **nʌ kyaleʔ wíꞏ** 'so again.' This sequence comprises four particles: **nʌ** 'now' (temporal), **kiʔ** 'actually' (emphatic), **aleʔ** 'again' (temporal), and **wíꞏ** (connective). The next two words are also particles and together they specify the location of the event, **éꞏnik nukwáꞏ** 'upstairs.' This utterance also has a noun, the English word **mattress**. It is not uncommon to find English nouns, especially for items that either have no Oneida word or where the Oneida word is a recent coining that has not become fully established. The excerpt in (4.2) has two clauses. The first begins in the connective particle **tahnúꞏ** 'and,' which is followed by the locative expression **tsiʔ nukwáꞏ** 'where.' The second clause in (4.2) begins with another locative expression, **tho nukwáꞏ** 'that's where.' In this excerpt Clifford Cornelius is talking about when the bed that he and his brothers and father were lying on broke in the middle of the night and it was the end of the bed where they had their heads that fell. Clauses that begin in **tsiʔ** and **tho** often co-occur in a *correlative* construction (section 8). The excerpt in (4.3) has three clauses: the first begins in the temporal particle **ókhnaʔ** 'and then,' the second begins in the indefinite expression **úhkaʔ ok** 'someone' (section 7.1), and the third is the clause **tsiʔ íꞏleʔ** 'where/as he is walking.' Locative and temporal expressions deserve far more space than can be devoted to them here. They usually include a locative or temporal particle, and often the verb has a prepronominal prefix: the **t-** cislocative, **y-** translocative, **tsh-** coincident, or **n-** partitive. Also, verbs preceded by the particle **tsiʔ** can have a locative or temporal function, and sometimes the interpretation as temporal versus locative is vague. For example, the **tsiʔ** clause in (4.3) could be interpreted locatively ('at, where') or temporally ('as').

(4.1)   **Nʌ kyaleʔ wíꞏ éꞏnik nukwáꞏ nyusahníhaweʔ mattress.**

nʌ kiʔ aleʔ wíꞏ   éꞏnik nukwáꞏ   n-y-usa-hni-haw-eʔ   mattress

so again   upstairs   PART-TRL-REP:FACT-3M.DU.A-take-PNC   mattress

'So then the two of them took the mattress upstairs again.'

Verland Cornelius, A Pig in the Window

(4.2)   **Tahnúꞏ tsiʔ nukwáꞏ yeyakwakuꞏhʌ́ꞏ tho nukwáꞏ yahúꞏsʌ<u>neʔ</u>.**

tahnúꞏ   tsiʔ nukwáꞏ   ye-yakwa-kuhʌ-ʔ   tho nukwáꞏ

and   where   TRL-1EX.PL.A-head.rest-STV   that's where

yahaʔ-w-aʔsʌʔ-neʔ

TRL:FACT-3Z/N.SG.A-fall-PNC

'And it's [the end] where we had our heads that fell.'

Clifford Cornelius, A Lifetime Working

(4.3)   **ókhnaʔ lothuꞏté úhkaʔ ok ohnaʔkʌ́ꞏshuʔ taꞏyʌ́ tsiʔ í<u>ꞏleʔ</u>.**

ókhnaʔ   lo-athute-ʔ   úhkaʔ ok   ohnaʔkʌ́ꞏshuʔ

and then   3M.SG.P-hear-STV   someone   all along behind

t-a-yʌ-e-ʔ   tsiʔ   i-hl-e-ʔ

CSL-FACT-3FI.A-walk-PNC   at/as   EPEN-3M.SG.A-walk-PRES

'and then he heard someone coming along behind him where/as he is walking.'

Norma Kennedy, My Father's Encounter

The definition of *utterance,* as used in this work, is dependent on the distribution of utterance-final forms. An utterance is any length of words—from one word to many, sometimes even what may translate into English as a paragraph—that ends with an utterance-final form. The excerpts in (4.2) and (4.3) end in utterance-final forms and so they are utterances. Not every Oneida word has a distinct utterance-final form (although most Oneida nouns and verbs do) and so sometimes an utterance is a stretch of spoken words that together are prosodically independent; they are followed by a longer pause and a significant pitch reset, such as the excerpts in (4.1), (4.4), and (4.5). The utterances in (4.4) and (4.5) don't have a verb, and the utterance in (4.5) consists just of particles (the speaker has been talking about a light that landed on a window sill and was unlike other lights in that it didn't illuminate the room). Whether utterances such as these should also be considered clauses depends on one's analysis of verbless structures.

(4.4) **yah ki? né· kánike? ká·slet.**
  yah ki?   né· kánike? ká·slet
  not indeed it's nowhere car
  'there were no cars anywhere.'

Olive Elm, Friday Nights

(4.5) **Ok ne? thikʌ́, yah nʌ? né·.**
  ok ne?   thikʌ́ yah nʌ? né·
  and as for that not that one
  'But not that one.'

Verland Cornelius, A Pig in the Window

In addition to referring to clauses and utterances, we refer to *constructions*. This is because often two or even three words have to occur together in order to convey a particular meaning (and the meaning cannot be derived from the meaning we attribute to the individual words in isolation). An example is the expression **úhka? ok** 'someone,' which is composed of **úhka?** 'who, anyone' and the particle **ok** 'only.' (Indefinite expressions such as **úhka? ok** are described in section 7.) Another example of a construction that consists of more than one word is negation, which requires (usually) the particle **yah** and a verb with the negative or contrastive prepronominal prefix (see section 5 for negation patterns). An interesting feature of multi-word constructions is that the two parts of the construction do not have to be next to each other, but can be interrupted by other words, mainly particles. We will see many examples of this in following sections.

4.2 Clauses as Arguments

Although it is not uncommon for an utterance to contain just one clause, it is far more common for an utterance to have two or more clauses. Speakers often connect one event or situation to another. For example, the meaning of a verb includes a 'who' and/or a 'what.' The 'who' and 'what' are semantic arguments of the verb and animate arguments are realized by the pronominal prefixes, as described in section 2.1. Semantic arguments of a verb can also be expressed by another clause. An example is given in (4.6). The main verb **wa?éhsane?** 'she finished' has two arguments. One of the arguments is the person who finished something, realized by the feminine-indefinite prefix **ye-/-e-** 'she.' The other argument is that which she finished; in (4.6) the clause **wa?utna?talu·ní·** 'she made bread' corresponds to the other argument. The argument clause, given in brackets, is simply *juxtaposed* to the main verb without any special marking. Another example of a juxtaposed argument clause occurs in the excerpt in (4.7). Here the clause **tʌshatilí·wahkwe?** 'they will sing again' is an argument of the main verb **tʌthutáhsawʌ?** 'they will start.'

(4.6)　**Nʌ kwí· né· ka?ikʌ́ wa?éhsane? [wa?utna?talu·ní·]**
　　　　nʌ kwí· né· ka?ikʌ́　wa?-ye-hsa?-e?　　　wa?-yu-at-na?tal-uni-?
　　　　so then　it's　this　FACT -3FI.A-finish-PNC　FACT-3FI.A-SRF-bread-make-PNC
　　　　'So then she finished making the bread'

Norma Kennedy, The Bird

(4.7)　**nʌ elhúwa? tʌthutáhsawʌ? [tʌshatilí·wahkwe?].**
　　　　nʌ　　elhúwa?　t-ʌ-t-hu-atahsaw-ʌ?　　　　t-ʌ-s-hati-lihwahkw-e?
　　　　then　right then　DL-FUT-CSL-3M.PL.A-start-PNC　DL-FUT-REP-3M.PL.A-sing-PNC
　　　　'then they will start to sing again.'

Mercy Doxtator, After a Loss

In some cases the verb in the argument clause has the OPTATIVE prefix. An example of an argument clause with an optative verb occurs in the excerpt in (4.8). (The optative prefix is represented as **aa** in the segmented version but written **a·** in the Oneida orthography.) In this case the situation described by the verb is one that is not seen as having taken place or existing; it may be a possible or even likely situation but it has not occurred and may never occur. In (4.8) the main verb is a negative verb; it is not unusual for optative clauses to occur with negative verbs since the negation entails that the action described by the optative verb cannot have happened. The third clause in this excerpt ('he could catch us') also has the optative prefix; this clause provides a possible, but unfulfilled, explanation for what was said in the first two clauses.

(4.8)　**Yah kwí· te?yakninú·wehse? [a·shakyatukóhtʌ?,]**
　　　　tá·t núwa? a·shukniye·ná·.
　　　　yah　kwí·　te?-yakni-nuhwe?-se?　　aa-shaky-atukoht-ʌ-?
　　　　not　　　　NEG-1EX.DU.A-like-HAB　OPT-1EX.DU>3M.SG-pass.by-BEN-PNC
　　　　tá·t núwa?　aa-shukni-yena-?
　　　　maybe　　　OPT-3M.SG>1DU-catch-PNC
　　　　'We don't like for us to pass him, maybe he'll catch us,'

Verland Cornelius, Ghosts, Flirts, and Scary Beings

Finally, argument clauses can begin in the particle **tsi?**, sometimes called a *subordinator* or *complementizer*. In this case the event is presented as something that is certain. An example is the bracketed clause in the excerpt in (4.9).

(4.9)   **Né·n lothu·té· thikʎ [tsiʔ úhkaʔ ok ohnaʔkʎ·shuʔ ta·yʎ·,]**
     né·n   lo-athute-ʔ   thikʎ tsiʔ úhkaʔ ok ohnaʔkʎ·shuʔ
     it's that 3M.SG.P-hear-STV that   that   someone along behind

     t-a-yʌ-e-ʔ
     CSL-FACT-3FI.A-walk-PNC
     'And so he heard someone coming along behind,'

Norma Kennedy, My Father's Encounter

Often a person or object is referred to with a clause, usually a description of a characteristic activity or attribute. Such clauses can be paraphrased as 'the one that, those that' and they also function as an argument of a (main) verb. Examples are given in (4.10) and (4.11). In (4.10) the verb **lónhahseʔ** 'he hires him' could be translated instead as 'he who hires him' and even more colloquially as 'his boss;' it further specifies an argument of the verb **wahʎ·luʔ** 'he said.' In (4.11) **kʌʔ nikatsyapslá·saʔ** 'the jobs are small' could be translated 'those that are small jobs' or just 'small jobs,' and it further specifies an argument of the verb **a·hoyo·tʎ·** 'he could work at, do.' Clauses whose function is to make reference to someone or something are called *internally-headed relative clauses*. Internally-headed relative clauses can either precede or follow the main verb while (other) argument clauses always follow the main clause.

(4.10)   **Nʌ kwí· n [lónhahseʔ] wahʎ·luʔ,**
     nʌ kwí· n   lo-nhaʔ-seʔ   wa-hʌ-ihlu-ʔ
     so then   3M.SG>3M.SG-hire-HAB   FACT-3M.SG.A-say-PNC
     'So then his boss said,'

Norma Kennedy, An Unwanted Passenger

(4.11)   **[kʌʔ nikatsyapslá·saʔ] a·hoyo·tʎ·,**
     kʌʔ   ni-ka-tsyap-sl-aʔ-saʔ   aa-ho-yotʌ-ʔ
     small PART-3Z/N.SG.A-job-NMZR-small-PL OPT-3M.SG.P-work-PNC
     'small jobs that [a man] might do,'

Clifford Cornelius, A Lifetime Working

An internally-headed relative clause can co-occur with an independent nominal. In the excerpt in (4.12) **tekahsi·núteʔ** is the internally-headed relative clause and **u·ták** 'pot, pail' is the nominal.

(4.12)   **[tekahsi·núteʔ] wí· u·ták waʔutnaʔtsyá·lʌʔ,**
     te-ka-hsin-ut-eʔ   wí· u·ták waʔ-yu-at-naʔtsy-a-hl-ʌʔ
     DL-3Z/N.SG.A-leg-attach-STV   pot FACT -3FI.A-SRF-pail-JN-set.down-PNC
     'she set a pot [on the stove], one with legs,'

Verland Cornelius, A Lifetime of Memories

We have tried to translate multi-clausal utterances so that they sound somewhat natural in English but we hope that the reader can appreciate that it is not always straightforward to know how to reflect the grammar of Oneida while also maintaining the flow of the narrative or the impact of what the speaker is telling us.

4.3 Introduction and Mention of Discourse Referents

The pronominal prefixes that are an obligatory part of the structure of verbs help to keep track of who the participants are in a situation, so nouns (or more precisely expressions that identify entities as opposed to situations) occur far less frequently in Oneida than in English. Then it is interesting to consider the possible function of nouns and other entity expressions when they do occur. One function is that they introduce and establish discourse referents— who or what will be talked about. We discuss the various ways in which discourse referents are introduced in this section. A second function is to contrast one referent with another, which we also discuss here. A third function is to keep straight multiple referents so that we know who is doing what; for example the two characters **Tá·wet** and **Kastes** are mentioned often in Mercy Doxtator's story *Kastes Buys a Face*.

Several discourse patterns are used to first mention the person or thing that will be the topic of the narrative or the conversation. One is a *presentational* structure that consists of a typical set of particles, such as **né· kwí· ka?ikʌ́** or **né· kati? wí· ka?ikʌ́** plus an expression that identifies the participant, the speaker's father in (4.13). Often this presentational structure is set off from the rest of the utterance with a prosodic break (represented by a comma).

(4.13) **Né· kati? wí· ka?ikʌ́ lake?níha kʌ́·, wahahni·nú· thikʌ́ lu·té· s kwí· teyehna?tatslatilútha? kʌ́·,**

    né· kati? wí·   ka?ikʌ́   lake?níha   kʌ́·   wa-ha-hninu-?   thikʌ́

    well then it's   this   my father   y'know   FACT-3M.SG.A-buy-PNC   that

    lu·té·   kʌs kwí·   te-ye-hna?tatsl-atilut-ha?   kʌ́·

    they say   customarily   DL-3FI.A-pocket-stretch-HAB   see

    'Well anyway my father, he bought an accordion, they say "people stretch a pocket",'

Mercy Doxtator, Why Dogs Don't Talk

A common strategy used for introducing a participant is with the verb **-yat-** 'name,' as in the excerpt in (4.14).

(4.14) **Ókhale? tsyeyá·tat tho yehe·yʌ́·se?, Marlene yutátyats,**

    ókhale?   ts-ye-ya?t-a-t   tho   yehe-yʌ-e-?se?   Marlene

    and   REP-3FI.A-body-JN-one[STV]   there   TRL-3FI.A-walk-HAB   Marlene

    yutat-yat-s

    3FI>3FI-name-HAB

    'And one person who was over there, Marlene is her name,'

Norma Kennedy, The Bean Game

Verbs whose meaning includes posture or movement are also used to first mention a participant and, in this case, the nominal typically comes after the verb. Examples of this are the excerpts in (4.15) and (4.16) with the verbs for 'crawl' and 'stand.'

(4.15) **thahatye·lʌ́· né· kʌʔ waté·sleʔ ótku̱ʔ.**

th-a-h-atyelʌ-ʔ   né· kʌʔ
CONTR-FACT-3M.SG.A-suddenly.surprised-PNC it's right here

w-ate-ʔsle-ʔ   o-atku-ʔ
3Z/N.SG.A-SRF-drag-PRES   NPF-snake-NSF
'suddenly he was taken aback, right there was crawling a snake.'

                                       Norma Kennedy, *How I Learned to Swear*

(4.16) **tho yakʌʔ í·lateʔ lukwé,**

tho   yakʌʔ   i-hla-t-eʔ   lukwé
there reportedly EPEN-3M.SG.A-stand-STV a man
'a man was standing there,'

                       Olive Elm, *Ghost Sightings at the Language Centre*

A clause without any noun or nominal can introduce a referent. In the excerpt in (4.17) someone has died and the only mention of that person is via the clause **oskánhe yukniyó·tehkweʔ** 'we used to work together.' In this case the verb is functioning as an entity expression (an *internally-headed relative clause*) and, as the translation suggests, it could be paraphrased 'a person I used to work with.'

(4.17) **né· tsiʔ kaʔikʌ́ wahlʌ́heyeʔ tshutayolhʌʔuhátiʔ oskánhe
yukniyó·tehkweʔ,**

né· tsiʔ kaʔikʌ́ wa-hl-ʌhey-eʔ   tshutayolhʌʔuhátiʔ   oskánhe
because this   FACT-3M.SG.A-die-PNC when it became morning   together

yukni-yoʔte-hkweʔ
1DU.P-work-PAST
'because a person I used to work with died this morning,'

                            Mercy Doxtator, *After a Loss*

Sometimes the referent involves two distinct items or sets of items, and then the words denoting the referents do not have to occur together. In (4.18) **katsihko·tú·** 'ovenbread' comes before the verb while **kháleʔ ohnʌná·taʔ** 'and potatoes' comes after it.

(4.18) **Swatyelʌ́ s nók thikʌ́ katsihko·tú· ʌyákwakeʔ kháleʔ ohnʌná·taʔ.**

swatyelʌ́   kʌs   nók   thikʌ́   ka-tsihkw-ot-u-ʔ
sometimes usually only   that   3Z/N.SG.A-fist-stand-DISTR-STV

ʌ-yakwa-k-eʔ   kháleʔ o-hnʌnaʔt-aʔ
FUT-1EX.PL.A-eat-PNC and   NPF-potato-NSF
'Sometimes all was had to eat was ovenbread, and potatoes.'

                           Pearl Cornelius, *Family and Friends*

Once a participant has been mentioned for the first time, he or she (or it) may not be mentioned for many clauses other than by pronominal prefixes on the verb. But sometimes a subsequent mention is made soon after the initial mention. Looking over these examples, it seems the referent is salient for the speaker or maybe has some special connection to the speaker. For example, once Norma Kennedy introduced the snake that bit her husband in the excerpt in (4.15) above, the word **ótku?** 'snake' occurs in the next five utterances of this story. The repeated mentions of 'snake' may be motivated by an intense dislike of snakes. Another example comes from Georgina Nicholas's story about growing up. In the first line of the excerpt in (4.19), Georgina introduces her great-grandmother (before the verb). After only two clauses she mentions her again in the next two clauses (after the verb in both these clauses); these two clauses are given on the second and third lines of the excerpt in (4.19). For the rest of the relatively long paragraph her great-grandmother is mentioned only via pronominal prefixes.

(4.19) **Lake?níha s lohsótha teyakwayá<u>she</u> . . .**
    lake?níha   kʌs   lohsótha   te-yakwa-yashe
    my father   customarily   his grandmother   DU-1EX.PL.A-be.together[STV]
    'my father's grandmother lived with us. . .'

né· s kwí· tashakolutahawíhtʌ? lohsó<u>tha</u>.
    né·   kʌs kwí·   t-a-shako-lut-a-hawi-ht-ʌ-?
    it's   customarily   CSL-FACT-3M.SG>3-tree,log-JN-bring-CAUS-BEN-PNC
    lohsótha
    his grandmother
    '[when he found a good tree for splints] he would bring it to his grandmother.'

Shekú kwí· tshiyakotshá·nit lohsótha,
    shekú   kwí·   tshi-yako-tshahnit   lohsótha
    still   COIN-3FI.P-industrious[STV]   his grandmother
    'His grandmother still worked hard,'

Georgina Nicholas, An Oneida Childhood

Subsequent mentions can occur after the verb, as in the excerpt in (4.19) from Georgina Nicholas's story, or before the verb, as in (4.20) below. This excerpt comes from Verland Cornelius's life story; it is the third mention of her grandmother in the opening paragraph.

(4.20) **Tahnú· s aksótha yakotsi?tsyaká·te? kʌs.**
    tahnú·   kʌs   ak-hsotha
    and   habitually   3FZ.SG>1SG-grandparent

    yako-tsi?tsy-a-ka?te-?   kʌs
    3FI.P-flower-JN-have.many-STV   habitually
    'And my grandmother had a lot of plants.'

Verland Cornelius, A Lifetime of Memories

In addition to introducing discourse referents, speakers may mention the referent with an overt nominal in order to focus the hearer's attention on the referent or to contrast one referent with another. Frequently a word occurs at or near the beginning of an utterance immediately before the assertion particle **né·** 'it's' or 'it's the case that.' This particle typically occurs at the very beginning of a clause, so putting a word before this particle highlights it. (In more technical terms, the word that occurs before the assertion particle is *left-detached*.) In the excerpt in (4.21) Pearl Cornelius has been telling Mercy Doxtator about how her brother thought he was making off with an apple when what he actually grabbed was a potato. Mercy asks 'a potato?' Pearl responds by putting **ohnʌná·taʔ** 'potato' at the beginning, before the assertion particle **né·**.

(4.21)   **Wá·lelheʔ né· kʌ n swahyo·wáneʔ,**

 wa-hl-elh-eʔ   né·   kʌ n   swahyo·wáneʔ
 FACT-3M.SG.A-think-PNC   it's   QUESTION   apple
 'He thought it was an apple,'

 ohnʌná·taʔ nʌʔ né·.

 o-hnʌnaʔt-aʔ   nʌʔ né·
 NPF-potato-NSF   that one
 'it was a potato.'

 Ohnʌná·taʔ.

 o-hnʌnaʔt-aʔ
 NPF-potato-NSF
 'A potato?'

 Hʌ́·, ohnʌná·taʔ né· lonʌskwʌhátiʔ.

 hʌ́·   o-hnʌnaʔt-aʔ   né·   lo-nʌskw-ʌ-hatye-ʔ
 yes   NPF-potato-NSF   it's   3M.SG.P-steal-STV-PROG-PRES
 'Yes, it's a potato he was stealing.'

Pearl Cornelius, Family and Friends

The excerpt in (4.22) is from a story about an old and sickly crow who needs to be fed by the younger crows. The young ones are contrasted with the usual situation where crows feed themselves.

(4.22)   **Nʌ kwí· kaʔikʌ́ lotithóskaʔ né· luwanu·túheʔ.**

 nʌ kwí·   kaʔikʌ́   lotithóskaʔ   né·   luwa-nutu-heʔ
 so then   this   young ones   it's   3>3M.SG-feed-HAB
 'So then these young ones, they were feeding him.'

Mildred Cutcut, The Crow

Another way of conveying contrast is with the use of the particles **nʌʔ né·** at the end of an utterance. Pearl Cornelius used this strategy in the second line of the excerpt in (4.21) above. Another example is the excerpt in (4.23) from an extended description about how different plants used to be grown.

(4.23) **Á·nuk, waʔakwaʔnukslotúniʔ s nʌʔ né·,**
    á·nuk   waʔ-yakw-aʔnuk-sl-ot-unyu-ʔ   kʌs   nʌʔ né·
    onion FACT-1EX.PL.A-onion-NMZR-stand-DISTR-PNC   habitually   those ones
    'Onions, we stood those,'

Georgina Nicholas, An Oneida Childhood

Speakers also use an overt nominal when they wish to *reactivate* a referent that was established and talked about earlier in the discourse. After the speaker has gone on to talk about a
different (but perhaps related) topic he or she returns to the original one. An example is
given in the excerpt in (4.24) from an episode about some bread that didn't turn out as an-
ticipated. The particles **ok neʔ** or **ok neʔn** or **ok wí n** at the beginning of an utterance often
occur in this function.

(4.24) **Ok wí· n akná·talok, yah ní· teʔwakanúhteʔ kátshaʔ né· nyehóti,**
    ok wí· n   ak-naʔtalok   yah   ní·   teʔ-wak-anuhte-ʔ
    and as for 1SG.POSS-bread   not   me   NEG-1SG.P-know-STV

    kátshaʔ   né·   n-ye-ho-atye
    where   it's   PART-TRL-3M.SG.P-throw[STV]
    'And as for my bread, I don't know where he got rid of it,'

Clifford Cornelius, A Lifetime Working

4.4 Mismatches between Verbal and Nominal Prefixes

The prefix that occurs on nouns and other entity expressions and the pronominal prefix on
the verb do not have to have the same person, number, and gender features, that is to say the
prefixes do not have to strictly match or "agree." These *mismatches* are not mistakes; rather
they are part of the regular distribution of pronominal prefixes. For example, when talking
of someone's mother the verb form that describes the actions of the mother will always have
the feminine-indefinite prefix, in spite of the fact that the different forms for 'mother' re-
quire feminine-zoic prefixes. Thus in (4.25) the verb has the feminine-indefinite agent prefix
ya-, while **aknulhá·** 'my mother' has the prefix **ak-** indicating a relation between feminine-
zoic and first person singular.

(4.25) **Waʔí·luʔ aknulhá·,**
    waʔ-ya-ihlu-ʔ   ak-nulhá·
    FACT-3FI.A-say-PNC   3FZ.SG>1SG-mother
    'My mother said,'

Mercy Doxtator, Why Dogs Don't Talk

Other mismatches occur when the relation between a verb and a nominal is one of *overlap*. There are two kinds of overlap. In one case, the prefix on the verb references two or
more participants but the nominal identifies only one of the participants; the other participant is included in the meaning of the prefix on the verb. In (4.26) the verb has the first person exclusive *dual* prefix ('he and I') but the nominal **laulhá·** 'he' refers to just one person.

(4.26)   **Nʌ kwí· laulhá· waʔákneʔ office,**
      nʌ kwí·   la-ulhá·   waʔ-yakn-e-ʔ   office
      so then   3M.SG.A-self   FACT-1EX.DU.A-walk-PNC   office
      'So then I went to the office with him,'

Clifford Cornelius, A Lifetime Working

Another example of this kind of overlap is given in (4.27). The verb has a plural prefix, but only the auntie is mentioned. So what the speaker is saying is that her auntie 'and them' (presumably the rest of the household) had a car.

(4.27)   **Ké·yaleʔ s né·n akwatauntieha tsiʔ lotiʔsléhtayʌʔ Model T,**
      k-ehyal-eʔ   kʌs   né·n   akw-at-auntieha   tsiʔ
      1SG.A-remember-STV   customarily   it's that   1SG.POSS-SRF-auntie   that

      loti-ʔsleht-a-yʌ-ʔ   Model T
      3M.DP.P-car-JN-have-STV   Model T
      'I remember that my auntie and them had a car, a Model T,'

Verland Cornelius, Ghosts, Flirts, and Scary Beings

The second kind of overlap is the opposite of the first kind. The verb mentions just one participant and so has a singular prefix, but the prefix on the nominal suggests two or more participants. The example in (4.28) is from a story about a little girl whose fingers are always bandaged and the sister who discovers why. The verb has the third person *singular* prefix, since it refers to the sister, but the nominal **tekyatʌhnu·téleʔ** has a *dual* prefix denoting the two in the sister relation, 'the one she is sisters with, her sister.'

(4.28)   **náleʔ waʔutkétskoʔ kaʔikʌ́ tekyatʌhnu·téleʔ.**
      nʌ aleʔ   waʔ-yu-at-ketskw-ʔ   kaʔikʌ́   te-ky-atʌhnutel-eʔ
      then again   FACT-3FI.A-SRF-raise-PNC   this   DU-3FZ.DU.A-siblings-STV
      'then her sister got up again.'

Norma Kennedy, The Girl with the Bandaged Fingers

5. Negation

The negation construction in Oneida consists of a negative particle **yah** and a prefix to the verb, either the NEGATIVE **teʔ-/te-** or the CONTRASTIVE **th-/thaʔ-**. The negative prefix occurs with verbs in the stative and habitual aspects, except before the **te-** dualic and **y-** translocative prefixes. The negative prefix has two forms: **te-** when the following pronominal prefix begins in **h**, and **teʔ-** everywhere else. An example of the negative prefix with a verb in the habitual aspect is given in (5.1). Note that other particles can occur after the negative particle **yah** and before the verb. In (5.1) the particle **e·só·** 'a lot' intervenes between **yah** and the verb.

(5.1)   **tahnú· yah e·só· tehatatíhah<u>kwe</u>ʔ.**
       tahnú·   yah   e·só·   te-h-atati-ha-hkweʔ
       and   not   lots   NEG-3M.SG.A-speak-HAB-PAST
       'he didn't used to talk a lot.'

Margaret Antone, Forecasting Things to Come

The contrastive prefix **th-/thaʔ-** occurs before the **te-** dualic and **y-** translocative prefixes, and with verbs in the punctual aspect. The contrastive prefix also has two forms: **thaʔ-** before the dualic prefix, and **th-** otherwise. An example with the contrastive before the dualic is the negation in (5.2).

(5.2)   **yah thaʔtewakatuhutsyoní, só·tsiʔ kano·lú·.**
       yah   thaʔ-te-wak-atuhutsyoni   só·tsiʔ   ka-nolu-ʔ
       not   CONTR-DL-1SG.P-want[STV]   too much   3Z/N.SG.A-expensive-STV
       'I don't want it, it's too expensive.'

Mercy Doxtator, Kastes Buys a Face

An example of the contrastive with the punctual aspect is given in (5.3). In the punctual aspect, the contrastive always occurs with the optative prefix. This is the only mode that occurs in the negation construction; there are no negative future or factual forms.

(5.3)   **Tahnú· yah s tha·yukwatkályaʔkse? tsiʔ niyo·lé· ʌtáktaʔ,**
       tahnú·   yah   kʌs   th-aa-yukw-at-kalyaʔk-hs-eʔ   tsiʔ niyo·lé·
       and   not   habitually   CONTR-OPT-1PL.P-SRF-pay-BEN-PNC   until
       ʌtáktaʔ
       Saturday
       'And we won't get paid until Saturday,'

Mercy Doxtator, All about Tobacco

Negation reveals an interesting feature of Oneida verb structure and that is that four of the prepronominal prefixes—**te-/teʔ-** negative, **th-/thaʔ-** contrastive, **n-** partitive, and **tsh-** coincident—occur in the same "slot," which means no two of the prefixes can occur in the same verb form. Consequently, a verb that requires the **n-** partitive or **tsh-** coincident prefix "loses" the partitive or coincident in the negative. For example, **-ot-/ -oht-** 'how, like, be so' requires the partitive, as in the excerpt in (5.4). But the negative of this verb does not have the partitive, as seen in the excerpt in (5.5). (In [5.5] the vowel plus the **ʔ** of the negative prefix is replaced by a stressed and lengthened vowel.)

(5.4)   **tho né· ni·yót tsiʔ wahoslʌhtáksʌʔ**
       tho   né·   ni-y-oht   tsiʔ   wa-ho-slʌhtaksʌ-ʔ
       that's   it's   PART-3Z/N.SG.A-be.so[STV]   that   FACT-3M.SG.P-dream-PNC
       'the way he dreamed it'

Mercy Doxtator, An Unusual Spittoon

(5.5)   **tshiwahu·níseʔ yah né· tho té·yot.**
tshiwahu·níseʔ   yah   né·   tho   teʔ-y-oht
a long time ago   not   it's   that's   NEG-3Z/N.SG.A-be.so[STV]
'a long time ago it wasn't like that.'

Pearl Cornelius, Family and Friends

Infrequently the particle **yah** occurs with a verb in the OPTATIVE mode rather than a verb with the negative or contrastive prefix. Examples of this are the next two excerpts. Perhaps this construction is used when the speaker is describing a situation that is somehow extraordinary. So in (5.6) those present expected an unusual visitor to be wearing an overcoat because it was so cold outside, and in (5.7) one might presume (incorrectly) that the ones telling stories would drink alcohol rather than just tea or coffee.

(5.6)   **yah kátshaʔ a·kí·luʔ tá·t kwaʔnyóh overcoat a·hotstúhakeʔ**
         tsiʔ seʔ niyotho·lé·,
yah   kátshaʔ   a·kí·luʔ   tá·t   kwaʔnyóh   overcoat
not   anywhere   I'd say   if   seems   overcoat

aa-ho-atst-u-hake-eʔ   tsiʔ   seʔ   ni-yo-athole-ʔ
OPT-3M.SG.P-use-STV-CONT-PNC   how   too   PART-3Z/N.SG.P-cold-STV
'no way I'd say for him to be wearing an overcoat [and] it was so cold,'

Mercy Doxtator, Some Woodcutters Get a Visitor

(5.7)   **Yah kiʔ nuwʌtú náhteʔ thikʌ́ aʔnyóh wí· oyá· a·honatstúhakeʔ wí·**
         tsiʔ latikalatúnyuhe̲ʔ.
yah   kiʔ   nuwʌtú   náhteʔ   thikʌ́   aʔnyóh   wí·   oyá·
not   actually   never   anything that   seems like   other

aa-hon-atst-u-hak-eʔ wí·   tsiʔ   lati-kalatu-nyu-heʔ
OPT-3M.DP.P-use-STV-CONT-PNC   as   3M.PL.A-tell.stories-DISTR-HAB
'Seems it was never for them to use anything else as they were telling stories.'

Pearl Cornelius, Family and Friends

Occasionally also, when the action or activity is clear from the discourse, the negative particle **yah** occurs without any verb. In the excerpt in (5.8) Hazel Cornelius is talking about how at weddings nowadays people don't say anything other than "Congratulations."

(5.8)   **Yah kwí· náhteʔ sʌ́haʔ isiʔ nú·.**
yah   kwí·   náhteʔ   sʌ́haʔ   isiʔ nú·
not   anything   more   yonder
'Nothing more.'

Hazel Cornelius, Starting Life Together

A noun or other nominal is negated with the negative particle **yah** before the nominal and the negative word **té·kʌ** after the nominal.[5]

(5.9) **yah seʔ isé· ok té·kʌ.**
  yah seʔ isé· ok teʔ-kʌ
  not too you only NEG-kʌ
  'it's not you only, you are not the only one.'

Spoken by Norma Kennedy

There are particles that occur in addition to, or in place of, the negative particle **yah**. The particle **nuwʌtú** 'ever, never' asserts that the situation described by the verb has not occurred even one time, although just as in English the assertion may not be literally true. **Nuwʌtú** is always located between **yah** and a negative verb.[6]

(5.10) **yah nuwʌtú tehʌ·tluʔ lakeʔníha.**
  yah nuwʌtú te-hʌ-iʔtlu-ʔ   lakeʔníha
  not never   NEG-3M.SG.A-sit-STV my father
  'my father was never home.'

Verland Cornelius, *A Pig in the Window*

The negative expectation particle **áhsu** '(not) yet' occurs in place of **yah** and with a negative verb or **té·kʌ**, as in the excerpts in (5.11) and (5.12).

(5.11) **áhsu kwahotokʌ́·u teʔyotéhsuʔ ókhnaʔ yaʔakwanáklateʔ.**
  áhsu   kwahotokʌ́·u teʔ-yo-ate-hsaʔ-u   ókhnaʔ
  not yet just for real NEG-3Z/N.SG.P-SRF-finish-STV and then
  y-aʔ-yakw-anaklat-eʔ
  TRL-FACT-1EX.PL.A-settle-PNC
  'it wasn't finished yet and already we moved in.'

Olive Elm, *Visits to My Auntie's*

(5.12) **nók tsiʔ áhsu kiʔ sixteen té·kʌ.**
  nók tsiʔ áhsu   kiʔ   sixteen teʔ-kʌ
  but   not yet actually sixteen NEG-kʌ
  'but I wasn't sixteen yet.'

Clifford Cornelius, *A Lifetime Working*

Negative commands are conveyed with the particle **tákʌʔ** and a verb with the FUTURE prefix. (Commands, or imperative forms, were discussed in section 2.1 on the structure of verbs.) An example of a negative command is given in (5.13). With the OPTATIVE prefix, the

---

[5] **Té·kʌ** looks like it is composed of the negative prefix **teʔ-** plus an element **kʌ**, which may be verbal in origin. A similar element, **ikʌ**, may also be present in the demonstrative particles **kaʔikʌ́** and **thikʌ́** and in the emphatic expression **kwahikʌ́** 'just really.'

[6] Outside negation, **nuwʌtú** occurs only in yes-no questions (section 6.2). An example provided by Norma Kennedy is **Nʌ kʌ nuwʌtú Tony Roma's yesatekhu·ní.** 'Have you ever eaten at Tony Roma's?' (ye-s-atekhuni TRL-2SG.P-eat[STV]).

particle **tákʌʔ** is used to make a strong suggestion, as in (5.14). In these two constructions, most of the time, the verb does not have the punctual aspect ending as is otherwise required when the verb has the future or optative prefix.[7]

(5.13) **Tákʌʔ nuwʌtú úhkaʔ ʌshehlolí kaʔikʌ́ tsiʔ nukyá·tawʌ̲ʔ̲.**
     tákʌʔ   nuwʌtú   úhkaʔ   ʌ-she-hloli   kaʔikʌ́   tsiʔ
     don't   never   anyone   FUT-2SG>3-tell   this   what
     n-aʔ-wak-yaʔt-awʌ-ʔ
     PART-FACT-1SG.P-body-happen-PNC
     'Don't you ever tell anyone what happened to me!'
Norma Kennedy, My Father's Encounter

(5.14) **tákʌʔ kwí·· só·tsiʔ ta·hutlakalé·last.**
     tákʌʔ   kwí·   só·tsiʔ   t-aa-hu-at-lakalehl-a-st
     don't   too much   DL-OPT-3M.PL.A-SRF-sound.noise-JN-CAUS
     'they shouldn't make too much noise.'
Mercy Doxtator, After a Loss

The particle **yáhtʌʔ** seems to be a kind of negative pro-form that substitutes for a (negative) clause. An example is given in (5.15).

(5.15) **utahséhtahkweʔ ok oniʔ n yáhtʌʔ,**
     uta-hs-ehtahkw-eʔ   ok oniʔ n   yáhtʌʔ
     CSL:OPT-2SG.A-believe-PNC   and or   not
     'you can believe it or not,'
Clifford Cornelius, A Lifetime Working

Finally, there are two expressions in Oneida that have the structure of negation, but don't have negative meaning. Each has two variants. The first expression is based on the verbs -ʌ- or -ʌʔ- 'happen' with the **y-** translocative prefix and it indicates necessity: **yah thya·ya·wʌ́· tsiʔ** and **yah thya·ya·wʌ́neʔ tsiʔ** 'it has to be, have to.' The other expression is based on the verb **-eʔne-/-eʔni-** 'evident' and indicates a great degree: **yah teʔwé·ne** or **yah teʔwé·ni** 'it's amazing, incredible.' A summary of negation patterns is given in Table 10.

(5.16) **Yah thya·ya·wʌ́· tsiʔ waʔkyenahninú·naʔ coal oil.**
     yah   th-y-aa-yaw-ʌ-ʔ   tsiʔ
     not   CONTR-TRL-OPT-3Z/N.SG.P-happen-PNC   that
     waʔ-k-yen-a-hninu-ʔn-a?   coal oil
     FACT-1SG.A-oil-JN-buy-DISL-PNC   coal oil
     'I have to go and buy coal oil.'
Norma Kennedy, A Scary Light

---

[7] Another construction where the punctual aspect suffix is not present is when a verb with the optative prefix follows forms of the verb **-elh-** 'want,' (e.g. **i·kélheʔ** 'I want' or **yah téhselheʔ** 'you don't want') as in, for example, **i·kélheʔ a·kathlolí** 'I want to tell.' The expected punctual aspect form is **a·kathlo·lí·**.

Verbal Negation	
yah 'not'	Verb with the negative prepronominal
yah nuwʌtú 'not ever, never'	prefix te(ʔ)- or the contrastive prepro-
áhsu 'not yet'	nominal prefix th(aʔ)-
tákʌʔ 'shouldn't, don't'	Verb with the future or the optative prepronominal prefix
Nominal Negation	
yah 'not'	té·kʌ
áhsu 'not yet'	

Table 10. Negation

(5.17) **Yah teʔwé·ni niyakotyaʔtahslu·ní.**
yah   teʔ-w-eʔni   ni-yako-at-yaʔt-a-hsluni
not   NEG-3Z/N.SG.A-evident[STV]   PART-3FI.P-SRF-body-JN-dress[STV]
'It's amazing how dressed up she was.'

Georgina Nicholas, The Flirt

6. Questions

Questions are generally of two types and are distinguished according to the expected answer. *Content* questions ask for information about a participant, or location, or anything beyond a simple 'yes' or 'no' answer. *Polar* or *yes-no* questions anticipate a 'yes' or 'no' answer.

6.1 Content Questions

Content questions in Oneida begin with one of several words depending on the kind of information the speaker is soliciting: **úhka?** 'who,' **náhte?** 'what,' **kátsha?** 'where,' **kánhke** 'when,' **tó·** in questions about measures or degree (how many, how long, how far, how big), and **oh** or **ot** for kind or manner (what kind, how). Note that **úhka? náhte?** is used alongside of **úhka?** for 'who.' Questions are exemplified in the excerpts in (6.1)–(6.6). **Kátsha?** is usually followed by the *classificatory* word **nú·**; and **tó·** is frequently followed by **nikú** in questions about amount, by **niyo·lé·** in questions about distance or extent, and by **náhe?** in questions about extent in time. (See section 8 for more about these classificatory words.) When they occur, classificatory words do not necessarily occur right after the question word; often other particles intervene.

(6.1) **úhka? né· náhte? yesalihwawí ta·hsekhahsyu·kó· aké·slet.**
úhka? né· náhte? yesa-lihw-awi   t-aa-hse-khahsyukw-?
who   it's what   3>2SG-matter-give[STV] DL-OPT-2SG.A-take.apart-PNC
ake-?sleht
1SG.POSS-car
'Who gave you permission to take apart my car?'

            Norma Kennedy, *How I Learned to Swear*

(6.2) **Náhte? wahetshlo·lí·.**
náhte? wa-hetsh-hloli-?
what   FACT-2SG>3M.SG-tell-PNC
'What did you tell him?'

            Mercy Doxtator, *A Man Tells Off His Boss*

(6.3) **Kátsha? nú· nisatayá·tu.**
kátsha? nú· ni-sa-atawya?t-u
where   PART-2SG.P-enter-STV
'Where did you go to school?'

            Pearl Cornelius, *Family and Friends*

(6.4) **Kánhke kati? né· ákte? nihawenú thikʌ́ latʌhninúhahkwe?.**
kánhke kati? né· ákte?   ni-haw-e-nu   thikʌ́
when   then   it's different PART-3M.SG.P-walk-STV   that
l-atʌhninu-ha-hkwe?
3M.SG.A-sell-HAB-PAST
'So when did that storekeeper go away from there for some place else?'

            Olive Elm, *The Dreamer*

(6.5) **Tó· s né· nikú latikálya?ks ne? thó·ne?.**
tó·   kʌs   né· nikú   lati-kalya?k-s   ne? thó·ne?
how   usually it's much   3M.PL.A-pay-HAB   at that time
'How much did they pay at that time?'

            Pearl Cornelius, *Family and Friends*

(6.6) **oh né· kati? nʌya·wʌ́·ne? ʌhseyʌtéhtane? aseayo·tʌ́·.**
oh   né· kati? n-ʌ-yaw-ʌ?-ne?   ʌ-hse-wyʌtehta?-ne?
how   it's then   PART-FUT-3Z/N.SG.P-happen-PNC   FUT-2SG.A-learn-PNC
aa-esa-yotʌ-?
OPT-2SG.P-work-PNC
'how will you get the experience to work?'

            Clifford Cornelius, *A Lifetime Working*

Náhte? plus a possessive form of the noun root **-lihw-** 'matter, business, affair, news,' **náhte? aolí·wa?**, is used to ask the question 'why.' **Náhte? aolí·wa?** is often reduced, as if written **náhte? alyá·** or even **náhte? alá·**. An excerpt that has a 'why' question is (6.7).

(6.7)　**náhte? kati? aolí·wa? tsi? yah nisé· tha·hsaté·sle?**
　　　　náhte?　kati?　ao-lihw-a?　　　　　　　tsi?　yah　nisé·
　　　　what　　well　3Z/N.SG.POSS-matter-NSF　that　not　you
　　　　th-aa-hs-ate-?sle-?
　　　　CONTR-OPT-2SG.A-SRF-drag-PNC
　　　　'well how come YOU're not crawling?'

Mercy Doxtator, My First Christmas Tree

Kátsha? 'where' plus the verb form **ka·yʌ́·** is used for asking 'which, which one?' An example is given in (6.8). The expected answer to this question is one of at least two alternatives and so this kind of question is called an *alternative* question. One answer to that question is the expression **kátsha? ok ka·yʌ́·** 'either one (or the other).'

(6.8)　**Kátsha? ka·yʌ́· ʌ·kátste?.**
　　　　kátsha?　ka-yʌ-?　　　　　　　　ʌ-k-atst-e?
　　　　where　　3Z/N.SG.A-put,lie-STV　FUT-1SG.A-use-PNC
　　　　'Which one will I use?'

Spoken by Norma Kennedy

(6.9)　**Kátsha? ki? ok wí· ka·yʌ́·.**
　　　　kátsha? ki? ok wí·　ka-yʌ-?
　　　　somewhere　　　　　3Z/N.SG.A-put,lie-STV
　　　　'One or the other.'

Pearl Cornelius talking to Mercy Doxtator

Finally, **tó·** occurs in clauses that have the structure of a question but the impact of an exclamation:

(6.10)　**tó· kátkʌs ka?ikʌ́,**
　　　　tó·　　k-at-kʌ-?s　　　　　　ka?ikʌ́
　　　　how　　1SG.A-SRF-see-BEN　this
　　　　'hey, how about I take a look!'

Mercy Doxtator, Beaver, Let's Trade Teeth!

6.2 Yes-No Questions

Yes-no questions, or *polar* questions, expect a 'yes' or 'no' answer and are formed with the question particle **kʌ**. The particle follows the first word or constituent in the utterance (or clause), so after a verb in (6.11), after a particle in (6.13) and (6.14), and after **úhka? ok** 'someone' in (6.15). The particle **kati?** can intervene between the first word or constituent and the question particle, as in (6.12).

(6.11)　**íhselhe? kʌ aétene?.**
　　　　i-hs-elh-e?　　　　kʌ　　　　　aa-etn-e-?
　　　　EPEN-2SG.A-want-STV　QUESTION　OPT-1IN.DU.A-walk-PNC
　　　　'do you want to go with me?'

Norma Kennedy, A Scary Light

(6.12)　**sniha·wí· kati? kʌ thok náhte? akowʌ́ yeksáh.**
　　　　sni-hawi-?　　　kati? kʌ　　　thok náhte?　ako-awʌ　　　　yeksá·
　　　　2DU.A-carry-STV　then　QUESTION　something　3FI.POSS-belonging　girl
　　　　'did you bring some belonging of the little girl's?'

Mercy Doxtator, The Spoiled Child

(6.13)　**nʌ kʌ yona?tala·lí.**
　　　　nʌ　　kʌ　　　　yo-na?tal-a-li
　　　　now　QUESTION　3Z/N.SG.P-bread-JN-ripe,cooked[STV]
　　　　'is the bread done?'

Norma Kennedy, The Bird

(6.14)　**né· kʌ ka?ikʌ́ tsi? ka·yʌ́· yo?nétskʌ,**
　　　　né·　kʌ　　　　ka?ikʌ́　tsi? ka·yʌ́·　　yo-?netskʌ
　　　　it's　QUESTION　this　　the one that　3Z/N.SG.P-loose[STV]
　　　　'is this the one [tooth] that's loose?'

Mercy Doxtator, Beaver, Let's Trade Teeth!

(6.15)　**úhka? ok kʌ náhte? tho yakawʌhe·yú.**
　　　　úhka? ok　kʌ　　　　tho　yakaw-ʌheyu
　　　　someone　QUESTION　there　3FI.P-die[STV]
　　　　'someone died there?'

Norma Kennedy, An Unwanted Passenger

Polar questions can solicit a 'yes' or 'no' answer to a negation. In this case the question begins in **yah kʌ**—the negative particle followed by the question particle. Examples are given in (6.16) and (6.17).

(6.16)　**yah kʌ te?satshanuní kóskos okúhsa? ʌ́hseke? ʌyólhʌne?.**
　　　　yah　kʌ　　　　te?-s-atshanuni　　　kóskos okúhsa?　ʌ-hse-k-e?
　　　　not　QUESTION　NEG-2SG.P-happy[STV]　pig　face　　　FUT-2SG.A-eat-PNC
　　　　ʌyólhʌne?
　　　　tomorrow
　　　　'you're not happy? you can eat pig face [head cheese] tomorrow.'

Verland Cornelius, A Pig in the Window

(6.17) **yah kʌ úhkaʔ teʔyakotsístayʌʔ a·huwatsistúthahseʔ,**
      yah   kʌ   úhkaʔ   teʔ-yako-tsist-a-yʌ-ʔ
      not   QUESTION   anyone   NEG-3FI.P-light-JN-have-STV

      aa-huwa-tsist-ut-hahs-eʔ
      OPT-3>3M.SG-light-attach-BEN-PNC
      'no one has a light for him?'

Mercy Doxtator, Some Woodcutters Get a Visitor

A negative polar question can include the particle **nuwʌtú** 'never, ever,' as in the next excerpt.

(6.18) **Yah katiʔ kʌ nisé· nuwʌtú isé· utayesatkʌʔsé·na?**
      yah   katiʔ   kʌ   nisé·   nuwʌtú   isé·
      not   well   QUESTION   you   ever   you

      uta-yes-at-kʌ-ʔse-hn-aʔ
      CSL:OPT-3>2SG-SRF-see-BEN-DISL-PNC
      'They don't ever come to see [visit] you?'

Spoken by Mercy Doxtator to Pearl Cornelius

Table 11 provides a summary of the different kinds of questions described in this section.

6.3 Embedded Questions

Clauses that have the structure of questions can occur after another clause; these are called *embedded questions*. An embedded question can report an inquiry, as in the excerpt in (6.19), where the embedded yes-no question 'is the bread done?' occurs after the verb for 'ask.' (Embedded questions are enclosed in square brackets in the excerpts below.) Most often in Oneida, however, an embedded question does not report an inquiry but corresponds to an argument of another verb. For example, in (6.20) the embedded question **tó· nikú latikályaʔks neʔ thó·neʔ** 'how much did they pay at that time?' is an argument of the verb 'I don't remember,' and what the speaker no longer remembers is an amount—the amount that would be the answer to 'how much did they pay back then?' And in (6.21) what the speaker says she doesn't know is the identity of a particular person—the person who gave her mother rides, or the answer to 'who gave her a ride?' Additional examples of embedded questions that correspond to an argument of the verb 'know' are given in (6.22) and (6.23).

(6.19) **nʌ kyaleʔ ʌtsyutatliʔwanu·tú·seʔ [nʌ kʌ yonaʔtala·lí.]**
      nʌ kyaleʔ   ʌ-ts-yutat-liʔwanutu-ʔs-eʔ   nʌ   kʌ
      again   FUT-REP-3FI>3FI-ask-BEN-PNC   now   QUESTION

      yo-naʔtal-a-li
      3Z/N.SG.P-bread-JN-ripe[STV]
      'she asked her again whether the bread is done.'

Norma Kennedy, The Bird

Content questions	
úhkaʔ or úhkaʔ náhteʔ	'who?'
náhteʔ	'what?'
kátshaʔ núˑ	'where?'
kátshaʔ kaˑyʌ́ˑ	'which one?'
kánhke	'when?'
tóˑ nikú	'how much?'
tóˑ niyoˑléˑ	'how far?'
tóˑ náheʔ	'how long?'
tóˑ plus a verb whose meaning includes measure	e.g. how big?, how expensive?
ot or oh niˑyót oh plus a verb whose meaning includes manner or kind	'what kind?'
Polar (yes-no) questions	
Word, constituent	kʌ
Word, constituent	kʌ nuwʌtú 'ever, never'
yah 'not'	kʌ plus a verb with te-/teʔ- negative or th-/thaʔ- contrastive prefix

Table 11. Questions

(6.20) **Yah teʔskéˑyaleʔ? [tóˑ nikú latikályaʔks neʔ thóˑneʔ,]**

yah teʔ-s-k-ehyahl-eʔ   tóˑ nikú   lati-kalyaʔk-s   neʔ thóˑneʔ

not NEG-REP-1SG.A-remember-STV how much 3M.PL.A-pay-HAB at that time

'I don't remember how much they paid at that time,

Norma Kennedy, My First Job in Tobacco

(6.21) **yah kiʔ teʔwakanúhteʔ? [úhkaʔ kʌs náhteʔ washakotiyaʔtítaneʔ,]**

yah kiʔ   teʔ-wak-anuhte-ʔ   úhkaʔ kʌs náhteʔ

not actually NEG-1SG.P-know-STV   who habitually

wa-shakoti-yaʔtitaʔ-neʔ

FACT-3M.DP>3FI-give.a.ride.to-PNC

'I don't know who gave her a ride,'

Verland Cornelius, A Lifetime of Memories

(6.22) **yah níˑ teʔwakanúhteʔ? [kátshaʔ nyehóti,]**

yah níˑ teʔ-wak-anuhte-ʔ   kátshaʔ n-ye-ho-atye

not me NEG-1SG.P-know-STV   where   PART-TRL-3M.SG.P-throw[STV]

'I don't know where he got rid of [my bread],'

Clifford Cornelius, A Lifetime Working

(6.23) **Yah teʔwakanúhteʔ [tho kʌ naʔteyotí·kat.]**
  yah te-wak-anuhte-ʔ   tho   kʌ   naʔ-te-yoti-ʔkat
  not   NEG-1SG.P-know-STV   that's QUESTION PART-DL-3FZ.DP.P-be.fast[STV]
  'I didn't know they could go so fast.'

Barbara Schuyler, *A Ghost on the Tracks*

Sometimes an embedded question consists just of the first word of the question and the rest of the question is inferred from something that preceded in the discourse.

(6.25) **nók tsiʔ yah kiʔ né· tha·hiná·tuʔ [úhkaʔ],**
  nók tsiʔ yah kiʔ   né· th-aa-hi-naʔtu-ʔ   úhkaʔ
  not   not actually it's CONTR-OPT-1SG>3M.SG-name-PNC   who
  'but I won't name who,'

Verland Cornelius, *A Lifetime of Memories*

(6.26) **Yah seʔ teʔyukwanúhteʔ [kánhke.]**
  yah seʔ teʔ-yukw-anuhte-ʔ   kánhke
  not too NEG-1PL.P-know-STV   when
  'We don't know at all when.'

Margaret Antone, *Forecasting Things to Come*

7. Indefinites

Words that occur in content questions (section 6.1) also occur in indefinite expressions. There are two kinds of indefinite expressions in Oneida. *Positive* indefinites, described in section 7.1, roughly correspond to English forms with 'some': 'someone,' 'something,' etc. *Negative* indefinites, described in section 7.2, roughly correspond to English forms with 'any' and 'no': 'anyone, not anyone, no one,' or 'anything, not anything, nothing,' etc. Note that the negative series is called negative because they occur in negative contexts (broadly speaking), not because the expressions themselves (necessarily) have a negative meaning.

7.1 Positive Indefinites

Words that begin questions (section 6.1) plus the particle **ok** (or **thok**) 'only' form expressions that correspond to the positive indefinite pronouns and other pro-forms in English: **úhkaʔ ok** 'someone,' **thok náhteʔ** 'something,' **kátshaʔ ok nú·** 'somewhere,' **kánhke ok** 'some time,' and **tó· ok** 'some' (amount, distance, size, etc.). **Úhkaʔ ok náhteʔ** occurs as well as **úhkaʔ ok** for 'someone.' **Thok náhteʔ** 'something' is pronounced by some speakers as if written **tok náhteʔ**, and **kátshaʔ ok nú·** 'somewhere,' when talking quickly, comes out sounding **sok nú·**. The combination **tó· ok** 'some' is most often pronounced and written **tó·k**. Examples of a few of these expressions are given in (7.1)–(7.3).

(7.1)　**teswashlíhʌ úhkaʔ ok ta·yʌ́·.**
　　　　te-swa-shlihʌ　　úhkaʔ ok　t-a-yʌ-e-ʔ
　　　　DL-2PL.P-hurry　　someone　CSL-FACT-3FI.A-walk-PNC
　　　　'hurry, someone is coming.

Barbara Schuyler, A Ghost on the Tracks

(7.2)　**Né·n, yahaya·kʌ́·neʔ thikʌ́ thok náhteʔ tho yehátaʔas.**
　　　　né·n　　y-a-ha-yakʌʔ-neʔ　　　　　　　thikʌ́　thok náhteʔ　tho
　　　　it's that　TRL-FACT-3M.SG.A-go.out-PNC　that　something　there

　　　　ye-ha-taʔ-as
　　　　TRL-3M.SG.A-put.in-HAB
　　　　'So he went out and he was putting something in [the car].'

Rose Antone, A Night Visitor

(7.3)　**tho yahyateʔsléhtayʌʔ tó·k niyo·lé·,**
　　　　tho　　y-a-hy-ate-ʔsleht-a-yʌ-ʔ　　　　　　　　tó· ok
　　　　there　TRL-FACT-3M.DU.A-SRF-vehicle-JN-put-PNC　some

　　　　ni-yo-le-ʔ
　　　　PART-3Z/N.SG.P-far-STV
　　　　'they parked the car some ways off [not too far away],'

Verland Cornelius, Ghosts, Flirts, and Scary Beings

The expression **thok náhteʔ** 'something' shows that **náhteʔ** was originally a classificatory word. **Thok náhteʔ** probably goes back to **ot ok náhteʔ**, where **ot** otherwise was used
in questions. **Ot** was followed by the particle **ok** to form the indefinite expression, and then
ot ok was followed by the classificatory word **náhteʔ**. To get from **ot ok náhteʔ** to **thok
náhteʔ** you have to know that consonants at the ends of words are "released" in Oneida,
which can be indicated with an **h** after the consonant; so **ot ok náhteʔ** would have been pronounced as if written **oth okh náhteʔ**. The vowel **o** of **oth** was dropped, and the first two
words have become one word and are written together, including the first **h**, thus **thok
náhteʔ**.[8]

Thok náhteʔ can co-occur with a nominal; for example, **atslunyákhwaʔ** 'dress' in the
excerpt in (7.4).

(7.4)　**Thok kʌs yakʌʔ náhteʔ atslunyákhwaʔ tho wahona·tí·,**
　　　　thok　　kʌs　　　yakʌʔ　　　náhteʔ　　atslunyákhwaʔ
　　　　some　habitually　reportedly　anything　clothing

　　　　tho　　wa-hon-aty-ʔ
　　　　there　FACT-3M.DP.P-drop.off-PNC
　　　　'They would leave some piece of clothing,'

Olive Elm, The Dreamer

---

[8] Additional evidence that **náhteʔ** was originally a classificatory word and not a question word is the fact that it is
the only question word that can occur with **tsiʔ** in free relative clauses (section 8).

The indefinite expression **kátsha? ok nú·** 'somewhere' is used also for approximation, 'about, around,' as in the excerpts in (7.5) and (7.6). Particle combinations such as **kátsha? ok nú·** can occur with other particles that interrupt the sequence. In the excerpt in (7.6), for example, the particle **ki?** 'actually' occurs between **kátsha?** and **ok**, and the particles **uhte** 'probably, supposedly' plus the connector **wí·** occur between **ok** and **nú·**.

(7.5)   **Ya·wét kyuhte wí· kátsha? ok nú· wísk yawʌ·lé·
        tsha?tewakohsliyá·ku.**

        ya·wét   kyuhte wí·   kátsha? ok nú·   wísk   yawʌ·lé·
        like   supposedly somewhere   five   teen

        tsha?-te-wak-ohsl-iya?k-u
        COIN-DL-1SG.P-winter-cross.over-STV
        'like I guess I was about fifteen years old.'

Norma Kennedy, My Father's Encounter

(7.6)   **Kátsha? ki? ok uhte wí· nú· tá·t núwa? yá·ya?k mile tsi? niyo·lé·
        thikʌ́ tyutʌhni·núhe?.**

        kátsha? ki? ok uhte wí·   nú·   tá·t núwa?   yá·ya?k mile
        somewhere   probably   where   maybe   six miles

        tsi? ni-yo-le-?   thikʌ́   t-yu-atʌ-hninu-he?
        how   PART-3Z/N.SG.P-far-STV   that   CSL-3FI.A-SRF-buy-HAB
        'It was probably about six miles to the store.'

Norma Kennedy, A Scary Light

Indefinites can be questioned, as in the following excerpt that contains two indefinite expressions, both preceding the yes-no question particle **kʌ**.

(7.7)   **thok kʌ náhte? niyawʌ́·u thikʌ́ ká·slet, úhka? ok kʌ náhte?
        tho yakawʌhe·yú.**

        thok   kʌ   náhte?   ni-yaw-ʌ?-u   thikʌ́   ká·slet
        something   QUESTION   (something)   PART-3Z/N.SG.P-happen-STV   that   car

        úhka? ok kʌ   náhte?   tho   yakaw-ʌheyu
        someone   QUESTION   (someone) there   3FI.P-die[STV]
        'something happened to that car? someone died there?'

Norma Kennedy, An Unwanted Passenger (earlier version)

7.2 Negative Indefinites

The expressions for 'no one' (or 'not anyone'), 'nothing' (or 'not anything'), 'nowhere' (or 'not anywhere') consist of a negation construction—either the negative particle **yah** plus a verb with the **te?-/te-** negative or **th-/tha?-** contrastive prefix, or a clause that begins in **tákʌ?** 'don't, shouldn't'—and a word otherwise used in questions. Examples with a negative verb are given in (7.8) and (7.9), and an example with **tákʌ?** is given in (7.10).[9]

---

[9] After **yah náhte?**, speakers on occasion omit the negative prefix on the verb: **Kwáh s kwí· yah náhte? yonúhtu?t** instead of **yah náhte? te?yonúhtu?t** 'it doesn't seem that long' (spoken by Pearl Cornelius to Mercy Doxtator). Or,

(7.8)   **né·n yah úhka? tehoke?tóhtu.**
né·n   yah   úhka?   te-ho-ke?toht-u
it's that not   anyone   NEG-3M.SG.P-appear-STV
'no one showed up.'

Barbara Schuyler, A Ghostly Experience

(7.9)   **Yah ki? ní· nuwʌtú náhte? te?yukyatkáthu í· khále? Masyha,**
yah ki?   ní· nuwʌtú náhte?   te?-yuky-atkatho-u   í·
not actually we   never   anything NEG-1DU.P-see-STV   me

khále?   Masyha
and   Mercy
'But the two of us never ever saw anything, me and Mercy,'

Olive Elm, Ghost Sightings at the Language Centre

(7.10)   **tákʌ? oni? náhte? ʌhsí·lu thikʌ́,**
tákʌ? oni?   náhte?   ʌ-hs-ihlu   thikʌ́
don't too   anything   FUT-2SG.A-say   that
'don't say anything,'

Olive Elm, Visits to My Auntie's

   There are two expressions for 'nowhere.' One is **yah kátsha?**, based on **kátsha?** 'where.'
The other is **yah kánike?**, which occurs only in a negative context. Examples are given in
(7.11) and (7.12). **Yah kátsha?** is occasionally used as a mild emphatic as well, as in the
excerpt in (7.13).

(7.11)   **kwáh yah kátsha? tehonathu·té· utayo?slehta·kálele?,**
kwáh   yah   kátsha?   te-hon-athute-?
just   not   anywhere   NEG-3M.DP.P-hear-STV

uta-yo-?sleht-a-kalel-e?
CSL:OPT-3Z/N.SG.P-vehicle-JN-sound-PNC
'they hadn't heard anywhere the sound of a vehicle,'

Mercy Doxtator, Some Woodcutters Get a Visitor

(7.12)   **ókhna? né· yah kánike? té·shla<u>te?</u>.**
ókhna?   né·   yah   kánike?   te?-s-hla-t-e?
and then   it's   not   anywhere   NEG-REP-3M.SG.A-stand-STV
'and then he [the man] wasn't anywhere anymore.'

Olive Elm, Ghost Sightings at the Language Centre

(7.13)   **Yah kwí· kátsha? thutayako?nikuhli·yó·ne?.**
yah kwí· kátsha?   th-uta-yako-?nikuhl-iyo-?-ne?
not   anywhere   CONTR-CSL:OPT-3FI.P-mind-good-INCH-PNC
'There was no satisfying her.'

Verland Cornelius, A Lifetime of Memories

---

yah náhte? wástak instead of **yah náhte? te?wástak** 'you're (literally, it's) useless' (spoken by Norma Kennedy).

In the examples so far the indefinite expression and the negation have occurred in the same clause, but very often the indefinite expression occurs in a different clause from the negation. Typically the negation clause comes first and the second clause, which begins with the indefinite expression, corresponds to an argument of the negative verb. The argument clauses are enclosed in square brackets in following excerpts.

(7.14)   **yah wí· téhselhe? [úhka? náhte? a·yukhikʌ́ ka?ikʌ́,]**
       yah wí· te-hs-elh-e?   úhka? náhte? aa-yukhi-kʌ   ka?ikʌ́
       not   NEG-2SG.A-want-STV   anyone   OPT-3>1DP-see this
       'you don't want anyone to see us,'
Mercy Doxtator, My First Christmas Tree

(7.15)   **yah te?waketshʌ́li [úhka? náhte? a·yakoyo·tʌ́·,]**
       yah te?-wake-tshʌly-u   úhka? náhte? aa-yako-yotʌ-?
       not   NEG-1SG.P-find-STV   anyone   OPT-3FI.P-work-PNC
       'I didn't find anyone to work,'
Norma Kennedy, My First Job in Tobacco

(7.16)   **yah tha·hakwe·ní· [náhte? usahʌ́·lu?.]**
       yah   th-aa-ha-kweni-?   náhte?   usa-hʌ-ihlu-?
       not   CONTR-OPT-3M.SG.A-able-PNC anything REP:OPT-3M.SG.A-say-PNC
       'he couldn't say anything,'
Verland Cornelius, Ghosts, Flirts, and Scary Beings

(7.17)   **yah se? né· te?kano·lú·se? [náhte? a·yekhwahni·nú·.]**
       yah se? né· te?-ka-nolu-?-se?   náhte?
       not   too it's NEG-3Z/N.SG.A-expensive-STV-PL anything
       aa-ye-khw-a-hninu-?
       OPT-3FI.A-food-JN-buy-PNC
       'it didn't cost a lot to buy groceries.'
Mercy Doxtator, All about Tobacco

Frequently negative indefinite expressions occur in conditional clauses with verbs that have the optative mode prefix. (In English, words like 'any, anyone, anything' that occur in negative contexts, in a broad sense of the term, are called *negative polarity items*.)[10]

(7.18)   **kwáh kwí· náhte? a·yukli?wanu·tú·se? khále? kwáh kwí· nók**
       "I s'pose,"
       kwáh kwí· náhte?   aa-yuk-li?wanutu-?s-e?   khále? kwáh kwí· nók
       just   anything OPT-3>1SG-ask-BEN-PNC and   just

---

[10] It is not the case that only negative indefinites occur in conditional contexts; for example, the positive indefinite **úhka? ok náhte?** was used in the following: **Tá·t a?nyóh úhka? ok náhte? yah te?tyakawelyʌ?tiyó tsi? tho íhse-hse?, yawelu?uháti?**. 'If it seems like someone doesn't like it that you're around, never mind' (Pearl Cornelius speaking to Mercy Doxtator).

I s'pose
I s'pose
'anything at all they would ask me, and just "I s'pose,"'

Clifford Cornelius, A Lifetime Working

(7.19) **tá·t kánhke náhteʔ na·hoyá·tawʌʔ**
tá·t kánhke náhteʔ   n-aa-ho-yaʔt-awʌ-ʔ
if when anything PART-OPT-3M.SG.P-body-happen-STV
'if ever anything happened to him'

Olive Elm, The Dreamer

(7.20) **úhkaʔ yah tha·yutawyaʔtá·naʔ**
úhkaʔ yah th-aa-yu-atawyaʔt-a-ʔn-aʔ
anyone not CONTR-OPT-3FI.A-go.to.school-JN-DISL-PNC
'[if] anyone wouldn't go to school'

Verland Cornelius, A Lifetime of Memories

(7.21) **úhkaʔ tho yaá·laweʔ utahuwánhaneʔ kih.**
úhkaʔ tho y-aa-hl-aw-eʔ
anyone there TRL-OPT-3M.SG.A-arrive-PNC

uta-huwa-nhaʔ-neʔ   kiʔ
CSL:OPT-3>3M.SG-hire-PNC   actually
'anyone who went there would be hired.'

Clifford Cornelius, A Lifetime Working

(7.22) **Kwáh núwaʔ nók úhkaʔ a·yutatliʔwanu·tú·seʔ a·yuta·tí·,**
kwáh núwaʔ nók úhkaʔ   aa-yutat-liʔwanutu-ʔs-eʔ   aa-yu-atati-ʔ
just now only anyone OPT-3FI>3FI-ask-BEN-PNC   OPT-3FI.A-speak-PNC
'Now it's just [if] they ask anyone to speak,'

Hazel Cornelius, Starting Life Together

Indefinite expressions are summarized in Table 12.

8. Free Relatives and Correlatives

The particle **tsiʔ** occurs in place of some of the words used in questions—specifically **tó·** 'how' (used for extent and amount), **kátshaʔ** 'where,' and (infrequently) **kánhke** 'when'— to introduce clauses that are sometimes called *free relative clauses*. A free relative clause co-occurs with a main clause and provides information about an argument (the 'who' or 'what') of the verb of the main clause, or a free relative clause may specify a relevant location, extent or manner. In free relatives, the particle **tsiʔ** is frequently followed by a *classificatory word*—a word that specifies location, extent, or manner: **nú·** or **nukwá·** for locations, **nikú** for amount, **niyo·lé·** for distance or extent, **náheʔ** for extent in time, and **ni·yót** for manner or kind. A free relative can also consist of **tsiʔ** plus **náhteʔ** 'what, anything' or **tsiʔ** plus a verb that begins in the **n-** partitive prefix and whose meaning has to do with size, extent, or

			Classificatory word	Gloss
	úhkaʔ	ok		'someone'
	ot = thok	ok	náhteʔ	'something'
	kátshaʔ	ok	nú·	'somewhere' 'around, about'
	kánhke	ok		'some time'
	tó· = tó·k	ok	nikú niyo·lé· náheʔ	'some amount, distance or extent, amount of time'
	úhkaʔ náhteʔ	Negative or conditional context		'anyone' 'anything'
yah tákʌʔ	úhkaʔ náhteʔ kátshaʔ kánikeʔ	Verb with teʔ-/te- negative or th-/thaʔ- contrastive prefix		'no one (not anyone)' 'nothing (not anything)' 'nowhere (not anywhere)' 'nowhere (not anywhere)'

Table 12. Indefinite expressions

manner. Verbs that take the **n-** partitive prefix and occur in free relative clauses include **-a-** '(be a) size,' **-oʔtʌ-** 'kind of,' and **-ʌʔ-/-yaʔtawʌʔ-** 'happen (in a particular way).' Excerpts that have a free relative clause are given in (8.1)–(8.5).

(8.1) **tho ʌhsetáliʔ [tsiʔ náhteʔ tesatuhutsyo·ní.]**
tho ʌ-hse-talyu-ʔ tsiʔ náhteʔ te-s-atuhutsyoni
there FUT-2SG.A-put.things.in-PNC that what DL-2SG.P-want[STV]
'you put all the things in there that [what] you want.'

Georgina Nicholas, An Oneida Childhood

(8.2) **ʌhunúhtuʔ kwí· [tsiʔ nú· nyʌhʌ·né·,]**
ʌ-hu-anuhtu-ʔ kwí· tsiʔ nú· n-y-ʌ-hʌn-e-ʔ
FUT-3M.PL.A-determine-PNC where PART-TRL-FUT-3M.PL.A-walk-PNC
'they can go where they want,'

Georgina Nicholas, An Oneida Childhood

(8.3) **kwáh oniʔ wakanúhteʔ [tsiʔ ni·yót tsiʔ yakotsluní,]**
kwáh oniʔ wak-anuhte-ʔ tsiʔ ni-y-oht
just even 1SG.P-know-STV that PART-3Z/N.SG.A-be.so[STV]
tsiʔ yako-atsluni
how 3FI.P-dress[STV]
'I even know how she was dressed,'

Olive Elm, Ghost Sightings at the Language Centre

(8.4) **wahathlolyániʔ [tsiʔ niyo·lé· nihonaʔku·níheʔ kaʔikʌ n lónhahseʔ.]**
wa-h-athloly-a-nyu-ʔ tsiʔ ni-yo-le-ʔ
FACT-3M.SG.A-tell-JN-DISTR-PNC that PART-3Z/N.SG.P-far-STV

ni-ho-na?kuni-he?   ka?ikʌ n   lo-nha?-se?
PART-3M.SG>3M.SG-make.mad-HAB   this   3M.SG>3M.SG-hire-HAB
'he told all about how much this guy who hired him was making him mad.'

Mercy Doxtator, A Man Tells Off His Boss

(8.5) **kwáh ké·yale? [tsi? nikahyatuhsló·tʌ,]**
kwáh   k-ehyahl-e?   tsi? ni-ka-hyatu-hsl-o?tʌ
just   1SG.A-remember-STV   that PART-3Z/N.SG.A-write-NMZR-kind.of[STV]
'I remember just the kind of paper it was,'

Olive Elm, Visits to My Auntie's

Certain combinations of **tsi?** plus a classificatory word occur so frequently that they also have a lexicalized, or fixed, meaning. So **tsi? niyo·lé·** and **tsi? náhe?** have the lexicalized meanings 'until' and 'while, during,' respectively. Excerpts with these meanings are given in (8.6) and (8.7). The lexicalization of **tsi? niyo·lé·** is also evident from the fact that in casual speech some speakers reduce **tsi? niyo·lé·** so that it sounds more like **tsyo?lé·**.

(8.6) **Nʌ kwí· nok u·tú· tho tyákwehse? tsi? niyo·lé· wahutenho·tú·.**
nʌ kwí· nok u·tú·   tho   t-yakw-e-?se?
so then it had to be there   CSL-1EX.PL.A-walk-HAB

tsi? niyo·lé·   wa-hu-atenhotu-?
until   FACT-3M.PL.A-close-PNC
'So then we had to stay there until they closed up.'

Barbara Schuyler, A Ghost on the Tracks

(8.7) **wá·s kwí· átste satnutolya?tá·na tsi? náhe? ʌkatna?talu·ní·.**
wá·s kwí· átste   s-atnutolya?t-a-?n-a?   tsi? náhe?
go   outside   2SG.A-play-JN-DISL-PNC   while

ʌ-k-at-na?tal-uni-?
FUT-1SG.A-SRF-bread-make-PNC
'go, go and play outside while I make some bread.'

Norma Kennedy, The Bird

The expression **tsi? nikú** is lexicalized with the meaning 'how much, a lot, all,' and **kwáh tsi? nikú** is used as a temporal expression 'how(ever) often, every (time), whenever.'

(8.8) **né· thikʌ́ tsi? nikú wa?kheste·líste?,**
né·   thikʌ́ tsi? nikú   wa?-khe-stelist-e?
it's   that   how much   FACT-1SG>3-laugh-PNC
'did I ever laugh at her,'

Norma Kennedy, The Bean Game

(8.9) **kwáh tsi? nikú tho yʌyáknewe? thikʌ́ khále?**
       knock knock knock knock, úhka? ok tho i·yʌ́·.
kwáh tsi? nikú   tho   y-ʌ-yakn-ew-e?   thikʌ́ khále?
just   how much   there TRL-FUT-1EX.DU.A-arrive-PNC   that   and

knock knock knock knock   úhkaʔ ok   tho   i-yʌ-e-ʔ
knock knock knock knock   someone   there EPEN-3FI.A-walk-PRES
'whenever the two of us got there, knock knock knock knock, someone is walking.'

Verland Cornelius, *Ghosts, Flirts, and Scary Beings*

Free relatives introduced by **tsiʔ ka·yʌ́·**, translated as 'the one that,' correspond to *relative clauses* in English and other languages. Relative clauses provide more information about a participant. In (8.10) the clause introduced by **tsiʔ ka·yʌ́·** elaborates on the third person masculine plural argument 'they' of the verb 'win.'

(8.10)   **Nʌ kwí· tho s yakʌʔ kwaʔnyóh wahutkwe·ní· tsiʔ ka·yʌ́· tehati·tʌ́heʔ;**
      nʌ kwí· tho   kʌs   yakʌʔ   kwaʔnyóh wa-hu-at-kweny-ʔ
      so then there habitually reportedly seems   FACT-3M.PL.A-SRF-able-PNC

      tsiʔ ka-yʌ-ʔ   te-hati-tʌ-heʔ
      that   3Z/N.SG.A-put,lie-STV   DL-3M.PL.A-fly-HAB
      'So then it seems that the ones that fly were winning;'

Ruben Cutcut, *Why the Bat Travels at Night*

The word **tsyoʔk**—from **tsiʔ** plus **ok** 'only'—can occur instead of **tsiʔ** in the free relative structures described above, and then the meaning involves a mix of different (kinds of) things, locations, etc. Excerpts with such expressions are (8.11)–(8.14).

(8.11)   **Kwáh s kwí· né· tsyoʔk náhteʔ kutu·níheʔ,**
      kwáh kʌs kwí· né· tsyoʔk náhteʔ   ku-atuni-heʔ
      just habitually it's different things, all kinds of things 3FZ.PL.A- make-HAB
      'They're making all kinds of things,'

Mercy Doxtator, *My Childhood*

(8.12)   **Nʌ kwí· kwáh tsyoʔk úhkaʔ waʔkheliʔwanu·tú·seʔ,**
      nʌ kwí· kwáh   tsyoʔk úhkaʔ   waʔ-khe-liʔwanutu-ʔs-eʔ
      so then just   different people, all kinds of people FACT-1SG>3-ask-BEN-PNC
      'I asked all kinds of people,'

Norma Kennedy, *How I Learned to Swear*

(8.13)   **kwáh s tsyoʔk nú· niyakwʌ́·tluʔ,**
      kwáh kʌs   tsyoʔk nú·   ni-yakwʌ-iʔtlu-ʔ
      just habitually   all over the place, everywhere PART-1EX.PL.A-dwell-STV
      'we lived all over,'

Mercy Doxtator, *All about Tobacco*

(8.14)   **Kwáh tsyoʔk nihotinʌskó·tʌ kʌ́·,**
      kwáh tsyoʔk   ni-hoti-nʌskw-oʔtʌ   kʌ́·
      just different, all kinds PART-3M.DP.P-animal-kind.of[STV]   y'know
      'They had all kinds of animals,'

Mercy Doxtator, *My Childhood*

The particle **tho**, which otherwise is used to specify a distal location or direction 'there, that way,' can occur in place of **tsi?** in free relative structures to link a location, extent, manner, etc. to a location, extent, manner, etc. mentioned earlier (*anaphoric* reference) or later (*cataphoric* reference). In (8.15) **tho nukwá·** 'that's where' is used anaphorically, referring to **ohná·kʌ?** 'in back, behind' uttered just previously in the same utterance. In (8.16) **tho ki? ok niyo·lé·** 'that's only how far' is also anaphoric; it states that a light came a certain distance and the exact location is given earlier in the story. Similarly in (8.17), the colour of the coat (black) is mentioned earlier in the story. But in (8.18) how much money the speaker had is specified by what immediately follows (enough to buy potato chips) and so the reference is cataphoric. (8.19) is a little different in that the size or age of the speaker is inferred from what we know about when people are old enough, more or less, to start working—that is, what we know about the world without being told directly in the story, and so the reference is *exophoric*.

(8.15) **tahnú· kʌs ohná·kʌ? nukwá· ne·né· wheelchair [tho nukwá· tkutawya?tákhwa?,]**

  tahnú· kʌs ohná·kʌ? nukwá· ne·né· wheelchair tho nukwá·
  and usually in back where it's that wheelchair that's where

  t-ku-atawya?t-a-hkw-ha?
  CSL-3FZ.PL.A-enter-JN-INST-HAB
  'and in the back, that's where they come in with a wheelchair,'

Olive Elm, Ghost Sightings at the Language Centre

(8.16) **tho ki? ok niyo·lé· thikʌ́ nuta·wé· thikʌ́ katsistotáti?.**

  tho ki? ok niyo·lé· thikʌ́ n-uta-w-e-?
  that's actually only how far that PART-CSL:FACT-3Z/N.SG.A-walk-PNC

  thikʌ́ katsistotáti?
  that light extended along
  'that's only how far that light came.'

Norma Kennedy, A Scary Light

(8.17) **Tahnú· [yah kwí· tho te?wahsohkó·tʌ ka?ikʌ́ n akwatyá·tawi?t] tshukyʌ·táne?.**

  tahnú· yah kwí· tho te?-w-ahsohkw-o?tʌ ka?ikʌ́ n
  and not thus NEG-3Z/N.SG.A-colour-kind.of[STV] this

  akw-atya?tawi?t tsh-uk-yʌta?-ne?
  1SG.POSS-coat COIN-FACT:1SG.P-obtain-PNC
  'And that wasn't the colour of my coat when I got it.'

Barbara Schuyler, Wintertime

(8.18) **Né· thikʌ́ [tho nikú wakhwístayʌ?] u·tú· kʌs potato chips wa?khni·nú·**

  né· thikʌ́ tho nikú wak-hwist-a-yʌ-?
  it's that that's how much 1SG.P-money-JN-have-STV

  wa?-w-atu-? kʌs potato chips wa?-k-hninu-?
  FACT-3Z/N.SG.A-possible-PNC habitually potato chips FACT-1SG.A-buy-PNC

'I had enough money that I could buy potato chips'

Olive Elm, Friday Nights

(8.19) **nʌ oniʔ ní· [tho ni·ká·] au·tú· aukyoʔtʌ́hsa<u>ʔ</u>.**
       nʌ   oniʔ   ní·   tho   ni-k-a-ʔ   aa-w-atu-ʔ
       and   too   me   thus PART-1SG.A-size-STV   OPT-3Z/N.SG.A-possible-PNC
       aa-wak-yoʔtʌ-hs-aʔ
       OPT-1SG.P-work-DISL-PNC
       'then I too was big [old] enough that I could go to work.'

Mercy Doxtator, All about Tobacco

Often one clause begins in **tho** and another begins in **tsiʔ** in a kind of *correlative* construction. The **tho** clause points to a situation and the **tsiʔ** clause elaborates. The **tsiʔ** clause and the **tho** clause in a correlative construction can occur in either order.

(8.20) **Tahnú· [tsiʔ nukwá· yeyakwaku·hʌ́·] [tho nukwá· yahú·sʌ<u>neʔ</u>.]**
       tahnú· tsiʔ nukwá· ye-yakwa-kuhʌ-ʔ
       and   where   TRL-1EX.PL.A-head.rest-STV
       tho nukwá·   yahaʔ-w-aʔsʌʔ-neʔ
       that's where TRL:FACT-3Z/N.SG.A-fall-PNC
       'And it's [the end] where we had our heads that fell.'

Clifford Cornelius, A Lifetime Working

(8.21) **[kwáh tsiʔ náhteʔ ʌhsatlʌ́nhahteʔ] [tho kiʔ nʌya·wʌ́<u>neʔ</u>.]**
       kwáh   tsiʔ náhteʔ   ʌ-hs-atlʌnhaʔt-eʔ
       just   what   FUT-2SG.A-wish-PNC
       tho   kiʔ   n-ʌ-yaw-ʌʔ-neʔ
       thus actually PART-FUT-3Z/N.SG.P-happen-PNC
       'whatever you wish for, that's what will happen.'

Norma Kennedy, A Wish Comes True

(8.22) **Né· kyuhte wí· [tho yaʔta·kaye·lí· kaʔikʌ́] [tsiʔ nikú onʌ́ waʔkata·tí<u>·</u>.]**
       né·   kyuhte wí· tho   yaʔ-t-aa-ka-yeli-ʔ   kaʔikʌ́
       it's supposedly that's TRL-DL-OPT-3Z/N.SG.A-enough-PNC this
       tsiʔ nikú   onʌ́   waʔ-k-atati-ʔ
       how much now   FACT-1SG.A-speak-PNC
       'I guess that will be enough how much I've talked.'

Mercy Doxtator, My Childhood

Certain other combinations of clauses could be considered correlatives. For example, (8.23) is a correlative with the quantity expression **sʌ́haʔ** 'more'.[11]

---

[11] Another possible correlative is a sequence of clauses that begin in the temporal particle **nʌ** 'now, then, when.' For example, **Né· kʌs nʌ waʔó·kalaweʔ nʌ waʔukwʌtá·whaʔ,** 'When it got dark and [then] we went to bed,' (Olive Elm, *Visits to My Auntie's*). However it is often unclear whether such sequences involve temporal subordination 'when . . . then . . .' or a sequence of events 'then . . . [and] then . . .'

(8.23)   **[kwáh tsiʔ nikú sʌ́haʔ lotiwilaká·teʔ] [sʌ́haʔ e·só· ohwístaʔ wahotiyʌ·tá·<u>neʔ</u>.]**

kwáh tsiʔ nikú   sʌ́haʔ   loti-wil-a-kaʔte-ʔ
however many   more   3M.DP.P-child-JN-have.many-STV

sʌ́haʔ   e·só·   o-hwist-aʔ   wa-hoti-yʌta?-neʔ
more   a lot   NPF-money-NSF   FACT-3M.DP.P-receive-PNC

'the more children they have the more money they will get.'

Verland Cornelius, A Lifetime of Memories

9. Counting

Oneida, and other Iroquoian languages, are unique in the extent to which verbs are used for counting. Different patterns are used depending on the amount (one, two, three or more) and whether what is counted is an animate being or an inanimate object.

9.1 Counting One

The state verb **-t** 'one' is used for talking about one item, be it an inanimate object or animate being. In this function **-t** requires the **s-** REPETITIVE prepronominal prefix and AGENT pronominal prefixes. An incorporated noun specifies what is being counted. In the excerpt in (9.1) the incorporated noun is **-saheʔt-** 'bean.' The incorporated noun is **-yaʔt-** 'body' for animates, as in the excerpts in (9.2) and (9.3). When inanimates are counted, the pronominal prefix is the ZOIC/NEUTER SINGULAR AGENT pronominal prefix; and when animates are counted, the prefix is MASCULINE, FEMININE-INDEFINITE, OR FEMININE-ZOIC, depending on the gender of the person or animal.[12]

(9.1)   **nʌ kiʔ ok wí· ukwa·tí· skasahé·tat.**
nʌ kiʔ ok wí·   waʔ-wak-aty-ʔ   s-ka-saheʔt-a-t
so right then   FACT-1SG.P-lose-PNC   REP-3Z/N.SG.A-bean-JN-one[STV]
'right away I lost one bean.'

Norma Kennedy, The Bean Game

(9.2)   **Né·n shayá·tat thikʌ́ waʔtyakyátlaneʔ,**
né·n   s-ha-yaʔt-a-t   thikʌ́   waʔ-t-yaky-atlaʔ-neʔ
it's that   REP-3M.SG.A-body-JN-one[STV]   that   FACT-DL-1EX.DU.A-meet-PNC
'And so I met this one man,'

Norma Kennedy, How I Learned to Swear

(9.3)   **Ókhaleʔ tsyeyá·tat tho yehe·yʌ́·seʔ,**
ókhaleʔ   ts-ye-yaʔt-a-t   tho   yehe-yʌ-e-ʔseʔ
and   REP-3FI.A-body-JN-one[STV]   there   TRL-3FI.A-walk-HAB

---

[12] Counting constructions are described in Koenig and Michelson (2010b) and Koenig and Michelson (2014). In these studies the clause that includes the counting verb is analyzed as an internally-headed relative clause (for example, 'the bean that is/amounts to one') to account for its relation to the main verb.

'And one person who was over there,'

Norma Kennedy, The Bean Game

The number word **úska** 'one' does not occur with the counting verb **-t**. However **úska** does occur occasionally on its own, especially with English nouns.

(9.4) **Úska ki? ok kwí· yonúhsute?,**
     úska?   ki?   ok   wí·   yo-nuhs-ut-e?
     one   actually only   3Z/N.SG.P-house-attach-STV
     'There was only one room,'

Georgina Nicholas, An Oneida Childhood

(9.5) **úska thikʌ́ stamp ʌhatiye·ná· kʌ́·,**
     úska?   thikʌ́   stamp   ʌ-hati-yena-?   kʌ́·
     one   that   stamp   FUT-3M.PL.A-grab.hold.of-PNC   y'know
     'they would take one stamp,'

Mercy Doxtator, My Childhood

9.2 Counting Two

Different constructions are used for counting two inanimates versus two animates. The state verb **-ke** 'be separate entities, amount to, be a certain amount' is used for inanimates. In the construction for counting two of something, **-ke** requires the **te-** DUALIC prepronominal prefix. What is being counted is expressed by an incorporated noun; in the excerpt in (9.6) the incorporated noun is **-nlaht-** 'leaf.' The verb is inflected with the FEMININE-ZOIC/NEUTER *singular* AGENT prefix, even though there are two items; as mentioned in the section on verb structure (section 2.1), dual and plural pronominal prefixes occur only with verbs that reference *animate* beings.

(9.6) **tá·t núwa? tekanláhtake ʌha·yá·ke? kʌ́h.**
     tá·t núwa?   te-ka-nlaht-a-ke
     maybe   DL-3Z/N.SG.A-leaf-JN-amount.to[STV]

     ʌ-ha-ya?k-e?   kʌ́
     FUT-3M.SG.A-detach-PNC   y'know
     'maybe he cut off two leaves.'

Mercy Doxtator, All about Tobacco

Two persons or animals are counted with forms based on the verb **-yashe** 'be together.' This verb always has the **te-** DUALIC prepronominal prefix. The pronominal prefix is the MASCULINE or FEMININE-ZOIC DUAL AGENT.

(9.7) **Tehniyáshe nihwánhaks,**
     te-hni-yashe   ni-hwanhak-s
     DL-3M.DU.A-together[STV]   3M.DU.A-tie-HAB
     'Two people were tying [tobacco leaves],'

Mercy Doxtator, All about Tobacco

(9.8) **Né· kwí· né· ka?ikʌ́ tekniyáshe otikstʌ́ha,**
  né· kwí·   né·   ka?ikʌ́   te-kni-yashe   oti-kstʌha
  so it's   it's   this   DL-3FZ.DU.A-together[STV]   3FZ.DP.P-old.person
  'So these two old ladies,'

Mercy Doxtator, *Berries and Bellies*

The **te-** DUALIC prefix plus a DUAL AGENT pronominal prefix can also be prefixed to the roots **-ukwe** 'person' and **-ksá·** 'child' to count two male or female persons or children.

(9.9) **né· thikʌ́ ísi? nukwá· íthnete? tehnukwé,**
  né·   thikʌ́   ísi? nukwá·   i-t-hn-et-e?   te-hni-ukwe
  it's that   right over there   EPEN-CSL-3M.DU.A-stand-STV   DL-3M.DU.A-person
  'there's two men standing right over there,'

Norma Kennedy, *How I Learned to Swear*

9.3 Counting Three or More

The root **-ke** 'be separate entities, amount to, be a certain amount' is used also for counting three or more inanimate entities. In this function **-ke** requires the **n-** PARTITIVE prepronominal prefix. A separate number word can give the exact amount. What is being counted is expressed by an incorporated noun, and the verb is inflected with the FEMININE-ZOIC/NEUTER *singular* AGENT prefix for the same reason that the singular prefix occurs for counting two objects, that is, dual and plural prefixes reference only *animate* arguments.

(9.10) **Áhsʌ nikanláhtake ʌtésku?.**
  áhsʌ   ni-ka-nlaht-a-ke   ʌ-te-sk-u-?
  three PART-3Z/N.SG.A-leaf-JN-amount.to[STV]   FUT-CSL-2SG>1SG-give-PNC
  'You're to hand me three leaves.'

Olive Elm, *Learning to Work in Tobacco*

An alternative construction for counting three or more inanimate entities consists of the word **nikú** 'amount' plus a number word.[13] An example of this structure is given in (9.11).

(9.11) **nʌ kʌs né· sʌ́ha? yah tha·kkwe·ní· áhsʌ nikú a·khla·kó· ónlahte?.**
  nʌ   kʌs   né·   sʌ́ha? yah   th-aa-k-kweny-?
  then   habitually   it's more   not   CONTR-OPT-1SG.A-able-PNC

  áhsʌ   nikú   aa-k-hl-a-kw-?   o-nlaht-e?
  three how much   OPT-1SG.A-set.down-JN-REV-PNC   NPF-leaf-NSF
  '(And then I would rush,) and even more I couldn't pick up three leaves.'

Olive Elm, *Learning to Work in Tobacco*

Three or more people are counted with the words **nihatí** for males or a group of males and females, and **nikutí** for a group consisting only of females.[14] An example with **nihatí** is

---

[13] The word **nikú** is probably from a root **-u-** plus the **n-** partitive prefix.
[14] These forms are probably based on a verb root **-i-** 'total' with the **n-** partitive prefix.

given in (9.12). **Nihatí** and **nikutí** are used only for the third person. The construction for the first person employs the verb root -u- 'be a certain amount' with the **n-** PARTITIVE pre-pronominal prefix and AGENT pronominal prefixes. An example is given in (9.13).

(9.12) **úksa yawʌ·lé· nihatí thikʌ́ tho yahʌ·néweʔ**
        úska yawʌ·lé·   nihatí   thikʌ́   tho   y-a-hʌn-ew-eʔ
        eleven   how many   that   there   TRL-FACT-3M.PL.A-arrive-PNC
        'eleven of them got there'

Norma Kennedy, *The Bean Game*

(9.13) **Tsiʔ nikú lotihwatsi·láyʌʔ, tsya·ták niyáki<u>ʔ</u>.**
        tsiʔ   nikú   loti-hwatsil-a-yʌ-ʔ   tsya·ták
        what   amount   3M.DP.P-family-JN-have-STV   seven
        ni-yaky-u-ʔ
        PART-1EX.PL.A-amount-STV
        'We were seven, that's how many children they had.'

Margaret Antone, *Forecasting Things to Come*

Tóhkaʔ 'a few' can occur instead of a number word in both the inanimate and animate constructions for counting three or more.

(9.14) **Tóhkaʔ s kwí· nikaya·láke waʔakwayʌ́<u>tho</u>ʔ.**
        tóhkaʔ   kʌs kwí·   ni-ka-yal-a-ke
        a few   habitually   PART-3Z/N.SG.A-bag-JN-amount.to[STV]
        waʔ-yakwa-yʌtho-ʔ
        FACT-1EX.PL.A-plant-PNC
        'We planted a few bags [of potatoes].'

Georgina Nicholas, *An Oneida Childhood*

(9.15) **tóhkaʔ kiʔ nikú atyá·tawiʔt ukyʌ·táneʔ**
        tóhkaʔ   kiʔ   nikú   atyá·tawiʔt   waʔ-wak-yʌtaʔ-neʔ
        a few   actually   how many   dress   FACT-1SG.P-obtain-PNC
        'I got a few dresses'

Norma Kennedy, *My First Job in Tobacco*

(9.16) **tóhkaʔ nʌ kiʔ nihatí tho latí·tluʔ,**
        tóhkaʔ   nʌ   kiʔ   nihatí   tho   lat-iʔtlu-ʔ
        a few   then   actually   how many   there   3M.PL.A-dwell-STV
        'there were a few of them living there,'

Mercy Doxtator, *My Childhood*

E·só· 'many, much, a lot' is occasionally used for talking about many inanimate entities, as in (9.17), but it more often occurs as an expression of degree (see section 10.1). It is based on the verb root -eso-, but the form **e·só·** has no pronominal prefix and so structurally it is a defective verb. (The root **-eso-** occassionally occurs as a regularly inflected verb form;

an example occurs in (10.18) in the section on degree.) The verb root **-nakle-** 'dwell, reside' also has the meaning 'be plentiful.' An excerpt with this verb is given in (9.18). The verb stem **-(i)tyohkwaná** 'big crowd' is used for many people. The stem can take the feminine-zoic/ neuter singular prefix, as in (9.19), or a plural prefix, as in (9.20).

(9.17) **e·só· yukwayʌthóhslu?,**
      e·só·   yukwa-yʌtho-hslu-?
      lots   1PL.P-plant-DISTR-STV
      'we have planted lots,'

Mercy Doxtator, All about Tobacco

(9.18) **katsyapslanákle? s latinolótshyus olihwakayú,**
      ka-tsyap-sl-a-nakle-?   kʌs
      3Z/N.SG.A-job-NMZR-JN-plentiful-STV   habitually

      lati-nol-ot-hsyu-s   olihwakayú
      3M.PL.A-corn.husk-stand-REV-HAB   old times
      'there were lots of jobs husking corn in the old days,'

Clifford Cornelius, A Lifetime Working

(9.19) **Kʌtyohkwaná ʌyakólyo?**
      kʌ-ityohkw-owanʌ   ʌ-yako-lyo-?
      3Z/N.SG.A-crowd-big[STV]   FUT-3FZ.SG>3-beat,kill-PNC
      'A lot of people will be killed'

Margaret Antone, Forecasting Things to Come

(9.20) **né·n só·tsi? yukwʌtyohkwaná, kayé kwí· niyáki?,**
      né·n   só·tsi?   yukwʌ-ityohkw-owanʌ kayé kwí·
      it's that   too much   1PL.P-crowd-big[STV]   four

      ni-yaky-u-?
      PART-1EX.PL.A-amount-STV
      'so we were too many, there were four of us,'

Clifford Cornelius, A Lifetime Working

The closest equivalent in Oneida of English 'all' (a *universal quantifier*) is **akwekú** 'all, every' from the verb stem **-kweku** 'all together, the whole of.' **Akwekú** occurs with both animates and inanimates (and often it is hard to tell, even from context, whether it applies to an animate or inanimate). In addition, the expressions **tsi? nikú** (or **kwáh tsi? nikú**) 'how much, whatever the amount' and **tsyo?k náhte?** (or **kwáh tsyo?k náhte?**) 'different things, all kinds of things,' described in section 8 on free relatives, are frequently used as (approximate) equivalents of English 'all (of an amount), the whole amount.'

(9.21) **nók tsi? akwekú kwí· swakatyesáhtu,**
      nók tsi? akwekú kwí· s-wak-atyes-a-ht-u
      but   all   REP-1SG.P-cheap-JN-CAUS-STV
      '(Then I made even more money,) but I wasted it all,'

Clifford Cornelius, A Lifetime Working

(9.22) **Thó·nʌ thikʌ́ nʌ akwekú ʌhutekhu·ní· n kahwa·tsíleʔ,**

thó·nʌ   thikʌ́   nʌ   akwekú   ʌ-hu-ate-khw-uni-ʔ n
and then   that   then   all   FUT-3M.PL.A-SRF-food-make-PNC

ka-hwatsil-eʔ
NPF-family-NSF

'And then all the family eat,'

Mercy Doxtator, After a Loss

(9.23) **kok né· náheʔ ókhnaʔ né· yahútshaʔahteʔ tsiʔ nikú yako·yʌ́· osahé·<u>ta</u>ʔ.**

kʌʔ ok né· náheʔ   ókhnaʔ   né·   yaha-w-at-hsaʔ-a-ht-eʔ
a little while   and then   it's TRL:FACT-3Z/N.SG.A-SRF-finish-JN-CAUS-PNC

tsiʔ nikú   yako-yʌ-ʔ   o-saheʔt-aʔ
how much   3FI.P-have-STV   NPF-bean-NSF

'in a little while all the beans she had got used up.'

Norma Kennedy, The Bean Game

9.4 Counting Possessed Entities

Counting can be combined with possession. The possessive structure consists of the stative aspect of a postural verb that selects PATIENT prefixes (see section 3 on possessive structures). An incorporated noun specifies the possessed entity. When there are two possessed entities, the number of entities is expressed by the DUALIC prepronominal prefix and by the number word **tékni** 'two.' In the example in (9.24) **tékni tehotiwi·láyʌʔ** tells us that they have two children and the form **teknukwé** 'two female persons' makes it clear that the two children are females, so they have two daughters. When there are more than two possessed entities, the number of entities is expressed by the PARTITIVE prefix and a number word that specifies exactly how many entities. An example is given in (9.25).[15]

(9.24) **tékni né· tehotiwi·láyʌʔ teknukwé**

tékni   né·   te-hoti-wil-a-yʌ-ʔ   te-kn-ukwe
two   it's   DL-3M.DP.P-child-JN-have-STV   DL-3FZ.DU.A-person

'they have two girls'

Mercy Doxtator, All about Tobacco

(9.25) **Né· kwí· aolí·waʔ nʌ kayé niwakwi·láyʌʔ.**

né· kwí· aolí·waʔ   nʌ   kayé   ni-wak-wil-a-yʌ-ʔ
so it's   the reason   now   four   PART-1SG.P-child-JN-have-STV

'That's why now I've got four children.'

Pearl Cornelius, Family and Friends

An alternative structure for two possessed animate entities is with the terms **tehniyáshe** 'two males, a male and a female' or **tekniyáshe** 'two females.' An example with **tehniyáshe**

---

[15] In these stories, owning two inanimate objects is never mentioned; however, the constructions for possessing inanimate entities is the same as those described with reference to (9.24) and (9.25).

is given in (9.26). Note that in this alternative strucuture the verb does not have the dualic prefix. Similarly, an alternative structure for three or more possessed animate entities is with **nihatí/nikutí** 'so many males/females.' An example is (9.27), and note that in this case the verb does not have the partitive prefix.

(9.26) **tehniyáshe s waknʌskwayʌ·táhkweʔ é·lhal.**
      tekniyáshe   kʌs   wak-nʌskw-a-yʌt-ahkweʔ   é·lhal
      two   habitually   1SG.P-pet.animal-JN-have-PAST   dog
      'I had two pet dogs.'

                               Mercy Doxtator, *My Dog Blackie*

(9.27) **nʌ kwí· áhsʌ nikutí lotiwi·láyʌʔ kaʔikʌ́ lónaʔ.**
      nʌ kwí·   áhsʌ   nikutí   loti-wil-a-yʌ-ʔ   kaʔikʌ́   lónaʔ
      so then   three   how many   3M.DP.P-child-JN-have-STV   this   man and wife
      'and then the couple had three daughters.'

                    Norma Kennedy, *The Girl with the Bandaged Fingers*

The meaning of the verb root **-kaʔte-** 'have many' entails both possession and quantity. The possessed entity is expressed either with an incorporated noun or an external noun, and the verb takes PATIENT prefixes. In the excerpt in (9.28) the root for 'flower' is incorporated, and in the excerpt in (9.29) the nominalized root for 'grandchild' is incorporated.

(9.28) **Tahnú· s aksótha yakotsiʔtsyaká·teʔ kʌs.**
      Tahnú·   kʌs   ak-hsotha   yako-tsiʔtsy-a-kaʔte-ʔ
      and   habitually   3FZ.SG>1SG-grandparent   3FI.P-flower-JN-have.many-STV
      kʌs
      habitually
      'And my grandmother had a lot of plants.'

                        Verland Cornelius, *A Lifetime of Memories*

(9.29) **Wakatleʔslaká·teʔ**
      wak-atleʔ-sl-a-kaʔte-ʔ
      1SG.P-grandchild-NMZR-JN-have.many-STV
      'I have a lot of grandchildren'

                      Clifford Cornelius, *A Lifetime Working*

Table 13 provides an overview of Oneida counting expressions.

9.5 Age and Time

Days, months, and years are counted with the constructions described in the previous sections; for example, **swʌhníslat** 'one day,' **tewʌhnislaké** 'two days,' **áhsʌ niwʌhnislaké** 'three days.' However, measuring hours and telling time, as well as specifying the age of a person, is accomplished with verbs whose meaning does not have to do with counting. Counting hours and telling time is done with the stem **-hwistaʔek-/-hwistaʔe-**, which consists of a verb root **-aʔek-/-aʔe-** 'strike, hit' and the incorporated noun root **-hwist-** 'metal.'

	one	two	three or more
Inanimate	**-t** 'one' plus s- repetitive, 3Z/N.SG.A prefix	**-ke** 'amount to' plus te- dualic, 3Z/N.SG.A prefix	**-ke** 'amount to' plus n- partitive, 3Z/N.SG.A prefix; plus number word or tóhka? 'a few, several'
			nikú 'amount' plus number word or tóhka? 'a few, several'
			akwekú 'all' kwáh tsi? nikú 'all, every' (kwáh) tsyo?k náhte? ' all kinds of, different things'
	Possession: Stative aspect of **-yʌ-** 'put, lie' plus te- dualic or n- partitive prefix, patient prefix, and a number word; **-ka?te-** 'have many' and patient prefix		
Animate	**-ya?tat** 'one' plus s- repetitive and agent prefix	**-yashe** plus te- dualic and dual agent prefix	nihatí (males, males & females) nikutí (females)
		-ksá· or **-ukwé** plus te- dualic and dual agent prefix	akwekú 'all' **-(i)tyohkwanʌ** 'large amount'
	Possession: Same structure with **-yʌ-** 'put, lie' as inanimates Alternatively, stative aspect of **-yʌ-** 'put, lie', and tehniyáshe/tekniyáshe (two) or nihatí/nikutí (three or more) but then no te- dualic or n- partitive prefix See also section 2.5 on kinship.		

Table 13. Counting expressions

With the PUNCTUAL aspect (9.30) the stem counts hours, and with the STATIVE aspect (9.31) the stem tells the time; as with count verbs the stem requires the **te-** DUALIC prefix for 'two' and the **n-** PARTITIVE prefix for three or more.[16]

(9.30) **swatyelʌ́ s tá·t núwa? a·kí·lu? tékni wa?tkahwistá·eke?**
       wa?akwatnúhtuhte?,

swatyelʌ́   kʌs   tá·t núwa? a·kí·lu? tékni
sometimes habitually maybe   I'd say two
wa?-t-ka-hwist-a?ek-e?   wa?-yakw-atnuhtu?t-e?
FACT-DL-3Z/N.SG.A-metal-strike-PNC   FACT-1EX.PL.A-wait-PNC
'sometimes I'd say we waited maybe two hours,'

Olive Elm, Learning to Work in Tobacco

(9.31) **kwáh kʌs ki? né· swatyelʌ́ s tékni teyohwistá·e ókhna? yukwáhsu?.**

kwáh kʌs   ki?   né· swatyelʌ́ kʌs   tékni
just habitually actually it's sometimes habitually two
te-yo-hwist-a?e   ókhna? yukwa-hs-u?
DL-3Z/N.SG.P-metal-strike[STV] and then 1PL.P-finish-STV

---

[16] There is no Oneida word for 'minute;' the borrowed word (from English) **minit** is used together with a number word, as in **wísk minit** 'five minutes' or **tóhka? ok minit** 'only a few minutes.'

'then sometimes by two o'clock we were done.'

Olive Elm, Learning to Work in Tobacco

The stem **-ohsliya?k-** is used for talking about someone's age; it is composed of the verb root **-yahya?k-/-iya?k-** 'cross over' and the incorporated noun root **-ohsl-** 'winter, year.' When used for telling age, **-ohsliya?k-** occurs with the **te-** DUALIC prefix; and since most often in these stories speakers are talking about their or someone else's age when something happened, the **tsha?-** COINCIDENT prefix is also present. An example with **-ohsliya?k-** is given in (9.32). Another verb that is used for specifing age is the stative aspect form of the verb **-e-** 'walk, go' plus the **t-** CISLOCATIVE prefix (literally, 'have come from somewhere'). An example of this verb is given in (9.33).

(9.32) **ó· tá·t núwa? kayé tsha?tewakohsliyá·ku.**
   ó· tá·t núwa? kayé tsha?-te-wak-ohsl-iya?k-u
   oh maybe four CONTR-DL-1SG.P-winter-cross.over-STV
   'oh, maybe when I was four years old.'

Rose Antone, A Night Visitor

(9.33) **wá·tlu? né· niwʌhní·take nityakawenú ókhna? né· sayaíheye?,**
   wá·tlu? né· ni-w-ʌhni?t-a-ke
   nine it's PART-3Z/N.SG.A-month-JN-amount.to[STV]

   ni-t-yakaw-e-nu   ókhna? né· s-a-ya-ihey-e?
   PART-CSL-3FI.P-walk-STV and then it's REP-FACT-3FI.A-die-PNC
   'she was nine months old and already she died,'

Hazel Cornelius, Starting Life Together

In addition to counting measures of time, one can talk about the frequency of an event. Forms for every day, year, month, etc. are based on the counting verb **-ke** 'be separate entities, amount to' with the TRANSLOCATIVE and DUALIC prefixes **ya?te-**, and optionally the **n-** PARTITIVE prefix. The relevant time period is expressed via an incorporated noun. This construction occurs most frequently for talking about 'every day,' as in (9.34).[17]

(9.34) **Kwáh kwí· nya?tewʌhnislaké thok náhte? wahaklihúnyʌ?**
   tsi? naákye<u>le</u>?.
   kwáh kwí· n-ya?-te-w-ʌhnisl-a-ke   thok náhte?
   just   PART-TRL-DL-3Z/N.SG.A-day-JN-amount.to[STV] something

   wa-hak-lihw-uny-ʌ-?   tsi? n-aa-k-yel-e?
   FACT-3M.SG>1SG-matter-make-BEN-PNC how PART-OPT-1SG.A-do-PNC
   'Every day he taught me something about how I should do it.'

Olive Elm, Learning to Work in Tobacco

Other frequency expressions are **úska útlatste?** 'one time, once upon a time', **nuwʌtú** 'never, ever,' **swatyelʌ́** 'sometimes,' **tyótkut** 'always,' **yeskʌhá** 'the last time,' and **yotká·te?** 'often.' The particle **oyá·** '(an)other' can also be used temporally 'another (time).'

---

[17] The expression **kwáh tsi? nikú** is also often used for 'every time,' as described in section 8.

10. Degree and Comparison

10.1 Degree

Degree is communicated in Oneida both with particles and with gestures. Gestures are used together with the particle **kʌh** and the longer (but less frequent) variant **kʌ́·tho** 'this (way), over here.' (As indicated by the translations, **kʌh/kʌ́·tho** otherwise has a locative meaning; see section 2.2.3.) This particle occurs with **nikú** 'amount' or with verbs that have to do with size, such as **-a-** plus **n-** partitive 'size,' **-es-/-us-** long,' or **-atte-** plus **t-** cislocative 'high,' to specify a degree; in this case the speaker must gesture or motion with one or both hands to show the relative amount or dimension, as in English 'yea big,' 'yea wide,' and so on. For example, someone might hold up four fingers and utter **kʌh ni·kú** 'this many, four.' In the excerpt in (10.1) Verland Cornelius describes the dimensions of a scary being; this example has both the variants **kʌh** and **kʌ́·tho**.

(10.1)   **kʌh yakʌʔ ni·yús kʌ́·tho wí· nityótte?**
       kʌh   yakʌʔ   ni-y-us   kʌ́·tho wí·
       this   reportedly PART-3Z/N.SG.A-long[STV] this

       ni-t-yo-atte-ʔ
       PART-CSL-3Z/N.SG.P-high-STV
       'it was this long and this high'

Verland Cornelius, Ghosts, Flirts, and Scary Beings

There are several other particles whose meaning has to do with a degree: **e·só·** 'many, much, a lot,' **só·tsiʔ** 'too (much),' **aʔé·** 'great,' **ostúha** 'a little,' and **kʌʔ nikúha** 'a little.' (Speakers joke that the longer you drag out the final vowel of **aʔé·** 'great' the greater the extent.) These are exemplified in the excerpts in (10.2)–(10.7). **E·só·** and **só·tsiʔ** can occur together, as in (10.4). The expression **kʌʔ nikúha** is made up of **nikú** 'how much, how many' and an ending that, together with the particle **kʌʔ**, means 'little, small.' This expression is hardly attested in these texts. 'A little' can also be expressed with **e·só·** 'much, many' and the negative form of the verb that occurs with **e·só·**, as in (10.7).

(10.2)   **Nʌ uhte wí· e·só· waʔukyatétshʌ̱ʔ.**
       nʌ   uhte wí·   e·só·   waʔ-yuky-atetshʌ-ʔ
       then supposedly much FACT-1DU.P-get.scared-PNC
       'Then I guess we got very scared.'

Verland Cornelius, Ghosts, Flirts, and Scary Beings

(10.3)   **só·tsiʔ kano·lú· kaʔikʌ́ n kóskos onu·tsí.**
       só·tsiʔ   ka-nolu-ʔ   kaʔikʌ́ n kóskos onutsí
       too much 3Z/N.SG.A-expensive-STV this   pig head
       'the pig head was so expensive.'

Mercy Doxtator, Kastes Buys a Face

(10.4)   **Tá·thuni? só·tsi? e·só· tʌyaknitha·lʌ́·,**
táthuni?   só·tsi?   e·só·   t-ʌ-yakni-thal-ʌ?
or   too much   lots   DL-FUT-1EX.DU.A-converse-PNC
'Or we will talk a whole lot,'

Olive Elm, *Learning to Work in Tobacco*

(10.5)   **Né· tsi? a?é· niwana?aló·tsla? lona?alo·lų́.**
né· tsi?   a?é·   ni-w-a-na?al-o(l)-?tsl-a-?
because   great   PART-3Z/N.SG.A-SRF-head-cover-NMZR-size-STV

lo-na?al-ol-u
3M.SG.P-head-cover-STV
'Because he had on a great big hat.'

Barbara Schuyler, *A Ghost on the Tracks*

(10.6)   **Nʌ kwí· né· ostúha ka?ikʌ́ wahotétshʌ?**
nʌ kwí·   né·   ostúha   ka?ikʌ́   wa-ho-atetshʌ-?
so then   it's   a little   this   FACT-3M.SG.P-get.scared-PNC
'Then he got scared a bit'

Norma Kennedy, *My Father's Encounter*

(10.7)   **tahnú· yah e·só· tehatatíhahkwe?.**
tahnú·   yah   e·só·   te-h-atati-ha-hkwe?
and   not   lots   NEG-3M.SG.A-talk-HAB-PAST
'and he didn't used to talk a lot.'

Margaret Antone, *Forecasting Things to Come*

An expression of intensity is the combination of **tsi?** plus a verb with the **n-** PARTITIVE prefix, as in those dialects of English where you can say 'she was *that* hungry, *how* she was hungry.' Examples are (10.8) and (10.9). **Tsi? nikú** 'how much' also functions this way, as in (10.10).

(10.8)   **Tahnú· yakʌ? tsi? niyutuhkályaʔks ka?ikʌ́ yeksáh.**
tahnú·   yakʌ?   tsi?   ni-yu-atuhkalyaʔk-s   ka?ikʌ́   yeksá·
and   reportedly   how   PART-3FI.A-hungry-HAB   this   girl
'And the little girl was really hungry.'

Norma Kennedy, *The Bird*

(10.9)   **ó·nista? tsi? na?akoná·khwʌ?.**
ó·nista?   tsi?   n-a?-ako-na?kwʌ-?
oh boy   how   PART-FACT-3FI.P-get.mad-PNC
'oh boy did she get mad.'

Verland Cornelius, *A Pig in the Window*

(10.10) **Á·, tsiʔ nikú washakwaste·lísteʔ s.**
    Á· tsiʔ nikú   wa-shakwa-stelist-eʔ   kʌs
    oh how much FACT-1EX.PL>3M.SG-laugh-PNC habitually
    'Oh, how much we laughed at him.'

Pearl Cornelius, Family and Friends

Finally, rather than talking about a greater or lesser degree, one can talk about *some* degree. The particle **kʌʔ**, in addition to its use as a locational expression 'right here' (section 2.2.3), indicates some specified extent, characterized by Norma Kennedy as "not a lot, not a little, but some." Lounsbury (1953, p. 98) describes it as: "A particle usually meaning *a certain* (way, amount, or kind)." Examples are given in (10.11)–(10.13). When the particle **kwáh** 'just' precedes, the implication is that the extent is on the small side.

(10.11) **Nʌ kwí· kwáh kʌʔ niyo·lé· kʌ́· nyahá·keʔ thikʌ́,**
    nʌ kwí· kwáh kʌʔ niyo·lé· kʌ́· n-yahaʔ-k-e-ʔ   thikʌ́
    so then just some distance y'know PART-TRL:FACT-1SG.A-walk-PNC that
    'So then I went on a [little] ways,'

Norma Kennedy, How I Learned to Swear

(10.12) **Nʌ kyaleʔ wí· waʔakyatwá·nikeʔ kʌʔ náheʔ**
    nʌ kyaleʔ wí· waʔ-yaky-atwaʔnik-eʔ   kʌʔ náheʔ
    so again   FACT-1EX.DL.A-shut.up-PNC some while
    'So then we would be quiet again for a while'

Olive Elm, Learning to Work in Tobacco

(10.13) **kwáh kʌʔ náheʔ nʌ waʔonuhsatalíhʌʔ,**
    kwáh kʌʔ náheʔ nʌ   waʔ-yo-nuhs-a-talihʌ-ʔ
    just some while then FACT-3Z/N.SG.P-house-JN-get.warm-PNC
    'in a [little] while the house warmed up,'

Clifford Cornelius, A Lifetime Working

The particle **kʌʔ** combines with **ok** 'only' to indicate a limited or small degree. When **kʌʔ ok** are adjacent (not interrupted by other particles), the combination is usually pronounced and written **kok**.

(10.14) **kok náheʔ oyá· tho sayuteʔsléhtayʌʔ.**
    kʌʔ ok náheʔ oyá·   tho   s-a-yu-ate-ʔsleht-a-yʌ-ʔ
    a little while another there REP-FACT-3FI.A-SRF-car-JN-put-PNC
    'in a little while someone else would stop.'

Georgina Nicholas, An Oneida Childhood

(10.15) **né·n sʌ́haʔ ok kʌʔ ok wí· nikatsístaʔ tho waʔkatsistá·laneʔ,**
    né·n   sʌ́haʔ ok   kʌʔ ok wí· ni-ka-tsist-a-ʔ   tho
    it's that nevertheless just small PART-3Z/N.SG.A-light-size-STV there

waʔ-ka-tsist-a-hl-a-ʔ-neʔ
FACT-3Z/N.SG.A-light-JN-set-JN-INCH-PNC
'nevertheless a small light landed there,'

Verland Cornelius, A Pig in the Window

10.2 Comparison 'more,' 'less'

The particle **sʌ́haʔ** 'more' and less frequently the particle combination **ísiʔ nú·** 'further' are used for 'more.'[18] In the excerpts in (10.16)–(10.18), all with **sʌ́haʔ**, the comparison is implicit and inferred from previous context. (An excerpt with **ísiʔ nú·** occurs later in this section.) In (10.16) the girl is older than she was before, in (10.17) the splints are better than those the speaker used previously, and in (10.18) the speaker made more money at this time as compared with the amount he made at an earlier time.

(10.16) **Né·n nʌ tshaʔutótyakeʔ thikʌ́, sʌ́haʔ tshaʔutótyakeʔ,**
     né·n   nʌ   tsh-aʔ-yu-atotyak-eʔ   thikʌ́ sʌ́haʔ
     it's that then CONTR-FACT-3FI.A-grow.up-PNC that   more

     tsh-aʔ-yu-atotyak-eʔ
     CONTR-FACT-3FI.A-grow.up-PNC
     'Then when she grew up, when she was more grown,'

Norma Kennedy, The Girl with the Bandaged Fingers

(10.17) **kʌʔ nukwá· sʌ́haʔ kaʔnuniyó né· íhsatst,**
     kʌʔ nukwá· sʌ́haʔ ka-ʔnun-iyo   né· i-hs-atst
     here   more   3Z/N.SG.A-splint-good[STV] it's EPEN-2SG.A-use
     'here are better splints, use them,'

Verland Cornelius, A Lifetime of Memories

(10.18) **Nʌ né· sʌ́haʔ yeswe·só· waʔkathwistu·ní·,**
     nʌ   né· sʌ́haʔ ye-s-w-eso-ʔ   waʔ-k-at-hwist-uni-ʔ
     then it's more TRL-REP-3Z/N.SG.A-lots-STV FACT-1SG.A-SRF-money-make-PNC
     'Then I made even more money,'

Clifford Cornelius, A Lifetime Working

Sʌ́haʔ can be modified by the degree particle **ostúha** 'a little,' as in the next excerpt.

(10.19) **ostúha sʌ́haʔ yaʔshakohnútlaneʔ.**
     ostúha sʌ́haʔ y-aʔ-shako-hnutl-a-ʔ-neʔ
     a little   more TRL-FACT-3M.SG>3-follow.after-JN-INCH-PNC
     'he's a little closer to catching up with her.'

Verland Cornelius, Ghosts, Flirts and Scary Beings

'Less than' is literally 'more a small amount,' as exemplified in the excerpt in (10.20).

---

[18] Literally, **ísiʔ nú·** is a locative expression consisting of the locative particle **ísiʔ** 'right there, yonder' and the classificatory word for locations **nú·**.

(10.20) **"tá·t" wahʌ́·luʔ "sanúhteʔ úhkaʔ ok náhteʔ sʌ́haʔ kʌʔ nikúha lo·yʌ́·**
        Grade six education,"

        tá·t wa-hʌ-ihlu-ʔ   s-anuhte-ʔ   kʌ   úhkaʔ ok náhteʔ
        if   FACT-3M.SG.A-say-PNC   2SG.P-know-STV QUESTION someone

        sʌ́haʔ kʌʔ nikúha   lo-yʌ-ʔ   Grade 6 education
        more a small amount 3M.SG.P-have-STV Grade 6 education
        '"if" he said "you know of someone who has less than a Grade 6 education,"'

Clifford Cornelius, A Lifetime Working

Comparison is expressed explicitly with a clause beginning in **tsiʔ ni·yót** 'the way it is, how it is.' The comparison clause usually follows the main clause. If the compared entity is mentioned with a pronoun, as in (10.21), the pronoun occurs right before **ni·yót**. Otherwise, the comparison occurs after **ni·yót**, as in (10.22) and (10.23). The excerpt in (10.23) exemplifies the alternative expression for 'more,' **ísiʔ nú·**.

(10.21) **sʌ́haʔ kiʔ né· kʌʔ nityakoyʌ́ha tsiʔ ní· ni·yót,**

        sʌ́haʔ kiʔ   né·   kʌʔ   ni-t-yako-yʌha   tsiʔ ní·
        more actually it's (young) PART-CSL-3FI.P-young as me

        ni-y-oht
        PART-3Z/N.SG.A-be.so[STV]
        'she was younger than me,'

Mercy Doxtator, Getting Hoyan

(10.22) **sʌ́haʔ laʔshátsteʔ tsiʔ né· ni·yót kaʔikʌ́ awéluʔuske̲ʔ̲.**

        sʌ́haʔ la-ʔshatste-ʔ   tsiʔ né· ni-y-oht   ka?ikʌ́
        more 3M.SG.A-strong-STV as   it's PART-3Z/N.SG.A-be.so[STV] this

        awéluʔuskeʔ
        witch
        'he was stronger than this witch.'

Norma Kennedy, My Father's Encounter

(10.23) **nók tsiʔ nʌ kiʔ né· ostúha ísiʔ ní· nú· wakanúhteʔ tsiʔ ni·yót**
        kwáh tshututáhsawʌ?,

        nók tsiʔ nʌ   kiʔ   né·   ostúha   ísiʔ   ní· nú·   wak-anuhte-ʔ
        but   then actually it's a little bit further me where 1SG.P-know-STV

        tsiʔ ni-y-oht   kwáh tsh-utu-tahsaw-ʌ?
        as   PART-3Z/N.SG.A-be.so[STV] just COIN-CSL:FACT: 3Z/N.SG.A-begin-PNC
        'but I knew a bit more than I did at the very beginning,'

Clifford Cornelius, A Lifetime Working

An explicit comparison can mention a specific point on a scale. In (10.24) the tobacco pile is more than five feet high, and in (10.25) butter costs less than a quarter.

(10.24) **a·kí·luʔ kyuhte wí· tá·t núwaʔ ísiʔ kyuhte wí· né· nú· five feet
na?tekayʌ·tés thikʌ́ oyú·kwaʔ kʌ́h.**

a·kí·luʔ kyuhte wí· tá·t núwaʔ ísiʔ kyuhte wí· né· nú· five feet
I'd say supposedly maybe further supposedly it's where five feet

na?-te-ka-yʌt-es thikʌ́ o-yu?kw-aʔ kʌ́·
PART-DL-3Z/N.SG.A-pile-long[STV] that NPF-tobacco-NSF see
'I'd say maybe over five feet is how high the pile of tobacco would be.'

Mercy Doxtator, All about Tobacco

(10.25) **Tahnú· neʔ thó·neʔ n owistóhsliʔ, wé·ni tsiʔ tékni sílu. Ok neʔn tá·t
sʌ́haʔ kʌʔ nikúha, tá·t núwaʔ twenty cents.**

tahnú· neʔ thó·neʔ n o-wisto-hsl-iʔ wé·ne tsiʔ tékni sílu ok neʔn
then at that time NPF-cold-NMZR-NSF evidently two bits but

tá·t sʌ́haʔ kʌʔ nikúha tá·t núwaʔ twenty cents
maybe more small amount maybe twenty cents
'And at that time, butter must have [cost] a quarter. But maybe even less, maybe 20
cents.'

Verland Cornelius, A Lifetime of Memories

11. Possibility and Necessity

Very often speakers qualify an event or situation that they are talking about by specifying
how likely they think it is that the event will occur, if the event is possible or necessary.
These expressions, among others, are part of what is called *modality*, and Oneida expresses
modality with both verbs and particles. Possibility and ability are expressed with the verbs
-atu- 'be possible, occur' and **-kweny-** 'able.' Necessity, and to some extent obligation, is
expressed with the verbs **-atu-** 'be possible, occur' and **-atuhutsyohu-** 'want, need, should,'
as well as the verb form **yah thya·ya·wʌ́·** 'it is necessary, it has to be.' Certainty is expressed by verbs such as **-anuhte-** 'know' and otherwise largely by particles. This section
will concentrate on the verbs that occur in expressions of modality. For particles (many of
which are verbal in origin) that relate to certainty or likelihood the reader is directed to section 2.2.2.

11.1 Possibility

Possibility is expressed both with **-atu-** 'be possible, occur' and **-kweny-** 'able.' Whether or
not a situation is deemed possible can be attributed to someone's inherent capabilities or to
external circumstances. The verb **-kweny-** 'able' is often used for a possibility that is due to
someone's inherent (physical) ability, as when the bat in the excerpt in (11.1) says that he is
able to walk (just like animals). This verb can be inflected with any of the prefixes that reference animate participants. In (11.1) **-kweny-** occurs with the first person singular agent
prefix **k-**.

(11.1) **ʌkkwe·ní· ʌkahtʌ·tí·,**
     ʌ-k-kweny-ʔ   ʌ-k-ahtʌty-ʔ
     FUT-1SG.A-able-PNC   FUT-1SG.A-leave,set.out-PNC
     'I am able to walk,'

Ruben Cutcut, Why the Bat Travels at Night

Most of the time the verb **-kweny-** is used when the possibility or ability is inherent, but occasionally it is used when the possibility is determined by someone else. In this case it is possible to interpret the meaning as involving obligation. This is suggested by the translation of the excerpt in (11.2).

(11.2) **né· kwí· né· ʌkkwe·ní· ʌkyʌtínyuhteʔ kiʔwáh.**
     né· kwí· né· ʌ-k-kweny-ʔ   ʌ-k-yʌt-inyuht-eʔ   kiʔwáh
     it's   it's FUT-1SG.A-able-PNC FUT-1SG.A-wood-bring.inside-PNC right
     'it would be up to me to bring wood inside.'

Georgina Nicholas, An Oneida Childhood

The verb **-atu-** 'be possible, occur' is the more usual verb when the possibility is due to circumstance. The verb usually occurs in the FUTURE or FACTUAL mode, and always with the feminine-zoic/neuter singular agent pronominal prefix, thus ʌwa·tú· (future) or u·tú· (factual). The verb in the clause after the -atu- clause specifies what it is that is possible. In (11.3), for example, Georgina Nicholas says that nowadays people can go into town to buy their groceries.

(11.3) **ʌwa·tú· oniʔ kanatá·ke ʌhutʌnaʔtslahninú·naʔ,**
     ʌ-w-atu-ʔ   oniʔ kanatá·ke
     FUT-3Z/N.SG.A-possible-PNC too   in town
     ʌ-hu-atʌnaʔtsl-a-hninu-ʔn-aʔ
     FUT-3M.PL.A-groceries-JN-buy-DISL-PNC
     'they can even go to town and buy groceries,'

Georgina Nicholas, An Oneida Childhood

A special kind of possibility is the possibility to *not* do something. This is expressed with **-atu-** (either future ʌwa·tú· or factual u·tú·) followed by a negative verb, so literally 'it's possible not to do something.' An example of this is (11.4); here Mercy Doxtator is telling us that her father didn't have to work ('it could be that he not work') for a while because her parents had saved some of the money they had made. In (11.5) Clifford Cornelius says that (back then) he could do without having to go to school and getting an education.

(11.4) **tó· kiʔ ok wí· náheʔ wé·ne u·tú· yah teshoyoʔtʌ́·u**
     tó· kiʔ ok wí· náheʔ wé·ne   waʔ-w-atu-ʔ
     some while only   evidently FACT-3Z/N.SG.A-possible-PNC
     yah te-s-ho-yoʔtʌ-ʔu
     not   NEG-REP-3M.SG.P-work-STV
     'I guess for a while it was possible for him not to work'

Mercy Doxtator, My Childhood

(11.5) **ʌwa·tú· yah tha·katáyahteʔ, don't have no education, ʌwa·tú· kiʔ ʌwakyo·tʌ́· sʌ́haʔ ok.**

ʌ-w-atu-ʔ	yah th-aa-k-atawyaʔt-eʔ
FUT-3Z/N.SG.A-possible-PNC	not CONTR-OPT-1SG.A-go.to.school-PNC

ʌ-w-atu-ʔ	kiʔ ʌ-wak-yotʌ-ʔ	sʌ́haʔ ok
FUT-3Z/N.SG.A-possible-PNC	actually FUT-1SG.P-work-PNC	anyway

'It was possible for me not to go to school, don't have no education, I could work nevertheless.'

Clifford Cornelius, A Lifetime Working

The verb **-atu-** can also indicate permission, although in these stories this use of **-atu-** is infrequent. The excerpt in (11.6), which comes from Mercy Doxtator's description of what happens after someone has passed on, may involve permission—in this case being allowed or permitted to eat after everyone else has been given the opportunity to eat. Otherwise permission is conveyed in Oneida with verbs whose meaning includes agreement or consent: **-athutat-** 'allow, consent, agree to, give permission,' **-lihwawi-** 'give permission,' **-atlihwisaʔ-** 'agree, talk over, plan,' **-naktot-** 'have time or opportunity.'

(11.6) **né· nʌ tsiʔ ka·yʌ́· yakotló·lu ʌwa·tú· né·n núwaʔ ʌshutekhu·ní·,**

né·	nʌ	tsiʔ ka·yʌ́·	yako-atlohl-u	ʌ-w-atu-ʔ	né·n
it's	then	the one that	3FI.P-watch-STV	FUT-3Z/N.SG.A-possible-PNC	it's that

núwaʔ	ʌ-s-hu-ate-khw-uni-ʔ
this time	FUT-REP-3M.PL.A-SRF-food-make-PNC

'then those who are looking on can eat next,'

Mercy Doxtator, After a Loss

NEGATIVE forms of both **-atu-** and **-kweny-** are used to talk about things that are not possible. Examples with the verb **-atu-** (**yah thau·tú·**) are given in (11.7) and (11.8). In (11.7) a mother and daughter couldn't eat right way because the mother had not baked any bread. In (11.8) this flirtatious fellow couldn't say anything because of the terrifying situation he found himself in. In these examples the absence of possibility, or rather the impossibility, is due to circumstance.

(11.7) **yah kwí· thau·tú· óksaʔ a·kyatekhu·ní·**

yah kwí·	th-aa-w-atu-ʔ	óksaʔ
not	CONTR-OPT-3Z/N.SG.A-possible-PNC	right away

aa-ky-ate-khw-uni-ʔ
OPT-3FZ.DU.A-SRF-food-make-PNC

'they couldn't eat right away'

Norma Kennedy, The Bird

(11.8) **Yah thau·tú· náhteʔ oniʔ né· usahʌ́·luʔ.**

yah	th-aa-w-atu-ʔ	náhteʔ	oniʔ	né·
not	CONTR-OPT-3Z/N.SG.A-possible-PNC	anything	even	it's

usa-hʌ-ihlu-ʔ
REP:OPT-3M.SG.A-say-PNC
'He couldn't even say anything.'

Verland Cornelius, Ghosts, Flirts, and Scary Beings

The negative of the verb **-kweny-** occurs when the inability is inherent, as in (11.9), but also quite often when it is due to circumstance, as in (11.10) and (11.11). In (11.10) the circumstance is the fact that the fellow saw a ghost. In (11.11) a situation—the speaker's mother leaving her daughter with a caretaker—was judged to be inappropriate. (It is interesting that in these stories the negative form of **-kweny-** occurs far more frequently than the non-negative form.)

(11.9) **yah né· tha·hatikwe·ní· ta·hati·tʌ́· thikʌ́ tho thʌ·né·seʔ,**
      yah   né·   th-aa-hati-kweny-ʔ   t-aa-hati-tʌ-ʔ   thikʌ́
      not   it's   CONTR-OPT-3M.PL.A-able-PNC   DL-OPT-3M.PL.A-fly-PNC   that

      tho   t-hʌn-e-ʔseʔ
      there   CSL-3M.PL.A-walk-HAB
      'they can't fly, those that are walking around over there [the animals],'

Ruben Cutcut, Why the Bat Travels at Night

(11.10) **yah tha·hakwe·ní· náhteʔ usahʌ́·luʔ.**
       yah   th-aa-ha-kweny-ʔ   náhteʔ   usa-hʌ-ihlu-ʔ
       not   CONTR-OPT-3M.SG.A-able-PNC   anything   REP:OPT-3M.SG.A-say-PNC
       'he couldn't say anything.'

Verland Cornelius, Ghosts, Flirts, and Scary Beings

(11.11) **Wahʌ́·luʔ, "yah kiʔ tha·kakwe·ní· thi·kʌ́."**
       wa-hʌ-ihlu-ʔ   yah   kiʔ   th-aa-ka-kweny-ʔ   thikʌ́
       FACT-3M.SG.A-say-PNC   not   actually   CONTR-OPT-3Z/N.SG.A-able-PNC   that
       'He said, "that won't do".'

Verland Cornelius, A Lifetime of Memories

11.2 Necessity

There are three constructions used to convey necessity. First, necessity can be expressed with the verb stems **-atuhutsyohs-/-atuhutsyoni-** (which has the benefactive suffix) or **-atuhutsyohu-**. The first stem is inflected with pronominal prefixes that reference animate participants, and these verb forms are translated as 'want' or 'need.' Often the want or need is inherent. So in (11.12), with the feminine-zoic non-singular prefix, we are told these ladies needed to go to the bathroom. The second stem is inflected with the default feminine-zoic/neuter singular prefix, and this verb is used for a strong suggestion or obligation ('should, supposed to'). For example, in (11.13) Rose Antone's mother says they "should" go elsewhere because she believes that leaving their haunted house is a *really* good idea. And in (11.14) Clifford Cornelius's father tells him he should have added baking powder when he was baking bread.

(11.12) **Nʌ kaʔikʌ́ kunukwé waʔtyonatuhútsyohseʔ ta·kutnuso·t<u>ʌ·</u>.**

nʌ   kaʔikʌ́   kun-ukwe   waʔ-t-yon-atuhutsyo-hs-eʔ
then   this   3FZ.PL.A-person   FACT-DL-3FZ.DP.P-need-BEN-PNC

t-aa-ku-atnusot-ʌʔ
CSL-OPT-3FZ.PL.A-urinate-PNC
'Then these girls needed to relieve themselves.'

Barbara Schuyler, A Ghost on the Tracks

(11.13) **teyotuhutsyóhu ákteʔ nú· nya·étowe<u>ʔ</u>.**

te-yo-atuhutsyohu   ákteʔ   nú·   n-y-aa-etw-e-ʔ
DL-3Z/N.SG.P-should[STV]   different where PART-TRL-OPT-1IN.PL.A-walk-PNC
'we should go some place else.'

Rose Antone, A Night Visitor

(11.14) **teyotuhutsyóhu baking powder sʌ́· yaesátyukeʔ**

te-yo-atuhutsyohu   b.p.   sʌ́·   y-aa-es-aty-u-k-eʔ
DL-3Z/N.SG.P-should[STV]   b.p.   also   TRL-OPT-2SG.P-add-STV-CONT-PNC
'you were supposed to put in baking powder too'

Clifford Cornelius, A Lifetime Working

The second construction used for necessity consists of the particle **nok** plus a form of the verb **-atu-** 'be possible, occur,' as in (11.15). And the third construction is the expression **yah thya·ya·wʌ́·**, which is a negative form of the verb root **-ʌ-** 'happen,' as in (11.16). These two constructions seem to be interchangeable.

(11.15) **nok ʌwa·tú· ʌyakwahninú·naʔ coal oil.**

né· ok   ʌ-w-atu-ʔ   ʌ-yakwa-hninu-ʔn-aʔ   coal oil
only   FUT-3Z/N.SG.A-possible-PNC   FUT-1EX.PL.A-buy-DISL-PNC   coal oil
'we have to go and buy coal oil.'

Norma Kennedy, A Scary Light

(11.16) **Yah thya·ya·wʌ́· tsiʔ Muncey yʌhʌ·<u>ké·</u>.**

yah   th-y-aa-yaw-ʌ-ʔ   tsiʔ   Muncey
not   CONTR-TRL-OPT-3Z/N.SG.P-happen-PNC   that   Muncey

yʌhʌ-k-e-ʔ
TRL:FUT-1SG.A-walk-PNC
'I have to go to Muncey.'

Norma Kennedy, A Scary Light

The construction **yah nok thau·tú·** is the negated form of **nok ʌwa·tú·** and it is used when the necessity is contradicted—that is, the event does not *have* to take place (or to put it slightly differently, it's not the case that it *must* occur). In the excerpt in (11.17), for example, Clifford Cornelius explains that long ago when he was doing ironwork one didn't need to have an education to do ironwork. It might be useful to compare the two negative structures involving the verb **-atu-**: **yah thau·tú·** and **yah nok thau·tú·**. **Yah thau·tú·** means absence of possibility ('can't'), as in (11.7) or (11.8) above, while **yah nok thau·tú·** means absence of necessity ('don't have to, don't need to'), as in (11.17).

(11.17) **Khále? nʌ kalístatsi? ukyo·tʌ́·, yah ki? nok thau·tú· kwahikʌ́**
        a·hahyatuhslayʌtelíhake? ne? thó·ne?.

        khále?   nʌ   kalístatsi?   wa?-wak-yotʌ-?
        and   then   iron   FACT-1SG.P-work-PNC

        yah ki?   nok   th-aa-w-atu-?   kwahikʌ́
        not   actually only CONTR-OPT-3Z/N.SG.A-possible-PNC just really

        aa-ha-hyatu-hsl-a-yʌteli-hak-e?   ne? thó·ne?
        OPT-3M.SG.A-write-NMZR-JN-know-CONT-PNC   at that time
        'And then I did ironwork, he [a person] didn't really need to have an education [to do ironwork] at that time.'

Clifford Cornelius, A Lifetime Working

The verbs **-atu-**, **-kweny-**, **-atuhutsyohu-** and **-atuhutsyohs-/-atuhutsyoni-** and their inflectional possibilities are summarized in Table 14.

12. Other Linkages between Clauses

Other possible relations between clauses include modification, purpose, condition, coordination, and the expression of cause or consequence. Some of these connections are introduced by a specific particle or set of particles some of the time, and some of the time the connection between clauses is inferred. Modification, for example, is expressed just by juxtaposing clauses. In the excerpt in (12.1) the radio, mentioned in the second clause, is described as being small in the first clause. In (12.2) the speaker, referenced on the verb of the first clause, says she has really long legs in the second clause.

(12.1) **Tahnú· kʌ? ok kʌs ni·wá· thikʌ́ yukni·yʌ́· watlʌnótha?,**
        tahnú· kʌ?   ok   kʌs   ni-w-a-?   thikʌ́
        and   small only habitually PART-3Z/N.SG.A-size-STV that

        yukni-yʌ-?   w-at-lʌn-ot-ha?
        1DU.P-have-STV   3Z/N.SG.A-SRF-song-stand-HAB
        'And we had just a small radio,'

Norma Kennedy, My First Job in Tobacco

(12.2) **tho wa?katítane? a?é· na?teksine·sú·se?,**
        tho   wa?-k-at-it-a-?-ne?   a?é·   na?-te-k-hsin-es-u-?se?
        there FACT-1SG.A-SRF-in-JN-INCH-PNC great PART-DL-1SG.A-leg-long-STV-PL
        'I would get in there [the buggy] with my great long legs,'

Olive Elm, Visits to My Auntie's

-kweny- (e.g. ʌkkweˑní· 'I can')	All pronom-inal prefixes	Possibility (obligation)
With negative (e.g. yah thaˑkkweˑní· 'I can't')		No possibility
-atu- (e.g. ʌwaˑtú· 'it can be, it's possible')	z/N prefix	Possibility
With negative (yah thauˑtú· 'it can't be')		No possibility
nok + -atu- (e.g. nok ʌwaˑtú· 'it has to be')		Necessity
With negative (yah nok thauˑtú· 'it doesn't have to be')		No necessity
-atuhutsyohs-/-atuhutsyoni- (e.g. tewakatuhutsyoní 'I want, I need')	All pronom-inal prefixes	Want, need
-atuhutsyohu- (teyotuhutysóhu 'should')	z/N prefix	Suggestion, obligation
yah thyaˑyaˑwʌ́· 'it has to be'		Necessity

Table 14. Expressions of possibility and necessity

A verb that identifies the purpose for an action is also juxtaposed; it can have the OPTA-TIVE prepronominal prefix, as in the excerpt in (12.3), but a purpose clause does not necessarily have the optative. For example, the excerpt in (12.4) has two purpose clauses; the first, 'to buy bread,' does not have the optative prefix while the second, 'for us to eat supper,' does.

(12.3) **ostúha kʌʔ nyahuwaˑyéleʔ ísiʔ aˑhátkwihteʔ,**

ostúha kʌʔ   n-y-a-huwa-yel-eʔ
a little here PART-TRL-FACT-3>3M.SG-touch-PNC

ísiʔ   aa-h-at-kwiʔt-eʔ
yonder   OPT-3M.SG.A-SRF-move.over-PNC

'she touched him a little so he would move over,'

Rose Antone, A Night Visitor

(12.4) **nok ʌwaˑtú· tyutʌhniˑnúheʔ aleʔ yʌhʌ́skeʔ ʌsknaʔtalahninúˑnaʔ**
          aˑyakwatekhuˑní· yoʔkáshʌ,

nok   ʌ-w-atu-ʔ   tyutʌhniˑnúheʔ aleʔ
only   FUT-3z/N.SG.A-possible-PNC   store   again

yʌhʌ-s-k-e-ʔ   ʌ-s-k-naʔtal-a-hninu-ʔn-aʔ
TRL:FUT-REP-1SG.A-walk-PNC   FUT-REP-1SG.A-bread-JN-buy-DISL-PNC

aa-yakw-ate-khw-uni-ʔ   yoʔkáshʌ
OPT-1EX.PL.A-SRF-food-make-PNC   evening

'I have to go to the store to buy bread for us to eat for supper,'

Clifford Cornelius, A Lifetime Working

Some of the particles and particle combinations that occur frequently to connect clauses are described in this section.

12.1 kanyó· ok 'so that'

The particle combination **kanyó· ok** 'so that, so long as' introduces clauses that denote result. *Resultative* clauses are exemplified in (12.5) and (12.6). **Kanyó·** otherwise occurs in the combination **kanyó· onʌ́** 'when, as soon as,' as in (12.7) and (12.8).

(12.5) **waʔukwayo·tʌ́·, kanyó· ok au·tú· a·yakwatnúhsi<u>ke</u>ʔ.**
waʔ-yukwa-yotʌ-ʔ   kanyó· ok   aa-w-atu-ʔ
FACT-1PL.P-work-PNC   so that   OPT-3Z/N.SG.A-possible-PNC

aa-yakwa-at-nuhs-ik-eʔ
OPT-1EX.PL.A-SRF-house-fill-PNC

'we worked, so that we could fill up the kill [kiln].'
Olive Elm, *Learning to Work in Tobacco*

(12.6) **Ehtá·ke ok nukwá· kanyu·tú· newspaper, kanyó· ok tákʌʔ úhkaʔ utayutkeʔto·t<u>ʌ́</u>.**
ehtá·ke   ok   nukwá·   ka-nyutu-ʔ   newspaper   kanyó· ok   tákʌʔ
below   only   where   3Z/N.SG.A-hang-STV   newspaper   so that   so as not

úhkaʔ   uta-yu-atkeʔtot-ʌʔ
anyone   CSL:OPT-3FI.A-peer,look-PNC

'The newspaper was hanging only on the bottom, so that no one could look in.'
Verland Cornelius, *A Pig in the Window*

(12.7) **He just disappeared kanyó· onʌ́ wahanutá·la<u>ne</u>ʔ.**
He just disappeared   kanyó· onʌ́   wa-ha-anutahlaʔ-neʔ
he just disappeared   as soon as   FACT-3M.SG.A-go.uphill-PNC

'He just disappeared as soon as he got to the top of the hill.'
Verland Cornelius, Ghosts, *Flirts, and Scary Beings*

(12.8) **Leamington ní· yʌhʌ·<u>ké</u>·. Kanyó· onʌ́ ʌwakatkályahk<u>se</u>ʔ.**
Leamington   ní·   yʌhʌ-k-e-ʔ   kanyó· onʌ́
Leamington   me   TRL:FUT-1SG.A-walk-PNC   as soon as

ʌ-wak-at-kalyaʔk-hs-eʔ
FUT-1SG.P-SRF-pay-BEN-PNC

'I'm going to Leamington. As soon as I get paid.'
Clifford Cornelius, *A Lifetime Working*

12.2 tá·t 'if, maybe, whether, or'

The particle **tá·t** 'if, maybe' introduces *conditional* clauses—a clause that describes a certain set of cirumstances that is prerequisite for another event or situation. The **tá·t** clause can occur before another clause, as in (12.9) and (12.10), or after another clause, as in (12.11) and (12.12).

(12.9)   **tá·t kánhke náhte? na·hoyá·tawʌ? tho kwí· nú· nyʌye·kó· wáh.**

tá·t   kánhke   náhte?   n-aa-ho-ya?tawʌ-?   tho kwí· nú·
if   when   anything   PART-OPT-3M.SG.P-happen-PNC   that's where

n-y-ʌ-ye-kw-?   wáh
PART-TRL-FUT-3FI.A-pick-PNC   right

'if ever anything happened to him she could get [the money] over there.'

Olive Elm, *The Dreamer*

(12.10)   **tá·t yah kʌ? tha·kitáklake? nʌ ʌséhsye? tákʌ? ʌsatétshʌ.**

tá·t   yah   kʌ?   th-aa-k-itakl-ak-e?   nʌ
if   not   right here   CONTR-OPT-1SG.A-lie-CONT-PNC   when

ʌ-se-hs-ye-?   tákʌ?   ʌ-s-atetshʌ
FUT-REP-2SG.A-awake-PNC   don't   FUT-2SG.P-become.afraid

'if I'm not lying right here when you wake up, don't be alarmed,'

Olive Elm, *The Dreamer*

(12.11)   **a·khehlo·lí· kwí· tá·t úhka? ok ʌ́tih.**

aa-khe-hloli-?   kwí·   tá·t   úhka? ok   ʌ-t-yʌ-e-?
OPT-1SG>3-tell-PNC   if   someone   FUT-CSL-3FI.A-walk-PNC

'I should tell them if someone is coming.'

Rose Antone, *A Ghost on the Tracks*

(12.12)   **ʌyesaná·khwahse? tá·t yah tha·shni·nú·.**

ʌ-yesa-na?khw-a-?s-e?   tá·t   yah   th-aa-hs-hninu-?
FUT-3>2SG-get.angry-JN-BEN-PNC   if   not   CONTR-OPT-2SG.A-buy-PNC

'they will get mad at you if you won't buy it.'

Verland Cornelius, *A Lifetime of Memories*

Expressions that include the particle **tá·t**—**tá·t núwa?, tá·thuni?, tá·tkʌ**—perhaps also involve condition, albeit weakly so. **Tá·t núwa?** 'maybe' describes an alternative, something that might happen if circumstances were otherwise. The combination **tá·thuni?** 'or, or maybe, otherwise' also denotes alternative. **Tá·thuni?** probably comes from **tá·t uni?/oni?** 'if too,' but this combination has been written in previous works as a single word and so it is here as well. **Tá·tkʌ**, also written as a single word but probably a combination of **tá·t** plus the yes-no question particle **kʌ**, is used when the speaker is not quite certain which of the alternatives is the correct one.

(12.13)   **tá·t núwa? ʌhuwahnútlane?.**

tá·t núwa?   ʌ-huwa-hnutl-a-?-ne?
maybe   FUT-3>3M.SG-follow.after-JN-INCH-PNC

'maybe they would catch up to him.'

Norma Kennedy, *My Father's Encounter*

(12.14) **Tá·thuni? anitskwahlákhwa? yé·se<u>le</u>?.**

tá·thuni?   an-itskw-a-hl-a-hkw-ha?   ye-?sle-?
or   SRF-haunches-JN-set-JN-INSTR-HAB   3FI.A-drag-STV
'Or someone is dragging the chair.'

Verland Cornelius, *A Pig in the Window*

(12.15) **kwa?nyóh yeksayʌtákhwa? tá·tkʌ yutslunyahkwahlákhwa? tho tká·nyote? thikʌ́,**

kwa?nyóh   ye-ks-a-yʌt-a-hkw-ha?   tá·tkʌ
seems like 3FI.A-dish-JN-put-JN-INSTR-HAB   or maybe

yu-at-hsluny-a-hkw-a-hl-a-hkw-ha?   tho   t-ka-hnyot-e?
3FI.A-SRF-dress-JN-INSTR-JN-set-JN-INSTR-HAB   there CSL-3Z/N.SG.A-stand-STV
'there was like this cupboard or maybe a dresser standing there,'

Norma Kennedy, *A Scary Hairy Adventure*

12.3 ati 'no matter, even though, although'

The particle **ati** occurs in contexts like the one in (12.16) where it is translated 'no matter' (cf. **ati ki?wáh** 'no matter, never mind'). **Ati** (or **ati tsi?**) also introduces *concessive* clauses, a clause that describes circumstances that are surprising or unusual given the content of the clause it co-occurs with. In this case, **ati** is translated 'even though, even if, although.' In (12.17) the **ati** clause follows another clause, and in (12.18) it comes before another clause.

(12.16) **ati né· úhka? á·ne? kih.**

ati   né· úhka?   aa-hn-e-?   ki?
no matter   it's anyone OPT-3M.DU.A-walk-PNC   actually
'he would go out with just anybody.'

Georgina Nicholas, *The Flirt*

(12.17) **nʌ kwí· ní· tsha?akwanakla·kó· ati tsi? tho s kwí· yukwahtʌ́ti,**

nʌ kwí· ní· tsh-a?-yakw-anaklakw-?   ati tsi?   tho
so then   us   CONTR-FACT-1EX.PL.A-move.away-PNC   even though there

kʌs kwí·   yukw-ahtʌty-u
habitually 1PL.P-leave.from-STV
'so then we moved away even though it was our home,'

Mercy Doxtator, *A Hairy Adventure*

(12.18) **Né· kati? aolí·wa? ati yokʌnolú yah ki? thya·ya·wʌ́· tsi? wa?ukwayo·tʌ́· tsi? niyo·lé· wa?akwatnúhsike?**

né· kati? aolí·wa?   ati   yo-kʌnol-u   yah ki? thya·ya·wʌ́· tsi?
well it's   the reason no matter 3Z/N.SG.P-rain-STV   it has to be   that

wa?-yukwa-yotʌ-?   tsi? niyo·lé·   wa?-yakw-at-nuhs-ik-e?
FACT-1PL.P-work-PNC   until   FACT-1EX.PL.A-SRF-house-fill-PNC
'That is why no matter if it's raining we have to work until we fill the kill'

Olive Elm, *Learning to Work in Tobacco*

12.4 khále?, tahnú· 'and'

The two particles **khále?** and **tahnú·** conjoin clauses, and in many cases they are inter-changeable. However only **khále?** conjoins nominals and more generally **khále?** seems to conjoin clauses whose content is parallel. **Tahnú·** more often begins a clause where the con-tent follows from something previous; so **tahnú·** could also be translated 'and so, and be-sides.' **Khále?** is a reduced variant of the relatively infrequent **ókhale?**, which does however reveal the probable etymology of the particle as a combination of the particles **ok** and **ale?** 'again.' In isolation **ok** is translated as 'only,' but note that **ok** can also mean 'and' or 'plus.' For example, **ok** occurs in numbers that involve addition, as in the excerpt in (12.21).

(12.19) **tsyatunhahni·lát khále? tsyatʌ?nikuhkátstat.**
    tsy-at-unh-a-hnil-a-t   khále?   tsy-atʌ-?nikuhkatstat
    2DU.A-SRF-life-JN-solid-JN-CAUS.INCH   and   2DU.A-SRF-endure
    'stick it out [persist] and don't give up.'
Clifford Cornelius, A Lifetime Working

(12.20) **Ó·, kwáh ki? kʌ? náhe? nʌ sahotiké·tohte?. Tahnú· wahsuti·yó.**
    ó·   kwáh   ki?   kʌ? náhe?   nʌ   s-a-hoti-ke?toht-e?
    oh   just   actually   a while   then   REP-FACT-3M.DP.P-Show.up-PNC
    tahnú·   w-ahsut-iyo
    and   3Z/N.SG.A-night-good[STV]
    'Oh, not too long and they showed up again. And it was a nice night.'
Verland Cornelius, Ghosts, Flirts, and Scary Beings

(12.21) **Skahwístat ok kayé sílu ukwatkálya?kse? swʌhníslat.**
    s-ka-hwist-a-t   ok   kayé   sílu
    REP-3Z/N.SG-A-metal-JN-one[STV]   and   four   bits
    ukw-at-kalya?k-hs-e?   s-w-ʌhnisl-a-t
    FACT:1SG.P-SRF-pay-BEN-PNC   REP-3Z/N.SG.A-day-JN-one[STV]
    'I got paid one dollar and fifty cents a day.'
Verland Cornelius, A Lifetime of Memories

12.5 nók tsi?, kwah nók (tsi?) 'but, only, just'

Nók tsi? 'but' (from **né· ok tsi?**) denotes contrast. An example with **nók tsi?** is the excerpt in (12.22). **Nók** occurs also in the combinations **kwáh nok** and **kwah nók tsi?**, which are translated as 'only, just' and involve restriction—'all so-and-so did,' or 'so-and-so did noth-ing but,' or even the archaic-sounding 'so-and-so but did.' Examples are given in (12.23) and (12.24). In some cases either an interpretation with 'but' or with 'only, just' is appropri-ate, as in (12.25).

(12.22) **nók tsi? yah ki? ní· nuwʌtú náhte? a·yukyatkáthu.**
    nók tsi?   yah   ki?   ní·   nuwʌtú   náhte?   aa-yuky-atkatho-u
    but   not   actually   us   never   OPT-1DU.P-see-STV

'but it was never for us to see anything.'

Olive Elm, *Ghost Sightings at the Language Centre*

(12.23) **kwah nók tsiʔ lotahúhsateʔ yokʌno·lṵ́.**
kwah nók tsiʔ   lo-atahuhsat-eʔ   yo-kʌnol-u
just only   3M.SG.P-listen-STV   3Z/N.SG.P-rain-STV
'he's just listening to it rain.'

Rose Antone, *A Night Visitor*

(12.24) **Kwah nók tsiʔ tho yʌséshlʌʔ,**
kwah nók tsiʔ   tho   y-ʌ-se-hs-hl-ʌʔ
just   there   TRL-FUT-REP-2SG.A-set-PNC
'All you do is set it down again over there,'

Mercy Doxtator, *Kastes Buys a Face*

(12.25) **Kwah nók tsiʔ tekahsinu·tṵ́·.**
kwah nók tsiʔ   te-ka-hsin-ut-u-ʔ
only   DL-3Z/N.SG.A-leg-attach-DISTR-STV
'But/only it had legs,'

Verland Cornelius, *Ghosts, Flirts, and Scary Beings*

12.6 né· tsiʔ 'because'

A clause that describes the circumstances that are the cause of a situation is introduced with **né· tsiʔ** 'because,' or by just **tsiʔ**, or by a combination of particles that includes **né· tsiʔ**, such as **né· wí· tsiʔ** in (12.26).

(12.26) **Nʌ s né· yakonúhtuʔks kaʔikʌ́ yeksá·, né· wí· tsiʔ niyutuhkályaʔks.**
nʌ   kʌs   né·   yako-nuhtuʔk-s   kaʔikʌ́   yeksá·
then   usually   it's   3FI.P-tire.of.waiting-HAB   this   girl

né· wí· tsiʔ   ni-yu-atuhkalyaʔk-s
because   PART-3FI.A-hungry-HAB
'Now the little girl was running out of patience, because she was so hungry.'

Norma Kennedy, *The Bird*

Appendix 1: List of Particles

This appendix is an alphabetical list of all the particles that occur in the stories with a reference to the sections in which they are mentioned. Some particles frequently are followed by another particle and typical combinations are given as well, indented, on the line below the particle. Sometimes these combinations do not differ much in meaning from the primary particle. The list gives about 160 particles. Though most of them can occur by themselves, they often occur in strings of two or more particles, and as many as eight. The number of possible combinations of particles is astounding, 2,060 in the stories and still counting!

áhsok 'all of a sudden, suddenly' 2.2.3
áhsu 'not yet' 2.2.3, 5.
ahsuhkʌ́ 'before when' 2.2.3
ákta? 'near, nearby, close to' 2.2.3
ákte? 'different' 2.2, 2.2.3
   akte? nú· 'different place, elsewhere, somewhere else'
akté·shu? 'different (places)' 2.2, 2.2.3
akwáh See: náhte? akwáh
akwekú 'all' 9.3
a·lé· 'sometimes, at times' 2.2.3
ale? 'again' 2.2, 2.2.3, 2.2.4, 4.1, 12.4
aolí·wa? See: náhte?
astéhtsi? 'morning, in the morning, early morning' 2.2.3
ati 'even though, although, no matter, never mind' 2.2.4, 12.3
   ati né· úhka? 'no matter who, just anyone,' ati ohnáhte? 'no matter what'
átskwe 'hey, how about it'
átste 'outside' 2.2.3
aya·wʌ́· '(I) hope so, (let's) hope so'
a?é· 'far, great' 2.2.3, 10.1
   a?é· niyo·lé· 'far away, far off,' a?é· nukwá· 'far away, way over there'
a?nyóh 'seems, seems like' 2.2.2
a?tsyók or wa?tsyók 'after a while' 2.2.3
ehnók 'a while ago' 2.2.3
ehtá·ke 'downstairs, below' 2.2.3

ehtá·ke nukwá· 'downstairs, below'
elʌ́ 'other side, other direction, across' 2.2.3
   elʌ́ nukwá· 'other side'
elhúwaʔ 'right then, recently' 2.2.3
   elhúwaʔ kʌʔ nahéhaʔ 'recently, just recently, a short while ago'
elók (from: elʌ́ ok) 'from side to side, back and forth' 2.2.3
   elók nukwá· 'from side to side'
é·nik or é·nike 'upstairs, above' 2.2.3, 4.1
e·só· 'many, much, a lot, lots' 5., 9.3, 10.1
hányo 'come on'
háoʔ 'come on, okay'
   háoʔ kiʔwáh 'come on, okay'
hʌ́· 'yes' 2.2
í· or ní· or niʔí· 'I, me, we, us' 2.2.1
ihéh traditional story opening 'Hark!'
isé· or nisé· or niʔi·sé· 'you' 2.2.1
ísiʔ 'right there, right over there, away' 2.2.3, 10.2
   ísiʔ nú· 'further, more,' ísiʔ nukwá· 'over there'
kaló· 'before, this (side)' 2.2.3
   kaló· ná·wati 'this side,' kaló· tsiʔ niyo·lé· 'before'
kánhke 'when' 6.1, 7.1, 8.
   kánhke ok 'sometime'
kánikeʔ 'nowhere' 7.2
kanyó· ok 'so that, so long as' 2.2.4, 12.1
kanyó· onʌ́ 'as soon as, when' 2.2.3, 12.1
katiʔ 'well, well then, then' 2.2.4, 4.3, 6.2
katokʌ́ 'certain'
kátshaʔ 'where' 6.1, 7.1, 7.2, 8.
   kátshaʔ nú· 'where,' kátshaʔ ok nú· 'somewhere,' kátshaʔ ka·yʌ́· 'which one'
kaʔikʌ́ 'this' 2.2.1, 2.2.3, 3.2, 4.3
kʌ or kʌ́h Question particle 2.2.1, 2.2.2, 6.2, 6.3, 7.1, 12.2
kʌh or kʌ́·tho 'here, over here, this way' 2.2.3, 10.1
   kʌh nú· 'here, over here, this way,' kʌh nukwá· 'here, over here, this way'
kʌs or s 'habitually, customarily, usually' 2.2.3
kʌ́·tho or kʌh 'here, over here, this way' 2.2.3, 10.1
kʌʔ A definite amount, degree, location, etc. 'not too little, not too much, some' 2.2.3, 10.1
   kʌʔ nú· 'right here, right there,' kʌʔ nukwá· 'right here, right there,' kʌʔ náheʔ 'some
   while,' kʌʔ nikúha 'a small amount,' kʌʔ niyo·lé· 'some distance, a ways' These often
   follow the particles kwáh and kwáh kʌs
kʌʔ ok or kok 'little, small' 10.1
   kʌʔ kiʔ ok wí· 'little, small,' kok náheʔ 'a little while'
kháleʔ 'and' 2.2.4, 12.4
khe·lé· 'I guess'
kiʔ 'actually, as a matter of fact' 2.2, 2.2.2, 4.1
kiʔwáh 'right, indeed' 2.2.2
kok See: kʌʔ ok

kwáh 'just, quite' 2.2.2, 2.2.3, 8. 9.3, 10.1, 12.5

The following examples of very common combinations are all translated, loosely, as 'just' or 'only': kwáh katiʔ wí·, kwáh kʌs, kwáh kʌs katiʔ wí·, kwáh kʌs kwí· né·, kwáh kʌs kwí· nók, kwáh kwí·, kwáh kyuhte wí·, kwáh né· nók, kwah nók tsiʔ, kwáh seʔ

kwáh ok onʌ́ 'just the same, still the same'

kwahikʌ́ or kwahikʌ́ tsiʔ 'just really' 2.2.2, 5.

kwahotokʌ́·u or kwáh kʌs otokʌ́·u 'just for real, truly' 2.2.2

kwaʔnyóh or kwaʔnyóh ok 'seems, seems just like' 2.2.2

kwí· connective particle (not translated) 2.2, 2.2.3, 2.2.4, 4.3

kyuhte wí·(from: kiʔ uhte wí·) 'I guess, supposedly, probably'

kyuniʔ (from: kiʔ uniʔ) 'too, also'

n uncertain function (not translated) 2.2.1

náheʔ Occurs in expressions to do with time 6.1, 8.

náhoht<u>eʔ</u>. Variant of náhteʔ that occurs at the end of an utterance.

náhteʔ 'what, anything' 2.2.1, 6.1, 7.1, 7.2, 8., 9.3

náhteʔ akwáh 'what exactly, what the heck,' náhteʔ aolí·waʔ 'why,' náhteʔ ni·yót 'how'

ná·ku 'under, underneath' 2.2.3

náleʔ (from: nʌ aleʔ) 'then, then again' 2.2.3

né· 'it's, it's the case that' 2.2.1, 2.2.4, 4.3, 12.5, 12.6

The following examples of very common combinations are all translated beginning in 'it's': né· katiʔ wí·, né· kʌs katiʔ wí·, né· kʌs kwí·, né· kʌs kwí· né·, né· kʌs kyuhte wí·, né· kʌs wí· tsiʔ, né· kiʔ né·, né· kyuhte wí·, né· oniʔ né·, né· s katiʔ wí·. Some also have more specific translations: né· aolí·waʔ 'it's the reason why,' né· kʌ 'is it?,' né· tsiʔ or né· wí· tsiʔ 'because'

ne·é· 'yes, yeah'

né·n 'it's that, so it's' 2.2.1

ne·né· 'it's that' See: né·

neʔ kʌ n 'you mean [so-and-so]?' 2.2.1

neʔ kʌ́h 'isn't it so' 2.2.2

neʔ thó·neʔ 'at that time' 2.2.3

nʌ 'now, then' 2.2, 2.2.3, 2.2.4, 4.1

nʌ katiʔ wí· 'so then, well then,' nʌ kyaleʔ wí· 'so again,' nʌ kiʔ ok wí· or nʌ kiʔ ok aleʔ wí· 'right then, right away, at once,' nʌ kiʔ 'already,' nʌ kiʔ né· 'at once, already,' nʌ kiʔwáh 'goodbye, so long,' nʌ kwí· 'so then,' nʌ sok wí· 'so THEN'

nʌʔ né· 'that one, as for that one' 2.2.1, 4.3

nʌʔú·waʔ or núwaʔ 'now, this time' 2.2.3

ní· 'I, me, we, us' 2.2.1

nikʌ́· 'let me see, let me think'

nikú Occurs in expressions of amount or frequency 6.1, 6.3, 8., 9.3, 10.1

nisé· 'you' 2.2.1

niyo·lé· Occurs in expressions of distance or extent 6.1, 8.

niʔí· 'I, me, we, us' 2.2.1

niʔí·<u>sé</u> 'you' 2.2.1

ni·yót 'how it is, so it is, the way it is' 6.1, 8., 10.2

ni·yót 'Look'it! Oh how it is!' (exclamation)

nók or nok 'only, just' 2.2.2, 2.2.4, 11.2, 12.5
  nók tsiʔ 'but'
nú· Occurs in expressions of location 2.2, 2.2.3, 2.3, 6.1, 7.1, 8., 10.2
nukwá· Occurs in expressions of location 2.2.3, 2.3, 4.1, 8.
núwaʔ or nʌʔú·waʔ 'now, this time, today' 2.2.3
nuwʌtú 'never, ever' 2.2.3, 5., 6.2, 9.5
oh Occurs in oh ni·yót 'what kind' 6.1
ohʌtú 'ahead, in front' 2.2.3
ohnáhteʔ See: náhteʔ
ohná·kʌʔ 'behind, in back' 2.2.3
  ohná·kʌʔ nukwá· 'behind'
ohnaʔkʌ́·shuʔ 'all along behind' 2.2.3
ok 'only' 2.2.1, 2.2.3, 2.2.4, 4.1, 4.3, 6.1, 6.2, 7.1, 8., 10.1, 12.1, 12.4, 12.5
  ok neʔ or ok neʔn or ok wí· n 'and as for'
o·ké· 'oh my'
ókhaleʔ 'and' See: kháleʔ
ókhnaʔ 'and then' 2.2.3, 2.2.4
óksaʔ 'right away' 2.2.3
  óksaʔ ok 'just right away'
olihwiyó tsiʔ 'a sure thing, for sure' 2.2.2
onʌ́ 'now, then' See: nʌ
onístaʔ 'darn, gosh'
oniʔ or uniʔ 'too, also' 2.2.4, 12.2
oskanʌ́ha 'slowly'
oskánhe 'together'
ostúha 'a little' 10.1, 10.2
  ostúha ok 'only a little'
ot ni·yót 'what kind' 6.1
ótyahkeʔ or ótyaʔk 'others, some'
oyá· 'other, another'
s See: kʌs
seʔ 'too' (emphatic) 2.2.2, 2.2.3
sʌ́· 'also' 2.2.4
sʌ́haʔ 'more' 8., 10.2
  sʌ́haʔ ok 'nevertheless, anyway'
shekólih 'hello, greetings'
shekú 'still, even' 2.2.3
sok (from: seʔ ok) 'only'
só·tsiʔ 'too much' 2.2, 10.1
  só·tsiʔ e·só· 'too much, too many'
swatyelʌ́ 'sometimes' 9.5
tá· 'oh'
táh 'no' 2.2
tahnú· 'and, and so, and besides' 2.2.4, 4.1, 12.4
tá·im 'no way'
tákʌʔ 'don't, shouldn't' 2.2.4, 5., 7.2

tá·t 'if, maybe' 2.2.4, 12.2

tá·t núwaʔ 'maybe' 2.2.2, 12.2

tá·thuniʔ 'or, or else' 2.2.4, 12.2

tá·tkʌ 'whether, maybe, if, either' 12.2

té·kʌ 'not' 5.

tetsyalú 'both'

the·tʌ́· 'yesterday' 2.2.3

thikʌ́ 'that' 2.2.1

tho 'there, that way, that's' 2.2, 2.2.3, 4.1, 8.

    tho nikú 'that much, enough,' tho niyo·lé· 'that far,' tho ni·yót 'that's how, that's the way,' tho nú· or tho nukwá· 'that's where' The *tho* in these expressions is often followed by katiʔ wí· (e.g. tho katiʔ wí· nikú) or by kiʔ (e.g. tho kiʔ ni·yót)

tho áleʔ 'almost time' 2.2.3

thóha 'almost' 2.2.3

thok 'that's only' 2.2.1, 7.1

    thok náhteʔ or tho kiʔ ok náhteʔ or tho kiʔ ok wí· náhteʔ 'something,' thok nikú 'that's only how much,' thok niyo·lé· or tho kiʔ ok niyo·lé· 'that's only how far'

thoʔnʌ́ or thó·nʌ 'and then' 2.2.3

tó 'how' 6.1, 6.3, 7.1, 8.

    tó· katiʔ náheʔ 'how long (time),' tó· nikú 'how much'

tóhkaʔ 'a few, several' 9.3

    tóhkaʔ ok 'only a few'

tó·k (from: tó· ok) 'some' (amount, distance) 7.1

to·káh 'I don't know' 2.2.2

toká·t 'if'

to·kʌ́skeʔ 'it's true, truly' 2.2.2

tshiwahu·níseʔ 'a long time ago' 2.2.3

tsiléhkwaʔ 'almost'

tsiʔ 'that' 2.2.4, 4.1, 4.2, 5., 8., 9.3, 10.1, 10.2, 12.3, 12.5, 12.6

    tsiʔ náheʔ 'during, since,' tsiʔ náhteʔ 'what, whatever,' tsiʔ nú· 'where,' tsiʔ nikú 'how much, how many, however many,' tsiʔ niyo·lé· 'how far, until,' tsiʔ ni·yót 'how it is, the way it is,' tsiʔ ka·yʌ́· 'the one that' These expressions are often preceded by kwáh.

tsyoʔk 'all kinds of, different' 8., 9.3

    tsyoʔk náhteʔ 'all kinds of things, different things,' tsyoʔk nú· or tsyoʔk nukwá· 'everywhere, all over the place,' tsyoʔk úhkaʔ 'everyone, all kinds of people' These expressions are often preceded by kwáh.

tú·skeʔ or to·kʌ́skeʔ 'truly, really' 2.2.2

tyótkut 'always' 9.5

úhkaʔ 'who, anyone' 2.2.1, 4.1, 6.1, 6.2, 7.1, 7.2

    úhkaʔ náhteʔ 'who,' úhkaʔ ok or úhkaʔ ok náhteʔ 'someone'

uhte 'supposedly, probably, I guess' 2.2.2

uniʔ or oniʔ 'too, also' 2.2.4, 12.2

ú·waʔ 'now, this time' 2.2.3

wahu·níseʔ 'a long time' 2.2.3

wé·ne or wé·ni 'evidently, must be, I guess' 2.2.2

    Also: wé·ne kwí· or wé·ne tsiʔ or wé·ne kwí· tsiʔ

wé·ne ki?wáh 'I suppose' 2.2.2
wí· connective particle (not translated) 2.2, 2.2.4
yah 'not' 2.2, 4.1, 5., 6.2, 7.2, 11.1, 11.2
  yah kátsha? 'nowhere, not anywhere,' yah náhte? 'nothing, not anything,' yah kánike?
  'nowhere,' yah nuwʌtú 'not ever, never,' yah se? 'no way,' yah úhka? 'no one, not anyone,' yah tho te?yo·lé· 'not that far,' yah tho té·ku 'not that much,' yah tho té·yot 'not
  that way'
yáhtʌ? 'no, not so' 5.
yakʌ? 'reportedly, they say' 2.2.2
yáts 'yikes, gosh, golly' 2.2
ya·wét 'like, kind of like' 2.2.2
yeskʌhá 'last time' 9.5
yotká·te? 'often' 9.5

Appendix 2: Segmented Texts

In this appendix we present three texts giving all the divisions within words that we could analyze. The first line, in bold, gives the Oneida language. Every Oneida line constitutes a prosodic unit. Periods occur after utterance-final forms, and commas occur at the end of lines when the following line resets to a higher pitch. Usually there is also a pause before a pitch reset. The second and third lines give the linguistic analysis, as was done in Part III. When a word's literal meaning doesn't translate obviously into English, we give the lexicalized meanings right below the linguistic analysis of the relevant word the first time the word occurs. Last there is a free English translation of the Oneida line. Table 15 gives references to utterances in the segmented texts that attest constructions described in Part III.

Barbara Schuyler, A Ghost on the Tracks

(1) **Kʌʔ tshityukwayʌ́·saʔ,**
kʌʔ tshi-t-yukwa-yʌ-ʔsaʔ
small COIN-CSL-1PL.P-young.person-PL
When we were teenagers—

i·kélheʔ a·kuka·látus kheʔkʌ́ha kháleʔ í· kháleʔ tekniyáshe ukwatʌló·slaʔ,

i-k-elh-eʔ	aa-ku-kal-a-tu-ʔs[19]	khe-ʔkʌha	kháleʔ
EPEN-1SG.A-want-STV	OPT-1SG>2SG-story-JN-erect-BEN	1SG>3-sibling	and
í·	kháleʔ	te-kni-yashe	ukw-atʌlo-ʔsl-aʔ
FIRST.PERSON and		DL-3FZ.DU.A-together[STV]	1PL.POSS-friend-NMZR-NSF

I want to tell you a story about my younger sister and me and our two friends,

Mack Irelandhné, Mack kháleʔ Dorothy Ireland lotiyʌ·táhkweʔ yutʌhni·nú<u>heʔ</u>.

Mack Ireland-hné	Mack	kháleʔ	Dorothy Ireland
Mack.Ireland-LOC	Mack	and	Dorothy Ireland

---

[19] This verb does not have the punctual aspect, which otheerwise is required in verbs that have a modal prepronominal prefix (factual, future, optative). As mentioned in footnote 7, sometimes optative verbs that follow forms of the verb **-elh-** 'want' lack the expected punctual aspect ending.

Construction	*A Ghost on the Tracks*	*Beaver, Let's Trade Teeth!*	*My First Job in Tobacco*
Possession	Alienable with 1PL.POSS prefix ukw- (1) (29); alienable with -yʌ-/ -yʌt- 'put, lie' and patient prefix (1)	Inalienable with 1SG.A prefix k- (2) (3); with agent prefix and -ot- 'stand' (4), -iyo- 'good' (15), -oʔtʌ- 'kind of' (17). Alienable with 1SG.POSS prefix ak(w)- (2) (8) (16); with patient prefix and -oʔtʌ- 'kind of' (17)	Alienable with patient prefix and -kaʔte- 'have many' (41), -yʌ- 'put, lie' (49); alienable with 2SG.POSS prefix sa- (46), with 1DU.POSS prefix uky- (47)
Argument clauses	optative verb (6) (18) tsiʔ clause (31)	juxtaposed clause (2) (3), optative verb (6) (19)	juxtaposed clause (43) (46) (47) (59), optative verb (47) (59)
Negation	yah plus negative prefix teʔ- (8) (11) (20) (24)	yah plus negative prefix teʔ- (6) (8) (18); yah teʔwé·ne 'it's incredible' (15)	yah plus negative prefix teʔ- (42) (48) (49) (59)
Questions	embedded yes-no (polar) question (20)	yes-no question (4) (7)	embedded question with tó· nikú 'how much (42), with náhteʔ 'what' (46); yes-no question (50)
Indefinites	úhkaʔ ok 'someone' (7) (9) (12) (15) (28), yah úhkaʔ 'no one' (8) (24), kátshaʔ ok 'about' (23)	yah náhteʔ 'not anything' (8)	
tsiʔ free relatives, tho clauses, corelatives	tho nú· 'that's where' (2), tsiʔ nú· 'where' (4) (21), tsiʔ náheʔ 'while' (24), tsiʔ niyo·lé· 'until' (27), tsyoʔk náhteʔ 'different things' (31), tsiʔ ni·yót 'how' (32), tho with n- partitive prefix and -awʌʔ- 'happen' (33)	correlative (1) (8) (15); relative clause with tsiʔ ka·yʌ́· (7); tho with n-partitive prefix and -yel- 'do' (12), -oʔtʌ- 'kind of' (17), -ʌʔ- 'happen' (18); tho nikú 'that much' (19)	tsiʔ nikú 'how many' (43), tho nikú 'how much' (45), tsiʔ nú· 'where' (52), relative clause with tsiʔ ka·yʌ́· (53), correlative (56)
Counting	tekniyáshe 'two' (females) (1); time with -hwist-aʔek- 'strike metal' (23)		-ke 'amount to' with partitive prefix and number word (43) (44); -t 'one' with repetitive prefix (43) (44)
Degree	só·tsiʔ 'too much' (11), aʔé· 'great' plus -a- 'size' (14), tsiʔ plus n- partitive prefix (18)	só·tsiʔ 'too much' (8) (18), tsiʔ plus n- partitive prefix (15)	e·só· 'much' (42), tsiʔ plus n- partitive prefix (41), kʌʔ ok and -a- 'size [small]' (49); superlative with t-cislocative prefix (53)
Possibility, necessity	Neccessity with nok u·tú· (3) (27), -atuhutsyohs- 'need' (6)		Possibility with ʌwa·tú· (50) (51)
Other linkages	nók tsiʔ 'but' (3), tahnú· 'and' (4) (8) (18) (33), tá·t 'if' (7), tá·t núwaʔ 'maybe' (11) (23), (né·) tsiʔ 'because' (14) (25), tá·thuniʔ 'or' (16) (31)	kháleʔ 'and' (2) (6) (15), tahnú· 'and (so)' (6) (15), né· tsiʔ 'because' (6) (15), nók tsiʔ 'but' (18)	nók tsiʔ 'but' (42), tahnú· 'and (so)' (44) (47) (48) (49), kháleʔ 'and' (54), kwáh kwí· nók 'just' (56)

Table 15. Constructions in segmented texts

loti-yʌt-ahkweʔ   yu-atʌ-hninu-heʔ
3M.DP.P-have-PAST   3FI.A-SRF-buy-HAB
                             store
at Mack Ireland's, Mack and Dorothy Ireland used to have a store.

(2) Tho nú· waʔákweht<u>e</u>ʔ.
tho nú·   waʔ-yakw-e-ht-eʔ
that's where   FACT-1EX.PL.A-walk-CAUS-PNC
That's where we went.

(3) Nók tsiʔ nok u·tú· kalistaʔkéshuʔ nya<u>ʔákowe</u>ʔ.
nók tsiʔ   nok   waʔ-w-atu-ʔ   ka-list-aʔke-shuʔ
but   FACT-3Z/N.SG.A-possible-PNC NPF-iron-LOC-DISTR
                                                railway tracks

n-y-aʔ-yakw-e-ʔ
PART-TRL-FACT-1EX.PL.A-walk-PNC
But we had to walk there on the railway tracks.

(4) Neʔ thó·neʔ nʌ tsiʔ kʌs nú· thyatʌhninúhahkweʔ kʌ́h,
neʔ thó·neʔ   nʌ   tsiʔ kʌs nú·   t-hy-atʌ-hninu-ha-hkweʔ   kʌ́·
at that time then   where   CSL-3M.DU.A-SRF-buy-HAB-PAST   y'know
At that time, where they used to have their store,

Ball Park kuwa·yáts,
Ball Park   kuwa-yat-s
Ball Park   3>3FZ.SG-name-HAB
it was called Ball Park [Road],

tahnú· kwáh kʌs tho áktaʔ kalistatáti<u>ʔ</u>.
tahnú· kwáh kʌs   tho   áktaʔ ka-list-atatye-ʔ
and   just   habitually there   near   3Z/N.SG.A-iron-extend-PRES
and the tracks went right by there.

(5) Nʌ kwí· tho nyaʔákweʔ thikʌ́ kalistaʔkéshuʔ,
nʌ kwí·   tho   n-y-aʔ-yakw-e-ʔ   thikʌ́   ka-list-aʔke-shuʔ
so then   there PART-TRL-FACT-1EX.PL.A-walk-PNC   that   NPF-iron-LOC-DISTR
So then we were walking on the tracks,

nʌ uhte tshaʔtewahsʌnʌ́ niyo·lé· niyukwe·n<u>ú</u>.
nʌ   uhte   tshaʔ-te-w-ahsʌnʌ   ni-yo-le-ʔ
then   supposedly COIN-DL-3Z/N.SG.A-middle[STV]   PART-3Z/N.SG.P-distance-STV

ni-yukw-e-nu
PART-1PL.P-walk-STV
and we had gone about halfway.

(6) **Nʌ kaʔikʌ́ kunukwé waʔtyonatuhútsyohseʔ ta·kutnuso·tʌ́·.**
nʌ   kaʔikʌ́   kun-ukwe   waʔ-t-yon-atuhutsyo-ʔs-eʔ
then this   3FZ.PL.A-person   FACT-DL-3FZ.DP.P-need-BEN-PNC

t-aa-ku-at-nusot-ʌʔ
DL-OPT-3FZ.PL.A-SRF-be.squating-PNC
Then these girls needed to relieve themselves.

(7) **Nʌ kwí·, í· kwí· tho i·kéteʔ waʔkatʌʔnikú·lalʌʔ,**
nʌ kwí·   í· kwí·   tho   i-ke-t-eʔ   waʔ-k-atʌ-ʔnikuhl-a-l-ʌʔ?
so then   FIRST.PERSON   there EPEN-1SG.A-stand-STV   FACT-1SG.A-SRF-mind-JN-on-PNC
So then I'm the one standing there keeping a lookout,

a·khehlo·líʔ kwíʔ tá·t úhkaʔ ok ʌ́tih.
aa-khe-hloli-ʔ   kwí·   tá·t   úhkaʔ ok   ʌ-t-yʌ-e-ʔ
OPT-1SG>3-tell-PNC if   someone   FUT-CSL-3FI.A-walk-PNC
to tell them if someone is coming.

(8) **Tahnú· tetyó·kalas wí·,**
tahnú·   te-t-yo-aʔkala-s   wí·
and   DL-CSL-3Z/N.SG.P-dark-HAB
And it was dark [night-time],

yah kwí· né· úhkaʔ tha·yutkáthoʔ.
yah   kwí·   né·   úhkaʔ   th-aa-yu-atkatho-ʔ
not   it's   anyone CONTR-OPT-3FI.A-see-PNC
nobody could see.

(9) **Yaʔkatkáthoʔ St. Thomas nukwá·,**
y-aʔ-k-atkatho-ʔ   St. Thomas   nukwá·
TRL-FACT-1SG.A-see-PNC   St. Thomas   direction
I looked over St. Thomas way,

nitwʌ·té· kaluhyá·ke nukwá·;
ni-t-w-ʌte-ʔ   ka-luhy-aʔke   nukwá·
PART-CSL-3Z/N.SG.A-bright-STV   NPF-sky-LOC   direction
the sky that way was bright;

nʌ waʔkhe·kʌ́· úhkaʔ ok ta·yʌ́·.
nʌ   waʔ-khe-kʌ-ʔ   úhkaʔ ok   t-a-yʌ-e-ʔ
then   FACT-1SG>3-see-PNC   someone   CSL-FACT-3FI.A-walk-PNC
then I saw someone coming.

(10) **Nʌ kwí· kwahotokʌ́·u waʔkatʌʔnikú·lalʌʔ.**
nʌ kwí·   kwahotokʌ́·u   waʔ-k-atʌ-ʔnikuhl-a-l-ʌʔ?
so then   just for real   FACT-1SG.A-SRF-mind-JN-on-PNC

So then I really watched out.

(11) **Tá·t núwaʔ ó· yah kiʔ só·tsiʔ teʔwi·nú̲.**

tá·t núwaʔ ó· yah kiʔ só·tsiʔ teʔ-w-inu

maybe   oh not actually too much NEG-3Z/N.SG.A-far[STV]

Maybe, oh, it wasn't too far.

(12) **Kaʔikʎ úhkaʔ ok tá·le̲ʔ.**

kaʔikʎ úhkaʔ ok t-a-hl-e-ʔ

this   someone CSL-FACT-3M.SG.A-walk-PNC

Someone was coming.

(13) **Wá·kelheʔ kiʔ ní·,**

waʔ-k-elh-eʔ   kiʔ   ní·

FACT-1SG.A-think-PNC actually FIRST.PERSON

I thought,

lukwé uh te̲.

l-ukwe   uhte

3M.SG.A-person probably

a man probably.

(14) **Né· tsiʔ aʔé· niwanaʔaló·tslaʔ lonaʔalo·lú̲.**

né· tsiʔ   aʔé·   ni-w-a-naʔal-o(l)-ʔtsl-aʔ

because great PART-3Z/N.SG.A-SRF-head-cover-NMZR-size.of[STV]

lo-a-naʔal-ol-u

3M.SG.P-SRF-head-cover-STV

he has on a hat

Because he had on a great big hat.

(15) **Nʌ sok wí· waʔtwakhʌ·léhteʔ waʔkí·luʔ,**

nʌ seʔ ok wí· waʔ-t-wak-hʌle-ht-eʔ   waʔ-k-ihlu-ʔ

so then too   FACT-DL-1SG.P-call.out-CAUS-PNC FACT-1SG.A-say-PNC

So then I yelled, I said,

"teswashlíhʌ úhkaʔ ok ta·yʎ̲·."

te-swa-shlihʌ   úhkaʔ ok t-a-yʌ-e-ʔ

DL-2PL.P-hurry   someone CSL-FACT-3FI.A-walk-PNC

"hurry, someone is coming."

(16) **"Tá·thuniʔ tá·le̲ʔ."**

tá·thuniʔ t-a-hl-e-ʔ

or   CSL-FACT-3M.SG.A-walk-PNC

"Or he is coming."

(17) **Nʌ sok wí· né· waʔtyakwaláhta<u>teʔ</u>.**
nʌ seʔ ok wí· né· waʔ-t-yakw-alahtat-eʔ
so then too it's FACT-DL-1EX.PL.A-run-PNC
So then we took off running.

(18) **Tahnú· tsiʔ niwʌto·lé· thikʌ́ tho ta·hsaláhtateʔ kalistaʔké<u>shuʔ</u>.**
tahnú· tsiʔ ni-w-ʌtole-ʔ thikʌ́ tho t-aa-hs-alahtat-eʔ
and how PART-3Z/N.SG.A-hard-STV that there DL-OPT-2SG.A-run-PNC
ka-list-aʔke-shuʔ
NPF-iron-LOC-DISTR
And it's really hard to run on railway tracks.

(19) **Niyoshno·lé· waʔukyaʔtu·tí<u>·</u>.**
ni-yo-shnole-ʔ waʔ-yuk-yaʔt-uty-ʔ
PART-3Z/N.SG.P-fast-STV FACT-3>1SG-body-discard-PNC
They left me behind real quick.

(20) **Yah teʔwakanúhteʔ tho kʌ naʔteyotí·kat.**
yah teʔ-wak-anuhte-ʔ tho kʌ naʔ-te-yoti-ʔkaht
not NEG-1SG.P-know-STV that's QUESTION PART-DL-3FZ.DP.P-move.fast[STV]
I didn't know they could go so fast.

(21) **Yaʔákwaweʔ kwí· tsiʔ nú· waʔukwehtuháti<u>ʔ</u>.**
y-aʔ-yakwa-w-eʔ kwí· tsiʔ nú· waʔ-yukw-e-ht-u-hatye-ʔ
TRL-FACT-1EX.PL.A-arrive-PNC where FACT-1PL.P-walk-CAUS-STV-PROG-PNC
So we got to where we were going.

(22) **Nʌ tho waʔakwatnúhtuh<u>teʔ</u>.**
nʌ tho waʔ-yakw-atnuhtuʔt-eʔ
then there FACT-1EX.PL.A-wait-PNC
Then we waited there.

(23) **Tá·t núwaʔ kátshaʔ ok tshaʔtewahsʌnʌ́ uhte waʔkahwistá·e<u>keʔ</u>.**
tá·t núwaʔ kátshaʔ ok tshaʔ-te-w-ahsʌnʌ uhte
maybe somewhere COIN-DL-3Z/N.SG.A-middle[STV] supposedly
waʔ-ka-hwist-aʔek-eʔ
FACT-3Z/N.SG.A-metal-strike-PNC
Maybe about half an hour.

(24) **Tsiʔ náheʔ tho yákweteʔ yukwatnuhtú·tu,**
tsiʔ náheʔ tho yakw-et-eʔ yukw-atnuhtuʔt-u
while there 1EX.PL.A-stand-STV 1PL.P-wait-STV
While we were standing waiting there,

né·n yah úhka? tehoke?tóhtu.

né·n   yah   úhka?   te?-ho-ke?to-ht-u
it's that   not   anyone   NEG-3M.SG.P-appear-CAUS-STV
nobody showed up.

(25) NΛ wa?ukwanehla·kó· thikΛ́ tsi? oyá· tha?a·wΛ́·.

nΛ   wa?-yukwa-nehlakw-?   thikΛ́   tsi?   oyá·
then   FACT-1PL.P-get.surprised-PNC   that   because   other

th-a?-yaw-Λ-?
CONTR-FACT-3Z/N.SG.P-happen-PNC
Then we were surprised because something out of the ordinary happened.

(26) NΛ wa?ukwatétsh̲Λ̲?.

nΛ   wa?-yukw-atetshΛ-?
then   FACT-1PL.P-get.scared-PNC
Then we got scared.

(27) NΛ kwí· nok u·tú· tho tyákwehse? tsi? niyo·lé· wahutenho·t̲ú̲·.

nΛ kwí·   nok   wa?-w-atu-?   tho   t-yakw-e-?se?
so then   FACT-3Z/N.SG.A-possible-PNC   there   CSL-1EX.PL.A-walk-HAB

tsi? niyo·lé·   wa-hu-ate-nhotu-?
until   FACT-3M.PL.A-SRF-close.door-PNC
So then we had to stay there until they closed up.

(28) NΛ kwí· úhka? ok sayukhiya?títa̲ne̲?.

nΛ kwí·   úhka? ok   s-a-yukhi-ya?t-it-a-?-ne?
so then   someone   REP-FACT-3>1DP-body-inside-JN-INCH-PNC
                  give a ride to
And then someone gave us a ride [home].

(29) Oyá· ukwatΛlo?sla?sh̲ú̲ha.

oyá·   ukw-atΛlo-?sl-a?-shuha
other   1PL.POSS-friend-NMZR-NSF-PL
Some of our other friends.

(30) Wé·ne kwí· tsi? wa?ukwatyánlu̲ne̲?.

wé·ne kwí·   tsi?   wa?-yukw-atyanlu-?-ne?
evidently   that   FACT-1PL.P-haunted-INCH-PNC
I guess we got haunted.

(31) Né· s yukhihlo·líhe? lotikstΛhokúha tsi? lutkáthos kΛs tá·thuni? lonathu·té· tsyo?k náhte? thikΛ́ kalistá·̲ke̲.

né·   kΛs   yukhi-hloli-he?   loti-kstΛh-okuha   tsi?   lu-atkatho-s   kΛs
it's   customarily   3>1DP-tell-HAB   3M.DP.P-old-PL   that   3M.PL.A-see-HAB   habitually

tá·thuni? lon-athute-? tsi? ok náhte? thikʌ́ ka-list-a?ke
or 3M.DP.P-hear-STV different things that NPF-iron-LOC
Some elders tell us that they used to see or hear things on the tracks.

(32) **Nʌ ki? yahá·kewe? tsi? ni·yót tsi? wa?kka·látu?.**

nʌ ki? yaha?-ke-w-e? tsi? ni-y-oht tsi?
then actually TRL:FACT-1SG.A-arrive-PNC at PART-3Z/N.SG.A-be.so[STV] that

wa?-k-kal-a-tu-?
FACT-1SG.A-story-JN-erect-PNC
Now I have arrived over there [at the end] of how I told the story.

(33) **Tahnú· kwáh kwí· otokʌ́·u ka?ikʌ́ tho niyukwaya?tawʌ́·u.**

tahnú· kwáh kwí· otokʌ́·u ka?ikʌ́ tho ni-yukwa-ya?t-awʌ?-u
and just for real this thus PART-1PL.P-body-happen-STV
And this really happened to us.

Mercy Doxtator, Beaver, Let's Trade Teeth!

(1) **Tsi? náhte? ʌkka·látu? kwahotokʌ́·u tho niyawʌ́·u.**

tsi? náhte? ʌ-k-kal-a-tu-? kwahotokʌ́·u tho
that what FUT-1SG.A-story-JN-erect-PNC just for real thus

ni-yaw-ʌ?-u
PART-3Z/N.SG.P-happen-STV
The story I will tell really happened.

(2) **Tshiwahu·níse? kʌ́· tshikeksá· ké·yale? s thikʌ́ nále? wa?o?nétskane? knawí·ke,**

tshiwahu·níse? kʌ́· tshi-ke-ksá? k-ehyahl-e? kʌs thikʌ́
long time ago y'know COIN-1SG.A-child 1SG.A-remember-STV customarily that

nʌ ale? wa?-yo-?netsk(ʌ)-a-?-ne? k-nawi-?ke
then again FACT-3Z/N.SG.P-loose-JN-INCH-PNC 1SG.A-tooth-LOC
A long time ago when I was a child I remember my tooth got loose,

nʌ thóha a·katnawilota·kó·,

nʌ thóha aa-k-at-nawil-ot-a-kw-?
then almost OPT-1SG.A-SRF-tooth-stand-JN-REV-PNC
lose a tooth
I was about to lose a tooth,

khále? aknulhá· ya?utáthʌle? akwatauntie.

khále? ak-nulhá? y-a?-yutat-hʌl-e? akw-at-auntie
and 3FZ.SG>1SG-mother TRL-FACT-3FI>3FI-summon-PNC 1SG.POSS-SRF-aunt
and my mother summoned my auntie.

(3) **Né· s thikʌ́ tho wá·yuweʔ kʌ́·,**

né·   kʌs   thikʌ́   tho   waʔ-yu-aw-eʔ   kʌ́·
it's   customarily   that   there   FACT-3FI.A-arrive-PNC   y'know

So she got there,

waʔutathlo·lí· kʌ́· náleʔ yoʔnétskʌ knawí·ke,

waʔ-yutat-hloli-ʔ   kʌ́·   nʌ aleʔ   yo-ʔnetskʌ   k-nawi-ʔke
FACT-3FI>3FI-tell-PNC   y'know   then again   3Z/N.SG.P-loose[STV]   1SG.A-tooth-LOC

and she [my mother] told her that my tooth was loose,

nʌ thóha a·katnawilota·kó·.

nʌ   thóha   aa-k-at-nawil-ot-a-kw-ʔ
now   almost   OPT-1SG.A-SRF-tooth-stand-JN-REV-PNC

I was about to lose a tooth.

(4) **Nʌ kiʔ ok wí· thikʌ́ tayúkhʌleʔ,**

nʌ kiʔ ok wí·   thikʌ́   t-a-yuk-hʌl-eʔ
right then   that   CSL-FACT-3>1SG-summon-PNC

Right away she called me over to her,

waʔí·luʔ, "ká·ts" waʔí·luʔ "kátkʌs thikʌ́,

waʔ-ya-ihlu-ʔ   ká·ts   waʔ-ya-ihlu-ʔ   k-at-kʌ-ʔs   thikʌ́
FACT-3FI.A-say-PNC   come here   FACT-3FI.A-say-PNC   1SG.A-SRF-see-BEN   that

she said, "come here," she said, "how about I take a look,

nʌ kʌ tú·skeʔ yoʔnétskʌ tsiʔ snawi·lóteʔ."

nʌ   kʌ   to·kʌ́skeʔ   yo-ʔnetskʌ   tsiʔ   hs-nawil-ot-eʔ
now   QUESTION   it's true   3Z/N.SG.P-loose[STV]   at   2SG.A-tooth-stand-STV

is it true you have a loose tooth?"

(5) **Waʔkí·luʔ "hʌ́· o·nʌ́."**

waʔ-k-ihlu-ʔ   hʌ́·   onʌ́
FACT-1SG.A-say-PNC   yes   now

I said, "yes."

(6) **Tahnú· s yah té·kelheʔ a·yuknawilotakó,**

tahnú·   kʌs   yah te?-k-elh-eʔ   aa-yuk-nawil-ot-a-kw-ʔ
and   customarily   not   NEG-1SG.A-want-STV   OPT-3>1SG-tooth-stand-JN-REV

And I didn't want my tooth to be pulled,

wá·kelheʔ né· tsiʔ yonuhwákteʔ,

waʔ-k-elh-eʔ   né· tsiʔ   yo-nuhwak-t-eʔ
FACT-1SG.A-think-PNC   because   3Z/N.SG.P-hurt-CAUS.INCH-STV

I thought because it hurts,

yah s kati? wí· óksa? té·kelhe? tho ya?tá·ktane? tsi? tyé·tlu? kʌ́h,

yah kʌs kati? wí· óksa? te?-k-elh-e? tho

not usually so then right away NEG-1SG.A-want-STV there

ya?-t-aa-k-t-a-?-ne? tsi? t-ye-i?tlu-? kʌ́·

TRL-DL-OPT-1SG.A-stand-JN-INCH-PNC at CSL-3FI.A-sit-STV y'know

so I didn't want to stand over there right away, where she was sitting,

khále? kwí· onʌ́ tho ya?téktane?.

khále? kwí· onʌ́ tho ya?-te-k-t-a-?-ne?

and then there TRL-DL-1SG.A-stand-JN-INCH-PNC

but then I did go stand over there.

(7) Nʌ kwí· wa?tkátskalawe? thikʌ́,

nʌ kwí· wa?-t-k-atskala?w-e? thikʌ́

so then FACT-DL-1SG.A-open.one's.mouth-PNC that

So then I opened my mouth,

ókhna? wa?í·lu?, "tó· kátkʌs ka?ikʌ́,

ókhna? wa?-ya-ihlu-? tó· k-at-kʌ-?s ka?ikʌ́

and then FACT-3FI.A-say-PNC how 1SG.A-SRF-see-BEN this

and then she said, "let me take a look,

né· kʌ ka?ikʌ́ tsi? ka·yʌ́· yo?nétskʌ,"

né· kʌ ka?ikʌ́ tsi? ka·yʌ́· yo-?netskʌ

it's QUESTION this the one that 3Z/N.SG.P-loose[STV]

is this the one that's loose?,"

wa?kí·lu? "né· wáh."

wa?-k-ihlu-? né· wáh

FACT-1SG.A-say-PNC it is indeed

I said "it's the one."

(8) Ókhna? né· wa?ehnyota·kó·,

ókhna? né· wa?-ye-hny-ot-a-kw-?

and then it's FACT-3FI.A-EMPTY-stand-JN-REV-PNC

pull [a tooth]

And then she pulled it out,

yah náhte? só·tsi? te?wakattokʌ́,

yah náhte? só·tsi? thye?-wak-attok-ʌ

not anything too much CONTR-1SG.P-perceive-STV

I didn't notice too much of anything,

ókhnaʔ né· tho tyéhaweʔ aknawi·lá·,
ókhnaʔ   né·   tho   t-ye-haw-eʔ   ak-nawil-aʔ
and then   it's   there   CSL-3FI.A-hold-STV   1SG.POSS-tooth-NSF
and then she was holding my tooth,

nʌ kwí· tayu·kú· kʌ́h.
nʌ kwí·   t-a-yuk-u-ʔ   kʌ́·
so then   CSL-FACT-3>1SG-give-PNC   y'know
so then she handed it to me.

(9) Waʔí·luʔ, "ʌhsya·kʌ́neʔ,"
waʔ-ya-ihlu-ʔ   ʌ-hs-yakʌʔ-neʔ
FACT-3FI.A-say-PNC   FUT-2SG.A-go.out-PNC
She said, "go out,"

waʔí·luʔ, "nʌ átste yaʔtʌ́staneʔ,
waʔ-ya-ihlu-ʔ   nʌ   átste   yaʔ-t-ʌ-hs-t-a-ʔ-neʔ
FACT-3FI.A-say-PNC   then   outside   TRL-DL-FUT-2SG.A-stand-JN-INCH-PNC
she said, "stand outside,"

ʌ́ti nukwá· nʌhsatye·lá·<u>teʔ</u>."
ʌ́tye nukwá·   n-ʌ-hs-at-yel-a-ʔt-eʔ
south   PART-FUT-2SG.A-SRF-do-JN-CAUS-PNC
                 turn to face a direction
and face south."

(10) "Thoʔnʌ́ ʌhsí·luʔ,
thoʔnʌ́   ʌ-hs-ihlu-ʔ
and then   FUT-2SG.A-say-PNC
"And then you will say,

'tsyoní·tuʔ tetyatatnawi·l<u>ú</u>'."
tsyoní·tuʔ   te-ty-atat-nawil-u
NOUN   DL-1IN.DU.A-REFL-tooth-give
'beaver, let us trade teeth!'"

(11) "Ókhnaʔ" waʔí·luʔ,
ókhnaʔ   waʔ-ya-ihlu-ʔ
and then   FACT-3FI.A-say-PNC
"And then" she said,

"ohná·kʌʔ nukwá· yʌsatí· thikʌ́ n onawi·lá· kʌ́h."
ohná·kʌʔ nukwá· y-ʌ-s-aty-ʔ   thikʌ́ = n   o-nawil-aʔ   kʌ́·
behind   TRL-FUT-2SG.P-throw-PNC   that   NPF-tooth-NSF   see
"throw the tooth behind you [over your shoulder]."

(12) Nʌ kwí· né· tho ná·kye<u>le</u>ʔ.
nʌ kwí· né· tho   n-aʔ-k-yel-eʔ
so then it's thus PART-FACT-1SG.A-do-PNC
So then that's what I did.

(13) Tho kwí· thikʌ́ wakyenawá·ku,
tho kwí· thikʌ́ wak-yenawaʔk-u
there   that   1SG.P-hold.onto-STV
I held onto it,

tho íkhaweʔ n onawi·lá·,
tho   i-k-haw-eʔ = n   o-nawil-aʔ
there EPEN-1SG.A-hold-STV   NPF-tooth-NSF
I held the tooth,

ókhnaʔ waʔkí·luʔ,
ókhnaʔ   waʔ-k-ihlu-ʔ
and then FACT-1SG.A-say-PNC
and then I said,

"tsyoní·tuʔ tetyatatnawi·l<u>ú</u>."
tsyoní·tuʔ te-ty-atat-nawil-u
NOUN   DL-1IN.DU.A-REFL-tooth-give
"beaver, let us trade teeth!"

(14) Ókhnaʔ ohná·kʌʔ nukwá· yahukwa·tí· kʌ́h.
ókhnaʔ   ohná·kʌʔ nukwá· yaha-wakw-aty-ʔ   kʌ́·
and then behind   TRL:FACT-1SG.P-throw-PNC   see
And then I threw it behind me.

(15) Né· s aolí·waʔ tho ni·yót tsiʔ yukhihlo·líheʔ,
né· kʌs   ao-lihw-aʔ   tho   ni-y-oht
it's customarily 3Z/N.SG.POSS-matter-NSF   that's   PART-3Z/N.SG.A-be.so[STV]
                                the reason

tsiʔ   yukhi-hloli-heʔ
that   3>1DP-tell-HAB
The reason that's the way it is, so they tell us,

né· wí· tsi? tsyoní·tu?,

né· wí· tsi?   tsyoní·tu?
because   NOUN

yah kwí· te?wé·ne tsi? na?tehanawili·yó·se? kʌ́·,

yah kwí· te?wé·ne tsi?   na?-te-ha-nawil-iyo-?se?   kʌ́·
it's incredible   what   PART-DL-3M.SG.A-tooth-nice-PL   y'know
is because it's incredible what nice teeth the beaver has,

tahnú· kwahikʌ́ tsi? owískla? ni·yót,

tahnú· kwahikʌ́   tsi?   o-wiskl-a?   ni-y-oht
and   just really   that   NPF-white-NSF   PART-3Z/N.SG.A-be.so[STV]
and they are really white,

khále? kwahotokʌ́·u tsi? lanawili·yó·se? ki?wáh.

khále? kwahotokʌ́·u tsi?   la-nawil-iyo-?se?   ki?wáh
and   just for real   that   3M.SG.A-tooth-nice-PL   right
and he has just really nice teeth.

(16) Né· s kwí· aolí·wa? thikʌ́ yu·té· akwatauntie kʌ́·,

né·   kʌs kwí·   ao-lihw-a?   thikʌ́   yu-ate-?
it's   customarily   3Z/N.SG.POSS-matter-NSF   that   3FI.A-say-STV

akw-at-auntie   kʌ́·
1SG.POSS-SRF-aunt   see
It's why my auntie said that,

né· thikʌ́ tʌtsyatatnawi·lú·,

né·   thikʌ́   t-ʌ-tsy-atat-nawil-u-?
it's   that   DL-FUT-2DU.A-REFL-tooth-give-PNC
that you two will trade teeth,

tho kati? ni·yót nʌ ʌsehsnawilo·táne?,

tho   kati?   ni-y-oht   ʌ-se-hs-nawil-ot-a-?-ne?
that's   so then   PART-3Z/N.SG.A-be.so[STV]   FUT-REP-2SG.A-tooth-stand-JN-INCH-PNC
                                                                              get a [new] tooth
that way you will get another tooth,

kwáh tshikʌ́ kanawiliyó kʌ́h.

kwáh   tshikʌ́   ka-nawil-iyo   kʌ́·
just   for real   3Z/N.SG.A-tooth-nice[STV]   see
a really nice tooth.

(17) **Né· kati? wí· ní· thikʌ́ tho niwakkaló·tʌ.**

né· kati? wí·   ní·   thikʌ́   tho   ni-wak-kal-o?tʌ
so anyway it's FIRST.PERSON that   that's PART-1SG.P-story-kind.of[STV]

So anyway that's the story I have.

(18) **Yah só·tsi? te?kaka·lés,**

yah só·tsi?   te?-ka-kal-es
not   too much   NEG-3Z/N.SG.A-story-long[STV]

It's not too long a story,

nók tsi? né· ki? kwahotokʌ́·u tho niyawʌ́·u.

nók tsi? né· ki?   kwahotokʌ́·u tho   ni-yaw-ʌ?-u
but   it's actually just for real thus   PART-3Z/N.SG.P-happen-STV

but it really happened.

(19) **Tho kati? wí· nikú ka?ikʌ́ wá·kelhe? a·kka·látu? kʌ́h.**

tho   kati? wí·   nikú   ka?ikʌ́   wa?-k-elh-e?
that's so anyway how much this   FACT-1SG.A-want-PNC

aa-k-kal-a-tu-?   kʌ́·
OPT-1SG.A-story-JN-erect -PNC   EH

That's all I wanted to tell.

Norma Kennedy, My First Job in Tobacco (partial)

(41) **Né· kwí· né· onʌ́ tutye·lʌ́hte? ukwatkálya?kse?,**

né· kwí· né· onʌ́   t-a-w-atyelʌht-e?   wa?-wakw-at-kalya?k-hs-e?
it's   it's now   CSL-FACT-3Z/N.SG.A-first-PNC   FACT-1SG.P-SRF-pay-BEN-PNC

So then was the first time I got paid,

onísta? uhte tsi? nuknehla·kó· wakhwistaká·<u>te?</u>.

onísta? uhte   tsi?   n-a?-wak-nehlakw-?
gosh   supposedly   how   PART-FACT-1SG.P-get.surprised-PNC

wak-hwist-a-ka?te-?
1SG.P-metal-JN-have.much-STV

gosh I was really surprised I had a lot of money.

(42) **Yah te?ské·yale? tó· nikú latikálya?ks ne? thó·ne?,**

yah   te?-s-k-ehyahl-e?   tó· nikú   lati-kalya?k-s   ne? thó·ne?
not   NEG-REP-1SG.A-remember-STV   how much   3M.PL.A-pay-HAB   at that time

I don't remember how much they paid at that time,

nók tsiʔ uknehla·kó· kiʔ tsiʔ e·só· ukwatkályahkseʔ.

nók tsiʔ   waʔ-wak-nehlakw-ʔ   kiʔ   tsiʔ   e·só·
but   FACT-1SG.P-get.surprised-PNC   actually   that   a lot

waʔ-wakw-at-kalyaʔk-hs-eʔ
FACT-1SG.P-SRF-pay-BEN-PNC

but I was surprised that I was paid a lot.

(43) **Wísk kwí· niwʌhnislaké thikʌ́ tsiʔ nikú ukyo·tʌ́·,**

wísk   kwí·   ni-w-ʌhnisl-a-ke   thikʌ́   tsiʔ nikú
five   PART-3Z/N.SG.A-day-JN-amount.to[STV]   that   how many

waʔ-wak-yotʌ-ʔ
FACT-1SG.P-work-PNC

I worked for five days,

**kwáh aʔnyóh sakehyá·laneʔ tékni yawʌ·lé· nikahwístake uhte i·kélheʔ thikʌ́
swʌhníslat neʔ thó·neʔ.**

kwáh   aʔnyóh   s-a-k-ehyahl-a-ʔ-neʔ   tékni   yawʌ·lé·
just   seems like   REP-FACT-1SG.A-remember-JN-INCH-PNC   two   teen

ni-ka-hwist-a-ke   uhte i·kélheʔ   thikʌ́
PART-3Z/N.SG.A-metal-JN-amount.to[STV]   I think   that

s-w-ʌhnisl-a-t   neʔ thó·neʔ
REP-3Z/N.SG.A-day-JN-one[STV]   at that time

I seem to remember it was like twelve dollars per day I think at that time.

(44) **Tahnú· wísk kwí· niwʌhnislaké ukyo·tʌ́·,**

tahnú·   wísk   kwí·   ni-w-ʌhnisl-a-ke   waʔ-wak-yotʌ-ʔ
and   five   PART-3Z/N.SG.A-day-JN-amount.to[STV]   FACT-1SG.P-work-PNC

And I worked five days,

tahnú· tékni yawʌ·lé· nikahwístake swʌhníslat.

tahnú·   tékni   yawʌ·lé·   ni-ka-hwist-a-ke
and   two   teen   PART-3Z/N.SG.A-metal-JN-amount.to[STV]

s-w-ʌhnisl-a-t
REP-3Z/N.SG.A-day-JN-one[STV]

and twelve dollars a day.

(45) **Tho kwí· nikú thikʌ́ ukwatkályahkseʔ.**

tho kwí·   nikú   thikʌ́   waʔ-wakw-at-kalyaʔk-hs-eʔ
that's   how much   that   FACT-1SG.P-SRF-pay-BEN-PNC

So that's how much I got paid.

(46) **Né·n, né· kiʔ thikʌ́ teknihatú·thne ukwatkályaʔkseʔ,**

né·n   né·   kiʔ   thikʌ́   teknihatú·thne   waʔ-wak-at-kalyaʔk-hs-eʔ
it's that   it's   actually   that   second   FACT-1SG.P-SRF-pay-BEN-PNC
So, then the second time I got paid,

nʌ kanatá·ke wá·nehteʔ aknulhá· kháleʔ lakeʔníha,

nʌ   ka-nat-aʔke   wa-hn-e-ht-eʔ   ak-nulháʔ   kháleʔ
then   NPF-town-LOC   FACT-3M.DU.A-walk-CAUS-PNC   3FZ.SG>1SG-mother   and
lake-ʔniha
3M.SG>1SG-father
my mother and father went uptown,

tho kwí· waʔuke·kwáhteʔ,
tho kwí·   waʔ-yuk-ekwaht-eʔ
that   FACT-3>1SG-invite-PNC
they invited me along,

wahʌ́·luʔ lakeʔníha,
wa-hʌ-ihlu-ʔ   lake-ʔniha
FACT-3M.SG.A-say-PNC   3M.SG>1SG-father
my father said,

"kʌʔ nukwá· n sahwístaʔ,"
kʌʔ nukwá·=n   sa-hwist-aʔ
here   2SG.POSS-metal-NSF
"here is your money,"

wahʌ́·luʔ, "í· kwí· ʌkha·wákeʔ,
wa-hʌ-ihlu-ʔ   í· kwí·   ʌ-k-haw-ak-eʔ
FACT-3M.SG.A-say-PNC   FIRST.PERSON   FUT-1SG-hold-CONT-PNC
he said, "I will hang onto it,

nók ʌskhlo·lí· nʌ náhteʔ ʌhsla·kó· ʌhsatathni·nú·seʔ."
nók   ʌ-sk-hloli-ʔ   nʌ   náhteʔ   ʌ-hs-lakw-ʔ
just   FUT-2SG>1SG-tell-PNC   then   what   FUT-2SG.A-choose-PNC
ʌ-hs-atat-hninu-ʔs-eʔ
FUT-2SG.A-REFL-buy-BEN-PNC
you just tell me what you choose that you will buy for yourself."

(47) **Tahnú· s kwí· yuknuʔwéskwaniheʔ lakeʔníha a·yakyatahúhsatateʔ thikʌ́ Cleveland Indians tehuttsihkwá·eks,**

tahnú·   kʌs kwí·   yukn-uʔweskwani-heʔ   lake-ʔniha   aa-yaky-atahuhsatat-eʔ
and   habitually   1DU.P-enjoy-HAB   3M.SG>1SG-father   OPT-1EX.DU.A-listen-PNC

thikʌ́ CI te-hu-at-tsihkw-aʔek-s
that CI DL-3M.PL.A-SRF-fist,knuckle,button-strike-HAB
And my father and I used to enjoy listening to the Cleveland Indians baseball games,

né· s thikʌ́ tekhénhes,
né· kʌs thikʌ́ te-khe-nhe-s
it's habituallly that DL-1SG>3-stick.up.for-HAB
I used to root for them,

né· kwí· ukyatteam.
né· kwí· uky-at-team
so it's 1DU.POSS-SRF-team
it was our team.

(48) **Tahnú· yah kwí· né· teʔyonuʔwéskwaniheʔ aknulhá· kháleʔ n teyakwatʌhnu·téleʔ a·kutahúhsatateʔ.**
tahnú· yah kwí· né· teʔ-yon-uʔweskwani-heʔ ak-nulhá? kháleʔ = n
and not it's NEG-3FZ.DP.P-enjoy-HAB 3FZ.SG>1SG-mother and

te-yakw-atʌhnutel-eʔ aa-ku-atahuhsatat-eʔ
DL-1EX.PL.A-siblings-STV OPT-3FZ.PL.A-listen-PNC
And my mother and my sisters didn't like to listen [to ball games].

(49) **Tahnú· kʌʔ ok kʌs ni·wá· thikʌ́ yukni·yʌ́· watlʌnóthaʔ,**
tahnú· kʌʔ ok kʌs ni-w-a-ʔ thikʌ́ yukni-yʌ-ʔ
and just PART-3Z/N.SG.A-size-STV that 1DU.P-have-STV

w-at-lʌn-ot-haʔ
3Z/N.SG.A-SRF-song-stand-HAB
radio
And we had just a small radio,

tahnú· yah kwí· akwáh teʔyoyáneleʔ.
tahnú· yah kwí· akwáh teʔ-yo-yanle-ʔ
and not especially NEG-3Z/N.SG.P-good-STV
and it wasn't very good.

(50) **Né· katiʔ wí· wahiliʔwanu·tú·seʔ, waʔkí·luʔ,**
né· katiʔ wí· wa-hi-liʔwanutu-ʔs-eʔ waʔ-k-ihlu-ʔ
well it's FACT-1SG>3M.SG-ask.about-BEN-PNC FACT-1SG.A-say-PNC
Well then I asked him, I said,

"ʌwa·tú· kʌ n oyá· usakhni·nú· watlʌnóthaʔ."
ʌ-w-atu-ʔ kʌ = n oyá· usa-k-hninu-ʔ
FUT-3Z/N.SG.A-possible-PNC QUESTION another REP:FACT-1SG.A-buy-PNC

w-at-lʌn-ot-haʔ
3Z/N.SG.A-SRF-song-stand-HAB
"can I buy another radio?"

(51) **Wahʌ́·luʔ, "kano·lú· kiʔ thikʌ́,**
wa-hʌ-ihlu-ʔ   ka-nolu-ʔ   kiʔ   thikʌ́
FACT-3M.SG.A-say-PNC   3Z/N/SG.A-expensive-STV   actually   that
He said, "it's expensive,"

ʌwa·tú· kwí·" wahʌ́·luʔ "tʌtyátyesteʔ kiʔwáh."
ʌ-w-atu-ʔ kwí·   wahʌ́·luʔ   t-ʌ-ty-at-yest-eʔ   kiʔwáh
FUT-3Z/N.SG.A-possible-PNC   he said   DL-FUT-1IN.DU.A-SRF-mix-PNC   right
he said "you and I can chip in, right."

(52) **Nʌ kiʔ ok wi· né· tho wahakyaʔtaha·wíhteʔ tsiʔ nú· thutʌhni·núheʔ watlʌnótha̱ʔ.**
nʌ kiʔ ok wí· né·   tho   wa-hak-yaʔt-a-hawi-ht-eʔ   tsiʔ nú·
right away   it's   there   FACT-3M.SG>1SG-body-JN-carry-CAUS-PNC   where

t-hu-atʌ-hninu-heʔ   w-at-lʌn-ot-haʔ
CSL-3M.PL.A-SRF-buy-HAB   3Z/N.SG.A-SRF-song-stand-HAB
So right away he took me to where they sold radios.

(53) **Laulhá· kwí· wahala·kó· tsiʔ ka·yʌ́· tyoyánele̱ʔ.**
la-ulháʔ kwí·   wa-ha-lakw-ʔ   tsiʔ ka·yʌ́·   t-yo-yanle-ʔ
3M.SG.P-self   FACT-3M.SG.A-choose-PNC   the one that   CSL-3Z/N.SG.P-good-STV
He was the one who chose the one that was the best.

(54) **Kháleʔ neʔ thó·neʔ battery kʌs kwí· né· wátstaʔ watlʌnótha̱ʔ.**
kháleʔ   neʔ thó·neʔ   battery   kʌs kwí·   né·   w-atst-haʔ
and   at that time   battery   habitually   it's   3Z/N.SG.A-use-HAB

w-at-lʌn-ot-haʔ
3Z/N.SG.A-SRF-song-stand-HAB
And at that time radios used batteries.

(55) **Nʌ kwí· né· wahakályahkeʔ kiʔwáh.**
nʌ kwí·   né·   wa-ha-kalyaʔk-eʔ   kiʔwáh
so then   it's   FACT-3M.SG.A-pay-PNC   right
So then he paid for it.

(56) **Kwáh kwí· né· nók sayákwaweʔ,**
kwáh kwí·   né· nók   s-a-yakwa-w-eʔ
just   it's   REP-FACT-1EX.PL.A-arrive-PNC
Just as soon as we got back again,

nʌ kiʔ ok wi· né· waʔthanahsu·tʌ́· kaʔikʌ́ watlʌnóthaʔ,

nʌ kiʔ ok wí·   né·   waʔ-t-ha-nahsut-ʌʔ   kaʔikʌ́   w-at-lʌn-ot-haʔ
right away   it's   FACT-DL-3M.SG.A-fasten-PNC   this   3Z/N.SG.A-SRF-song-stand-HAB
right away he hooked up the radio,

ókhnaʔ tho nú· yahlotálhoʔ tsiʔ nú· naʔtehuttsihkwá·eks.

ókhnaʔ   tho nú·   y-a-hl-otalho-ʔ   tsiʔ nú·
and then   that's where   TRL-FACT-3M.SG.A-snag-PNC   where

te-hu-at-tsihkw-aʔek-s
DL-3M.PL.A-SRF-fist,knuckle,button-strike-HAB
and then he turned it to [the station] where they were playing ball.

(57) **Tehuttsihkwá·eks kwí· neʔ thó·neʔ yoʔkalásh<u>ʌ</u>.**

te-hu-at-tsihkw-aʔek-s kwí·   neʔ thó·neʔ   yoʔkaláshʌ
DL-3M.PL.A-SRF-fist,knuckle,button-strike-HAB   at that time   evening
They were playing ball that evening.

(58) **Nʌ kiʔ ok wi· né· tho waʔakyátiʔ waʔakyatahúhsatate<u>ʔ</u>.**

nʌ kiʔ ok wí·   né·   tho   waʔ-yaky-at-yʌ-ʔ   waʔ-yaky-atahuhsatat-eʔ
right away   it's   there   FACT-1EX.DU.A-SRF-put-STV   FACT-1EX.DU.A-listen-PNC
                                sit down
Right away the two of us sat down and we listened.

(59) **Ok neʔn aknulhá· kháleʔ n teyakwatʌhnu·téleʔ,**

ok neʔn   ak-nulhá?   kháleʔ=n   te-yaky-atʌhnutel-eʔ
and as for   3FZ.SG>1SG-mother   and   DL-1EX.DU.A-siblings-STV
And my mother and my sisters,

oyá· kwí· né· náhteʔ waʔtyotiʔnikulha·lʌ́·,

oyá· kwí· né·   náhteʔ   waʔ-t-yoti-ʔnikulhal-ʌʔ
other   it's   what   FACT-DL-3FZ.DP.P-bother.with-PNC
they got into something else,

yah seʔ né· teʔyonuʔwéskwaniheʔ a·kutahúhsatateʔ tehuttsihkwá·eks.

yah   seʔ   né·   teʔ-yon-uʔweskwani-heʔ   aa-ku-atahuhsatat-eʔ
not   too   it's   NEG-3FZ.DP.P-enjoy-HAB   OPT-FZ.PL.A-listen-PNC

te-hu-at-tsihkw-aʔek-s
DL-3M.PL.A-SRF-fist,knuckle,button-strike-HAB
they didn't like to listen to ball games.

References

Below are the references cited in this work. There are many more excellent sources that discuss Oneida and other Iroquoian languages. An annotated bibliography that includes a range of works is Michelson (2011).

Abbott, Clifford. (1982, 1983). Bear Stories, Ukwehuwehnéha Onúhkwaht (Oneida Medicine), Witch Stories, Animal Fables. Oneida Tribe of Indians of Wisconsin.

Abbott, Clifford. (1984). Two Feminine Genders in Oneida. Anthropological Linguistics, 26, 125-37.

Abbott, Clifford. (2000). Languages of the World/Materials 301: Oneida. Muenchen: Lincom Europa.

Abbott, Clifford. (2006). Oneida Teaching Grammar. Retrieved from http:// www.uwgb.edu/ Oneida/Grammar.html

Abbott, Clifford, Christjohn, Amos & Hinton, Maria. (1996). An Oneida Dictionary. Oneida Tribe of Indians of Wisconsin. (Online version available at http://www.uwgb.edu/Oneida/ Dictionary.html)

Antone, Angela, et al. (1981). Tekalihwathé:tha'. London, ON: Centre for the Research and Teaching of Canadian Languages, Department of Anthropology, University of Western Ontario.

Campisi, Jack. (1979). Oneida. In Bruce G. Trigger (Ed.), Handbook of North American Indians, Vol 17: Northeast (481-90). Washington, DC: Smithsonian Institution.

Chafe, Wallace. (1994). Discourse, Consciousness and Time: The Flow and Displacement of Conscious Experience in Speaking and Writing. Chicago, IL: University of Chicago Press.

Chafe, Wallace. (2015). A Grammar of the Seneca Language. Oakland, CA: University of California Press.

Chafe, Wallace, & Snow, Lena. (1980). The Bird. In Marianne Mithun and Hanni Woodbury (Eds.), Northern Iroquoian Texts (96-103). Chicago, IL: University of Chicago Press.

Cornelius, Marla, et al. (1985). Tsi' Niyukwalihó:tʌ. London, ON: Centre for the Research and Teaching of Canadian Languages, Department of Anthropology, University of Western Ontario.

Koenig, Jean-Pierre, & Michelson, Karin. (2010a). Argument Structure of Oneida Kinship Terms. International Journal of American Linguistics, 76, 169-205.

Koenig, Jean-Pierre, & Michelson, Karin. (2010b). How to Quantify Over Entities in Iroquoian (Oneida). Paper presented at the Annual meeting of the Society for the Study of Indigenous Languages of the Americas, Baltimore, Maryland.

Koenig, Jean-Pierre, & Michelson, Karin. (2014). Deconstructing SYNtax. In Stefan Müller (Ed.), Proceedings of the 21th International Conference on Head-Driven Phrase Structure Grammar (114-34). Stanford, CA: CSLI Publications.

Koenig, Jean-Pierre, & Michelson, Karin. (2015). Morphological complexity à la Oneida. In M. Baerman, D. Brown, & G. Corbett (Eds.), Understanding and measuring morphological complexity (69-92). Oxford: Oxford University Press.

Lounsbury, Floyd G. (1942). Phonology of the Oneida Language. (MA thesis). University of Wisconsin, Madison, WI.

Lounsbury, Floyd G. (1953). Oneida Verb Morphology. Yale University Publications in Anthropology, 48. New Haven, CT: Yale University. (Reprinted by Human Relations Area Files Press, 1976.)

Michelson, Karin, & Nicholas, Georgina. (1981). Three Stories in Oneida. (Georgina Nicholas, Teller and Trans.). National Museum of Man Mercury Series, Canadian Ethnology Service Paper No. 73. Ottawa: National Museums of Canada.

Michelson, Karin. (1988). A Comparative Study of Lake-Iroquoian Accent. Dordrecht: Reidel.

Michelson, Karin. (2011). Iroquoian Languages. Oxford Bibliographies Online: Linguistics. Mark Aronoff (Ed.). New York, NY: Oxford University Press. Retrieved from http://www.oxfordbibliographies.com/view/document/obo-9780199772810/obo-9780199772810-0023.xml

Michelson, Karin. (2015). Gender in Oneida. In Marlis Hellinger and Heiko Motschenbacher (Eds.), Gender Across Languages (Vol. IV) (277-301). Amsterdam: John Benjamins Press.

Michelson, Karin, & Doxtator, Mercy. (2002). Oneida-English/English-Oneida Dictionary. Toronto: University of Toronto Press.

Michelson, Karin, & Price, Catherine. (2011). Native Languages Resource Guide: Oneida, Cayuga, and Mohawk. Ontario Ministry of Education.

Sapir, Edward. (1911). The problem of noun incorporation in American languages. American Anthropologist, n.s., 13, 250-82.

Index

active verb, 343-5, 353
additive particle, 358, 359
agent prefixes, 346-53, 360, 362, 369-71, 380,
    403-5, 410, 417, 436
alienable possession, 366-71
alternative question, 388
anaphoric reference, 358, 401
animate verbal arguments, 347, 353-4, 373,
    403-10, 417, 420
argument clause, 373-5, 396
argument of a verb, 346-7, 353-5, 373, 390,
    397, 400, 405
assertion particle, 357, 379

benefactive suffix, 343, 420

cataphoric reference, 401
causative suffix, 343, 364
cause, 422, 428
cislocative prepronominal prefix, 276, 355,
    372, 411, 412, 423
classificatory word, 6, 386, 393, 397-9, 415
coincident prepronominal prefix, 355, 372,
    382, 411
complementizer particle, 374
conditional clauses, 396, 398, 424
connective particles, 6, 355, 356, 359, 372,
    431, 434
consequence, 422
consessive clauses, 426
content questions, 386-8, 391
continuative suffix, 345
contrastive prepronominal prefix, 355, 373,
    381-3, 386, 391, 394, 398
correlative construction, 372, 402-3

default prefix, 345, 354, 420
demonstrative words, 356-7, 384
dislocative suffix, 343
distributive ending, 356, 361, 363
distributive suffix, 343
dualic prepronominal prefix, 355, 381, 404-5,
    408-11
dyadic verb, 346-7

embedded question, 390-2
emphatic particles, 358, 372, 395
entity expression, 362, 376, 377, 380
epistemic particles, 357
eventive verb, 343
evidential particles, 357-8
exclamations, 356, 358, 388
exclusive, 345-6, 380
exophoric reference, 401

factual prefix, 344, 348, 352, 355, 382, 418
feminine gender, 345-6, 355
feminine-indefinite, 345-7, 355, 362, 374,
    380, 403
feminine-zoic gender, 345-7, 349, 354-5, 360,
    362, 380, 403, 404, 405, 407, 418, 420
first person pronoun, 356
free relative clause, 397-8, 400, 401, 407
future prefix, 5, 344, 345, 355, 382, 384-5,
    386, 418

gender, in pronominal prefixes, 345, 346, 355,
    380, 403

habitual aspect, 343-4, 345, 353, 362, 381

imperative, 343, 344-5, 384
inalienable possession, 366, 369-71
inanimate verbal arguments, 345, 346, 347, 353, 354, 403-7, 410
inchoative suffix, 343
inclusive, 5, 345-6, 348, 370
indefinite expressions, 356, 372, 373, 392-8
indefinite reference, 345-6, 355
instrumental suffix, 343, 362
internally-headed relative clause, 362, 375, 377, 403
interrogative pronouns, 356
intransitive pronominal prefix, 347

juxtaposed clause, 374, 422, 423

kinship terms, 343, 36-6

left-detached nominal, 379
lexicalized expressions, 5, 364, 399, 435
locational particles, 356, 358, 372, 414
locative suffix or ending, 13, 361, 363, 370, 371

masculine gender, 345-7, 349, 353, 355, 360, 365, 360,365, 400, 403, 404
mismatches, pronominals, 380-1
modal prepronominal prefixes, 344, 355, 435
modality, 417
modification, 422
Mohawk, 357
monadic verb, 346
motion verb, 344

negative expectation particle, 384
negative indefinite, 392, 394-97
negative particle, 356, 373, 381, 383-4, 386, 389, 391, 394, 398, 418, 419, 421, 423
negative polarity item, 396
negative prepronominal prefix, 348, 355, 373, 381-4, 386, 394, 398, 418, 419, 421, 423
neuter gender, 345, 354-5, 360, 362, 403-5, 407, 418, 420
nominalizer suffix, 13, 361, 366
noun, incorporated, 5, 343, 362-71, 403-5, 408, 409, 411

noun prefix, 359-63
noun suffix, 359-63, 367, 371
number, in pronominal prefixes, 345-6, 380
number words, 404-406, 408 410

objective pronominal prefix, 347
Onondaga, 356, 357
optative prefix, 344, 345, 355, 374, 382, 383, 384-6, 396, 423, 435
overlap, pronominals, 380-1

particle, definition, 356
partitive prepronominal prefix, 6, 355, 372, 382, 397-8, 405-6, 408-413
past suffix, 345
patient prefixes, 347, 353, 356, 360, 366, 367, 369, 371, 408, 409, 410
person, in pronominal prefixes, 345-6, 380
plural ending, 345, 360, 363
polar questions, 386, 388-91
positive indefinite, 392-4
possessive prefix, 13, 360, 367-8, 370, 371
posture verbs, 366, 369, 370, 377, 408
present, in motion verbs 344
presentational structure, 376
progressive suffix, 343
punctual aspect, 343, 344, 345, 353, 355, 382, 385, 410
purpose clauses, 421, 423

question particle, 358, 388, 389, 394, 425
questions, words used in content questions, 356, 386-7, 392, 397

reactivation of discourse referent, 380
reflexive prefix, 343
relative clause, 400
repetitive prepronominal prefix, 276, 355, 403 410
result clauses, 424
reversative suffix, 343

second person pronoun, 356
semi-reflexive prefix, 5, 13, 343, 362
Seneca, 357

state verb, 343-5, 353, 364, 367, 369, 371,
    404
stative aspect, 343-5, 353, 362, 363, 366, 367,
    370, 371, 382, 408, 410, 411
stative verb See: state verb
subjective pronominal prefix, 347
subordinator particle, 374

tag expression, 358
temporal particles, 356, 358-9, 372, 399, 411
third person pronoun, 356, 357
transitive pronominal prefix, 347, 350, 355,
    365
translocative prepronominal prefix, 355, 372,
    381, 382, 385, 411
triadic verb, 346

universal quantifier, 407

yes-no questions, 384, 386, 388-91

Printed in the USA
CPSIA information can be obtained
at www.ICGtesting.com
JSHW062004061223
53161JS00003B/9

9 781442 628335